GRIGORI SVIRSKI
A HISTORY OF POST-WAR SOVIET WRITING:

The Literature of Moral Opposition

**Translated and Edited by
Robert Dessaix and Michael Ulman**

Ardis   Ann Arbor

The Russian edition of this book was published in 1979 by Overseas Publications Interchange, Ltd., 40 Elsham Road, London, England. The text of this translation has been abridged by the editors, who also made a variety of small corrections in dates and quotations. The Russian edition contains a Russian-language bibliography, which those who read some Russian may want to consult. The English-language bibliography in this translation was provided by the editors of Ardis Publishers. The photographs on pages 2, 76, 444, 445, and 448 are from the author's collection; all others are from the photographic library of Ardis.

A History of Post-War Soviet Writing
English translation by Robert Dessaix and Michael Ulman

Library of Congress Cataloging in Publication Data

Svirskii, Grigorii, 1921-
    A history of post-war Soviet writing.

    Translation of: Na lobnom meste.
    Bibliography: p.
    1. Authors, Russian—20th century. 2. Dissidents—
Soviet Union. 3. Russian literature—20th century—
History and criticism. I. Title.
PG2998.D5S9313   891.7'09'0044   81-1492
ISBN 0-88233-449-2   AACR2

PART I □□□□ HEROES OF THE FIRING-SQUAD YEARS

PART II □□□□ CHERRY-PLUM BLOOMS IN TBILISI

PART III □□□□ THE SOLZHENITSYN DECADE

LIST OF ILLUSTRATIONS

PART I

HEROES OF THE FIRING-SQUAD YEARS

1. THE STATE STARTS AN AVALANCHE

It was in 1946 that I first found myself inside the half-open gates of the Union of Writers of the U.S.S.R. In the middle of the small green courtyard, I saw Rodin's Thinker, frozen on his rock in an attitude of endless concentration. I felt great happiness at the thought that my soldiering days were a thing of the past and that I was one of those for whom thinking was a natural condition.

With a smile to greet my new life, I strode towards the door behind which a committee which worked with young writers ('young writers'— just imagine!) was waiting to discuss with me my first prose opus.

In the doorway I looked back at the strained, bent back of the Thinker, eternal and beautiful in his concentration. Now, thirty years later, I would say in the *torment* of concentration.

The years of the pogroms were behind us, as were the years of hard-won successes and cruel defeats.

What exactly is the literature of moral resistance, this tortured yet not fatally wounded body of works which are my very flesh and blood? Will it stand mute and unfathomable before history, a twentieth-century Russian sphinx? or will it be heard? As is generally recognized, modern Soviet literature is like an iceberg: above the surface it is smooth and shining, subject to censorship and often Aesopian, while beneath the surface we have samizdat covered in sharp and sometimes formless outcrops. The literature of today is indivisible, however Soviet criticism might chop it up into transparent, orthodox cubes. It is no longer possible to crush it through slander and repression—it is the history of whole generations of people who "thought differently", prepared for the sake of their convictions to go to prison and into special psychiatric hospitals

"Art," said Boris Pasternak, "is the record of the displacement of reality produced by feeling." It is not difficult to understand how unthinkably heretical these words sounded within the walls of the Union of Writers where every inch in the displacement of reality is determined not by the creator's feeling but by official directives.

In looking back over the past thirty years, it is glaringly obvious how shallow, gray and improbably featureless the tide of books flowing into the 350,000 libraries of the Soviet Union is, what little connection it has with literature, how degrading it is and destructive to spiritual values.

However, even during the firing-squad years under Stalin, there were writers who did not surrender their inner freedom and in the sight of all stepped forward to meet the bullet.

Some of these writers are very well-known in the West: Boris Pasternak, Anna Akhmatova, Marina Tsvetaeva, Osip Mandelstam, Mikhail

Bulgakov, Andrei Platonov, and one or two others. Over the past few years—indeed, over the past quarter of a century—modern Russian literature has been represented in the West above all by these famed writers. They have saved the honor of Russian literature in the Soviet period.

A burning problem arises, however. The average Soviet reader was not acquainted with these names—in some cases microscopic editions of their works, and in other cases complete suppression, defamation and imprisonment had had their effect. Even in Professor L. Timofeyev's textbook for philological students, *Soviet Literature*, there is not a single mention in over 400 pages of either Akhmatova, Pasternak, Babel, Zamyatin, Zoshchenko, or Pilnyak, whose penetrating "Tale of an Unextinguished Moon," concerning the knifing to death by a surgeon of a commander called Gavrilov—read: Frunze—Stalin did not forgive.

But if this is the case, if the average Soviet reader was unacquainted with the majority of Russian writers of the Soviet period studied in the West, and sometimes did not even know their names, who, then, served as a moral support for several generations of people who "thought differently"? Nobel prize-winners Aleksandr Solzhenitsyn and Andrei Sakharov did not appear on the scene until later. The students who protested against the bloody invasion of Hungary and gathered on Mayakovsky Square, the generation herded into special psychiatric hospitals and camps in the Mordvinian Autonomous Region and Siberia, the fearless generation of dissidents, may scarcely have even heard of Solzhenitsyn and Sakharov. In that case, who was it that gave spiritual strength to these generations? Who are the modern Russian writers who worked heroically in hellish conditions with executions and pogroms going on around them and saved thousands and possibly millions of people from disillusionment, cynicism and compromise?

After the Second World War I remember that our favorite books were Hemingway's *A Farewell to Arms* and Remarque's *All Quiet on the Western Front*. What attracted us was the truthfulness in the small details, in the accounts of the filth of the trenches, with which we ourselves were still in a sense soiled.

Yet the essential part remained alien to us. In Remarque's *Return* one of the heroes goes back to the battle-field where his friends had remained and there shoots himself. It was a return to the dead.

We were no lost generation. We lived with a sense of victory, a sense of a people who had crushed fascism. Among the friends I remember from the war and the university there was no one who suffered from an inner vacuum or a feeling of being superfluous.

Then suddenly, in the mid-sixties, twenty years after the war against the fascists, we heard in Moscow the first strains of a song now known in every corner of Russia, a song about the soldiers who had fallen and now risen from their graves. They rose to the trumpet's call: "If Russia calls her dead, then things are bad..." The soldiers rose from their graves in their

12

crosses and stripes to sing: "We look and see that there's been a mistake." From thousands upon thousands of tape-recorders in engineers' and workers' hostels came the amazing words: "there's been a mistake, and it's all been for nothing." I remember the strained, sometimes stunned young faces of those listening to the song. And our generation, and those that followed, accepted the thoughts and feelings of Alexander Galich's heroes as their own. Had we then become a lost generation? We looked around us with horror. What, then, had happened to Russia? Why did whole generations feel rejected and lost?

Once upon a time when a traveller journeyed across Russia he would see through his window, above the hayricks and the hills, the stations and the towns, the glistening cupolas of the churches. Everyone would notice them and watch them go by. Nowadays, if you travel south through Kharkov or north to Arkhangelsk, it is the death-dealing giants which soar skywards above the earth, it is the steel-gray of the radar installations and rocket-launchers which dominate the city skylines. The god of the present State system in Russia is the nuclear missile. This god has plunged the twentieth century into terror of a kind never before known on earth. In Russia it has deepened the everyday, perennial fear of the cudgel.

In the dying days of the Stalinist era, the poet Nikolai Glazkov, one of the persecuted talents, wrote:

> *I watch life from under a table.*
> *Twentieth century, extraordinary century—*
> *The more interesting it is for the historian,*
> *The sadder for our contemporary...*

As if in confirmation of his words, we have the endless rumblings of "localized" wars: Korea, Vietnam, the clank of Soviet tanks in Hungary, Czechoslovakia, Sinai and on the Golan Heights.

There was, however, a year in which fear seemed to abate in Russia, as chronic illness abates for a while. This was the first year after the war, the year with whose events this book began. Deafened by the roar of cele-bratory rockets and fusillades we began to realize with horror what was really going on, just as Alexander Solzhenitsyn suddenly realized, lying on the bare earth floor of the divisional counter-espionage post. Or like the Rostov writer Vladimir Fomenko, shy, mild-mannered, kindly Fomenko, who religiously believed that "there must be a good reason for putting people in jail."

On 14th August 1946 many people began to realize something was wrong. On that day the intoxicating feeling of victory disappeared. From the heights of the edifice of State the first stone was rolled, starting the ava-lance which was to bury beneath it almost an entire literary generation. This first stone had the most prosaic of names: the Resolution of the Central

13

Committee of the Communist Party of the Soviet Union on the journals *Zvezda (The Star)* and *Leningrad*. As is well-known, in it Akhmatova's verse and Zoshchenko's stories were declared "a danger to the state."

Were Stalin and Zhdanov seeking to protect themselves from Akhmatova and Zoshchenko? Heavens above! Millions had been taken off to camps in Black Marias. They could have easily taken away two more and finished them off as they had Mandelstam and Babel. They could have taken reprisals quietly... but no. Instead they staged a "sabre dance," a menacing Caucasian dance performed with a dagger clenched between the teeth. "I'll kiss you or cut your throat, as the fancy takes me."

The whole world started to find hurried explanations for this inexplicable event: "Leningrad has always been a window on the West," explained Walter Vickery, "it is no accident that it was Leningrad which was attacked to prevent them looking at the West."[1] Others regarded the Central Committee's resolution on Zoshchenko and Akhmatova as "an isolated case," a blow struck just at Akhmatova and Zoshchenko.

What was the cause of the Stalinist hysteria of 1946—the real cause, which has, alas, remained hidden from the view of investigators?

During the war I realized that the most terrifying thing was not an attack, or a battle, but the minutes, even the seconds, before an aircraft enters the flak, when you can see the black or white puffs of smoke, but still haven't reached them, although you're about to any second. You can smell the powder and feel the tearing of the plane's metal skin... Your heart sinks.

How surprised I was on my return from the war to read the following lines by a young poet who at that time was completely unknown:

> *Going to their death they sing,*
> *To see it makes you want to weep.*
> *The most fearful hour in battle*
> *Is when you're waiting for an attack.*
>
> *I seem to be a magnet*
> *Attracting shells.*
> *There's an explosion—a lieutenant wheezes,*
> *And death again passes by.*
>
> *But we can wait no longer,*
> *And a numb hostility*
> *Takes us across the trenches,*
> *Puncturing necks with bayonets.*
>
> *The fight was brief.*

And then—
We downed the icy vodka,
And with a knife I dug out
    from under my nails
Someone else's blood.

The author of these lines, which were written in 1942, was Semyon Gudzenko. He read them to Ilya Ehrenburg and Ehrenburg had them published. He rang the secretary of the Union of Writers, Alexei Surkov. "This isn't something you can just dream up!" Ehrenburg told him, "you must have used a bayonet yourself to talk about digging out someone else's blood from under your nails."

The truth about the war had hardly begun to make its way into the pages of the newspapers and journals when the Party leadership's first cry of "Enough!" was heard. Military themes had been adequately reflected in literature and now it was time to reflect peaceful constructive labor.

Gudzenko replied to the Party's cry with verses published only after his death. They were verses which he read before student audiences and which turned out to be a challenge to Stalin's commands, something of which he had no suspicion at the time:

Every poet has his native province,
Forgiving him his errors and his sins,
Small grievances he's occasioned, slight offense,
In return for truthful verses.

I also have a faithful native province
Not able to be found on any map.
My strict and frank, my distant province
Is war.

The Party press again and again demanded the abandonment of war themes. Concern should be shown, it said, for those who had returned from the field of battle and their wounds should not be reopened. Gudzenko replied to the "humanists" in 1945 in his poem "My Generation":

Don't pity us—after all we pitied no one,
As before God we're blameless before our commanders.
On the living, coats went brown with blood and clay,
On the graves of the dead pale blue flowers bloomed.

Don't pity us—after all we pitied no one,
Whoever's gone into the attack or shared his last crust
Will understand this truth—it came to us in the dug-outs

15

> *and slit-trenches*
> *To argue in a low, hoarse whining voice.*

This then is the root of the matter: the truth, the unadorned truth, not an episode, not a chance detail, was to be the goal of the generation returned from the war! This is what frightened and panicked those in authority. A literary generation had come of age which had sworn as if on the Bible: "The truth, the whole truth, and nothing but the truth."

> *I now rip anger from my carefree soul*
> *Like bandages...*
> *The battle goes on amidst the smoke and firing...*
> *You can lie down dead in the fight,*
> *But dare not leave yourself a single line*
> *Or keep for yourself a single heartbeat.*

(Gudzenko wrote these lines in Stalingrad in 1943.)

Several years went by and more profound talents began to appear. Suddenly the voice of Alexander Mezhirov was heard. Mezhirov had been an infantryman and driver at the front.

> *We're lying in a bunch at Ladoga,*
> *Our guns are firing on our own side.*
> *They should be shooting at the enemy*
> *But they're fallen short, overshot, fallen short—*
> *We're firing on our own side.*
>
> *Our officers try to comfort us,*
> *Our great Motherland loves us....*
> *Our guns are chopping up our own side,*
> *It's fallen short, overshot, fallen short—*
> *We're firing on our own side.*

These verses understandably soon became a symbol of all that was happening in the country, a symbol of the literary pogroms, repression and grievances:

> *It's fallen short, overshot, fallen short—*
> *We're firing on our own side.*

In the first year after the war, prose was elevated to a more prominent position in literature. In 1946 the brilliant war stories of Emmanuil Kazakevich and Viktor Nekrasov appeared one after another on the literary horizon. Here was the truth, the unadorned truth, destroying the falsity in the sketches of such writers as Boris Polevoy and Konstantin Simonov.

There were attempts to compromise this unadorned truth. It was called "degraded" and "trench-truth." But the truth did not yield. It kept shining with all its old brilliance.

At this point the writer in Russia was like an attacking infantryman: he had little talent and needed strong arms to push himself up from the ground. If he had no strength in his arms or courage in his heart, no matter how talented he was, he would stay lying in the dirt, afraid to lift his head or speak out!

Stalin was frightened not only by instances of insubordination in literature and in life, but even more so by Russia's historical experience. Close on the heels of the defeat of Napoleon had come the Decembrist revolt. Ryleyev's ballads had first been heard by a small circle of people, but the author together with his readers and friends had soon turned up on the Senate Square. Revolt had never been confined to literature.

The Decembrists had been a handful of individuals, Napoleon had been defeated by serfs, but now millions had been involved intelligently and in full awareness of what they were doing.

Zoshchenko, Akhmatova and half the Union of Writers could have been carted off to the camps, and would have been, if there had been any point in doing so. However, it was impossible to send away or even to identify in advance the huge stream of young people who had sworn to live and write in accordance with the dictates of their conscience. They took their oath in the name of their friends who had perished, and sometimes been murdered.

We knew a lot—too much, in fact, and therefore had become dangerous. We knew not only what life was like "under the yoke of capitalism" (the Berlin Wall came later.) That was not the point—we also knew what life was like under a different kind of yoke.

In the war I was no more than a junior officer. As far as the progress of the war was concerned, my horizons were severely limited. All the same, I saw thirty thousand men—two Siberian divisions—sacrificed near Moscow for the sake of five charred fireplaces, all that was left of a burnt-out village, just because the commander had told Stalin that the village had been taken. Soon after that this particular battle-field became one of our aerodomes, and for two whole days and nights we dragged frozen bodies off to the sides (*podsnezhniki*, or "snowdrops," they were called) so that the planes could take off and land.

Everyone knew, indeed could see for himself, that the penal battalions were being wiped out. Above the Arctic Circle, in the rugged Musta-Tunturi mountain range, the prison-soldiers were being finished off as surely as if they had been mown down by a firing squad. For four years in a row they had stormed one mountain to the cry of "Forward! For our native land and Stalin!" fully aware that the German heavy artillery had the mountain in its sights and that to try to take it head-on was senseless. For four years retreat was allowed only when there was no one left to retreat. Then a new party of prisoners would be sent up and it would all begin again. The few who somehow happened to survive had their papers stamped in red: "redeemed in blood."

In what way was Musta-Tunturi different from the brick factory in Vorkuta where for years on end political prisoners were shot and their bodies kept in stacks?

There is not a soldier from the front who did not witness the destruction of people through the obtuseness of the commanders, their heartlessness and utter indifference towards the common man. It is well-known that Stalin's stubbornness alone was responsible for the death of 750,000 men surrounded by the Germans at Kharkov.

From the regime's point of view, there was too much that the literature born on the battle-field could relate. Thousands of new writers and poets could say with Semyon Gudzenko:

> *I now rip anger from my carefree soul*
> *Like bandages...*

Stalin decided to give everyone a fright. In 1946 he had had his first stroke. What images came to haunt this murderer of millions at that time?

And so began the veritable rockfall of terrifying decisions: to bury everyone once and for all, so that there should be no question of insurrection, and in particular to bury those who were not publicly acknowledged, people nurturing their designs in silence, people it was impossible to send the Black Maria to pick up.

But a watch cannot be kept on everybody! One of Stalin's favorite books was Alexei Tolstoy's *Peter the First.* Now Stalin was afraid of a "revolt of the Streltzy" on the part of those who had returned from the front. Up to his neck in blood, he was terrified of a revolt like the one against Peter.

He thought he could see the beginnings of this revolt in the literature of unadorned truth, with which I shall commence this attempt at an investigative study.

First of all I must speak about those who, during those terrible years of the firing squads, rushed forward to meet the fire.

2. EMMANUIL KAZAKEVICH

When I met Kazakevich for the first time, I was struck by the lack of animation in his face, which was still as a death-mask. His eyes were piercingly attentive, sad and wise. His pupils behind the thick lenses of his spectacles seemed huge and wide, as if in horror. I often recall his eyes. They are a symbol to me of Kazakevich's fate as a writer.

His first story, "The Star," appeared in 1947. After the official optimism of Alexei Tolstoy's sketches in *Pravda*, the half-truths of Boris Gorbatov's Donbass sketches, after all the "lightening-conductor" plays written at Stalin's express command, such as Alexander Korneychuk's "The Front" (Stalin was trying to shift the blame onto the military commanders he had shot)—after all these half-truths and conscious falsities Kazakevich's short tale appeared to herald a new literary trend. There was no end to the enthusiasm of some and the fearfulness of others. The combination of profound poetry and truth gave the critics grounds to exclaim: "Kazakevich's star has risen."

The Soviet press made attempts to limit the significance of the story, swamping it in nonsensical stereotyped official praise.

However, the press did not succeed in representing "The Star" as being a piece of patriotic reading-matter on the war of the kind distributed by the pulp digest *Roman-gazeta*. "The Star" stood out clearly by virtue of its bitter tone in poetry. From its very first note it had the sound of a requiem: "Advancing, the division penetrated a boundless forest, and was swallowed up by it."

The almost fairytale-like melodiousness of the opening recalled the tales of the ruin of the Russian land, Prince Igor's army setting out under a bad omen (a black sun) and Yaroslavna's bitter plaint with its poetic inversion and metaphoric quality in *The Tale of Igor's Campaign*. Everything about this story is a poet's work.

> *Putting on his camouflage coat, tying up all the cords tightly— at the ankles, over the stomach, under the chin and at the back of the neck— the scout cuts himself off from wordly cares, from his superiors, or his memories. He ties grenades and a knife to his belt and puts a pistol inside the front of his coat. In this way he repudiates all human regulations and puts himself outside the law, relying from now on only himself.*
>
> *Like a bird of the forest, he has no name. He would be perfectly well able to relinquish even human speech, limiting himself to bird-calls in order to pass messages to his comrades. He merges with the fields, the woods, the gullies, becoming the spirit of these spaces—a*

dangerous spirit, lying in wait, nurturing in the depths of his mind only one thought: his task.

And so begins the age-old game in which there are only two players: man and death. (p.46)*

Literary officialdom pricked up its ears like a pack of hunting dogs. The call came: "To heel!" but they broke their leashes. It must be admitted that they had a fine sense of smell. Deep inside the book, as in a ship's hold, lay the terrible truth about the Stalin era, which has only now been noticed and generally recognized, since the appearance of Aleksandr Solzhenitsyn's *Gulag Archipelago.*

Here is an example which occurs almost in passing early in the book:

Travkin led his detachment to a lonely house on a rise. The door was opened by an old woman... she looked exactly like one of those old Ukrainian women from around Kiev or Chernigov, in numberless coarse linen skirts, with small, veined, dried-up hands. The only difference was in the unfriendly glint in her piercing eyes...

'A bandit's old lady, if ever I saw one,' muttered one of the scouts.

He was half right. The old woman's younger son had indeed followed the path of banditry into the woods. The elder one, however, had joined the Red partisans. While the bandit's mother remained in hostile silence, the partisan's mother hospitably opened the door of her cottage to the men. After giving the scouts some fried fat and some kvass in a clay jug, the partisan's mother gave way to the bandit's mother, who sat down with a glowering look at her loom, which took up half the room.

"A bandit's old lady..." Who were the young men who, although born of the same mother, followed the "bandit's path," in contrast to their own brothers? Who were the young Ukrainians—the "zapadniki" or "westerners"—who greeted the Soviet tanks with such a lack of enthusiasm, as did later the Hungarians, the Croats and the Czechs?

Even in those days faint rumors reached us of strange armed detachments which cut down both Germans and Russians. And there was a terrible fact of which we are all aware: that the Soviet Union acknowledged no prisoners! Stalin said that there were no Soviet prisoners, only traitors.

Yet, soon after the outbreak of the war, the Germans surrounded whole armies—millions of soldiers! The only ones evacuated from Mozyr were we airmen—the rest were ordered to hold out till the last man. Not far from

---

*Page numbers refer to Russian-language editions listed in the Bibliography.

Volkolamsk we liberated a camp which had only been in existence for two months, and the people who walked out of it were mere shadows in rags. We shook rusks for them out of our gas mask cases and they pounced on them like dogs on a bone. Were they traitors?

It is not those wretches who betrayed their native land, but their calculating native land which betrayed them and three times no less.

Aleksandr Solzhenitsyn was to say on this subject somewhat later:

The first time she betrayed them through incompetence, on the field of battle. It was prisoners of war whose bodies had received the enemy's blows and stopped the Wehrmacht. The second time she betrayed them heartlessly, leaving them to die in captivity. The third time she betrayed them without conscience, enticing them back with maternal love ("The Motherland forgives you! The Motherland is calling you!"), then throwing a rope around their necks as they crossed the border.

We seem to have witnessed so many vile things in the eleven hundred years of our existence as a state, but has there ever been an abomination afflicting millions to equal the betrayal of our own fighting men and the declaration that they were traitors?

This is why the nostrils of our literary watch-dogs began to quiver. They sensed what was concealed behind this strange "bandit's old lady."

They were very much afraid that the book's millions of readers ("The Star" was published in millions of copies) would pause for a moment on meeting this "bandit's old lady" and ask themselves: now, it's all one family, one peasant family which you couldn't even divide up with an axe; so why are the two brothers shooting at one another?"

This is how it is in any great literature. It is like currents in a strait. On the surface there is a layer of warm water, while below it is a completely different icy one, flowing right at the very bottom in the opposite direction.

An even franker, more obvious image, is provided in "The Star" by the investigating officer from the military prosecutor's office, Yeskin, who turns out to be correct in his suspicions about Mamochkin, the scout, failing to return the peasants' horses to the village.

Why does the reader hate this investigator so much? The pock-marked, self-confident Yeskin and rowdyish Mamochkin are not significant in themselves. What is significant is the precise moment in the narrative at which Yeskin appears.

The more threateningly death hangs over the scouts, the more thickly the bullets fly over the heads of Travkin, Mamochkin and Anikanov, who have become heroes extraordinary, the closer creeps the Soviet military tribunal in the shape of a merciless pock-marked pedant, ready, should his victims try to spring from death's grasp, to quickly tighten the noose.

How hateful these "millstones of justice" must have become, grinding through hundreds of soldiers and officers day after day, just as they were to grind through Solzhenitsyn. And what a risk it was for the author to order the narrative in the way he did.

Gogol once lamented: "the pen keeps poking into forbidden places." Kazakevich's pen had quickly veered around, like a compass needle towards the north, in an impermissible direction, mortally dangerous for an author. It pointed to a more pressing danger threatening the Soviet people from the rear, reminding it that it was not free in this war of liberation. His story "Two Men in the Steppes," which came out a year later—a year of mounting reprisals against members of the intelligentsia—was definite proof that for the author of "The Star" "Yeskinism" was secretly his main theme, arrived at as a result of his own painful experience. The heroes of Kazakevich's new story were a young lieutenant, Ogarkov and *the blind cruelty of the Stalin period*—a military tribunal which had sentenced Ogarkov to be shot.

Ogarkov is the head of a chemical warfare unit. However, in the general confusion, he is sent off urgently with a parcel to be delivered to one of the divisions, and, being a city-bred man, loses his way in the woods and fails to deliver the parcel. There are no grave consequences as a result, but for the moment the author leaves this question aside. He is more immediately concerned with the fact that Ogarkov is sitting in a dug-out waiting to be shot. From here on the narrative strays from the foreordained path of socialist realism and takes on a quality which is totally unaccustomed in officially sanctioned literature.

The Germans advance, the Russian front-line is moved back, and in the confusion Ogarkov and the soldier guarding him are simply *forgotten* and remain in a sort of no man's land. The Germans have rumbled by somewhere to one side and there is no trace of the Soviet troops at all. So the condemned man and his guard Dzhurabayev attempt to make their way back to their own side. At first Dzhurabayev pushes his condemned prisoner along with a bayonet in his back, then walks alongside him and finally fights alongside him. Dzhurabayev is wounded, and Ogarkov carries him on his shoulders. Then, when Dzhurabayev dies, Ogarkov takes his gun and papers, and together with the remnants of other units trying to break out of the German encirclement, finally reaches his own side, which to all intents and purposes had executed him.

Dzhurabayev, the soldier guarding Ogarkov, is as simple as the wind or the grass in the fields. He has the sharp ear of someone brought up in the steppes, he hears many things apart from the distant gunfire. "A crow on a poplar suddenly fell silent, perhaps it had flown away or gone to sleep. Not far away in the thick wheat there was a soft rustling noise where gophers or field-mice were running about. The chirring of crowds of insects was getting louder and louder." (106)

Our man from the steppes is kind and just. The guard commander had hinted that he should shoot Ogarkov if anything should happen, but Dzhurabayev did not take the hint and possibly did not even understand it. Instead, he shared his kasha with the condemned man, although it was brought for him alone.

Towards evening, when the sun is behind them, Ogarkov, slowly making his way eastwards, sees Dzhurabayev's shadow beside him. He feels deep dislike for this shadow, almost hatred. *Not for Dzhurabayev, but for his shadow.*

However, on a human level, quite a different relationship grows up between the two men "He could shoot me," thinks Ogarkov. "Why doesn't he?" "You have a sleep, I won't escape...I promise you..."

They go on further together, and find themselves in the middle of a skirmish where an unknown infantry lieutenant recognizes Ogarkov as an officer, pushes a machine-gun into his arms and sends him off to reconnoitre. Ogarkov thinks briefly of escape but then he thinks about the young soldier he has been given to assist him, who has unquestioning trust in him, and he thinks about the lieutenant who pushed the machine-gun into his arms. "It was much more the faith in him on the part of these men he had chanced upon than fear of Dzhurabayev's finely attuned senses and stubborness that made Ogarkov get up and go back."

He walks on towards his court-martial, "carrying the machine-gun in front of him like some fragile article belonging to someone else. His arms soon got tired, and, stealing a glance at Dzhurabayev, he rested the machine-gun on his belt.

"Suddenly Dzhurabayev asked him: 'Were you in the Komsomol?' 'Yes,' Ogarkov answered. 'Ay-ay-ay!' said Dzhurabayev woefully, meaning by this disapproval, surprise and pity."

When Ogarkov is quite alone, he is as free as a bird. His feelings are unexpected. He has lost the cursed shadow, but at the same time he has lost Dzhurabayev who had become his comrade-in-arms. He feels deprived of support and a visible goal.

However, Kazakevich would not have been the great master of the narrative he was if he had not put new temptations in the path of his condemned man, Ogarkov. These take the form of a comely peasant girl Maria, who has no objections to his staying with her, and her young neighbor, a deserter who made it back to his home and whose voice can be heard singing in the neighboring yard:

> *The golden days are beginning*
> *Of the pitch-black love of a thief.*
> *Oh, my black steeds!*

The neighbor invites Ogarkov to drink a bottle of home-brew with him and begin a new life. Ogarkov does not drink with him and tries not to listen to the drunken voice sobbing:

> *We'll flee the cursed chase,*
> *Do not sob, my sweet...* (113)

All the bridges have been blown up, but all the same Ogarkov steers a boat towards his waiting executioners, leaving the warm-hearted and affectionate Maria on the opposite bank of the river.

This is not the book's finale, but the finale of the theme so mortally dangerous for the author:

> *The boat was carried forward, and soon Ogarkov found himself in the middle of the river. The solitary figure of the woman on the bank disappeared from view.*
>
> *Looking around him, Ogarkov felt in his heart a feeling of extraordinary freedom and even happiness...*
>
> *And he wanted his mother and Dzhurabayev to see him, if only for an instant. And if little Valya, the chemistry instructor, was still alive, well, he wanted her to see him too. And the commander of the sapper battalion, and the snub-nosed lieutenant. He wanted them all to see that he wasn't a miserable fugitive.* (135)

Why was this theme of Ogarkov's return to army headquarters and his court-martial mortally dangerous for the author? Because what Kazakevich, the fearless front-line scout, was saying at a time when mass executions by firing-squad were Stalin's established policy was that *patriots were being shot, people who were faithful to Russia, to Soviet Russia, to their last breath.*

If this had been all Kazakevich said, it would still have been quite sufficient ground for having him killed. But he did not stop there. He also made a deep study of the other side to everyday life—the shadow. Not one of Kazakevich's characters believes in the humanity of the tribunal's decisions, not a single one. Nor does the author himself, "... some of the youngest officers accused the tribunal of harshness and bureaucratic pedantry."

In Yuli Daniel's "Moscow Calling" the Soviet government institutes a "Day of Open Murder." Daniel wrote this during the Khrushchev years of "liberalism"—yet it is common knowledge that his fate was to be sent to the camps. Kazakevich spoke to us not of days, but of *years* and *decades* of open murder. And he spoke of it—and it does not cease to astonish me— in 1948.

However, the question remains: is the "shadow" the tribunals? This is the notion Kazakevich's characters came to accept but not the author himself. In what could be described as an act of self-sacrifice, he proves that it is not the tribunals.

All members of the tribunal are prey to a fear of their own capacity for pity. Dzhurabayev, after fighting beside Ogarkov for the first time, becomes fond of Ogarkov. "And feeling this," the author writes, "he decided to take swift and cruel measures. He led him further, forcing himself to say: 'You come to headquarters!.'"

Dzhurabayev is of little account. The president of the tribunal, a large, stern woman with major's tabs on her collar, whose son had been killed not long before (he had been rather like Ogarkov), "looking at the tall fair-haired young lieutenant, felt a gnawing pain for one second, which she immediately squashed."

Who or what is the author's target, if it suddenly turns out that the whole tribunal, from the president to the guard Dzhurabayev, is constantly striving to stamp out all that is natural and human in itself? So they too have one eye on the shadow bearing down on them. This, then, turns out to be what the front-line scout Kazakevich was determined to write and have published at a time of mass terror.

Yet he did not stop here. Emmanuil Kazakevich spoke frankly of a worse misfortune: millions of Ogarkovs still believed in the justice of that barbarian epoch, still believed that there was a reason for imprisoning and shooting all those people. When they dragged lieutenant Ogarkov off to be executed, in effect without a trial or investigation, he considered it quite just, as he did the sentence itself. "He started to tremble, violently, helplessly. The trembling soon stopped and was replaced by dead numbness. No, he had nothing to say to the tribunal. Everything that was to happen had to happen because it was just."

It was also just that he should be shot standing beside a Baptist whose faith forbade him to take up arms. The Baptist was not about to ask for leniency if people like Ogarkov were being shot. It was only just before his death that he could not help asking Ogarkov with whom he was locked up in the dug-out: "You're one of them, on the Soviet side, what are you here for?"

Ogarkov had no doubts about the justice of the punishment being meted out to him even when he saw in the eyes of the president of the tribunal—before his case had been considered—an open hostility which surprised him. There was no point in expecting mercy here, and Ogarkov, "without reading it, signed everything he was asked to." If Ogarkov had realized that it was all a fantastic lie, would he not merely have said to himself, like millions of his contemporaries: "When wood's chopped, chips fly!"?

This is when the shadow made its presence felt, hanging densely over a whole generation and darkening its consciousness. A quarter of a century before *The Gulag Archipelago*, Emmanuil Kazakevich spoke, and, as we have seen, spoke forthrightly, of the black shadow of *The Gulag Archipelago*

25

over the country, over every one of its inhabitants.

Stalin was incensed, as not only Kazakevich was to find out. This is mentioned in the samizdat publication *Political Diary* which recently came out in the West.

It is hard to say what saved Kazakevich in that bloody year during which all his older friends from the days before the war when he was living in Birobidzhan and just starting out as a Jewish poet were arrested and then shot. He was left with the faint hope that he might be let off if he wrote a "truthful work." A year later, in 1949, in a race against time, he completed the novel *Spring on the Oder*, a fat book written in accordance with all the canons of socialist realism. The novel was awarded the Stalin prize and translated without delay into various foreign languages.

Physically Kazakevich had been saved. But the writer was no more, although he continued to write book after book.[3] His last shining hour came in 1956 when he became one of the editors of the miscellaneous collection *Literaturnaya Moskva (Literary Moscow)*, which was then in the vanguard of literary non-conformism. He died in 1962, just a few months before Solzhenitsyn's *A Day in the Life of Ivan Densiovich* came out.

Now, as I write about this genuine talent, stifled, not in a prison-camp barrack, but on the other side of the barbed-wire in a comfortable writers' apartment house, I constantly recall his face, as motionless as a death-mask and seem to see before me as in real life his piercingly attentive eyes, sad and wise, wide with horror behind the thick lenses of his spectacles.

3. VIKTOR NEKRASOV

Viktor Platonovich Nekrasov is possibly an even more surprising phenomenon than Emmanuil Kazakevich. His book *In the Trenches of Stalingrad*, which appeared in 1946, comprises a whole literary epoch in itself, and epochs, as we know, cannot be cut out of history even by a Glavlit circular.

The manuscript written on pages out of an exercise book and signed with the unknown name V. Nekrasov, by an amazing stroke of luck found its way straight to the apartment of V. Keller-Aleksandrov, who was on the editorial board of *Novy Mir (New World)*. The windows in this strange hermit's apartment were still covered with blackout-blinds from the war years, although the war had ended long before. It was as if he were screening off the Stalinist "peacetime," trying to live in the past, in some lofty regions of the mind.

Keller, a thin, ill, eccentric man, was a genius when it came to questions of style. It was to him that Aleksandr Tvardovsky first read his verse, listening to his advice and trusting in his ear.

I still remember Keller's excited falsetto over the crackling telephone: "I've come up with a manuscript. Just fished it out of the pile of stuff that had come in. It's the *real thing*."

There in Keller's apartment on god-forsaken Third Tverskaya-Yamskaya Street, barricaded in behind a triply-bolted door, I made the acquaintance of the swarthy young man of few words with sunken cheeks and a tough, mocking voice. He introduced himself as "Viktor, or just Vika" and then introduced the hero from his book, a young man with a boxer's build, called in the book Chumak, who was even more taciturn than Nekrasov.

It was an astounding period when authors would bring their wounded, but miraculously still-surviving heroes home to spend the night and busy themselves with their needs, and editors would "place" not only manuscripts but also authors, who were sometimes starving, homeless, wearing crumpled overcoats with holes burnt through them.

Keller had the manuscript typed out and persuaded Alexander Tvardovsky to read it. On reading it he straight away rang Vsevolod Vishnevsky, who had just discovered Kazakevich. The manuscript they had lit upon was talented in a wholly spontaneous way. It its verbal texture it is in complete contrast to Kazakevich's prose. There are almost no poetic tropes, none of his agitated, metaphoric prose which loses so much if retold in its bare story-line. Viktor Nekrasov's prose style is businesslike, often dry, like a diary.

Yet it is a writer's diary. All sense organs are called upon: "The rain had stopped, not a sound from the Germans. There was a smell of rotting

27

fowl's droppings. Igor and I were lying beside the left-hand machine-gun" (33). The smell of fowls' droppings gives rise to a whole range of feelings in the reader: the bullets must be whistling near peasant cottages; nearby, in a cellar or simply flattened on the cottage floors, are lying children and old women, shuddering at every shot.

What originality there is in Viktor Nekrasov's characterization. We see Maksimov, a chief staff officer, approaching. We do not even know his rank. He is a smartly dressed man with a dry manner, that is about all we know. Then suddenly we read: "At his approach everyone fell silent. In order not to appear idle—the instinctive desire to look busy in the presence of a chief staff officer—everyone crowded around the map-boards and felt for something in their pockets."

We should all know who it is who starts bustling around in this way, It is front-line infantry officers who have just been leading men into the attack, fighting at bayonet point, men in coats spattered with blood, afraid of neither God nor the devil. Afraid of neither God nor the devil, but afraid of the chief staff officer! As you can see, almost nothing is said about the officer, yet everything is said.

And not only about him. The chief staff officer is in a bad mood. He reprimands one officer for not doing up his shirt pocket and another for petty irregularities in his uniform. His questions are answered by first battalion commander Shiryayev. A section of Shiryayev's blue vest is showing from behind his open collar. "It was strange that Maksimov did not reprove him" (7), the author remarks as if in surprise. Everything is immediately clear. Shiryayev is a support, someone to rely on. He is forgiven even this. One sentence slipped in in passing becomes an element in the characterization.

Nekrasov often makes use of this device of presenting a point of view through other characters, which creates an impression with maximum effect. For example, there is a completely wordless scene in the story in which the front is being rolled back and the soldiers are retreating. The reader does not see the soldiers however, but something else: "In the doorways stand women—silent, their heavy, rough arms hanging straight at their sides. They stand in front of every house, watching us pass by. No one runs after us. They all stand and watch."

In the Trenches of Stalingrad is as multilayered as the very earth. I shall attempt to examine it like a geologist, layer after layer, going down deeper and deeper, down to the most secret, forbidden and mortally dangerous one.

On the surface, the narrative concerns the battle at Stalingrad and how heroism becomes a fact of everyday life, something which the press of the day was totally occupied with. Admittedly, the press tried to spend as little time as possible on strikingly authentic details of the kind Nekrasov supplies: "there are now a hundred men in the regiment, not more." Instead of two to three thousand... bayonets ready for action.

Here is another example. Preparations are under way for an attack and a crowd of observers arrives. Someone in command asks, taking out a little notebook: ' "And what resources do you have at your disposal?"

"I don't have resources at my disposal, I have a small group of men," Shiryayev blurted out. "The attack will be carried out by fourteen men."

Nekrasov's characters at times take even greater liberties. An electrical engineer at the Stalingrad thermal electric power-station, Georgy Akimovich—not, admittedly, a soldier—says very bluntly: "How can we fight the Germans?... The Germans came all the way from Berlin to Stalingrad without walking an inch, and here we are, lying in the trenches in jackets and overalls with 1891 model .375 rifles."

"What does all that mean?"

"It means we don't know how to fight."

"What do you mean—'don't know how,' Georgy Akimovich?"

"Knowing how to fight means being able to get from Berlin to the Volga" (83).

Later, the same universally respected character says:

> When we were up against Napoleon we also retreated, all the way to Moscow. But then we were losing only territory and in any case only a narrow strip of it. And Napoleon gained nothing except snow and burnt-out villages. But now it's different. We've lost the Ukraine and the Kuban, so we haven't got any grain. We've lost the Donbass— no coal. Baku's been cut off. Dneprostroy has been destroyed, thou- ands of factories are in German hands... Do we have the strength to overcome all that? Do you think we do?

For exactly this kind of notion, expressed in a private letter, Aleksandr Solzhenitsyn was thrown into the Gulag, and not so very long ago. Yet in the example from Nekrasov it was by no means just a question of a personal letter.

Superficially the narrative is about the inhumanity of wars, which, according to the Leninist conception, can of course be divided into just and unjust wars.

> I remember one of our men who had been killed. He was lying on his back with his arms flung out and a cigarette butt sticking to his lip. A small cigarette butt still smoking. This was the most terrible thing I saw in the whole war. More terrible than the towns destroyed, the bellies slit open, the arms and legs torn off. Those arms flung out and the cigarette on his lip. A minute before there had been life there, thoughts, desires. Now, only death.

The bombing starts. The soldiers hurriedly hide, "then clamber out, and if anyone has been killed, they bury them right there on the bank in the bomb-craters. They take the wounded to the medical unit. And they do it all calmly, with breaks for a smoke and a few jokes." *Murder had become a fact of everyday life.* They laugh, dig a grave, have a smoke and dig another grave.

This has the quality of an everyday occurrence in the stone age when men attacked mammoths with stones and were cheered if they were successful, even if somebody later had to be buried.

Let us now penetrate further, beyond the superficial level of the narrative.

Lieutenant Kerzhenetsev, who is modelled on the author, has an orderly called Valega, a remarkable young man, kind-hearted and brave. "He never talks about himself," Nekrasov writes. "All I know is that he has no mother or father... He was tried for some offense or other, he doesn't say what. He went to prison. He was let out ahead of time. He went to the war as a volunteer... " Simple-hearted Valega is one of the most attractive soldier figures in Soviet literature. Yet Valega was in prison. Who was not in danger of being imprisomed in Russia?

Nekrasov and Kazakevich, who up to this point had never set eyes on each other, were drawn to the same tragic theme from different sides and different fronts.

"A spade is as much a weapon as a rifle," says an officer cheerfully in *The Trenches of Stalingrad* to the men gathered on the river bank, "and should anyone, God forbid, lose his spade, pick or even wire-cutters, he'll be immediately courtmartialled. The men listened attentively and cut their names in the handles. They went to bed with their spades under their heads." Kazakevich brilliantly described a man being sentenced to the firing-squad for failing to deliver a parcel. Nekrasov broadens the scope: you can be shot for losing a spade, or even a pick.

Naturally enough, Valega, having served his time in prison, is by no means as simple as was thought. They pass a post with the sign "Stalingrad 6 km." The post is leaning to one side and the sign is pointing straight to the sky. "'The road to paradise,' says Valega gloomily. He turns out not to lack a sense of humor, either. I didn't know that." 'The simplest Soviet soldier, as simple as it is possible to be, is sharp-sighted, sensitive and vulnerable. This theme, approached from the point of view of lieutenant Kerzhentsev, is examined more and more closely, deeply and comprehensively.

Young men such as Valega are insulted, angered and on occasion go to pieces as a result of not only the constant intimidation but many other factors, such as, for example, the usual falsified dispatches. According to the dispatches, the enemy loses three times more and the Soviet side three times less than is really so. "On one occasion a Messerschmitt was shot down in the area of our regiment," relates Nekrasov. "Who shot it down is not known, but in the evening dispatches of *all three* batallions it was noted: 'An enemy aircraft was brought down by accurate machine-gun fire from units of the regiment.'" Consequently, three aircraft were brought down.

The atmosphere of continual lies and confusion becomes so dense at times that it even overcomes such steadfast types as Shiryayev. Once in a dugout, after a drop of vodka, he opens right up and frankly asks Kerzhentsev: "Tell me, was it ever like this in your experience during a retreat? They're saying it's all over... Everything's gone to pieces, there's nothing left. Did you ever see anything like this before? I did once see something like it..."

It causes no surprise if on occasion some soldiers lag behind in a march and then make off for their own villages (if there are villages left to go back to); Shiryayev is forced to brandish his pistol threateningly at some company commanders: "If we lose just one more man, I'll use this pistol." But it is not only soldiers who escape. An officer, Kaluzhsky, suddenly goes missing, together with a cart and a soldier. They do not drive off during an onslaught of the German panzer columns. They simply want to stay alive. "The monolith of the people," as was then the accepted phrase, was undermined, over a long period, by a stream of things battering against it: by the terror, by the ruined condition of the peasantry and by the endless "feast during the plague" in certain generals' dug-outs, hung with rugs and furnished by their aides-de-camp with so-called "campwives" (PPZh: pokhodno-polevye zheny). The desertion of Kaluzhsky, whose duties are in the rear services, supplying the upper echelons with "all the necessities" is a reflection of the disorder, callousness and self-interest at the top. Nothing affects a man as much as the example of the highest in command. Yet the majority does not run away but stays to fight to the last, although they are no better treated as a result.

We have finally reached the depths of the sub-text, which, we should note, is sometimes so obvious that the critics were struck dumb. Even to conjecture such a sub-text was like committing suicide, let alone to speak of it openly. As I have mentioned, Kharkov was Stalin's shame. The second advance at Kharkov, undertaken on Stalin's personal, and furious orders, against all the considered advice from military headquarters, led to the loss of 750,000 men. After the disaster at Kharkov, according to Marshal Bagramian, Stalin gave up direct control of operations, finally leaving them to the specialists.

In short, Kharkov was Stalin's sore spot, the Achilles heel of the genius of all times and peoples. Who would dare touch it? Viktor Nekrasov. "We must change this map of Korsakov's," he writes. "We didn't even use the new, crisp one with the big tentacled blob of Kharkov like an octopus in the left-hand corner" (13). But this is only an aside.

In a friend's dugout, "a lamp is smoking, made out of a flattened cartridge. On the wall, cut out of a newspaper, is a picture of Stalin and another young, curly-haired man with a pleasant, open face.

" 'Who is that?'

'Jack London.'

'Do you like Jack London?'

'Everyone likes him. You can't help liking him.' "

There is almost a whole page about what a fine man Jack London is, whereas Stalin is not mentioned once. Sensing that he was putting himself in a dangerous position, the author added: "There's something genuine about him [Jack London]. Even Lenin was fond of him. Krupskaya used to read Jack London to him" (138). This is almost the perfect excuse.

However, Nekrasov will not let the subject alone. The friend who had the pictures hanging on his wall, dies, and the author takes Jack London's picture from the empty dugout and hangs it in his own. "I hung London's picture above the table below the mirror." What about Stalin's picture? It stays in the abandoned dugout. Lietuenant Kerzhentsev does not take it for himself. The picture is useless. There are quite a few such episodes, and each one of them filled the hearts of the generals in charge of persuasion and punishment with quiet horror.

There was no more heretical notion at that time than the one that it was not Stalin's genius, but the mountains of corpses of Russian soldiers and, in the end, the Second Front which brought about victory.

Nekrasov expresses these ideas cautiously, it is true, as if in some doubt, like the soldiers, as to whether or not what happened in Africa could be considered a second front. He does, however, note: "In a speech on 6th November Stalin made his prophetic promise: 'It will one day be our turn to celebrate!' On 7th the allies landed in Algiers and Oran. On 13th November the Germans bombed Stalingrad for the last time, and flew away. There was a silence in the air which was incomprehensible, unfamiliar, and utterly astonishing. The Fritz had clearly run out of breath" (217-8).

Without beating about the bush for a single moment, he writes:

> Shiryayev says, without looking up: "What a strong will he's got, all the same... My God.'
>
> "Who do you mean? I don't understand."
>
> "Stalin, of course, He's been shouldering this burden for almost two years. For all of us, remember. It's all right for you. You sit in your dugout, smoke the odd cigarette, and if you don't like it, you crawl out, swear at everyone, sometimes brandish a gun... And what about him? All he's got is a map with little flags on it. It's an impossible task... Just take a look... he's got a hold on all of us."

The official critics took such fright that initially they approached the book as if it were a time-bomb.

"He's got a hold on all of us." What did the author mean when he wrote that? What was he hinting at? No one dared say it publicly, but everyone was thinking about just one thing, discussing it in whispers in the publishing houses and in the Union of Writers: it has been made clear, in black and white: "brandishing a gun."

So, according to Nekrasov, it means that Stalin has a hold on us through military tribunals, defense detachments of the NKVD, executions in front of the ranks and on the march, and battalion commanders' guns. In a word, by means of terror.

Those who had carried out the punishments knew how many millions of soldiers they had had shot and thrown into camps, both during the war and after it, when the echelons of wretched prisoners of war began to return, and how many millions had been left to rot from cold and hunger. But the official papers from the military tribunals were kept under lock and key, stamped "SS" (*Sovershenno sekretno*)—top secret.

What was to be done? Put the author on trial—in secret, of course, and quickly take the book out of circulation? Or simply not notice? It was entirely up to the powers-that-be. At any rate, a cautious, gradual campaign of abuse was begun in the press, and, during discussions and in the offices of the highly placed, the ominous words "as if" in such common usage among judicial investigators and Party-affiliated critics began to be heard. "As if" he had a hold on us through fear, or the firing squad.

Viktor Nekrasov was awarded the Stalin Prize for *In the Trenches of Stalingrad*. The reason was that bulldog-like Vsevolod Vishnevsky, enraged, had roused everybody, realizing that if he gave in to Fadeyev who had crossed Nekrasov off the list of those put up for the Stalin Prize, the young writer would be pilloried and his own head would roll. Nekrasov has vivid memories of that time. " 'You know, Stalin himself put you up for it,' Vsevelod Vishnevsky once told me, shutting the door and unplugging the telephone. Vishnevsky was editor of the journal *Znamya (The Banner)* in which I had published. "On the last night. The type had to be reset in the newspapers.'

However, such a heretical text was not republished anywhere. It remained as it was only in the tenth issue of *Znamya* for 1946. The mountain of prize-winning editions which followed buried the dangerous original version once and for all. Just one year later, in the 1947 edition put out by *Moskovsky rabochiy*, a publishing house directed by the well-intentioned Chagin, whose protege Sergei Esenin had been, certain changes had been made: the fateful phrase "has got a hold on us all" had been clarified: "Just take a look here—he's holding... holding... the whole front." And although the novel came out in a separate edition two years after the end of the war, the editor, for safety's sake, gave Shiryayev a little extra faith and perspicacity: "and he [Stalin] will lead us to victory. You'll see, he'll lead us to victory."

If the *Znamya* text and the 1947 text are compared, it becomes apparent that the latter has been rewritten, indeed plowed over, by the editor. Viktor Nekrasov even gave a whistle in surprise when not long ago I showed him the two texts. At that time the author of the first text would not have suspected that anyone would dare to "improve" him in such a way.

Now, with the passage of years, one realizes very clearly that Viktor Nekrasov was literally walking along a knife-edge. He did not omit a single dangerous theme, not a single one...

At a time when the orgy of Stalin's official chauvinism was under way, the author purposely introduced a principal character with the name of Farber and even described in detail how this Farber "felt his inadequacy especially keenly." Admittedly, Farber at once edged the conversation in a different direction, claiming that he was envious of Shiryayev's strength and agility.

However, in order to ensure that the reader—the thoughtful reader—did not allow himself to be edged in a different direction and remained aware of the trend of the subtext, Nekrasov describes a conversation between Kerzhentsev and the bluntly truthful scout Chumak: "Tell me about the tanks. What's the name of that second fellow who scored a hit?" asks Kershentsev. "Korf," answers Chumak. "A private?" "Yes." "Was it his first tank?" asked Kerzhentsev, pursuing the question. "No, his fourth. The first three were near Kastornaya." "Any decoration?" "No." "Why not?" "Buggered if I know. A case was put up..." Nekrasov is fearlessly informing us, in 1946 of all years, that people with non-Russian names fighting the fascists were sometimes in an uncomfortable position.

At this new deep level almost everything is a matter of allusion, innuendo, seemingly chance retorts, comprehensible, it should be added, to everyone in Russia thirsting for the truth.

In these scenes Viktor Nekrasov attained his full stature as a Russian writer and as a Russian with an ardent loathing for the Great Russian chauvinism whipped up by Stalin. This was the Nekrasov who was later to stir up the whole country with his public protest against the Kievan Pompadours intending to turn Baby Yar into a Park of Culture and Rest.

"A bell has been erected in Buchenwald," he wrote in *Literaturnaya gazeta* in 1959, "whose tolling is meant to warn against any repetition of what happened. And in Kiev? Is there to be dancing on the graves of those who were shot?"

As the book comes to its conclusion, the reader finds himself penetrating into depths of the sub-text which the critics did not simply tip-toe around, but fled around with their eyes screwed up tightly.

Is it by accident that the concluding episode in the book is the bloody slaughter staged by the dim-witted chief of staff Abrosimov, a cruel, hysterical man? This is the last emotional, psychological blow struck. Its place in the narrative is calculated with the same precision with which the sapper Kerzhentsev defused bombs—one false move and you're dead.

Shiryayev is preparing an assault. The enemy is so close that the Germans and Russians are using the same lines of communication. Shiryayev and Kerzhentsev decide to blow up the defensive works dividing the passages and force their way into the German trenches without emerging on the surface where they would be at the mercy of the German guns firing at point-blank range.

As they reach the section they are to blow up, Abrosimov runs up to them.

He was breathing heavily and licking his parched lips with his tongue.

"Well, are you bastards going to fight or not?"

"Yes, we are," answered Shiryayev calmly. "Let me explain."

Abrasimov went crimson.

"I'll do the explaining..." He clutched his holster.

"Forward into the attack! ... Aren't you attacking?"

"The attack's misfired because..."

"I'm not asking why..." and he suddenly went wild again and waved his gun in the air. "Forward into the attack! I'll shoot you for cowardice—why aren't you carrying out orders^"

I thought he was going to collapse in convulsions.

"All officers forward! You, forward! I'll show you how to save your skins... You think you can just sit in the trenches..."

Almost immediately we were laid flat by machine-gun fire. The man running at my side fell flat immediately, his arms flung out wide in front of him.

The Germans did not fall silent for a second. You could make out quite distinctly the gunner turning the machine-gun, fan-like, from right to left, from left to right.

When we take into account the numerous episodes such as the map of Kharkov, the pictures of Stalin and Jack London, Shiryayev's remarks the "He's got a hold on us all..." and others, we realize that in those terrible years Viktor Nekrasov was passing judgment on something no one could presume to judge—Stalin's methods and Stalin's disciples, personified by Abrosimov. He alludes transparently—too transparently for his own survival—to those to whom Russia was obliged for the death of twenty million people.

On the surface we have the destructiveness and harmfulness of every-day experience and popular heroism, and at the bottom we have the deeply hidden revolt against the misanthropic idea of the "cog-man," to whose health "the great organizer of our victories, comrade Stalin" had just drunk a toast.

If I may be permitted to compare the courage of the two writers, Kazakevich and Nekrasov, both pressing forward to brave the fire, I think that the army scout Kazakevich realized more clearly what was awaiting him. In those days Nekrasov reminded me of a carefree young Kievan lad running out of a forest into a meadow, not fully realizing yet that the meadow was actually a mine-field.

But it is Nekrasov who proved the stronger. Kazakevich was broken, whereas Nekrasov was not, right up until the last. When they tore the pen out of his hand, withdrew from circulation and impounded everything he had written, and twisted his arm, he broke free and emigrated. He broke free to carry on the fight.

Here I should like to put a full stop. It is tempting to put one. But in that case, the main question would remain in the dark, a question which no commentator on the literature of resistance has the right to circumvent, especially a commentator on works which were published in the dying days of the Stalin era when almost everyone felt he was in a column of political prisoners—"left, right, left, right, there's no escape, the guards will shoot without warning." The question is: how could books such as these appear at all? To what measures, intentionall or half-consciously, did their authors have recourse to get around the censors? Not just the literary editors, but also the reactionary military censors—all books concerning the war were sent without exception not just to the usual political censors, Glavlit, but to the military ones as well, to prevent the author or poet letting slip some military secret (or so it was claimed). How did anti-Stalin books manage to break through the defense lines of Stalinist censorship?

The authors had their own simple devices of which the thoughtful Russian reader was well aware.

The devices were simple, unsubtle, as simple and unsubtle as the clearly stated prohibitions, or as a barbed-wire fence:

1. *No generalization*

How can there be any question of generalization, when things are different for us from what they are for other people? Viktor Nekrasov seems to ask us, with his tough smile, as if to forestall criticism. "Our regiment is out of luck. We've only been here for a bloody month and a half and we've got no men left and no guns." Naturally, everything is going fine for other people: "A long column of vehicles went by with small anti-tank guns bouncing over the pot-holes. The vehicles had an unusually well-made look about them...*The weren't ours*... Tanned, bearded faces were looking out."

And soon afterwards, when life has become completely unbearable for Nekrasov's characters, and the countryside is the tormenting, depressing countryside of the steppes, and "the heat is so stupefying it addles the brain, new units appeared on their way to the front, well turned-out, with submachine guns and helmets. The officers were wearing squeaky yellow rifleslings and new map-cases smacked against their sides. The Siberians gave us a slightly ironical look."

Everything was obviously in these green-helmeted Siberians' favor... Even the heat was in their favor. They were not us.

2 *Show the leading role of the Party*

When it came to this question, Stalin did not even spare his favorite, Alexander Fadeyev, making him rewrite his novel *The Young Guard*. In its original version the novel calumnied many people, especially one of the leaders of the Young Guard, the heroic Tretyakevich (the traitor Stakhovich in the novel) but after it had been rewritten it became boundlessly mendacious: the Krasnodon Party underground which was in fact betrayed by the Gestapo within hours of the German occupation, was reborn at the behest of Fadeyev's pen and took up its leading role again.

In what way did Viktor Nekrasov, officer in the trenches, writing his first book in a military hospital, perceive the danger? Apparently not so much rationally as "with a Russian's flogged back," to use the classic expression, he sensed beforehand the rusty barbed-wire of censorship and attempted to defeat it with minimal losses for the artistic fabric of his story.

> *"Things are bloody awful," said one of the men we met, briefly, "the regiment's in a corner."*
> *We said nothing.*
> *"The major's been killed... so has the commissar."*

Twelve pages later we read again, unexpectedly: "I heard the major and the commissar were killed." Five pages later we read again, apropos of nothing at all: "They say the major and the commissar have been killed." Yet the restive Nekrasov cannot hold out against external pressure and immediately adds: "The commissar was killed. Maksimov seems to have been surrounded. It's a pity about him, he was a bright lad. An engineer, after..." So it turns out that although the commissar was killed no one is sorry about him, the representative of the Party leadership, but they are sorry for Maksimov, who was a bright lad.

It would have been better if Nekrasov had not been forced to make insertions. However, the demand that there be a Party commissar involved in the battles was beyond discussion. Either there was a commissar or the manuscript would never become a book.

But Nekrasov does not stop there. He cannot resist saying a few words about so-called "Observers." He describes the following striking scene:

> *It was crowded in the cellar, you couldn't even turn around. There were two representatives of the political section. One was from divisional headquarters. The regimental communications chief. They were observers. I understood the necessity for their presence, but they irritated me.*

Finally, Kerzhentsev asks everyone not taking part in the attack to leave the dugout.

> *The captain's 'the observer' eyes became round. He put aside the newspaper.*
>
> *"Why?"*
>
> *"Because."*
>
> *"I would ask you to remember that I am your superior."*
>
> *"I remember, but I'm asking you to leave, that's all."*
>
> *"Am I in your way?"*
>
> *"Yes, you are."*
>
> *"In what way?"*
>
> *"By being here. By smoking. Can't you see what's happening? We can't breathe. I think I'm beginning to sound stupid..."*

The captain does not go away, but the author has taken the bit between his teeth.

> *"So you intend staying here, do you?"*
>
> *"Yes, that's my intention."*
>
> *"And will you also attack the hill with us?"*
>
> *He looked at me fixedly, without blinking, for a few seconds. Then he made a show of getting up, neatly folding his newspaper, and putting it in his map-case. Turning to me, slowly and carefully pronouncing each word, he said:*
>
> *"Very well. We'll discuss this further elsewhere." And he started crawling out through the slit trench. On the way he caught his bag on a nail and for a long time could not detach it.* (160)

For the reader, this is no longer a mere "detail."

"They're fine chaps," remarks the author in passing, about the representatives of the political section, "they realize that questions are out of place at this moment, and quietly go about their own business."

The "fine chaps," naturally, have a good laugh as they watch the captain trying to detach himself from the nail. They're human beings!... "I had nothing against them," Kerzhentsev-Nekrasov adds hurriedly. "But I couldn't just send out the captain. They laughed understandingly and, wishing us good luck, went out.

"We immediately felt freer in the dugout."

In the same good-humored way, he tells the story of Senechka, the regiment's political "agitator," the lowliest worker in the political propaganda outfit, a common soldier like everyone else. Senechka makes a dummy of Hitler and hoists it above the parapet, the Germans shoot at Hitler and and the soldiers have a good laugh. They said that Nekrasov would not get away with sending the Party representatives out of the dug-out, and that Senechka could not swing the balance in his favor.

No other Soviet writer had the courage to write what Nekrasov did

—not a single one! Six hundred Soviet writers at that time were either in prison-camps or else already buried with a prison tag on their ankle. Viktor Nekrasov had the courage.

3. *Vice is punished, virtue triumphs*

... or, as the Minister of Culture N. Furtseva was to formulate it rather simple-mindedly: *the ending must be good.*

In Nekrasov's story, chief of staff Abrosimov, after the attack for which he was criminally to blame, is tried and sent to a punititive battalion. That is as it should be, and it is unthinkable for it to be otherwise.

However, from the reader's point of view, this is not a real part of the story. Evil is not extirpated: those not shot by the Nazis are killed off by the Abrosimovs, by stupidity, fear, hysteria, callousness and the right to "clutch the holster."

How was "Two Men in the Steppe," which revealed the truth of the Stalin era, received in the West? Was it at least noticed that more had been said in the story than the author had meant to say? Was it noticed, for example, that Kerzhentsev-Nekrasov's opposites, both the admirable Shiryayev and the criminal Abrosimov, had the right to execute without trial—"to brandish a gun"—and by no means only during combat? (Court-martialling was used to intimidate characters of secondary importance only.)

It was Konstantin Simonov, Secretary of the Union of Writers of the USSR, who was elevated at that time to the position of official favorite. He was sent on a trip to America along with quantities of his doctored Stalinist fiction. (Simonov's artistic method has been accurately described, on the basis of the way he has operated over the last twenty-five years, as "being the first to rush into a field cleared of mines.") The newspapers gave all the glory to Simonov. Yet his novel *Days and Nights* was essentially a smoke-screen.

The whole thing was a successful maneuver engineered by the Propaganda Section of the Central Committee of the CPSU. Even in the United States, where there were people following the latest works in Soviet literature with sympathetic interest, comments such as this were made: "Towards the end of the year Victor Nekrasov's novel *Stalingrad* appeared, although to a large extent it repeats and reinforces the mood of Simonov's *Days and Nights...*" They had separated the wheat from the chaff, as the saying goes.

4. UP AGAINST THE MEASURING STICK: V. PANOVA PARDONED, V. GROSSMAN CONDEMNED, MASS EXECUTION OF JEWISH WRITERS, ELECTION OF ILYA EHRENBURG

"How are you getting on?" I once asked the writer K. in the winter of 1949. He was in fact doing well, and is to this day.

"The same as everyone else!" he replied with that liveliness natives of Odessa have. "With my back up against the measuring stick." We were walking across the deserted Moskvoretsky Bridge with the icy wind whistling around us. Looking around from time to time to see if we were being overheard, he explained what he meant. In a concentration camp near Weimar there was a measuring stick on the wall with an opening in it for a gun-barrel. The prisoner would be stood up against it as if to measure his height. Then he would be shot in the back of the neck. "I'm in the same position. You publish something. You're stood up against the measuring stick. You wait in a cold sweat to see whether they're measuring you for a prize—first, second or third—or whether a shot will ring out."

Vera Panova was stood up against this measuring stick. Her novel, *Kruzhilikha* (1947) is unlikely to be remembered by literary historians for its excellence as a work of art. It will remain however a landmark in the history of courageous and honest social thought.

Vera Panova is no longer with us and there is no one to separate the wheat from the chaff—the flabby publicistic insertions prompted by fear or the obligatory social realist *heppi-end* (happy ending) in which virtue triumphs. This is a pity. In *Kruzhilikha* Panova drew close to Nekrasov and Kazakevich.

The first time I had a conversation with Panova was one night in the gardens of the writers' retreat house in Koktebel in 1966. My routine skirmish with Party officials in Moscow was just over. The woman on duty that night brought me a note. It was from Vera Panova. I went to the gardens as if to a tryst.

"What are you doing?" she asked urgently. "What you're up against is so huge. They'll run right over you and not even look back..." Her lips were trembling and her face was bloodless and white. It was the face of someone who was frightened to death. I was stunned. Who would not have been?

When one looks carefully at Vera Panova's portrait one realizes that she is a person of complexity and strength. There is a direct, penetrating look in her gray eyes. It is an unyielding, imperious look. It was strange that she should have been in such a state at that time, in 1966, when both Stalin and Khrushchev had been swept away and, as it seemed, neither she nor anyone else was under any particular threat. Perhaps she had never been

41

as fearless as people had thought. If so, this only made her determination to tread forbidden paths all the more courageous.

In 1948, she forced the thoughtful reader to reflect on the *new class.* This was long before Djilas came out with his world-renowned study of the new class. This "leading"class of bureaucrats ruining the country was first whispered about in university lecture-halls—as was natural in a country where the expressions "class warfare" and "class hatred" had been appearing in newspapers and heard over the airwaves for half a century. There was some attempt, admittedly, as a precautionary measure, not to use the word "class" in such an unusual context.

In 1944 Panova was living in the Urals in a city which had always been called Perm and was then renamed Molotov. In a suburb of Perm called Motovilihka there are gigantic factories. Here in Motovilikha Vera Panova began her novel *Kruzhilikha.* "Although I had written a number of things in my time," she tells in her autobiography, "it was here that I realized for the first time how difficult a writer's work is, and how sweet."

The first note struck in *Kruzhilikha* is this: Uzdechkin, a trade union leader, declares in the presence of the city authorities: "Common consent counts for nothing here. What we have is a *director's autocracy.*" This reference to an autocratic director (the book's main character) at a time of Stalinist autocracy was not a coincidence or accidental allusion: all the leaders in *Kruzhilikha* are petty autocrats. Even the chief engineer, Vladimir Ippolitovich "was capable of dismissing a man without warning or explanation, for the slightest act of carelessness, some trivial oversight, or simply a whim."

But let us begin with the main character, the almost legendary hero Listopad. Listopad's autocratic nature is brought to light purposefully and masterfully by means of the device of *laying bare*, on all sides and all levels. He cannot bear Uzdechkin. "Listopad was told that Uzdechkin had suffered a great misfortune: his wife had gone to the front as a medical orderly, and had been killed at the very beginning of the war. He had been left with two little girls, an older boy, his brother-in-law and his sick and aged mother-in-law. In his domestic life Uzdechkin was a martyr. Listopad was indifferent to these stories because he did not like Uzdechkin."

That is straightforward. But that is not all there is to it. Listopad is not indifferent only to the fate of people he finds unpleasant. He loves his young wife Klavdia. Misfortune strikes when Klavdia dies during childbirth. She leaves some diaries which she kept in shorthand so that no one could read them. At his request, Listopad's secretary deciphers the diaries, and it transpires that Klavdia was desperately lonely. She lived with a man for whom she did not really exist. "I come last," she wrote, for no one but herself. "If I die, he'll get by without me perfectly well."

Once, when he comes back from the factory and goes straight to sleep, Klavdia asks him out loud if perhaps he does not love her. "I was happy without you, with you I am unhappy... Why did you marry me?... Forgive me if I am asking more than I should, but I can't live without happiness." These are the last lines in Klavdia's diary. Listopad's secretary does not show them to the great potentate—why disturb his Excellency?

It is possible that Listopad actually did not love his young wife, who was so far removed from his all-consuming concerns. Such situations do arise. However, he really does love his mother, of that there is no doubt. He often remembers her and his childhood, the village and the haymaking, as bright spots, feast-days, as it were, in a hard life. He is very excited at the prospect of his mother's arrival on a visit. When she arrives he asks her to spend the whole summer with him. "The summer? There's no doubt about you, Sashko!" his mother answers, surprised. "The harvest starts in two weeks, I'm head of the kolkhoz—although you haven't asked me anything about it, or about Oleksy either." (Oleksy is his blind step-father.)

In each chapter Panova confronts Listopad with people who are close to him. As we have seen, he is intolerant of Uzdechkin. Towards his wife he is inattentive—it is not by accident that her diary is deciphered only after her death. Panova, however, goes all the way. Listopad is no less inattentive and indifferent to those closest to him—to his mother and his step-father—than he is to Uzdechkin. He cannot even bring himself to ask his mother about her life and whether she has need of anything.

Vera Panova, it appears, was taking a searching look at the positive hero of the Stalinist era, the darling of the Party, the hero of whom the Party regional committee and Moscow were so proud. And what did she choose to accentuate, what did she consider the dominant strain in this type, his very core? What did she choose to describe in rich detail, with abundant talent and merciless precision? *The hero's callousness and inhumanity and what we might call his moral deafness.* Those who are most drawn to Listopad and happiest with him are the swindlers—his driver, Mirzoyev, for instance, who takes generous liberties with the director's car and lives in clover, and the representatives of the Party machine who, like the swindler Morzoyev, idolize him and shield him as much as they can, while living like kings themselves. Are they too, then, criminally self-interested? Do they find his power convenient, even if it is immoral and inhumane?

Naturally, Panova is unable to touch on these questions directly. For this reason Ryabukhin, the enormously powerful Party Secretary at the factory, abuses Listopad just to observe the niceties: "You're a selfish bastard, you know, but I like you—God knows why." Looking for a path through the mine-field of her own creation, Panova thinks up an amusing motif: Ryabukhin suffered shell-shock during the war and went blind temporarily, and when he could first see again, "all the faces around him appeared beautiful."

The representative of the people is Lukashin, an ex-soldier, utterly honest, quiet-mannered, hard-working and unrecognized in terms of medals and decorations. Panova constantly emphasizes that it is Lukashin who is the personification of the people in *Kruzhilikha*. In her autobiography which came out in 1968, twenty years after *Kruzhilikha* was published, she speaks of it directly: "While Listopad and Uzdechkin are fighting each other, Lukashin is always right there, not getting involved in the argument, but reminding them: "Comrades, comrades, I am here too..."

His voice goes unheeded, of course. Lukashin is a kind of "Tyorkin in the other world," who appeared in this world long before Tvardovsky's work of this name came out. But Panova's is an unsmiling, sad Tyorkin.

Yet the novel seems to have been written according to the canons of socialist realism. Consequently there must be some realistic motivation for the people's voicelessness. Just why does Lukashin not fight evil? Is he powerless in the face of moral turpitude? What exactly is wrong with the hero who personified the people? "He was butted by a cow when he was a child," answer the people from his village (250). What did Vera Panova mean by this: the Tartar invasion, the Revolution, the years of terror and mass deportation of the peasantry? She leaves a space for the reader's imagination to fill in.

The author tells how Listopad and his ilk are held aloft by the mass of the people; by the rural and semi-rural working people, eternally holding their peace; by an intelligentsia accustomed to arbitrary rule; and by the indomitable Uzdechkin, the character who brings on, and completes, the disclosure of the moral bankruptcy of the period. All of a sudden it becomes plain that the heroically honest, incorruptible Uzdechkin, guardian of the people, militant defender of the kitchen-garden and the pension, a respected man, elected by the people, is as heard-hearted as his opposite, Listopad, the Stalinist hero.

Admittedly, Uzdechkin's hardness is not something reasoned out consciously or cynically like Listopad's—Listopad declares that it is important to know how to live "in clover." It is in his heart that Uzdechkin is hard, his tortured heart, weary from being pestered on all sides, from the debasement of hunger and poverty, both on the land and in the factory. He is hard-hearted even to Tolik, his dead wife's little brother, who silently cries at his relatives' lack of concern. It is perhaps this image of Uzdechkin, a sick, suffering man, "promoted by his people" according to his merits to a responsible position, which constitutes Panova's heaviest blow at the system which dries up and deadens even people such as him.

And Ryabukhin, the Party luminary, symbol of the Party at the factory, who bathes all Kruzhilikha in light and speaks in some kind of monstrous, half-peasant, half-official goobledygook is hard-hearted too. In fact, every single one of those who run Kruzhilikha is callous and merciless towards those close to him. Objectively speaking, their affinity to one another, like Nekrasov's antiheroes', is the product of the cruel times they lived in. This was the truth of the epoch as Vera Panova saw it and described it from 1944 to 1947, years of mass reprisals.

Naturally, attempts were made to take reprisals against her without delay. In the satirical weekly *Krokodil (The Crocodile)* a mocking feuilleton entitled "Speshilikha" (a play on the words "Kruzhilikha" and "speshka"—rush) appeared in which *Kruzhilikha* was completely demolished. Panova was a Stalin Prize-winner (for her story "Fellow Travellers") and the tone *Krokodil* adopted was not customarily adopted with Stalin Prize-winners. At times it was impossible to make any courageous gesture at all. It was obvious that the attack had been inspired by the Propaganda Section of the Party's Central Committee, if not by someone at a higher level. Publication of Panova's works was brought to a halt. At public lectures "members of the public" began to ask questions such as: How long will this Panova's odious slander be tolerated? Why is Panova still at large, since she has slandered the people and the Party?

Panova did not wait for the Black Maria to arrive. She was well aware how these things were handled in autocratic Russia. She wrote a letter addressed to the "highest name" in the land, and, through Alexander Poskryobyshev, Stalin's secretary, succeeded in having it delivered to Stalin. As a rule Stalin did not respond to writers' complaints, although he made a small number of exceptions as in the case of Gorky, Bulgakov and a few others. But he could on occasion be "responsive" to the appeals of women writers. Not long before Panova, Vera Inber had sought his protection, and he had "protected her from attempts to cause her harm." Like an Eastern despot, Stalin did not regard women as having equal rights with men. Nor, of course, was he afraid of them. Just as Kazakevich was, of course, a broken man after the attack on his "Two Men in the Steppe," Panova was a changed woman after *Kruzhilikha* appeared. As late as the sixties her lips would tremble whenever she thought of the State machine which had raised her to such heights by means of a prize.

Panova's victory was certainly a strange one. Two years after being awarded the Stalin Prize for her novel *Kruzhilikha* an abusive "letter to the editor" appeared in the press. This was a recognized form of punitive action. Then on 21 September 1950 in an article called "The writer's skill" Vera Panova, Stalin Prize-winner, was forced to defend herself from speeches made at public meetings by "prominent lathe-operators" who for some reason could not forgive her, not the lathe-turner in her novel, but the high official, Listopad. It became more and more difficult to speak out against these prominent lathe-turners as it did against Vsevolod Kochetov, who was at that time still far from prominent. The criticism of *Kruzhilikha* was such that it seemed to be about an entirely different book. Indeed the book actually appeared to be changing from day to day.[5]

It was not Panova's book which had changed—the times had changed, and they had changed with Stalinist abruptness. This was most evident in the devastating assault on Vasily Grossman's novel *In a Just Cause* published in *Novy Mir* in 1952.

To all appearances it was a novel about the war and nothing else. However, from time to time themes showed through which had been aired for the first time in post-war literature by Vera Panova and were intolerable to Stalin—themes touching on the social stratification in Soviet society. Here are two illustrative episodes.

Colonel Krymov is on his way to the front. He drives up to a crossing crammed with people fleeing from the Germans. At the crossing a general "opened the door of his car and shouted at the crowd striding across the bridge: 'Where do you think you're going? Get out of the road! Let me through!' "

"An old peasant, leaning on the mud-guard of the car, said with unusual good humor but just a slight note of reproach, as he would to another peasant: 'Where do we think we're going? You can see for yourself—we're going the same place you're going. Everyone wants to stay alive...' "

"And there was something in the good-natured way this peasant fleeing from the Germans spoke which made the general hurriedly slam the door without saying anything."

Now the panic starts, and there is a ruthless rush for the crossing. Krymov, although he is going to the front and not away from it, and therefore has right of way, stamps his foot and yells at the driver to go faster. This is how Grossman describes this seemingly unremarkable event:

> There were two Red Army soldiers standing on a flat pontoon leaning against the planking of the bridge. Even the sappers and the men controlling the crossing considered these men's work difficult because they came under fire more and got hit by more fragments than those working on the bank. You just couldn't protect yourself from the fragments working in the middle of the river on thin-sided pontoons.
>
> When Krymov called out impatiently to the driver, one of the men on the pontoon said to the other: "The easy way?" He had in mind, apparently, not just those who travelled at their ease in civilian vehicles, but those who were looking for an easy way out of the war so that they could have a nice long life.
>
> Without any hint of condemnation, the second man agreed: "He's in a hurry to stay alive."

What an uproar followed the appearance of Grossman's novel. Newspaper headlines cried: "On an erroneous path!" The well-known pogrom organizer Mikhail Bubennov sent a letter to Stalin about Grossman's novel. This episode, one of hundreds, is interesting because it points straight to the ultimate organizer of all political murders. The whole country wrote to Stalin. Tortured and bleeding, Russia turned to her torturer for the truth and protection. Whole mail-vans of letters were sent to Stalin. No government office could deal with such an enormous flood, and a large number of the letters was burnt. I was told about this in shocked amazement by a literary friend of mine and at that time serving in the Kremlin guard. Although it was many years later, his voice still shook with emotion as he told me how thousands of *unopened* envelopes bearing the sacred name and address of "Comrade Joseph Vissarionovich Stalin, The Kremlin, Moscow" were thrown into the fire. But Mikhail Bubennov's letter reached Stalin's desk the very day he sent it. At *Pravda*, where the letter was quickly sent from the Kremlin, they were afraid to touch the text, even to the extent of putting in a comma which should have been there. They later said with the ecstasy of loyal subjects: "it wasn't Bubennov's version any longer." After Stalin himself had read it with a pencil in his hand, it was already an historical, inviolable text like the national anthem.

Novy mir, which had published Grossman's novel, quickly dissociated itself from its author and made protestations of sorrow and remorse. The irony is that this happened on 5 March 1953, the day Stalin died, while Fadeyev went into a rage demanding that the guilty be crucified three weeks after the tyrant's death, on 28 March. Stalin had inspired a fear which was to last for decades.

Vasily Grossman was torn to shreds, as Solzhenitsyn was to be years later. Some time later all seventeen copies of the manuscript of the second part of his novel about Stalingrad were seized and impounded. This was more than he could endure. Not long after he died of cancer, although he managed to strike a last blow at his tormentors in a work which came out after his death, "Forever Flowing." We shall speak of this story later.

Vasily Grossman's tragic experience saved from destruction the manuscripts of many Soviet writers writing in secret and nurturing hopes for the future. They hid their manuscripts safely away again. For Grossman there was no mercy. The trials and the mass murder of writers writing in Yiddish had recently taken place. These facts are so well-known that I would not spend time on them if it were not for one circumstance which has gone unnoticed by literary scholars. While fiercely hating one group of writers, the literary establishment wiped out a completely different group, on the basis of their social or ethnic connections. Stalin, for example, was infuriated by certain Russian writers, including many not of Russian origin. Pilnyak, Babel, Grossman and Kazakevich, for example, at times directed all their creative energies against the butcher's dictatorship, although not always consciously. Yet in his chauvinism and antisemitism, Stalin angrily executed not the seditious writers but loyal Jewish poets and writers such as

Perets Markish, Fefer and Kvitko who had in fact glorified the Stalin epoch, the Kolkhozes and the shock-brigades. On 12 August 1952, on Stalin's orders, large numbers of Yiddish writers and poets, loyal to the regime and members of the Jewish Antifascist Committee, were taken off to camp and shot. This was an unexpected *quid pro quo.*

"A great writer is like a second government," Solzhenitsyn was fond of repeating. Ilya Ehrenburg found such a burden beyond him and did not take it on. Both his personality and his works were complicated, contradictory and, with few exceptions, bore all the signs of appeasement and compromise. His efforts were directed at surviving. However, the pogrom victims had no one else to turn to—Stalin did not reply to them—and so they wrote to Ehrenburg. His dacha at Novy Iyerusalim (New Jerusalem) outside Moscow was crammed full, almost up to the roof with letters from those who had been trampled on and abused. What could he do? He published an article in *Pravda,* begging people not to be surprised at the spiritual unity of those being attacked: "If tomorrow persecution were to begin of people with red hair or snub noses, we would witness the uniting together of people with red hair and snub noses." He passed on to the Central Committee of the Communist Party several horrifying letters including, as I remember, one from the neighbors of a Russian woman who was a cleaner. On reading in the newspaper that her husband was an "evil cosmopolitan," she went mad and axed to death her cosmopolitan husband, monster that he was with his non-Russian blood, and their three children. In the snowy depths of Russia, where it was the custom to believe the printed word, tragedies more terrible than Shakespeare's were being enacted.

Yet even Ehrenburg's timid intervention provoked the fury of the professional murderers. At a meeting of newspaper editors, the Director of the Cultural Section of the Central Committee of the Party Golovenchenko announced to resounding applause that "this morning, enemy of the people, cosmopolitan No.1, Ilya Ehrenburg was arrested." However, Golovenchenko had been in too much of a hurry and had not checked his information. Such haste was unforgiveable—Stalin did not like the machine to run on ahead. One of the editors rang Ehrenburg's apartment from the meeting and found him home. Ehrenburg in his turn rang Stalin and demanded that he be allowed to speak to him, and the recent winner of the International Stalin Prize was not refused his request. Golovenchenko suffered a heart-attack in his office on Staraya Square and it was then that Lev Kassil's witticism made the rounds of Moscow: "so *they* too have heart-attacks."

The mountains of letters and the streams of sorrow had some effect for Ilya Ehrenburg found the strength to stand firm and disobey Stalin.

On 30 April 1953, the day the "doctor murderers" were to be hanged on the traditional Lobnoye mesto, or place of execution, on Red Square, while newly-build barracks in Siberia, Kazakhstan and the Hungry Steppe were awaiting the arrival of the deported Jewish population of the USSR, there was a gathering of so-called "State-Jews" (Jews with responsible positions in State organizations) at the *Pravda* offices. They were to sign their names to an article approving of the deportation of all Jews, including babes in arms, in order to "save them from the people's wrath."

Lev Kassil, who followed the poet Dolmatovsky, the Party historian Mints and others, in signing this document ("Well, what else could we do?" he grumbled sadly), tells how Ehrenburg got up and, staggering over people's feet, made his way out of the room. He was the only one there who did not sign. Everyone looked at him in horror as if he were someone falling out of the window of a sky-scraper. Ilya Ehrenburg later gave an account of what he had gone through during those minutes when he first decided to oppose Stalin's will—that is to say, to die. "I thought they'd get me right there at the door of the conference room, but I looked, and there was no one in the corridor. They'll be in the cloakroom, then, I thought. No, they just gave me my coat. I went out and told the driver: 'Take me to the dacha by the longest route.' " In the car Ehrenburg wrote a letter which was to be his last will and testament, never for a moment doubting that they would come for him at the dacha.

That day Ehrenburg committed the greatest act of self-sacrifice of his life: he voluntarily chose death. However, perhaps because it was not reported to Stalin that someone had dared oppose his plan, Ehrenburg stayed alive. Towards the end of his life his moral fibre stiffened and this casts a more favorable light over his life as a whole.

5. THE HATCHET-MEN

The appearance of a courageous book in the USSR is like the escape of a dangerous prisoner from jail. The alarm is sounded, the chase begins, the dogs are set loose. Successful escapes, as we have seen, are rare, and the remaining prisoners are locked up even more securely. The First All-Union Conference of Young Writers was called in 1947 as part of this process. The Secretaries of the Central Committee of the Komsomol made their offices on Staraya Square available to the delegates, and no expense was spared. The quiet crowd of young people in fresh loose-fitting shirts sat and looked up at the imposingly handsome figure of Alexander Fadeyev with his graying temples as he revealed to them the very basis of socialist realism: "We must show Soviet man truthfully and show him as he *ought to be*, throwing light on his future." He rustled his sheets of paper as he rustled them throughout these years, at plenary sessions and conferences; after the first State-directed hail of rocks he was promoted to General Secretary, in place of the Leningrad poet of the blockade, Nikolay Tikhonov, who had not been firm enough. "An apple, as it is found in nature, is a rather bitter fruit. An apple grown in a garden is both a real apple and at the same time as an apple should be," declared Fadayev, theorizing in an inspired and captivating way.

Ten years later on 19 April, 1956, in a speech he made at the preparatory conference for the Plenum of the Union of Writers he no longer had recourse to metaphors. He worded his confession confusedly, hiding behind stereotyped phrases from the newspapers. The uncorrected, straightforward stenographic record of the conference, which could be read in great secrecy in the Union of Writers a year later, bears eloquent testimony to this fact.

"There is a need to declare fully what the consequences of the cult of personality were," he said, "the cult which led to the attempt to inculcate a Party spirit (*partiynost*) by force..."

At this point Fadayev had only twenty days to live. Twenty days later he put a bullet in his temple. He had the determination to shoot himself in the head but not to be truthful, even then. "I was asked to go to *Pravda* one night. When I got there, Pospelov simply said to me: 'Comrade Stalin has given us the urgent assignment of smashing the cosmopolitan group...' The *Pravda* article was put together as ordered and written in twenty-four hours."

Many people knew what the actual truth was; even Fadayev did not particularly seek to conceal it when speaking privately. I first heard what really happened from the theater critic Iosif Yuzovsky. I remember clearly the well-fingered pages of the journal *Theatr* containing the sparkling articles

Yuzovsky had written—or Yuz, as his friends called him. I also have a very clear memory of Yuz himself, a small, wizened man like a kindly gnome. On one memorable occasion at Maleyevka Yuz skied off one morning into the forest, stripped to the waist with a rucksack on his back. He lost his sense of direction, however, and spent fourteen hours skiing around in the forest trying not to freeze to death. In vain we looked for him all that day, calling out his name and hallooing. There was no answering call. Night had fallen before he made his way back to the writers' house. My first sight of him then will always stay with me: there he was out in the fierce frost in his knitted cap, a look of desperation on his face, tuning off the ski-track across the snow towards us.

I have another memory of him from a later period. It was also at Maleyevka and we were standing beside the enormous radio-receiver trying to catch the news. With soundless steps the critic Kornely Zelinsky, a literary hyena with a saccharine-sweet air of civility and all the right connections came up to us. "What are you tuning into?" he asked, trying to appear as casual as possible. "Something from abroad?"

"It's not dying that terrifies me," Yuzovsky said suddenly. "What terrifies me is that the very people who tormented you all your life will be the ones to make fine speeches at your graveside..."

Zelinsky slipped away as soundlessly as he had appeared and several years later, just as Yuz had foreseen, he made a touching speech at Yuz's graveside.

Like everyone else, Fadeyev was very fond of Yuz, with his cheerfulness and frankness. The two of them met unexpectedly in February 1949 in snow-blocked Pyatnitsky Street, face to face, the executioner and his victim. There was Fadeyev, crimson-faced, breathing out wine fumes and radiating well-being, and Yuzovsky, frail and starving, branded "a saboteur" and "bandit of the pen" by the newspapers of the day and expecting to be arrested at any moment. They slipped slightly on the ice, stopped and stared at each other. Then Fadeyev suggested to his old friend that they go to a cafe where they joined the red-nosed habituals crowding round the high tables. Having drunk enough vodka for two—half a liter— with the "rootless cosmpolitan," he disclosed in an apologetic way how serious the matter was and that he pitied Iosif with all his heart.

And that is how the matter stood. A few militant hacks—Sofronov, Gribachev, Surov, Bubennov and others—had written Stalin a letter saying that the group of "antipatriotic" literary critics was hindering the development of truly Russian, patriotic drama. The letter had been passed on to Stalin immediately, like Bubennov's letter about Vassily Grossman, and one can only guess who actually initiated it. "Yuz, what could I say to Joseph Vissarionovich in reply?" Fadeyev exclaimed guiltily, gulping down his vodka, "what could I say?"

Seven years later while addressing a meeting in the well-trained voice of a professional preacher, he was to say: "In the *Pravda* article [on Yuzovsky and others] there was a touch of chauvinism." Sitting directly in front of Fadeyev in the front row on that occasion was Vassily Grossman. His face bore an expression of stony contempt. Fadeyev glanced fleetingly along the rows, then his lips parted as if he had scalded them:

> *There's another example. The affair of Grossman's novel... We coerced him, twisted his arm, but he is an intelligent fellow, he realizes that it doesn't depend on us... It is quite clear that there have been excesses in the fight against cosmopolitanism right across the ideological front... And if Sholokhov accuses Fadeyev and Surkov of acting like sergeant-majors, then the question arises as to whether this is not a way of shielding yet more sergeant-majors.*
>
> *Yashin wrote* Alyona Fomina. *He wept as he wrote it. He said: "I can't bear to look at what's happening in the rural areas." [Fadeyev was not telling the exact truth here. Yashin actually wept when the editors cut the verses on poverty in the Vologda countryside out of his poem.] We've ended up with a platform of untruths on which it is impossible to create anything sensible... Literature and art cannot exist on a basis of lies. If an attempt were made to force anyone to read the record of the '1949' 13th Plenum and then read aloud his speech again now, no one would have the courage to do it, for fear the audience would eat him alive. I am referring to Shkerin, Belik, Kirsanov and Perventsev—who fulminated against everyone.*
>
> *I am well aware of the fact that Meyerhold's and Tairov's theaters were closed. Meyerhold's theater was closed because there were two depositions made to the effect that Meyerhold was a French spy... We must unswaddle our brains and say that it's time we freely criticized the mistakes that have been make... These are my thoughts in rough form... You understand that one is now thinking over one's life...*

Fadeyev fell silent and would have liked to leave the dais. But the audience was waiting to hear what he would say next, especially the writers who had just returned from the camps, with their burning eyes and sunken cheeks chafed by the Siberian winds. Amongst them was Yuri Dombrovsky, a nervous, shy man and Makaryev, a silent, bony man who had just publicly called Fadeyev a scoundrel. Soon after this, seeing that nothing was changing, Makaryev hanged himself. But in those days he still demanded justice, and Fadeyev forced himself to say what could no longer be hidden. The former political prisoners there would not have allowed it.

"This whole question is bound up with the group system: Gribachev and Surov make up one group which still exists. There's more than one group at *Oktyabr* (October)." Someone in the audience called out: "That's right, more than one!" Fadeyev forced himself to continue. "We've grown so accustomed to living in groups that we made no effort, and indeed did not have strength, to climb higher[?!]. I was called in by the Security people and asked what I thought of Kirshon when he was arrested. I said that Yagoda, Averbakh and Kirshon were all of a kind.[6] I was used to thinking like that. But my reply could have been a fateful one for Kirshon."

On 13 May that year (1956) Alexander Fadeyev shot himself at his dacha in Peredelkino after sending letters to a number of friends, letters which were quickly intercepted by the State Security service. When I heard that he had committed suicide, I immediately went to the Union of Writers, where I heard hardly a word of regret from anyone. "It wasn't a hunter we heard firing yesterday in the forest," said the older writer N. to Alexander Galich the same day, "It was him.. Shot himself like a dog. In front of the child," he added angrily. "He might at least have gone out into the forest."

In shooting himself when he had "thought over his life," Fadeyev provoked the fury of the Politburo. "He shot at us! At each one of us!" roared Klement Voroshilov, "the first Red officer," as our generation used to sing.

As youngsters filling the auditorium at the First Youth Conference in March 1947 we were, of course, in no position to know that from the village of Peredelkino alone, where writers had their dachas, twenty of Russia's best-known writers had been thrown into the Gulag to die and be tortured, and that the arrest of every single one of them had been authorized by Alexander Fadeyev and in some cases, even instigated by him.

He knew when reprisals were coming. The day before the ageing writer Yuri Libedinsky's apartment was searched, Fadeyev hurried there and was let in by an elderly relative. (The Libedinskys were not at home, but the old lady recognized Fadeyev and so was not concerned.) He rifled through all the papers in the writer's study until he at last found what he had been looking for: the packet containing his correspondence with Libedinsky, to whom, he Fadeyev, owed his fame. It had been Libedinsky who had first "discovered" the young provincial writer "Sasha" Fadeyev and helped him to move to Moscow and get his writings published. The packet of letters in the study of Libedinsky who was a marked man could have compromised Fadeyev, the blameless General Secretary. As a matter of fact, although his house was searched from top to bottom the next day, Libedinsky was not arrested. They confined themselves to Averbakh and Kirshon. The rest were taken one by one a little later.

We participants in the Youth Conference had, of course, not the slightest inkling of the fact that for Alexander Fadeyev, the truth—the naked, unadorned truth—resembled death, and we listened to him as to an oracle. The oracle was admittedly embarrassed when one of us (I do not now remember who) asked him later during a refreshment break in the canteen where we were drinking vodka like "real writers,": "Alexander

Alexandrovich, what would you do if some young writer were to come and put a slim book called *The Rout* on your desk, and if it were *The Rout* as you wrote it, with a tragic ending and with that sniveller Mechik dashing about all over the place although he's supposed to be a Red partisan, and the main hero having a non-Russian name Levinson—what would you do? Would you publish this new writer's talented work? Tell us the truth or don't say anything!" Fadeyev gave a strained smile, blushed right down to his neck, quickly downed his cognac and, as he walked away, forced himself to say: "I'm afraid not." Episodes such as this brought us down to earth, saving us from the high-flown blather being passed off as "new literary concepts" and from the flattery of bureaucrats which could turn to anger at any moment.

All the same, we almost believed Fadeyev, as did the whole country as it repeated Fadeyev's discovery about apples "in nature" and "grown in the garden." If Fadeyev had not had the legendary biography of the partisan in the Far East behind him and the reputation of being "almost a Tolstoy," he would scarcely have been able to inflict the devastating blow on our generation that he did.

The harm this "almost Tolstoy" did to our generation of writers from the front can only be compared in its extent with that done by Konstantin Simonov. I remember how, after the war, Simonov was showered with flowers at Moscow University, although his "comforting" wartime poetry was already on the wane: "Wait for me, I shall return/Just keep waiting..." I had been attracted to him ever since the battle at Khalin-Gol. In the midst of the drum-rolls of "art" glorifying the coming war—in which little of our blood would be shed and even that would be on other's territory, naturally— a human voice was suddenly heard. It belonged to a poet I did not then know, bending over a dead soldiers notebook:

> *He'd written down carefully in a corner*
> *His mother's address and his wife's:*
> *He believed in victory, yet knew*
> *Not everyone would come back from the war.*

During the action above the Arctic Circle, Konstantin Simonov, dressed in his short fur coat, went to the north coast of Norway on a torpedo boat to drop a landing force. No, Simonov was no "Almost Tolstoy," but someone dear to us, a soldier-poet.

Then suddenly I saw this "dear" man in the Oak Room of the Writers' Club on Vorovsky Street, next to the restaurant from which came appetizing smells. Here the crushing of Jewish writers took place to the clink of dishes and shouts of "Another bottle of Stolichnaya!" At the leading lights' table stood Anatoly Surov, a small, lame man with a swollen red face. From time to time he hiccupped drunkenly and rapped his walking-stick threateningly.

It was his habit to rap his walking-stick in a restaurant. However he never used the newspaper term "cosmopolitan" there, preferring to drawl with menacing relish: "Bring us a couple of yids for starters! I'll soon polish them off!" And then he would rap his walking-stick for the whole room to hear.

Now, standing at the table covered in green cloth, he was shouting about the cosmopolitans, "alien by blood and in spirit," who did not allow the genuine Russian to come into his own. Standing next to him was Simonov, sober and well-bred, vaguely twisting his trimmed moustache (it was what we called a "Stalinki" moustache) and giving an ironic smile. You could sense that he was somewhat shocked by the presence of the drunken lame pig beside him, but what he was was little different from what Anatoly Surov was bellowing beside him.

Not long before, *Pravda* had attacked him for his story "Smoke of the Fatherland," and Simonov had told one of my acquaintances: "Today I ceased being a good fairy." There was a note of caution in his voice. I am not sure that he understood at that time Stalin's simple approach: "good fairies" lack diligence—how much more reliable they are when dangled on strings.

Although a philology student and author of one book, I was completely ignorant of the "course of modern history." "Why are they together?" I wondered, looking at Surov and Simonov, although Simonov had already written the play *An Alien Shadow* about evil American scientists whom no Soviet scientist is allowed to meet and who steal an antibacterial virus under the guise of scientific cooperation.

Two or three years later, I no longer asked myself such naive questions. The change came after I had been summoned by Alexander Fadeyev to come for a "talk." But it was definitive after the meeting at *Literaturnaya gazeta* at which the so-called Bershadsky affair was discussed.

Rudolf Bershadsky was head of the *feuilleton* department of *Literaturnaya gazeta*. During the hysteria brought on by the reports of the "doctor's plot" several enthusiasts, among whom Shaposhnikova had a prominent role (Shaposhnikova was a long-time MGB informer and later joined the editorial board of the monthly *Moskva*), broke into Bershadsky's desk at night. There they found two pieces attacking the doctors, which Bershadsky had not had published. "In these historical times," Shaposhikova proclaimed loudly, "when *Pravda* and *Izvestiia* are continually publishing materials on these murderers, these Vovsis and Etingers, *Literaturnaya gazeta* has remained tight-lipped." Then it all started in earnest. "Imperialist intelligence agent!" "Judas sells his country for 30 pieces of silver!" "Saboteur!" The terminology had been refined over many years.

Rudolf Bershadsky appeared at the podium at a Party meeting, bent and half dead. During the war he had been commander of an artillery battalion. He had gone all the way from Stalingrad to Berlin with his guns. He had been wounded and gone deaf from shell-shock, and still had dozens of fragments in his body. His chest was covered in decorations. The silence in the room was becoming oppressive. It seemed that at any moment someone would call out: "Comrades, we've got the wrong man. There's been a mistake."

Then Konstantin Simonov rose from his seat, genteel and resourceful as ever, and "saved the situation." As if lost in thought, and pronouncing his r's softly in the French manner, he made a speech which many of us will not forget until the day we die. For almost a month afterwards, Moscow literary circles could talk of nothing else.

"Yes," said Simonov, his voice showing the strain of the pain he felt and the difficulty of his decision to put aside his party for the man who was at his mercy, "Bershadsky did indeed fight bravely. He personally put several tanks out of action... His valour was written up in the military newspapers. I know that." Here the editor-in-chief off *Literaturnaya gazeta* was silent for a moment before striking the final blow: "Yes, he fought bravely! But for what ideals?" Simonov then really lashed out. Bershadsky's ideals were, of course, cosmopolitan ones.

Bershadsky was arrested forthwith. This happened three days before Stalin died. Six months later he was released "in view of the absence of corpus delicti." He went to the Union of Writers, where the elegant Simonov was delivering a paper on Soviet literature to an audience of Moscow schoolteachers. The self-effacing school-teachers were crowded towards the rear and the first three rows were empty. Wearing his prison jacket, Rudolf Bershadsky sat down in the middle of the first row. Simonov went pale, took a sip of water, trying to stop his teeth from knocking against the glass, and finished his speech in praise of the achievements of Soviet literature.

We now come to an astounding, and possibly unique, circumstance. With the exception of Fadeyev, Simonov and two or three others to whom we shall return, the Stalinist pogroms of 1946-1953 were basically carried out by "well-known writers" who never wrote.

Anatoly Surov, a semi-literate anti-Semite who was perpetually drunk and never hid his prejudices, was one. A special commission of the Union of Writers subsequently established that he had never written a single line. Ironically, it was a certain Ya. Varshavsky, a starving "cosmopolitan" expelled from every writer's organization, who had been "ghosting" for him. Surov had hired him "for creative purposes." Surov lost his authorship and his rights as a writer were never reinstated. Naturally, he was not allowed to go to waste and was given a managerial position in the All-Union Radio Commission.

Arkady Perventsev was a no less ominous figure. Mayakovsky's cousin, he was a huge, shaven-headed insolent man who some said looked as if he might have been a dushegubka driver.* His first book, *Kochubey*, which came out in 1937, was completely rewritten by the literary editor—everyone in Moscow knew about it. Artistically it was so superior to all his other illiterate hack works that it was perfectly obvious that *Kochubey* had been written by someone else. How many people were put in prison by this non-writer, who was always screaming at talented academic critics about "cosmopolitan" writers: "How long will they go undermining the edifice of Soviet drama with those little rodents' teeth of theirs, those poisonous, plague-carrying teeth they've got?"

Orest Maltsev was a fictitious character to the point where in the column in the Union of Writers directory for Stalin Prize winners which lists what the Stalin Prize was awarded for there is simply a dash. His book *A Yugoslav Tragedy* is well-known, however, as is the red-headed war invalid Volodya Gurvich, son of one of the founders of the American Communist Party, first of all dismissed from his place of work at the instigation of the MVD and then expelled with his mother from Moscow as a parasite. In order not to die of starvation, Gurvich leapt at the first job to come his way and wrote this novel which had been commissioned for Orest Maltsev, all about the "bloody dog Tito." When peace was made with Tito, the book was removed from all Soviet libraries and Orest Maltsev turned out to be the Stalin Prize Winner for literature, without writing a line.

These non-writers became a kind of *oprichnina* or administrative elite in the service of Fadeyeev and Simonov. Never before in the history of Russia had an *oprichninia* inflicted such losses on culture.

"There were more than six hundred of them—completely innocent writers whom the Union obediently allowed to go to their fate in the prisons and camps," writes Solzhenitsyn in his letter to the Fourth Congress of the Union of Writers, repeating the official figures made public by the Union of Writers itself. When he wrote these lines Solzhenitsyn was still obviously not aware of the whole truth. The Union of Writers not only "allowed" writers and critics to go to prison, it actually pushed them into prison. And of those returning from penal servitude in exile it demanded silence or betrayal. And this, alas, is not just a bad dream.

A whole team of "Simonovites" (N. Drozdov, prose editor on Simonov's *Novy mir*, together with his associates) rewrote from scratch the rather loosely written manuscript of V. Azhayev, a former prisoner. It had been published by a provincial publishing house. The author had turned the real-life concentration-camp commandant Barabanov, greatly feared by both prisoners and guards, into Batmanov, hero of freedom Soviet style. Simonov eagerly lent his support to the lie: after all the corrections that were made, the major pipeline as before is laid not by wretched, starving, half-dead political prisoners, whom the author betrayed, but by exceptionally happy Soviet citizens. Simonov looked through the completed manuscript with a vigilant eye, on the look out for any remaining allusions to camp life, unnecessary psychological associations and so on. Vasily Azhayev, the quiet, sickly political prisoner was praised to the skies for his silence. For his silence and his timidity he was appointed editor-in-chief of the show-case journal *Sovetskaya literatura (Soviet Literature)* which was published in various foreign languages and where, as is well known, the editor-in-chief made no decisions.

Thanks to Konstantin Simonov, Azhayev's "Gulag Archipelago" became a world-famous apotheosis of free labor in a free country in the form of the novel *Far from Moscow*, which caused quite a sensation and was awarded the Stalin Prize (First Class).

As we can see, the Simonovs of the Soviet Union not only pushed writers into prison, but, if necessary, quickly created on their behalf or as a form of "assistance" to them "a new socialist epic," and then set up a loud drumming to cover the escape of a few brave souls among the writers from the columns of prisoners. They wanted the courageous to be forgotten, and the sooner the better. And it must be said that these Simonov's succeeded.

––––––––––––

*dushegubka—a war-time execution chamber on wheels. Prisoners were sealed in the back of the vehicle which was then driven around until they had all been asphyxiated by the exhaust fumes which were forced into the closed chamber.

6. SAMIZDAT UNDER STALIN (1945-53)

It would at first appear senseless to speak of samizdat in the post-war years, under Stalin. What samizdat could there have been during years of total terror, when people were put in prison and even shot not only for some heretical line in a poem or story, but for an anecdote, an allusion or a smile! Indeed, people were shot for no reason at all, and the older generation is still prey to the old numbing fear.

Could samizdat have come into being at a time when its authors were condemned men and its readers almost condemned men themselves? The answer would seem clearly to be that it could not have. Yet, nonetheless, it did exist.

Amongst students in Moscow, for example, typed copies of poems were always circulating. The poems were always anonymous, and the content sometimes completely innocent. You would only know who had written a particular poem when the person giving it to you said under his breath: "This is Marina Tsvetaeva."

Everyone would take Tsvetaeva and read her, sometimes even during lectures, because they at least knew her name from the truncated modern literature course in which a few lines were devoted to her, lines beginning with something negative such as "she did not recognize," "did not agree," "could not accept" and so on. The pages would pass along the rows in the Hall of Communism, the lecture-hall in which something obediently lawful and as long drawn out as a yawn would be being taught.

I remember the shock I felt when I read one poem of Tsvetaeva's the first year after the war, written out in a rather childish hand on a crumpled page out of an exercise-book:

> *Longing for my native land! Turmoil long since exposed!*
> *It's all utterly the same to me now here I am utterly alone,*
> *Or over what stones I wander with my market bag homewards*
> *   like barracks or a hospital...*
> *All houses are strange to me, all temples empty,*
> *   And nothing matters, it's all one.*
> *Yet if a tree should loom upon my path, if above all a rowan*
> *   tree!...*

Later, whole generations who had preserved some spiritual values despite the onslaught of Stalinism knew these lines by heart. But for those of us who had grown up under the hermetically sealed glass dome of a terror-based system, they were a revelation. Let me explain why.

We had just returned from the war. We had seen punitive battalions in action during the war and some of us had been in them. Others had fathers and brothers who were taken away in 1937. At any rate, by this time we knew that there were people—wonderful people—who had been slandered, abused and hidden away in prisons. Naturally, we began to look at emigres in a new light, particularly those who were poets and writers, and to ask ourselves if they had not shared the fate of those who had served in the punitive battalions or the so-called "enemies of the people." Had they also been slandered?

When I hesitantly asked those who had given me Tsvetaeva's "Longing for my native land..." to read if I could have something else, they handed me barely legible—probably the sixth or seventh—copies of the verse of Tsvetaeva and Osip Mandelstam, without the poets' names on them.

We had a particularly keen sense of the actuality and the strange normality of the violence done to talented people after 1948-9: these were the years when our favorite teachers were expelled from the university. Those who came to the fore were the cynical and carping critics such as the chairman of the Department of Western Literature, Roman Samarin, or the long-time provocateur Professor Elsberg, formerly secretary to Kamenev.

As youngsters in 1937, we had been deceived. It had not been a difficult thing to do. Now everything was different. We ourselves were different. Violence was being done not to far off "saboteurs" we did not know, but to dedicated old men we loved with academic caps and chalky elbows, always ready to take trouble over our problems, sitting patiently with us until midnight if necessary.

I remember with great clarity the evenings and nights I spent at Gelendzhik, the university rest house on the Black Sea. It is a damp night and there is a smell of seaweed in the air. The sea is not far away. Five or six people who trust each other are huddled in little groups. The border guards chase the students off the beach, shouting: "It's out of bounds! After ten at night the beach is a forbidden area!" Yet the students keep trickling back into the forbidden zone, closer to the surf and the sound of the gleaming water, and there they take turns at reciting poetry. It goes on far into the night. Some of them turn out to remember all of Gumilev.

Before the war I had known young people who could recite the whole of Pushkin off by heart or pick up and carry on with any of Lermontov's poetry from any point. And now, only five or six years later, the same young people were for some reason reciting there in the night not Pushkin or Lermontov any longer, poets they had "done" as part of the official syllabus, although they still remembered them, but Gumilev and Tsvetaeva—above all Gumilev. Their youthful voices could be heard reciting their verses for one, two or even three hours at a stretch. One would pick up where the other left off, carrying on from the middle of a line forgotten half-way through. In the face of everything, poems which had been withdrawn from all the libraries and to all intents and purposes had been rooted out of the hearts of entire generations, could again be heard on the damp night air. There were verses about distant seas and sea-captains:

> ... discoverers of new lands
> who are not afraid of hurricanes
> and know what eddies and sandbars are,
> whose breasts are covered not with the dust of lost charts
> but encrusted with sea-salt,
> who mark their daring paths
> on tattered maps with a quill.

The student reciting these lines had only to fall silent momentarily or pause to catch his breath and the lines would immediately be taken up by ringing, enraptured voices:

> Let the sea rage and lash,
> And the crests of the waves reach the sky,
> None will tremble before the storm
> Nor furl his sails.
>
> Arms such as these are not given to cowards,
> Nor are these sharp assured eyes
> Whose glance can suddenly launch a frigate
> Against puny enemy craft,
>
> And strike the gigantic whale
> With well-aimed bullet or iron harpoon,
> And spot the guarding light of beacons
> In the many-starred night.

These romantic lines were invested with all the young men's most deeply held hopes and vows. They were colored with a profound and sometimes insanely courageous sub-text, which was no longer romantic, but realistic and charged with self-sacrifice. These young men were preparing themselves for battle, in the name of their teachers and of the truth they dreamt of defending.

I remember rushing from the train down to the sea, thinking to plunge straight into it. Then I heard these verses being recited in excited, impetuous tones like a confession:

> I know I am not your equal,
> I have come from another land,
> And it is not the guitar I love

But the untamed song of the zurna.

I do not read my verse
In halls and drawing-rooms
To sedate gowns and jackets
But to dragons, waterfalls and clouds.

At this point the young man reciting noticed me standing there in my navy jacket. Realizing he did not know me, he broke off. Someone jumped up, ready to rush off into the darkness, but then someone said in a deep voice: "He's one of us, he's from our faculty." Then the young man who had been reciting took a deep breath and cried out again to the surrounding darkness:

I shall not die on a bed
Attended by notary or doctor,
But in some wild crevasse
Smothered in thick ivy...

A young girl burst into tears and began to sob her heart out. The others tried to calm her and led her away, holding her up and I asked what was wrong with her.

I need not have asked. As I have just mentioned, mass arrests were taking place at the university. A number of teachers as well as quite a few students were thrown into prison. Some of our number were among them. On one occasion a few of them were walking around Moscow with some Albanian students, and one of my friends Sergey Matveyev nodded in the direction of the Kremlin and said: "I suppose you think they lead an idyllic life in there. Don't worry, they have their disputes to settle in there, too." The Albanians, with their devoutly dogmatic attitudes, were horrified and reported Matveyev's words to the Secretary of the University Party Committee. Students from our year began to disappear one by one. It turned out that the MGB had cooked up a whole student conspiracy in the student dormitory on Stromynka Street—a terrorist conspiracy, naturally. One of those arrested was this girl's brother.

When her sobbing died away, we were quiet for a long time, feeling deeply depressed. Then one of us began reciting again, at first in a low voice, then louder and louder, reciting the lines which reflected our thoughts and mood so closely:

He stands before the blazing furnace
A small old man.
His untroubled gaze seems humble
As he blinks his reddish eyelids.

64

All his workmates have fallen asleep
And only he is still awake.
He is still busy casting the bullet
Which will tear me away from the earth.

The boy fell silent, and this time no one picked up the lines. What Gumilev had foreseen was terrifyingly real. As it had turned out, it was not about his own fate alone that he had written his poem "The Worker."

Everyone was dispirited and quiet; then, in a scarcely audible voice, the boy went on:

> *The bullet he's cast will whistle*
> *Over the gray-haired, foam-flecked Dvina,*
> *The bullet he's cast will seek out*
> *My breast, it will come for me.*
> > *I shall fall in deathly anguish*
> > *And glimpse the past in waking dream*
> > *My blood will spurt out in a stream*
> > *Onto the dry, dusty, trampled grass.*
> *The Lord will reward me in full measure*
> *For my brief and bitter span...*
> *This is the work of the small old man*
> *In a light-grey smock.*

In place of Bagritsky's and Mikhail Svetlov's pre-war romantic verse we naturally turned to Gumilev's bold and bitter romantic poetry, unprompted by anything except what life itself had taught us.

Then it was Marina Tsvetaeva who had become our very breath of life:

> *They all lie in a row,*
> *No line can divide them.*
> *You look and see just soldiers.*
> *Where are ours and where are theirs?*
>
> *He was white and became red,*
> *Crimsoned by blood.*
> *He was red and became white,*
> *Whitened by death.*

Later, in class, we could pass around philosophy abstracts in which the height of sedition was Spinoza:

*government which attempts to control minds is accounted tyrannical,
and it is considered an abuse of sovereignty and usurpation of the
rights of subjects, to seek to prescribe what shall be accepted as true,
or rejected as false...*

(A Theologico-Political Treatise, ch. 20)

I remember being shown Spinoza surreptitiously, with the cover concealed and the heretical passage indicated with a finger-nail mark. Poor Baruch Spinoza! Originally he had been banished by the rabbis, and now he had become a heretic in an epoch which exterminated rabbis. Spinoza now took his place beside the forbidden Voloshin and the incomprehensible Pasternak.

The main body of this samizdat literature was not to come back to us until eight or ten years had passed, and by then it was to be quite different— the samizdat of former political prisoners' manuscripts rejected by the publishers. There was to be a whole stream of these former prisoners' manuscripts, which was to seep through to the West only in small trickles. But at that time, under Stalin, when Solzhenitsyn, Evgenia Ginzburg and Varlam Shalamov were still languishing in labor camps, it was Gumilev and Tsvetaeva, Voloshin and Pasternak who sustained us. This is why the verse of academic poets such as Esenin-Volpin, for example, which poured forth in unending streams and was taken up and recited without delay, was quite naturally regarded as just risky mischief-making.

Samizdat, which was born in the terrible years of Stalinist terror, was elevated to the position normally occupied by the classics. This is what determined its significance and its lasting influence.

PART II

THE CHERRY-PLUM BLOOMS IN TBILISI...

1. THE RESUSCITATION OF SOCIAL THOUGHT

Resuscitation is, of course, primarily a medical term. Although it is a very difficult process, experience shows that it is by no means always out of the question.

It would hardly be an exaggeration to say that despite the campaign of intimidation, the widespread resuscitation of social thought began to take place at all levels of the population.

Although the very memory of it is shameful and ludicrous, the fact is, if we are to be serious and ruthlessly objective about it, that the intellectual level of the average so-called *"intelligent"* or member of the intelligentsia approximated that of the almost illiterate workers of 1905 who went to the Winter Palace to see their "little father the tsar"—*tsar-batyushka*—saying: "Our little father the tsar does not know the truth. They're hiding the truth from him." It is in such thoughts and feelings, sometimes secretly nurtured, that an explanation can be found for the crush on Moscow's Trubnaya Square in which thousands of faithful subjects were trampled to death, trying to see Stalin's body lying in state, and for the tears of apparently thinking, intellectually mature people. Living in Russia, especially during Stalin's last year, was like living in a deep well. It was as if the whole nation had been dropped down a well and there it existed in utter darkness, deprived of outside information, except for what had been filtered or "ideologically intensified," as Russia's brainwashing experts would have it.

I remember a neighbor of mine who worked in some office on a beggarly salary coming running in, his eyes wide with fright, muttering: "What's gone wrong? What's going to happen? They've ordered Beria's portrait to be taken down! Lavrenty Pavlovich Beria's!" The people on our street, half-drunk because it was the weekend, were by and large indifferent to the news and cynical about it. In both drunken and sober voices they bawled:

> The cherry-plum blooms in Tbilisi
> Not for Lavrenty Pavlovich
> But for Kliment Yefremovich
> And Vyacheslav Mikhailovich.

Vyacheslav Mikhailovich Skryabin, whose Party nickname was Molotov, was still in power. They were to sing ditties about his fall four years later, with the same cynicism and utter indifference. The only ones to get a terrible fright were the former Party-line critics, inquisitors, informers and hangmen.

Literaturnaya gazeta, cowardly like all bullies, was thrown into great consternation. Not long before, for example, it had been trampling the Leningrad writer Yuri German into the mud. It made such a commotion about his short story "Sub-lieutenant in the Medical Corps," which had been partially published in *Zvezda*, and had a doctor with the Jewish sounding name of Levin in it, that it was hurriedly decided not to publish the rest of it, and the type was broken up. Then all of a sudden there appeared in the same *Literaturnaya gazeta* a laudatory three-column article in honor of the "great writer" Yuri German. His praises were sung as if he had been Shakespeare in an anniversary year, without any mention, of course, of how they had so recently been hounding him. Vassily Grossman, it is true, had not yet been reinstated. They had only got as far as Yuri German, who had not attracted Stalin's special attention. However, it was perfectly obvious that a few cogs in the smoothly functioning mechanism of the State had come too loose.

Vladimir Yermilov, chief editor of *Literaturnaya gazeta* and the persecutor of dozens of writers—"from Mayakovsky to Tvardovsky," as they used to say in the Union of Writers—suddenly began to lavish praise on Tvardovsky and heap abuse on his own friends, writers from the MGB such as Vassily Ardamatsky. Vassily Ardamatsky would scarcely have been worth mentioning if he had not later become, together with Lev Nikulin, a leading "anti-writer." Such writers, with their upside-down morality and their praise of lies, treachery and murder (so long as they were "to the glory of the Revolution," of course) merit our special attention, and we shall return to them.

Then something unexpected happened. The mass reader was not capable of switching over to the new wave-length with such rapidity. He remembered the tenor of the abusive articles from yesterday's newspapers and was confused. The mass reader was not a hardened cynic and demanded some explanation. As readers—especially retired colonels—kept reminding *Literaturnaya gazeta*, literature was about "what ought to be" and not "what was."

In answer to these readers there appeared an ironical article under the light-hearted heading: "Where did the writer see such broken-down old horses?" The article, which was purportedly written by a kolkhoz chairman, was an attack on an "antipatriotic" writer who was supposed to have mentioned noticing a skinny horse in the field. The horse was just skin and bones, which was not at all typical, because as everyone knew and as the song on the radio went, in the USSR "our horses are well-fed, their hooves ring out..."

Literaturnaya gazeta, in fright, began taking upon itself the urgent task of re-educating the reader whom it had itself first led by the nose into the jungle of false theories—for example, the "lack of conflict" theory and the primacy of the positive hero. This was a moment of clarity for *Literaturnaya gazeta*—it was a *lucidum intervallum*, as the wits amongst the older writers who had had a classical education called it—that is to say, a madman's period of lucidity.

During this period of lucidity *Literaturnaya gazeta* even attempted to pour shame on the Soviet writers who had published the article "Finding Sobakin" which had caused quite a sensation at the time. (Sobakin was a wretched "internal reviewer" who read manuscripts received by the publisher and who was always ready to demolish any manuscript which had not found favor with a publishing house.)

The *lucidum intervallum* continued for the required period of time. At Yermilov's dacha there was an iron plaque on the wall with the inscription: "Beware of savage dog." Someone scratched in underneath with a nail: "and unprincipled." The plaque had to be taken down straight away.

That was not the end of the switching of attitudes, however. Stalinist methods of falsifying social thought, which were so deeply ingrained, broke out again like a scarlet fever rash. At this time Fyodor Panfyorov's appallingly bad novel *Mother Volga* was being discussed. *Literaturnaya gazeta* published a selection of readers' letters about it. There were thirteen letters in favor of it, and a few less which were critical of it. In short, it was just a run-of-the-mill sort of book with nothing about it to cause a hue and cry. What an awkward position *Literaturnaya gazeta* found itself in when it came to light that it had received more than a thousand angrily critical letters and only thirteen approving of the novel. The overwhelming negative response had been concealed, while the thirteen positive letters had all been printed as "the people's opinion."

But it was no longer possible to conceal everything. People began to criticize the works of "antiliterature" loudly, and especially Babayevsky's novel *Cavalier of the Gold Star*. The falseness of such books became glaringly obvious after the September Plenum of the Central Committee of the Communist Party in 1953 when it was revealed that there were then fewer cows in the USSR than there had been during the reign of Nicholas II. Revelations such as this, which were to become rarer and rarer, led not only to the collapse of so-called "village" anti-literature, which loudly proclaimed abundance at a time of famine, but led to tragedy for certain gifted writers such as Sergei Antonov. His undoubtedly talented stories about country life, with their folkloric overtones, imbued with the grassy smells of the countryside, were written through the eyes of a holiday-maker staying at his dacha. They made no claim to generalized truthfulness. Yet this talented writer could not forgive himself for having tried to get away with mere folksy tales, and for a long time he was silent.

By way of contrast, nationalistic writers raised their voices, at least at first. The famous Dagestani poet Rasul Gamzatov became interested in the tragedy of Shamil's betrayal by Russia and demanded that a monument be erected to him. Later at a writers' congress he made a congratulatory speech to Russian writers which made the chairman Sergei Mikhalkov leap from his seat as if he had sat on a nail.

"I congratulate Russian writers," he intoned slowly into the microphone,

71

"the first among equals, on behalf of the Dagestani people, the second-last among equals."

Emmanuil Kazakevich brought back an anecdote from Hungary which was evidence of the fact that for many nations the Soviet Union's great power status really stuck in the throat. A pact is concluded between the USSR and Hungary on freedom of navigation on the Danube—for the Russians up and down the river, and for the Hungarians across it. He never failed to add that he heard the anecdote in the Budapest regional committee of the Party.

Alas, the political anecdotes which flooded Russia during the time of stagnation remained just that—anecdotes. The State security service, which had struck such terror into people's hearts, was not interested in creative literature in those times of frightened confusion and insight.

Immediately after Stalin's death, in fact almost the following day, the rustling of the pages of samizdat became louder. Whatever survived the purges of 1937 and was still lying in hiding-places was copied and disseminated stealthily all around the country. It is interesting to inquire into the question of what sort of thing became samizdat after Stalin's death in March 1953, apart from the verse of Gumilev and Tsvetaeva which was widely known only in university circles. What did the new samizdat consist of?

However paradoxical it may seem, the fact is the subject of the new samizdat was none other than Lenin. I remember reading that year for the first time a copy of Lenin's letter to Dmitry Kurski, People's Commissar for Justice, written out on a page from an exercise book. In it he urged the "establishment and legalization of terror"... "without hypocrisy, straightforwardly"... "it must be organized on as wide a footing as possible."

It turned out that the letter had been printed earlier, but for our generation it was a new discovery. We read with enormous interest about things which had always been hidden from us. I remember being greatly struck by the words of Vera Zasulich, published in Russia on 26 November 1917. There were the words of the member of the Narodnaya volya movement who shot the city governor. She was considered a heroine even under Stalin and had an assured place in the history of the Russian liberation movement. Suddenly it came to light that this heroine of the people had said the following:

The freedom of the printed word can only be defended against Lenin and his accomplices by action. It is impossible to make them see reason or to frighten them. Lenin is trying to frighten us socialists by portraying our fighting against his sovereign power as a fight "in the ranks of the bourgeoisie" against the workers, soldiers and other masses. But this is as much a lie as all the rest... we're fighting not against the masses, but against the lies they're being entangled in... Through their tireless fight Russians will prove—to themselves, and

72

that is very important—that there are not only despots and slaves in Russia but also citizens... [1]

We were thunder-struck at such revelations. Clambering up the slippery, slimy walls out of the airless well of Stalinism, we looked out for the first time on horizons whose existence we had not even guessed at. What were we to do? How could we almost quickly and sensibly make sense of what was going on when all the relevant documents were still locked up in the "spetskhran" or special depository of the Lenin Library, just as they had been under Stalin. Naturally we turned to Dostoevsky and Pasternak. We read and re-read *The Devils* and the story of the double agent Azef. These books had ceased to be just fiction for us.

We young writers found what we wrote was being constantly rejected by the editors, although a few things occasionally got through unexpectedly, as I shall relate later. We were forced to be extraordinarily active because in the main we knew perfectly well that neither Fadeyev, nor Simonov, nor Surkov, nor Katayev would protect us from brutal attack. For many years we had anxiously waited for the sound of the voice of the respected and venerable Soviet "classic" writers, who had become something akin to the icons of Soviet literature. We hurriedly opened our newspapers, believing that in that year of shocks and sharp changes no one could stop Leonov, Gladkov, Fedin or Paustovsky, for example, from uniting against the enslaving curse of our literature—Soviet censorship. However, the "neoclassics" were silent.

There was, admittedly, a rumor about an audacious act on the part of the writer Stepan Zlobin. Zlobin, who had been the leader of a revolt in a German extermination camp during the war, deserves special mention and indeed a special place in the history of modern Russian literature. On one occasion Zlobin was invited as a writer and historian to an editorial meeting at *Politizdat*. Among those present were tried and true members of the Institute of Marx, Engels and Lenin, who proceeded to eliminate from the projected publication list for the next few years some books about participants in the Revolution who had been killed by Stalin. One revolutionary was excluded as a deviationist and two as partial Trotskyites. The list was becoming rather thin. Zlobin put up his hand and asked the main stickler for purity present, who the main Trotskyite was. There was at first some confusion, then the answer came that it was of course Trotsky. "Not at all," said Zlobin. "The main Trotskyite was Stalin." The jealous defender of Party purity lurched forward in his seat and would have fallen right off if others had not held him up. It was three generations since Russia had heard the like.

But this was only the expression of a personal opinion and one that did not of course get published. Who would be the first to take a step like this in print? Several generations were waiting for the bold spirit who would

73

first throw a stone into the putrid bog, provoke discussion, abuse and some serious reinterpretation of life. Let him just begin the process!

In any event, it was Ilya Ehrenburg who began it. In the tenth issue of the monthly *Znamya* for 1953 there appeared an article by Ehrenburg with the innocent title "On the Writer's Work." This issue was read until it fell apart, as was everything that was heretical yet close to the truth. "Every society knows an epoch of artistic flowering," wrote Enrenburg. "Such periods are called the noon of literature. At present Soviet society is still passing through the early morning." What a fool's paradise we had been living in! For thirty years the press had been daily pounding us with phrases such as "under the sun of the Stalinist epoch" and "on the sunny side of the world." Whole generations had been brought up on these clichés and believed that they lived under a benevolent sun, or at least under the benevolent sun of Stalin's constitution. It now turned out that the dawn had just begun to appear. Did this mean, then, that the Stalinist era had been a period of darkness?

"There is an area," Ehrenburg went on, "of which the writer should have a deeper understanding than his fellow citizens and contemporaries: man's inner world." But it was the Central Committee of the Communist Party of the Soviet Union which was supposed to have a deeper understanding of everything than anyone else and which issued all the directives on art. Yet now, according to Ehrenburg, "the writer should not be bringing up the rear, he is more like a scout than a clerk back at headquarters. He does not copy things out or summarize, he is out discovering." This was a revolt! Revolt against the ignorant, enslaving control of censorship and against Golovenchenko's successors in the Central Committee. "A writer cannot correct his heroes' lives," Ehrenburg stated categorically, "as a proof-reader might correct proofs for a book."

Less than six months later his novel *The Thaw* appeared. It was essentially the continuation of the same heretical article. Its main negative hero was the factory manager Zhuravlyov, a bureaucrat somewhat akin to Listopad in Panova's *Kruzhilikha*. This new Listopad urges people "to look less on the dark side of things, then there will be fewer sides all around." He refuses to made a truck available for a woman in childbirth, saying: "That's not what trucks are for."

There is an artist in the book called Pukhov, a cynic who has wasted away his talent (a theme treated by Gogol in his story "The Portrait" which is about the tragedy of the artist who strives to accommodate his client's taste.) There is also a heroine called Lena who leaves the negative hero Zhuravlyov for the gray but positive character Koroteyev. None of this was new in Russian literature. Ehrenburg had not discovered anything new. The story is perhaps one of Ehrenburg's weakest. Even his fragmented, contrastive style, so appropriate in his scorching publicistic writings, is somehow flabby and colorless in *The Thaw*.

The question arises as to why, if the characters in *The Thaw* are not new and the story-line is a well-used and elementary one, this artistically weak book became a symbol of its time and a phenomenon of the years of transition? Why did its critics attack it as if it represented some exceptional danger?

At the end of the book a storm is whipped up which sweeps Zhuravlyov off his pedestal and "the thaw" begins. Ehrenburg made this word the title of his novel and it acquired a symbolic meaning. All Russia was saying "it's the thaw" while all the obscurantists from Molotov to Sholokhov were claiming that nothing had happened, that everything was just fine, except for a few separate shortcomings.

Ehrenburg had given thinking Russia an exact and graphic definition of the period: it was a thaw. As might have been expected, everyone from Sholokhov to Simonov soon began to tear Ehrenburg to shreds. Ehrenburg's reply to his critics was firstly a preface to a book by Babel which was immediately suppressed, and secondly his last, and possibly best work, *People, Years, Life*. Whole chapters of the book were taken out by the censors and subsequently made their way into samizdat. Ehrenburg's contribution to the process of spiritual awakening in the Russia of the post-Stalin years is difficult to overestimate.

However it was not Ehrenburg who delivered the heaviest blow to Stalinism. The hero of 1953 was another writer entirely, a former police investigator in Irkutsk who took a stand against the arbitrary use of power. He took a death-defying risk, accusing the powers-that-be in the press of being "liars." He put his case so cleverly, clearly and unambiguously that Ehrenburg, author of the seditious article "On the Writer's Work," was almost forgotten. His name was Vladimir Pomerantsev.

2. THE HEROIC ACHIEVEMENT OF VLADIMIR POMERANTSEV

Valdimir Pomerantsev, the first person to break out of the stagnant morass of Stalinism, was a small, quietly spoken man of almost painful modesty. He had an unhurried manner and went about even in the cruellest frosts in just a light woollen jacket. "I'm from Irkutsk," he would say with a shy smile. "I'm used to not giving in to the cold." His lasting achievement was to have a sketch published in the twelfth issue of *Novy mir* for 1953 with the prosaic title "On Sincerity in Literature." It came out only two months after Ehrenburg's well-aimed article in the October issue of *Znamya*.

No sooner had the December issue of *Novy mir* gone on sale than all thinking circles in Russia were talking about Vladimir Pomerantsev. But first let me say something about a side of his life which is little-known and no less heroic than his article uncovering the lies of the epoch.

Pomerantsev had studied jurisprudence and as a young man had worked as an investigator in the isolated parts of Siberia. He then left law, indeed fled from it as one flees from falsehood and hypocrisy. However, many of his fellow students had become well-known public prosecutors and judges, and, through meeting him from time to time, these friends from younger days were so impressed by the principled stand he took that they were continually freeing innocent prisoners. At his own expense he would travel to distant towns and talk to frightened witnesses and get to the truth.

On my first visit to his house on a quiet little street not far from the Stalinskaya subway station, he had two young men with him with shaven heads and wearing quilted prison jackets. They were musicians who had been sentenced to twelve years each in the camps and had in fact come straight from the camp.

A month after they had received this terrible sentence Pomerantsev found out the truth about what had happened. Tired after a concert, they had not wanted to play at the wedding of the chairman of the city council. A messenger from the great man himself had insisted that they play, and finally one of the musicians had said: "Listen, we only play at funerals. Now if your chairman were to kick the bucket..."

They came for them the next morning. They didn't bother fabricating any political justification for it—times were different. They were convicted of gang rape, which was not an uncommon occurrence at that time in that area, and sentenced to serve out their whole term without remission.

Pomerantsev got hold of all the papers documenting the city authorities' revenge. He obtained the removal of the public prosecutor who had used the gang rape case to have the young men unjustly imprisoned.

However, the battle to have the young musicians freed from prison went on for five years. While in the camp, one of them, a violinist, got frost-

77

bite in his fingers which were then amputated, while another went blind. They were "pensioned off" as invalids. A third one could not bear the suffering and hanged himself. Only two came out of the camp after five years inside. And the first thing they did on getting out was to go to see their liberator, Vladimir Pomerantsev.

Over the years all sorts of people gained their freedom through Pomerantsev's self-sacrificing efforts: factory workers, young men from the country, geologists, kolkhoz chairmen. On his birthday, guests would fly in from as far away as Petropavlovsk in Kamchatka and Magadan, sometimes just for the day. As they raised their glasses to toast this health, many would wipe a tear or two from their eyes.

In December 1953 Pomerantsev sounded the alarm. His investigatory sketch "On Sincerity in Literature," which liars and falsifiers so much wanted to eliminate from the history of literature, lies before me as I write. "Insincerity is artificiality in the creation of something... The history of art and the first principles of psychology cry out against artificiality in the writing of novels and plays." In the Central Committee they realized very quickly that it was socialist realism he had in mind. Socialist realism consisted of nothing but a schematized, prescribed approach and artificiality.

It was the main "varnishing" devices in Soviet literature which came under fire in his article: a) the crudest—the fabrication of universal well-being and prosperity (Babayevsky, Antonov, Pyryev's films such as *The Kuban Cossacks*); b) the subtler device—no obvious falsehood. The pork in aspic and roast goose are absent from "kolkhoz life," but the negative and unpleasant aspects are passed over in silence; c) the basest and most cunning of all—working out a story-line so that all the more problematical questions and all thematic depth remain to one side, untouched. "The distortion here is in the arbitrary choice of subject matter," said Pomerantsev.

In the wake of Pomerantsev's article there surfaced in Moscow a story which was half anecdote and half perceptive analysis of what socialist realism was in fact, all about. According to the anecdote, there once lived a cruel tsar called Nebuchadnezzar, who was lame in one leg and had only one eye. The court painter depicted him as a knight of magnificent proportions with eyes shining with courage. He was executed for "varnishing reality." A second painter was summoned who naturally was all too aware of what happened to the first. He depicted the terrible tsar exactly as he was, lame and one-eyed, and he too was executed, "for culminating reality." The third one summoned drew the terrible tsar side-on. The tsar was kneeling, and screwed up one eye as he took aim with a bow and arrow. There was no distortion. It was his bad eye that the tsar had screwed up, and his short leg was doubled up. The tsar as hunter was the very picture of agility and vigor. There was nothing false about it. There was also nothing true about it. The teller of this tale usually ended it by saying that the frightened and trembling artist who had at the last moment hit upon the method of foreshortening his subject was the progenitor of socialist realism.

This anecdote was soon being told all over Moscow and soon afterwards all over the country. It was told in the universities, in the Union of Writers, at high-level meetings and even at the innumerable high-security scientific research institutes and engineering institutes where the technocratic elite snorted with mirth when they heard all about it.

So Pomerantsev's sharp, talented article, in giving voice to feelings which had been building up for a long time, began to change the moral climate of the country. But Pomerantsev went further. "Writers not only can, have but do have, and obligation to reject all devices and methods designed to obviate contradictions and difficult problems." A real writer will never seek to suppress problems.

Pomerantsev tells of a case from his law experience when he was sent to a far-flung kolkhoz in Zaozerye which was beyond the reach of the authorities. It was run by a real virago, a widow who had got the kolkhoz on its feet, and saved numbers of people from starvation, but not always by irreproachable means from the point of view of the law. She ran a homemade liquor still, for example, and used the brew to pay off the carpenters and fishermen who helped make the kolkhoz prosperous. The public prosecutor demanded that an action be brought against the widow immediately, and that she be sent to prison, despite the fact that she had saved scores of children from death. It was then that Pomerantsev gave up his job in the public prosecutor's office. In years to come he was several times to go to the rescue of just such kolkhoz chairmen.

"Frankness must be bold," he demanded in the article published in *Novy mir*. "Don't write until you're white hot. Don't think about the public prosecutor." This was remarkable advice, coming from a former investigator in the public prosecutor's office.

He naturally has no mercy for the smug, untalented establishment writers who "beat us" when we are suffering and defenseless "with empty, dried-up phrases." But Pomerantsev has a particular score to settle with critics. "It's not sounds we hear coming from the critics," he writes angrily, "just echoes... It is poor when the critic has no suggestions to make, but waits for suggestions to be made to him." "We know the names of many writers and know their books, but we have no idea what literature owes them or what they have given it."

"Our critics," Pomerantsev goes on indignantly, "are afraid of counting some modern Soviet writers as part of our literary heritage... and they are afraid of disregarding those who have been swept upwards on some paper glider and are held aloft on gusts of wind or by strings."

In each paragraph and in each line Pomerantsev was aiming telling blows at his opponents. "What does 'playing safe' on the part of our editors mean?" he asked. "It means at least ten different vices: egotism, cowardice, blind pragmatism, favoring lack of content and other things, including moral baseness." Yet people shake hands warmly with these cowardly editors and invite them to dinner. They should be boycotted and shunned by honest people. Writers should be writing about real passions and suffering. "The enrichment of themes seems to me the most urgent necessity in literature."

It is apparent that literature was "mobilized" in some sense immediately after Stalin's death—the very same year, in fact, although there was still no thought of sweeping Stalin from his pedestal. Indeed, on the contrary, Yermilov and his ilk were still glorifying the Stalin epoch. Yet genuine writers moved into the attack against the entrenched positions still occupied by the Stalinists.

As will be readily understood, Pomerantsev's attack on Stalinism was held against him to the end of his days. Scores of excellent stories he had written remained buried in drawers. This was a real crime against literature, because Vladimir Pomerantsev was a talented and penetrating writer.

His story "The Carp," for example, which was suppressed by the censors, is unforgettable. It is worth touching on this story which was not passed for publication by the censors despite the fact that merely to recount it does not do justice to the masterful way in which it is written. A phone-call is received in the manager's office of a fish enterprise to the effect that the Kremlin wants some carp. Thinking that it must be Stalin himself asking for the carp, one of the functionaries rushes off in a panic to a distant fish farm where he knows carp are still raised. It is deepest winter. None of the farm workers is willing to try to fish the carp out from under the ice, so the Secretary of the Party regional committee and the functionary break a hole in the ice and stand up to their knees in the icy water carrying out the task the State had given them—catching some carp. The functionary brings back a few carp, but falls seriously ill. It soon comes to light that it was not Stalin who wanted them at all, but General Vlaslik, the guard commander. His mother has come to visit him from the country and is upset because the fish in Moscow are all salt-water fish, and her son could do with a nice fresh-water carp. The General decides to make his mother happy and rings the ministry on the Kremlin telephone—the so-called "vert-ushka" or direct line. Pomerantsev tries to make us see that fear and obsequiousness had reached such a point that on receiving a call from the Kremlin a man was ready to kill himself, his relatives and anyone else for that matter, just to come up to the mark. He subsequently becomes an invalid, is spurned by his wife and rejected by his children. Having in a sense given his life for the Stalin epoch, his high government official asks himself, and those around him: "I'm an invalid, I get an invalid's pension. There are war invalids. There are work invalids. What sort of invalid am I?"

Pomerantsev's sharply drawn, vibrant stories passed from hand to hand. The censors removed them from his published collections, which were dry, colorless books. They were less books than excerpts from books. Works such as "The Implacable Notary" (1960) and "The Werewolf" (1961) made their way into print in a distorted form. The latter is about a remote Siberian village where officials sent from the city, and indeed any enemies, are killed by tying them to a deer's back and chasing the frightened deer into the forest undergrowth where it tries to get rid of the screaming, bloodied burden on its back by scraping against trees. In 1965 *An Unhurried Conversation* came out, mutilated by the censors just like his earlier works. Pomerantsev made an attempt to publish the stories which were the product of so much suffering in a collection called *House of Stories.* He died the very day the type for his long-awaited book was broken up.

It was Valentina Karpova, chief editor of the *Sovetsky pisatel* publishing house, who caused his death. When she heard that the editor of an associated publishing house had been rebuked by the Central Committee for putting out one of Pomerantsev's books, she stopped the printing-presses in Tula, where, among other things, *House of Stories* was being printed. Over the telephone, Karpova told Pomerantsev that she would take a fresh look at his book. Pomerantsev, who was ill and weakened by suffering and had already had two heart-attacks, realized what the cowardly and over-vigilant editor's implacably severe tone meant. Dropping the telephone, he fell down gasping. He was taken to the hospital where he died.

Together with many other writers, I attended his funeral. I had no intention of making a speech, I just wept—we had been friends all our lives. It was the official mourners who were invited to speak, the same people who had hounded him into his grave. What foresight Yuzovsky had had! "There's nothing terrible about dying," he had said and his words seared my memory, "what is terrible is that those who persecuted you will make fine speeches at your graveside." Pomerantsev had also foreseen this. He had given his wife the strictest instructions before he died that his coffin was on no account to be ceremonially displayed in the Writers' Club. He did not want to be in the presence of unclean spirits. But the wretches pursued him to the end. They hurried to the crematorium with a small wreath wound onto wire—it is a wonder it was not barbed wire. Having meted out their punishment, the *Sovetsky pisatel* representatives assumed sorrowing, deeply shocked expressions.

This was intolerable. Pushing forward, I asked permission to speak, not in the name of a publishing house or the commission on the literary heritage, but of the writer's friends. They tried to edge me away and a broad-backed man in a leather coat began to force me back, but it is not so simple to cause a scene at a funeral to the quiet, sorrowing strains of Chopin and in front of the bereft family I began to speak and no one interrupted me—no one dared. I told everyone who had killed Vladimir Pomerantsev. As a result, the murderer's name was at least known to Moscow literary circles. "In the galaxy of the martyrs to Russian literature," I said beside the coffin, "the star of Vladimir Pomerantsev has now begun to shine."

After Pomerantsev's brilliant breakthrough with his prosaically named article "On Sincerity in Literature," the chief editor of *Novy mir*, Aleksandr Tvardovsky, was removed from his post, although not, it is true, for the last time. Konstantin Simonov was appointed chief editor, himself to be removed in his turn after *Novy mir* published Dudintsev's heretical novel *Not by Bread Alone*.

Aleksey Surkov raged and fulminated at various plenary meetings that "in place of the concept of the Party line in literature, Pomerantsev has given pride of place to 'sincerity.'" And if "the Party line" and "sincerity" were suddenly declared to be synonymous, then where would Surkov be? Pensioned off.

It was not the "utterly sincere" Aleksey Surkov who was continually harassed and dragged from office to office, but Vladimir Pomerantsev, who once angrily told the powerful Polikarpov, head of the Cultural Section of the Central Committee of the Communist Party: "We're not going to come to any understanding, you and I, comrade Polikarpov, because you don't need freedom, whereas I do."

Freedom was as necessary to the courageous and talented Valdimir Pomerantsev as air. That is why he was killed.

3. THE SCAFFOLD DECKED WITH FLOWERS

Vladimir Pomerantsev's achievement bore abundant fruit. It galvanized all those who still had some conscience. A whole new militantly critical literature appeared, together with new names that all thoughtful Russians spoke of with gratitude.

Among them was Fyodor Abramov who became one of the most interesting prose writers about the darker sides of country life. Mark Shcheglov was another. We were students together when he was a sickly young man on crutches but possessed of irrepressible spiritual strength. Everyone was fond of him. Up to that time no one had ridiculed that living corpse Leonid Leonov so cleverly and so bravely as Shcheglov. In his novel *The Russian Forest* Leonov had portrayed a scoundrel by the name of Gratsiansky and, fearing a drubbing from the State, Leonov attempted to attribute Gratsiansky's origins to his experience in the tsarist secret police and abroad. Soviet reality, supposedly, could not have produced scoundrels of this kind. What a lashing he was given by Shcheglov, a highly-talented critic for a quarter of a century who was doomed from the outset.

Both Fyodor Abramov and Mark Shcheglov were the products of *Novy mir*, fresh young growth in the devastated forest of incorruptible criticism. They were followed by some venerable names: the poetess Olga Berggolts, heroine of the Leningrad blockade, whose assault on the murderous elements in Soviet society took the form of an article with the straightforward, hard-hitting title of "Against the Liquidation of Lyrical Poetry"; the sea-faring playwright Aleksandr Kron, who ridiculed the misunderstandings which frightened Soviet dramatists tried to pass off as "conflicts"; there was the much maligned poet Ilya Selvinsky who published a famous protest in *Literaturnaya gazeta* in which he compared Soviet writers and critics to members of an orchestra: some are given rosin so that the sound of their instruments carries a long way, and others are not, so that they can only be heard in the first three rows of the stalls.

Two of the hangmen from 1949 were speedily removed from the secretariat of the Union of Writers: Gribachev and Sofronov. At first they disappeared as completely as Pushkin's "stone guest," but then they turned up again at close quarters: one was editor-in-chief of the showcase periodical *Sovetsky Soyuz (Soviet Union)* and the other editor of *Ogonyok (The Spark)*, a magazine which in the Soviet Union is principally found in hairdressers' salons.

"Our armored train stands waiting in the siding," as the rather bitter joke went at the Union of Writers (the words were from Svetlov's poem "Kakhovka"), indicating the general presentiment that something unpleasant was about to happen. And not without justification. Stalinism could not abide the truth, and by degrees the moral atmosphere was polluted by a flood of dishonest works such as Alexander Shteyn's play *A Personal Affair* (*Teatr*, No. 2, 1954).

The play's heroine, Maryana, does not want to join the Party. "Why not?" asks her father, Khlebnikov, who himself survived the Stalinist butchers only by a miracle.

"Not until you're rehabilitated, father, I just can't," his daughter replies.

Her father pushes her aside, and stands up and shouts at her: "What do you mean, you can't? Are you nursing a grudge or something?" Maryana says nothing. "Who have you got a grudge against? The Party?" Naturally Maryana says nothing. But her father is not giving in without a fight. "I'm asking you who you've got a grudge against."

Maryana murmurs something which is meant to sound stupid, and mentions her present state of mind. Her father now gets very worked up and says in an impassioned, apoplectic monologue: "What would my life have been without the Party? It was my very life-blood." And so on and so forth. In conclusion he says: "It's shameful!"

Dishonest works such as this, in all genres, occupied the Soviet stage and pushed out the genuine, analytical art of artistic discovery.

However, this was insufficient to save the hangmen. In order to save the hangmen, it was necessary to erect a constantly functioning scaffold, on which talent could be strung up. The country did not have to wait long, since it had been assembled long ago, before 17 August 1934. It was on this day that Maksim Gorky opened the First Congress of Writers, declaring in tones of exalted enthusiasm that they had gathered together with writers from abroad "in a country where Stalin's iron will is untiringly and miraculously at work." According to the report in *Pravda*, at this point Gorky had to interrupt "an explosion of enthusiasm."

Alexander Fadeyev informed the audience with true inspiration how astonishingly deep the meaning of a word could be and took as an example the word "friendship." For instance, there was the friendship which bound the Party leaders. More precisely this was an "iron" friendship, he said. "Iron will," "iron friendship"—yet this was only three months before Kirov was murdered. This was truly a new kind of friendship.

Alexei Surkov did not grasp the full significance of Fadeyev's comparison of friendship and iron and was annoyed that the question of hate had been forgotten at the First Congress. Like the crafty old fox he was he sensed what was going to happen. He wanted blood, but without any euphemisms or poetic turns of phrase.

Twenty years passed between the First and Second Congresses, and as everyone now knows, these were twenty years of iron friendship of a kind Russia, throughout centuries of bloody history, had not yet known. Once more the scaffold was rolled out, decked with flowers, entwined with garlands and even illuminated. This happened on 16 December 1954, the day the Second Congress of Writers was opened. I attended the Second Congress from the second day to the last in the naive hope that literature would be given a new lease of life. When I first went into the Hall of Columns in the House of Unions, I was tempted to believe for a moment that everything had indeed changed. The walls of the House of Unions were covered in cartoons of a kind which would have been impossible a year earlier, let alone eighteen months when Stalin was alive. One of them showed a sluttish, sneaky-looking girl with the pointed, cringing features of an informer. The next one showed her faceless silhouette wearing a red Komsomol necktie. The first cartoon bore the caption: "This is Liza—Liza Lickspittle" (*Liza—podliza*.) Under the second: "This is Liza in the *Detgiz* version." (*Detgiz* publishes children's books.)

Nearby, covering a whole wall, was a drawing showing the head of Kornei Chukovsky. The first impressions of life of almost every child in Russia were formed under the influence of Chukovsky's *Moydodyr*. For a long time he was in disgrace, especially when this letter to Repin begging him not to return to Stalin's Russia was found (and sent to the appropriate authorities) at Repin's dacha. And now here was a cartoon caricaturing in a good natured way long-nosed Kornei Chukovsky. Underneath was the playful caption: "Nashdodur."[2]

The proceedings were opened by Olga Forsh, by then an elderly writer, a clever woman and a member of the intelligentsia. She had a malicious streak. Referring to the representative of the Central Committee at the Congress, she said in the foyer: "You call that a face? It's an udder."

Up on the dais she quavered her way through something written on a piece of paper given her by Konstantin Fedin as he helped her to the dais, bending down to her respectfully as he did so. The speech, which had obviously been prepared by the "udder" in the foyer, was completely devoid of ideas. What a tragedy it is when a nation's people of conscience, intelligence and talent are reduced to mouthing the words on scraps of paper from some government office! A good third of the audience got up noisily and started out of the corridors.

Then suddenly there was a movement in the opposite direction. I remember clearly how the writers poured back into the hall finishing their sandwiches as they came. The reason was that the poet of the Leningrad blockade, Olga Berggolts, was about to speak. Her pale, drained, suffering face and scarcely audible, faltering voice caused something akin to panic amongst the official party: Berggolts had started speaking about the writer's right to self-expression. Without self-expression, she said, there could be neither writers nor literature. Then suddenly turning to the trembling official figures on the dais, she said with the weariness and chronic anguish of the eternal political prisoner: "But you don't need any of this... You don't need literature. You need just one writer, and even then..."

Neither I nor my neighbors could catch the last word. "And even then..." what? (The word was also omitted from the official record, together with quite a lot of other material.) We started asking everyone in turn: "And even then... what?"

Olga Berggolts herself no longer remembered. She was sitting in a corner of the cafeteria, pouring herself glass after glass of vodka with a trembling hand, trying to escape, even if just temporarily, from the terrible world where literature was led publicly onto the scaffold, as in times past when the tsars' assassins were led to the scaffold.

Who could blame this heroine of the Leningrad blockade? There had been all the sleepless nights of interrogation, the camps, the blockade, the execution of her husband, the poet Boris Kornilov, and the failure to punish his murderer, the informer Lesyuchevsky, who after the war, thanks to his denunciations of others, was put in charge of the *Sovetsky pisatel* publishing house; then there was the strangulation of post-war literature, whose mouth was stuffed up in a special way like a prisoner's before he is shot. All this was too much for the frail little woman with the ashen face.

Thanks to the efforts of many, the text of Olga Berggolts' speech was eventually published in its complete form. *Literaturnaya gazeta* was forced to reproduce exactly Berggolts' outburst of self-expression, including the final words: "You need just one writer, and even then a deceased one."

The first to recognize the danger of this concept of self-expression was Aleksandr Fadeyev—his services were valued with good reason. His immediate reaction was that "it's decadents who use that sort of terminology."

Self-expression! It was essentially self-expression that Pomerantsev had been demanding. If free rein were given to "self-expression," thoughts and feelings would take precedent over Party line. This alarmed the Congress big-wigs so much that they did not allow Konstantin Paustovsky to speak. As early as 1947 he had demanded of us that we never give up the feeling of inner freedom, for without it there could be no literature. He had almost immediately come down with an attack of asthma and had been helped to a divan where he had lain wheezing: "The feeling of inner freedom... without it there can be no..." Pushkin was the first in Russia to speak of "secret freedom," an expression picked up and passed on by Blok. In his poem "The Prophet" Pushkin has given us the complete blueprint for action. Konstantin Paustovsky, leader of a prose writers' seminar, had not been able to bequeath to us the feeling of "secret freedom." It had been impossible even to pronounce the words "secret freedom" except in private. Secret from whom? They would have quickly asked. And to what end? However, even we raw beginners had understood what Paustovsky had wanted to tell us—reserved, careful Paustovsky, who had avoided politics for decades.

The old toadies on the Congress presidium were well aware of the sort of ideas which were Paustovsky's very life-blood. One of their stooges in the audience called out: "Let's finish there!" Everybody was already tired of the chatter and the speechifying volcanoes spewing forth cotton-wool.

No less than thirty-two Moscow writers immediately declined to speak in Paustovsky's place. Alexander Bek announced this for the whole hall to hear in order to shame the Congress chairmen. A vain hope! Not a shadow of discomfort passed over the faces of Surkov, Simonov or Korneichuk, that inseparable threesome of literary proceedings. Only a businesslike expression and a sense of the importance to the State of their mission could be observed on their faces.

I remember how Paustovsky, realizing that he would not be allowed to speak, stood up in the middle of the hall, bent over as if something were weighing him down, and then slowly walked out, tapping the floor with his cane. There was complete silence, even among those up on the dais. The tapping seemed to be getting louder. It rang in my ears for a long time—tap! tap! tap!

That was the first time it really came home to me: what is this Congress? It's really a scaffold on wheels. It had stood out in the shed for twenty years unneeded—they had used other, more modern methods to kill people, but now it was needed again, and it was decorated with fresh flowers and rolled out, so that literature should not even think of trying any "self-expression."

As before, on innumerable occasions, the literature of moral resistance had been shown the soap-smeared rope. And yet again it refused to be intimidated.

A decision was then taken to deceive it. It was publicly announced that henceforth and for all time writers themselves would be in charge of literature. The Party functionary Dmitry Polikarpov, Zhdanov's right-hand man and a figure detested by most writers, changed jobs. Until this move, he had been installed in the famous Rostov house in Moscow where the Union of Writers had been founded and where he gave audience to the suffering. Now he was ensconced in the gray Central Committee building where he was in charge of the whole range of Soviet culture. Before he left, he managed to rid the courtyard of the Union of Writers of Rodin's magnificent Thinker. The stone thinker was a living reproach.

4. THE COBBLESTONE—THE PROLETARIAT'S WEAPON

Olga Berggolts' "self expression" had been held up to shame, Vladimir Pomerantsev and his longing for sincerity had been thrown overboard, and Ilya Ehrenburg's novel *The Thaw* had been trampled into the dust. Now in 1955 the leadership of the Union of Writers made attempts to preserve the ideology and tactics of the scorched earth policy. This meant that there was not to be a single article or book which diverged in its conceptions even a fraction of an inch from the mandatory Party line, the peremptory shouts and orders of the Secretaries of the Party Central Committee. A scorched earth policy means that there is just one single point of view, a single opinion about everything in the world, particularly the inner life. In a word, scorched earth tactics mean fascism.

Then suddenly strange winds blew up, coming at first, possibly, from the uprisings spreading through the camps. At first they were put down with tanks and then the camps were reorganized. In the camps people demanded one thing—the truth, on behalf of the whole country. These new, biting winds sometimes overcame Stalin's enthusiastic apprentices, allowing the first timid literary protests to survive.

It was publicistic literature which first raised its head. Like a literary scout, it precedes the main body of prose. Prose demands time. Publicistic literature is like a stone on the roadway. The writer overcomes his fear and lets fly with it. "The cobblestone is the proletariat's weapon"—these words are inscribed on the base of a "masterpiece" of socialist realism, a sculpture showing a worker reaching in anger and desperation for a cobblestone.

My own prose writings, like those of Vladimir Pomerantsev and other friends, lay for decades untouched in drawers and in publishers' cupboards, losing their freshness. On other occasions the manuscript got so cut about as to be unreadable. We were willy-nilly being pushed to the point of throwing stones.

One day in 1954 I went to *Literaturnaya gazeta* with an article. It was an ordinary sort of article, not very long. The theme, admittedly, was taboo: about how people were being taught to stop thinking in departments of Marxism at the universities. It is quite possible that what first prompted me to write it was Pomerantsev's article, which for me was the first flash of light in the darkness. I wrote it at the beginning of 1954 and eventually managed to get it published, however paradoxically, in the semi-official Central Committee journal *Partiynaya zhizn (Party Life)* (1955, no. 24). This was an organ of instruction whose every word was law for the Party machine.

I went from editor to editor, from desk to desk, with this article for two solid years. Some looked at me as if I was the village idiot, others as if I was a dangerous inventor pestering them with some new kind of infernal machine under my arm. However, sometimes it was discussed and even commented favorably upon, and on these occasions I would go to pick it up after being called urgently by phone and listen to polite explanations to the effect that it would be better *for me* to put it aside until times were different.

Then someone on the staff of *Literaturnaya gazeta* was bold enough, not to have it printed—the run-of-the-mill Soviet journalist has never had the right to make decisions of that kind—but to give a report on it at a meeting of the editorial board. It was at a time when nothing was very clear and consequently no one dared object to it aloud, in case he was taken for a reactionary. So the article was sent off to be set up.

It was only later in the quiet of their offices, alone with their fears, that they really took a thorough look at it. A week later I was told that the article was what was wanted and that it was "correct," but that it would be better not to base it on the situation at Moscow University because this could have undesirable repercussions abroad at a time when the University was celebrating its jubilee. It would be better, I was told, to take some quiet provincial tertiary institution and strip *it* naked before the whole world, showing it up as an exception typical only of some out-of-the-way place. This was not a suggestion but a condition of publication.

I had never been to Odessa and had intended for a long time to take a look at the city Babel and Paustovsky came from, and so I chose Odessa. At the University there everything was the same as in Moscow, down to the last detail. On the second or third day I happened upon the class which became the basis of my study. At any rate, this class became the thread I pulled on to unravel the whole ball. I shall describe what happened in some detail because this question of mass-mindlessness and credulity is a basic one for an understanding of Russia. It was a philosophy seminar on aesthetics, conducted by an old professor, an erudite, intelligent man with a sceptical set to his mouth. A paper was read by a fourth-year student, a philologist by the name of Podgayets, a much-decorated war hero who had lost a leg, a serious man with an open, good-natured face. He analyzed certain plays which were at that time being attacked in all the newspapers. He also attacked them, naturally, but not in such quarrelsome terms as the newspapers. He spoke more decorously, discussing the imagery and arguing his points and using the whole arsenal of philosophical terminology. In other words, he slated the plays, but in almost scholarly fashion, with references to Hegel and the Young Hegelians, as well as to Marx-Engels-Lenin, of course. He ridiculed the "no-conflict" theory which was so prevalent at the time. A good student, and a thoughtful man.

The professor was very pleased with him, and asked, as is usual, if there were any questions. For some reason there were none. As a guest

I sat quietly at the back. Then hesitantly I raised my hand and asked which of the plays he had just analyzed so skillfully he had seen performed. He answered that he had not been able to see the plays because they had not been put on in Odessa. Then I made myself put up my hand again and ask which of the plays he had read. I thought I knew what the answer would be, and I felt ashamed at asking, but business was business. Flushing slightly, he answered that he had not read the plays either. The professor made a feeble attempt to object, and waved his hands around in protest, but Podgayets stubbornly repeated in all honesty: "No, I haven't read them." Then he looked at me with his bright eyes with their hard core of incomprehension and exclaimed: "What's wrong with that? There have been so many reviews written on these plays! In every newspaper! In every journal! There aren't any other opinions!"

Before me stood a man who had reached his fourth year at the university and could participate in a philosophy seminar presenting a scholarly analysis of a topic while remaining firmly convinced that in a scholarly analysis it is permissible to rely not on the powers of one's own mind, on one's own knowledge or ability, but on someone else's opinion, especially a "leading" opinion.

How many misfortunes Russia has seen, how much blood has been spilt, how many betrayals have been called noble acts because young people have been taught to stop thinking for themselves. They have been duped, turned into well-behaved parrots who vote and shoot without thinking about what they're doing.

I started thinking about the following questions as I began unravelling the ball: Were the teachers stupid? Not at all. Both the professor taking the seminar and the head of the department were intelligent people. What then was happening? If all the intelligent people came together and formed a fellowship of fools and begot children after their own likeness, what would the end result be?

It turned out that the academics in Odessa, like their colleagues in the humanities in tertiary institutions in Moscow, were living in terror, as before. The terror of the "thirties had not been forgotten or overcome, the period when saying anything that was not completely lifeless was called 'ad-libbing,' while whatever was new or independent was immediately decried and declared a 'hostile thrust.'"

Since that time there have been at least six generations of students. They have come to the university as inquisitive youths with a thousand why's on their lips, and by the end of their fifth year there, deprived of the opportunity to seek or compare, fed like peasant babies on pap and pacified with dummies, they have joined in the pseudo-scientific phrasemongering. Their brains have grown numb. Podgayets in his honesty and millions of other Podgayetses in every corner of the USSR have not even suspected that they have been cruelly and criminally deceived. They had first been

91

disarmed and then bound hand and foot.

My article caused panic and horror, even on the part of my supporter at *Literaturnaya gazeta*. However, it was too late to retreat and it was sent for approval to Vitaly Ozerov, the deputy editor-in chief, now editor-in-chief of the theoretical monthly *Voprosy literatury (Problems of literature)*, whose title is popularly shortened to *Vopli (Screams)*. The old *Pravda* man and boss of Soviet critics did not have a moment's hesitation. "Teaching them to stop thinking? No such problem has developed," he declared, looking away from me at an empty corner.

I remember flaring up and saying: "You know, we trembled with fear for thirty years. Can't you find the strength to overcome that fear? If you can't, then who can?" The old truth-lover blushed, and, taking the article, wrote across it in a firm hand: "To be set up," and gave me a lucid look.

However, he put the article in an issue which he was not responsible for. The editor-in-chief, S.S. Smirnov, who was responsible for it, put a thick red line through the article, and Vitaly Ozerov just threw up his arms as if to say: "I tried to be brave and honest, but alas! ..."

Several days later I received instructions to appear at the Sretenka Street police station, room 7. I arrived puzzled. At the duty desk there were a few foul-mouthed, drunken women and there was a disgusting smell of vomit in the air. I was taken straight to a separate room where the senior lieutenant who got up to greet me was a youthful looking man with the ruddy cheeks of a good Komsomol member. Politely he said: "We're not the police. We're State Security."

For the next four hours or so he asked me in the minutest detail about who I was friendly with, who I spent my time with, what I wrote and what I thought. I knew very well what the politeness of interrogators could turn into, although the firing-squad era had passed. I gave the names of two of my most orthodox acquaintances, whose combined ages came to 150. Then I fell silent. He gave a sign and asked why I visited so-and-so... former camp-inmates used to go there, he said, people who were resentful and sick. They were not always responsible for what they said, whereas I was. I had not the vaguest idea what was going on.

Apparently the period for having my soul bared was over. The senior lieutenant went away and came back with some heavy types in civilian clothing. They looked at me closely for a long time and then finally one of them said in a relaxed, fatherly voice: "Your record looks fairly clean, and your friends, as far as we can make out, are all right. Why do you write this sort of stuff... about teaching people to stop thinking... eh? Real science fiction. Revolt of the slaves, eh? You'd better be careful, my lad!"

"So that's what I owe all this to," I thought in astonishment. There was only one thing I could do—complain. But to whom could I complain about the editor-in-chief of *Literaturnaya gazeta* who had a direct line to the Kremlin on his desk? I went to see Dmitry Polikarpov, former Secretary of the Union of Writers and at that time on the Central Committee of the Party. A word from him could stop the presses, cut up or bury articles. Anything important was checked out with him first—the editors were petrified of him.

He carefully read the article and said that he had no objections to it, but that it was impossible for him, as a responsible member of the Central Committee, to force the chief editor of *Literaturnaya gazeta* to print what he did not want to print. Literature was now in the hands of the writers themselves. Like Vitaly Ozerov, he then looked at me with a saint-like expression in his eyes.

I wandered out of his office worn out and depressed by the hypocrisy which lay on me like a grave-stone. I set off down the corridor with my exit pass in one hand and the galley proof of my ill-fated article in the other. It was a long corridor and I wandered along reading whatever caught my eye, as a city-dweller does. Mostly it was name-plates, but then I suddenly noticed a sign covered in blue glass which said: "Editor-in-chief, *Partiynaya zhizn (Party Life)*." "Well, since I'm here, why not knock?" I thought. Filled with new determination I knocked. The editor took the galley proof in hands trembling with rage and immediately began to read it, no doubt because it was not simply a manuscript but was set out like a newspaper article.

When he had read it through, he took off his spectacles and said the unthinkable: "You can't imagine how badly we need an article like this..." I was simply stunned—it was so unexpected. He went on in a business-like manner: "We'll use it in the next issue. I'll send it off to be set up."

Here I began to panic. It was over six months since I had written it. Someone might have died in Odessa since then, or things might have changed. I had better go and take a look.

"Certainly," he said. "Can you fly to Odessa straight away? So we can get it into the next issue."

A telephone call was made from the Central Committee reserving me a seat on the plane. Only one was reserved, but four were kept for me, just in case. I was travelling like the merchant in Ostrovsky's play—four carriages for one man.

In Odessa I witnessed a radical change of a kind which it is important to understand if we are to get some idea of the moral atmosphere of the epoch. Just six months earlier I had been in Odessa with papers showing I was on official business for *Literaturnaya gazeta* and had found it easy to make friends. I now tried to make the same kind of friendly contacts, and found that it was out of the question. People talked to me as if they thought I might shoot them in the stomach while we were talking. They were openly afraid of me and could barely bring themselves to speak to me. What was wrong? It took me some time to realize. This time my credentials were quite different. They were stamped in big red letters with the initials of the Central

Committee of the Communist Party of the Soviet Union. In smaller letters underneath was: "*Partiynaya shizn*, organ of the Central Committee of the C.P.S.U."

So I was not simply anybody any more. I was "from there," someone you could not argue with, or speak frankly to. I could suddenly see for myself now that people coming "from there" were as a rule unable to grasp the real situation because they heard only what they wanted to hear.

I remember to this day the stammering of the director of the regional publishing house and the frozen, jelly-like eyes of the rector of the University, who was numb with fear of saying the wrong thing. It was painful to watch. It was both absurd and terrible at the same time.

When my article appeared on the Moscow newsstands, its title had been changed by a member of the editorial board who was on the Central Committee. All mention of a "Department of Marxism" had been bashfully removed from the heading, although it had been left in the body of the article. It now bore the more academic title of "Breeding an Unthinkable Approach." The final paragraph was also an editorial contribution.

Thus there appeared in the semi-official organ of the Central Committee an article reporting how for years, indeed for decades, in the departments of Marxism-Leninism, Dialectical Materialism and Political Economy—in fact all the most strongly Party-oriented departments, students had been taught to stop thinking. So that these few pages might see the light of day I had spent two years of my life. Yet all my cobblestone, thrown in desperation, did was rattle a few sleepy windows—nothing more.

No one could understand how the article had gotten published. And, quite frankly, no one was more astounded that I was. Yet the explanation turned out to be quite simple. The issue in which the article appeared came out at the end of December 1955. It was only six weeks or so before the Twentieth Party Congress at which Stalin would be declared the murderer of millions and it would sink through to the thickest schoolboy in the land that, as Galich's song has it: "Our father turned out to be no father, but a bitch."

The Twentieth Congress was opened in winter, right at the beginning of 1956, and in the gray Central Committee building they already knew what was being prepared, and they were in a hurry to get in step. I was unaware of this, as was the country as a whole, but they knew.

A couple of weeks earlier, or six months later, such a "seditious" article would never have appeared. It would have been declared slanderous and anti-Party. What of prose of a more extended kind, written over many years and bearing in its depths the same basic theme? Could it break through to the reader?

Ilya Ehrenburg, Vladimir Pomerantsev and Olga Berggolts had been the first to assail the butchers with whatever came to hand. They could not wait. After them came our generation—the soldiers back from the war.

Even before the Twentieth Congress, publicistic literature had gained a small bridgehead.

It was in this atmosphere of hopes and fears, of concealed confrontation and open threats, that a Moscow writers' organization began to put together, with great difficulty, a collection of poetry and prose called *Literary Moscow* which was to represent a whole epoch in Russia's spiritual life.

1956 was the year of anti-Stalinism only in a manner of speaking. The "year" lasted from the end of the Twentieth Congress in the second half of February, when Khrushchev's speech in closed session opened the eyes of the whole world to the true nature of our "leader and teacher," until 30 June 1956, when the Central Committee started to beat a retreat. At a meeting in Moscow Anastas Mikoyan was soon to be heard berating members of the intelligentsia for "trying to stir up the elements."

All the same, Russian literature managed to have its say. As in 1953, for a very short space of time it achieved total mobilization. It was *Literary Moscow* which first attracted everyone's attention. Although it was an enormous volume, it did not contain even a third of the material prepared for it. Banned after the appearance of the second volume, *Literary Moscow* became not just a landmark in Russia's social and literary life, but a pinnacle heroically reached only after many losses. The greatest losses were the early death of Emmanuil Kazakevich who had nothing left to hope for after the routing of *Literary Moscow*, and the long isolation and illness of the writer and poet Aleksandr Yashin. When Yashin died, still unbroken, his funeral was held in the cemetery of his native village of Bludnovo in the Vologda district to the wailing and sermons of mourners from several northern villages. The funeral was conducted as if it were that of the last defender of the peasants.

However, all that was to come later. At the time, early in 1956, as I leafed through the first volume, which had just been passed for publication, I was delighted to see that among the editors were Konstantin Paustovsky, who in the past had always avoided open conflict with the authorities, and Emmanuil Kazakevich who had survived all the violent assaults directed at him and had again thrown himself into the fray, at least as an editor. Serving with Paustovsky and Kazakevich were Aleksandr Bek, Venyamin Kaverin, and Vladimir Tendryakov, each one of whom is a beacon in Russian post-war literature.

In the preparation of the first volume, there was a need to exercise some home-spun diplomacy, a touch of old-style politesse. When the editorial board was presented with something of an uncompromisingly explosive character, it would put it aside on the grounds that the first issue must present an almost "cloudless" picture, and be inoffensively round. "They mustn't take fright at what we're doing, otherwise they'll ban it... They'll have to get used to us first and see that we're not rebels and not robbers who sound like nightingales..." The first volume really was round and smooth... like a cannon-ball. That is why some shied away from it.

However, the important thing about this smooth first volume is that there were pearls to be found in the enormous pile of "official dung" made up of articles by people in authority such as Konstantin Fedin, Yevtushenko's empty verse and some sterile, although not always untalented, prose, including Kazakevich's novel *House on the Square*, which was hobbled by the constrictions of socialist realism.

The pearls attracted wide attention, as was only to be expected at a time when the scorched earth policy was being pursued with the greatest ferocity and the one or two break-throughs mentioned above in the publicistic area were the exceptions that proved the rule.

By 1956 the field of literature had indeed been reduced to burnt-out stubble. In the higher education establishments Professor L.I. Timofeyev's notorious literature textbook, mentioned above and put out by *Uchpedgiz* as early as 1946, was still in use. Only two peasant poets—for some reason a rare phenomenon in a peasant country—appeared intact in it: Isakovsky and Tvardovsky. Esenin also reappeared in it, which was counted a historical victory of some kind. A third of Russian literature—the most probing, thoughtful and talented part—had disappeared from view.

It was not now the custom to attack this suppressed body of literature, because that would have attracted too much attention. It was simply not mentioned, discarded—to all intents and purposes destroyed. This was the Stalinist version of the fascist practice of burning books. In the final analysis, it is unimportant whether the books were burnt on a public square to the jubilant shouts of the crowd, or hauled off to paper factories secretly at night to be chopped up into noodle-like strips and thrown into vats. A few copies were left to be kept in the special depository at the Lenin Library, where they are available only to specialists on presentation of special documents, but on no account were they available to students. So as far as the bored mass of the reading public was concerned, a third of Russian literature remained just a heap of ashes.

Literary Moscow made what was virtually a new start. It had a freshness and liveliness about it, especially in its poetry. It brought the reader the truth he had been thirsting for. The poems of Margarita Aliger and Nikolai Zabolotsky, who had returned from the concentration camps in poor health and in the last stages of exhaustion, attracted wide attention. In Margarita Aliger's verse the truth about the war seemed to come to life in all its vividness, a quality which seemed to have been lost after the first books by Kazakevich and Nekrasov.

> *In Eastern Siberia is the village of Kukoy,*
> *A handful of huts above a river in the taiga.*
> *On the rise beyond the village are fields and meadows*
> *And beyond them, like a wall, the taiga.*
> > *In forty-one when the enemy was advancing*
> > *The village farewelled a platoon of fathers and husbands,*

A platoon of Siberian soldiers as they left their dear taiga...
Not one came back.

...No weddings are celebrated here, no children are born,
Life is without adornment, without adventure.
The villagers put out the lights very early,
The accordion is never played in Kukoy,
There are no parties, no fun,
Just the sorrowing of widows which has lasted for years.
        So what are my thoughts dwelling on?
On the passing of the years of youth,
Which can never have warmth blown into them or be brought
                                                        back,
And on our common lot, Kukoy,
My strong, wise friend.

In it a Soviet poet, famous and seemingly without any worries, suddenly writes about sharing the fate of the village of Kukoy, which had in effect been wiped out by the enemy. It is well-known how the Siberians were slaughtered near Moscow—and not only near Moscow.

I remember the strong jolt this poem gave me when I first read it. It stayed with me mainly because it was the first breath of fresh air for a long time. Later I heard poems which were artistically stronger and more full of life than this one, but this was the first gulp of fresh air in the stifling atmosphere of censorship then prevailing.

Nikolai Zabolotsky's verse provided a similar breath of fresh air and similarly gave poetic expression to the truth—and his poetry was of a very high standard. Zabolotsky was a great Russian poet. After his return in a state of utter exhaustion from the camp, Zabolotsky published little of his own verse but more and more often published his translations from the Georgian. He lived outside Moscow, at first without the right to go into Moscow itself. Moscow was the territory of the man who had denounced him, Nikolai Lesyuchevsky, director of the *Sovetsky pisatel* publishing house. We were afraid that Zabolotsky, who had fallen silent in his corner in the forest, would never regain his strength and vigor. He turned out to be completing a new book of verse. On what subject?

Starling, let me have a corner
To live in your old starling-house.
I'll pledge you my soul
For your sky-blue snowdrops.

Spring is whistling and muttering,
The poplars are in water up to their knees,

The maples are waking from their sleep
To flap their leaves like butterflies.

There is such a mess in the fields
And the streams are in such a muddle
That if you leave your attic
You can't rush at break-neck speed into the copse.

I am certainly one to try it,
But a wandering butterfly whispered to me
That whoever is noisy in spring
Has no voice left by summer.

Turn to face the universe,
Celebrating the sky-blue snowdrops
And journey across the spring fields
With the unconscious starling.

Another poem in the same vein is "Morning":

Lovers break off their conversations,
The last starling flies away,
All day long the silhouettes of crimson hearts
Fall from the maples.

Autumn, what have you done to us?
The earth is freezing in red gold.
The flame of sorrow is whistling underfoot,
Stirring the piles of leaves.

The mood of these poems is not a transient or a chance one. It makes itself felt again in "The Cranes":

The cranes flew in a long triangle,
Lost in the depths of the sky...

...Stretching out his silver wings
The leader led his small tribe
Across the whole wide vault of the sky
To the valley of abundance.

But when a lake, transparent to the bottom,
Flashed beneath their wings,
A gaping black gun-muzzle
Was lifted from the bushes towards them.

100

A beam of fire struck the bird's heart,
The quick flame flared and went out
And a piece of wondrous grandeur
Collapsed on us from the heights.

These lines may give some impression of the thoughts and feelings which seized the spent body of Russian poetry as epochs came apart at the seams. For some generations one age, the age of terror, had come to an end and a new one had begun which made it possible, over the graves of one's friends, to give meaning to the times they lived in and to one's place in the endlessly cruel and bloody stream.

During these memorable days the flood began of shattered people in ill-fitting, crumpled jackets, with bloodless lips and burning eyes. They got down from the train with their plywood cases in their hands at the North Station in Moscow and were carried by the crowd out onto Komsomol Square—the very name seemed a mockery of them. Some had spent seventeen years in the camps, others even more. No one met them, except occasionally an old woman, weeping loudly as if she were not welcoming but saying farewell to a son or brother.

Naturally, all those poets who had remained poets, and particularly the great poets (and cowards do not become great poets in Russia because of the circumstances under which poetry has to exist there) went forward to meet this stream of shattered people with burning eyes in which there was a new spark of hope.

We were not surprised that there also appeared in *Literary Moscow* a new canto called "Childhood Friend" from Tvardovsky's epic poem "Vista beyond Vista" ("Za dalyu dal") in which one of Russia's most prominent poets, recognized as such by the country's leaders, joined those striding forward to greet those whom the leaders had thought were dead and buried long ago, and now tried not to notice. This canto is in the descriptive mode like much of Tvardovsky's poetry. Nevertheless I shall quote a few verses to remind the reader of Tvardovsky's attitude to those he walked with shoulder to shoulder until he died.

No sooner talk of wisdom—
When wood's chopped, chips fly, they say...
But no reward for such a fate
Is yet envisaged.

A pity... Anyway, here's a story
Which is very simple to tell.
Our train and one from the other direction
Were standing at Tayshet station in the taiga.

101

A man I usually held onto in my memory
Among my other losses
Like a border-line
Was there, alive—there he was.

I was not mistaken although
He'd worn that quilted jacket for years.
It was him! And he recognized me.
He shouldered his way towards me...

And a shameful feeling of fear
Of misfortune came for a moment...
But we were already shaking each other
By the shoulders and hands, saying "My old pal!"

"Old pal!" No suffering is stupid.
The whistle will blow either for him or me.
So after seventeen years apart—
Five minutes together.

The two streams of people could not be separated, even in literature. Admittedly, only Tvardovsky could be permitted this.

At this point where for the first time the officially recognized stream of Russian poetry met the stream from the camps, I must say to those lovers of Russian poetry who are always saying, as if under some kind of spell, that politics do not interest them, that in Russia man, the living human soul, is the victim of politics. For many centuries politics has trampled this living soul under the boots of soldiers and prison warders. This is the reason the most profound lyric poetry, the purest creation of modern Russian poets, as we have seen in the case of Nikolai Zabolotsky, is at the same time political. It is fearful of politics, yet political.

In the same first volume of *Literary Moscow* there was a story by the talented writer Sergei Antonov called "The Questionnaire." As already mentioned, at one time Antonov's antipathy to politics led to his writing placid country tales while people in the countryside were dying from starvation. Many readers could not forgive Antonov this. Indeed, he did not forgive himself.

In "The Questionnaire" his main concern was to depict a callous manager for whom the answer to the question in the questionnaire "Were you at any time in occupied territory?", a question which at that time could blacken the applicant's record irrevocably, was more important than the applicant himself. In choosing the theme of hard-heartedness, Antonov was punishing himself, but the reader no longer had any faith in the writer who had once forgotten people for the sake of a few likes of folkloric melodiousness.

No mention was made of him at literary discussions, as if the subject were a shameful one.

All this—the village of Kukoy, the starling which lost consciousness, the starling which heard nothing of the woes of earth, and the meeting with the old friend on the station platform at Tayshet—all this was to be found in the first "overly cautious" volume, which was to be proof, as Bek imagined with his usual naïveté, of the editors' loyalty and law-abiding principles.

The real explosion, which was to rock the whole country, was not long in coming. It came the same year, 1956, as the Stalinists, frightened to death by the Hungarian uprising, finally lost their patience. The second volume of *Literary Moscow* was passed for publication in December 1956.

6. THE YEAR OF ANTI-STALINISM: FRESH INSIGHTS
The second—and last—volume of *LITERARY MOSCOW*

1. Alexander Yashin sounds the alarm

It took just six months for the times to change, and to change decisively. At a reception at the Chinese Embassy, Nikita Khrushchev again declared himself a Stalinist. However, it was too late to ban the second volume of *Literary Moscow*. When it appeared, the whole country started talking about Alexander Yashin's story "Levers."

Yashin was a former peasant from the Vologda region whose ties with his native village remained strong all his life. He was a poet much in favor with the State, a Stalin Prize winner, a native son—in short, he "belonged." He was the last person the Stalinists expected this sort of thing from. This story cost Yashin his life, or at least shortened it, bringing a multitude of misfortunes on his family.

Yahsin's "Levers" underpinned stories by Yuri Nagibin and Nikolai Zhdanov which I shall discuss later. His story rang an alarm-bell which made some people look up and listen and others act. Yet it is a simple story, which does not at first sight appear to be a call to action.

It is a story which no student of modern Russian literature should fail to acquaint himself with. It is a distillation of the wrongs not only of the past, but also of the present, and the future. It shows the sufferings of Russia crushed by arbitrary rule, with people deprived not only of the right to act, but also of the right to think—in other words, the right to a normal human existence which is inconceivable without the right to think about life.

It is not difficult to imagine how soldiers can be turned into "levers" and sent to fight the Czechs, for example. A soldier has sworn allegiance. He is ordered to shoot, and he shoots. The alternative is to be court-martialled or commit suicide—which also happened in Prague. Nor is it difficult to understand how Party functionaries become "levers." It is in the nature of their work. By way of compensation they enjoy a great number of privileges, not to mention a double salary. If they sell their independence, they do so consciously.

But how could the peasants, the mass of the people, become "levers"? This had not been discussed in Russia for a long, long time. "The people are silent—as Pushkin tells us in *Boris Godunov*. And by its silence, Yashin seemed to be adding, it was furthering the ruin of the countryside and arbitrary rule—villainy, in a word. Yashin did not resort to Aesopian devices, but spelt it out in black and white.

This was perhaps the first post-war example of "folk" prose—earthy, solid, undiluted by the sometimes insipid, colorless language of the cities—

entering the mainstream of Russian literature after a break of a quarter of a century. This "folk" prose became a continuing basis for a whole stream in post-war Soviet literature, later to be called "village prose" (*derevenskaya proza*).

The story opens on a note which is almost symbolic in its everyday quality. Four men are sitting in the kolkhoz office smoking. There is so much smoke in the room it is almost impossible to breathe. Even the radio seems to be crackling because of all the smoke. The men can hardly even see each other through it. One of them says to the man next to him who is dropping live ash on himself: "If you burn your beard off, the cows won't be afraid of you any more." Unperturbed, his neighbor replies: "If they're not afraid any more, they might give more milk." They do not appear to be talking about anything important, just trifles. But in fact there is nothing trifling about this conversation. It introduces us to the main theme which the reader absorbs without realizing that it is the main theme.

Then comes another everyday scene from country life, again nothing out of the ordinary. It is an official aspect inasmuch as it is set in the kolkhoz office. The scene is in half-light. Here and there are posters and banners in honor of some special day—but they have been up all year. There is a list of kolkhoz members on the wall showing the number of work days to their credit, and an empty blackboard divided into two equal parts. At the top of one side is written "Black" (here are written the names of those with a bad work record.) The board itself is black like the kolkhoz members' life, but it is customary to consider one side "red" (which has connotations of "beautiful" in Russian)—there is an order from above to that effect.

An atmosphere of expectancy slowly builds up although nothing is directly said about it. Smoke, the blackboard, random snatches of conversation. There is no sugar in the village. Not that there is any complaint about it! One of the men sitting smoking says that the store manager "threw in a couple of kilos for me. Is he afraid of something, do you think?" The other says: "Of course he's afraid of something. I'm the new store manager now." The narrator explains that this man was made store manager because he joined the Party. When he joined a few months earlier he began expressing his opinion that all positions of authority in the kolkhoz should be occupied by Communists. How simple, how naively simple everything is. Once he has his Party card, he starts getting extra supplies. They now recall that the old store manager was caught stealing, which they had not known before. The new Communist store manager buys a fountain pen and starts wearing a tie. He joins the kolkhoz managers.

The atmosphere clears, despite the smoke. The main theme now starts to come through more and more strongly. "All right, so he too it [sugar] ," said Shchukin after a moment's consideration. "But where's there any justice anyway? What happens to the sugar? Where's the soap and everything?" Another one of the men jokes: "What does justice matter to you? You're

106

the store manager!"

Someone intones in a business-like way: "We must do the right thing. Everything depends on doing the right thing. Only I don't understand what's going on in this district. We're told to plan from below. Let the kolkhoz decide itself what it's best to sow and what not to sow—but they don't approve our plan. Three times they refused to pass it, then passed their own plan and insisted on it, too."

The conversation becomes deeper, passing from sugar and cows to the subject of how people's hands are tied.

"There's justice for you. They don't trust us," says one of the characters. "Around here justice is made one of the directors so that it doesn't get upset or open its mouth," says another kolkhoznik and throws his cigarette butt into a pot. Shchukin the storeman gets his word in: "Do you mean to say that justice is only needed for meetings and public holidays, like criticism and self-criticism, and that it doesn't have any application to what we actually do."

And so the conversation goes on. It is a normal conversation among people who are sick of lies, although some people, like the store manager, are already managing to turn the situation to their own advantage. How easy it is to argue convincingly that since it is the Party which is in power and I am in the Party I am in power, so give me a post!

This utterly normal, confidential conversation between men from the same kolkhoz ends with one of the characters, who has visited the district boss, reporting what he said to him: "What are you doing to us, I said. The kolkhoz won't agree to changing the plan for the third time. You talk them into it," he said. "We talked you round when the kolkhozes were being set up, now you talk the others round. Implement the Party line. You're now our levers in the countryside."

This is the first mention of the word "levers." What is its meaning? How is it used? Why are people called "levers"? Obviously so that official lies and unrealizable plans, ruinous plans, might triumph, so that the crops their grandfathers sowed and harvested for generations might not be sown, but instead what Moscow decided should be allotted to the different regions and districts.

How then could a district committee Secretary function? If he were honest, he would send off a protest and put his head on the block. If he were not honest, the system itself would pick him out like high-quality grain. Like attracts like. "He doesn't come out in the open with the people," the same kolkhoznik says of the district committee Secretary. "He knows full well that everyone in the kolkhoz gets a hundred grams per working day. Yet he keeps saying: 'Each year the value of a day's work grows and the people's well-being increases.' We haven't got any cows left on the kolkhoz, but he says: 'Each year the kolkhoz live-stock sector grows and strengthens.' He says to tell people that they're living badly for this reason or that at the moment, but they will live better—and then they'll work more willingly." But the district committee Secretary is lying.

If we consider that he lies not in his own words but in words taken from the speeches of the State's leaders such as Khrushchev and Bulganin, using official State-sanctioned stereotyped phrases, we can easily understand the enormous risk Alexander Yashin was running in his determination to make a break with the deeply-rooted State system of lies. His break is a complete one. He sees right to the heart of his subject.

> *Giving a small cough but remaining bent over, one of the men looked up and said somewhat hoarsely: "The top men in the district have forgotten how to talk to the people, they're ashamed. They under-tand what's going on but they're afraid to make a move. What do they mean—talk us round?...They expect us to be levers...They see the houses boarded up in the village but don't want to say anything about it out loud. The only thing they're worried about is that they should have nice round figures in the reports.*

The lamp starts to flicker and someone makes the casual remark: "Blast it, it'll go out without air. A lamp needs air too."

It is a friendly, frank conversation, all the more impressively true to life because of the casual details: the smoke, the black-board one half of which it is obligatory to regard as "red," the lamp which *also* needs air.

Suddenly there is a noise in the cottage. An old woman's voice is heard crying out behind the big Russian stove: "Where do you think you're dropping your ash, you old carcass? You don't have to clean up!" The men are startled and look at each other. "Are you still here, Martha? What are you there for?" "You know what for! I'm watching you! You'll set fire to the office and I'll be dragged off to court. The broom's dry and you could easily drop a spark—God preserve us!" "Just go home!" "I'll go when I'm good and ready."

The men's conversation breaks off as if they feel guilty about something. For a long time they sit smoking in silence. When they start exchanging brief remarks again, the remarks are empty, not about anything or directed at anyone.

Finally, one of them, Shchukin, who has still not got used to his managerial position and is at heart still an ordinary kolhoznik, suddenly cannot help bursting out into loud laughter: "What a fright she gave us, damn her!" They all exchange glances and also burst into laughter. "Gave us a fright all right, the old devil, roaring at us from behind the stove like that. I thought it was the boss himself come to catch us at it... The way we got a fright, you'd think we were little boys stealing apples."

Laughter lightens the atmosphere and people begin to feel normal again. "What are we afraid of?" says Pyotr Kuzmich in a thoughtful and slightly sad way, "It is ourselves we're afraid of."

"It's ourselves we're afraid of." So that is the way things are. So this is what Russia has been brought to—not bureaucratic Russia, but grass-roots Russia, the mass of the people in whom everyone from Dostoevsky to the populists have put their trust, the true, peasant Russia untouched by lies. And it is a peasant poet with a Vologda way of speaking and thinking who tells us how frightened the peasant workers are, the Vologda peasants who stayed out of reach of the Tartar hordes and Genghis Khan. But not out of reach of Stalin and Khrushchev.

A woman teacher they have been waiting for arrives and the Party meeting they have gathered for begins. Sitting down, the teacher complains about the lack of wood at the school.

"We'll leave business till later," the chairman interrupts her. "First we must conduct the meeting. There's a long-standing requirement by the district committee that there should be two meetings a month, and we haven't managed to have a single meeting. How are we going to account for ourselves?"

Our despairing author's intent is now clearer. The proceedings at the Party meeting are wholly unnecessary. The meeting is not being held to attend to any business, but for the sake of making a report. This is an attack on the very foundations of the bureaucratic machine which without all this fuss would soon end up on the scrap heap.

Old Martha from behind the stove, who is not a Party member, the depths of Russia incarnate, and hope of the populists, has no difficulty in grasping what is going on. When they try to make her leave, she does not protest or kick up a fuss. Nor does she call the Party worker an old carcass this time, either, in her familiar, peasant way. "Carry on, carry on, I understand, I'm off." This is no longer an area of life where Martha has a right to say her piece, but a closed Party meeting.

The author is barely able to withhold his anger and irony. If it had been any stronger, it would have been virtually suicidal. "The earthy, natural element vanished entirely and the action shifted into another world, a complicated setting which was not wholly customary or comprehensible to these simple, warm-hearted people."

At this point a strange misprint made things worse. The author presumably meant to say that after Shchukin was appointed store manager, "there were no ordinary kolkhozniks left in the Party organization." (In Russian the difference lies in one letter: "ryadovykh kolkhoznikov i part-organizatsii ne bylo.") "That's not a chance misprint, but a deliberately malicious act—an act of sabotage!" claimed the frightened literary bureaucrats, playing safe.

The meeting, of course, drifts on in a flow of verbal garbage: "...this was not foreseen and allowed to take its own course... Explanatory work was not taken up with the masses and consequently they were not convinced..." Although the young Communist Shchukin sits in his corner making ironical remarks under his breath at the expense of the empty verbiage to which he is not accustomed, it is soon made plain to him who *is* experienced and in his element here. "All right, let him have his say. That's the way it's done! Piotr Kuzmich is carrying out his duties. That's the way it's done at the district level, and that's the way we do it. Like master, like man." They quieted down, ready to vote for whatever is necessary. "That's the way it's done!" Not long ago they were people, now they are people no longer, but levers.

The lifeless official part is over and some young people burst into the room, impatient to begin a party—the room serves as both office and club for the kolkhoz, there being only one "official" building in the village. They fling open the windows. "It's so smoky in here," the girls cry.

It turns out that the smoke was no ordinary smoke, but Party smoke. Russia is smothered with smoke, stupefied with smoke, to the point of nausea and giddiness. When the poet's pen is guided by suffering and courage, his images have great strength. This poet had the determination to cry out for all Russia to hear: "We have been silent long enough!" We're people, not levers!"

2. Yuri Nagibin, Nikolai Zhdanov, Nikolai Zabolotsky, Alexander Kron

Alexander Yashin's "Levers," which aroused such lively interest among thinking people in Russia, could scarcely have appeared at all if it had been the only piece in the second volume of *Literary Moscow* attempting to throw some light on the "new class" of usurpers and destroyers. Apart from Yashin's story, which was as far-reaching as Russia's misfortune itself, there was also a story by Yuri Nagibin called "A Light in the Window."

Nastia, a maid in a rest house, keeps an empty room clean and tidy in readiness for "the big man," should he decide to turn up. There are rooms like this in every rest house and sanatorium, however unprepossessing, just in case "the big man" arrives—some government minister or factory manager, a Central Committee or district committee Secretary—every rest house has its own "big man." Sweeping out these uninhabited rooms and seeing the cramped conditions all around, Nastia is patient for a year and then she throws caution to the winds, ignores the ban on using the rooms, turns on the light, invites the janitor's children and a few friends in and settles down in front of the television as if she owned the place.

Seeing the light in the window of the room set aside for the "big man," the manager naturally hauls Nastia over the coals. As Nagibin describes it, there grows in the manager as he abuses Nastia "a sensation of intolerable self-disgust which penetrated right down to his fingertips."

Nagibin's story was almost as sharp-edged as Yashin's and possibly even more poetic. However, the impression it made on our generation in terms of its forcefulness and deep significance cannot be compared with the impression made by "Levers."

In the same issue of *Literary Moscow* there appeared a story by the Moscow writer Nikolai Zhdanov called "A Trip Home." The mother of an important Moscow big-wig, Varygin, dies at home in her village and her son goes home for the funeral. He returns to a world which he imagined no longer existed—a world of want. The furniture is rough, the old samovar is coming unsoldered. The junk in the room acquires a new significance in that it casts a different light on the visitor himself. The cracked and useless samovar lies on its side just like the visiting big-wig from Moscow. He, too, has come unstuck on his journey and is useless to anybody in his native village.

His mother waited for her son for many years, but he cut himself off not only from his village but also from his mother. He speaks a different language from the people in the village as if he came from another country. The following conversation takes place between a peasant woman who knew his mother and the former peasant lad:

> *"Was she waiting for me to come?" he asked.*
>
> *"This year she didn't talk about it, but that summer when you promised to come she was very impatient for you to come. She kept saying: 'Any time now, any time now.' Then she quieted down. But she wasn't hurt about it, no. She understood how hard it is for a busy man to get away. I dare say you've gone farther than anyone else from our village."*

After making some tea, she puts the cup in front of him and sits down at the table.

> *"What I wanted to ask you is this," she went on. "Have they done the right thing by us or not? This year we sowed hemp, seventy-four hectares of it. The hemp had just flowered when the spring crops ripened. We wanted to harvest it and then stack it, but we were told to get on with the threshing and send it off. But if you don't bring hemp in at the right time, you won't get any seed."*
>
> *"She thinks there's something I can do about it," thought Varygin in dismay, trying to remember what was involved in harvesting hemp and where the bit about the seed came in. But he could not remember.*
>
> *Aloud he said: "It's a political question. The State must always come first for us. Everything depends on the level of consciousness of the masses." He fell silent, feeling that he had said the wrong thing.*

If even Varygin was able to feel it, how much more able was the reader. The reader had been surrounded by Varygins for a long time. He had met them in Vera Panova's work after the war. Panova's Listopad was drawn more cautiously, but then times were different. There is nothing cautious about the way Varygin is drawn. He is not only callous, but does not even understand the language of the people, as if he were from another world. The only things he is left with are a feeling of guilt and the peasant woman's question: "Have they done the right thing by us?"

Nikolai Zabolotsky appeared again in the second volume. There was a whole collection of poems by this poet who had come to life again. One of his poems includes these three stanzas:

> As winter first advances,
> Wandering above the spacious Neva
> We compare summer's glow
> With leaves strewn along the shore
> > But I'm a lover of old poplars
> > Which try not to throw from their branches
> > Their dry rusted shirt of mail
> > Until winter's first blizzard.
> How shall I describe the similarity between us?
> Like a poplar, I'm not young either,
> And I too need a coat of mail
> To meet winter's approach and its deadly cold.

This poem clearly needs no commentary. This is the poetry of a master who did not believe in the warmth or even in the thaw which everyone believed had arrived. This great poet died like this, still frozen, in anguish that he had no protective armor to help him bear the cold. There were other poems like this in *Literary Moscow* and more came out later.

It was in the same issue of *Literary Moscow* that Ilya Ehrenburg introduced Marina Tsvetaeva to Soviet readers. It really was a case of introducing her as a new writer because by this time whole generations of readers had never even heard her name. After all, who would have dared tell them about a poet who had come back to her native land and then hanged herself?

This was a real break-through, a piercing of the ban which had sealed her off. Everyone hastened to make his contribution.

> My verses about youth and death
> —Unread verses!—
> Strewn about in the dust of shops
> (Where no one picked them up or does so now!)
> My verses, like precious wines,
> Will have their turn.

112

It was with these lines written by Tsvetaeva at the age of twenty that Ehrenburg opened his article on Tsvetaeva's poetry.

Ehrenburg, too, was in some haste. Tsvetaeva had perished as had her books and as had so many of Russia's best poets before her. Ehrenburg himself was not young and therefore he felt a sense of urgency. And Tsvetaeva had wanted to give voice to the same things he had wanted to express for many years:

> *I refuse to be*
> *In the Bedlam of non-people,*
> *There I refuse to live.*
> *With the wolves on the squares*
> *I refuse to howl.*

Of course, Ehrenburg explained, Tsvetaeva is talking about Fascism here—of the German variety. Up to this time Khrushchev alone was allowed to mention Stalinism, and only then in closed session at a Congress barred to the public.

It is to *Literary Moscow* that we are indebted for turning Russia's attention to this unknown poet. If *Literary Moscow* had achieved nothing else, apart from making Tsvetaeva's name known, it would have achieved much. But it did more—it went onto the offensive.

The editors seemed to have bided their time and then gone into the attack by publishing a number of critical essays and articles among which the most forceful was the playwright Alexander Kron's article about the destruction of the country's theatrical life. In it he accused the powers-that-be of "painting over existing contradictions" under the banner of "consolidation." It was indeed a despicable slogan, demanding as it did that writers unite with their hangmen. "There is no greater untruth than that the so-called no-conflict theory was the brain-child of creative artists," Kron wrote. "You might as well claim that it was the biologists' idea to ban the teachings of Darwin." In this way there was no direct accusation directed at the Party Central Committee. The artistic intelligentsia had successfully stormed new heights.

Kron wrote of an editor who regarded himself as a kind of watchdog: "It appears that as in the army a book has both a commander and a political commissar." "Art knows only one legitimate hierarchy," he wrote, "that of talent."

It is not hard to imagine the reaction to these words on the part of those at the top of the literary hierarchy—all the Surkovs, Fedins, Gribachevs and Korneichuks. There was a malicious joke circulating at Korneichuk's expense to the effect that if he wrote something good, he would sign it in full "Kornei Chukovsky" but if it was rubbish he would feel ashamed and shorten it to "Korneichuk."

"That is how the hierarchy is established among playwrights," Kron went on relentlessly. "There are general survey articles, signed by people no one has ever heard of—but this is of no importance since they are written in the people's name. "The people know and love such writers as..." "Such writers are not carrying out their duty to the people..." "Such plays have received some recognition among the people..." "The people rejects such plays as..." This magic formula, which obviates all necessity for arguing the case, is accompanied by a list of writers and plays.

The readers of Kron's article laughed, and of course nothing is as deadly as laughter. It was not something harmless that it was aimed at, however, but Stalinism, which knew how to crouch down on the ground like a mad dog and then suddenly spring up and bite. Kron was well aware of this, as were all the editors, and although he was well-known and the recipient of a number of honors, he still found the courage to say "I am attacking." "If drama is regarded as part of the greater body of Soviet literature, then there are no serious grounds for herding it into a cell," he concluded.

Kron's article caused the same panic as Yashin's article. Quite by chance I happened to be in the office of Nadezhda Chertova, Secretary of the Moscow Party organization, when Lesiuchevsky, director of the *Sovetsky pisatel* publishing house, rang her about the forthcoming discussion of *Literary Moscow*. It was a case of one hangman ringing another. On Chertova's desk lay the proofs of the third issue of *Literary Moscow* which was in fact fated not to appear. I shall never forget her shouting into the telephone: "We'll adopt an iron-fisted attitude to the discussion." Literature, of course, does not thrive on iron. The vocabulary of these mentors of literature, of course, does not thrive on iron. The vocabulary of these mentors of literature and poetry is noteworthy. Over the years a special, lethal, violent vocabulary had been developed, the language of informers and those who carried out the sentences. The choice of language speaks volumes in itself, regardless of how it is dressed up.

Khrushchev was horrified by the Hungarian uprising and convinced, as only an ignoramus can be, that it was all the fault of writers—of the Petofi Circle in Hungary, and of the Moscow writers in Russia, and this led to an increase in the power and arrogance of the innumerable Chertovas and Lesiuchevskys. They regarded *Literary Moscow* as a rattlesnake which had slithered into their comfortable apartments. The most poisonous of all was, of course, Yashin's "Levers." They hammered away at it at all the meetings and set all the hacks onto it, all the modern Bulgarins and Greches. All the levers were pulled, all the stops were out.

How Russia's Party-appointed leaders took fright at Yashin's little tale! They started rushing off to the Central Committee, dredging up the old Stalinist terminology such as "ideological sabotage," the hot-lines to the Kremlin started buzzing, messengers ran back and forth as if a war had started and the enemy had to be repulsed immediately, today, for tomorrow would be too late.

With Russia's reading public Yashin's story had a stunning success. It helped many to stand up straight and acquire some realization of what was actually going on. It even allowed some to think things through to their conclusion. This was not an easy thing to do for people crushed by years of disinformation. It was this story which struck the heaviest blow, despite the insertions of the "co-author"—the pock-marks of the age—designed to soften the blow.

These pock-marks simply went unnoticed. After all, who could hold it against a writer if he did not want to be dragged straight off to the Lubianka away from his wife and six children, a writer who was also a talented poet, the support of a warm, close-knit family in the peasant tradition. The authorities soon made it their business to try to smash this family, something they did not take long to do. But we shall return to this point later.

Until I read "Levers" I was not personally acquainted with Yashin. His epic poem *Alyona Fomina*, for which he received the Stalin Prize and which was mutilated by the censors, had not disposed me to try to know him. When I had read "Levers," I went up to him in the Union of Writers, shook his hand and congratulated him. We went down to the cafeteria together and got talking. I told him about my concerns, how I had spent two years "bashing away" at my article on how students were taught to stop thinking in departments of Marxism and was now wondering how many years I would have to keep bashing away at my novel on the same theme. We became friends and it transpired that we were concerned about the same things and felt the same way about them. Later, when I was expelled from the Party for my stand against censorship and Stalinism, he was called to give evidence at a high level, and was witness in my defense.

Alexander Yashin's fate was a tragic one. After "Levers" he was constantly under attack and being threatened. However Yashin would just spread his elbows on the rostrum and say with a knowing smile, as if he were just some country bumpkin: "I thought you'd thank me, but instead of that I'm really copping it from you." But it was pointless for him to pretend to be a country bumpkin. His smile was too frank, his eyes with their cunning peasant's squint too piercingly intelligent.

He kept on writing and did not retreat. A few things got into print, but most of his stories and poems stayed in his desk drawers. That is why in the later stories such as "My Rowanberries" and "A Vologda Wedding" (*Novy mir*, no 4, 1965 and no. 12, 1969) where he refuses to yield, he is so fresh and interesting.

Although his most valuable works have probably not been published, he still died a victor.

7. THE YEAR OF ANTI-STALINISM—THE FALL: DANIL GRANIN AND HIS STORY "ONE'S OWN OPINION"

Following in the footsteps of the fearless *Literary Moscow*, which had only a few months to go before being smashed, *Novy mir* moved into the attack. It goes without saying that Konstantin Simonov, who was then editor of the journal, would never have been the first to make a move. But when things came to the boil so suddenly, he could not stay silent, nor did he want to. He, too, apparently believed in the possibility of change, all the more so since he had great sympathy, and had had all his life, for men of courage, a sympathy which as a rule he kept to himself. When attempts were made after "Levers" came out to starve Yashin to death, he sent his wife a thousand rubles. Since he was a millionaire, this was no great sacrifice for him, but for some reason no other millionaire writers sent a penny. Deeply moved and with tears in her eyes, Yashin's wife later told me about Simonov's gift which helped the family to survive. But this was later.

At the end of the summer, it appeared that a new era had arrived. In a single issue of *Novy mir* Danil Granin's story "One's Own Opinion" and the final part of Vladimir Dudintsev's novel *Not by Bread Alone* came out. Vladimir Tendryakov's work "Potholes" had appeared earlier. It was artistically of a higher standard and in some ways more profound than the other works of the anti-Stalinist period.

The time of hope had lasted just one year, and even then not a full year as we have seen. The coming of autumn was accompanied not only by the crimson in the woods but the blood of the Hungarian insurgents whom Khrushchev was convinced had been urged to revolt by the iniquitous writers in the Petofi Circle.

After the executions in Hungary, it was the Soviet protesters in the literary field, despite the fact that they had barely appeared on the scene, who first came under the blows of the State's fist.

Apart from the three works mentioned above, other works were published which are well worth some examination. L. Kabo's story "On a Hard March" is particularly worth mentioning. It is about people from a school trying to break free from the lies and dogmatism ensnaring it. There are others in the same vein. However, it is in the first three stories by Yashin, Nagibin and Granin that the anti-Stalinist tendency found its most clear-cut expression. It is of no importance whether Stalin's name is mentioned in them or not—they all attack Stalinism, crushingly, boldly and from different angles.

To return to Granin's "One's Own Opinion": a young scientist, Olkhovsky, is bold enough to oppose the theories of the academician Stroyev, who is no less influential in the technological sciences then Lysenko was in biology. Olkhovsky comes forward with a technical invention designed to save an enormous amount of fuel. However, as so often happens, the invention is based on a principle which overturns a classic work in the field, that of the academician Stroyev.

The acting director of the institute agrees with Olkhovsky's theory and inwardly praises him for his invention. But he knows that it is not enough to "hold this or that particular opinion"—in addition one must also hold an appropriate position. He, Minayev, is still just the acting director. When I am made the permanent director, he tells himself, then of course I'll help Olkhovsky. Meanwhile he does nothing and Olkhovsky makes a complaint to the district committee. Minayev informs the district committee that Olkhovsky is a trouble-maker and no attention should be paid to his complaints. The deputy minister to whom Olkhovsky has given his manuscript returns it to Minayev for his consideration. Everything is taking its normal course. The person you make a complaint against is the one who ends up considering your complaint. Little wonder "Don't spit into the wind" is Russia's most wide-spread saying at the present time. Time passes and Minayev becomes the permanent director of the institute, but nothing changes. "I must get established first," he thinks.

This psychological portrait of a bureaucrat with responsibilities for scientific research—and research in other areas—scrambling up the ladder is drawn with great precision. I have often heard my university colleagues say the same thing as they move up the ladder—"first I must get established," that is to say, I must not go against the current until I am strong and invulnerable. But who in Russia is invulnerable?

Another reason Minayev is in no hurry to support Olkhovsky is that he has been openly and sharply critical of Loktev, an instructor at the Party city committee, a dim-witted bureaucrat with a "dead, disused sort of face." Olkhovsky characterizes the city committee's attitude to the affair as "corpse-like indifference to living thought."

Minayev is even sorry for Olkhovsky. "Because of his lack of talent," writes the narrator, "Loktev let no act of opposition to him go unpunished." Deep down Minayev is envious of Olkhovsky's unencumbered freedom. But he lets him down yet again.

This is what people began to write about in Russia as soon as Stalin had been swept off his pedestal: city and regional committee instructors who are untalented, envious scoundrels, yet in whose presence everyone walks on tip-toe. This all comes out as the story develops.

Minayev, the director of the institute, instructs one of his young assistants at the institute to "prepare a final decision" on Olkhovsky's case. Although he is wholly on Olkhovsky's side, the young man prepares the sort of paper which is expected of him, completely demolishing Olkhovsky. "Why did you write a paper like this," Minayev asks him shamelessly, "when it is at variance with your own opinion? Why are you acting like Molchalin?"

It is understandable that Molchalin from Griboyedov's play *Woe from Wit* should have come to mind—Molchalin accommodated "everyone without exception/the doorman, the yardman, to avoid unpleasantness,/the doorman's dog, to make her sweet-tempered." This is how Minayev punishes both himself and his assistant, appearing to us in the process as an arrogant cynic.

But the young assistant is a match for Minayev. He is ready for whatever blows might come. "I've written it as you want it so that one day I can write as I consider necessary," he says, looking Minayev firmly in the eye. This is the same philosophy as Minayev's: I shall be brave and principled "when I get established."

Thus everybody is now against Olkhovsky, against "living thought," despite its enormous value to everyone. This is not some heresy about restructuring society, but an idea for restructuring an engine, providing savings which will strengthen the State, the Soviet State, even if it is backward and retrograde.

All the same, a thought or a man who is not quite lifeless is a threat to the city committee instructor Loktev. He has no intention of supporting Olkhovsky either now or later when "he has consolidated his position." He is a Party apparatchik, a grave-digger without illusions or a hint of self-deception. It is observably true that the sort of people who joined the Party machine were as a rule engineers without any future in technology, ambitious but indolent men devoid of any talent, and the half-educated, for whom any affirmation of life is a threat. Naturally, the apparatchik Lotkev demands Olkhovsky's immediate dismissal and expulsion from the city to an outlying district.

It now suddenly seems to Minayev that all his established concepts in life have been reversed. It is not the inventor making advances in life who is important, but this powerful reactionary. Everything in life now rests on him. This is how Granin describes the new feeling which comes over Minayev, director of the scientific institute:

> The river was crammed with the last ice moving down it. In places the river was all white as if it were frozen over. Chunks of ice were being pushed up against the granite piers of the bridge, cracking gently, and the jagged blocks swirled around and disappeared under the arches. Leaning out over the railing, Minayev looked downwards. The ice seemed to be standing still and the bridge to be moving. There was a draft of cold air coming up from the black water, and he could hear the ringing of the long glittering crystal shapes as they broke against the granite and sank, glinting, beneath the surface. Minayev pushed himself back from the railing with some effort... He felt old and permanently weary. Suddenly he could see himself from the outside—a flabby, bald man with a swollen face, crossing a bridge with

119

his hat held tightly in one hand. God, how quickly he'd aged! When did it happen? He, Volodya Minayev, school choir leader, secretary of the faculty Party cell... He was suddenly terrified—was he really already an old man?

It had taken many years and many humiliations for the scientist to force himself to look at things in this way: it is the bridge which is moving, not the river or the ice.

Granin describes the disintegration of a personality with extreme perspicacity, through the eyes of Minayev himself, who:

remembered his humiliating powerlessness when the chief engineer had listened to his impassioned speech as he sipped his tea and then said, purposely getting his name wrong: "Listen, Linyaev, if you make a nuisance of yourself again with this nonsense, I'll kick you out of the factory. You can go now." He and his friends had tried to resist further and had gone and made representations, but all in vain. They could have wasted three, five or ten years on a hopeless battle and still not won anything in the end. There were three of them. First one was dismissed from the factory, then another. Then it was Minayev's turn. He pretended to submit. He consoled himself that it was only for a first time. He had to make a detour, become independent, gain some authority first, and then smash these bureaucrats. He had moved towards his goal with clenched teeth. He was appointed deputy head of his section. He trained himself to be patient and silent in the name of the day when he could do what had to be done...

How many Olkhovskys there were left on the path behind him!... Untiringly, like an ant, he had built up his position, trying to make it even stronger. Why? What had he gained? The higher he climbed, the less he was himself.

The story ends with an exposure. The main action takes place in a railway-carriage in which Minayev is returning to Leningrad after betraying Olkhovsky yet again. He has betrayed him at the ministry in Moscow because Stroyev is needed by the institute in connection with quite different matters. He can help them get certain things and push certain things through. Minayev looks out at the night through the window and can see only his own reflection in the glass.

Against the dense blackness of the night the double panes mirrored the heavy figure in striped pyjamas, the puffy face with the cigarette in a corner of the tightly closed mouth, and beyond it another more blurred figure covered in bright spots of rain. As it touched the cold glass, the cigarette smoke turned into blue-gray clinging tendrils.

From the black depths outside the window the young Minayev looked in through the tendrils at him, in the wet cap and worn jacket of his student years. Water streamed down his pale cheeks and scrawny chicken's neck. "You see, you're putting it off again, you useless wretch. What a pitiful sight you are." "You have to take the facts of a situation into account, it's all very well having great ideas when you don't know what life's about, but life's something I know inside out." "You promised to be yourself. You said that when you were made director and got established, then..." "What a naive young boy you are! You'd think a director was God. Now if I worked in the ministry..."

There was a third Minayev as well, who listened to the old Minayev, reassuring the young one, confidently proving that what had happened had been unavoidable, promising to help Olkhovsky as soon as circumstances were right, knowing all along that they never would be. He would always play tricks with himself and keep playing the same endless game, lacking the strength to tear himself free from the grasp of his own double-mindedness. He would always find some justification. He would always strive to be honest tomorrow...

It is this inner monologue which is the climax of the story. Here Granin ripped the covers off the "new class," affirming yet again that the so-called technocrats of the USSR in whom some put certain hopes were in the main morally degenerate and in practical terms no different from the repressive functionaries in the Party machine, except that their methods of self-justification were more refined.

8. THE YEAR OF ANTI-STALINISM—A STORMY FALL: VLADIMIR DUDINTSEV AND *NOT BY BREAD ALONE*

No one was indifferent to Vladimir Dudintsev's novel *Not by Bread Alone*. It was perhaps Dudintsev, together with Granin and some others, who made the most decisive attempt to suggest new perspectives to the reading public.

The need for this could not have been more urgent. It was in that year, 1956, that the land of "victorious socialism" saw its first disturbances and strikes in Moscow. This happened when crane-drivers and metal-workers at the enormous Sharikopodshipnik ball-bearing factory came out on strike. I lived for many years in Sharikopodshipnikov Street right beside the factory, went to school in the neighborhood and departed for the war from there. Naturally I wasted no time in going to the court to hear the case against the young strikers. As can easily be imagined, they were not charged with striking—how could there be strikes in a workers' and peasants' State?—but for hooliganism. One of the young men had got hold of the section head, an arrogant man and a thief, and shaken him bodily.

I could see with my own eyes how tense the courtroom was. In answer to the magistrate's threat to have an old worker who had made a comment from the body of the hall removed, the whole courtroom called out in one voice: "We'll all leave!" There were about a thousand workers crowded into the courtroom and I remember the militiamen huddling against the walls as if a gale had just blown up. After the case had been heard and the crowds had dispersed, the magistrate was taken out through a rear door.

People now tried to make some sense of their existence, having suddenly seen that their "workers' State" was as hostile to the working man as it had been under Stalin. Consequently, it is not difficult to see why Dudintsev, despite the uneven quality of his book, found himself at the center of public attention.

Dudintsev is unlikely, as I see it, to come to rest on "time's sandbanks" as Solzhenitsyn or Tendryakov, author of "Potholes," most assuredly will. Like Vera Panova's novel *Kruzhilikha*, whose main value was in its depiction of Listopad, Dudintsev's novel will no doubt find a place in the history of Russian social thought. This is particularly true of the character of Drozdov who is similar in some ways to Listopad.

However, since the times were different and the firing-squad era had passed, it was possible to discuss the Listopads seriously. The depiction of Drozdov was a crushing blow to and merciless exposure of "Stalin's falcons." Drozdov is depicted not only from the narrator's point of view, but also in passages of self-analysis and by surrounding him with physical objects which are no less revealing in terms of his character than his self-analysis.

We shall attempt to throw some light on the devices the author makes use of to create this character whose name became a household word for several generations. Let us examine these devices page by page.

Drozdov, who was by no means stupid, had his own theory, which allowed him to stride fearlessly forward, taking part in the discussion of questions about which he understood very little.

The difficulties of a leader's great task did not frighten him, but on the contrary attracted him. He even had his own theory on the matter. He considered it necessary always to experience growth pangs, stretch higher and just fail to reach the goal. A job should always be slightly beyond one's abilities.

As early as the very first pages the author directs his fire at issues which are by no means insignificant. The "cult of incompetence" is in a way the ultimate basis on which the bureaucracy rests, a bureaucracy ready when the "Party's call" comes to take over the management of anything at all—today a bath-house, tomorrow culture, the day after tomorrow aircraft construction. Dudintsev takes the bull by the horns, as they say.

Drozdov is, of course, a man of little education. As the author does not fail to point out he misspells the word "guarantee" in a memorandum.

Drozdov long ago convinced himself that it was almost his hereditary right to be a leader, as if he had been born not in a peasant hut but a boyar's palace. Outwardly he tries not to act according to his convictions. However the narrator's sarcasm only aids the reader in recognizing the familiar features of an establishment figure: "Drozdov was a small man dressed in a shiny leather coat of a chocolate-brown color with a white astrakhan collar and a hat of the same grayish-white astrakhan fur."

Lies are a way of life in the Drozdov family—telephone-callers are always told, according to his express instructions, that "he is not at home." It is on this note that the self-revelation of the hero begins. He commands that lies be considered the truth and that everyone act accordingly.

In the early pages of the novel we are still unaware of this character's purpose in the novel, but we already know almost all there is to know about him. Up to this point Drozdov has been a man of few words—it is the objects surrounding him which are eloquent. Drozdov "walked around his enormous desk on which gleamed his black Kasly cast-iron ink-stand made from tokens of hetman's power. There were two maces, a massive seal and a tall Cossack hetman's staff... all weighty and heavily significant objects." When the white astrakhan hat is also taken into account, a very full picture is formed of the feelings this little man wanted to produce in his inferiors.

Drozdov is not at all as simple as he seems. His grandeur is by no means merely a matter of irony. He knows how to inspire respect for himself in the town and even gives reason for the townspeople to speak of him with

124

admiration. He knows exactly who is popularly despised and willingly and inventively mocks the hated functionary in question. For example, Bashashkin, the warehouse manager, is in the habit of making everyone walk through an enormous puddle in the roadway to get to his office. Drozdov notices Bashashkin's visitors making their way to his office up to their knees in water and orders his driver to drive right into the middle of the puddle. Then, opening the door of his van, he calls out brightly to Bashashkin. "Bashashkin stood some way off shifting from foot to foot, then was forced to come up to the van dressed in his yellow boots to stand in the puddle for half and hour listening to Drozdov's unhurried instructions for doing a stocktake of the fuel. The next day a high wooden walkway was built in front of Bashashkin's warehouse."

The whole town has a laugh at Bashashkin's expense. Drozdov knows the way to the heart of the simple man who for centuries has lived in the hope that "the master will come and settle the dispute."[3] The master really does drive up and settle the dispute.

Drozdov's wife is much younger than he is and he inspires respect for himself in her with his convincingly solemn speeches to which it is hard to voice objections. "I am one of those who produce material values. The chief spiritual value in our time is the ability to work well, to create as many necessary things as possible. Our work forms the economic base of the country," he explains proudly. The respect of those around him helps him to become convinced of his own rightness.

However, the author takes us more and more often into Drozdov's home, behind the smoke-screen of cheaply bought popularity, to sense again how inhumane his main habits and principles are. An example is his theory of self-isolation. Dudintsev is ruthless with Drozdov who considers, for example, that ordinary people should not be invited into the house. After all, things he has rightfully earned would only make them feel envious, yet why should he refuse the rewards of being a director?

It took Dudintsev to show us that the new class had not only been reborn but that its rebirth was accompanied by a special theory of "self-isolation," which it considered necessary in the interests of the cause. This was no Listopad remembering with joy the haymaking and his kith and kin in the village.

For all that, Drozdov is no fool and deep inside he knows his true worth, so that when his wife accuses him of vanity and showing-off, he tells her half in jest and half seriously: "The Communist system will keep me out, of course. I've got scales and barnacles from the past growing all over me. But as a builder of Communism I'm acceptable, I'm right on top."

Khlebnikov said that mankind is divided into inventors and acquisitors. The acquisitors seized power on earth long ago. So that Russia should not be an exception, the inventors, as everyone knows, were all shot—even the geniuses Korolyov and Tupolev only survived by accident and all their lives they were mindful of the fact that one fine day, as Korolyov used to say, they would be taken and "popped off without an obituary."

While Panova's Listopad was a kind of strange exception—and Panova did not link him to anything wide—Dudintsev goes further, fearing nothing, or so it seemed at the beginning, at any rate. After all, it was not Moscow in 1937 during the terror, but 1956, "the late Rehabilitance," as Muscovites wrily joked. The author fearlessly follows up all leads, all links and intermediaries allowing Drozdov to sweep up the civil service staircase.

Drozdov is not alone in the capital where he arrives so grandly. Present with him is the invisible city of Kitezh and its inhabitants, the highly educated parasites and murderers headed by their chief, Avidyev, director of the institute. The inhabitants of this invisible Kitezh could hardly have held out for long if they had not been propped up by the deputy minister himself, Shutikov, and Shutikov in his turn by the minister himself. As far as Shutikov is concerned, an inventor is something outrageous and unnatural. An inventor who arrives with all his bits of paper and starts making demands of some kind, in the face of the Kitezhans' opposition—or at least without their support—well, Shutikov just can't take this sort of thing seriously. When an inventor called Lopatkin manages by chance to get through to the minister, with the help of a secretary he knows, Shutikov looks at him as if he were a miraculous apparition. When the minister summons him he says: "Have you ever seen salmon jumping up a waterfall? No?"

Shutikov understands perfectly well that truth is on the side of Lopatkin, although he signs and sets in motion the plan submitted by the Kitezhans because it has been put forward by Avdiyev himself. It is not the project itself which is important to him, but the question of who is backing it and how influential the people he is helping now are, people who one day in their turn will help him.

Drozdov, who has been appointed section head in the ministry, has landed in the right place and soon grasps the situation. Together with the others, he demolishes Lopatkin's project, just as he had before back in his little town of Muzga where he was the local dictator.

Granin's Olkhovsky was destroyed, and now it was Lopatkin's turn. Suddenly, different writers, having no connection with each other coming from different parts of the country, with different backgrounds, views and life-styles, were describing not only similar situations, but were perceptively choosing practically identical situations and characters. How sick and tired everyone had become of the pseudo-socialist routine, the callousness and vindictiveness of the bureaucrats, which were so close in spirit to the Mafia's bloody "protection" system. The Mafia is not concerned whether someone is right or wrong. It shoots when it is to its own advantage or in the interests of self-preservation. It is merciless towards whoever breaks its own laws. In essence, this is what Dudintsev is talking about also, explaining why not only in literature but even in the technical field a new discovery must remain unused even though it could bring enormous and immediate profits. What interest does the Mafia have in the welfare of the State or people! It is the Mafia!

Drozdov, as a man of advanced ideas, thinks up a theory of the rational murder of inventors. After all, they only hinder planned development. Progressive theories are the very air he breathes!

The Mafia has a real need to gain a firm foothold amid the red sea of socialist banners and to take on the colors of the State flag. "If the personality gets in the way," as the psychiatrists at the Serbsky Institute say nowadays, "why not extinguish that personality?"

The novel has an uncomplicated lyrical theme as well. Drozdov's wife Nadia sees with what contempt her husband treats Lopatkin whom she knew at the school where they once taught together, and courageously helps the luckless young inventor. She first becomes his friend and then eventually his wife. The lyrical theme serves here as a sort of "auxiliary engine."

As we have seen, it was not the lyrical element which interested the author. "The cult of personality" has not disappeared but, on the contrary, has penetrated every pore. Every branch of science, every factory and government office has its own thought-extinguishing "cult." The author thus gives an answer to the question of what is happening in Russia at present, why any thought which has not received the authorities' stamp of approval is immediately declared "dissident thought" (*inakomyslie*). Such is the structure of any bureaucratic system. It is just that the inhumanity of Stalinism gives it the additional possibility of bloody reprisals in its campaign against "dissident thought."

The death of the secondary character, the inventor Busko, serves to underline even more strongly the hopelessness of the battle of human thought with the mindless State rumbling like a tank over the landscape, crushing out all life.

Lopatkin is very stubborn. Well, so much the worse for him! A way is found to dispose of him to everyone's complete satisfaction. It is the way Lysenko disposed of his academic opponents: he had them put in prisons from which they did not return. Lopatkin is convicted of a breach of secrecy after he involves Nadia in his project without first getting official permission for her to have access to official secrets. He is arrested and sentenced to eight years in prison. So Lopatkin disappears in the Gulag Archipelago like Lysenko's victim the academician Nikolai Vavilov and thousands upon thousands of other scientists and engineers. Here we have the truth about the age and the truth about the flag which is not only symbolically blood-red.

The novel originally finished here, at the end of Part Three. However, if the author had left it at that, the book would never have been published for it was a challenge not only to the moral world of Stalinism "which was no more," but at the same time to the theory of socialist realism, one of the main theories thought up by the ideological Drozdovs. In 1956 the censors would not have allowed the publication of a *Woe from Wit* based on material from a socialist society. That "wit" could lead to "woe" in an era of victorious socialism was unthinkable!

Possibly on Simonov's advice, Dudintsev wrote a fourth part to the novel which was not without some verisimilitude, at least superficially. It was not beyond the realms of possibility that an investigator such as Badyn might exist. Badyn will not accept the sentence Lopatkin has received, writes a submission giving his own opinion and then—and this is more in the realms of fantasy—fights, while Stalin is still in power, for the annulment of Lopatkin's sentence. The scientist Galitsky from the military institute could also have existed. He builds Lopatkin's machine while the latter is in prison. Admittedly, if he had existed, Galitsky would have been more likely to have had Lopatkin transferred to one of the special prisons for scientists described by Solzhenitsyn, but in 1956 the depiction of such a turn of events was still impossible.

When Dudintsev had concocted the mandatory and false Part Four of his novel, Simonov was still editor-in-chief of *Novy mir*. He was stunned by the revelations at the Twentieth Congress and took the risk of publishing *Not by Bread Alone*. And although later he dissociated himself from his own actions, the deed was done. The mark of Cain on the brow of the Soviet bureaucracy was there to see for anyone who did not actually close his eyes to it.

9. A CLASSIC OF THE YEAR OF ANTI-STALINISM: VLADIMIR TENDRYAKOV'S "POTHOLES"

Many methods have been thought up of turning a book which has come out into something non-existent. The main ones applied in Russia have been vilification and the maintenance of complete silence on the subject of the book in question. Some of the books, the less dangerous ones, have been abused and censured. Dudintsev's novel is an example of this. But the most dangerous ones have been removed from the libraries, ignored in the press, or praised in *Literaturnaya gazeta* in such a way that the reader loses all desire to even open the book. Meanwhile, the reasons for the book's being written are kept secret.

The best books were sometimes quite unknown in the depths of the country, even to literature teachers. This was true of Tendryakov's story "Potholes," although it was translated in the West almost immediately, in 1957.

As many people are now fortunately aware, Vladimir Tendryakov is not only one of the most talented of modern writers, but also one of Russia's most staunchly honest writers. As a member of the editorial board of *Literary Moscow*, he was against any compromise.

The action in "Potholes" unfolds in a small town cut off by prolonged rain from the rest of the country. During the rain salt and kerosene disappear from the shops, there are no more film-shows at the House of Culture, and letters arrive three months late. It is fifty kilometers from the rain-swept forest settlement to the nearest railway station.

The driver Vasya Dergachev goes to the roadhouse "to catch a few bream," as he puts it, before making the long trip to the station. "Catching bream" means picking up passengers for the trip. In these backwoods a driver is the sole sovereign of a tiny kingdom—his automobile. Everyone who enters his territory must pay tribute. There is an abundance of "bream" of all sorts: the director of the machinery and tractor station Knyazhev, whose own car has broken down, an old woman with a big basket, a junior lieutenant taking his young wife away from her native village, and finally a strapping young man around whom the web of the story-line is about to be woven.

Right from the start the reader falls under the spell of Tendryakov's prose. The old woman with her basket full of eggs makes room for herself in the car and pushes her neighbor unceremoniously: "Goodness, how you've spread yourself out! You're as thin as a rake, but look at the space you're taking up—you're like a great fat old woman! Move over, come on, move over—there we are!"

The lieutenant naturally attempts to assume command and cut a bit of a figure in front of his young wife: "You sit here, Natasha. Stretch your legs out this way. Come on, everyone, squash up a bit! No, we'll sit here like this... and stand the suitcases upright."

The road is perceived as a symbol of Russia as a wasteland of impassable roads and misery.

> *What a road, what a road!*
> *The deep wheel ruts, just like crevices in the mud, puddles like small ponds with cunning snares hidden beneath the surface of the murky water, kilometer after kilometer churned and plowed up by all sorts of different types—here was proof for all to see of the impotent rage of the passing cars.*
>
> *Oh, what a road, what a road!—it was the eternal bane of the whole Gustoy Bor district. Generation after generation of cars grew old before their time on it, destroyed by the ruts and potholes, and the engulfing mud.*

The nightmarish, impassable condition of the road lies in wait for everyone. Page after page is devoted to the description of the terrible road, producing a sense of its symbolic nature as the road Russia is taking. This is a sense which stays with the reader. On this road it is an inch by inch battle.

At one point on the road the driver starts day-dreaming. He can already see himself overcoming the various obstructions and difficult sections on the road ahead. This is, of course, a simple and common literary device for setting the scene—the driver is lost in his rosy day-dreams and the reader is prevented from thinking about any mishap that might occur. But then the accident happens: the car turns over on its side on Tyrkin Hill.

The carload of unfortunate passengers now begins to take on a life of its own. Each passenger, to whom the author has devoted two or three sentences at the beginning, starts to suffer in conformity with his character. And with what precision and insight Tendryakov draws the character of each one!

The lieutenant starts shouting: "Who entrusted you with the task of transporting people? You're no driver! You shouldn't be let near a cart, let alone a car!" He keeps on shouting for quite a time while attempts are made to calm him down. Then all of a sudden the old peasant woman who has lost everything she had with her, smashed and broken in the accident, says: "The officer is upset about his cases."

At this point a muffled groan is heard coming from underneath the overturned car. The old woman is the first to hear the groan and starts jabbering: "Saints in heaven! Holy Fathers! Mother of God! The boy's been hurt! I swear to God he has. Just lie still, my poor thing, don't try to move... Please help, someone! Hurry, go and get help!"

130

They want to get the injured boy out from under the car which has crushed him, and again the lieutenant says in his commanding voice: "We mustn't move him... It's important from a legal point of view that we leave everything just as it is." How perceptively Tendryakov notes the dehumanizing aspect of military arrogance.

The others carry the injured man away on a stretcher. Disgraced, the lieutenant stands for a moment, then, feeling shamed by the others, rushes after to help carry the stretcher. The peasant woman's attitude to him immediately changes. They continue to abuse him, but now more through inertia. "So it got to him." "His conscience got to him." "That girl of his has got a soft heart." "These smart types always get the cream." But they behave quite differently. "The old woman, sighing as she tied up her empty basket with a kerchief, got up and went over to the case which had burst open. 'Oh, dear! His things have been thrown out all over the place. Come on, let's pick them up. I suppose he'd got them together for his little nest, too. Oh, dearie me!'"

There is not a single superfluous detail in the story. At the very beginning there is a description of a length of wire which is wound around the sides of the car. Its purpose in the story is not clear, yet it is on this piece of wire that the young man catches his boot as he tries to jump out of the car. As a result he is crushed. Again, as the State official gets into the car, a few lines are devoted to a description of his coat which, as things turn out, is to be a very necessary piece of equipment—it is used in place of the canvas for the stretcher on which the young man is carried.

At this point the drama is heightened and the narrative acquires still greater depth. At the scene of the accident, Knyazhev, the director of the Machinery and Tractor Station, joins the others in carrying the stretcher and shows himself to be efficient, courageous and humane. The injured man can only be saved if a tractor can tow him on a sled through all the mud to the hospital. Knyazhev is approached as he sits in his director's chair to ask for his assistance. These pages are the most significant in the story:

> *Knyazhev stood up from his desk. He was wearing the same shirt as he had been wearing when he helped carry the injured man and behind him on the wall hung his dirty, wet coat...*
>
> *"Nikolai Yegorovich," Vasya began, "things look bad. We must get him to the town hospital in Gustoy Bor to be operated on. The doctor's assistant has rushed off to ring the surgeon."*
>
> *Knyazhev made a regretful smacking sound with his lips, but made no reply...*
>
> *Vasya felt awkward not on his own account, but on Knyazhev's. Knyazhev was frowning and not letting Vasya see his eyes.*
>
> *"You must let us have the tractor. It's the only way out," said the lieutenant firmly, standing behind Vasya.*

"The tractor? Ye-e-es, well... The tractor isn't a transport vehicle you see, but a work vehicle. I can't possibly let you use the property of the State for purposes it's not meant to be used for."

"Nikolai Yegorovich! Vasya felt the blood rushing to his face. "A man is dying! It's not up to me to tell you this. We need a tractor and trailer. Unless you let us have it, he'll die..."

"Nikolai Yegorovich!" Vasya was on the point of bursting into tears. "The tractor isn't needed for shifting bricks or timber. Do you really think anyone would say anything against you for giving us the tractor to save someone from dying?

"I can't take the risk. It would upset the work schedules. I'd be leaving the kolkhoz without a vehicle. No, my friends, I'd get no pats on the back for that."

As they were going out, Knyazhev blurted out after them: "I helped get him out, I carried out my civic duty..."

As an ordinary man, Knyazhev is humane and reliable, whereas a director of the Machine and Tractor Station he is a soulless "lever." The lever in an inhuman system is a theme which is brought out unerringly in the best works of Soviet literature.

Tendryakov pursues this theme in a most interesting way. Vasya, the driver, and the lieutenant decide to make a complaint about Knyazhev's inhumane stand. To whom should they complain? In the first instance, to a representative of the power of the Soviets. After some searching they find the chairman of the village soviet, in the expectation that he will bring Knyazhev to his senses in the name of a higher power. They arrive at his house which is an annex made of logs on the main village soviet building. He appears as soon as they knock. After listening to their story he shakes his head sorrowfully. "If I say anything, he'll just tell me that Soviet power at the district level is much bigger than I am, so get lost and don't kick up a fuss... Nikolai Yegorovich has a lot of power around here and the rest of us don't count for anything."

They they go off to look for the militia. The militia, after all, is exactly the same as the State. The State will not allow Knyazhev to just let a man die.

The lieutenant heatedly explains to the divisional inspector that by not letting them have a tractor, Knyazhev is causing someone's death.

"Right!" says the inspector, breaking into the lieutenant's heated speech. "I'll explain the position point by point. I have no right to requisition the tractor. Without written instructions, any such action on my part would be illegal."

"Let's go," says Vasya angrily to the lieutenant.

"Wait there!" [The inspector stops them.] "We have to look into

*the business of the accident yet and uncover the guilty party. It's
my duty to detain the driver, sit down and slowly go over it all point
by point and draw up a report."*

*Vasya froze in the doorway, but the lieutenant turned around
sharply and said quietly and clearly: "You can draw it up on your
own fat face. You put a report before a human being... Let's go!"*

The militiaman is evidently ready only to draw up an indictment,
not to save a human being.

The general conclusion everyone comes to is that Knyazhevs cannot
be broken down. Almost imperceptibly as far as the reader is concerned,
Tendryakov has moved from speaking about Knyazhev to speaking about
Knyazhevs, in the plural. " 'Why bother trying to talk the Knyazhevs round.
I'd like to march him off to the public prosecutor's office!' fumed the lieutenant. 'It's hopeless, we'll never break him down. Let's think how to get
the boy out.' "

After rushing all over the village and raising a storm, the lieutenant
finds the Party secretary and rouses all the Communists at the Machinery
and Tractor Station to action. With the help, if it can be called that, of the
Party organization, they get hold of a tractor—but not soon enough. The
Party's help is in vain, just as if it had never existed. They set off for the
hospital with the injured youth on a sled attached to the tractor, but are
too late. When the doctor's assistant pulls back his eyelids, she sees he
is already dead. Some considerable time later the surgeon, who has been
called from the district hospital, arrives on the scene after making his way
there on foot through the mud. When he has heard what happened, echoing
the author, he brands Knyazhev as a "bureaucrat... a bureaucrat who has
grown into a murderer!"

Tendryakov's "Potholes" may be considered the most profound and
merciless work to come out during the last twenty years in the Soviet Union.
It can be compared with works such as Sergei Zalygin's "On the Irtysh,"
which we shall come to later. But is it just about the fact that there are still
"bureaucrats who have grown into murderers" in the USSR? While it is about
this, Dudintsev and other writers deal with the same subject. In Tendryakov's
work a deeper thematic level is uncovered. A new class of people has appeared which has usurped the people's property and made capital out of
words such as "the people's" and "the State's." In Knyazhev's words: "I
can't possibly let you use the property of the State for purposes it wasn't
intended for." The new class uses what it takes from the people, what was
for common use, against the people, even when it is a question of someone's
life or death.

This was the first time writers had spoken so directly and so convincingly in an artistic sense of the power elite's deadly hostility towards the
ordinary man.

There were moves to nominate Tendryakov for the Lenin Prize, but only on condition that he dissociate himself from *Literary Moscow* and state that he "had nothing in common with all the Kazakeviches and Aligers." But Tendryakov refused to dissociate himself and consequently for a long time no further attention was paid to him.

Nowadays Tendryakov, who is one of the most talented "folk" writers in Russia, is not only little known in the West but beginning to be forgotten by many in the USSR also, although his works are sometimes republished and he occasionally receives some conventional praise, more in the form of lip-service.

Unlike other writers of his stature, he is never mentioned in the press, gives no addresses at congresses and even refuses to sign the "collective" letters from writers expressing anger on various prescribed subjects. He has not signed a single letter of this type. As a result, he can hardly expect to be the object of official praise.

10. A TIME OF VAIN HOPES: CULTURAL LIFE AFTER THE TWENTIETH CONGRESS

In the years of de-Stalinization, Russian culture sprang unexpectedly to life in a variety of ways just like the scorched, cracked steppe after a long drought. First came Russian prose, then other branches of literature. Drama, painting and sculpture came to life, full of vitality, talent, intelligence and daring. It really was a time of hopes—vain ones, as became clear later. But only later. At the time, many of us hoped that the direct, angry exposure of the crimes of Stalinism which had horrified the world would not allow the hangmen who had gone into hiding to return to their rounds, their blood-drenched rounds of murder, both of people and culture.

It was our hope that a new era was dawning and that mankind retained a few crumbs of conscience. "Conscience is a sharp-taloned beast, clawing the heart" wrote Pushkin, and at that time more than ever before we had cause to recall his words. It is incredible how willing we were to take comfort in lines of poetry! And there was now an abundance of poetry—new, young poetry was bursting forth in waterfalls, in geysers.

Yet no more than two or three years later these excited and seemingly sincere poets suddenly disappeared like dandelion flocks blown away by the wind. Years later some began to complain like Yevtushenko: "We're dwarf birches,/We thought out clever poses..." Poetic thought lost its clarity and definition, becoming blurred like a picture on the screen losing its focus. We shall return to the poets of the period later in order to present them in an integrated way and show their overall development.

One Moscow director used to say that theaters had a dog's life-span. Twelve years and a theater reached old age. The only theaters which could hold sway for fifty years were the Moscow Arts Theater and others which were kept uselessly in existence thanks to injections of help from the State.

New theaters exploded into life like fire-crackers, deafening and delighting the public with plays with names such as *The Naked King*. The words "Naked King" were hurriedly written up on bill-boards and fences all over the city. It was in this way that the first season of the youth theater *The Contemporary* was announced. *The Contemporary* did not have an easy time forming, pushing its way up like grass through asphalt. Its actors worked long hours by day in various jobs and rehearsed at night. No one knew whether it would succeed in keeping going, whether it would be allowed to irk the authorities right in the center of Moscow on Mayakovsky Square, which was to become well-known somewhat later for its seditious gatherings. No one really believed that these suspicious semi-outcasts from the Ministry of Culture would survive.

Then suddenly the public was stunned by *The Naked King*. The play was by the Leningrad playwright Evgeny Shvarts and was an adaptation of motifs drawn from several of Andersen's fairytales. That good-humored, peace-loving teller of fairytales would no doubt have been astounded if he had known how his words, pasted up on the fences of the city, would resound around Moscow.

It was impossible at that time to describe Stalin in more precise terms than Shvarts' version of Andersen did. Crowds would gather at the entrance to the theater in numbers which in the West would no doubt be seen only at championship sporting events. I well remember how the audience roared with laughter as they watched it, the young girls, students from the university, screaming with delight and applauding, and people repeating in the corridors and apartments at the university the words of the lame prime minister in the play: "Excuse my bluntness, your majesty, but you are a genius!" The Minister for Tender Feelings became an obligatory character in all student skits. He was very like the poet Zakharchenko, editor of the journal *Tekhnika molodyozhi (Technology for Youth)*—a tall, trembling man famous for having produced a sycophantic documentary film entitled *Our Nikita Sergeevich* just before Nikita Sergeevich Khrushchev fell from power. *The Naked King* swept over us like a cleansing storm. As Marx once said: "By laughing people leave the past behind."

Nikolai Akimov, director at the Leningrad Comedy Theater, put on Daniil Al's and Lev Rakov's play *More Dangerous than the Enemy*. It was about an idiot of a manager, a Party appointee, who hears that reforms are about to take place in Moscow and fools will be thrown out. Without waiting for written instructions from above, the management of the local concern immediately look for a fool to dismiss post haste—and to made a report. In charge of the operation is, of course, the head of personnel, a functionary of military bearing who, when he receives visitors, is accustomed to calling out not "Come in!" but "Bring him in!" and who, to the amusement of the audience, first locks up the drawers of his desk as befits an interrogator. Naturally, he soon finds the fool the management needs, someone whose qualities do not fit in with his high calling. He turns out to be the plumber. The plumber is dismissed although he is desperately needed: the central heating radiators are not working and water is leaking from them everywhere. At this period the number of retired interrogators was multiplying at a rat-like rate and this particular theatrical rat-interrogator, created with a deep knowledge of the subject, was an excellent adjunct to the Naked King in Shvarts' play.

The times had so decisively changed that it was difficult to realize that quite recently, in 1954, the courageous Moscow playwright Leonid Zorin's play *The Guests*, about degenerate bureaucrats, had been vilified as counterrevolutionary. Later, to the vast amusement of the audience, Zorin's play *Dion* was put on at the Vakhtangov theater on the Arbat. To the amusement of the audience, the Roman emperor Claudius, bald and stout and very like Nikita Khrushchev, strutted around the stage revelling in the faithfulness of his subjects: "Oh, how loyal you are to me!"

Some playwrights came to the fore who were not afraid to touch on important and sensitive themes. For several years in a row the main auditorium of the Red Army Theater in Moscow was full to overflowing with audiences who had come to see Alexander Volodin's play *The Girl at the Factory*. The heroine of the play was an ordinary worker, Zhenka Shulzhenko, who rebels against the routine of lies and the "show" put on by the so-called workers' representatives. Plays such as this sounded the death-knell of the false "production" novels which had shown "his Excellency the working class" as happy, wise and constantly sober.

A little later at the Gorky Drama Theater in Leningrad Gorky's play *The Philistines (Meshchane)* was put on. It had been put on thousands of times in theaters all over the country. However, this time the producer was Tovstonogov and the audience gasped with shock: in all previous performances the hero, the engineer Nil, had been the prophet of the future, "stormy petrel of the revolution," as Gorky had depicted him. His famous proclamation that "rights aren't given, rights are taken" corresponded to the official concept of Bolshevism. Now Tovstonogov's proletarian Nil—the future of Russia—suddenly became an undisguised mass butcher. When he pronounced the words everyone had known since childhood in his arrogant, pushing way—"rights aren't given, rights are taken"—the audience froze with horror. Why had they not seen it before, why had they not realized that this super-positive hero Nil would trample all laws underfoot and in accord with his "revolutionary conscience" would shoot and strangle a third of Russia. What Russia had recently gone through and was going through cast a completely different light on Nil the Bolshevik.

Tovstonogov also put on Griboedov's *Woe from Wit*. This play in verse is known to every Soviet schoolboy. It is a classic, a part of Russian history. Suddenly Famusov appeared on stage as a malevolent modern bureaucrat from the Stalinist era, while above the stage a crimson placard could be seen bearing a quotation which was not from the classics of Marxism at all. It was a desperate cry from Pushkin: "What a trick the devil played on me to have me born in Russia with intelligence and talent."

Khrushchev was later specially brought to the theater by the Leningrad authorities to crush out Tovstongov's hotbed of wickedness. When he read Pushkin's words—doubtless for the first time in his life—he flew into a rage and ordered the placard to be torn down immediately. He then returned to the Kremlin, convinced that sedition had been rooted out in Leningrad once and for all. Khrushchev was not able to reach the aesthetic heights necessary to understand the producer's interpretation of the play, especially since towards the end of the day on his trips around Russia he was as a rule incoherent from alcohol. The Party secretaries en route used to fill him up with vodka to the point where he was capable of making the type of drunken revelations with which he regaled the workers of Murmansk and Bratsk and which have become legendary.

At first Khrushchev's complete lack of culture helped the country's withered culture to stand up on its rickety legs and gain some strength, or enough strength at least for some young youthful student ensembles to begin appearing rather than being smothered at birth. It was under these conditions that the beginning of the director Liubimov's famous Theater on the Taganka were fostered at the Shchukin Theater School. It was later to become one of the best-known theaters in Moscow. Just as some theaters are associated with their actors—the old Moscow Arts Theater, for example, with its constellation of talented actors—so the Theater on the Taganka was known for its producer. We all used to go to see Liubimov as people had gone to the Moscow Arts Theater to see the actors Kachalov, Moskvin and Ktorov.

Luibimov and his associates began moderately seditiously with the production of Brecht's *Good Woman of Setzuan,* which is about a fallen woman who is a better person than everyone else and who for that reason becomes one of the chosen of the gods. At a time when love conflicts were regarded as apolitical and therefore harmful, it even seemed brave to many people to put on a play such as this. It was staged by Liubimov with such feeling and such unpretentious simplicity that it became quite a talking-point, and it was decided not to send the students away to theaters outside Moscow, as is usually done, but to turn the final year students into a theater company. As I remember, the students received some assistance from Konstantin Simonov, who was hastening to gain the reputation of a progressive. However, as soon as the theater was formed, it showed its true purpose—it showed its teeth. One of the performances which followed was of Esenin's *Pugachev,* which is about rebellion and in praise of rebellion. As the play opened, the audience saw a place of execution constructed downstage, a birch-wood platform with the executioner's axe stuck in it and actors standing on either side dressed in rags and holding candles for the dead. This scene was both the play's prologue and epilogue. All the play's action took place on a stage ringed with a chain and against a background of burning candles and the axe stuck in the scaffold, while in the center of the stage writhed the runaway convict Khlopusha, played by gloomy, husky-voiced Vysotsky; and the fact that the man writhing in chains was none other than freedom-loving, hard-drinking Vysotsky, gave the performance the awesomely powerful stamp of authenticity. This was what Russia had been like and what Russia was still like. Would it ever be different?

In the same theater Brecht's *Galileo* was also put on. His old Galileo also sounded horrifyingly modern. The inquisitors with their fat ugly faces like those of Stalinist bureaucrats made short work of dissident thinking. Their methods could have led you to suppose that despite their black medieval garb they had received their instructions in the Moscow city committee of the Party.

All these defiant theaters gave expression to our general feelings, our fear, our anger, our impatience. The stormy audience reactions, especially at the Taganka, can easily be imagined. It was particularly noticeable at the Taganka because the autitorium was tiny, incredibly so for a Moscow theater—indeed, this was obviously the only reason the theater was tolerated. In a country stupefied by countless millions of copies of magazines and films, it was regarded as not really existing at all.

However, these old plays alone were an insufficient repository for all our passions and hopes, so, like mushrooms after rain, satirical companies began to appear. For example, there was The Little Blue Bird under the direction of Viktor Dragunsky, an actor, a writer for children, and the Leningrad company Let's Not! under the direction of the brilliant, although sometimes cantankerous, playwright Yuli Rest.

I remember how amused my Moscow writer friends used to be by the skits they put on. The audience reaction to the uncomplicated action was what one would expect in a children's theater where the children actually participate in the proceedings. And what was taking place really was astounding. Take, for example, the following skit. The scene is a doctor's surgery. The patient is an old man, a historian. Since he is in excellent health, the doctor asks him in amazement how he has managed to retain his cast-iron constitution into old age. The historian explains. The historians did away with Dostoevsky—he was an obscurantist and anyway incorrectly reflected the dialectic. "And that was right," says the actor with conviction. And now they have been told to extol him again because he's a classic, the pride of Russian literature. "And that is right too!" says the historian to the audience, provocatively, as if to say "You won't catch me out!" "Then we did away with Babel—well, he was enemy, and a nationalist, too. And that was right! Then not long ago they said he could be published because the time had come. And that was right too!" This is all said with the same expression of dim-witted infallibility. The actor then recounts dozens of examples of the Party's everyday hypocrisy which has led to all sorts of things—and not only in the literary world—being first extirpated and then praised to the skies. His constant and steadfast refrain is: "And that was right!" He concludes the account of his unprincipled, erratic life with a speech which brings the house down: "Did anyone ever waiver? I certainly didn't waiver! If I did, then the Party Line and I waivered together. So no one waivered... And that is right, too!"

Another of the sketches has an editor working on a manuscript which he has to get into shape in a hurry. The type-setters are ready for it. He takes an enormous pair of shears and cuts off the corners of the manuscript—"to round it off nicely."

Another is called "Blowing the critical whistle." On one side stands an important-looking Party type while a critic holds the floor, laying into various writers. He tears Tolstoy, Dostoevsky and Chekhov to pieces. After Chekhov he pronounces Kochetov's name. The Party type immediately blows a police whistle. This outrage must be stopped! You can't attack Kochetov. The critic is off again, calling *The Lay of Igor's Host* a forgery and utterly demolishing the entire seventeenth century. But as soon as he comes to Kochetov, the whistle blows again. Kochetov's cast of "untouchables" was not, of course, about to collapse as a result of any criticism. Later the Central Committee applied its own drastic police methods to afford protection to this "caste." Yet the fact that someone had started speaking openly about the existence of this caste of untouchables evoked not just joy but a feeling of being released from slavery.

There is an old traditional round dance in which the dancers move towards each other in two rows. One row chants: "We sowed the millet (*proso*), we sowed it" and the other chants: "And we'll trample your millet, we'll trample it." Now, on the stage of the Central Literary Club, two rows moved towards each other. One rather straggly row made up of writers shouted: "We sowed the prose (*prozu*), we sowed it" and the well-ordered column of critics advanced, spiritedly shouting: "And we'll trample your prose, we'll trample it."

Yes, those were days of hope and joy, apprehensive joy. This joy was dimmed, however, by the death of the critic Mark Shcheglov. He suffered from tuberculosis of the bone and walked on crutches. He was a man of quite amazing strength and fortitude, and was in a position to become the most important critic in present-day Russia. The overriding reason for his death was that no one cared about him. The authorities did not heed him, and he even posed a threat to them. If anyone was not clear about this, Alexei Surkov was always ready to explain in exactly what way.

He was supposed to be under the constant supervision of the doctors under all circumstances. Yet this same much-abused, "unneeded" Shcheglov was not given the necessary authorization to go to the writers' retreat house to rest and he was forced to go to the south as an "unofficial" tourist on a completely unorganized footing. There, far from his doctors, he contracted meningitis and died. The wretches in power sighed with relief. Mark Shcheglov had been unrelenting in his opposition to those in authority.

If it was Arkady Belinkov, imprisoned while still a student, who was the pride of Soviet literary studies (and he was even recommended for the Lenin Prize for his brilliant book on Tynianov), it was Mark Shcheglov who was the hope of modern Russian literary criticism.

Shcheglov's critical essays show more talent than anything else in recent years in Soviet criticism. It is to be hoped that his article on Leonov's *Russian Forest* in particular will be published in the West, together with others of his articles from *Novy mir*. We believed at the time that a sort of Shcheglov period had arrived—hence the particular pain his death caused, a pain I still felt although we were not close friends. If I am ever asked if the one-time poet Alexei Surkov can be forgiven, my simple answer will be: Mark Shcheglov!

11. THE HATCHET-MEN

There was no more sinister hatchet-man during that period than the one-time poet Alexei Surkov who once declared out loud for all to hear: "This Renaissance must be suppressed."

Alexander Fadeyev shot himself. Even worse, Konstantin Simonov published Dudintsev and then absented himself in comfortable exile in Tashkent for a year. Alexei Surkov felt that his hour had come.

Yashin's and Dudintsev's sudden escape from the ranks of the social-ist realists, and what was virtually the mass defection of writers "beyond the bounds of what is permitted" gave the country's rulers such a fright that books containing criticism of the "new class" of power-wielding bureau-crats disappeared for a long time. The Hungarian uprising only added fuel to the flames.

To do battle with these writers—to whip them into line—the Party dispatched a punitive squad made up of men Khrushchev dubbed "the tommy-gunners." When the alarm signal went or the Central Committee rang the bell, these tommy-gunners would spring into action against a danger-ous book, or the refractory speech of some free-thinking writer—against whatever they were ordered to attack. As Paustovsky once said about a certain type of literary hero, "they never have doubts or waver and never make a mistake because they have an empty heart." This campaign was governed by just such an "empty heart," and this is no mere literary image or exercise in hyperbole.

For twenty years the view that the Soviet intelligentsia is divided into liberals and conservatives has held sway. This stereotyped notion is still the prevailing one in both newspapers and specialist studies in the West. Yet even twenty years ago the artistic intelligentsia was no longer polarized in this way. The blood of the camp inmates even seeped through to the top brass of the Union of Writers in the old Rostov mansion on Gertsen Street, even those born blind began to see. What Russia was left with was not "lib-erals" and "conservatives," but people of conscience and mercenaries—those who had their price.

Even Vsevolod Kochetov, the conservative par excellence, who gave his name to a whole obscurantist stream in literature for which the term "Kochetovism" was coined, said in 1961 to a young writer whose manuscript he was returning: "You talk in your story about a maximum wage for Party members and proper appointment by election... You want to open the floodgates... We've gone too far along the way for there to be any thought of going back... We've gone through that station."

Kochetov the conservative simply sold himself, "leant on Polikarpov," as we used to say. But he did not lean on Polikarpov as Simonov had done—

for this reason that he was transferred to Moscow in 1961 to be editor-in-chief of the journal *Oktiabr (October)* together with a handful of similar "conservatives" in the hope that they would provide some kind of counter-balance to *Novy mir*. The Kochetovites could not of course provide a counterbalance because they lacked the requisite talent. Talented people do not serve the conservative cause except out of fear.

After February 1956 writers in Russia were not, I repeat, divided into liberals and conservatives. For this reason the following excerpts from a speech Surkov gave at a meeting of the Moscow intelligentsia in the field of the arts deserve attention. He was seeking to crush the "Renaissance" which was then still in its infancy. Surkov—and there is no "emptier heart" than he—who was spokesman for the Central Committee and the KGB at one and the same time, launched into a harangue full of borrowed official jargon:

> There have been calls in the press, sometimes open and some-times veiled, to reject socialist realism as the basic creative method in Soviet literature. If, some years ago, the experiments of such literary and artistic figures as Meyerhold, Tairov, Bulgakov and Babel were hushed up, in more recent times certain critics and literateurs have gone to the other extreme, magnifying these theatrical and literary figures' experiments in the artistic field and offering them a general amnesty, despite their real mistakes and errors. Attempts have been made to canonize Boris Pasternak and certain other poets writing in a similar vein. With much ado Marina Tsvetaeva was almost elevated to the rank of Russia's most outstanding twentieth-century poet.

He, Alexei Surkov, Secretary of the Union of Writers of the USSR, was not about to tolerate any meddling with the Table of Ranks! You never knew where you might end up in the hierarchy if you did.

The first sputnik had just been launched and Aleksei Surkov was quick to harness it to his cause:

> When I was in Italy I had an interesting conversation with a certain Italian literary figure... "When you criticized Dudintsev" [this anonymous literary figure is supposed to have said to Surkov] "I thought you hadn't liked the ugly truth shown in the book. But then the sputnik appeared in space and its appearance just did not tally with the picture of Soviet society and Soviet science as Dudintsev had depicted them. The sputnik sowed doubts in my mind."
> (*Literaturnaya gazeta*, 28 November 1957.)

Stalin had used Valery Chkalov's and Valentina Grizodubova's heroic flights as a cover for mass executions. Surkov decided to go a step further—to use the burnt-out sputnik in the sky as a smoke-screen for a pogrom on earth.

In Russia Surkov's painstaking zeal produced disdainful amusement. Everyone had read Dudintsev and had found it to be a book not about technical backwardness but about the degeneracy of those in power, all the Drozdovs, Shutikovs, Avdiyevs and Surkovs. It was also about ideological collapse—and this was where, indeed it was only here, that the book was dangerous to the new class.

Having hounded the talented Mark Shcheglov to death and slandered Dudintsev, Kaverin and Granin, Surkov tried to strike even Ilf and Petrov's works *The Twelve Chairs* and *The Golden Calf* out of Soviet literature by preventing them from being republished. I remember him calling these books, loved by several generations of readers, *Ostap Bender's Journey in the Land of Fools*. As far as I am aware, there was not a single talented work Surkov did not viciously attack during those years. He tore writers to shreds not because he had to but because he wanted to, taking revenge on talent for his own sterility as a writer.

The frank and verbatim record of his speech at the 1956 meeting, with which I had the opportunity of acquainting myself, provides undeniable evidence of the kind of man we were dealing with.

> *A very delicate situation has arisen in Russian literature of a kind which is not observable in a single (writers') organization in the world. In the case of the Moscow 'organization, we find that over forty percent of the writers are not of Russian origin. (In fact, twenty-one percent—G.S.) In matters such as literature and art, a few of the finer points need to be pointed out. This is not a question of racism... I am not saying this just because I have to give an address, it's something I wanted to speak about, something we feel very a-cutely...*

["We" of course, means Khrushchev—the piper calls the tune.]

> *As a result of this situation in Russian literature the Russian national element is being effaced from the language and from our imagery. This is particularly reflected in the fact that the translation of poetry into Russian is wholly in the hands of people of non-Russian origin... In many conversations I have with people I hear the remark that there is a spiritual life in the USA which doesn't exist here, although these vulgar philistines don't realize that in the USA there are more severe limitations than here, that Howard Fast is not banned but is made to live under such conditions that his books are actually physically read by almost nobody...*

The Party must be able to believe that literature is capable of lending the Party a helping hand and that it isn't just a collection of dead souls, an assemblage of boasters.

Surkov was not speaking just on his own behalf, as became obvious when he threatened nothing more nor less than the disbandment of the Union of Writers if it did not quiet down.

Nikolai B. gets up and starts pulling Fadeyev to pieces and telling me what to do, as if he were a modern Tolstoy and I were a cab-driver from Tverskaya Street... At the coming Plenary Session of the Union of Writers we shall have to consider what we're to do with the Union of Writers.

It was then that Alexander Tvardovsky called Surkov "a syrupy hyena." When Tvardovsky died, his family asked Surkov not to attend the funeral. But it was just as Yuzovsky had predicted. Surkov made a speech at the funeral ceremony, stretching out his white proletarian hands towards the coffin. Several people got up and left. Solzhenitsyn, who was sitting beside Tvardovsky's widow, could not tolerate this sanctimonious performmance. "Now the whole twelve honorable Secretaries arrived on the scene. There in the guard of honor were the same lifeless flaccid men who had whooped as they hunted him down. It has been like that here for a long time, ever since Pushkin. When he dies, a poet falls into the hands of his enemies, who promptly take over the body and fall over themselves making stirring speeches."

What law was operating to turn one-time poets and untalented playwrights such as Sofronov into "tommy-gunners" of the right? It is possible that the authorities made no attempt to make use of talented writers to prop themselves up, to seize for their own purposes those who were at hand? They certainly did. The Central Committee understood full well that no one trusted the untalented, and knew that Surkov's followers at the Literary Institute had been facetiously christened "surkovaya massa" (a play on the words "syrkovaya massa"—a lump of cottage cheese). For many years the Central Committee sought some maestro, some authority or talented individual who could effectively muzzle Russian literature. The first man the punitive forces tried to recruit after the war was none other than Boris Pasternak. This happened shortly after the publication of the State-inspired libellous attacks on Zoshchenko and Akhmatova. Some unknown, polite gentleman of military bearing wearing civilian clothes appeared at Pasternak's house and asked him on behalf of the government to join the campaign against Anna Akhmatova and to hold up her "unpatriotic poetry" to shame.

"What do you mean!? How can I? We're friends—old friends!" he said, frightened and waving his hands about. He kept talking in this vein for some time and then one of the emissaries of the State got up and said coldly and threateningly: "As a matter of fact, the people doesn't understand your verse, either."

"Quite right! Quite right!" cried Pasternak joyfully. "Your Trotsky said the same thing!" The "art experts" rushed out of the house as if they were being pursued.

They left Pasternak alone after that. They let the ever-willing Surkov worry about him. Soon afterwards Surkov wrote a devastating article, accusing Pasternak of being an alien and quoting the following well-known lines from his poetry to bring the point home:

> *Shielding my muffled face with my palm,*
> *I cry through the window to the children in the yard:*
> *"Tell me, good children,*
> *What millenium is it out there?"*

On 29 August 1957 the Union of Writers of the Russian Federation was set up. In setting it up, Khrushchev set the tone by declaring: "Sobolev who is not a Party member is closer to us than Aliger who is."

The Party leaders' bureaucratic thinking was fully reflected in the Central Committee's decision: in order to stifle the Moscow organization, it was decided to create another organization superior to it. A handful of old Stalinist informers, chosen for the task somewhat at random—all the Gribachevs, Sofronovs and Alekseyevs were there—was dispatched to man the new superior organization which then set to work.

The new policy of the thugs in the Secretariat of the Union of Writers of the Russian Federation was exemplified in the following way: the Union of Writers of the Russian Federation immediately accepted into membership six hundred literary bureaucrats from areas outside Moscow—directors of regional publishing houses and editors of Party publications. In Moscow the political editor of *Pravda*, Yuri Zhukov, who wreaked violence on everyone and everything, became a member of the Union of Writers of the Russian Federation and subsequently its director.

Bureaucrats were taken in en masse, to add weight, so that the scales would tip very decidedly in the direction of conformism and Stalinist practice, and so that Paustovsky, Tendryakov, Kaverin and 150 other writers with progressive views should never again be in a position to win not just a majority, but even a measure of approval. The tommy-gunners saw their main job as keeping out alien elements and protecting their own.

The Secretariat of the Union of Writers of the Russian Federation did not, of course, ratify the expulsion of Elsberg from the Union. Elsberg had been exposed as an informer. Elsberg was sent away for eighteen months to Tashkent, following in Simonov's footsteps, until passions cooled. It was the young poet Fyodor Belkin who was now pushed forward into a position of prominence. Gribachev and others wrote ecstatic prefaces in his books. He was given the honor of being published in New Year editions of the newspapers. For example, the following lines of a poem by Belkin were published in the New Year issue of *Literaturnaya gazeta* for 1959:

> *What we say in our hearts is repeated in work,*
> *We speed further along Ilyich's path.*
> *We trust the Party, its deeds we can see,*
> *We walk with the Party, shoulder to shoulder.*

I quote this wooden verse in particular because there is an interesting story attached to it.

Fyodor Belkin, who as a good guard dog had attacked Margarita Aliger and Ehrenburg and had even gone so far as to call Pushkin "an invention of the urban intelligentsia," let himself go to the point where he decided to repeat all his violently repressive ideas for the benefit of television viewers. Here he had a set-back. An old investigator from Minsk happened to be staying in a Moscow hotel where he saw Fyodor Belkin's television appearance. He was shocked to see on the screen the man he had been looking for for fifteen years, chief of the Nazi district police who had personally shot hundreds of partisans and Jews in the area. People could now not help noticing the striking similarity of the orders issued by Hitler's police and Khrushchev's ideological decrees. A man who was an executioner—a "tommy gunner"—for both Hitler and Khrushchev—turned out to be someone who had received the blessing of the State. This, then, was the course modern Russian history was taking. Right at the top was an "empty heart."

12. ISAAK BABEL RESURRECTED

At a time when the government was conducting a campaign of vilification against the books inspired by the year of anti-Stalinism, an article whose appearance at first glance seemed inexplicable was published in *Literaturnaya gazeta*. The newspaper had been ordered to exhume Babel.

Babel, of course, had perished in the Stalinist camps. He had no sooner been rehabilitated and republished when suddenly he was reconsigned to oblivion as a traitor. Liutov, a character modelled on the author in his *Red Army Cavalry*, was now compared with Mechik from Fadeyev's novel *The Rout*, who was a key figure in the destruction of a partisan detachment. Later the hostile attacks in the newspapers found their way into the area of so-called serious research.

What was the reason? Did the right hand not know what the left was doing? It certainly did know. It transpired that the Stalinist machine had made a crude miscalculation. While attacks were being made on the new works by Dudintsev, Granin, Yashin and others under the scorched earth policy, the classical works of Soviet literature started to come into their own again. At one time they had been suppressed together with their authors, but now, in the years following the revelation of the truth about Stalin, the classics were resurrected and republished, and in 1957, after interminable delays, Isaak Babel was published again. Andrei Platonov came out almost at the same time, and eventually Mikhail Bulgakov. "Sedition" had been pushed out of the door, but came back in through the window. The literary hatchet-men tried to grab it but were too late. At once out of the bottle, the genie helped to fortify the new generations inwardly.

The resuscitated Babel came out with a preface by Ehrenburg.

> *At a time when romans-fleuves were being written, at a time of verbal inflation, Babel above all, feared verbosity. He was a realist in the most precise sense of that word. His short story "Gedali" grew out of a few remarks in his diary: "A Jew, small, a philosopher. A shop beyond the imagination—Dickens, brooms and gold slippers. His philosophy: everyone claims to be fighting for the truth, but they're all robbers..."*

Ehrenburg's preface to the 1965 edition of Babel's work—the second posthumous edition—was torn out of the books ready for distribution on the grounds that it was counter-revolutionary. A new preface was inserted, this time written by Lidia Polyak, which began with the sentence: "It is not easy to write about Babel!" That was an understatement. "The main question Babel asks, his main themes," Polyak bravely admitted at the end of

149

her article, "is whether a man has a right to be violent during a revolution, whether he has the right to be inhuman in the name of truth and humanity." She even quoted a diary entry from 1920: "Budyonny's men are bringing Communism, an old woman is crying."

The short story "Gedali" represents the main spiritual nerve in Babel's writings. Later Pasternak was to pose the same questions in *Doctor Zhivago*: is the revolution justified if it leaves in its wake millions of corpses and the tears and despair of tens of millions, if ceaseless butchery carries off the flower of the nation and if power usually ends up in the bloodstained hands of those who behave most despicably? This theme is clear enough without further development. It is worth considering here something that even Babel was not conscious of in all its ramifications, for all his wisdom. After all, history imposes limits on the perception of people living at a certain time in a certain place.

In his story "The Road to Brody," in which Budyonny's men destroy hives which do not belong to them and steal the honey, Babel writes: "From the chronicle of everyday evil, I feel a tightness inside which never lets up, like heartburn." Squadron commander Trunov in the story of the same name, who shoots one of his own men, is cruel and malicious. In "The Letter," an early story in the collection, the young peasant lad Kurdyukov, one of Budyonny's men, leaves his beloved horse behind at home and asks his mother with the solicitude of someone brought up in the country not to forget to wash the horse's front legs with soap. He then informs her laconically that they had "finished old Dad off"—meaning his own father who had been serving under the Whites. In general, this young Red Army soldier is quite a philosopher, delivering himself of opinions such as that "the rear has no feelings for those at the front—it's full of traitors and yids, just like under the old regime." In the story "Berestechko" an old man is suspected of being a traitor, so the cossack "Kudrya pulled out his dagger with his right hand and carefully, without bespattering himself, cut the old man's throat." Another of Budyonny's men, Matvei Pavlichenko, happily tells the story in "The Life and Adventures of Matvei Pavlichenko" of how he trampled a landowner called Nikitinsky to death: "What I say is this—by shooting someone all you do is get rid of him, shooting him is an act of kindness... But I don't spare myself, sometimes I'll trample on someone for more than an hour, I want to know what life is really about here."

But perhaps all this is merely the elemental cruelty of hardened soldiers, the bestiality of the dregs of society? Alas, these everyday acts of violence were actively encouraged by the revolutionary leadership and the heroic figures of the period. In the story "The Brigade Commander" Budyonny tells the brigade commander, Kolesnikov, to drive the Poles out of a certain small town. " 'If you try to make a run for it, I'll have you shot,' he said and, smiling, looked in the direction of the head of the Special Section.

'Right,' said the head of the Special Section."

Budyonny's "I'll have you shot" and his smile are even more terrifying than the crude sadism of those serving under him. For Russia they bode a new bout of self-destruction of unheard-of dimensions. It comes through clearly in the ease with which he says "I'll have you shot" and in the calm way the head of the Special Section replies "Right."

Kolesnikov drives out the Poles and rides into the captured town. Babel describes it as follows: "That night I could see in the way Kolesnikov sat in the saddle the imperious indifference of a Tartar khan."

The authors of prefaces and studies about Babel mention the contrasts in everyday reality described by him and that the juxtaposition of such contrasts was one of his principal literary devices. And so it was, but it was also a means of talking about the pain wracking his heart in a way which would strike home powerfully.

The spectacle of the Tartar khans gathering strength terrified Babel. These newly arisen khans showed utter contempt not only for the enemy but for their own fathers and brothers, the village peasants. In the story "The Remount Officer," in which he retains the main character's real name, Babel describes how some peasants come to complain about their treatment. They cannot plow because their horses have been taken away from them. The chief staff officer comes out onto the porch and "shielding his inflamed eyes with his hand, he listens with apparent attention to the peasants'" complaints. But his attentiveness is nothing more than a ploy. Like any well disciplined and over-tired clerk, he knows how to stop his brain functioning completely during idle moments. During these few moments of blessed absence of thought our staff officer cranks up his worn-out motor." This was now happening as he listened to the peasants.

At the end of the story there appears a character call Dyakov whose origin can be found in Babel's notebooks: "A Communist... cunning, a liar, a very picturesque figure." Dyakov has not the slightest intention of looking into the peasants' complaints: "with an operatic flourish of his cloak, he disappeared into the staff building."

There is no love lost between the new Tartar khans and the *intelligenty*. The khans do nothing to lessen the soldiers' contempt for them or to stop them dealing with them however they wish. "What a nasty little type you are!" exclaims Savitsky, Divisional Commander in "My First Goose." "You've been sent along with inquiries being made," he says to the narrator, "and people who wear specs get their throat cut around here." Afonka Bida who shoots his fatally wounded comrade, turns to the narrator who could not bring himself to shoot a man and says: "You types in specs pity a man the way a cat pities a mouse." "You want to live without enemies," the Squadron commander Baulin accuses an *intelligent*. "Isn't that what you're working towards—living without enemies?"

It is more than the narrator can stand. In "The Evening" he goes back

151

to the *Red Cavalryman* publishers where he sits and agonizes. "I was mulling over the class war in my confused poet's brain when Galin came in, the whites of his eyes flashing. [Galin belonged to the publishing house—G.S.] 'Galin,' I said, overcome with self-pity and loneliness, 'I'm sick, I'm obviously finished, and I'm tired of my life in this cavalry of ours.' "

When Budyonny made a vicious attack on Babel,[7] it was Gorky who came to his defense. "Babel has painted his characters more vividly and more truthfully than Gogol painted his Zaporozhian Cossacks," Gorky wrote in *Pravda.*[8] "It is impossible to criticize such works as Babel's *Red Cavalry* from atop a horse's back," asserted Gorky.

However, Babel did not consider that he had given any special coloring to his characters. "I have just reported what I saw when I was with Budyonny," he declared, well aware of the effect his words have.[9] "I'm not capable of inventing things... The motto on my shield is Authenticity."[10]

But in that case was this unvarnished, and at times vicious, "unbalanced" authenticity still socialist realism? And if so, how was Gorky's position, given that he was the father of socialist realism, to be explained to the people? Critics were put in an awkward position and came up with the following explanation: "What Gorky had to say about Babel's Romantic idealization and vivid depiction of the soldiers' characters is still valid. The Romantic idealization finds expression in the way the cavalrymen, for all their faults, have the aura of men fighting for abstract justice for all mankind, for a vital truth whose meaning is not yet clear."[11]

Some time later the meaning of the vital truth became quite clear. As Evgenia Ginzburg bitterly remarks in her book *Into the Whirlwind* looking at her former ideological enemies, now political prisoners as she is, sharing her cell: "How relative all human systems of thought are and, on the contrary, how absolute is the terrible suffering people condemn one another to."

After his *Red Army Cavalry*, Babel had his *Odessa Tales* and "Sundown" published. When these stories are read one after the other, one is struck by the similarity on the moral plane of the cavalrymen and the Odessa bandits. In "The Father" from *Odessa Tales*, the head of the Odessa bandits Froim Grach sits in the doorway of a brothel waiting for his future son-in-law. "My respects, Grach," said Ivan Fiver, "there's a woman banging on the door at your place..." It was Froim Grach's daughter Basya banging on the door. She had to be married off. The man she was to marry happened to be at the brothel. "The brothel-keeper drew up a chair for Grach to sit on and he sank into an attitude of indefinite expectancy. He waited patiently like a peasant in a government office. On the other side of the wall Katyusha was moaning and breaking into ripples of laughter." Froim Grach waited until one o'clock in the morning and then went in to have a little talk with Benya Krik, the enviable bridegroom to be.

There is an episode in the story "The Widow" in *The Red Army Cavalry* which seems at first to be quite different. Shevelyov, a regimental commander, is dying. Beside sits his wife Sasha and Lyovka, the divisional commander's driver, chewing on a piece of meat. "When he had finished the meat, Lyovka licked his lips and pulled Sasha away into a hollow. 'Sasha,' he said, 'we may as well be hung for a sheep as a lamb. Come on, Sasha, give in. I'll do anything for you. He's had his day, Sasha...' Close by the commander listens to all this, still clinging to life.

In moral terms, is there any difference between Budyonny's cavalryman and the head of the Odessa bandits? It should be noted that the Odessa bandits did not touch the poor and only robbed the city's rich. "The lining on the stolen purses is made of tears," as they used to say. Can the same thing be said of Budyonny's men? On this point we have the most exact and authoritative testimony possible. Ordzhonikidze and Tukhachevsky reported to Lenin and Kamenev: "Beginning with Voronezh, the cavalry received no wages and had no proper supply arrangements. Consequently it was forced to assure its own food supply and under the conditions of overcrowding customary in the cavalry this inevitably led to some suffering on the part of the local population."[12]

Behind these cautious official phrases—"forced to assure its own food supply" and "inevitably led to some suffering on the part of the local population" lies a multitude of unavoidable, planned "everyday crimes": old men brutally cut down, arson, atrocities perpetrated against both the Russian and Ukrainian population and on hapless Jewish communities butchered by both the Polish Whites and the Cossack Reds.

The groundwork had been laid, and after that things could only develop with gathering strength. There was the brutal arbitrariness of the khans, accustomed, as we have seen, to execute or show mercy as the spirit moved them, as both an example and an encouragement to the men. The invisible standard flying above the troops was a call to "expropriate the expropriators," an incomprehensible slogan which the political workers translated in a way which was much more to the point: "Plunder the plunderers!"

The cavalrymen were now and then joined by Makhno's and other Cossack atamans' bands of outlaws. The bandits and part-time bandits would join the Reds or leave them with equal ease. Their differences were political and depended on the atamans. There was nothing moral about them. As far as morality was concerned, Afonka Bida summed it up in his comment on what had happened in Volyn where beehives and people alike had been hacked to pieces: "The bees can put up with it, we're doing it for their own good."

"Human cruelty is ineradicable," Babel lamented.[13] The agony of the peasants continued for a long time still to find its way into art and even films, which were controlled by the State with particular thoroughness: "The Whites came and robbed us, then the Reds came and the same thing happened, you see... How can a poor peasant get away from it?"[14]

There is another difference that stands out between Budyonny's cavalrymen and the Odessa thieves as Babel describes them. The Odessa bandits are brave, as are the cavalrymen, but the Odessa bandits are also clever and possess a brilliant talent for improvisation. The wedding in "The King" is a case in point. The bandits are enjoying themselves at the wedding while the new police captain, acting on the principle that a new broom sweeps clean, decides to organize a raid and catch all the thieves in Odessa at one fell swoop. But the policemen on their way to catch Benya Krik's associates have not gone more than fifteen paces from the police-station when it bursts into flames. The idea was Benya's.

> *The policemen, their backsides wobbling, were running up and down the smoke-filled staircases and throwing boxes out of the windows... Although the firemen were filled with zeal, it turned out that there was no water in the nearest tap. The police captain—the broom which was to sweep clean—stood on the footpath opposite chewing at his moustache, which had found its way into his mouth. The new broom stood there motionless.*
>
> *As he passed the police officer, Benya saluted him in military fashion. "The very best of health to you, your Honor," he said sympathetically. "What do you say to this misfortune? It's really shocking..." He stared at the burning building, shook his head and smacked his lips. "Dear, oh dear, oh dear!"*

With their "code of honor" and "honor among thieves" and their implacable attitude towards informers, for whom they could always spare a bullet, Babel's picturesque bandits were simply old-fashioned. Old one-eyed Froim Grach, the real head of Odessa's forty thousand thieves, could not have imagined that he would just be shot, without a trial or an investigation, when he came to the Cheka for discussions. He thought they would ask him respectfully to be seated, offer him a cognac and then later take him out the back way. He could not have imagined that the motive for killing him could be that "we represent the power of the State and a man like you is not needed in the society of the future."[15]

Borovoy, who works for the Cheka, is also confused, knowing that Grach is a legend and that there is no one else like him. The narrator is obviously also confused, It took fifty years for a clear realization to form amongst the succeeding generations of Cheka and KGB prisoners of what the real motives for preventative murder were. "Under the fascists, apparently, the Mafia ceased to exist. It could not have been otherwise. Whether the dictatorship is that of one person or that of a Party administrative oligarchy, it considers organized crime as its own prerogative and brooks no rivals."[16]

As we have seen, if Babel's bandits were morally akin to Budyonny's Cossacks, and murder and plunder were the order of the day for both, they cannot be compared with the all-powerful State. In this regard, they were simply knights of honor.

In the 1936 *Goslitizdat* edition of Babel's stories, two stories "With Old Man Makhno" and "Ivan and Marya" were published. In post-war editions they were left out. Why? Six of Makhno's horsemen are raping a woman. Kikin, the young lad holding the wretched woman by the head, tries to reassure her: six is nothing, sometimes up to twenty of them do it. This young lad keeps asking to be allowed to have a turn as well—some of them have already had a second go. But when he is given permission, he refuses. "No thanks, Matvei Vasilevich, I said, I don't want to go after Vaska, I might regret it for the rest of my life."[17]

This story, which is masterful in both the choice of narrator—the naive and rather stupid boy—and in the structure of the language, and which is terrifying by virtue of the very ordinariness of the events narrated in it, is the only one from the whole cycle of Babel's war stories which has been forgotten and well and truly buried, although the earnest claim continued to be made to the effect that what had been described in the story had not only taken place on Makhno's side.

As I. Smirin has aptly remarked, the Odessa tales are imbued with the "irony of the pathetic."[18] There is much truth in this. With very few exceptions, all Babel's prose is imbued with the irony of the pathetic. Despite the truth of this, the fact mentioned at the beginning of this chapter should not be lost sight of: *The Red Army Cavalry* was not the same book for a reader in the "fifties as it had been even for the author himself, who had been very much under the influence of the legendary nature of the cavalrymen. For a quarter of a century the whole of Russia proudly sang: 'We're the Red cavalry and the singers of heroic tales/Tell of our brave deeds.' " The fury of the awakened elements both terrified and attracted the writer, while historical perspectives were still shrouded in the bitter smoke of revolutionary illusions and atrocities made legitimate in the name of the bright future.

The illusions floated away and the terror strengthened. It is possibly this fact rather than the simple overthrowing of the literary traditions of the early years of the century, the traditions of Bely and Remizov, which explains the re-working of the early stories. Budyonny and his henchmen attacked not with swords but with anonymous letters. In order to forestall the fate awaiting him, Babel was even forced to sing the praises of Joseph Stalin, the wise old man Gedali's sworn enemy, at the First Congress of Writers. Nonetheless, it is perfectly obvious that although, like Blok, Babel at first accepted the Revolution, he hastily stepped back from it once he had seen it face to face. Neither of these great Russian writers could bear the Revolution's "everyday crimes," and while one died, the other fell silent for many years.

There is another aspect to Babel's writings which should be kept in mind if Babel is to be properly understood. This is the pity for the peasant held in such contempt by the conquering bloodthirsty hordes, pity for the hapless *intelligent*, for the butchered, plundered Polish Jews, the pitying love for the simple people tormented by war and pillage, which became an emotional motif running through all Babel's writings.

It was this deep compassion which led him to take up the theme of the annihilation of the peasantry, a theme with fateful consequences for Babel. For more than a quarter of a century the NKVD-MGB kept Babel's extraordinarily talented prose hidden from Russian readers. Now Babel is seen as the originator of a whole stream of works in Russian literature concerned with the peasantry, a stream which only resurfaced and reestablished itself after the war thanks to Yashin's "Levers."

PART III

THE SOLZHENITSYN DECADE

1. 1961-62: THE DOORS ARE AJAR

At the very beginning of the sixties a new kind of literature began to push its way past the censors. Apart from its own value as literature, it was important in that it prepared the way for Solzhenitsyn, creating an atmosphere in society which was receptive to Solzhenitsyn and severely weakening the hold of prevalent dogmas and intolerant attitudes.

In considering this new trend in Russian literature, we must turn first to *Pages from Tarusa*. Young Russians do not know this work at all because it has long since disappeared from library shelves. This talented collection of literary and artistic contributions which was compiled in Tarusa and published in Kaluga in 1961 was regarded by the authorities as a public danger.

The editor-in-chief of this collection, its creator and guiding spirit was Konstantin Paustovsky, a man who never forgave betrayal, cowardice or compromise. On occasion he would show his contempt for informers quite openly. He once asked the writer Lev Nikulin in a voice which was soft but loud enough for those standing around to hear: "Cain, where is Abel? Nikulin, where is Babel?"

Paustovsky did not stop at mocking remarks or angry outbursts at those he regarded as scoundrels. He had a well-defined positive program of action which he started to put into effect at the first opportunity. *Pages from Tarusa* was not just another book with birch trees on the dustjacket. *Literary Moscow* had been banned. *Pages from Tarusa* was Paustovsky's counter-attack, a breach in the new wall of censorship.

The first ideas for the collection were worked out in the fall of 1958 at a writers' retreat in Yalta when Paustovsky realized that to do nothing was as good as being dead. Not that he had been unaware of this before, but now in Yalta a plan of action crystallized in his mind.

I shall never forget that fall in Yalta. The fierce heat had abated. In the hills there was a pleasantly drowsy aroma of warm pine-needles. Our thoughts were far from rainy Moscow until we were roused from our drowsy resort-town existence by a telegram from Paustovsky announcing his arrival in his familiar mocking style. When he came into the building, he cast an eye over the red and blue velvet door curtains and said, addressing no one in particular: "A nice jolly second-rate sort of place!" That evening, when it was learnt that the writer Vasily Smirnov who had been active in the suppression of *Literary Moscow* was to arrive, Paustovsky called out for the whole dining-room to hear in tones of mock panic: "Better blow up the wells and head for the hills!"

A few days later there was a report on the radio about the launching of the sputnik with the dog aboard. It was announced that the dog would not return to earth but would be burnt up on re-entry in the dense layers of the earth's atmosphere. That day as we were climbing up into the hills away from the sea, with Ilya Selvinsky ahead of us panting and walking backwards (he maintained it was easier on the heart) Paustovsky stopped, looked up at the sky and said: "It's a shame about the dog. They should have put the Secretariat of the Union of Writers in the sputnik." He did not say another word all the way to the top. When we got back he said to Selvinsky who was drenched with perspiration: "Then you wouldn't have had to walk backwards in your declining years."

He was by no means alone in his fury and his determination to take some action. Even Ilya Selvinsky, who was far from appearing a rebellious spirit now, unexpectedly organized an evening at which poets read their seditious verse, some of which had been printed but most of which had not seen the light of day. Reading his own verse, he would read a little and then swallow something for his heart. It was such a joy and a surprise to find that he had remained true to his rebellious youth that for a long time we would not let him stop reading. He had been taken prisoner, but not killed.

Selvinsky pointed to his heart and read in farewell his poem "On My Anniversary," which has still not been published and remains among his papers:

> *My chairman was a viper,*
> *My publisher was a hare,*
> *My critic was a bear...*
> *If you want to be a Soviet writer*
> *You have to be in the best of health!*

The aroma of warm pine-needles, the courage of Selvinsky who was so ill, and our enthusiastic applause even brought on a "fit of sincerity" in the poet Mikhail Dudin, a Party type who was later to become a leading figure amongst the Leningrad writers. He began reading his poem from 1956 about an underground forest fire. A fire sweeps through the forest unseen, destroying the trees' roots, leaving the forest still standing but dead, although outwardly it is still green and alive. "And what sort of ground are *we* standing on?" he blurted out. Olga Forsh, who had a commanding presence despite her eighty-five years and did not mince her words, looked at him in astonishment. This was not the Dudin she knew. Alexander Yashin strode across to him impetuously and shook his hand. How quickly their paths were to part. Meanwhile there was an illusory "balance of power" in force.

At about two-o'clock in the morning someone started screaming in a wild, heart-rending voice. I rushed out onto the stairs in my pyjamas, thinking that there had been an accident. There I saw Vasily Smirnov, with whom I was to have several encounters later, in a terribly agitated state from all his shouting. This small, bony man with colorless, frozen features was shaking his fists at Yashin and repeating in a frenzied way: "You've sold out to the yids, sold out to the yids!" He only recovered his self-control when he saw the large crowd of half-dressed people standing around.

Two days earlier, Shambadal, the aging translator of Sholom-Aleichem, a small, thin-necked man always brimming over with enthusiasm, rather like a character from Sholom-Aleichem's works, had been reading his new works in the foyer. Vasily Smirnov had made a point of walking around the crowd of people listening, giving them a wide berth. I remember him circling higher and higher up the staircase above the foyer, sticking to the railing as if to show that he wouldn't touch those yid-lovers with a barge-pole. The screwball behavior of the "iron chancellor," as he had been christened, had caused great amusement, but after his performance that night he no longer seemed quite so funny.

The next morning Paustovsky called me over. "Did you hear what happened? What an original interpretation of Yashin's 'Levers,' he remarked sarcastically. "You'd never have thought it possible." He was silent for a moment and then said in a changed, hoarse voice: "Well-poisoners!"

We went down into the town. Paustovsky said that writers were obviously in for a bad time. Smirnov spent all his time in the cultural section of the Central Committee. "What Khrushchev is thinking, the iron chancellor is saying. If someone like him gets into a position of power... The journals are under siege. We have to make a breach. We have to use our own voices."

Paustovsky prepared his breach of the blockade very thoroughly, with an eye to the way of thinking of our masters, the Party bureaucracy. This is why *Pages from Tarusa* contains so many "TV spot announcements," as I call them, which are exaggeratedly orthodox and meant to divert the attention of the authorities. The introduction, for example, is like the quintessential lead article from *Pravda*: "The grand program for the building of Communism, revealed to humanity in the new program of the Communist Party of the Soviet Union..." and so on.

Apart from the impressive-sounding introduction there are quite a few production sketches printed in arrestingly large type which immediately attracts attention. This was done especially for the "master's eye," which dislikes small print. For example, Paustovsky describes in tones of endearment some of the more unusual inhabitants of Tarusa, flying in the teeth of the cutting remarks of those who scoff at provincial towns. Cunningly, Paustovsky first sings the praises of the stove-setter, the locksmith and the carpenter. The stove-setter is a master of his craft, setting stoves speedily in his own special way, the lock-smith is so dexterous that he was even able to fix a broken denture for an old man with a piece of wire, while words alone cannot express his admiration for the carpenter, who enjoys making bird-houses and bird-cages. Then, almost in passing, Paustovsky mentions that not long before he died the poet Nikolai Zabolotsky lived in Tarusa, and that the famous artists, Polenov, Krymov and Borisov-Musatov also lived and worked there. It was in Tarusa that Marina Tsvetaeva spent her child-hood. She dedicated some of her verses to Tarusa and many of them were published for the first time in *Pages from Tarusa*, as was her story "Kiril-lovny" in which she implores fate: "I should like to lie in the... cemetery in Tarusa, under an elder-bush... Paris, May, 1934." But this is all in small print, whereas the stove-setter, the locksmith and the carpenter are all de-scribed in large print. Everything of importance, everything it was the original purpose of the book to say, every last line of it, was in small print. What a comment it is on the conditions that one of Russia's great creative talents found himself working under that he should have been forced to play such a shabby trick in order that what he had created might see the light of day.

Thanks to Paustovsky, Soviet readers were reacquainted with Ivan Bunin, who had become virtually unknown since he emigrated. All we had of his was the occasional slim little volume of stories which were meant to illustrate rural poverty—under the tsars, of course—or the tragic fate of the personality in a world of injustice in "The Gentleman from San Francisco." That was all. We did not really know Bunin at all. Some even thought that two or three stories were all he had written.

Pages from Tarusa also contained a beautifully written sketch by Paustovsky about Yuri Olesha. Even those who had never met Olesha had the feeling as they read it that this irrepressible, somewhat old-fashioned man, who was like a wise old bird, was present with them like an old friend.

I once had the good fortune to see Olesha. How well I remember this tall, very thin man with the face of a tame, emaciated lion who had forgotten that he was capable if not of eating his trainer then at least of giving him a good fright. I saw Olesha at a moment of quiet joy for him, a moment he loved to talk about. After many years his *Three Fat Men* had just been republished.

"I stood beside the cash-register, listening to its ring. It was like music to my ears. People kept coming up and saying: 'Eighty-seven kopeks,' 'eighty-seven kopeks,' 'eighty-seven kopeks.' Then suddenly I heard the assistant call out to the cashier: 'Don't put any more Olesha's through!' " There is one detail which has crept into this story of Olesha's as faithfully reproduced in a sketch by the late Boris Yampolsky[1] which is not quite right. Olesha, always shy and proud, did not go so far as to stand around near the cash-register. He stood with his eyes closed at the far side of the shop near the door, rocking slightly as if in a strong wind. You would not have thought he was interested in the cash-register at all.

I stopped for a moment beside him, thinking that he was ill. But there were no signs of suffering on his earthy-colored face with its sunken cheeks. It bore rather an expression of inspired dreaminess. He was standing listen-ing to young and old voices calling out continually "eighty-seven kopeks." I am glad that Yampolsky's sketch about Olesha, "Long live the world with-out me," did not just disappear like so much else.

162

For many years, Olesha, one of Russia's most talented writers, lived quite literally the life of a beggar. Waitresses at the National Hotel restaurant in Moscow used to give him something to eat out of the goodness of their hearts. He never had any money, yet drank more and more. Olesha could almost always be found in the National restaurant. We were also regular patrons of the National, which is, of course, right in the center of Moscow and much frequented by foreigners. Yampolsky had once said to us on hearing our rather risky arguments in the Writers' Club: "Listen, if you want to go to a nice place where you can sit and say whatever you like, go to the National. It's looked after by the foreign department of the KGB, which isn't interested in what Soviet citizens say. All the tables have microphones but no one will pay any attention to what you say—you're looked after by a different department." We had laughed, as I remember, not quite believing in such a division of labor, but afterwards we quite often dropped into the National. Olesha would always come over and sit with us for a chat and a glass or two. When he died, the Union of Writers attempted to reimburse the waitresses for the debts Olesha had run up but they took offense. "Do you think we don't know who Yuri Olesha was?" one of them exclaimed.

Although it was absolutely forbidden to do so, Paustovsky even managed to allude to the circumstances Olesha lived in for so many years. "He died quite recently, and his fine face is quite unforgettable. It was the face of a man lost in thought right in front of us. Nor can I forget the little red rose in a buttonhole of his old jacket. *I saw him wearing that jacket for many years.*" (My italics—G.S.)

There are also inspired sketches about Blok and Lugovskoy by Paustovsky in *Pages from Tarusa*. Even sketches such as these could not be published in the official press.

Pages from Tarusa saw the beginnings of the literary careers of many poets and prose-writers and among them was Bulat Okudzhava. It was in this collection that Okudzhava took the first step in establishing himself as a writer with his penetrating story about the war called "Lots of Luck, Kid!" In it the truth about the war is seen throught the eyes of an eighteen-year old schoolboy.

The opening has a seemingly naive, boyishly playful ring to it. It sets the tone for this story of a schoolboy who was sent off to the war without any moral or physical preparation and who survives quite by chance. This was a landmark of great importance for Okudzhava. His story helped him become known, even if not very widely, and opened up new possibilities for him, providing him with a new public. The rest he achieved himself with his songs. It is difficult to say whether he would have succeeded in making such rapid progress if it had not been for the publication of "Lots of Luck, Kid!" which lent some legitimacy to his position and gave him some claim to the public's attention and the right to take his place on the

163

theater stage.

Yuri Kazakov is another writer who first became known to a wider public through *Pages from Tarusa*. Three of his stories were published in it. Stylistically and thematically, this poetic writer has much in common with Paustovsky and to some extent with Prishvin. Kazakov's works have been republished many times, but he would scarcely have become so widely known as a writer if it had not been for Paustovsky.

However, it was the prose of a writer called Boris Balter which had the greatest impact. His story "Three from One Town" was the first work he had had published. Later it appeared again in the monthly *Yunost (Youth)* with a few additions, as if to confirm that its appearance in the seditious *Pages from Tarusa* had not been merely a historical error.

"Three from One Town" tells the poetic account of some romantic young boys from a seaside town who are just finishing school and are about to go into the army. It is set in the menacing pre-war years of 1939 and 1940 and has a confidential ring to it—it could be your neighbor or school friend telling it.

The boys are drafted into the army before they have even left school. Their parents are against it. Even a neighbor to whom they come to complain about their parents suddenly says: "They shouldn't be taking you off like that. You went to school for ten years—that's more than at the grammar-school in the old days. No one who finished grammar-school went off to be an officer. Only idiots did."

The boys are angry. They share all the prejudices of their time. "Vitka, why haven't you hanged yourself yet?" asked Sashka. "Why should I?" "If I had a father like yours I'd have hanged myself five times and drowned myself twice." "Your mother's no better." "My mother's a different kettle of fish. She comes from the petty bourgeoisie. She's allowed to be like that. She's backward in her way of thinking."

The boys have their attachments and their enemies. although not personal ones. It was too early to have personal enemies, One of these enemies is the tin-smith. "The tin-smith was our personal enemy. Why we did not know. He hadn't done us any harm and we'd never said a single word to him. But all the same he was our enemy, it was something we felt, and we despised him for his double life" (91). The point is that when the tin-smith makes the acquaintance of young women holidaying in the town, he passes himself off as a sea captain. Vitka particularly despises him. Whenever the boys meet him out with some woman, Vitka cannot stop himself saying: "What parasites some people are. You can't get a primus mended anywhere, while they're out enjoying themselves."

The young heroes have an intolerance for everything which is not as crystal-pure as they are themselves. They are even intolerant of those who think differently from themselves—here the times they lived in had played a nasty trick on them. On one occasion they discuss the still-born Soviet constitution which they religiously believe in and according to which everyone has the right to vote. Vitka does not agree with such liberalism. Why should everyone be allowed to vote? "People like old Tin-smith should be drowned in the sea, not given the right to vote," he says. Intolerance brought much unhappiness to that generation, but there is no mention of that in Balter's clear, vivid story. His concern is to relate how pure and naive his contemporaries were as they went off to that war of extermination from which so few returned.

Balter was followed in *Pages from Tarusa* by the poet Naum Korzhavin. His real name was Mandel. He had once been one of the most talented students at the Literary Institute. His authority there had been indisputable to the point where some of the Institute's humorists had invented a new scale for evaluating poetry called the mandel scale. The poems of all the different poets were evaluated at one mandel, two mandels, a half mandel and so on. Sometimes Mandel's own poems would only rate a quarter mandel.

Even at that early stage Mandel had written a cycle of historical poems which was not of course published and in which at one point he described the 14th century Muscovite prince Ivan Kalita in the following terms:

> To the eye you were rather repulsive,
> And by nature base. But it makes no matter.
> Your path in life turned out to be
> Historically progressive.

For these lines or similar ones, Mandel went straight from the Literary Institute into exile. He was a happy and rare exception among the orthodox and obedient young writers of the day. Like Arkady Belinkov, he saw through Stalinism while Stalin was still in power. This is described in faithful detail in his autobiography which has now been published in the West.[2] Although Korzhavin had been known to some earlier, it was through *Pages from Tarusa* that he first reached a wider public.

New works by well-known poets such as David Samoylov and Boris Slutsky also appeared in the collection. Zabolotsky, too, was represented by some previously unpublished poems. In one of them this great and persecuted poet wrote the following audacious lines:

> Joining together madness and sense
> We'll build a house amid the deserts of meaning...

It was also in *Pages from Tarusa* that we came across Vladimir Maximov as a prose-writer for the first time. His story "Settling the Land" is mercilessly truthful. Maximov is above all uncompromising towards himself. Few writers would have the determination to punish themselves through their hero as he did for his own moral blindness.

The main character joins a small expedition going up a river in the Siberian taiga with all its boulders and shoals. Apart from the hero there are two other workers in the expedition: Dimka, a young lad who has been amnestied and who "only wakes up so he can take a few swigs from the flask," and Tikhon, a peasant from near Vologda who is always signing up for expeditions, a taciturn man without ties, concerned only with his kit-bag.

A few days out the narrator writes a letter to his guardian at the children's home with whom he keeps in touch. He describes his companions on the expedition in the following terms: "What people! My God, I used to despise heroes—heroes only exist in bad novels—but if there were just one self-respecting man among them. You couldn't possibly say that they 'battle for existence.' They don't battle, they just potter around in their own filth, pushing their fellows away from the trough as hard as they can." It is with thoughts and feelings such as these that the hero sets off up the river under the leadership of Kolpakov, who comes from the area and also takes on a gypsy and his heavily pregnant wife.

Events develop simply and tragically. Dimka and Khristina the gypsy's wife fall in love. The gypsy overhears the lovers talking together and the next time the boat capsizes he does not swim to safety, although he is an excellent swimmer. He remains on the bottom of the river in the taiga. Dimka, and the narrator, realize that the gypsy committed suicide. Although Dimka swims to safety, he soon dies from exposure.

The expedition is stranded. There is no one to row the boat and no supplies. Kolpakov and the narrator leave Tikhon and the pregnant Khristina in a dug-out and set off through the taiga for help. Kolpakov does not make it. When the rescuers arrive on the scene they find that Tikhon has crawled off into the taiga to die—he could no longer walk. He said to Khristina: "I'll go away because I'll start smelling when I die here and you'll be too weak to drag me away."

It seems that on setting out on the expedition everyone in fact had an affirmative view of life, had his pride and was devoted to his chance companions, and the young narrator has a complete change of heart. Everyone turns out to be quite different from his first conception of them. In his very first story Maximov discovers the fine qualities people may possess although they sometimes go unrecognized in everyday circumstances. "Settling the Land" can be seen as a stepping-stone to more important works, even though the quality of Maximov's more substantial works remains uneven.

Maximov emigrated to the West. In going into exile in the West he sought to preserve the sense of inner freedom without which, as Paustovsky was convinced, a writer cannot exist. The fate of some or the other contributors to *Pages from Tarusa* is also significant. Bulat Okudzhava, whose lyrical songs sustained people all over the country, became Russia's darling.

As a mark of their gratitude, hundreds of Party bureaucrats pounced on him greedily, trying to deprive him of his last crust of bread, and in fact, to finish him off.

Yuri Kazakov, of whom Paustovsky was so fond, began to drink heavily and fell silent for many years. Boris Balter's fate was more tragic: this wounded war hero and former regimental commander could not withstand the persistent carping criticism and attacks on the film based on his book *Three from One Town* and he died after suffering two strokes. The reason he was not spared such vicious attacks at Party meetings is that he signed a letter protesting against the practice of holding closed political trials in Russia. He wanted no more than trials conducted according to the principles of justice—and suffered the fatal consequences. Naum Korzhavin (Mandel) did not sign this letter. His poems were found in the desks of some students who were arrested, opponents of any restoration of Stalinism. This was quite enough to have him banished from Russia. The more talented the contributor to *Pages from Tarusa*, the more severely he was dealt with. When the fate of those established writers and poets such as Tsvetaeva and Zabolotsky whose work appeared in the collection is taken into consideration as well, the fate of Russian literature in the Soviet period becomes only too evident. Whoever had a deep love for Russia, whoever held Russia more dear than life itself, was cast into prison or sent into exile.

The exceptional achievement of *Pages from Tarusa* was to help create in Russia the special conditions which produced a certain tolerance of the truth on the part of the authorities. Yet this collection was not the only factor involved. Of some importance here was a story by Veniamin Kaverin published in the second issue of *Novy mir* for 1962 called "Seven Pairs that are Unclean." It was to serve as a kind of bridge in terms of its themes to the writings of Solzhenitsyn, whose first published work, the story "One Day in the Life of Ivan Denisovich," came out in the same journal nine months later.

What is striking about Kaverin's story is the authenticity of the details about camp life, details which were so little known before Solzhenitsyn. Kaverin describes prisoners being loaded onto a ship. They are made to kneel on one leg and are then counted. In the ship's hold it is the common criminals who, as usually happened, rule the roost. A robber named Alemasov, the chief of the criminals, decides to seize the ship, the *Onega*, and take it to Norway. In making their preparations, the criminal gang terrorizes the political prisoners. Then all of a sudden an aircraft with black crosses on it appears over the ship as it makes its way across the White Sea. A sentry is killed in the attack and falls into the hold. This is how the political prisoners find out that the war has started. Alemasov decides that the war will make it easier to seize the ship, but things turn out quite differently. A feeling of fear for Russia grips even those who have had some sympathy for Alemasov and the seizure of the ship becomes impossible. When the political prisoners are unloaded in the area threatened by the German advance, they immediately join in the fighting after first shooting Alemasov.

There are echoes of Kazakevich's "Two Men in the Steppe" in Kaverin's story. It had taken fifteen years for the theme which had so infuriated Stalin to break through again, the theme of the savage repression of those patriotic people who were faithful to their native land to their last breath. The same theme appeared in Tvardovsky's works, in Olga Berggolts' and in Galina Nikolaeva's.

Political prisoners, some of whom had talent, were not returning to write about what they had experienced. Books were also coming out by well-established writers which gave people pause for thought. Foremost among these books which roused and heartened the reading public was perhaps Pavel Nilin's story "Cruelty." It came out not long after the Twentieth Party Congress.

Nilin's hero Venya Malyshev works in the Criminal Investigation Department and is firmly convinced that Soviet power has no need of deception. Believing in the innocence of a peasant called Lazar Baukin, he gives him a chance to escape from prison. As he had promised, Baukin, together with others from his village, capture the leader of a robber band and bring him to Malyshev in the town. However, the chief of the Criminal Investigation Department gives an order for the robber chief, Baukin and some other peasants to be shot so as to assure himself and Malyshev of the credit for catching the dangerous robber. Even before this tragedy unfolds, Malyshev has an argument with a Party journalist with Security connections called Uzelkov who maintains that to have a "conscience" is to uphold "Christian morality" which is something foreign to Bolsheviks. This argument echoes themes found in Babel's "Gedali" and many other stories. This is not surprising because it was essentially an argument about the fate and the ruin of Russia which had believed, if only for a short time, in Smerdykov's morality—if there is no God, then all is permitted. After Baukin and the others from his village have been shot, Malyshev commits suicide.

In her writings Galina Nikolayeva accuses the Security service of exercising power arbitrarily. Veniamin Kaverin also attacks the informers whose slander is "full of a multitude of sins—a reliance on ignorance, and a bogus truthfulness in the details, and a terrible logic to their falsehoods, a logic which it is almost impossible to understand but which stabs you in the heart."

The only writer who really approaches the same level of truthfulness as Nilin does is Valentin Ovechkin, who once attempted to kill himself by shooting himself in the temple with a hunting rifle. In one of his short stories, "A Hard Spring" (1956), which caused quite a sensation at the time, a character called Kholodov, a Party Secretary who once worked for the KGB. Vy force of habit, he still writes denunciations. As Ovechkin writes: "However much you feed a wolf, he still looks towards the forest."

Where does this deeply-rooted habit of informing on others come from? It is second nature to people like Kholodov. How could he have become accustomed to having the right to slander others?

It was Nilin's story "Cruelty" which was to provide the answers to these burning questions. The point is that the action takes place at the beginning of the "twenties, that is to say, when Lenin was still alive." The organization of the terror is not yet Stalin's responsibility. And although Nilin could not write about it openly and could not take the step Grossman did in his story *Forever Flowing*, published abroad after appearing in samizdat, still the very period in which action takes place in his story affirms that honest people who found themselves in the hands of the Security service were forced to shoot themselves both in the early twenties under Lenin and in the thirties and forties during Stalin's reign of terror.

Mention must be made of the high literary standard achieved by the writers during these years. This was the period when Vasily Aksenov's story "Half-way to the Moon" came out, as well as Tendryakov's "Three, Seven, Ace" and Yashin's "Vologda Wedding." These and certain other writers drew liberally on the resources of contemporary spoken Russian for their stories, the peasant and partly underworld slang which was so much the fashion in the cities. They taught the purists among their readers not to isolate themselves from the modern urban slang. At the same time, they made it easier for readers to accept Solzhenitsyn's prose and prepared them for Solzhenitsyn's themes by presenting their own with such profundity and from such unusual angles.

The way was open for Solzhenitsyn. Ahead of him lay any number of chance circumstances which would decide his fate, but they were essentially of an administrative or bureaucratic nature. Literature carried out its mission, regardless.

One question of extreme importance in any discussion of modern Russian culture remains. Why did these particular years, 1961 and 1962 become years when the "doors were ajar" for the literature of resistance? In December 1962 Khrushchev closed the door again firmly. What was the reason for the authorities' two years of benevolence?

In the first place, the old fear of the truth-seeking soldier returning from the war had passed. In the second place, the fear of the rebel writer had also begun to diminish. First of all there had been the Soviet sputnik and then they had put a man in space. By comparison with a ballistic missile, of what account were the insurgents from Herzen Street in Moscow? If necessary, they could be gotten rid of very quickly. For a short time the Soviet authorities really were in the grip of a kind of "cosmic" benevolence.

In a speech he made to writers in May 1959, Khrushchev took an almost liberal stance. In answer to Vadim Kozhevnikov's obsequious call to the Central Committee to "guide us," Khrushchev said: "It is difficult to come to a decision about what to print and what not to print... This is why

I ask you, comrades, not to put the burden of this decision on the government, but to decide it for yourselves in a comradely fashion..." Hardly anyone apart from the editor of *Novy mir,* Alexander Tvardovsky, took advantage of this rare opportunity, this unbelievable crack in the wall cutting us off from inner freedom, which existed for over two years.

The factors leading up to the appearance of Solzhenitsyn on the literary scene were therefore various—literary, political and even cosmic. They prepared the way for the voice of the lost generations, the lost land of Russia to ring out, a voice which could not be ignored.

2. THE MORTAL AND IMMORTAL SOLZHENITSYN

When Solzhenitsyn first stepped onto Western soil, I was watching the event on television. On seeing his hard face with its exhausted, aloof expression and the beard ruffled by the wind, I went quite cold. "That's not Solzhenitsyn!" I said to those watching with me. "See, it doesn't even look like him! At this very moment the real Solzhenitsyn is in the Lubyanka being burnt with cigarettes on the chest and taunted. They've sent us his double, an agent. He'll go around making speeches for a month or two, compromising Solzhenitsyn both by what he says and what he doesn't say, and then Solzhenitsyn's wife will arrive and he'll just vanish, and the Soviet government will seemingly have had nothing to do with it." I rang people in several European capitals raising the alarm and shouting down the telephone: "It's not him! It's not him! The real Solzhenitsyn is still in the Lubyanka!" Fortunately I was mistaken. The arrival of his wife put an end to my fears.

However, when later I got to know him—and I do not mean just the great portrayer of contemporary life and the twentieth-century archpriest Avvakum cursing and conquering an atomic-age State, but the philosopher and futurologist as well—I again had the feeling that this was not Solzhenitsyn. It was as if someone else had been substituted for the author of *The First Circle* although I had no doubt it was not the KGB who had made the substitution. They had obviously not been able to make up their minds to take this step, or else had not obtained approval from above.

Why does this strange feeling that this is not Solzhenitsyn keep coming back to me? There are, of course, mountains of books and articles on the works of Solzhenitsyn. Donald Fiene's book *Alexander Solzhenitsyn: International Bibliography of Writings by and about Him* (Ann Arbor, 1973) contains 2,465 items and by now the number must have increased enormously. It is not my purpose here to spend time looking at this body of research or to take up contentious points with any of the researchers. My purpose is quite different: to examine Solzhenitsyn's times and the shift in public consciousness and in literature which Solzhenitsyn's appearance caused. Not wishing to go over old ground, I shall particularly concentrate on the writer's personality and the extent I found it to be consistent. There is something fanatically obsessive about this personality rising psychologically above the graves of millions and having its roots deep in the spirit of the Russian schismatics who immolated themselves in isolated corners of the land for the sake of true faith.

It was at the end of 1961 that I saw Alexander Solzhenitsyn for the first time. I was in the prose section of the *Novy mir* office returning a manuscript I had been given to look at in my capacity as a reader. Sitting there on a squeaky chair in a corner of the passageway, which is where writers just starting out were kept waiting, was an author I did not know. In his hands he held a cheap cardboard folder. Across from him sat one of the editors, Anna Samoylovna Berzer, working at her desk. Some of us used to call this small, thin woman "litmus paper" because at times when things looked black she would be dismissed from *Novy mir*, and at times of greater liberality brought back again.

My unknown author's fingers were not nervously rapping on the cardboard folder in his lap, and he showed no impatience. This was an author who had received a reply, someone who had been lucky or at least given some hope. His fresh, beardless face, which was no longer young, was glowing, although not with joy but with hard-won contentment. His face had a defenselessness and openness about it which seemed to beg forgiveness for any intrusion. "He has a soft face," as Akhmatova said at the time.

A soft face, a cloth cap and a cheap gray suit from a country store. He looked just the same when I saw him again in 1967. This was when I had my first conversation with him outside one of the writers' premises in Moscow where he had come, not trusting the post, to deliver by hand to some writers his address to the Writers' Congress due to open three or four days later. The wind was blowing the bottom of his cheap jacket up around him, making his unpressed cotton trousers flap. He was already a world-famous figure. His epoch-making stories "One Day in the Life of Ivan Denisovich" and "Matryona's Home" had been published long since. It was the latter which made the greater contribution to his recognition among writers. "The theme at work in this story was unheard-of before," said some of our venerable cowards, "it's a frightening theme, like an explosion right at your feet. Still, obviously we have a great talent here." Although everyone had recognized him as an important writer, outwardly he remained the same slightly stooped country school-teacher from a small town outside Moscow. Lev Kopelev told me that Solzhenitsyn was then living on just seventy-five kopeks a day.

When did his face start to change? Perhaps when he began to grow a beard, possibly so that his face would not look so soft and defenseless? However, his features only acquired their expression of inflexibility, severity and hardness after the Writers' Congress. He was left with a sense of betrayal' when his letter was not read and he realized that a life in prison-camps may be ahead of him, hand to hand combat with arbitrary power, the refined brutality of jailers and the power of the atomic-age State. He seemed to foresee his second eight-year term in prison.

It was during this period that official lecturers and bureaucrats from the Union of Writers initiated their frenzied campaign of lies against Solzhenitsyn. Either that year or the next a lecturer from Moscow spoke to workers at a factory in Ryazan where Solzhenitsyn lived, painting him in such black colors, using phrases such as "betrayed us for dollars," "slanderous attacks on the workers' State" and "sold himself," that the young workers, after a few drops of vodka for courage, set off to "deal with" Solzhenitsyn. When they got to his small house on a quiet street in the city, they found he was not at home and were met instead by polite old ladies. Everything about the house—the worn curtains in the windows, the shabby furniture—convinced them that Solzhenitsyn was living in desperate poverty and after looking about them in confusion and perplexity they went away quietly.

On one occasion in about 1970 I noticed a car with a special antenna and the KGB prefix MOTs in front of its registration number parked outside Lev Kopelev's door into our building. (We lived in the same apartment block.) It was obviously listening in to some conversation. Cars of this type which are called the "mobile patrol" used to stand often outside our block "protecting writers from foreign correspondents," taking photographs of people going in and out and "averting the possibility of communication." We had a fair idea of their number-plates which were distinguished by the prefix MOTs. However, this particular black Volga was equipped with an additional antenna and had four men sitting in it all the time, tense and motionless like shop dummies. I concluded that Kopelev, who was a specialist in German literature and married to a specialist in American literature, must have been entertaining foreign guests as usual. His guests were usually American or German university professors, although he was sometimes visited by young post-graduate students from the United States, England and Germany who would talk frankly and freely. I immediately went over to his apartment to warn him that their conversation was being listened to. In our apartment block people normally opened their doors straight away without asking who was there. This time, after a pause, someone asked: "Who is it?" I said who I was and the door was opened. When I came into Kopelev's study, a room lined with books from ceiling to floor, I saw Alexander Solzhenitsyn sitting in a corner noting something down on a notepad.

As I remember, they were talking about Heinrich Boll who was supposed to be coming to Moscow. I nodded towards the window and Kopelev said affably with an ironic smile: "We're old jailbirds." Then in a louder, animated voice he said:"Would you like to hear a new joke? There was this beautiful girl..." I was the only one who laughed. It was as if I had been paid to. As I laughed, I kept looking towards the window as if it were not a large window in an apartment block but a spy-hole in a prison cell with the guard's eye glued to it on the other side. Solzhenitsyn gave a small smile, just with his lips, more at the effort Kopelev had put into the telling of the joke than at the joke itself. His lips then took on their usual implacable, hard expression.

I had several such chance encounters with Solzhenitsyn, either in Kopelev's apartment or on Aeroportovskaya Street, near the writers' apartment blocks. I remember with great clarity that he never spoke about himself on such occasions. Every time he would ask me about myself. One meeting I remember particularly clearly. It was just near the underground station and Solzhenitsyn was no doubt on his way to see Kopelev again. That morning I had been expelled from the Party, which I had joined during the war. The decision to expel me was a final one taken at the highest levels in the Committee chaired by A. Pelshe. Pelshe was a member of the Politbureau of the Central Committee of the Communist Party, a small, dried-up, white-faced Latvian who had saved his own skin during the Stalin years at the terrible price of losing every ounce of humanity left in him. He was rather like a deaf old man who can only hear when his hearing-aid is switched on. If he wants to hear what is being said to him he turns it on, but if he does not, he turns it off.

My expulsion had taken all morning and I had been treated with great contempt by the whole Committee. I was expelled for a speech I had given at the Union of Writers in which, among other things, I had spoken approvingly of Solzhenitsyn.[3] When I referred to Solzhenitsyn as a great writer, Pelshe listened to me with his hearing-aid switched off, as it were. His clear light-blue eyes, roamed absently around the room. The other members of the Committee sat tensely erect like hounds straining at the leash. There was a firm directive on Solzhenitsyn and consequently there could not be two opinions on the subject. If a Party member ignored something such as this... My fate was decided—indeed, had been decided well beforehand. The man who was up for expulsion just ahead of me, and who was given a reprieve at the last moment, whispered to me as he swept past me in the corridor: "They'll murder you!"

Solzhenitsyn listened to me carefully and asked a few questions about my future. There was nothing sentimental about his attitude, unlike the attitude of some of the older writers who would embrace me and listen to my story with tears in their eyes. He just touched my shoulder and said a few words the gist of which was "Don't give way!" I distinctly remember the expression on his face and my own feelings and thoughts at that moment. He stood very straight like an officer serving in line, as if he had never had the stooped figure of a country school-teacher or book-keeper. He stood erect with straightened shoulders against whatever wind might blow. This was late in the fall of 1968, a terrible year marked by the Soviet tanks rumbling into Czechoslovakia. We had just been mourning the demise of "socialism with a human face."

Solzhenitsyn was wearing a new overcoat with a fur collar. The fur seemed to me of an expensive kind and the coat itself fit for a lord ["barskoye"]. This was the word which came to mind and although it is a pejorative term to me, I felt no condemnation at all for him. On the contrary, I felt joy. He was being hounded and attacked in every newspaper and at meetings all over the country—for a single word in support of him you were dismissed from your place of work and deprived of your last crust. All my joints were aching as if I had been put through a wringer, just for telling

174

some high-ranking scoundrels: "We'll all die—I shall and so will you—and rot away without a trace, but he will remain, like Russia herself." They were not just trying to kill him off but to create a lifeless desert all around him. Yet here he was looking just splendid, refreshed, almost well-groomed, with his thick, neatly trimmed beard and white face showing over the top of his expensive fur collar. He looked like some imperious lord—regardless of everything. When I said goodbye, I still felt knocked around, even my muscles were aching as if I had just been whipped, but I felt an inner satisfaction, a quiet joy: "They're not going to get the better of him, they're not going to break him."

As usual, I had not asked any questions. There were so many people hanging around Solzhenitsyn—to some of them one could take no exception, but some of them aroused suspicion—that I think he talked freely and openly only with his old prison friends, such as Lev Kopelev.

As is well known, Lev Kopelev was the prototype for Lev Rubin in *The First Circle*. Having been a political prisoner, Kopelev was able to work in the midst of noise and commotion. He would sit working on a manuscript with the radio blaring over by the window. "The music cuts out the noise of the dump-trucks," he used to say by way of explanation.

It is my vivid memory of this exceptional man, now cut off from me by the barbed-wire ringing the great prison-camp which is Russia, which allowed me to come to some conclusions about the relationship of the documentary and imaginary elements in Solzhenitsyn's prose. The direction his inventiveness, or conjectures, took give a much fuller picture than biographical data or the memoirs of his contemporaries could give of the author's personality.

The theme is a wide one. Now that Lev Kopelev's autobiography *To Be Preserved Forever* and Dmitry Panin's autobiography *Sologdin's Notes* have been published, it will no doubt receive the renewed attention of researchers. These books have made it possible to study with painstaking, scientific thoroughness the question of the extent to which invention corresponds to the truth and the lives of Solzhenitsyn's characters to the lives of their models. Was verisimilitude sacrificed for the sake of the actual biographical facts or was the opposite the case? Sologdin, for example, bears little resemblance to the real Panin whom I have met and Panin is a Roman Catholic and a fanatical proponent of reform.

Solzhenitsyn does not hesitate to transform real life in accordance with his own moral and religious outlook. He never feels bound by the facts. If necessary, he will concoct a character out of four or five actual people. This was the case with Ruska Doronin in *The First Circle* who becomes an informer in order to find out who the informer in the "sharashka" or special prison is. He finds out on pay-day when all the informers receive 147 roubles. According to P. Herzenberg, one of those Doronin was modelled on, three different prisoners were models for Doronin. He looks like a prisoner called Gusev, shares the emotional experiences of a certain Vitkovsky, while his character, his actions and adventures are modelled on those of Perets Herzenberg, who was in prison with Solzhenitsyn from 1948 to 1951.

Herzenberg's wife Tanya, a former lecturer at Riga University, recalls a conversation she and her husband had with Solzhenitsyn in May 1956 during which he advised them to emigrate to Israel. "If I were a Jew," he told her, "I'd become a Zionist." This conversation has great significance for any attempt to understand Solzhenitsyn's world-view at a time when it had still not been clearly formulated. At that time he already had some sympathy for nationalism and approved of the views of nationalists.

The similarity between Solzhenitsyn's characters and people from real life ends with Doronin-Herzenberg, as far as I can establish. As soon as the facts cease to correspond to his artistic intentions, Solzhenitsyn brushes them aside with the determination of a man who is in no doubt about why he has taken up his pen.

The main character in almost all Solzhenitsyn's works is Ivan Denisovich, the man of the people who bears all burdens and guides the destiny of Russia. There were innumerable Ivan Denisoviches in the camps. Flaubert once said that there was an Emma Bovary weeping in twenty French towns, and Solzhenitsyn could no less justifiably say that his Ivan Denisovich was carrying his cross in every camp in Russia, even if the camp were an ordinary Russian town and not surrounded with machine-guns.

How does his Ivan Denisovich happen to be in a "sharashka," one of the privileged camps for scientists and engineers? In *The First Circle*, for instance, there is the "peasant Spiridon," the guard, a fifty-year-old Russian, as Solzhenitsyn emphasizes, in the chapter called "The Traitor Prince." When Rubin and the other erudite prisoners put the prince on trial with nervous hilarity, "the peasant Spiridon smiles slily." In fact, as Kopelev told me, there was no such person as this Spiridon, a symbol of conscience and fate. There was a janitor called Rodion, as Kopelev remembers. He was a stooge and an informer, as janitors have been for generations in Russia. But this did not fit in with Solzhenitsyn's intentions, so a character called Spiridon was created, a man of the people, invented because Solzhenitsyn, with Russian blood in his veins and drawing his strength from the Russian people, could not do without a Russian peasant called Spiridon. He could not do without an ideal which would flow through his works like a healing stream, although this peasant ideal might at times appear under different names and have different characteristics. One cannot help wondering if Solzhenitsyn has not in fact idealized the people—the people which now numbs its brain with drink in the most terrifying way in an attempt to avoid thinking about how it lives.

A people which has lived for centuries in grinding poverty, buffeted by all sorts of invasions, groaning, figuratively speaking, under an endless Tartar yoke, while remaining in some essential sense good and sensitive to

176

human suffering, scarcely needs any idealization.

The hero of Solzhenitsyn's prose is Solzhenitsyn himself. Does this not cast a new and sharp light on the personality of the author? This is particularly true of *The First Circle* where Rubin, Sologdin and Doronin are all complete characters and only Nerzhin, the main character is not rounded off.

As Professor Zhekulin has correctly observed,[4] Rodion Nemov in *The Love-Girl and the Innocent*, Gleb Nerzhin in *The First Circle*, Oleg Kostoglotov in *Cancer Ward*, Alex Koriel in "Candles in the Wind" and Ivan Denisovich himself are all Solzhenitsyn. Kostoglotov with his self-confidence and abrupt manners learnt how to live from the simple peasant Ivan Denisovich Shukhov, absorbing his qualities. The progression from searching, doubting Nerzhin to confident Kostoglotov, "a political prisoner ["zek"] through and through," was only possible when Ivan Denisovich became Solzhenitsyn's alter ego. Finally, the narrator in "Matryona's Home" is a cursory sketch of Kostoglotov soon after his return to normal life when the narrator feels drawn back to the heart of old Russia where Solzhenitsyn himself at first wanted to bury himself.

Does not an awareness of this hero-centered approach resolve many of the misunderstandings which have provoked such violent attacks in the Western press and among Orthodox priests, Jewish nationalists and European social democrats, not to mention Andropov's henchmen in the KGB network?

Solzhenitsyn has every right to take a hero-centered approach in his fiction, but it goes further than a question of literary method. Just as our shortcomings are sometimes said to be the enlargement of our virtues, so the hero-centered structure of Solzhenitsyn's fiction may be said to be just one aspect of his whole hero-centered world-view. Figuratively speaking, he has returned to the Ptolemaic system, maintaining that the sun goes around the earth.

"Can we and dare we describe all the vileness in which we lived which is not so different from that of today?" Solzhenitsyn writes. "If this vileness is not fully exposed, we are left with lies. This is why I believe that in the thirties, forties and fifties we had no literature. Unless it tells the whole truth, it is not literature."[5] Kazakevich, Nekrasov, Yashin, Tendryakov, Paustovsky, Babel, Zoshchenko, Pasternak, Zabolotsky—these creators of great literature certainly existed. It is Solzhenitsyn who did not exist, either as a writer or a reader, during those years—after all, you cannot do much reading in the trenches or in the Gulag Archipelago.

Solzhenitsyn is throwing the baby out with the bath-water. This has necessarily left its mark on his deeply interesting book *The Calf and the Oak*, which was written by a literary Ptolemy who, for all his greatness, imagined himself at the center of the universe. It must be said in Solzhenitsyn's defense that our literature contained a lot of superfluous "water"—sometimes muddy, sometimes syrupy, but oceans of it. Yet does the chronicle of our literature really not begin before 1962 when "One Day in the Life of Ivan Denisovich" appeared? And are the "concerned writers" from the rural areas and their works, "mainly from the post-Solzhenitsyn period,"[6] really worth no more than a cursory glance? It is above all in *The Calf and the Oak* that Solzhenitsyn's outstanding characteristic as a writer is crystallized—a writer whose native element is prose and only prose. What Solzhenitsyn the publicist affirms, Solzhenitsyn the prose-writer immediately denies, and with immeasurable conviction. For example, Solzhenitsyn is sharply critical of the recent emigres who, he claims, are alien to Russia and have left her to her misfortune. Solzhenitsyn the publicist raged at them in open letters, public addresses and comments reported in the newspapers. Yet Solzhenitsyn the writer, with the fearless frankness we associate with him, tells us in *The Calf and the Oak* how he agonized at night in his cell in the Leforovo prison wondering if he would be thrown out of the country the next day and asking himself why he had not emigrated in 1970 when he could have left through Stockholm and why he had allowed himself to end up in prison again. After all, "the way was open to me to follow my predecessors into that old-world domain of writers... But instead I refused to allow myself that now impenetrable life and refused to allow my great life's work to be written, and spent three more years without a roof over my head and had come back to prison to die. And I regretted it, I regretted not having gone in 1970."

Almost all the intellectuals among the recent emigres are people who have got out of prison or escaped the threat of prison or the mad-house, fleeing the KGB or Party interrogators, years of slanderous attacks and discrimination, fear for their children who would be made to pay for their parents' unorthodox thoughts, and the impossibility of creating their "great life's work." Almost every single one of the dissidents left behind him a Lefortovo inexpressibly darker than anything Solzhenitsyn experienced during the nights he spent there. Solzhenitsyn enjoyed the world's protection—and was saved from further misery. Ordinary dissidents were shot, hanged, starved to death, driven mad—and more often than not in complete obscurity.

Blessed is the escaped convict, and blessed are Solzhenitsyn's confessional writings, even when interspersed with his memoirs and speeches which at times, almost in passing, give more definition to our picture of Solzhenitsyn the publicist and futurologist. However, his prison writings have lately given rise to false rumors and attacks both in the West and the East, and at first glance attacks of a serious nature.

In fact there are no impenetrable barriers between the two genres. A writer is not a submarine divided up into watertight compartments. Did not Solzhenitsyn, the militantly Orthodox publicist, give all his great works from "One Day in the Life of Ivan Denisovich" to the *Gulag Archipelago* a nationalistic bias even if he was not conscious of doing so?

In Russia there are many different ethnic groups. How right I. Shafarevich was when he said that "in times of turmoil it is unlikely that class hatred will serve as the match which sets our house ablaze. However, national hatreds certainly could. The underground tremors which are now making themselves felt give some idea of the tremendously destructive force they could become once they surface."[7]

Out of all the claims being made and all the questions being asked of Solzhenitsyn at present, this is why I have chosen this one: is the immortal author of "One Day in the Life of Ivan Denisovich," *Cancer Ward*, *The First Circle*, and the *Gulag Archipelago* a chauvinist? Is he anti-semitic? If he is a chauvinist, then he is an *immortal* rabble-rouser and provocateur. As the author of *Hostages* and books about State chauvinism in Russia and a researcher into "friendship of the peoples" in the Soviet Union, I feel obliged to devote some attention to this question. Indeed, I am rarely allowed to avoid it—I do not recall a single public address or lecture I have given without being asked this question. If Solzhenitsyn's writings are those of a writer sowing dissension or even in a small degree those of a rabble-rouser, then we have all been mistaken about Solzhenitsyn and he really is not who we thought he was.

When Solzhenitsyn was in Russia and his life was in danger, I considered it my duty as a man and a writer to do what I could to shield him from abuse and wrongful accusations, even if there were things I would have liked to reproach him with. When a man is standing on a railroad track and a train is speeding towards him, it is absurd to start telling him that one trouser-leg is higher than the other or that his shirt is hanging out—he has to be dragged off the rails and rescued. Fortunately Solzhenitsyn is no longer under threat. Now we are in a position to discuss everything relating to him quite calmly.

The impact of the second part of the *Gulag Archipelago* cannot be doubted, and impact is an important aspect to any literary work. The persecutors among the Jews are portrayed in relief, forcefully—even portraits are drawn of them to strengthen the impression, whereas the victims among the Jews are mentioned more at random. The books balance, to borrow an expression from accounting, but the impact is quite different.

In various parts of the world including Russia and France voices have been raised, sometimes by anti-Semites but also by ordinary philistines and yes-men, claiming that "it's all the Jews' " fault—the Revolution, everything..." Then, from the other side, a persistent rumor started to circulate to the effect that Solzhenitsyn was a hardened anti-Semite and actually a "Soviet man" who had escaped from prison but had carried his prison away with him. To close our eyes to these opinions would be imprudent, if not culpable.

It is impossible to counteract this slander on Solzhenitsyn merely by writing articles white-washing him, by adding up the number of positive and negative characters in his works according to their national origins as one cyberneticist tried to do recently in a paper entitled "A Vicious Circle

179

of Insults," or by any other statistical calculations of this kind, because such approaches, however well-meant, fail to take into account the principal component of a work of literature—the impact.

There certainly were things which Solzhenitsyn failed to consider, as if they simply had not happened. For example, the central events of the October Revolution alone carried off 600,000 Jews, mainly big business-men and small ones still subject to expropriation. 600,000 is 10 per cent of the Jewish population of Russia at the time. Subsequently, almost all chabad rabbis and the rabbis of other branches of Judaism, of which there were always a great number, were killed or thrown into prison. In the twen-ties all Bund members were seized as were later all Zionists and other Jewish workers and craftsmen who had partially organized themselves into trade unions. As a percentage of the Jewish population, the number of people arrested and killed was enormous.

Not only ordinary Jews were attacked, but also people who performed religious functions. For example, when I was filling out forms for the Air Force I wrote that my grandfather on my mother's side "had cut fowls' throats and for that been deprived of the right to vote." When the officers came to this line, they had a good laugh. It had not been so amusing, how-ever, when my grandfather and his whole family—wife, and six daughters with their husbands and children—had been thrown out of their apartment just because he "cut fowls' throats." Fifteen years earlier in 1914 my great-grandfather, who had been one of "Nicholas' soldiers,"[9] was thrown out of his house in the Vilno region together with his enormous family on the basis of a decree by the Grand Prince Nikolai Nikolaievich ordering the deportation of all Jews from a 400-kilometer zone along the front as "po-tential German spies." Yet my great-grandfather had shed his blood for Russia as early as the first seige of Sebastopol and had decorations for his twenty-five years' service to the tsar and the Fatherland and had even been rewarded with a plot of land near Vilno, the same piece of land he was thrown off of after it had been surrounded by a detachment of Cossacks. What a vicious circle of insults!

There is no doubt that Solzhenitsyn had the right to write as he did. As Tolstoy put it, every writer has his "idea that hurts," and Solzhenitsyn is no exception. For him the sufferings of the Russian people and the Russian church mean more—hurt more—than the sufferings of the Jewish people or the followers of the Jewish religion.

In my own case, I took up the defense of friends in Russia on many occasions without making any distinction between them on grounds of nationality, not even in the way I thought of them. Most of them were Russians, but they included Jews, Ukrainians and Lithuanians. I took up the cause of the Crimean Tartars as a people. However, I wrote a documen-tary novel called *Hostages* about the growth of State anti-semitism in Russia and the bitter experience of Russian Jewry because this was what caused me pain in Tolstoi's sense. The fact that I did not write a book about the extermination of the Crimean Tartars despite my denunciation of their exterminators does not mean that I am at heart anti-Tartar or that there is even the faintest whiff of anti-Tartar feeling in my attitude. God knows, the Crimean Tartars' tragedy is my own tragedy. However, the "idea that hurts" me is a single one, as it must be at a given historical moment as a work matures in a writer's mind and fully occupies it.

In that case, how is it that I am not anti-Tartar but Solzhenitsyn is supposed to be anti-semitic? The author of *The First Circle* and the *Gulag Archipelago* is not to blame for the fact that there were not other Solzhenitsyns to write about the sufferings and victims of other nationalities with the same impact as he wrote about the Russians and in that way redress the balance. The problem is that there is only one Solzhenitsyn and it is this rather than anything else which has given rise to the shift in public opinion.

Every writer has the right to write about the thing that gives him pain—he is not some kind of department store where every conceivable kind of merchandise is on show.

There is no need to defend Solzhenitsyn. The need is rather to affirm his right to say what he has said. It is an author's sacred prerogative. There is particularly no need to compare Solzhenitsyn to Gorky, as Rutman has done in his article "A Vicious Circle of Insults," finding the two writers' views on the endless sufferings of the Jewish people incompatible. It is fashionable at present in the West to refer to Gorky in derogatory terms. As the originator, during the Stalinist terror, of the instructive saying "If the enemy doesn't surrender, he's exterminated," he partly deserves the modern judgment passed on him. He supported Stalinism and was exterminated by it. (On this question, see the memoirs of the painter Yuri Annenkov, which relate the facts concerning Stalin's poisoning of Gorky, facts which are familiar to many in Russia.) However, it is senseless to weigh Solzhenitsyn and Gorky up against one another, whatever Solzhenitsyn's attitude to the tragedy of Gorky.

The point is that Gorky must be weighed in the balance together with others such as Korolenko, Herzen and Saltykov-Shchedrin, who referrred in "Unfinished Conversations" to the tragedy of the Jews in these perceptive terms: "Even the raising of the level of education, as the experience of the anti-semitic movement in Germany shows, does not tangibly improve the situation." What then needs to be done "in order to bring about the final humanization of humanity? When will it occur?" It must be remembered that Saltykov-Shchedrin wrote this almost a hundred years before the gas ovens and Auschwitz.

This is why there is little purpose in elaborating a new theory in Solzhenitsyn's "defense" to prove that he was right and Gorky was wrong on the so-called nationality question. If a comparison is to be made at all, it must be not only, and not so much, with Gorky as with all the socially sensitive classical authors of the nineteenth and twentieth centuries and above all with Korolenko, Herzen and Saltykov-Shchedrin.

If we desire a bright future for Russia with her many nationalities, we must think through all these questions very thoroughly. Otherwise the bloodshed will never be stopped.

There are two Solzhenitsyns. There is the immortal author of "One Day in the Life of Ivan Denisovich," "Matryona's Home," *The First Circle, Cancer Ward* and the *Gulag Archipelago*. This is the Solzhenitsyn who is responsible for an advance in literature and in social consciousness and gave rise to a whole new direction in Russian art. This is the man who gave birth to the Solzhenitsyn period. Then there is the frail mortal, the morbidly subjective writer in a frenzy of pain and despair at the impasse Russia finds herself in. The immortal author is not in opposition to Saltykov-Shchedrin, Korolenko or any of the other socially concerned writers fighting for Russia. He stands beside them and always will. Solzhenitsyn the frail mortal is another question.

The hero-centered approach in Solzhenitsyn's writings is in fact only one aspect of his much praised personality. It made itself felt in his emotional futurology, and in his aggressive publicistic writings which are not always completely thought through. This is something we shall return to.

3. TWO FRONTS: WAR AND PRISON

Literature is a guerilla war. Wherever there is resistance, a front is formed. When the authorities began in panic to take counter measures, a samizdat front of rejected manuscripts was thrown up. This happened long before Solzhenitsyn.

A couple of years after the death of our great "leader and teacher," *Novy mir* received a manuscript from a former Chekist. I was allowed to skim through a few pages of the manuscript which was entitled "Yezhov in Sverdlovsk." According to the manuscript, which was the first in a whole stream of such articles, "the iron-hearted People's Commissar" Yezhov arrived in Sverdlovsk and called a meeting of State Security operatives. Sverdlovsk had not reached the target Yezhov had allotted it, and was making a poor job of rooting out enemies of the people. The People's Commissar thumped the table with his fist. He had hardly sat down when a young man wearing a blouse called a *stalinka* made his way to the podium. He was an NKVD operative and had an open peasant's face. He gave his name and his mother's address. In his hands he carried a small case. Still holding it, he took the microphone to announce in a firm, low, emotional voice that people were being exterminated in Sverdlovsk who were patriots, true to their native land. He then began to describe how people had been tortured. He was not allowed to finish. He was dragged from the podium with his hands held behind his back. He was shot without further ado in the courtyard. Then another young man got up also carrying a small case. The best they expected evidently was to be sent to prison. He said he shared the views of his comrade and could confirm that faithful Leninists were being exterminated. Ten minutes later he was also shot in the same courtyard. There were no more protesters.

The story of Venya Malyshev told by Pavel Nilin in his story "Cruelty" thus swiftly received documentary corroboration, although Nilin could not have known anything about this rejected manuscript. *Novy mir* was no longer what it had been under Tvardovsky. Simonov had just assumed control of it. The manuscript was sent back to the provinces as were hundreds and even thousands of similar examples of documentary "prison prose." There was such a flood of manuscripts of this kind coming into the different journals—Khrushchev said that 10,000 manuscripts on the prison-camp theme had been received by Soviet periodicals—that they did not know what to do with them all.

If the author was a professional writer, the manuscript was not always sent back. It was sent off "for consultations" and often arrived back with several pages missing. In my own case, a whole chapter dealing with Malenkov's hypocritical appeal to the effect that "we need Gogols and Saltykov-

Shchedrins" vanished from a manuscript I had sent in. It had obviously found its way to Room Seven at the militia: in Russia there were still no copying machines so they had to take the actual page out of the manuscript.

Friends of mine also "lost" pages from their manuscripts. However, it was Vasily Grossman who suffered the most in this way. Grossman told how his novel about Stalingrad was confiscated. The novel was denounced to the Central Committee by Vadim Kozhevnikov, who at the time was the editor-in-chief of the monthly *Znamya*. Two men appeared out of the blue one day at Grossman's apartment on Begovaya Street and said in the matter-of-fact way of plumbers who had come to fix a leaking tap: "We've come for your novel."

The inquiry at the KGB was conducted precisely as it was twenty years later when they were looking for Solzhenitsyn's *Gulag Archipelago*. They found Grossman's typist, a woman who suffered from ill health, and put her on the "conveyor." The "conveyor" treatment consists of subjecting the person being investigated to a series of interrogators who are changed around in shifts. The whole investigation department, one after another, questions and torments the wretched victim who has not been charged with any offense, sometimes for twenty or even forty hours at a stretch, until he passes out, goes mad, dies or makes a confession. Under the "conveyor" treatment, they eventually extracted a confession from the typist. She revealed how many copies had been typed and who had helped. The KGB operational groups then mounted a widespread operation. All over the USSR they searched the apartments of Grossman's relatives, friends and acquaintances, and confiscated all copies of the manuscript, drafts, notebooks and even typewriter ribbons.

Grossman was called in to the KGB and asked with concealed mockery: "Well, have we got everything?" "Yes," said Grossman inaudibly. The KGB man gave an unpleasant laugh and said: "It doesn't pay to be secretive with us." He then produced the seventeenth and final copy. It had been hidden with a cousin in a distant city.

Suslov, Secretary of the Central Committee, agreed to see Grossman, who was grief-stricken by what had happened. "This isn't what we expect from you at all," he said politely, almost affably, offering Grossman some tea. "A book like that might be published in two or three hundred years, perhaps... But at the present time discussions about whether or not the October Revolution was necessary are out of the question."

Other writers began to avoid Grossman, as if he were a leper. The talented writer Boris Yampolsky, who had lost all his friends in 1937, was terrified of going into his neighbor's apartment, knowing he was under surveillance. However, he overcame his fear—and was practically the only one to do so—visited Grossman and then meticulously encoded his notes and left for posterity a record of Grossman's statement made just before he died: "I've been hanged in a gateway."[10] At least it was not the KGB's gateway. Despite the wave of searches, drafts of some chapters of the novel remained in the hands of friends and editors and eventually arrived in the West.[11] More importantly, several days before he died, he finished the story "Forever Flowing" and thereby managed to deliver a last blow to his murderers virtually from his coffin.

The biologist Zhores Medvedev did not wait for them to come for his manuscript. No stranger to scientific method and precise calculations, he quickly took his manuscript around to the apartments of different scientists and friends and to various editors.

Not surprisingly, the authorities had the Kaluga Psychiatric hospital in store for him. His manuscript dealt with the destruction of the biological sciences in the USSR and the many years of Lysenko's murderous reign. His was the first manuscript to be widely distributed across the country.

By coincidence Khrushchev's approval of Solzhenitsyn's themes and the success of Medvedev's distribution methods, which obviated the necessity for a printing press, came at the same time and had irreversible consequences.

The battle with official lies was joined by more and more new authors, among whom a little later were General Grigorenko and Zhores Medvedev's brother Roy who wrote a probing work investigating the crimes committed by Stalin.

During these years Muscovites used to carry manuscripts around in string-bags and other small carrying bags. Samizdat is weighty and voluminous. It was read even by people who as a rule hardly ever opened a book. Writers and historians suddenly found themselves in the position of judges of the Supreme Court, disclosing the details of crimes unheard-of in history, including the crimes of the Supreme Court of the USSR. Readers hardly had time to absorb Roy Medvedev's enormous work before the historian A. Nekrich's book *1941* was going the rounds. This was an honest book which on account of its very honesty had been removed from circulation. Then the writer Mark Popovsky's manuscript appeared in samizdat. Popovsky wrote about the fate of academician Nikolai Vavilov who fell victim to the murderous Lysenko and his supporters. Mark Popovsky managed to track down denunciations signed by these supporters. Later still the historian Grigory Pomeranets' brilliant essay on the fate of Russia appeared, followed by the manuscript of a story entitled "Apartment no. 13" by the talented writer Anna Valtseva. The quality of this story can be judged by the fact that after it had been published in the monthly *Moskva*, even though in such a shortened form that it was virtually ruined, the editor-in-chief Nikolai Aratov was dismissed from his post. Aratov had himself been a professional writer, but in his place a colonel from the Political Administration was appointed. He is said to have been responsible for establishing two new categories of literature: there were "Ay-ay-ay" ("Boy-oh-boy") manuscripts and "not ay-ay-ay" manuscripts.

When the colonel rang the alarm, a cry of shock and disapproval (not ay-ay-ay") went up all around. This happened in particular when the banned novels by Solzhenitsyn began circulating illegally and then Nadezhda Mandelstam's memoirs *Hope Against Hope*. People read them at night, in trains and at work, covering up the pages of the manuscript with official papers.

The authorities were greatly disturbed by the veritable Niagara of samizdat which was unleashed. The wife of a famous dramatist was detained near a writer's apartment block carrying a heavy bundle. It turned out to contain nothing but fresh laundry. The sharp young men in hats employed searching suspicious persons were recalled and replaced.

The journals were flooded with samizdat—and the journals were vital to those engaged in samizdat even if they knew they would never have anything published in them. The journals were a kind of railway station for samizdat because once a manuscript reached a journal it could go anywhere, the author was not responsible. The editor's mark on the manuscript absolved the author of all blame.

It was decided to dam up the flow according to the rules laid down in Saltykov-Shchedrin's *Glupov* or *Town of Fools* by blocking it up with dung. Work was started on 10 February 1966.

The details of the trial of Daniel and Sinyavsky are well-known in the West. Yet the view Soviet writers had of the trial is curious. They were of course completely uninformed, or rather disinformed, about what was going on, and only those who had been "checked" were allowed to attend the trial and even then only one session so that no one could form a consistent picture of the whole thing. However, afterwards these observers would gather in the Writers' Club around the tables in the restaurant and, surrounded by a crowd of writers who had not passed scrutiny and who were even sometimes suspect in their views, they tried to piece together a general picture of what had taken place. The exchanges that took place were sometimes quite unexpected. "They're just escapees," said the critic Sh. with disdain, referring to the two writers standing trial. "They dug a tunnel under no man's land and started crawling to the West." The older writer who was quietly sipping his coffee suddenly said: "And how else can you escape?" The whole Club erupted in wild laughter which was too nervous to be entirely natural.

The fate of Sinyavsky and Daniel concerned us deeply, especially when we finally became acquainted with the full text of the verdict. The brutal cynicism of the verdict incensed everyone. For example, referring to his story "The Hands," the authorities accused Daniel of calling for revenge for the violence "supposedly" wreaked on the people by Soviet power. Everyone, young and old, was shocked by this "supposedly." Did this mean that six hundred writers had not died in the camps but had only supposedly died? At the Twentieth Party Congress it was admitted that millions of innocent people had been brutally slaughtered. Had that now only supposedly happened? Could we never get away from these "as ifs" and "supposedlys" in official statements?

Returning from the court hearings, the writers were now more willing to tell us in whispers about Daniel's bravery and forthrightness. Without mincing his words, he told the court from the dock that "the country is on the eve of the establishment of a second cult of personality."

The pile-up of official dung was washed away and the river surged forward again. This constituted the principal failure of the grandees of the *Town of Fools*, although as usual what worried them was that aspect of the whole affair which could not be pushed under the carpet—the campaign raging in the Western press.

The Writers' Club filled with athletic, broad-shouldered young men no one knew and the discussion of the trial was transferred to the writers' apartments. Only Arkady Sakhnin, a journalist with KGB connections, kept grumbling loudly at the Club that "they should have nabbed them for a currency offense, not for what they'd written." Literature was apparently not subject to the processes of law.

Sinyavsky's article "On Socialist Realism" was whisked off by samizdat and widely dispersed around the Soviet Union, although the main idea in the article that "in its heroes, content and spirit socialist realism is much closer to the eighteenth century in Russian literature than the nineteenth" was a commonplace at university seminars at the end of the forties. It inspired these seminars which were led by professors who perished one after the other and gave some sense to the secret discussions which were composed of allusions and insights. The stale smoke-filled air of our university seminar rooms and smoking-rooms would have wafted off without trace if it had not turned into the "stolen air," to borrow a phrase from Mandelstam, of Sinyavsky's talented essay on Russian classicism with a Komsomol badge. The essay became a real source of joy, as did his second study of Yevtushenko's poem "Bratsk Hydro-Electric Station." As a researcher and essayist, Sinyavsky unfailingly attracted the attention of the thinking population of Russia, as did Daniel as a prose writer. My reservations about Sinyavsky's fiction which I consider to be little more than a mish-mash of borrowings from other Russian and Western writers garnished with irony are, however, considerable.

Yuri Daniel has also attracted the attention of Western students of Russian literature, chained as he is by history to Andrei Sinyavsky. In *Moscow Calling* written in 1961 the Soviet government declares Day of Open Murder as well as Miners' Day, Builders' Day and others. This led to discussions in the West about the underground man to whom the Soviet authorities were awarding a special day of celebration. It was not this which struck Russian readers, however. From our point of view, the underground man's celebrations had been going on for decades. We had watched him wreaking havoc in Russian culture, ruining the kolkhozes through drunkenness and killing the innocent. What shocked us was the terrible picture of Russia's future presaged in Daniel's work, as for example in his perceptive and psychologically exact description of the various reactions to the Day of Open Murder in the different Soviet republics: in the law-abiding Ukraine "it was accepted as an official directive with black-lists compiled in advance; in Central Asia it was a day of carnage, with the wholesale murder of Russians; and in the Baltic republics it was totally ignored and no one was murdered at all."

Although Daniel's prose possesses the qualities of vision and precision, in my opinion he reaches the heights of his artistic skill and achieves his fullest self-expression in his later "Verse from Captivity." This is the verse of a mercilessly honest and successful poet. They are the product of suffering in the torture-chamber which "stifles its cry with its teeth." Prison-camp literature from Solzhenitsyn onwards does not so much speak about the prison guards as treat them with contempt. They are only referred to by such undignified names as "popka" (Polly Parrot) and "vertukhai" ("screw"). What indeed is there to say about people set on you like dogs? "One foot out of line" and you're dead. They are nothing but murderers.

Daniel looked at his murderer and say that he, a poet, was being guarded from people by

> *Not a robot or lowering numbskull...*
> *Not a murderer in love with lead,*
> *But a frail bespectacled green youth*
> *In boots and forage cap.*
> *Hey! You in the tower! Boy in the tower!*
> *How did this terrible thing happen to you?*
> *You must've glanced at good books*
> *Before being sent here.*
> *Rejecting outright evil*
> *Is a matter of good taste.*
> *Listen, what year are you from?*
> *How did you end up in that tower?*

These lines about a deceived generation echo the suffering of the writer and poet Emmanuil Kazakevich whose lieutenant Ogarkov from "Two Men in the Steppes," a man as pure as the driven snow, "signed everything without thinking about it," even his own death warrant. Kazakevich's bitter theme was taken up by another poet twenty years later.

However, in those twenty years of totalitarian rule a lot of water flowed under the bridge. Dzhurabayev's guard duties are now borne by Daniel's Ogarkov, "a bespectacled greenhorn." This then is where Ogarkov, the heart and soul of honesty, ended up after twenty-five years of State hypocrisy—in a prison watch-tower from which he can shoot down anyone he wishes with impunity. The poet asks him:

And what if I climb the wire
Painfully, again and again stifling my cry with my teeth?
What if I get to no-man's land? If I want
You to disappear right away, vanish?
Will you be up to rendering this service?
>*Come on, decide! You're sick too*
>*Of this God-forsaken hole in the steppes.*
>*You get leave for sure*
>*And go to Moscow to see your mother and sister*

And you won't recall me hanging on the wire
Upside-down like a quaver.

It is a simple task to convince a peasant from some far-flung part of the country who can scarcely read and write of anything you like. But where did the young men go who had "glanced at good books"—and why?

A terrible new theme, more dangerous than the searing mushroom of an atomic explosion, cast its shadow over Russia. Whom would the Ogarkovs of the seventies follow? Whom would they shoot and crush under their tanks? The whole world desperately wanted to be friends with them, but they stayed in their watch-tower, the watch-tower Fadeyev was so fond of mentioning in his speeches. We were "in the watch-tower of history, the watch-tower of time, the watch-tower of the only correct teaching." Would they too look at the world through the apertures in their watch-towers? Or would something worse happen? Would an inner cynicism or emptiness be revealed in these werewolves who from boredom or a secret attachment to their work, would hum romances about the poets they had finished off:

>*Not our great-grandchildren, not our descendants*
>*But today's dregs*
>*Quote Pasternak*
>*On a sign from above.*

Daniel was concerned much less about his own fate than about the fate of "the boy in the watch-tower" who had accepted his duties as an executioner as something unavoidable, the boy who was forced to gun down a world which did not believe that such a thing was possible. The poet is little concerned with himself and his own hard fate, in fact it was not until A. Marchenko's book *My Testimony* came out that we really learnt just what trials Daniel went through. What causes him pain is the sight of the boys in boots pushing back the "weeping women" who had come from far away with rucksacks on their backs, "rucksacks of unspent passion,/Rucksacks of years of anguish."

His despair derives from the all-pervading viciousness and hate, and also from the mind-numbing camp slang. Daniel's verse about the new camp and soldiers' slang, the language of despair and slavery, still awaits research.

The Soviet government chose L. Smirnov as the judge for Sinyavsky's and Daniel's trial, a fine-looking man with a fair complexion and the manners of a man from the educated classes. Evidence on questions of style was presented to the court by the country's greatest expert on stylistics, V.V. Vinogradov, an academician and *intelligent* of the greatest refinement. His task was to adduce evidence that the texts were indeed Sinyavsky's. (Admittedly, Vinogradov stipulated beforehand that his name with all its intelligentsia connotations should not be mentioned at the trial.) Zoya Kedrina, mentioned above, no less a refined member of the intelligentsia and supposedly representing "the people," was also proud of her blue blood and her ancestors' high education. All the country's "culture reserves" were enlisted. Yet they conducted the case like a lot of bootmakers. For the second half of the trial Daniel was hidden away in solitary confinement in Vladimir prison. Only those they have reason to fear are locked up in Vladimir prison, those who present some danger even in a camp because there the thinking, courageous person is surrounded by dozens and sometimes even hundreds of people seeking the truth.

It is not surprising that the jailers feared the poet Yuli Daniel who swore the following oath when he was in Ozyorny camp in the Mordvinian ASSR in 1968 and the "boys in the watch-tower" had begun to crush the Czechs under their tanks:

> *We shall not now dare*
> *Lie to the notebook page,*
> *It's now more than we can bear*
> *To round off corners with rosy colors.*
> *We need no idyll, no pastoral,*
> *No anthem without words.*
> *We are fated to remember everything*
> *And tell others.*

In the third quarter of the century, two streams of poetry merged: the stream from the guerilla front and the stream from the war. The verse of the infantryman Gudzenko and the political prisoner Daniel ended up side by side.

Their generation was cut to pieces and scattered. Some were praised as valorous defenders of the Motherland, others were pilloried as her enemies. Yet their thoughts and feelings were identical, and sometimes expressed in identical terms.

During the decade of Solzhenitsyn, who was front-line soldier and political prisoner at one and the same time, both the "fronts" our generation fought on—the military and the prison camp—rallied to the one banner.

4. THE TWO-YEAR RENAISSANCE: EVGENIA GINZBURG AND VAR-LAM SHALAMOV

The indignation in the Western press over the ideological "trial" in Moscow and the exhortations of governments of all shades which felt somewhat awkward at having to deal with a group of Count Benkendorfs risen from the grave, led to a change in the psychological climate in the USSR which lasted for two years. Fingers had been burnt at the trial. They even stopped "calling in" writers over the manuscripts which the winds of samizdat scattered to the four corners of Russia. The hatchet-men fell silent and for the first time we tasted freedom, a concept half-forgotten in Russia from time immemorial.

Two years of semi-freedom—730 days—this was quite enough time for the genie to escape from the bottle, and what a wise genie it was. "So you pillory writers for publishing under pseudonyms and for secretly sending their manuscripts to the West? You call them turncoats and cowards? Very well, then! We'll write under our own names, openly, and give what we write to others to read—to anyone who wants to read it!"

The atomic-age State, which had terrified the world and itself, was not ready for this massive turn-about in psychological tactics on the part of its subjects. Suddenly there were people reading works in public and people writing tracts and open letters to the literary journals. Even the samizdat distributors stopped making strenuous efforts to disguise who they were. An example is the mathematician Yulius Telesin who at that time lived in Moscow, although now he has left the Soviet Union and there is no reason to conceal his identity. It was his custom to turn up at friends' apartments "rustling leaves"—carrying sheets of samizdat under the lining of his overcoat or jacket. He used to be called in Russian not "prints datsky" (Prince of Denmark) but "prints samizdatsky" (Prince of Samizdat).

In his memoirs, put together after he had left the Soviet Union, he makes particular mention of an interesting aspect to his activities—the perplexity the punitive machine was thrown into. "Before the routine search of my home began," writes Telesin, "the investigator turned to me with the suggestion that I 'voluntarily hand over the samizdat.' I replied that if it were a question of arms or narcotics, I would understand what was wanted of me, but that the precise legal sense of the concept "samizdat" was unknown to me and that I simply did not know what he was looking for." According to Telesin, the investigator was lost for a reply. "Evidently even the legal profession eventually found it necessary to define this wide concept with precision," writes Telesin. The judge at the first "pure samizdat" show trial in May 1969, Labrova, had a specific purpose in asking almost every witness what he understood by the term samizdat. At this trial I. Burmistrovich was accused of disseminating works which "besmirched" the Soviet State and social order. Burmistrovich was chosen because the investigators found that he was giving the works of Daniel and Sinyavsky to others to read, that is to say, works which had been branded as "besmirching the State" by the court.

As is well-known, the law in the Soviet Union is not governed by precedent, as it is in England. This was possibly the first time in Soviet juridical practice that a court had had recourse to precedent as a basis for a new series of trials since in the Soviet criminal code the concept of samizdat does not exist.

The constant concern of Soviet legal theoreticians over a period of fifty years had been how to justify the arbitrary rule of the hatchet-men, but now they were either paralyzed by indecision or, after Central Committee criticism, thrown into a state of hysteria. In the first issue of *Molodoi kommunist (Young Communist)* for 1969, Major General A. Maygin declared that "so-called samizdat" was directly instigated by Western agencies. This had a menacing ring to it—ten years of solitary confinement. However, no mention was made of Western agencies at Burmistrovich's trial.

While the courts were trying to decide what to do about the question— and their indecision lasted for over ten years, from about 1963 to 1973 when the USSR became a party to the International Copyright Convention in order to crush samizdat—and writers were intimidated and hounded outside the courts, samizdat literature really burgeoned in an unprecedented manner. In houses everywhere typewriters started clacking. Hidden in briefcases and shopping bags, "prison prose" manuscripts flowed out across the country. The best of these works, as it turned out, went far beyond the bounds of the so-called "prison genre." Literature was on the march again with the same sort of determination it had displayed in 1956 after the de-Stalinization Party Congress. The only difference was that whereas in 1956, which was a year of hope, prison prose and labor-camp prose had waited to appear in official publications, this time it did not. It immediately became samizdat.

Students of samizdat should note here that samizdat made its appearance in the USSR in two unequal bursts. First of all came the works of well-known authors such as Solzhenitsyn and Grossman which were widely disseminated in the Soviet Union and only then found their way abroad. The magic of these famous names was highly effective. Then came the samizdat of completely unknown young authors who were first published abroad and only then, if they had enjoyed some success, did their manuscripts find their way into samizdat in the Soviet Union. Andrei Amalrik is a case in point.

Andrei Amalrik was one who received nourishment and encouragement from samizdat, although literary samizdat appeared in the West, with few exceptions, later than Amalrik's books. Sinyavsky, Daniel and Tarsis were also not known in samizdat form in the USSR before they were published in the West. These two streams intermingled and mutually enriched each other.

Apart from Solzhenitsyn's prison writings, undoubtedly one of the most talented books about the Gulag is Evgenia Ginzburg-Aksenova's *Into the Whirlwind* which paints a particularly harrowing picture of the women's camps. Part I has now been published in many countries around the world, although not, of course, in the Soviet Union.

I made Evgenia Ginzburg's acquaintance under somewhat strange circumstances. I had an elected and totally unimportant position as an inspector, together with a few other writers, on the board of the *Sovetsky pisatel* housing cooperative. I was told that after seventeen years in the camps and in exile, Evgenia Ginzburg now found herself in Lvov in very reduced circumstances. Her husband had died and she was now quite alone and had nowhere to live in Moscow. At the next board meeting, I proposed that we offer her an apartment in the writers' apartment block. I did not doubt for a moment that there could be any objection because there was not a single writer on the board who had not read her manuscripts. However, a certain Mikhail Z. rose to his feet, one of the older generation of writers, specializing in the "romantic komsomol" genre, and stated the official point of view in uncompromising terms: that Evgenia Ginsburg could not be given an apartment because she was not a member of the Union of Writers and could not become one—at the present time because she had not published anything. There was a heavy silence, then completely on impulse I called out: "It's you, my romantic friend, who should have been in prison all these years and not Evgenia Ginzburg. By mistake she went to prison instead of you. And this is all the thanks she gets!" People started laughing, shouting things out and coughing. There were calls to put it to the vote. The outcome was unanimous—with the exception of our stubborn and now crimson romantic: Evgenia Ginsburg was to be given the apartment.

The next day a woman with wide cheek-bones and black hair like a gypsy's knocked on my door at home. Right there in the doorway she said: "I'm Vasily Aksenov's mother—that's right, Evgenia Ginzburg." We became good friends. I could talk for hours about Evgenia Ginzburg, and about her bitter wit which sustained her during times of both trouble and joy. I remember on one occasion she said to me, blushing like a young girl: "Grisha, don't hold it against me, will you, but I'm getting married. It's for the third time, I know, and I'm rather old to be a bride—I'm nearly sixty-four. Yes, I know what an important step it is to take. When the friend I shared the cell with in Yaroslav died, she was just left lying on the floor for a week before they carted her off. At least when you're married, someone will bury you straight away when you die!"

When she settled into her apartment in the writer's block, she acquired a sort of blind faith in my enterprising organizational ability, something I in fact, completely lacked, and kept hinting that I should have an escalator built in the Aeroportovskaya underground station. She said it was needed for aged writers and political prisoners who had great trouble with the stairs. "We've been so knocked about, we'll just drop dead, unless we have an escalator. Our hearts can't stand it."

Evgenia Ginzburg and I were neighbors for seven years in that apartment block, sharing our misfortunes and our happiness, and sending parcels to her daughter in Siberia where she claimed the shops were completely empty. At night we used to go for walks together around the streets in our neighborhood, as far as possible from the writer's blocks which were bristling with microphones.

"I'm gradually learning to overcome my fears," she said once with a little smile. "I can't bear being left alone in a locked room. Yesterday someone went out locking the door from the outside and you can't imagine how I banged on the door and cried out, just as I did in that cell in Yaroslavl. So this morning I tried an experiment. I sent my husband off for some bread, put the key in his pocket and shut myself in. I sat there shaking with fear and trying to overcome it."

She finds that poetry lifts her spirits and helps her to survive. She used to read poetry in her cell, in the train, and in the transit camps—particularly Pushkin and Blok, Selvinsky and Pasternak.

There are many literary allusions and associations in Evgenia Ginzburg's works, perhaps even more than in Sinyavsky's. However, they are of quite a different kind from those in Sinyavsky's writings. She captures the psychological atmosphere of a women's camp, the genuine flavor of camp life, if living in that hell can be called "life." As she draws them, the characters are distinctive and original. Every observation is perceptive, the outcome of her own suffering, etched in blood, as it were.

The literary associations in Evgenia Ginzburg's works are an element which enriches the main character. Literature here means inner freedom which the author emphasizes to the greatest degree and speaks of in her own prison verse when she writes: "I have something you have not the power to take away." In *Into the Whirlwind* we find the masterful prose of a humanist poet. The author's optimistic Foreword could certainly put the reader on his guard if he did not know the saying coined by the orientalist Professor M. Zand, a saying which gained wide currency in Moscow and which is a key to many courageous and seemingly contradictory manuscripts from the USSR. "You must learn to dance on this side of the bars," said Zand. "In the East this is the privilege of wise men."

It is not easy to "dance on this side of the bars" for an author recording for the generations to come the cacophony of "Van Seven" containing mothers and sisters dreaming of their children until suddenly time, like Bulgakov's Woland, gives them a glimpse of what the future holds for dreamers.

In "Van Seven" there are two levels of perception which shed a sinister, deathly light. We learn that the journey Van Seven is on for most of its passengers is their last journey. Yet these condemned people joke, sing and read poetry. The horror of their situation becomes a joke, it provokes laughter. This two-levelled approach is not just a device, but the very essence of Evgenia Ginzburg herself and her buoyant character. When she was waiting to be shot, she curled her hair on her finger and powdered her nose with tooth powder, remarking to herself with a bitter laugh as she did these familiar things: "There's nothing surprising about it. Charlotte Corday made herself pretty before she was guillotined."

Right from the outset the book is characterized by the naked truth of wartime writings from the front: "I didn't sign the false accusations, but mainly because they didn't beat me. My case was over before they started to apply the 'special methods' on a large scale." "Thoughts of my children took away all my courage." Evgenia Ginzburg is merciless towards herself, the Stalinist prisoners and the Socialist Revolutionaries who refused to accept cigarettes from her because she had never been "in opposition." Although she is an atheist, she does not hide the fact that when her life was in danger she was supported by the great staunchness of the believers among the peasant women. On one occasion these women refused to work at Easter and they were forced to take off their shoes and stand in the freezing water covering the ice on the lake. "They stood barefooted on the ice and continued to sing prayers, while we, throwing down our tools, rushed sobbing and crying from one armed guard to another, begging them and trying to talk them into doing something."

There were in all three great literary talents who survived Stalin's camps to describe their experience: Solzhenitsyn, Ginzburg and Shalamov. I saw Shalamov only once. I was looking for someone in the Union of Writers and glanced into the conference hall where a meeting was taking place. On the speaker's rostrum stood a man with a completely fixed expression on his face. He appeared dried up and curiously dark and frozen like a blackened tree. I noticed he did not touch the desk as if it were not there or else disgustingly dirty. Among those on the rostrum was Ilya Ehrenburg looking exhausted and damp with perspiration. He was twitching nervously, which made his grey hair ruffle up like a cock's comb and then flop over again.

Ehrenburg was trying to get up and go quietly out, but the man standing at the desk without touching it suddenly called out in a weighty, authoritative manner: "Don't leave your seat, Ilya Grigoryevich!" and Ehrenburg huddled back in his seat as if the weight of the frosty voice had crushed him into it.

If I had known anything at all about Shalamov then, I would have put off all the things I had to do and stayed where I was, but Shalamov was at the time still unknown to me. When I did not find the man I was looking for, I backed out of the stuffy, smoke-filled room. I have since learnt that what Shalamov was speaking about on that occasion was the punishment meted out to the writers of his generation. What he had to say was menacingly unorthodox and Ehrenburg tried to avoid having to listen. The best chapters were at that time being chopped out of his own book *People, Years, Life* by the censors—the chapters on Meyerhold and Tairov, for example—although he had defended them in the Central Committee. However, he was not allowed to leave. Writers returning from the camps where they had been political prisoners were uncovering a new page in the history of Russian literature and Ehrenburg did not dare, and did not wish, to oppose this revelation.

Varlam Shalamov's figure, appearing as it does to be hewn from a chunk of eternal ice in which he had frozen, is no less unusual than his works. In style and tone there is a sharp distinction between Shalamov's and Evgenia Ginzburg's or Alexander Solzhenitsyn's writings. Complementing Solzhenitsyn's, Shalamov presents a picture of his own unsmiling world comprising the farthest reaches of Russia's prison-camps where he is firmly convinced man is worse than a beast, more merciless than a beast, more terrifying than a beast.

It was truth and not perfect style that was required of Shalamov, and in each new story he uncovered new pages of truth about convict life with such power, that even former political prisoners who had not witnessed such things were struck dumb. The truth revealed by Shalamov shocks because it is described by an artist, described with such skill, as they used to say in the nineteenth century, that the skill is invisible.

Shalamov speaks sparingly but vividly about himself. "I was born in Vologda and spent my childhood there. Here over the centuries as a result of the banishment to the area of so many protesters, rebels and different critics by the tsars, a sort of sediment built up and a particular moral climate was formed which was at a higher level than any city in Russia." All the same, for some reason Vologda never rebelled against Soviet power. Yaroslavl and the north were ablaze with revolt but Vologda was quiet. In 1919 Kedrov, who was in command of the northern front, had two hundred hostages shot there. Kedrov was the incarnation of Shigalyov, and his coming was foretold by Dostoevsky in *The Devils*. To justify what he had done he referred to a letter Lenin had sent him in which he had written: "please show no weakness."

An echo of that mass execution so many years ago almost had fatal consequences for Shalamov. One of the hostages shot in 1919 was a local chemistry teacher. As a result, Shalamov did not even know the formula for water and it was only by chance that his examiner, a former political prisoner, not believing that anyone could be quite so ignorant about chemistry, gave him a bare pass in the subject, thus making it possible for him to enroll in courses enabling him to become a doctor's assistant and consequently survive. The story is told in "The Examination" (*Novy zhurnal*, no. 102). "I was exiled during the war for declaring that Bunin was a Russian classic." This was the second or third time the indomitable rebel from Vologda had been "punished."

Perhaps his most profound work is the story "The Second-hand Book-seller" (*Novy Zhurnal*, no. 110). Two men are rattling along a road in Kolyma in a truck, knocking against each other because the road is so rough. They are political prisoners and are being taken to the medical assistant's course mentioned above. Shalamov calls this companion Fleming because he was the only one in the course who knew that it was Fleming who had discovered penicillin.

Fleming is a former Chekist and NKVD agent and he talks about the trials in the thirties and the use of "chemical methods" to break the will of the prominent people on trial. "The secret of the trials was the secret of pharmacology." (These were apparently the beginnings of Russia's special "psychiatric hospitals.") Fleming is a secret police agent with aesthetic pretensions, however. It is a source of pride to him that he had something to do with the "Gumilev Affair." It is from Fleming that we learn that the principal informant on the "artistic intelligentsia" in the Union of Writers was Major-General Ignatev, the author of the book *Fifty Years of Service* which caused such a sensation at the time. "Fifty years of service, and forty years in the Soviet secret service," says Fleming, putting it more exactly.

I remember General Ignatev taking his seat at meetings in the Union of Writers not too far from the rostrum so that he could hear everything and applauding the speakers, his hands moving slowly in their white kid gloves. Surkov and Fadeyev were always extremely respectful towards him, and in my innocence I thought they were impressed by his breeding, which they lacked, and his erudition as a polyglot.

"Yes, I am in good health," Fleming writes in his last letter to Shalamov, "but is the society I'm living in healthy?"

Shalamov's stories flew round Russia, especially during the two years when writers were not jailed for what they wrote. Now his stories have been published in *Novy zhurnal* in New York, and in publishing them this journal has perhaps made its greatest contribution to Russian resistance literature.

In being saved from destruction, Varlam Shalamov's writings preserve in large measure the truth about an important aspect of Soviet reality, although his truth is cruel and sometimes unbearably so. His stories grip the reader with a feeling of hopelessness. Truly, Shalamov has been frozen by his experience in the Gulag Archipelago for the rest of his life. He is like a blackened tree, struck by lightening, which will never again become green. Yet without the figure of Shalamov the truth is incomplete.*

––––––––––––

* Shalamov's stories were first published in *Novy zhurnal* (no. 85, December 1966). They have since been published in a separate edition by Overseas Publications Interchange Ltd., London, 1978.

5. THE FLOOD OF PRISON SAMIZDAT

In no other country is there such an abundance of prison literature as there is in Russia. Only Russia has nurtured so many millions of dreamers brought to their senses by the heavy fist of the secret service investigator. In just the last six or seven years a whole collection of prison literature has flowed into Western publishing houses including, quite apart from the works of Solzhenitsyn, Ginzburg, and Shalamov, Eduard Kuznetsov's *Diaries*, Anatoly Marchenko's *Testimony*, Valentin Moroz's *Report from the Beria Reservation*, Dmitry Panin's *Sologdin's Notes* and books by the Socialist Revolutionary Ekaterina Olitskaya, the Zionist Abram Shifrin and many others. In general, the West scarcely noticed this flood of books, as it had earlier scarcely noticed the forty books about the camps published in Russian, until Solzhenitsyn's *Gulag Archipelago* became known.

The most outstanding of these books is Eduard Kuznetsov's *Diaries*. We shall come back to this book by the philosopher and martyr Kuznetsov in the chapters on nationalism.

The most disappointing of the books is perhaps Dmitry Panin's *Sologdin's Notes*. What I found disappointing about it was its tendency to try to be both edifying and prophetic. For some reason Panin decided to bore the West rather than his countrymen in Moscow with his edifying comments and prophecies. This is a disease many specialists in their own field succumb to. They begin to consider themselves competent in all fields and on all questions. For example, the famous missile expert F. is always giving peremptory advice on economics and politics, the engineer Mikulin imagines himself an innovator in medical theory and insists that everyone who wants to be healthy should ground themselves at night—if they will just hold on to an earthen pipe they will have no problems. Psychiatrists are familiar with this omniscience mania but it ceases to be so amusing when it grips dictators. Panin's edifying instructions and prophecies are not dangerous.

All the same it is scarcely possible to ignore one of his philosophical conclusions in which he virtually joins his tormentors.

Panin, a good engineer and a courageous man, immortalized by Solzhenitsyn in the character of Sologdin in *The First Circle*, concludes from his sufferings, backed up by historical experience, that a "harmful layer" in Russian society is to blame for the country's woes. This "harmful layer" is the intelligentsia. "The Russian intelligentsia not only formed the revolutionary parties and gave direction to their activities, but also formed the views of many ordinary people." The intelligentsia led them to rise against the monarchy and in doing so plunged Russia into a bloody nightmare.

Without wishing to enter into a dispute with Dmitry Panin on worldviews on which my views are not impartial, I would like to cite the opinion of the philosopher Fyodor Stepun, who is by no means a Marxist and has lived in exile in the West. In his analysis of the causes of the Revolution, Stepun considers the monarchy itself mainly to blame because it did not put the most educated segment of Russian society at the service of the people but drove it underground. By its stupidity, the 9th of January executions it ordered and the cult of Rasputin which it fostered, it aroused the hostility of almost everyone.

There is no real point in spending time on the errors to be found in the prison writings on their formal side, and the skill or lack of it on the part of authors. In these prison writings it is not the how but the what which is more important.

We shall attempt by juxtaposing documentary sources—and virtually all prison writings may be considered documentary sources—to make a comparison between the immorality of Stalin's terrible autocratic rule and the morality of today when, according to official statements, "Leninist norms have been reinstated." As we progress in our study of Russian literature, we shall look around us carefully and make use of the rich documentary evidence available.

To what extent over the last quarter of a century have such aspects of Soviet life as the courts, the regime, the educational institutions, relations between the different nationalities, religious tolerance and official secrecy really undergone a change? What does the new morality consist of, if it is new? Did society change on awakening from the horror of mass terror? Did it become more healthy or less healthy and more cynical? On these subjects prison literature gives us abundant food for thought.

We shall take as the first texts for our comparison, those dealing with:

Representatives of Soviet law:

Under Stalin:
Solzhenitsyn: "It is not the judge who judges—he simply receives his salary. It is the directives from above which pass judgment. In 1937 the directive was either for ten years, twenty years, or the death penalty. In 1949 it was for twenty-five years all around. The legal machine was just a rubber-stamp." (*Gulag Archipelago*)

After the reinstatement of Leninist norms:
Kuznetsov, 1970: "The public prosecutor demanded the death penalty for Dymshits and me... I had not the slightest doubt that the sentence of the court would fully meet the prosecutor's wishes. A big political game was being played in which our fates were not taken into consideration at all. We were not even pawns in the game—the pawns were the judges and the prosecutor." (*Diaries*)

The murder of prisoners in the camps:

Under Stalin:
There is no need for further quotations from literary sources.

After the reinstatement of Leninist norms:

Kuznetsov: "At the end of the summer of 1964 I saw Romashov brutally murdered. I could also mention Ivan Kochubey and Nikolay Tomashuk who were killed by soldiers practically in the middle of the settlement but it's impossible to mention everyone."

Marchenko: from the chapter "Richardas' Story" about the murder of Lithuanian students. An officer says to an injured student before finishing him off: "Free Lithuania! Just start crawling and I'll give you independence." (*My Testimony*)

Moroz: "The minimum calorie intake to avert starvation [according to Unesco statistics] is 2,400. Below that mental and physical degradation results." "In the cell I am in [in 1967] the "upper" norm is 2020 calories, and sometimes we only get as few as 1324." (*Report from the Beria Reservation*)

The graph of State morality:

Under Stalin:

Panin: "The criminals' lack of anything to smoke pushes them to become informers. They go to see the 'godfather' [supervisor]: 'We're at our wits' end. Please give us something to smoke. We want to turn in a counter-revolutionary. He's spreading propaganda and abusing the rules.' 'First, let's take a statement, and then we'll light up.' "

After the reinstatement of Leninist norms:

Marchenko: A prisoner called Budrovsky, who has denounced Marchenko, has collected his pay, which consists of sweets and biscuts for his denunciation. "Where did you get them?" "It's from when I was in Ashkhabad, in the prison there. One of the investigators used to allow me to get them." "He hasn't got me a single kopeck, I don't know why." "He decides who has behaved well. The superintendent doesn't give out parcels from home for nothing, he said, you have to earn them." "I know what that means."
Moroz: Major Sverdlov tells Danil Shumuk who was arrested in 1957: " ' If you agree to cooperate with us, I'll tear up the warrant for your arrest and the record of your interrogation here in front of you...' Shumuk went back to Siberia to do ten years' hard labor for remaining an honest man."

The Fruits of State morality:

After the reinstatement of Leninist norms:

Marchenko: the amateur choir of Polizeis [collaborators with the Germans] is singing the songs "The Party is our helmsman" and "Lenin is always with you." The audience laughs and makes whooping noises. The supervisors shout: "Back to the cells for disruptive behavior!" "Once they sang 'The Bells of Buchenwald' but for some reason the authorities did not like it."

Moroz: "Captain Krut, in charge of the Ukrainian KGB in the Mordvinian camps, said to me: 'What have you got against Stalin? On the whole he deserves the highest appreciation.' "
  " 'When we had Stalin, we had order.' Captain Volodin's words, uttered during the interrogation of Masyutko in Lvov, give a better idea than volumes of written evidence could do of the reasons the KGB came into being and of the role it now carries out."

Relations between the nationalities in the USSR—so-called "friendship of the peoples":

Under Stalin:

Panin: "Several times the Chekists made clumsy attempts to provoke prisoners of different nationalities to butcher each other. They were banking on the feud brewing between the Banderists and the Muslims [the Chechens, Ingush, Tartars and Azerbaijanis]. The most strenuous efforts to organize this St. Bartholomew's Eve were made by the head of the supervisory section lieutenant Machekhovsky, the Chekist who had served with Kovpak's partisans."

After the reinstatement of Leninist norms:

Marchenko: "They try to recruit soldiers from the national minorities or from the more distant republics (but not from the Baltic republics) as guards in the Mordvinian camp, the sort of men who have a poor command of Russian."

Vladimir Bukovsky, in an open letter to Aleksei Kosygin, Chairman of the Council of Ministers: "In April 1975 a conversation took place in concentration camp VS 389/35 in the Urals between the assistant commandant of VS 389 Captain Sharikov and my friend Chekalin. Sharikov made unambiguous attempts to implant chauvinist attitudes in Chekalin, demanding that as a Russian he break off all contact with Jews, Ukrainians and so on. I am a Russian. It is painful to me that chauvinism should be preached at an official level in my country and russification should have been elevated to the status of official State policy. It is painful to me that Russia should be a prison-house of nations on a greater scale than was the case sixty years ago for there are no voluntary inmates in prison" (*Russkaya mysl,* Paris 15 January, 1976).

Mockery of religion:

Under Stalin:

Evgenia Ginzburg's example of women being forced barefoot onto the ice for refusing to work at Easter.

After the reinstatement of Leninist norms:

Marchenko: "When a believer in the prison goes to a doctor he is told: "Why are you putting your name down for an appointment? Make an appointment with your God, let him heal you.'

Moroz: "Fyodor Vyzrov, an Ossete, was a thief. Then he became a Jehovah's Witness and stopped thieving. His instructor told him: 'You should have stayed a thief.' D. Panin was right when he stated: 'Camps are the marrow of Soviet society.'

Changes in the camps over a quarter of a century:

Marchenko: "Instead of Stalin's portrait on the wall in the superintendent's office there was Lenin's and on the opposite wall, right across from Lenin, looking him straight in the eye, was Khrushchev's."

Some of the soldiers are ashamed of the job they are performing.

"They do not even write home that they are prison guards. Sometimes you would get talking to a soldier like this and if he was convinced that you would not give him away, he would tell you quite frankly what he thought about the camps and his work in them. 'In a year I'll get out of it, and it can go to the devil for all I care.' "

Some of the legal investigators would express themselves as frankly as the soldiers. The head of the "investigatory isolation block," Major Gorshkov, says to Kuznetsov: "Why do you keep on about the law? You talk like a woman who's just got married. Now you're a sensible man, aren't you? You must know that it's the spirit of the law that counts, not the letter."

Moroz: "Behind the closed doors of the KGB offices a different view of socialist legality exists. When Levko Lukyanenko asked the Lvov KGB interrogator Captain Denisov why there was such an article as Article 7 which guarantees each Republic the right of secession from the USSR' Denisov replied: 'That's for foreign consumption.' "

Political prisoners and common criminals:

Under Stalin:

In the works of Solzhenitsyn, Evgenia Ginzburg, Panin and others, the common criminals are "socially close" to the regime. The political prisoners are the enemies of the people, whom those who are "socially allied" are free to treat as contemptuously as they wish.
Solzhenitsyn: "Criminal: 'Go and wash, then, my fascist sirs!' "

After the reinstatement of Leninist norms:

Marchenko: "The criminals get themselves transferred to the political camp more or less at will. There's a legend in the criminal camps that the politicals enjoy quite bearable conditions, are better fed and do lighter work."

"I saw two former criminal prisoners who were then politicals, nicknamed Musa and Mazay. On their foreheads and cheeks they had tattooed: 'Communists are butchers' and 'Communists drink the people's blood.' Later I met a lot of political prisoners with slogans like these imprinted on their faces. The most common ones were 'Khrushchev's slave' and 'Slave of the CPSU' written across their foreheads."
That the criminals should help the writers in prison in any way was a fantastic idea. "Daniel's right arm had been broken and knitted together badly—it was a war wound. So he had to be given hard labor of the most strenuous kind. The authorities calculated that he would be completely knocked out by the hellish conditions and ask for easier work. Then he would be easy to handle. He could write for the camp newspaper—and so on."
"Daniel made no request to them for lighter work and all our own politicals helped him as much as they could... They started calling men from our brigade [mostly made up of criminals— G.S.] in to the KGB."
"Who is helping Daniel with his work?"
"We're all helping."
"Why?"
"One lad with a quick tongue thought of a reply: 'It's written in that moral code of yours—one man is another man's friend, comrade and brother.' Everyone in the camp grew to love [Daniel]. He quite unconsciously became a focal point for the various divergent groups and national groupings."

The main new development at that time was the striving on the part of those being judged—the "criminals"— for publicity and on the part of those judging them for secrecy and keeping the whole affair in the dark. The werewolves—as the Soviet press liked to call them, using a term introduced after the trial of Sinyavsky and Daniel—as time was to prove, were State offences. Two collections of documents present convincing evidence of this: *The Chain Reaction* about Galanskov and Ginzburg and *Red Square at Noon* about the demonstration on Red Square and the trial of the demonstrators, compiled by Natalia Gorbanevskaya.

The protesters began speaking openly, while the regime went underground. This tendency on the part of the regime became more and more evident. After burning their fingers over the trial of Sinyavsky and Daniel, the authorities made an effort not to put writers on trial any more but to send them out of the country (in the case of Galich, Maximov, Nekrasov and others), or to kill them, for example by giving them poison cigarettes (Voinovich) or by some other violent means at the entrances to the writers' apartment blocks, which they said had become favorite meeting places for hooligans. In *Hostages* I described how the daughter of the actor Mikhoels, who was himself one of Stalin's victims, was hit on the head with a piece of iron piping at the entrance to her own apartment block. A second before she was struck someone in a hat with a red band cried out: "That's her!" In May 1976 news was received about an attack on a friend from my university days, Konstantin Bogatyryov, who had been in prison under Stalin. This was the second attempt at dealing with him without due process of law in the space of a few years. "E. Bonner-Sakharova passed on the news to the West by telephone: 'The well-known translator Konstantin Bogatyryov was brutally beaten up by unknown persons at the entrance to his apartment block on Aeroportovskaya Street. He is known for his translations of Rilke and Böll and is a member of the German PEN Club. He is in a hospital in critical condition with a broken temporal bone and other injuries.' "[12] Bogatyrov never left the hospital.

"The KGB behaves according to the code of the criminal world, which of course avoids publicity," as the Medvedev brothers have remarked. It could not be otherwise. The general line remained the same. Valentin Moroz expresses this more exactly and graphically in his chapter "Orgy on the ruins of the personality," where he writes: "Stalin did not recognize cybernetics. Yet he rendered mankind an outstanding service in this field: he invented the programmed man. Stalin was the creator of the cog."

In 1946 in *The Trenches of Stalingrad* Viktor Nekrasov had protested against turning people into cogs. Twenty years later the historian Valentin Moroz who had been forced into the trenches of a different war gave evidence of the orgy on the ruins of the personality:

"A generation of people grew up, born of fear, and on the ruins of the personality an empire of cogs was established... A cog shoots at anyone and then on command fights for peace... This empty human being is the main accusation to be made against despotism and also its inescapable fruit." Stepnyak-Kravchinsky wrote: "It is worse than a plague. A plague kills at random, whereas despotism chooses its victims from the flower of the nation."

Censored literature posed the painful question and samizdat answered it openly, even from behind prison bars.

This was the beginning of a new process of the influence of officially censored literature and samizdat on one another, an influence felt not so much in terms of form as in terms of the fearless ideas expressed. This influence is all the more unequivocal since many books by professional writers well-known in Russia suddenly disappeared as if they had been swallowed up by the earth itself, only to reappear as the forbidden fruit called samizdat or tamizdat ("published over there"—in the West).

6. ESTABLISHED WRITERS REDUCED TO SAMIZDAT: VASILY GROSSMAN, ALEXANDER BEK, LYDIA CHUKOVSKAYA

I. VASILY GROSSMAN

The flow of prison writings which made it possible for some comparison to be made between the morality under Stalin and in the present day revealed the depths to which Soviet society had sunk, the camps being "a mirror on Russia."

The books about the camps of today in some sense primed the canvases of the professional writers whose pictures took on a different aspect, becoming a background to the works of artists who produced a revolution in the thinking of whole generations, even of the older generation whose ideas would never have been jolted by the samizdat of unknown writers. Many of the old Communists, even those who had been prisoners in the camps, refused to admit to themselves that the regime was spiritually bankrupt. They were only too willing to adopt the State's mumbled dictum about a "return to Leninist norms." Such people who had imbibed respect for authority with their mothers' milk could only be made to look at themselves in a completely impartial light by someone they recognized as a Soviet patriot, a figure of authority, a knight without fear or blemish.

For many people it was the older writers Vasily Grossman, Alexander Bek, and Lydia Chukovskaya, who had been thrown back on samizdat, who became these figures of authority. Of these, it was perhaps Vasily Grossman who was most successful in uprooting the illusions and lies which were entrenched in the widest circles of the Soviet intelligentsia.

He knew that he was dying and had no time to lose. He wrote the now widely known *Forever Flowing*. The confiscation of his novel *In a Just Cause* and the cynical words of the Central Committee Secretary Suslov to the effect that his novel "could be published in two or three hundred years" left no doubt that a decision had been made to destroy him.

What sort of man was Vasily Grossman who has been feared by the Soviet leadership like the plague? I only saw him a few times, and we did not so much as exchange greetings. Unlike Paustovsky, he had no disciples and lived alone, especially in his later years after his novel had been confiscated. My main impression of him as a man was formed at an evening at the Union of Writers devoted to his memory. It took place in December 1969, just five years after his death. The evening was kept a secret—no one was informed that it was to take place. I found out about it quite by chance, as did most of those filling the smaller hall in the Union of Writers. At exactly the same time in the main hall a performance by the best actors, singers and musicians in the USSR began. This was a deliberate attempt to draw people

Soviet leadership like the plague? I only saw him a few times, and we did not so much as exchange greetings. Unlike Paustovsky, he had no disciples and lived alone, especially in his latter years after his novel had been confiscated. My main impression of him as a man was formed at an evening at the Union of Writers devoted to his memory. It took place in December 1969, just five years after his death. The evening was kept secret—no one was informed that it was to take place. I found out about it quite by chance, as did most of those filling the smaller hall in the Union of Writers. At exactly the same time in the main hall a performance by the best actors, singers and musicians in the USSR began. This was a deliberate attempt to draw people away from the smaller hall where there were said to be just a few old men muttering about something or other.

After chairman Konstantin Simonov's rather frosty introductory address, General Ortenberg, war-time editor-in-chief of the newspaper *Krasnaya zvezda (Red Star)*, took the floor. He either did not notice or chose to ignore the organizers' nervousness. He said what he thought with a soldier's directness. He said that Vasily Grossman had been modest to the point of bashfulness and excessively stubborn. As time was to show, stubbornness had been one of his most needed qualities. The General did not, of course, have *Forever Flowing* in mind, and had possibly not even heard of it. He told how Grossman, on returning from Stalingrad where he had been both in the trenches and at headquarters, had asked him, the editor for two or three months to write a report of his experiences. This was unheard-of. Correspondents were given two or three hours to get a dispatch in and most of them telephoned their material in. And here was Grossman asking for two or three months! The General was deeply indignant, but acting on some instinct he suppressed his general's self-esteem and gave him the time he had asked for.

Thus in 1942 Grossman's war story *The People Are Immortal* appeared and immediately set the tone for literature from the front. It did not of course contain the whole truth, which was still inadmissable even eighteen years later, but the false cheeriness of all the Polevoys and the juggling with figures indulged in by people like Korneichuk stopped flooding the newspapers.

Grossman's war sketches brought him fame throughout the length and breadth of Russia. He won the hearts of refined members of the intelligentsia, men from the front and the families of those who had died, who learnt first from Grossman's writings of the hell which had carried off those close to them.

The unstinting praise of Grossman by this retired general provoked slight panic. It had not been foreseen. Simonov lost no time in giving the floor to the vultures. The vultures had never unmasked themselves so openly as on that occasion as they recalled how Grossman had behaved towards them. Evgeny Dolmatovsky called Grossman an irritable, unpleasant, stonily unsociable man. Naturally he was reserved towards a scoundrel and informer like Dolmatovsky! The cartoonist Boris Yefim, a broken, unctious man of stout build and brother of the murdered journalist Mikhail Koltsov, said with a candor which was obvious to all: "Grossman was impossible to work with. He couldn't bear a single word of falsehood." At this even Simonov could not help smiling, which he tried to cover up by working his lips and pulling down his moustache.

It was only at the very end of the evening that a friend of Grossman's was allowed to take the microphone. A friend had to be allowed to speak to avoid a scandal. This was the critic Fyodor Levin, a constant victim of literary pogroms. His reddened cheeks shaking with anger, he looked straight at the Dolmatovskys in the audience and told them in a weary, calm voice that Vasily Grossman had been a faithful friend, although he had never imposed on, and had been rather shy with his friends. He had been a charming and very witty man, the life and soul of any gathering. It was only just before he died that he had become taciturn and reserved. The officials on the rostrum shrank with fright and dismay as they listened to Levin. Attempts had been made to have Levin shot during the war on the basis of a false denunciation by the poet A. Kovalenkov.

During the purging of the cosmopolitans Fyodor Levin had been quickly reminded that he had not liked Makarenko's book *Flags on the Towers*. "You killed Makarenko!" screamed the professional hangmen. Now as they sat huddled at their table on the rostrum they were half dead with fear that Levin might call each of them by name. Several years later when Levin's coffin was on display at the Writers' Club, a young man with a pale intellectual face stood weeping convulsively beside it. Levin had not had a son, and the literary scholar Etkind asked in a whisper who he was. "It's the son of the military investigator who saved Levin from execution," he was told. "Later both families became firm friends." This proud, benevolent man with Pickwickian cheeks and a prophet's eyes was never afraid of the highly placed bureaucrats, even the most dangerous of them, those who frequented the Lubyanka. And he did not yield to them now.

Levin's low, droning voice became drier and lost its benevolence. "The Board of the Union of Writers made a decision to publish Grossman's collected works. However, they are not published. From year to year the living push out the dead." Then, as he cast his wise eyes filled with sadness over us, he said: "There is much sense in the saying that dogs are afraid of even a dead lion."

Simonov hurriedly closed this half-secret "evening in memory of Vasily Grossman," ignoring someone's raised hand and the fact that the list of those wishing to speak had not been exhausted. Dogs are indeed afraid of even a dead lion.

The hero of Grossman's story *Forever Flowing*, Ivan Grigoryevich, is returning from a camp. There are three others with him in the train compartment: two well-to-do civil servants from government offices in the capital and a works supervisor who is somewhat the worse for drink and whose frank tales make the civil servants angry. These two comfortable civil servants with their self-interested "blindness" and ill-temper in fact display in an original way the characteristics of Nikolai Andreyevich, the main character's brother, a colorless, frightened man with a job in a scientific institution, a careful man devoid of malice who nevertheless has found that the purge in the sciences has worked to his advantage. He has been moved up to take the place of the talented people who have been victimized. But there was a particularly base kind of fear apart from fear of hunger, torture and hard labor in Siberia to which he was subject—and Grossman makes it clear that he shared it with the Russian civil service as a whole: he was afraid of being given red caviar instead of the black variety. "This base 'visceral' fear was encouraged by his youthful dreams during the years of war Communism—if he could just avoid doubting, just vote without concern for the implications, just sign whatever he was asked to. Yes, it was fear for his own skin which kept up his ideological strength."

This generalized portrayal of the civil servants serves as a contrast to the character of Ivan, who is returning from the camps. Predictably this is in conformity with all the traditional canons of drama. However, at this point Grossman breaks with these canons. His structure is more complex, more ruthless and more unexpected. Starting with Chapter Seven, entitled "Who is to blame? Who will take responsibility?", this becomes quite obvious.

However, strangely enough, in this chapter about informers and defamers in which the author mercilessly castigates the informers and turns them inside out like rag dolls, he pronounces no sentence on them, and is almost sorry for these Judases in his concern to understand them. He wanted people to look up and beyond the more immediate questions. There is nothing accidental about this inserted chapter about informers who were victims of circumstances, repulsive victims perhaps, but still victims. This is another step in the progression of the narrative towards the sources of evil. Here a completely different theme is introduced, or at least a different angle on the theme, a different cross-section of society. The chapters about the famine Stalin organized in the Ukraine in the thirties are called "Cemetary of the Diehards."

> The district released a plan—giving the number of kulaks... but the village soviets had their own lists,

the woman who has fallen in love with Ivan relates:

> They took people on the basis of these lists... the trouble was not that the lists were sometimes drawn up by rogues—there were more honest

210

people involved than rogues—but that what was done was evil and wrong on both counts. The main thing is that these lists were a crime, they were unjust...

It is a simple woman, letting a room to a former camp prisoner who comes to this heretical, and from the viewpoint of official morality, hostile conclusion. Like so many people in Russia, she has begun to think:

Why did I just freeze up? After all, people were suffering so terribly, the things they did to them! And I used to say that they weren't people, that they were just a lot of kulaks. What a word they thought up for them! Was it really Lenin who invented it? What terrible suffering he permitted. In order to kill them, they had to declare that kulaks weren't people. It's not true. They were people, people! That's what I've begun to realize—they were all people.

It is on the lips of this disenchanted woman that the mechanism of total deception is unmasked in its terrifying, all-pervading simplicity: the regime simply juggled with words. The hangmen's ruse was a patent one: today one lot of people is not people, and the next day another lot. During those years, the "others" were not only the kulaks.

We thought that there was no worse fate than the kulaks'. We were wrong. The axe fell on the peasants, young and old alike, wherever they might be. The famine came and killed them. Who gave the go-ahead for this mass murder? I often wonder if it was really Stalin. I don't think there has ever been an order like that given as long as Russia has existed. No order like that was ever given by the tsar or the Tartars or the Germans during the occupation. The order was to starve to death the peasants in the Ukraine, on the Don, in the Kuban, them and their children. All the seed stocks were to be taken. They looked for grain as if it were bombs or guns... That's when I realized that for Soviet power the main thing was the plan and people were just nothing.

I doubt that many pages are to be found anywhere in world literature to match these for their horror and their extraordinarily penetrating, mind-numbing effect on the reader. Even in barbarian times the enemy was not treated as harshly as in our own times the Russian peasantry, the country's age-old providers, were treated. Is it any wonder that for decades now Russia has had to scratch about for its grain in other people's granaries?

The woman's confessional manner in explaining her views and the painful way she arrived at the truth and freed herself, together with so many others in Russia, from the delusions of the Stalin period, bear witness more clearly perhaps than anything else can to Grossman's ability to keep his hand constantly on Russia's spiritual pulse.

> *A howl went up in the village—it saw that it was going to die. Everyone was howling—it wasn't a question of reasoning it out, or of what they felt inside, it was as natural as leaves rustling in the wind or straw squeaking. One NKVD man said to me: "Do you know what your villages are called in the district? The cemetery of diehards."*
>
> *Old people used to tell about the famines under Nicholas. Then everyone used to help, lending money, opening canteens. In the cities peasants used to beg alms and the students used to collect donations. But under the worker-peasant government no one gave any grain, all the roads were blocked off by barriers and troops, the militia, the NKVD. They wouldn't let the starving leave their villages, you couldn't get near a town. No bread for the country's real bread-winners.*

It now becomes horrifyingly plain, perhaps for the first time, just how contrary to the interests of the people the regime which arose under the people's banner is.

Everything that the author has written constitutes a terrible condemnation of the main instigator of the evil, the universal evil which befell Russia, washing over it like gigantic tidal waves sweeping away every living thing from the shores.

"When he argued, Lenin did not seek the truth, but victory... All his abilities were harnessed to one aim—to seize power," Grossman, the student of Lenin, tells us. "The essence of such people lies in their fanatical belief in the omnipotence of the surgeon's knife. The surgeon's knife is the great theoretician, the philosophical leader of the twentieth century."

Grossman argues convincingly that if we want to understand Lenin, we must know the history of Russia. On the one hand there are the prophecies of Gogol, Chaadayev, Belinsky and Dostoevsky. Russia is a winged troika before which all nations and countries will draw back. Yet the same Chaadayev brilliantly discerned a striking feature in Russian history: "the gradual enslavement of our peasantry under serfdom is nothing but the strictly logical consequence of our history." Again he wrote: "Progress is basically the progress in human freedom." And in Russia? History confirms Chaadayev's perception: the abrogation of St. George's Day, Peter I's conversion of so-called "idlers" into serfs, the rise of State serfdom, Catherine II's introduction of serfdom to the Ukraine. If social development in the West produced a growth in freedom, in Russia it produced a growth in slavery.

Grossman arrives at a conclusion which flows from Chaadayev's perception and the experience of the twentieth century: "the Russian soul is a thousand-year-old slave." "What can the world expect from a thousand-year-old slave if it becomes all-powerful?"

This was enough for the vengeful sword to fall on Grossman. It was a

Soviet sword in the form of the Central Committee of the CPSU and the KGB who at first made vain attempts to declare *Forever Flowing* a forgery. The telephone in his widow's apartment did not stop ringing. The Central Committee demanded that she make a statement for publication in the press. She might not have been able to withstand the threats that were made if it had not been for the poet L., a friend of her husband's, whom she rang for advice. Knowing that he was speaking not only to his friend's widow but also to the evesdroppers from the State Security service, L. exclaimed heatedly: "How can we lie to our government?! Chapters from the book have already appeared in *Znamya*, don't you remember?"

Grossman's widow agreed with a sigh and the Central Committee forbade the publication of the *Collected Works* of Vasily Grossman.

As well as the Soviet sword, an anti-Soviet sword in Paris came flashing down on Grossman. Arkady Stolypin, son of the tsarist minister, accused Grossman of repeating the ideas of "that great writer Nekrasov."[13]

It should not be imagined that the Central Committee and the KGB were angered only by the anti-Lenin pages in Grossman's story. From the point of view of present-day Soviet politics of terrifying the world with its military might, a much more heretical opinion than the disrespectful attitude to Lenin was the opinion that "Russia is a thousand-year-old slave."

Perhaps Stolypin's son was right when he spoke of the inexactness of Grossman's image of Lenin as the "bridegroom" whom Russia preferred to others. Actually, it was not Lenin Russia gave its preference to, but the Socialist Revolutionaries. However, Lenin dismissed the Constituent Assembly together with the Socialist Revolutionaries. And what was Russia's reaction? It followed the master of the moment and submitted to fear and demagogy. The age-old traditions of slavery won the day. Stolypin was quite willing to admit that the Estonians were "eternal slaves" and that the Latvians were ready to sell themselves into slavery at any time, but the "Russian soul"—never!

The fact that the views of Russian chauvinists, both Soviet and anti-Soviet, were identical on this question is to my way of thinking the most terrifying, and utterly unexplored, hope-destroying circumstance for Russia.

Twentieth-century messianism, inflated at the beginning by the idea of a "world conflagration" ("On the mountain we shall fan the flames/Of the world conflagration onto the bourgeois") and then by Stalinism with its chauvinism grafted onto the mass of the people lacking any sense of justice, has become a real danger. Vasily Grossman is by no means exaggerating when he warns that the tragedy of Russia—the Leninist synthesis of lack of freedom and socialism—could become the tragedy of the whole world.

"The power of State nationalism and the rabid nationalism of the mass of the people, deprived of freedom and human dignity, have become the new linchpin, a new type of thermonuclear warhead, and have determined the fate of the twentieth century."

II. ALEXANDER BEK

In 1943 Alexander Bek wrote his story "Volokolamsk Highway" and took the manuscript to a publisher. It was wartime and there was a food shortage. His wife gave him a milk-can and told him to bring some milk back from Moscow. "And don't forget it in the train," she reminded him as he was leaving. Bek did not forget the milk-can but he did forget his manuscript, leaving it on the seat in the train. He lost his completed manuscript.

Bek returned to the front. He went around the dug-outs and trenches of the characters from his book, sometimes on his elbows and knees. Some of them he found in a hospital. He himself was almost killed during an artillery bombardment. Eventually he rewrote his story.

Ten years later, Bek, now the famous author of "Vokoloamsk Highway" and other books, a prize-winning and apparently successful writer, was standing in the doorway of the glittering main hall of the House of Unions in Moscow, the former Noblemen's Assembly building. He was in a state of indecision. Inside the Second Congress of Soviet Writers was in progress and he could hear the drowsy hum of the proceedings. He could not decide whether to deliver his address to the Congress or to keep out of harm's way. But when Konstantin Paustovsky, on whom the Moscow writers had been pinning their hopes, was refused permission to speak, Bek, who had now decided not to speak but to go away quietly and submissively, started calling out in his hoarse, indistinct but still quite audible voice that it was outrageous. As I mentioned before, thirty-one Moscow writers followed Bek's lead and made their protest by declining to speak in Paustovsky's place.

For all his kindness, sensitivity and absent-mindedness, which sometimes made him appear to be living in another world, at crucial moments Bek could display a courage and irrepressible energy which seemed foreign to his nature. "I belong to the 1937 generation," he used to say. "I'm tired of being afraid." But I remember an occasion in 1969 when he was so afraid that his hands shook. The Union of Writers had unexpectedly decided to send me on a trip to the far north to write something of an orthodox nature and earn forgiveness for my reprehensible actions. When he heard about it, Bek rushed round to see me—we lived near each other—and he was scarcely inside the door before he was loudly trying to convince me not to go under any circumstances. "They're only sending you so they can kill you," he said, trying to make me see reason. "It's more awkward to kill you in Moscow, but there they'll set some hoodlum onto you and he'll bash you over the head with a water-pipe wrapped in newspaper and that'll be the end of you. Grisha, you don't know what they're like! I'm afraid of them! Scared to death of them!"

And now this deeply frightened man who had lost almost all his friends in 1937 wrote a courageous book, every line of which he staunchly defended, refusing to take out an episode which Demichev himself, Secretary of the

Central Committee of the Party, asked him to remove. Then when he saw that his manuscript was going to be disfigured and emasculated anyway he gave it to samizdat, realizing that that was the only way it would ever come out in an unmutilated form.

Bek was dissatisfied with the books which had made him famous and wanted to begin a new cycle of works whose epigraph would be Emmanuil Kazakevich's words: "At the end of the iron age the conquerors are put on trial." He sought out former political prisoners who had known the People's Commissar for Heavy Industry, Sergo Ordzhonikidze, the only People's Commissar during the thirties who had protested against the terror and was killed as a result. Bek did not manage to complete the projected cycle, but he did write the first pages of it. In the eleventh issue of *Novy mir* for 1965, a notice appeared about the forthcoming publication of Bek's *A New Appointment*. The type for the book was set but it did not appear. Why? Bek kept "within the bounds of what was permitted" as he always did. Many of the episodes were toned down and others were severely cut back in anticipation of the Glavlit censors' "ever-watchful eye." What is the explanation for the fact that when it was not printed the manuscript was disseminated around the country with as little delay as Grossman's, despite the fact that as a manuscript meant for publication it did not contain, and could not contain, any really deep examination of the causes of Russia's tragedy?

The main character in the book is Onisimov, People's Commissar for tank building, a man without a single flaw, even a hidden one as his student friends had said of him. This flawless, legendary character is dismissed from his post as People's Commissar and sent as ambassador to some backwater called Tishland (a play on the Russian word "tish"—tranquility).

Bek begins the narrative of events from the end. The reader is immediately intrigued and wants to know why this flawless hero has been dismissed.

What sort of man is this hero from the Stalinist era who is so devoid of self-interest, so irreprochable in his personal life, a man who has never killed anyone, and on the contrary once sent Stalin a bold report protesting against arrests in his industry on the grounds that there were no saboteurs there? His character is revealed retrospectively at an unhurried pace without undue pathos or pressure but with deadly effect.

There is no hint of opulence in the way Onisimov lives. His apartment is uncomfortable and empty apart from the furniture officially allotted to him. His wife is a rather cold woman, one of the period's activists. Up to their necks in work, passion is the least of their concerns. They married "not for love but for reasons of ideological kinship, as it were." His whole life is dedicated to the building up of industry and the glory of the Soviet Union and then suddenly he is dismissed. He collapses in a faint. "Case of clash [sshibka]" is the doctor's verdict somewhat later. "A clash" occurs when one thinks one thing but is forced to do something else, against one's own convictions. Onisimov does violence to his own inclinations and finds justifications for what has happend. "I am the Party's soldier," he says. He castigates himself but again acts contrary to his own inner urgings.

Onisimov cannot remember a year without its "clashes." Beria was his enemy and he was always secretly afraid of him. Full of fear he would go to Politburo meetings expecting to be arrested. Stalin had toyed with him for a while, like a cat with a mouse, and then enjoying the effect the appointment produced, had made him People's Commissar. In his new position Onisimov was forced to support bogus inventors and adventurers if this was what Stalin wanted because he was "the Party's soldier." There were many such "clashes," painful ones which destroyed his personality. Finally, Onisimov learnt to slip away from dangerous thoughts in the simplest of ways: by saying to himself "it's none of my business, it doesn't concern me, it's not for me to judge."

His brother Vanya, whom he loves, dies in prison, but the learned Onisimov even then remains as firm as a rock—it is not for him to judge. At home talking to his son he finds himself incapable of speaking frankly. The inner corrosion goes deeper. He sees himself supporting the advancement of passive, obedient people, because like his idol Stalin, he "does not tolerate objections." He awards a complete rogue a promotion simply because he knows how to hold his tongue: "a piece of machinery shouldn't blabber."

Time molds this flawless character. He could not have been anything else in an "iron age" as the writer convincingly shows in an episode which is based on fact. This episode is so noteworthy that I shall quote it in an abriged form. It largely determined the fate of the book and the fate of the author.

Zinaida Garvilovna's muffled voice could be heard coming from the large study. [Zinaida is Orzbonikidze's wife.]   There was someone else's voice as well... Sergo stood up quickly and said: "Excuse me please." He left the room. For a moment or two Onisimov sat there alone, paying no attention to the voices in the other room. Then Sergo started speaking loudly and excitedly. The other man answered calmly and even perhaps in measured tones. Could it be Stalin? They were speaking in Georgian. Onisimov did not know a word of Georgian so fortunately could not find himself in the position of eavesdropping. All the same, he felt he had to go away without delay because the conversation in the other room seemed to be getting more and more heated. How should he leave? The only way out was through the study. Onisimov got up and strode through the doorway.

Sergo continued speaking in an impassioned way. He was almost shouting. His pallor had changed to a crimson flush with an unhealthy blue tinge to it. He was gesticulating wildly, trying to prove something to Stalin and reproaching him with something. Stalin, in the soldier's

*uniform he unfailingly wore, was standing with his hands folded over
his stomach.*

*Onisimov tried to pass by without saying anything, but Stalin
stopped him. "Comrade Onisimov. I imagine you must have heard
us talking here?"*

"I'm sorry, I didn't know..."

*"Of course, these things happen... But which of us do you agree
with? With Comrade Sergo or with me?"*

"Comrade Stalin, I don't understand Georgian."

*Stalin let this sentence pass as if it had not been spoken. Looking
hard at Onisimov from under his low brow, and without raising his
voice in the slightest, he said again even more slowly: "So with whom
are you in agreement? With him?" Stalin paused. "Or with me?"*

*Onisimov did not dare look at Sergo again. He was compelled
by some force which was almost instinctual and quicker than thought...*

Onisimov, the man without a single flaw, betrays his dear friend Sergo.
In this year of terror, he wants to stay alive, that is all. This is when what
was possibly the most crippling "clash" occurs. Compared to this one, the
others pale into insignificance.

Needless to say, Demichev, the Central Committee Secretary in charge
of ideology, demanded that this episode be taken out. Not only this one,
but above all this one. The same evening I met Bek. As was our habit, we
went as far away as possible from the writers' apartment blocks and wandered
among the dark shapes of the blocks which were still being built, standing
like ruined buildings during the war.

"If I take it out, then what, I ask you, will be left?" Bek mumbled
in his subdued, suffering voice. "What did I write it for, I ask you?"

Bek refused to take out everything that he was "advised" to take out.
Not that he was anxious to get the reputation of being a stirrer. As always,
he wanted to remain "within the bounds of what is permitted," but rather
what was permitted by the de-Stalinization Congress.

Bek was not one to wriggle out of things or take a few steps backwards
the way politicians do. In details he would retreat and recut his cloth, suffering as his hero did from "clashes." But when it came to essentials—"am I
a prostitute or what?"

So the book went into samizdat and then to the West. I know no other
book which paints a portrait of the Stalinist Guard, the best of whom lifted
up Russia's industry on their own shoulders, including atomic industry,
with the objectivity and depth which comes only with authentic and painful experience. This gave it its power to strip the masks off things which had
previously been concealed and its lasting significance.

The narrator does not forgive Onisimov, and this was understood by
those whose decision it was whether or not to allow the book to be published.

It was no accident that when Demichev promised Bek that his book would be published, the chairman of the Council of Ministers, Alexei Kosygin, suddenly intervened—as far as I am aware this was his first intervention in literary affairs.

In his book Bek does not forgive "Stalin's falcons," and this is the real reason for the campaign against the book, not the complaints of Tevosian's widow who made a tremendous commotion claiming that Onisimov was modelled on her husband. The untiring crusade of Tevosian's widow turned out to be nothing more than a convenient pretext. This is shown by the fact that the book's fate was not altered when Bek, tormented to the limit of his endurance, added the character of Tevosian in a brief episode, portraying him as a noble figure who warned Onisimov that Beria would be telephoning him.

When you come to the last page in the book, you cannot help remembering Nikolai Andreevich, the biologist of mediocre ability from Grossman's *Forever Flowing*, a pathetic time-server who long ago convinced himself of the rational march of history which had cleared away a place for "him, Nikolai Andreevich."

All the enthusiasts and iron-willed leaders of the period, all these "ardent workers," actually needed oceans of blood in order to strike fear into the heart of Russia. Without this fear, Russia would not have tolerated them for a moment.

It cannot be necessary to explain further why Bek's book was rejected and ended up as samizdat, despite the fact that he had won all sorts of prizes and was one of Russia's best-known and most loved writers, in many ways the darling of his times. He died, like his hero, from a "clash." However, in contrast to his hero, he did not retreat. In order not to retreat, this old and ailing man had need of real courage and, more than that, a readiness for self-sacrifice. This is no exaggeration. I spent a large part of the war at Vayenga aerodome in the Arctic where the torpedo bomber pilots flew out of. They were virtually suicide missions. I know that there is no one who is immune to fear. But in the war people had no choice. A military command had to be carried out. No one could give Alexander Bek a command, only he could do that.

This mild-mannered, absent-minded, defenseless and shy man was called upon to show far more strength of will than the glorious Heroes of the Soviet Union whose portraits decorate every Soviet military establishment. He simply could not act in any other way than he did. He was a deeply honest man who had the misfortune to begin his writing career in the same terrible year for Russia that Kirov was shot on Stalin's orders. From that moment on the nightmare of mass executions did not cease for a single hour.

Bek successfully defended his last and principal work. However, he paid for his success with his life as Vasily Grossman did. He soon contracted cancer and died.

III. LYDIA CHUKOVSKAYA

Chukovskaya chose as the epigraph to *Going Under* a line from Tolstoi: "A man's morals can be seen in his attitude to words." Illuminating her narrative with this idea of Tolstoi's, Chukovskaya plunges beneath the surface, as it were, into the depths of the Soviet writer's inner world of fear and distortion caused by the regime. The theme of this book which is so much a product of her own bitter experience, is Stalinism and the written word. Lydia Chukovskaya dared to sharply criticize Mikhail Sholokov's a-morality, the falsehoods in *Literaturnaya gazeta* and elsewhere. She became the cultural conscience of the country and in our conscienceless times that is no small thing.

Naturally a story written by a woman such as this could not fail to attract attention, or at least the intelligentsia's attention, because the intelligentsia knew the power of words—both their healing and death-dealing power.

Litvinovka in *Going Under* is a so-called "dom tvorchestva"—a place where writers may go to write in peaceful surroundings, not far from Moscow. Its real name is Maleyevka. There are places of this kind outside Kiev and Yerevan in Armenia. Indeed, they are to be found everywhere, as are the ubiquitous, attentive "sister-housekeepers" ("affectionate pretense is one of their duties," writes Chukovskaya). Everywhere too is to be found the unique categorization of the guests, not according to rank or income—there would be nothing unique about that—but according to views. An honest writer will not find himself sitting next to Alexander Chakovsky, for example. Writers who are for sale would not dare to sit at the same table with Kaverin and would avoid Lydia Chukovskaya. That is an unwritten rule in these institutions. People only mix with people of like views.

The narrator in *Going Under* makes friends with a man named Bilibin, a writer who has been in the camps. Her friendship with Bilibin, who has himself suffered deeply, leads her to dream about her husband, Alyosha, who was sentenced to ten years in prison without right of correspondence. She has never forgotten Alyosha and feels in some way to blame for what happened to him. In what way is she to blame? "Today I realized what the matter is," she writes. "I am alive, that's what it is."

Old memories come flooding in and she cannot remain indifferent to them.

Despite the stream of prison literature, and Solzhenitsyn's and Shalamov's books in particular, what Lydia Chukovskaya has written on the prison theme is original. Prison is seen here from a different angle. A line of women stands freezing in the cold all night outside in the Big House (the Leningrad Security headquarters). In the middle of the crush of women in line is a young Finnish woman with a baby. The baby has just died, right there in the line. Although she is almost out of her mind, she tells no one that her child has died so that no one tries to push her out of the line and so that she can get to the window behind which there is someone sitting who knows where her husband is. A commandant with a casual air appears, looking as if he were just made up to be a jailer. The keys hanging on his belt clank heavily. His revolver holster is undone. In her mind the narrator goes over the words she will have to say quickly when she gets to the window. "I know from experience that as soon as I see the face and eyes of the man sitting at the big table going through the cards with the names of people arrested on them, an insuperable feeling of the pointlessness of saying anything at all seizes me." It seizes her this time as well. The window is quickly closed. All she can see in front of her is a crooked plywood door with the notice "Exit here" on it.

How drawn she feels in her hapless situation to Bilibin who has been in prison himself. Bilibin is more and more open with her. Once she comes back after a walk thinking about him and feeling "hungry, cheerful and for some reason, not unhappy." Bilibin tells her, "apprehensively glancing at the door and then for some reason at the ceiling" that "ten years without right of correspondence" means the death penalty, so her husband is long dead.

Bilibin tells her about his prison friends and about how they suffered in mines and froze in the forests chopping wood. He has the memory of a professional writer. He even remembers the stutter of his close friend, buried in the camp cemetery.

While he is in Litvinovka Bilibin finishes a novel he has been working on. It has almost been accepted for publication in the monthly *Znamya*. Bilibin talks about his experiences and writes, writes and talks. Eventually the manuscript is ready, and he takes it to the narrator to read. It now becomes clear that Bilibin is an amalgam of all the unfortunate, broken writers who have betrayed their comrades. People who had been in prison once were afraid of being sent back again. This is why almost all of them— the gifted writer Yaroslav Smelyakov, and the modestly competent Alexandr Rekemchuk, Yury Smirnov, a quiet man of mediocre talent, and of course the much praised Vasily Azhayev who was the first to succumb to dissipation—destroyed with their own hands their *Gulag Archipelagos*. Later there were many more of these shattered Rekemchuks who became lackeys and drunkards, writing about the hell they had lived through in the camps as if it had been a period of happy, healthy labor in complete freedom.

This is the type of manuscript Bilibin's turns out to be. "I had several times in my life had occasion to feel grief," the narrator writes. "But this was the first time I had experienced shame. Bilibin came in.

"You're a coward," I said. "No, you're something worse. You're a

false witness." He started to get up. "You're a liar... Good-bye. Why did you not have the dignity to keep silent? Just not say anything. Surely out of respect for the people you buried you could have found some other way of earning a crust of bread. Without resorting to your forest and your mine and that child, and your friend's stutter?" He went out... I once counted how many paces it was from his door to mine. It was nineteen. But now it had become nineteen miles, not one less, nineteen centuries.

Lydia Chukovskaya rose to do battle for the Word. The Word had deceived millions and is still a terrible weapon, possibly even more terrible than the atomic bomb or nerve gas. She attacks not only the hangmen, but also those of their victims who have become their accomplices. They are no different from the hangmen, and she hates them just as fiercely, and has even more contempt for them than she has for the hangmen.

Lydia Chukovskaya is one of the few who restrained the weak from compromising with arbitrary rule. She did not allow anyone to forget the wisdom of Tolstoi's words: "A man's morals can be seen in his attitude to words." Of course, this did not mean that scoundrels stopped being themselves. They concealed themselves, not daring to lift their heads for a time. But honest people felt stronger. Solzhenitsyn's decade had arrived, suffusing what was being written with a special kind of strength and raising the standard of honesty.

It was convincingly evident to the writers of the day that the State treats those who are not afraid of it differently. Power lives like a parasite off fear and people's cowardice. "This is what makes them afraid!" Solzhenitsyn exclaimed once, shaking his massive fist. Lydia Chukovskaya's voice rang out with even greater strength, and honest people felt stronger.

7. THE WORLD OF MODERN RUSSIAN SCIENCE FICTION AND TRAGIC NATURALISM

In the history of censored literature, the rise and fall of science fiction represents one of Aesop's more unexpected inventions. Realistic literature was denied access to the printing press and it found itself, from Solzhenitsyn to Bek, Lydia Chukovskaya and other new writers, in a trap. It was cut off as surely as if a fire-break had been made around it. It then turned into science fiction, breaking free from the earth and soaring away like a bird from a hunter.

In its new form the literature of resistance was not immediately recognized for what it was. Science fiction was customairly regarded as just "reading matter." For years it had been making the Tungus meteorite out to be a spaceship from another planet and taking its readers on trips to Venus. This was all quite acceptable.

In 1964 an article was published in *Literaturnaya gazeta* saying that science fiction in the USSR was a cinderella. The authorities were not opposed to the idea of giving science fiction the green light. The idea was to distract the reader from Solzhenitsyn's themes.

However, the hatchet-men were led astray by their ignorance. The science fiction writers made no secret of their intentions. Stanislav Lem said that the future interested him only as a scientist. "As a writer I am concerned only with the present, the contemporary world." The Strugatsky brothers were no less frank. "What attracts us about science fiction is the fact that it is the ideal, and for the moment the only literary means which allows us to broach the most important problems of today." If they had only stayed just theorists! But they went further. Beginning in 1966 with the story "The Hellenic Secret," the Strugatsky brothers moved from utopian science fiction to fantastic writing of a social and philosophical kind. It is not difficult to decipher their allegories and symbols of the triumph of evil over downtrodden man.

Did Russian readers understand the Strugatsky brothers? Did they take them to their hearts? In 1966 the journal *Science Fiction (Fantastika)* conducted a survey. The most popular writers in the genre turned out to be the Polish writer Lem, the Strugatsky brothers Boris and Arkady and the American writer Ray Bradbury. The officially lauded and by no means untalented writer I. Yefremov was relegated, together with his descriptions of a Communist tomorrow, to eleventh place.

The Strugatsky brothers entered the arena fearlessly. Prison-camp literature had been unanimous in its condemnation of the so-called OSO "troikas." (OSO stands for "osobogo soveshchaniya"—special commission). These "troikas" had passed sentence on millions of people including Evgenia

Ginzburg, Varlam Shalmov and many other authors I have examined here or left out for different reasons. Every Russian reader will remember these mechanical judges and their cold, expressionless eyes like those of frozen pike. Then suddenly the word "troika" arose again in the fantastic genre in the title of the Strugatsky's story "Tale of a Troika." The manuscript was shunted around many journals before finally being printed in the backwoods journal *Angara* in Irkutsk (1968, No. 4-5). This issue was quickly taken out of circulation and the editors of *Angara* were dismissed "for political shortsightedness."

One of the Strugatskys' philosophical works, "The Snail on a Slope," was relegated to the pages of the Ulan-Ude (Siberia) journal (*Baikal*, 1968, No. 1-2) and subsequently it too was taken out of circulation and the editors were punished and dismissed. Their next book *The Ugly Swans*, which was rejected by all Soviet editors, eventually circulated as samizdat and later came out in the West. Their earlier story "It's Hard to be a God" was translated into English and the Strugatsky brothers became well-known abroad. At the same time they also fell into disgrace with the State. Unfortunately, nowadays in Russia these two things are as inseparable as Siamese twins.

Here are the lines from "Tale of a Troika" which so frightened the almighty atomic-age State:

> *Footsteps were heard in the reception room... and the whole Troika appeared in the room, all four of them... The wheels of the machine began turning. The first case was announced, that of old Edelweis Petrovich the inventor. They dealt with him quickly. "Death," roared Lavr Fedotovich.*
>
> *The others who then came before the Troika in turn were Konstantin, who came from another planet, Kuzka the pterodactyl, and the lizard Lizka who had refused to leave his lake, forcing the commission to go to Cow's Bog. The commission had been attacked by insects and the commandant was found guilty of preparing a terrorist act!*

Unadulterated fantasy, obviously!

Konstantin, the representative of another planet, is an even more fantastic character. He wants peace but at the same time asks for assistance to return to his own planet. In other words, he naively wants detente. The Troika's response to this is as follows: "The existing psychological gap does not allow us to form a correct impression of your aims in coming here. We do not understand why *you* need friendship and cooperation with us." The decision taken is one properly taken by the State: "Any ship coming within range of our means of destruction will be destroyed without warning."

Further on more things occur in the spirit of Lavr Fedotovich's "Death"! The positive heroes try to interfere in the Troika's thought processes with the help of a special apparatus, a remoralizator. " 'It's not

224

working,' Edik said to me bitterly... 'Things are bad, Sasha... These sewer-diggers have no morals.' "

It is a dirty white goat which furnishes the definitive picture of the latest Troika of leaders. The goat is brought along by a woodsman called Feofil.

> "This is Khlebovvodov," said the goat [referring to one of the Troika members']. "He doesn't have a profession as such... He has been abroad... forty-two countries. He boasted and scrounged everywhere he went. His distinguishing characteristic is his great social adaptability and ability to survive, based on stupidity as a matter of principle and a constant striving to be more orthodox than the orthodox..."
>
> "Tell us something," Feofil asked Khlebovvodov.
>
> "Mistakes were made," Khlebovvodov said quickly. "People aren't saints. Even old ladies make mistakes. Even a horse with four legs stumbles. Whoever doesn't work doesn't eat..."
>
> "Right, right," said Feofil. "And will you make more mistakes?"
>
> "Never!" said Khlebovvodov firmly.

Even in realist literature there have been few more laconic and scientifically exact portraits of orthodox Party types. The goat jumped over the heads of the realists.

The conversation the goat and the forester Feofil have with the second member of the Troika is quite short:

> "What is your attitude to false witness?" asked Feofil.
>
> "I'm afraid that that term is rather old-fashioned," said Farfurkis. "We don't use it."
>
> "What is his attitude to false testimony?" Feofil asked the goat.
>
> "It never comes to that," said the goat. "He always religiously believes in his own testimony."
>
> "Well, what are lies, really?" said Farfurkis. "Lies are the negation or distortion of facts. But what is a fact. In the conditions of our incredibly complicated life can we actually speak of facts."

However, the goat has scarcely begun to question the presiding member of the Troika Lavr Fedotovich when Khlebovvodov summons the militia. The fiendish goat does not wait for the arrival of the militia and the prosecutor, and makes off.

The goat should have expected this to happen. How dare she criticize the ruling Troika and Lavr Fedotovich Vunyykov himself, who speaks like Podgorny and other government officials: "We're obliged to announce... We're obliged to emphasize... We're obliged to assure you." He also acts only in the name of the people: "The people will thank us if we carry out these tasks even more energetically than in the past. The people will not forgive us if we do not carry out these tasks even more energetically than in the past." "Pull down that blind!... The people don't want it up."

Of course, the people do not want works such as these, and as we have seen the Central Committee showed no mercy to the editors who failed to realize in time why these famous writers had turned up with their manuscripts in Siberia.

Their second work, "Snail on a Slope," caused no less consternation among the authorities than the first one. The innocent fantastic genre had now become right before the eyes of the political leaders an extremely dangerous Trojan horse. The fantastic genre had not been so transparent in its meaning for a long time in Russia. There is much more to this profound and despairing story than satire. It is possibly one of the saddest books in modern times.

Above the precipice at the edge of a mysterious forest rises the Directorate. The forest represents life and all its complications, and the Directorate, the incredibly ignorant management of the forest. "Ignorance excretes into the forest. Ignorance always defecates into something."

The relations of the authorities with the populace are abundantly clear. Beatrisa, an official in the group organizing relief for the impoverished populations, complains: "All our detachments have to do is appear in the vicinity of a village and they abandon their homes and all their belongings and go away... We have tried to give them proper clothing. One died and two fell ill... I think we should capture their children and organize special schools for them."

The main character, Perets, dreams of nothing other than breaking free from the clutches of the Directorate which is always eradicating and ensnaring things. He goes to see the Director with the secret hope of being able to obtain leave. As he awaits his turn, the following highly significant exchange takes place:

> The secretary said: "Perets, the Director will see you now."
> Perets was surprised. "Now? But there are three ahead of me."
> The secretary raised her voice. "Employee Perets, the Director will see you now."
> "Wants to argue about it," someone muttered.
> "People like that should be sent packing," someone else said loudly. "Given a good drubbing and sent packing."
> "He knows what's coming," a few people in the waiting-room said. "There's no use trying to wriggle your way out of it."
> "To think we put up with someone like that!"
> "You may have to put up with him. It's the first time I've seen him."

A fantastic episode, almost phantasmagorical, yet no more so than reality itself. Thousands upon thousands of such episodes actually occurred: the defamation of Pasternak and Solzhenitsyn by people who had never even held a copy of their books in their hands but who applauded all sorts of murders and *Pravda* editorials even when they called, as one did, for the shedding of "gallons of the blood of the enemies of the people." As a result of the unending nightmare and senselessness of what was happening, people stopped thinking.

"I live in a world which someone has invented." says poor Perets in horror, without trying to find an explanation for it. " 'I long to understand—it's a kind of sickness,' Perets suddenly thought. 'That's what's the matter with me—I'm sick with the longing to understand,' "

Eventually Perets can no longer bear his mechanical existence under the watchful eye of the official in charge of eradication, Domoroshchiner, and he makes his escape by jumping out of a car into a slushy bog. He wanders across the bog, almost drowning in the mire and hoping to find some people somewhere. "To start with, just kind people... I mustn't get any grand ideas..." He stumbles upon a colony of talking automatons. He flees from them at such breakneck speed that by accident he wins a race being organized by the Directorate. He is congratulated with embraces, and bathed by the drivers' paramour, the sweet-natured Alevtina.

Then the leap into despair begins, a leap which throws light on many things, including the authors' world-view and possibly their "angry protests" against the publication of their manuscripts abroad.

Either because he won the race or simply by mistake, Perets is appointed Director, the most important man in the whole soul-destroying Directorate. Perets, an intellectual and nihilist, suffering from a longing for understanding, assumes supreme power. He is so shocked that for a long time he cannot take in what has happened. Domoroshchiner has difficulty in getting him into the Director's office which has been empty for several hours. Domoroshchiner needs the Director's authority to carry out his eradication work. On the Director's desk is a diary with notes about bulldozers and other machines.

" 'To hell with bulldozers,' thought Perets. 'That's it—no bulldozers, no eradication sawmills... I'll blow them all up!' ... He thought of what the Directorate was... and realized that there were a lot of things which should be blown up. Too many. 'Any fool can blow things up,' he thought."

Perets takes a long time to get the Director's safe open. This is the repository of great secrets. He swings open the heavy armor-plated door. "On the inside the door was covered in obscene pictures from a men's magazine while the safe itself turned out to be almost empty. Perets found a pince-nez with the left lens cracked." The broken pince-nez becomes an allusion to and almost a symbol of the Directorate. Admittedly, the safe also contains a pistol, kept clean and in good order, with a single cartridge in the barrel." This is apparently meant for Directors who cannot meet the high responsibilities of their post. It is an emergency exit for those who are morbidly conscience-stricken.

However, Perets is sick with a longing for understanding, and not with fits of acute conscience. This is now a different Perets. " 'I must say power does have its advantages,' he thought." All the more so in view of the fact that Domoroshchiner has prepared all the necessary papers and Alevtina who gave him his bath has typed them out. Perets refuses to sign routine correspondence and when he is begged to sign something at least—if not these papers, then some other ones—he dictates his Directive No. 1: "To workers in the Eradication group: to eradicate themselves in the shortest time possible... Let them throw themselves off the precipice... or shoot themselves... today..."

When she has written down the Director's order, Alevtina grows quiet and then gives her approval. " 'That's right,' she said. 'It's even more progressive that way... Listen, sweetest, if you don't like one of the directives, then don't give it, but do give another one. Here you've given me one and I have nothing else to ask of you...' " As for Domoroshchiner, he is ecstatic. " 'A stroke of genius," he said quietly, pushing Perets towards the desk, 'brilliant. I have no doubt it will go down in history...' Perets backed away from him as if he had been a gigantic centipede, stumbled against the table and knocked Tanhauser over onto Venus."

This is apparently what happens in the world when power falls into the hands of "progressives," even such intelligent and kind-hearted ones as Perets, battlers for freedom, passionate opponents of those bent on eradication. However, amongst the impedimenta of power, the pince-nez with the cracked lens reminiscent of Faggot Korovyov's satanic pince-nez in Bulgakov's *Master and Margarita*, lies awaiting for them. Routine sucks them in like a bog and yet again evil reigns, calling itself this time progressive.

Although the Solzhenitsyn era filled many writers' sails with wind, it could not teach them to maintain a firm course. Indeed, can one ask of every writer that maturity Solzhenitsyn acquired from his experiences in the labor camps?

The critical edge of the Strugatskys' fantastic writings became blunted. It was corroded mainly by the heroes' scepticism and cynicism which reflected the authors' own state of mind. They were buried alive by Glavlit and did not even utter a cry of protest as the earth blocked their mouths.

Their story "The Ugly Swans" is imbued with perhaps even deeper despair than the others. The story-line as usual is fantastic way beyond the bounds of possibility: the town mayor starts a round-up of people who wear spectacles. These "slimies," as they are called, are put in a special leprosarium. A leprosarium for "goggles" is a step forward, abreast with the times.

There is a revolt in the leprosarium and the rebels are joined by the children of the city who have fled their homes. Their parents naturally rush off to "rescue" their children. They are stopped at the gates of the leprosarium by a powerful voice coming over the loudspeaker: "What can you give your children? Look at yourselves! You brought them into the world and are now deforming them after your own image and likeness." It is scarcely a convincing argument. The spectacle-wearers win, the old regime flees—first the leaders, then the middle-class philistines who naturally blame the rebels for everything, and finally the army. In other words, the authors are inviting the reader into a frankly utopian world of impossibly successful revolutions which save children.

However, in this world of utopian bliss and fabulous transformations there also lives a talented singer, a lover of wine and women and a well-known poet. His name is Viktor Banev and he delivers his daring verses in youth clubs to his own accompaniment on the banjo. The narrator's attitude to him is one of ironic benevolence. We join him on a journey he makes throught the unfortunate land and it soon becomes clear why it is Banev we travel with.

The book begins like a detective story. Some people are trying to ensnare one of the bespectacled men in a trap and bundle him into a police car. Finally, they succeed. Viktor Banev is disgusted by such happenings. "How did he fall into their trap?" he asks his beloved Diana.

"The mayor sets them up, the bastard..."

"What have the slimies done to them?"

"You have to hate somebody... In some places they hate Jews, in other places Negroes and here it's slimies."

"It's revolting... It's the same with the State. Wherever you go things are rotten."

Banev tries to do something. He takes the trap and goes to the police where he demands an investigation. The city has extraordinary laws. Until there has been a statement from the victim, it is considered that there has been no crime. (This is a direct allusion to the extraordinary Criminal Code of the Russian Republic and the "scholarly and practical commentaries' on it. Fantasy and real life go again, hand in hand.) Although Banev continues to rebel and from time to time to seek the truth, there are many things he does not bother about. He becomes a cynic—you have to live, after all—and when Diana asks him about his creative techniques, for example, at what point he inserts into his books the element of "national consciousness" without which the State has no need of his books, Banev explains with a wry smile: "First of all I saturate my mind with national consciousness— I read the President's speeches, learn the old heroic sagas off by heart, go to patriotic meetings. Then when I start vomiting—not just feeling sick, but actually vomiting—I start writing."

Naturally, Banev drinks. He will drink with anyone at any time, with progressives and security agents. Eventually he attracts the notice of the President himself. In this fantastic city everything depends on the President. "Countries which the President liked waged just wars in the name of their peoples' democracy. Countries the President for whatever reason did not like waged wars of aggression."

" 'Victor,' the President says to Banev whom he has summoned, 'do you want to keep getting your bread and butter as before? Then stop your strumming.' ... His Excellency was alluding to my performances with my banjo in the youth clubs."

This time the President lets Banev off lightly, but the mayor intervenes and proposes that as a popular poet and a favorite of the young people he make a public stand against the spectacle-wearers. This will be a strain on his conscience, but all the same...

Someone of experience whispers to Banev: "Sell yourself easily and for a high price—the more honest the writer, the more dearly the powers-that-be must buy his services."

Perhaps Banev would have sold himself just as many had before him, but he finds himself being asked as a poet to speak to the children in a school. He grinds out the usual sort of thing and then suddenly hears in reply words which the reader realizes do not come from the children but from the authors, words addressed straight at the generation holding the reins of power or else grovelling at the feet of those in power: "You have eaten yourselves up, you have dissipated yourselves on wrangling among yourselves, on lies and battles with lies which you carry on while dreaming up new lies." "You simply cannot believe that you are already dead men and have created a world with your own hands which has now become your own tombstone. You have rotted in trenches, blown yourselves up under tanks—and who has benefited from it?"

Banev is panic-stricken. "Why should they respect me for all that? For attacking tanks with a naked sword? Only idiots put up with a government which got its army into a situation like that. Destroying the old world and building a new one on its bones is a very old idea, and it has never led to the desired results. You can't wipe out cruelty by cruelty."

The idea that violence cannot end violence was shared by many writers—Pasternak wrote about it and now the Strugatskys. Where does it lead? It leads Banev to despair. He even "composes" a song which actually belongs to Vysotsky, one of Russia's most popular bards, who has now been virtually tamed.

> I've had enough, I'm fed up to the teeth,
> I've even begun to tire of songs,
> I'd like to lie on the bottom like a submarine,

Out of range of their direction-finder.

But that is here in the real world. In the fictional world of social utopias the spectacle-wearers conquer the city. We are familiar with this denouement from "The Snail on the Slope" where Perets becomes Director. Admittedly he does not wear glasses but they are there waiting for him all the same, in the safe.

The theme of the historical victory of progressive forces has its humorous aspects in this early work. Banev is glad about their victory but is deeply distressed that the new chiefs have turned rum and whisky into water. "They're undermining the very basis of society, the corner-stone," he fumes. "Damned kill-joys..." He has not expected that progress would mean this. "Another new rule. The newer rule, the worse it is, as everyone knows."

The shift towards deeper pessimism in the general outlook of talented writers such as the Strugatsky brothers reflects the present-day pessimism of the great mass of the Soviet intelligentsia intimidated by the open trials and the arrest of dissident thinkers. It has taken refuge in the prudent argument that "the new is always worse. Power is power. The present lot at least won't start a mass terror campaign..." Sakharov and A. Ginzburg follow their path and the Strugatskys theirs. Let us not underestimate their merits. They deserve recognition for what they have managed to do. After Solzhenitsyn was banned and prison writings and realistic literature with a sharply critical punch to it were also banned, science fiction or the fantastic took upon itself a dangerous burden and bore it self-sacrificingly for two years. Millions of devotees unexpectedly found themselves in the very center of a social storm and untold millions of readers may have seen through the unaccustomed "down to earth" science fiction of the Strugatsky brothers. They deserve recognition for achieving more than could have been expected. As a result of their last books being anathematized in the USSR, their critical basis and their angry caustic exposures, received prominence. There is a law of reaction operating in banned literature. Its critical impact is strengthened, the more furiously the authorities try to contain it, the stronger it grows.

In the story "The Ugly Swans" there is a line about a drinking session in which the poet Banev is taking part as usual. "We won't get drunk," says one of the characters. "we'll just drink, like half the population. It's the other half which gets drunk—well, good luck to them." It is now time to turn to this second half of the population which drinks itself into a stupor, sometimes every day. However, we shall not say simply "good luck to them" but shall try to understand how this hard-drinking half of Russia lives.

231

As it happens, a book has been written by a talented representative of this hard-drinking half of the population, a works supervisor by the name of Venedict Erofeev. It is *Moscow-Petushki* which the author has ironically called a "poem." This authentic and stark testimony to the degradation of an enormous section of the Russian people circulates as samizdat in Russia where it is avidly read.

Moscow-Petushki is an ironic, tragic and poetic work yet at the same time it is full of naturalistic detail. It would seem to be the complete opposite of a fantastic work in the sense in which life itself is fantastic. To a Russian reader the very first lines smack of sedition. The narrator tells how he has never seen the Kremlin although he has been all over Moscow. He always means to have a look at it but for some reason or another always ends up in the Kursk railway station restaurant or a bar instead.

This book is really a tragic epic poem. There is no strong story-line. Venya works near Moscow's Sheremetyevo airport. "We would unwind a cable off a drum and put the cable under the ground. Then we'd have a drink. The next day we'd get the cable from the day before out from under the ground and throw it out because of course it would be all wet..." Venya, who is a brigade leader, keeps a graph of the drinking bouts and the amount drunk in a day. "The graphs are interesting... One of them has Himalayas, Tyrolean Alps, Baku promontories and even the top of the Kremlin wall in it, which I might add I have never seen..." These graphs are submitted as the brigade's production graphs.

Venya takes a local train from Moscow to Petushki where he drinks, both "on his own initiative" and with his neighbors. He shares his experience in mixing drinks with such names as Balm of Gilead, Silvern Lily, and Komsomol Girl's Tear. However, he prizes above all others a cocktail called Bitch's Innards which is made up of Zhiguli beer, Sadko the Wealthy Guest hair shampoo, a remedy for dandruff and sweaty feet, and an insecticide. This is left to ferment for a week on a base of cigar tobacco of various sorts, then served.

However, these pages with their Rabelaisian overtones do no more than introduce the theme. In the conversations and musings that follow the whole history of Russia is told by Venya to the accompaniment of drunken bouts which border on the fantastic. It is at this level that we find some similarity between the works of Erofeev and the Strugatskys, works which are otherwise very different from one another in style, genre and subject-matter.

In Venya's drunken, or seemingly drunken, ramblings all the Revolution's sacred cows are mocked and derided—all the cliches from Party addresses, all the stereotypes of present-day thinking, the habitual mindlessness and apathy, the whole traumatized psychology of a wretched people, and especially careerism, the root cause of many woes.

Venya is dismissed from his position as brigade leader on account of his "inebriation graphs." "I now triumphantly declare: never again to the end of my days will I do anything to repeat my sad experiment in rising up the ladder. I shall remain at the bottom and from the bottom I shall spit at your social ladder, one gobbet for each step. You have to be a bugger hewn out of pure steel from head to foot to climb up that ladder. Well, I'm not like that." When it is taken into account that Stalin once said the same thing about Dzerzhinsky—that he was hewn out of pure steel from head to foot—and before Stalin Herzen had described the Decembrists in these terms, then the full caustic force of Venya's analogies is clear.

Although a son of the people through and through, he treats his drunken flesh and blood with contempt. "O freedom and equality! O brotherhood and dependents... O blessed time in the life of my people—the time from the opening to the closing of the stores." Venya Erofeev spares neither himself nor his own people whom he meets at work, in the liquor stores and in the train. He enters a carriage after drinking out on the carriage platform. It is full of people who:

> *looked at me almost apathetically with round, apparently vacant eyes... I like the fact that people in my country have such empty, protruding eyes. This inspires me with a feeling of rightful pride. You can imagine what sort of eyes people "over there" have, where everything is a matter of buying and selling... deeply hidden, concealed, avaricious and frightened eyes... Devaluation, unemployment, poverty. They look at you sullenly, with never-ending worry and pain— they're the sort of eyes they have in the world of Ready Cash!*
>
> *But what eyes my people have! They're always bulging, but without any expression at all, completely lacking in any sense— but for all that what strength there is in them, what spiritual power! These eyes will not sell anything, nothing at all, and will not buy anything. Whatever happens to my country—in times of doubt, times of onerous decision-making, in times of trials and tribulations, these eyes will not blink. To them everything is manna from heaven...*

The grimaces of Aesop are terrible, but even more terrible is this look of hopelessness. At times it seems that it is the look of someone in a raving delirium which is the last resort of the thinking man. Cynicism and frenzy drive Venya to his death. He is apparently killed when his head is smashed against the Kremlin wall.

The juxtaposing of the Strugatskys' fantastic writings and Erofeev's purposely earth-bound, naturalistically based tragic and poetic prose produces the clearest possible evidence that literary forms, even when belonging to widely disparate genres, have the same content in Russia today—they represent an angry protest against those who are bringing the Russian land to ruin, bringing the shortages of grain upon it and what is even more terrible, bringing it to the point of mindlessness and despair. This comparison of the writings of the Strugatskys and Erofeev also demonstrates that this second half of Russia about which the Strugatskys' intellectual heroes said "and good luck to them" is not dead but alive and plunged in anguished, angry, desperate thought.

8. THE LAST ATTEMPT TO BREAK FREE FROM THE YOKE OF CEN—SORSHIP: THE GENRE OF WRITERS' SPEECHES

The noose of censorship was being quietly tightened all the time. This was being done without resorting to the processes of law. Most of what was being written remained buried in desk drawers. The times demanded a new strategy for breaking through the barriers of censorship: writers' speeches. This strategy was not put into effect straight away because people still nurtured the hope that things would change. They did not believe either rationally or in their hearts that evil of such dimensions could go unpunished.

However, the events were to make it plain that this was not the case. The well-known informer Professor Elsberg of Moscow University suddenly reappeared on the pages of *Literaturnaya gazeta* giving writers lessons in morality and humanism. He was elevated to the rank of chief theoretician at the Gorky Institute of World Literature. A neighbor of mine in my apartment block, an old critic and former political prisoner, sent to the camps as a result of a denunciation by Elsberg, said to me one evening while we were out walking that if Elsberg was now writing about morality then the only thing left for him to do was to die. And die he did—the following morning.

The human conscience found what was happening unbearable. Quite unexpectedly the opinions and criticisms of well-known writers, even when expressed in a small circle of acquaintances, at a small meeting or in one of the rooms at the Literary Club where most meetings were of an informal kind, turned up in samizdat.

As we have seen, it began with Konstantin Paustovsky's address. Copies of his address on Dudintsev's novel *Not by Bread Alone* circulated all over Moscow and then to every corner of the country and were read like proclamations. They were still not considered to be strictly prohibited material and were read in trams, at work, in clubs and lines outside shops. People snapped them up the way they snap up newspapers with sensational news in them in the West. The path free speech was to take had now been marked out.

A short while later, Mikhail Romm, the famous director of several well-known films about Lenin, held in high esteem in Russia, was taking part in a closed discussion and said what he thought about the obscurantist Kochetov who had just been appointed editor of the journal *Oktyabr* by the Party Central Committee. Without mincing his words Romm went even further: he explained the fascist import of the literary pogroms which were taking place. His speech quickly became available to readers all over Russia through samizdat.

Few artists went through the shattering experience Romm did. His last film, a documentary called *The Ordinary Face of Fascism* reached the screens with difficulty. The audience laughed nervously as it watched it. In Hitler as he did the rounds of art galleries, striking all manner of poses, his arm stretched out like a prophet's, full face and in profile, the audience could see Russia's own home-grown Fuhrers Stalin and Nikita Khrushchev who had just been ranting at an art exibition on the Manezh Square. Never before had Russian "socialism" been shown so talentedly and so obviously, as far as millions were concerned, to be Nazism's brother. Naturally whatever Mikhail Romm said and wherever he said it immediately became known all over the country and supported the moral climate surrounding the open militant refusal to accept iniquity.

Viktor Nekrasov lent him his support from where he was in the south of the country. This was the period when he publicly castigated Kiev's civic leaders for their plan to turn Babi Yar into a place of merriment and diversion. The ranks of Romm, Nekrasov and others were soon joined by the writer Frida Vigdorova, a small woman of almost morbid timidity. At the Union of Writers it was said that the transformation that had taken place in her was striking. Her tomes devoted to the upbringing of young Komsomol members were considered so orthodox in their approach that their author was made a delegate to the regional soviet. Whenever she spoke about her young heroes or saw people from the electorate in her office she would glow with elation.

However, the regional committee of the Party made a serious miscalculation where Vigdorova was concerned. She was a woman of conscience not only within the framework laid down by the regional committee. She not only reconciled families, came to the defense of battered wives and mothers who came to her to complain, not only found apartments for workers' families living eight or even twelve to a room, but she also dropped everything to go to the trial of Iosif Brodsky, who had been accused of parasitism.

She had come to the defense of the innocent before. When the Leningrad scholar I. Serman and his wife the writer R. Zernova were thrown into prison under Stalin, she risked her own life to fight for their release.

On another occasion she defended in the press a schoolboy who had been the victim of a campaign of lies. When she was asked at the highest level what this boy was to her, on the assumption that no one would defend with such passion and stubbornness someone they had no connection with, she replied, "He is a person to me."

It was a tremendously difficult task for her to make a record of the trial of the poet Iosif Brodsky which began in Leningrad in February 1964, two years before the trial of Sinyavsky and Daniel. The judge Savelyeva shouted to Vigdorova "Stop taking notes!" Vigdorova replies: "I would like to request permission to take notes, your Honor." "No," said Savelyeva. "I am a journalist," said Vigdorova," "a member of the Union of Writers. I write on education. I ask your permission to take notes." The judge replied: "I don't know what you're writing down. Stop writing!" Calls came from the public gallery for her notes to be taken from her. Nevertheless, Vigdorova took a record of the whole trial including all the judge's remarks, giving some concept of what was really going on and the atmosphere of police intimidation and violence which accompanied the court hearings. The world learnt that in these days of "freedom" under Khrushchev when even Alexander Solzhenitsyn was being published, conversations such as the following could take place with poets in a Soviet court:

Judge (to Brodsky): What is your occupation?

Brodsky: I am a poet and a translator. I consider...

Judge: No "I considers." Stand up straight! Don't lean against the wall! Look at the court! Address the court in a proper fashion! (To Vigdorova: Stop writing immediately or else I'll have you removed.)

This trial was one of the first outrages committed by Soviet justice upon free thought—in this case poetic thought—since the death of Stalin. Prompted by circumstances and her own conscience, Vigdorova found herself drawn into the spiritual crusade of the young people. Later Alexander Ginzburg came to her for support and he did not come in vain. The world was to become aware of Ginzburg only after his trial which became known in the history of the resistance as the trial of Ginzburg-Galanskov.

This determined and deeply honest woman Vigdorova appears to have suffered the same sort of fatal "clash" that Alexander Bek described in his last book. Ideas inculcated since childhood tell you one thing while your conscience tells you something else. Bek's hero Onisimov died from just such a "clash" and Bek himself died not long afterwards of cancer. It was as if he had foreseen what was going to happen to him. Vigdorova seems to have been the victim of a similar "clash." She saw again with her own eyes the evil reality of the age of the police state which she had thought was coming to an end. A deeply moral person, believing with all her heart in the victory of the truth and that "difficult happiness,"as one of her last books is called, she was so shattered by what she experienced in the courtroom at Brodsky's trial that after he and other young protesters were sentenced she could not go on living. The horror she felt at this new victory of "Leninist norms" was too much for her and two or three years later she died.

Just a few days before she died, she had a visit from a writer who was a member of the Party executive committee—a completely hardened character. He was not at first allowed to see her. He then said that he had something of extreme importance to explain to her. In tears he asked her forgiveness. It turned out that he had to propose that Vigdorova be expelled from the Union of Writers. Only her death saved her from expulsion from the Union of Writers and from villification in the press. The significance of writers such as Frida Vigdorova is enormous. It is not just a matter of what they wrote but of their fate, the ordeals they suffered. They hurled themselves unarmed at the State. As a rule children follow their parent's deeds rather than their words, particularly if their parents have paid for nobility of spirit with death.

Stepan Zlobin was a historian and the author of historical novels such as *Salvat Yulayev, Bunyan Island* and *Stepan Razin.* His best books were about rebels. His influence on the ideas of young writers was enormous and I have described it in *Hostages* (260-264).

In 1941, although he was suffering from tuberculosis, Zlobin demanded that he be sent to the front. He was not sent. He then joined the Moscow irregulars and went to the front on his own initiative. They fought the German tanks with one rifle for every three men. The tanks crossed their lines and Zlobin found himself a prisoner of war. Behind the barbed wire of the German concentration camp Zlobin became one of the resistance leaders. He saved hundreds of captured escapees from the firing squad by switching the numbers on their shirts for the numbers of prisoners who had died of hunger. Later he also took every opportunity available to save "writers' captive minds," as he sometimes put it. Eventually Zlobin, like Paustovsky, was no longer allowed to make public addresses because each time he would make insulting remarks about the "leading writers" being "rotten stumps," "muggers" and "generals who were out-generalling the generals." When he was no longer allowed to speak, he began to make use of the two or three minutes permitted for procedural comments to deliver his "knockout blows" —for example, on the question of who to send to some conference.

Once after demanding the removal of Vasily Ardamatsky's name from the order paper—Ardamatsky had KGB connections—Zlobin turned to Leonid Sobolev, Alexei Surkov and other "leaders" who were presiding and who had just arrived from the Kremlin where they had assured Khrushchev of their faithfulness to the Party line, and said in a calm, hoarse voice: "This is something which you who stand in a greedy throng beside the throne— it doesn't matter which throne—cannot understand." Naturally the whole of Moscow knew what he had said the next day.

Fortunately, despite persecution and mass executions, there is no shortage of honest people in Russia. I have only named a few of them. In Leningrad students hung on every word of Professor Etkind whose courses attracted Iosif Brodsky at one time. The Leningrad critic A. Makedonov became very well-known for his pithy contributions to discussions at the Union of Writers, as did Stepan Zlobin for his. While a political prisoner in one of Stalin's concentration camps in Ukhta, ill and suffering from the cold, Makedonov concluded a lecture on Chekhov with the following words: "Chekhov died in 1904 a free man. If he had lived to our times, he would be here with us, behind the barbed wire of a camp." I went to Ukhta in 1970. Old people still remember his presence among them there as a high point of their lives.

I remember very well the feeling of having been orphaned which overcame me when Zlobin died in 1964. In October 1965 the whole ideological machine of the Central Committee and the State Security turned up at the Union of Writers led by its chief, Central Committee Secretary Demichev, whose presence always boded ill. After overcoming my fear that I might never return home again, I publicly accused them of pursuing a policy of State chauvinism and arbitrary rule. I spoke with the force I did mostly because Stepan Zlobin was no longer with us. If he could not speak out, who would? I called the censor a "literary OSO" ("special commission") and said things to those persecuting us which no one but Zlobin usually permitted himself to say.

Before Solzhenitsyn's publicistic writings appeared, our bitter and angry outbursts were essentially episodic. Solzhenitsyn's arrival on the scene gave rise to a new and mighty wave we all rode up on. We then tried to defend Solzhenitsyn and so in spite of everything were obliged to stay on the same lofty plane as Solzhenitsyn, at least in terms of fearlessness. There was no place for wavering or equivocation after he had applied Pushkin's dictum— "They only know how to love the dead"—to Soviet rulers.

The Moscow writer Georgy Vladimov who was keeping the manuscript of his story "Faithful Ruslan" aside for a more propitious moment attacked the hatchet-men with great directness: "Are we a nation of tell-tales, scum and stooges, or are we a great people?" he asked angrily.

The talented Leningrad writer and former navigator Konetsky wrote with great force: "With contempt for myself I am forced to say that censorship and its oppression of my artistic consciousness have had an irreversible effect on my thinking and my work as a writer. Even before you write anything down, the inner censor says the notorious words: 'It won't get past them.'" In the year in which we are celebrating the fiftieth anniversary of Soviet power the arbitrary rule and tyranny of censorship have reached their apogee, which is nothing less than desecration of the spirit."

Dozens of writers said the same thing. Before Solzhenitsyn had written his letter, few had the determination to do so. It is possible that hundreds of writers made their choice only after coming to terms at that time with the bitter truth of the age they lived in: "they only know how to love the dead."

The Union of Writers was now polarized as never before into two separate and deeply hostile groups—the writers and the hatchet-men.

9. THE HATCHET-MEN

There was great commotion at the Union of Writers. Secretaries, cloakroom attendants and representatives of the literary bureaucracy were rushing about everywhere. In an access of zeal the head of the Secret Section of the Union of Writers, a retired security officer with only one arm, slipped on the wooden stairs and tumbled to the bottom. Gromov, in charge of the Drama and Theater Section, a rather frail man with sunken cheeks, swept the doorman aside and flung the door wide open. The reason for all this commotion was that two large black cars had drawn up at the entrance.

Looking out of my second-storey window, all I could see was the sparkling wet roofs of two limousines obviously connected with affairs of state. "Who's the mysterious visitor?" I asked a writer who had just given me a petition to sign protesting against the resurrection of closed trials. "Oh," he said, with a dismissive, offhand gesture, "it's the stuffed eagle."

In a few moments this lifeless stuffed eagle, with its glassy, vacant light-colored eyes, went past and I was struck by how exact writers can be in their derogatory descriptions. Konstantin Fedin, General Secretary of the Union of Writers, with his dessicated, almost mummified features, his once proud profile and this predatory nose, reminded me of nothing more than one of those stuffed eagles you find in a school biology laboratory which has just been wiped down with a wet cloth and now stands with its features carefully smoothed down, shining with a kind of lifeless pride.

I do not like cold writers. This is why Fedin was never one of my favorite authors. All the same, when I first crossed the threshold of the Union of Writers, I felt the kind of respect for him which one feels for those who are masters of their craft, be they bricklayers or writers. Even when people began to treat him like an icon, I kept saying for a long time to those who were opposed to it or envious of him: "He's a master of his craft. If some lickspittles want to call him a classic, it's not his fault."

All the same I was surprised by the intensity of the contempt for him which the older writers did nothing to hide. For some reason they always began their stories about him with the one about his evacuation. As a "classic," he was given the middle bunk in the railway carriage. He would arrange himself on it and start sprinkling himself with some powder against bedbugs and other parasites. Underneath him were writers not numbered among the classics, sitting jammed up against one another. Fedin's insect powder would drift down onto them in thick clouds, onto their pitiful wartime food and onto their children. Fedin did not acknowledge their protests, as if there had been no one at all below him. He was above such things.

As a rule I regarded stories of this kind as examples of the kind of ill-will which sometimes surrounded successful writers like a choking cloud.

This remained my attitude until I became acquainted with the details of Marina Tsvetaeva's untimely death. I learned that just before she committed suicide, in her misery and despair, Tsvetaeva had gone to Chistopol where, figuratively speaking, the more prominent evacuated writers had pitched their tents. She went to both Fedin and Aseyev to ask for help—in vain. She then returned to her God-forsaken Elabuga and slipped a noose around her neck. When I learnt about this, I realized that the story about the clouds of powder raining down on those below had not been made up. Fedin had also screened himself off from the weeping Tsvetaeva. Later he was to turn away from Boris Pasternak, Alexander Solzhenitsyn, Alexander Tvardovsky, Sinyavsky and Daniel—anyone singled out by the powers-that-be—with the same insouciance. He knew how to deal with whatever was bothering him or causing irritation—just sprinkle himself with some strong-smelling potion and he was safe. However, we should not begin at the end.

Moral turpitude was increasing everywhere, leaving its mark on everyone. In this respect Konstantin Fedin was no worse than other writers from the thirties avid for recognition and success. Certainly, he killed off the main hero of his novel *Cities and Years* which brought him fame, the representative of the Russian intelligentsia Andrei Startsev. He killed him off like a dog. In killing Startsev, the positive hero Kurt, according to the narrator, "did everything for Andrei which a comrade, friend and artist should have done." An artist has an obligation to destroy a friend who has put the personal above the common good. This was the high-water mark of the "flood of amorality" in the liberal twenties. Everyone appears to have adhered to it. In his play *Lyubov Yarovaya* which was staged with resounding success by MKhAT the writer Trenyov has his heroine betray her husband, a colonel in the White Guard. In *The Forty-first* the painter Boris Lavrenyov puts a rifle in the hands of the heroine and pulls the trigger, killing her lover for the heinous crime of "thinking differently." Sholokhov depicts fratricide as the height of justice. Only Babel experienced any disquiet at the Revolution's immorality. Like his character Gedali, he showed no enthusiasm for the fact that one of his heroes, one of Budyonny's men, could cut his own father's throat, even if he was a White. The "chronicle of everyday crimes" caused him anguish. The chronicle of the twenties merged quite naturally with the chronicle of the thirties as the children rejected their fathers and mothers when the latter turned out to be "enemies of the people."

This endless chronicle of sanguinary deeds must have occasioned Konstantin Fedin some remorse as well. It could not have done otherwise—after all, a man is not born a beast of prey. However, Fedin had no wish to be parted from the comforts he enjoyed and hung on with clawing, ageing hands. I well remember Fedin crying out in anger and fright when told of the ·new ruling of the Literary Foundation making writers repair their dachas at their own expense: "At least let us die in peace!" It was becoming more and more difficult to live out one's days in comfort. It had to be paid for.

When it was decided by the Central Committee to put Daniel and Sinyavsky on trial and to intimidate Soviet writers once and for all, Fedin pleaded illness. Since the mountain would not go to Mohammed, Leonid Brezhnev and his colleagues from the Politburo went to see Fedin, now the General Secretary of the Union of Writers, at his dacha in Peredelkino. The township was cordoned off as if it had been infected with cholera. Around Fedin's old, well-kept dacha stood big black cars like tanks. Fedin greeted his guests warmly as brothers and like-minded people. Of course, he did not oppose the trial of the writers—how could they have thought such a thing! They should be tried with all the rigor of Revolutionary law! Why provoke unnecessary friction with the authorities when it would be simpler to dust himself with powder—it would not be the first time. Not long before he had applied his remedy when called upon to show some support for Paustovsky, Tendryakov, Kazakevich, Aliger and Bek, "the unpacified mountain folk" as he ironically referred to them.

How the powder flew around when Solzhenitsyn was under fire. Even his closest friends, those who had known him since the days of the Serapion Brothers, a literary brotherhood which had rejected State supervision of literature, found this too much to take. "Whose side are we on?" these former Serapion Brothers asked, conscious of the effect their words would have. "We're on the hermit Serapion's side." It was a long time since any of them had sworn faithfulness to Serapion. Those of them who had not been shot had lived side by side with Fedin and forgiven him much. This time they did not forgive him. In anger Kaverin wrote to him:

> We have known each other for forty-eight years, Kostya. We were friends when we were young. We have the right to judge each other. It is more than a right, it is a duty... How could you have not just failed to support but actually suppressed Literary Moscow, a periodical which our literature badly needed. After all, on the eve of the mass meeting of writers at the Film Actors' Club you gave this publication your support. With your dangerously treacherous speech already written and in your pocket, you praised our work... Your name was greeted at Paustovsky's 75th birthday celebrations with complete silence and with good reason. It would not surprise me if now after the banning at your insistence of Solzhenitsyn's Cancer Ward, for which the type had already been set at Novy mir, your first public appearance were greeted with whistling and foot-stamping... There is not a single publisher or literary enterprise which would deny that Markov and Voronkov were in favor of publishing Cancer Ward and that the type was only broken up because you spoke out so firmly against it...

You have taken a responsibility on yourself without apparently being aware of its enormity and significance... Without suspecting it yourself, perhaps you are becoming the focus of acrimony, indignation and discontent in literary circles...[15]

"Without suspecting it..." Is it possible that Fedin had been forcing writers' heads into the noose for twenty-five years without suspecting that this was arousing ill-feeling? Is it possible that after doing nothing to save Marina Tsvetaeva from suicide, betraying Pasternak and dozens of other writers, he had no suspicion of the indignation and resentment which had sprung up around him? Can he have trampled Russian literature into the ground yet not had some inkling of the discontent this caused? Even if Konstantin Fedin had been born a deaf-mute, he could not have helped having some suspicion of it. Feeling the vacuum surrounding him for years and enjoying the company of no one but a few "ladies of State" such as Braynina his personal biographer or Karpova, editor-in-chief and censor at the Writers' Publishing House, people who were only immune from contempt and disdain in Fedin's house.

It was not by chance that Alexander Tvardovsky who like Kaverin tried to save Solzhenitsyn for a wide Russian readership closed his extremely reserved letter to Fedin with words filled with despondency: "As I have said, I end my letter without any particular hope that it will have any favorable practical effect." The practical effect of a hangman's labor has been well-known to Russia for centuries.

When Fedin writes a personal letter, he sends the original to the addressee and the carbon copy to TsGALI (the Central State Museum of Literature and Art). When he starts measuring himself up for history like this, it becomes amusing. However, when he uses "bug powder" to screen himself off from all that is genuine and deserving of pride in Russian literature, and herds Russia's greatest poets and writers onto the scaffold, it ceases to be a laughing matter.

I have been an unwilling listener to Fedin's base and empty speeches on dozens of occasions. There is only one occasion which merits our attention here. At the entrance of the writers' retreat house in Peredelkino, Fedin once ran into the youthful-looking, impulsive writer Yelizar Maltsev. Maltsev, who should not be confused with the notorious Orest Maltsev, the supposed author of *A Yugoslav Tragedy*, was once honored with the post of head of the writers' Party Committee. He was Fedin's pupil. At the Literary Institute, Fedin had been his tutor, his supreme inspiration and mentor. It was Fedin who had thought up his literary pseudonym. Maltsev's real name is Pupko, which in Russian has undignified umbilical connotations. Yelizary Pupko decided to call himself Yelizar Bolshov ("large"). When he asked his beloved teacher's advice, Fedin took one look at his small, thick-set, round-faced pupil who was just beginning to put on some weight and exclaimed good-humoredly: "You're no Bolshov! You're a Maltsev" ("small"). Thus Yelizar Pupko became Yelizar Maltsev, a well-known prose-writer in Russia, the author of successful novels about labor, screen-plays and the libretto of the opera *With All My Heart* which has been performed at the Bolshoi Theater. He was even a Stalin Prize-winner. (Tvardovsky did not like Maltsev and never printed anything he wrote, although he sometimes wrote on themes popular with *Novy mir* writers.)

Maltsev met his teacher at the entrance to the house. It was the period when *Novy mir* was under strong attack. This attack could not have occurred without Fedin's concurrence. The Central Committee would not have had Tvardovsky dismissed unless Fedin had sanctioned the dismissal. Fedin smiled at his pupil from afar, but Maltsev barred his way and asked him angrily and sharply if he knew what he was doing. "It's not just *Novy mir* you've killed, it's a whole direction in Russian literature. You've trampled it to death. You'll never live down the shame of what you've done." Fedin's lips started to tremble, although they were still contorted in a pathetic smile. He tried to slip past, but Maltsev did not let him until he had finished speaking his mind.

I have never known anyone who was hated at the Union of Writers as fiercely and unanimously as Fedin. He was despised by those on the left and on the right and by the fence-sitters who were ready to love everyone and everything if it was in their interests. Even the old draft-horses in the "hangmen's guild" Gribachev and Sofronov, even Kochetov and Surkov were despised less. What could you expect of such incompetents suddenly elevated to high positions by chance? They were just ordinary guard-dogs, nothing more, ready to pounce on whoever they were ordered to.

Konstantin Fedin did not become a hatchet-man through dire need. No one was in a position to force him or to deprive him of his means of livelihood. They simply realized in the Central Committee that a man with his empty, icy eyes was ready to commit any deed, so long as he, a figure of world renown, was not bothered by the nasty bed-bugs ordinary people brought with them.

Incomprehensible though it may seem, during the Stalinist period of bloodshed Fedin never lost his reputation for being a decent man. He was never actually one of the established participants in the campaigns of character assassination, nor was he one of the NKVD's "literary consultants." In fact, he maintained a disdainful distance from the cohorts of Fadeyevs and Yermilovs. Why then should former Serapion Brother Konstantin Fedin, a Soviet neoclassic of the most majestic decrepitude, have suddenly degenerated in this way at a time when neither Stalin, Molotov or even Khrushchev were any longer on the scene and he need have had no fear that anyone would take away from him his gentleman's estate or any of the other trappings of comfort supplied by the Literary Foundation, even if there were a coup d'etat. How can this catastrophic disintegration of the personality be explained?

Above all the explanation lies in the impoverishment or even loss of his talent. As the Moscow critic L. has put it so aptly, one could only read his last lengthy novel *The Fire* to the end if sentenced to do so by a military tribunal. Sensitive readers of *Novy mir*, in which it appeared, simply tried to ignore the dying embers of Fedin's *Fire*. The loss of talent is the main reason and follows the pattern of decline observable in other writers such as Leonid Leonov, of whom Gorky was once incautious enough to say that "his talent would last a lifetime," and Leonid Sobolev, the author of *Major Repairs* Part I (Part II was never written). Writers of whom it can be said in the words of the old saying, that "they have much ambition but little ammunition," are legion. Experience has shown that it is from the ranks of those whose talent is on the wane that the chief hatchet-men are drawn.

There are, however, examples to the contrary. Gorky's friend Fyodor Gladkov, for instance, did not become a collaborator. Age brought no increase in talent to him. He was remembered in school textbooks for his early novel *Cement*, not for his later stories. All the same, Gladkov refused to play the hangmen's bloody games with them right up to the end.

Apart from all the traditional reasons, there are also individual destructive forces at work, driving a man into the abyss. Most commentators on modern Soviet literature leave aside the conflicts arising within writers' families, perhaps because their causes are so often diffuse, subjective and open to argument. However, the home front is obviously of great importance in determining the course of a writer's life. It is vital to take into consideration such factors as the personal antagonisms and principles of those close to him and whether they restrain him from dishonest actions or, on the contrary, prevail upon him to commit them by asking: "What will your children have to eat tomorrow otherwise?"

One of the factors which greatly hastened the moral transformation of Konstantin Fedin into the spineless, arrogant and malevolent character he was to become was the death of his first wife D. According to what various writers and their children who lived in close proximity to the Fedins for decades have told me, she was a forthright, honest woman who, they assured me, would never have forgiven him the base acts he later committed. She was not just honest but courageous to a rare degree: she would make a point of speaking in public to the wives and children of wirters who had been executed and of helping them. The granddaughter of the writers Bergelson who was murdered by Stalin told me that when she was eight years old she could not understand why her mother would stand talking to D. for such a long time. "D. would call out to us and we would stop there, sometimes in the middle of the courtyard with a blizzard blowing. I would be numb with cold while my mother would keep talking on and on to D. about trifles or nothing at all and would not let me run inside. It was only later that I became conscious of D.'s heroism. There at the well in the courtyard of the writers' block on Lavrushensky Lane we could be seen from every window... by those who shied away from us like the plague and by the janitors who were informers."

When D. died, Fedin stopped feeling ashamed about what he was doing. The only thing that now mattered was to be allowed to die in peace.

It was often the case that the elite surrounding the chief of the hatchetmen of the day included writers who in fact did not exist as writers. The poet Mikhail Svetlov, a broken but witty man who was never wholly sober and who earned his livelihood by translating from the languages of various nationalities in the USSR, was once stopped in the Writers' Club by a Turkmen, a stout man bereft of any literary talent, who proceeded to reproach him in faulty Russian for completely mistranslating his verse. Svetlov had added a new idea about which a rather dangerous controversy arose in *Literaturnaya gazeta.* "If you make a fuss," said Svetlov cheerily, being slightly tipsy, "I'll translate you back into your own language."

There have been many examples of such "literary grandees" suddenly appearing, created by skillful Russian translator-poets. A need arose at one time for folk poets to write poems praising Stalin. Poets doubling as translators "created" Dzhambul and Suleyman Stalsky. Present-day Dzhambuls are not expected to indulge in unstinting praise of anyone but to take part in the persecution of talented writers. Certain extremely wealthy landowners and owners of large flocks of sheep in the Central Asian republics—literary *bais*, as they are called—have given their support at writers' congresses in Moscow to all sorty of obscurantist skullduggery.

Svetlov devised a little game on the basis of this strange policy regarding national cultures. You turn to any page of the Directory of the Union of Writers and look through the list of names on the page. (The Directory contains some 7000 names.) If you can name what even one of the writers on the page has written, you win. If not, you buy Svetlov a glass of vodka. As a result of this game Svetlov has practically drunk himself to death. It is no wonder. What have Abdumomunov, Shapirov, Musrepov, Karbabayev and all the rest ever written? What have these people, elevated to positions of power as Secretaries, Party organizers and editors, given the world? What are they famous for? Even in their own republics? The most you can expect is to find occasionally, in some bibliographical listings, the faded names of their insignificant publications, which have long since passed into oblivion.

This game contrived by Svetlov is one he can hardly ever lose. These cruel *oprichniki* who inspire such fear in their contemporaries, remain essentially anonymous, however many medals and crosses they are awarded. Even if one of them should chance to write a book which hits the market at the right psychological moment, like Korneichuk or Vadim Kozhevnikov, it would all the same be because, as Kaverin has so aptly put it, "a writer who throws a noose around another writer's neck will find a place in history unconnected with his own work and wholly dependent on what his victim wrote."

PART IV

THE MISERY OF THE PEASANTS

1. BABEL'S *VELIKAYA KRINITSA*

It was the peasantry which bore the brunt of Russia's woes on its shoulders—in the trenches and the prisons, at home and in exile. But there was one misfortune which struck the peasantry particularly: agricultural ruin. This was the result of forced collectivization. Fifty years later Russia has still not recovered from it and buys grain wherever it can. The terrible experiences of the peasant population have naturally given birth to a particular literature and antiliterature, from Sholokhov to Babayevsky and the modern "smoke-screen writers" such as Mikhail Alekseyev and Georgy Radov. Russia has been literally flooded with a constant stream of this antiliterature. Sholokhov's *Virgin Soil Upturned* and Babayevsky's *Cavalier of the Gold Star* came out in editions of millions. In many Soviet libraries Sholokhov's and Babayevsky's books are calculated not by the number of copies but by meters of shelf-space. "We have eight meters of Sholokhov and a meter and a half of Babayevsky," I was told in one district reading room. Antiliterature was created by the State as a weapon in its punitive campaign. We shall deal with it in its proper place.

The literature concerned with the plight of the peasant population suffered the same fate as the countryside itself. It was exterminated by all possible means—starvation, Siberia, and the bullet. It was scattered to the four winds. Even published works which had become well-known disappeared overnight. This was true of Babel's works.

It appeared that all Babel's works had vanished quite irrevocably, together with their author. Then some ten years ago certain pages were uncovered and, strange as it may seem, published. They display Babel's talent at its most brilliant and now allow us to sketch in the outline of that authentic literary process which began spontaneously and was cut off with true Stalinist ferocity.

The fuss associated with Babel's name must have been obvious even to the most casual reader of Soviet publications. For a quarter of a century all mention of his name was suppressed, then he was published twice in twenty years in Moscow although not without much gnashing of teeth and the banning of Ehrenburg's uncongenial preface. This fuss constituted a belated rebuttal of Max Eastman's, Gleb Struve's and other commentators' remarks about Babel's silence. "Babel is ours and no one else's," declared the Soviet journals in a flurry of indignation. It was the evil Sovietologists who had dreamed up the notion that Babel "had become disenchanted and apparently stopped writing and fallen silent."[1] The police-report language and the use of the word "apparently" make it difficult to trust the statements of the former Middle East specialist A. Belyayev who suddenly became an expert on Isaak Babel.

Despite his repellently legalistic style, Belyayev, Babel's strenuous supporter, is not mistaken about Babel. He quite properly quotes Fyodor Levin, Babel's friend and researcher into his life and works: "The impression may be gained that [Babel] worked and wrote very little. However, this is not so. Babel worked extraordinarily hard and persistently. As he mentioned several times in his letters, he sometimes worked until he was worn out and developed a headache. However, he did not finish everything that he started and stored away what he did finish 'to ripen.' "[2]

Belyayev, who, as we must not forget, was Babel's stalwart supporter, goes on to provide a detailed list of Babel's works from his last period. "In 1927 Babel finished his play *Sunset* and in the same year he scripted two films, *The Chinese Mill* and *Benya Krik*. In the "thirties he worked on a novel about Chekists and wrote the story 'The Great Cavalry'..." and so on. Belyayev is obviously well-informed. He knows both what appeared in print and what could have appeared but did not. Why did it not appear? It was still over ten years before he was arrested and he would have had time to publish what he had to say about the Chekists and the Great Cavalry. "Babel was ruthless in his demands on both himself and his work," writes Belyayev zealously. "In a letter to V. Polonsky he admitted: "I will not submit a manuscript a moment before I consider it is ready." Nothing could characterize the very essence of the difficulty of Babel's fate better than these words. His artistic talent was of an original kind and his works were limited to one, or more precisely, two themes. He had exhausted them in his stories about the Red Army Cavalry and in his *Odessa Tales* he experienced an acute creative crisis."

This is why the security agent's device of using the word "apparently" as Belyayev did is so infuriating. It conceals the mocking cynicism of the old-world merchant who said: "I'll kill you, then light a candle for the repose of your soul—a hundred-rouble one!" The point is that Babel never wrote a story entitled "The Great Cavalry." I would have taken it to be a misprint if Belyayev had not gone on to base his notion of Babel's works being limited to just two themes on this "misprint," and if he had not attempted to use Babel's exacting attitude to his work to protect his murderers who are still concerned to make sure that Babel's later works continue to lie "ripening" on the shelf.

The "very essence" of his work was by no means confined to two themes. This is a grave falsehood. There was a third theme which was certainly the dominant one in the thirties. This was the theme for which Babel was killed and his archives confiscated. This is the theme he worked into his tragic novel *Velikaya Krinitsa* which Belyayev has renamed *The Great Cavalry (Velikaya konnitsa)*, presumably with the aim of erasing all trace of it. It is the theme of the great misery of the peasantry and the great violence done by the State to the countryside.

It unexpectedly transpired that certain chapters of the novel *Velikaya*

Krinitsa or *Velikaya Staritsa* had survived in the form of typewritten copies which Babel had evidently given to friends to read. Despite the fact that it was so dangerous to keep books or manuscripts by "enemies of the people," these friends did not destroy these chapters. This only came to light twenty-seven years after Babel was arrested. In the *Selected Works* of Babel which came out in 1966 with Ehrenburg's preface a chapter from the novel appeared under the title "Gapa Guzhva." The book was published in the mining town of Kemerovo. Thus Babel's chapter, from a book which had been suppressed by the NKVD and lain "ripening" for so many years, now "broke through" to Russian readers by the same means the disgraced Strugatsky brothers and many other Moscow and Leningrad writers had used, trying to escape the State's all-seeing eye by publishing in the journals of Siberia, the Baikal area, Kuzbass and sometimes even farther afield. Different generations used the same methods. However, even in Kemerevo, a provincial town far from the capital, the chapter "Kolyvushka" from *Velikaya Krinitsa* could not be published. It took the terrible Tashkent earthquake for the genuine unabridged Babel to reach the readers.

This is how it happened. Immediately after the Tashkent earthquake, when every city in Russia was taking in orphaned children and gifts and donations were pouring into Tashkent, writers from Moscow, Leningrad and some other cities decided to make a gift of their own. They brought out in Tashkent an issue of the journal *Zvezda Vostoka (Star of the East)*, for which they received no payment. Only the very best poems and stories were chosen for it. Someone—perhaps it was Ehrenburg—offered Babel's "Kolyvushka" as a contribution.* You don't look a gift horse in the mouth, as they say, and besides, the authorities had other things to worry about—half the city was housed in tents, water was being carted around in large tanks and bodies were still being found under the ruins. Now Babel's "Kolyvushka," also in its way once buried under the rubble by other "earthquakes," resurfaced.

This issue of *Zvezda Vostoka* has long since become a bibliographical rarity. It is not available to the broad reading public. For this reason I shall quote from it unsparingly in my examination of it, particularly since the appearance of this small work, taking up as it does only three and a half pages, really can be compared to the miracle of resurrection from the dead.

The subject-matter of this literary miracle is as ancient as the Tartar invasion. Outsiders break into a peasant household and set about destroying it. In modern terminology the process is called *raskulachivaniye*—dispossession of the kulaks. The women are taken away to internment and where possible, the men are killed. The narrator does not conceal where his sympathies lie; they are on the side of the peasant Ivan Kolyvushka from the very first line. It is not by chance that his name ends in the hypocristic

---

* The chapters rescued from oblivion were published in the West a year earlier: Isaak Babel, *The Lonely Years, 1925-1939*, New York, 1964.

suffix *ushka*. He is by no means a "blood-sucker and exploiter" but simply a hard-working peasant. Either he or his family has made everything they have with their own hands.

Here is the opening of "Kolyvushka":

> *Four men strode into Ivan Kolyvushka's yard: Ivashko, the Regional Council representative, Yevdokim Nazarenko the head of the village soviet, Zhitnyak, the chairman of the kolkhoz which had just been formed and Andriyan Morinets. Andriyan moved like a tower which has just started to walk. Clutching a bursting canvas briefcase to his thigh, Ivashko rushed past the barns and darted straight into the house. On dark-colored spinning-wheels at the window Ivan's wife and two daughters were spinning thread. With their hair tied in kerchiefs, their long sleeveless cloaks and small clean bare feet they looked like nuns. Between the towels and the cheap mirrors hung photographs of ensigns in the imperial army, school-teachers and city folk at their summer house. Ivan followed his guests into the house and took off his hat. "How much tax does he pay?" asked Ivashko, turning round.*
>
> *The headman Yevdokim, his hands stuck in his pockets, watched the spinning-wheel flying round... "In this State," said Yevdokim, "you give up everything, comrade... In this State, it's impossible not to give up everything..."*
>
> *Above the guests the whitewashed walls came together in a low, warm dome. Everything in the room—the flowers in lamp-chimneys, the flat cupboards and the polished benches—reflected a painful cleanliness. Ivashko leapt up and rushed towards the door with his briefcase flapping.*
>
> *Kolyvushka stepped after him. "Comrade," he said, "will there be an order issued about me or what?"*
>
> *Tymysh the cheerful bailiff appeared in a flash at the gate. He strode after Ivashko along the muddy village street, measuring out the paces with his long legs. Ivan signalled to him and caught him by the sleeve. The cheerful pole of a man bent over and opened his may which was filled with his raspberry-colored tongue and set with pearls. "We're sending you away..."*
>
> *And on his long crane's legs Tymysh rushed after his chief.*

The poetic qualities of this passage set it apart from other parts of the narrative. Babel's main poetic device here obviously consists of depicting the peasant world as immobile and frozen and the intruders as bustling and agitated. Everything in the peasant milieu is immobile—the old photographs, the towels and cheap mirrors hanging on the wall. The image of the whitewashed dome strengthens the sense of immobility. Every word and image impresses on the reader this sense of immobility. It is the immobility which precedes death. It is tinged with sorrow. The spinning-wheel has taken on a dark hue and the women are like nuns. Even the dome has a monastic quality about it. The life lived under its brooding weight is that of an anchorite or recluse. Later on we see the mother wearing "a shroud." The dark-colored spinning wheel, the nuns, dome and shroud make up the world Babel has constructed here, a world frozen in a kind of grief-stricken, stony severity and the sensations of approaching death. The description which sums up the scene in the room is nothing short of brilliant: "painful cleanliness."

We find here the two great sources of strain in a peasant's life merged into one: firstly, the almost superhuman strain of his patient unending toil (we find the same thing later in the writings of Sergei Zalygin, whose hero Stepan Chauzov dreams of buying a third horse but does not because if he did his wife would not survive); and secondly, the awareness of death as always ready to strike. Everything in the room—even the cupboards and the benches—seem to sense their doom. The world of the peasant is frozen in an attitude of painful, hopeless petrification.

The other dominant force—the element of destruction—is described by Babel as disorganized, almost senseless, agitated movement. Ivashko "rushed with his briefcase flapping," "darted straight into the house," "restlessly pressed his foot against the floor-boards," clutched a bursting canvas briefcase to his thigh" and "leapt up." Andriyan Morinets, by way of contrast, is "enormous in an inhuman way" and "moved like a tower which has just started to walk." Everything here is crooked, inhuman, larger than life or bustling. Ivashko shouted, "his arms swinging." Tymysh "measured out the paces with his long legs." And this comes straight after the description of painful cleanliness of those who are doomed.

Curiously, once inside the invaders feel somehow unsure of themselves, despite the fact that on the face of it might is on their side. They have the lethal might of Stalin's orders to back them up and of an army which has already bloodily suppressed several peasant uprisings—they simply enter and take possession once and for all. Nevertheless, their arrival is depicted in terms of agitated, mindless dashing about.

Something unheard-of in Soviet literature is to be observed here: the victors are shown to be non-people. Forty years later one of Galich's characters was to call his prison-guards "whorish non-people" ("kurvy-nelyudi"). Babel sensed their approach in the twenties. It is the world of the spirits of Russian folklore which assume power and the non-human which throws restraint to the winds.

Ivan Kolyvushka comes into his house and "takes off his hat." Then he follows Ivashko off timidly. Even before half a page has been read, the strength of the poetic sub-text is clearly felt to lie in the contrast of the eternal which is being destroyed and the bustling commotion of the band of intruders. The intruders who burst in are bandits, non-people, although the walls of the peasant house still enfold them under their warm dome in welcome. The peasantry in Russia is meek, thirsting for humanity and indulgence as if it were to blame for something. "Please forgive us if all is not as it should be," they say, even when unreservedly glad to see someone. Over the evil spirits broods a warm dome.

Tragically, whatever is warm and alive can be killed, sometimes with impunity, yet the world of evil spirits lives on, full of vitality.

In the first lines of the story the narrator makes his position quite clear. The contrast between the two forces or elements is completed in the comparison between the agitated motion of Tymysh's stork-like legs and the stock-still legs of a horse laden with wheat, the peasant's source of wealth for centuries.

We now come to the second page of "Kolyvushka" which I am examining separately only for the purposes of delineating the story's structure more clearly. Since the text is not available to the reader elsewhere, I quote it at length with just a few deletions.

A harnessed horse was standing in Ivan's yard. The red reins had been thrown over some sacks of wheat. Next to the overhanging lime-tree in the middle of the yard was a stump with an ax sticking out of it. Ivan touched his cap with his hand, shifted it and sat down. The mare dragged the sledge over to him and stuck out her tongue curling it into a pipe shape. The mare was in foal and her belly was drawn tight. She playfully got hold of his padded shoulder and pulled at it. Ivan was looking down at his feet. The trampled snow lay around the stump in ripples. Bending over, Kolyvushka pulled out the ax, held it suspended for a moment in the air then hit the horse with it across the forehead. One ear flew off, the other jerked up, then flattened itself. The mare bellowed and bolted. The sledge turned over and the wheat was strewn across the snow in swirling streaks. The horse was rearing up and down on its forelegs and tossing back its muzzle. At the barn she got caught up in the teeth of the harrow. Her eyes looked out from behind a flowing curtain of blood. She began to make a plaintive singing sound. Her foal turned inside her and a vein on her belly swelled.

"Let's be friends," said Ivan, stretching out his hand to her, "let's be friends, my beauty..."

... The horse's ear was hanging off, her eyes were twisted to one side, with gleaming rings of blood around them, and her neck and muzzle made one straight line. Her upper lip was drawn back in despair. She pulled on the breast-band and moved, dragging the bounding harrow behind her. Ivan drew the ax round behind his back. The blow hit her between the eyes and as the animal collapsed the foal turned again. Ivan walked once around the yard then went up to the

barn and rolled the winnower outside. His strokes were wide and
slow as he smashed the machine, and twisted the ax in the fine mesh
of the wheels and the drum. His wife, wearing a long cloak, appeared
on the porch. "Mother," Ivan heard her call in a far-away voice,
"Mother, he's destroying everything."

The door opened. An old woman wearing sackcloth trousers
came out of the house, leaning on a stick. Her yellowing hair lay
against her cheeks, covering the pockmarks in them. Her smock hung
like a shroud on her flat body. The old woman walked onto the snow
in her shaggy stockings.

Taking the ax from him, she said to her son: "Have you for-
gotten your father, you killer? Have you forgotten your convict bro-
thers?"

The neighbors gathered in the yard. The peasants stood in a semi-
circle and looked away. Some woman darted forward and started
shrieking. "Get hold of yourself, you slut," her husband said to her.

Ivan stood leaning against the wall. His rasping breathing was
being carried around the yard...

"I'm a man," he suddenly said to those around him, "I'm a man,
I belong to this village... Haven't you ever seen a man before?"

This then is the second part of the narrative—an ax in hands which have abandoned all hope, the destruction of a home, a family, a world— self-extermination. The only ones who are flourishing are the non-people.

Only a line and a half is devoted to the destruction of the machine while half a page is given over to the sufferings of the horse. Babel is no sadist, so why does he describe the horse's heart-rending sufferings at such length, and in such naturalistic detail? The crux of the matter is not the horse itself although the peasant household relies heavily on the horse. Its force here is not so much an economic one as the force of something living, something held dear and inseparable from life itself. It is a circle of blood, not only in the economic sense but in the biological sense also. It is the circle of peasant life. While the horse is being killed, her foal stirs inside her. The Russian word Ivan uses when he stretches out his hand to her in seeming reconciliation is "dochka"—literally "daughter." The horse's terrible suffering is a measure of the pain caused by what is happening, as is Ivan's own pain. Ivan Kolyvushka takes form almost in a physically tangible sense through his horse's suffering.

The seal of death lies on everything. The figure of the mother stepping onto the snow in her shaggy stockings suddenly becomes the very personification of death. Death clothed in a shroud takes away the ax and restores order. Bowing to death, Ivan becomes quiet. His heavy breath floats around the yard. He begins to perceive the horror of what he has done—he has killed his own "daughter."

The patriarchal family is collapsing. The mother still has the power in her hands. She makes her son stop. What is the point of this? Babel reveals the deep-lying meaning of what has happened: Ivan Kolyvushka's revolt is madness. Pushkin wrote in horror of revolt in Russia: "May God preserve us from seeing a revolt in Russia—it will be senseless and merciless!" A century later nothing had changed, particularly human nature, the dead and the living.

The most direct personification of life is the mare in foal. This is not just life but the poetry of life. "She made a plaintive singing sound."

Kolyvushka, half-dead and demented with grief, had still hoped that something would happen and "stepped" after Ivashko—he did not stride. Then he killed his horse and her foal and finally froze inwardly. The women are also dead in a sense, having inwardly frozen. "The sleds slipped out of the gates of Kloyvushka's house. The women were sitting on bales like frozen birds... They drove round the edge of the village and sank out of sight in the flat snowy wasteland. The wind was rumpling the snow underneath and moaning in the wasteland, spreading blue waves. A tin sky hung above them. The sparkling sky was strung with a jeweled net..."

Even for Babel, author of *Red Army Cavalry* and *Odessa Tales*, the laconic style, the use of metaphors, the precision and the historical sense given to the deep levels of the story mark a high point in his art.

As it is constructed, the story brings out the rigidity seizing the peasants and their world as death approaches and then the final rigor mortis. We have the nuns, the shroud, the dome and the pockmarks in the cheeks. The women bury themselves almost according to monastic rites. Kolyvushka buries himself with an ax in his hand. He breaks the meek solemnity and says something which could never have been expected of him: "I'm a man."

These are not the words of a philosopher. It is not Satin speaking, Gorky's high-flown thinker from the "lower depths." It is a peasant speaking, someone who to all appearances does not think about such matters. It is a line which is bursting with tragedy. A man has killed his horse which is like a "daughter" to him and has nothing left and only then says what he has to say. He cannot help himself. The words escape him like a moan: "I'm a man, I belong to this village... Haven't you ever seen a man before?"

It then becomes evident that he is surrounded by compassion: the other peasants look away. This simple detail uncovers a deep moral significance. When one of the women starts shrieking, her husband pulls her up sharply.

The scene concludes with the depiction of the landscape swallowing everything up. Babel's acute sense of what was artistically right prevented him from mentioning the "frozen birds" again. Nothing apart from the tin sky strung with a net of stars above the village is needed.

The third page of the story exhibits some continuity in its structure althought it has its own particular aspects as well. The theme of the paralysis of the peasant world is built up. The peasants are shown to be frozen in an attitude of rigidity. Even the peasant "troika" running the kolkhoz meeting which Ivashko uses to shield himself is the very image of silence. It is a Stalinist OSO or special commission of the kind formed all over Russia "in the people's name" to cover up reprisals. However, there are not enough lawyers to go round in the countryside, so people like the simple farm-laborer Movchun ("the Silent One") are brought in to help out, people who sometimes cannot even sign their own name. They work under the instructions of the ever-busy Ivashko.

However, Babel goes further. The village has suffered a blow from which, like Kolyvushka's horse, it will not recover. Hundreds of thousands of peasants were massacred on the spot in the USSR at that time. Eight million of them were forced into special trains guarded by soldiers with machine-guns on the platform of each carriage, to be tipped out into the Siberian taiga to suffer in appalling conditions or to die. Later whole nationalities were dealt with in this fashion—the Crimean Tartars, the Kalmyks, the Chechens and the Meskhetians from Georgia.

The village accepts the blow with a sense of doom. Babel describes its acceptance of its fate with great bitterness. The village assembly is described like a mystery play. It is reminiscent of a religious procession waiting in expectation of justice in a frenzy of faith and in silence. Those presiding are hushed, as if a wave of silence had passed over the gathering. "A breaker rolled splashing over Velikaya Staritsa. The crowd surged along the shattered street. The legless were carried along in front. An invisible banner fluttered over the crowd." This is an apocalyptic scene, the end of the world.

But it is an apocalypse on a village scale. It is characterized by the mute cowering of the morally pure, the mad and the ignorant.

> People rushed up to the village soviet and came to a halt standing in rows. In the middle of the crowd a circle was revealed, a circle of scuffed snow, an empty place like the one left for the priest in a procession. In the middle of the circle stood Kolyvushka with his loose shirt hanging out underneath his waistcoat. His head was white. The night had silvered his gypsy's crown. Not one black hair remained. Snowflakes like weak birds carried by the wind floated along under the now warm sky.

Like the "warm dome" and "painful cleanliness," the "now warm sky" is a key description of inner moral completeness, a key to the beginning.

An old man lifts up his hands and says: "Tell us, Ivan, tell the people what's troubling you." However, it is not this timid interjection from the old man "with broken legs," as Babel notes apparently in passing, which breaks the oppressive silence. The silence is broken by a whisper from Kolyvushka, whose hair has gone white overnight. He addresses his fellow villagers using the old term *mir*. " 'Mir, where are you forcing me to go?... I was born among you...' A grumbling crept along the rows."

What sort of grumbling is it? Those grumbling are the people like the ignorant peasant laborer Movchun. They have been deceived, although they are pure in heart. One of them is Morinets. "Although the cry could not break out of his powerful body, his low voice shook: 'Let him keep working ... He won't be any trouble.'"

Babel emphasizes the physical effort Morinets had to make to get the words out. It is a peasant's last word. It contains the foundation of everything. It contains a judgment on a dehumanized policy. It is the judgment of the very peasants in whose name the most terrible crime in Russian history was unleashed.

Babel's contrastive device, so essential to his art, comes to the fore again. On the one hand, the peasants are silent, Kolyvushka whispers—the life forces are silent. On the other hand, the hobgoblins and evil spirits hold forth at great length in their place—the hunch-back Zhitnyak, chairman of the newly formed Kolkhoz, which actually came into being on the orders of Ivashko from the Regional Council and Ivashko. Only three paragraphs are devoted to Zhitnyak's phrase-mongering and Ivashko's bellowing, but the impression is given that they are endless. They cannot be read without hatred being roused for these ranting murderers. There is nothing to them but an unappeased appetite for empty reasoning. They sarcastically proclaim like newspaper stereotypes: "Our State is utterly insatiable."

Stalinist hypocrisy was quickly grasped by all the Zhitnyaks and Ivashkos. It was not they who were insatiable and cruel but, as they saw it, the State, the people as a whole, whose protectors they had declared themselves to be. The narrator has this insatiability accentuated in an ironical way: Zhitnyak the hunch-back is talking about a woman he has spent the night with, which he is boasting about: "We stuffed ourselves like pigs until we broke wind." Theirs is the power of out-and-out hooligans and jail-birds who although they are still unsure of themselves are triumphant.

On reading this chapter with the title "Kolyvushka," we readily sense its main poetic import, and not just rationally but with our feelings: the living are doomed and the world of evil spirits is triumphant. This is the prism which refracts the story into its various strands.

Babel finished his story in 1930. It was only the second year of Stalin's first Five Year Plan. Incredible as it may seem, the principal crimes were still ahead. In 1930 Babel foresaw the ever increasing fear that was to come of the executioners for their victims, and their hatred of them. He predicted the whole Stalinist amorality complex which is still triumphant in Russia. Babel foresaw and depicted in his writings the Soviet psychological phenomenon of hatred on the part of the dead underworld spirits for life, their fear of the living, the thinking, the human. "You've come to put us up against the wall," Zhitnyak says to Kolyvushka after hearing the people say "let him work." "You've come to tyrannize over us with that white head of yours, and to make us suffer. Only we're not going to suffer..."

Zhitnyak is of course a provocateur. As later literature would confirm, this was in the nature of Stalinism. He shouts at Kolyvushka that he has gone to get a shot-gun. The reason for this frenzied outburst is that he wants to have a chance to shoot him himself without fear of punishment. " 'You ought to be killed... I'm going to get my pistol. I'll finish you off.' The hunchback rushed off to get his gun on his thin splayed legs.' "

If it were not for the wild winds of Stalinism blowing behind him, he would be nothing and fall to pieces.

Babel portrays what is monstrous with a sense of the grotesque. Otherwise it would not have been possible to portray it fully, and the extent of the atrocities committed by the State in the land of victorious socialism would have been practically inconceivable.

In resorting to the grotesque, Babel does not go beyond the bounds of realism at any point. He measures it out with consummate skill.

The chapter from *Velikaya Krinitsa* called "Gapa Guzhva" in the Kemerovo collection is no less profound than "Kolyvushka" although the schemes showing the eradication of the Russian peasantry would seem to be less detailed and striking. When compared with "Kolyvushka" it becomes sinister. Ivashko turns out to have been insufficiently ferocious. We learn that he has been "swept up" ("zameli"). This was one of the everyday euphemisms for "arrested" in those years. At the time of the mass terror campaign a flood of cynical jargon words came into everyday speech, taking the place of responsible expressions whose full import was apparent. During the Civil War, as Maximilian Voloshin has related, dozens of jargon words appeared as synonyms for the word "rasstrelyat" ("to shoot," "to execute by shooting"). The ordinariness of killing was soon expressed in the ordinary casual type of word which made the terrible criminal essence of the times less evident. Words such as "razmenyat" ("to exchange"), "otpravit k Kukhoninu" ("to send to Kukhonin"), "shlyoput" ("to smack"), "koknut" ("to crack") and "pustit nalevo" ("to push to the left") began to be used. The same thing happened in the thirties. The new wave of killings gave rise to a new wave of words expressing cynicism and indifference.

After Ivashko has been "swept up," a replacement is appointed. This is the "Voronkov judge" who is said to have put "nine gentlemen in the cooler... Next morning they were to be sent to Sakhalin Island." The next morning, however, they are found hanging by their belts from beams. All the same the judge organizes a kolkhoz in Voronkov within twenty-four hours. This is the turn events take.

The only person to dare mock the judge is the irrepressible and fearless Gapa Guzhva. "She's not a woman, that widow of ours, she's a devil," they say of her with respect.

Gapa Guzhva behaves audaciously towards the judge, asking him, for example, if it is true that everyone at the kolkhoz will be sleeping under

261

the same blanket. "Her eyes were laughing in her calm face. 'I'm against it, this sleeping altogether in a bunch. What we like is sleeping in twos and a drop of vodka...' " Then she goes off to dance at a wedding where she smashes a barn with a boathook. Then she goes again to the judge. She staggers into his house and wants to know how whores will be treated under complete communism. "They'll disappear," he says. "But will whores be able to live or not?" "Yes, they will," he replies, "but it will be a different kind of life, a better one." "The woman stared at the corner with unseeing eyes. She touched the necklace on her breast. 'Thank you for what you've said..' "

The last sentence in the story is as follows: "The translucent clouds swept low. Silence spread over Velikaya Krinitsa, over the flat, icy graveyard of the wasteland of the night in the country."

The footnote "1930" at the bottom of the page provides a final shock. The night enveloping the village is a grave-yard. It is hardly surprising that in Belyayev's article "Velikaya Krinitsa" becomes "Velikaya Konnitsa" ("The Great Cavalry"). The murderers are still trying to deceive history.

More than a quarter of a century separates Babel's brilliant description of the ruination of Russia from the next landmark, Sergei Zalygin's story "On the Irtysh," which was the first to return courageously to the bloody theme of the smashing of the Russian peasantry.

2. SERGEI ZALYGIN: "ON THE IRTYSH"

The continuity in characters, motifs, situations and observations in the books by Babel and Zalygin are such that the deep moral aspects of the catastrophe which hit the Russian peasantry and which was so vitiated by Stalinist antiliterature are brought right to the surface.

A detailed portrait of Stepan Chauzov, the main character in Zalygin's story "On the Irtysh," is presented right from the start. The grain confiscated from Alexander Udartsev's granary is on fire. Chauzov is trying to put out the fire from the most dangerous position—the roof. The peasants attempting to put it out from below are worried about him. "He'll burn alive!" they say to one another. "Nothing easier," someone agrees. Every now and again someone asks anxiously: "Is he still alive or what?"

Stepan is strong and smart and respected by the other peasants in his village. When a group of them was approaching a river-crossing one day and they were coming to a dangerous slope "one let him go ahead, and then another, and when Stepan looked around, he saw that he was riding ahead of everyone. Well, if that was the way it was to be..."

Zalygin's reasons for making Stepan Chauzov the focus for this tragic narrative is obvious. Chauzov represents the peasant's conscience and quick wits. Pavel Pechura, the only Party member in the village, has him appointed kolkhoz chairman. Even the young investigator sent from the city to look into the grain fire immediately realizes what sort of man it is he has to deal with. In addition, it transpires that Chauzov fought against Kolchak during the Civil War.

The investigator believes Chauzov and is right in doing so, but Chauzov does not have much faith in the investigator. He has a deep-rooted distrust, inherited from his father and grandfather before him, of city people, and especially of the authorities and of investigators. And he understands that this one is not a mere investigator but a legal official. This was Siberia where outsiders' prying eyes had never been liked. Vladimir Pomerantsev has a story about how the inhabitants of an isolated Siberian village strapped investigators and other men from the city to the backs of deer and then hit the deer with switches across the belly to make them bolt off into the forest with their human burden and try to rub them off against tree trunks.

Although old Udartsev tries to kill Stepan when they are pulling out the burning grain, Stepan takes no legal action against him. As far as he is concerned, the legal official is more dangerous than old Udartsev because he is incomprehensible to him. Coming away from the investigator he tells the others: "I think I've fought him off, men." Indeed he has. It is not the investigator who presents a danger to Stepan. The village is like an upturned ants' nest. The peasants are being driven to the kolkhoz. They are not

263

resisting but a few things give them cause for apprehension. "At the moment bad feelings are kept to one side," says Stepan's wife, "but what will it be like in the kolkhoz? If someone in the kolkhoz is spiteful and greedy it will affect everyone. All will suffer." Another wise old peasant called Nechay is also worried: "I worked out... how I'd harness the horse and drive by the smithy and get a nail I need from the blacksmith. But how did it turn out? You'll decide what to do and leave me to carry out the orders... In a year you'll decide you like giving orders."

The peasants' observations as they sit together talking in the office are very much to the point and not without their humorous side: "Well, men, there shouldn't be any war, anyway... So long as they keep calling me a petty bourgeois in the newspaper, there won't be any war. Before a war breaks out, they always call us heroes." Then suddenly the conversation becomes more serious. "It's the easiest thing in the world, sending the kulaks off into the wilds past Tobolsk or Turukhan... But where is it going to stop?" Nechay asks. "Tell me, Fofan, who knows where they'll draw the line?"

Zalygin's was the first work since Babel's in which a peasant foresees the senseless cruelty which surrounds power. Times were different although things did not get worse. As the poet has said: "Times have been worse but not more vile." In many ways Babel's Kolyvushka carry out acts which are strikingly similar. Kolyvushka kills his horse so that the non-people should not get hold of it and Alexander Udartsev sets fire to his grain. Udartsev's humane side is not mentioned at all. The terms used to describe him are legal ones, framed like a death sentence, although by its very nature literature does not tolerate death sentences without a wide-ranging examination of the case and the right of appeal.

The only character in whose defense Zalygin raises his voice is Stepan Chauzov who according to spiteful and slanderous reports is socially allied to the kulak. This provides the clearest possible evidence of the present-day morality of a society in which the extermination of eight million peasants is officially regarded as an unimpeachably correct act. "There were, of course, occasional shortcomings"...

Zalygin has no direct quarrel with the official morality, or to put it more precisely, with the legitimized immorality of the State. However, despite all his cautiousness, the reader cannot help being struck by the similarity in what he and Babel describe. In Babel the figures in authority display a repulsive agitation in all their actions. Zalygin's kolkhoz chairman Pechura is something of a buffoon whose arms almost reach his knees and are always swinging all over the place." Babel's chairman talks in cliches taken from the newspapers as does Zalygin's: "At this point in time we must pass through a certain period... as we take these strides and progress we attain a life of the greatest happiness."

There is one change. Zalygin has lessened the enthusiasm of the authorities and increased their cynicism. "I repeat whatever is being said at the regional level, only louder. Then they stay happy and say what a conscientious chairman I am." Of his hands the narrator tells us: "His hands were long and thin, not a peasant's hands, somehow not deft hands... Pavel was not a man of the soil, not cast in the peasant mold."

He is aware of this himself and for this reason has Stepan Chauzov appointed chairman. However, he does not want Chauzov to become a time-server for the non-people, shutting up when he is told and agreeing when he is told. This is the source of all his woes.

Chauzov, like everyone else in the village except Pechura, does not surrender every last ounce of grain and the matter is brought up at a meeting of the "troika" working on "the complete exposure of the kulaks." The lawyer and the first chairman of the Committee for the Poor Koryakin are members of the troika. Koryakin is no peasant but one of those at the top. He demands that Chauzov be considered a kulak. The lawyer protests vehemently and Koryakin starts to get threatening: "You won't divert me from the course set by Stalin!" He does, indeed, faithfully follow the course set by Stalin. With the aim of compromising Chauzov, he sends him a scurrilous peasant called Egorka Gilyov who whispers to him that Udartsev is making out that he, Chauzov, set fire to the grain. Chauzov ignores the provocation and does not go to see Udartsev. This is enough for Koryakin. "Chauzov didn't go to see Udartsev, that's true. But he didn't say that Udartsev was implicated in it." The act of provocation has been thought out with typically insensate Stalinist cruelty. If Chauzov had gone to see Udartsev, he would have been doomed, and if he cannot be lured out, he is still doomed—for not informing.

While this is going on Koryakin says to the investigator in a private conversation: " 'You know what a drop of water is like in spring... no dirt in it, not a speck—pure as a baby's tear.' He patted the investigator's shoulder. 'That's the sort of ideology we're creating now.' "

A great deception was being implemented all over the country—in Siberia, the Ukraine and the Kuban. Stepan Chauzov is not in a position to go into the ramifications of this deception although he is being surrounded like a wolf. He feels that he is being surrounded but does not know what to do about it.

"Who do you think I should go after with this chisel, eh?" Stepan asks Egorka Gilyov, who has been sent on his errand by Koryakin. "If Soviet power sent an officer in a cockaded hat with epaulettes and a cannon after me, I'd soon put a few dents in him, I can tell you. But who am I going to hit out at as it is? Pavel Pechura? or Feofan? Soviet power uses peasant hands to do its work for it. And no one can shoot it down or push it aside. I'm not my own children's enemy when Soviet power promises them life. Who am I to beat up, then?"

The peasants do not know how to hide from their misfortune. They have "history" explained to them and cross themselves to ward it off: "God save us from history... Can't we just live a bit without history? It's always creeping ahead of you." "History isn't a horse you can pull this way or that, you know."

Babel's peasants were all "Movchuns" who only grumbled. Zalygin's peasants are philosophers. This may be the result of the fact that the book was written some thirty-five years after Babel's and the author has passed the wisdom of today's peasantry off as the wisdom of the peasants of 1929 and 1930. It is not beyond the bounds of possibility all the same that Zalygin's characters are no more complex than Siberians actually are. They are peculiar people.

"Peasants had lived in the town for hundreds of years, since the distant past, almost since the time of Yermak. They were free peasants and fugitives from the Demidov factories in the Urals, from Russian provincial areas. They kept accumulating their stock of peasant wisdom, handing it down from grandfather to great-grandson, and the line of these ideas stretched right to the door of Stepan Chauzov."

Nowadays in the seventies a man in a State official's cap journeying down the Enisei river is afraid to go far from a landing place into the taiga because 'in the taiga it's the law of the bear' as the saying goes. And if he is a fisheries inspector then he stays very close to base, something I myself have had occasion to witness.

Nechay brings Stepan, who is to be deported, a box of nails, hoping they might be of some use. That is all this wise old philosopher can do to help. He asks Mitya, from his own village, now in charge: "Is it true that Stepan Chauzov, one of our own peasants, is a kulak and enemy of the people?"

"No," said Mitya. "Chauzov isn't an actual kulak,"

"Then why are you actually deporting him?"

"Life is being completely transformed, comrade Nechay. When the wood is chopped, chips fly."

Mitya religiously believes that Stepan's wife's tears are the last she will weep. "In five years or so perhaps the class war will be over and complete justice will be established. And then there will never be any more tears."

Even Mitya, for all his fanatical enthusiasm, feels the immorality of the Stalinist saying about the wood and the chips. He makes wretched attempts to help Chauzov and to save his wife and children. "Klavdia Petrovna," he tells her, "inasmuch as your origins are in a completely different social stratum, you could make an application... You could stay here, and even keep the children with you." Klavdia replies that although she once looked after him, fed him and mended his trousers for him, it was all in vain because he, Mitya, has no soul. (In some sense Zalygin is passing judgment on himself here.) Since Mitya made his prediction that five years would elapse and all tears would be wiped away, thirty-five have passed. Time has revealed the terrible true meaning of the Stalinist expression that when the wood is chopped chips fly.

Zalygin does not dare to humanize the figure of Udartsev or to try to understand his pain. They are after all not people but kulaks. Vasily Grossman, who died the year "On the Irtysh" came out replied to this in his story "Forever Flowing" very simply: "They are people." The immorality of present times is fully uncovered, times in which the mention of class opponents in humane terms in the literature of a classless society is not allowed.

The comparisons with Babel are very striking. Babel's women "were sitting on bales like frozen birds" as they drove away from the village. In "On the Irtysh" Zalygin writes that Olga Udartseva's "soul seemed to have been nipped by the frost." When they send Chauzov away, his little children sit on bundles and their mother makes them drink cold milk to give them strength for the trip. "They drank some and she made them drink more. Now they're sitting in a stupor from all the milk."

The Chauzovs are taken away. The other peasants stand at the gates watching. One of the women starts howling and others shout at her to "shut up." This is an echo of Babel's "get a hold of yourself, you slut."

The last sentence in "On the Irtysh" harks back to Koryakin's "ideology" which was as pure as a drop of water in spring. "It was the first dripping of the thaw for the year. The icicles hung from the roofs and the fat drops tinkled as they smacked the ice—drip-drip, drip-drip!"

Few writers could be more different from each other in terms of their experience, their principles of characterization and their style than Babel and Zalygin, author of the huge, calculatedly conformist novels *Altay Paths*, *Salty Gully* and others. Yet it transpires that when a modern writer who is striving to adapt himself to society and to survive suddenly determines to tell the truth, even with certain reservations, at greater length than necessary and with a positive hero (the legal official) whom no one listens to but who is called in the press "a true representative of the party," he feels obliged to tie up at the wharf of literature beside a ship of some size. If the wharf is crowded, he pushes up against another big ship and they are then viewed as being together.

Our generation from which Babel's "Velikaya Krinitsa" was concealed was shaken by Zalygin's "On the Irtysh." His story revealed for all those whose conscience was still intact a theme which bled like a wound. At the time it seemed to us that the truth about the destruction of the countryside in the thirties had come to light for the first time in his story. There would be nothing else to say if it were not for the fact that the Soviet critics afforded "On the Irtysh" their patronage. The main concern of Soviet critics was that the literary Table of Ranks should not be touched and that Sholokhov should not be infuriated by Zalygin's story. They felt constrained to manoeuvre so that they could run with the hares on the Irtysh and hunt with the hounds on the Don. "Stepan Chauzov's drama"—this was how deportation to Siberia and the death of eight million peasants were termed—

"ultimately results from the fact that there was no one in the village of Krutye Luki corresponding to Sholokhov's Davydov."[3]

However, since no one, neither the critic nor his readers, believed any more in heroes such as Sholokhov's Davydov, well-intentioned critics were concerned to protect "On the Irtysh" from attacks from above and did so by claiming that what distinguished Zalygin's honest book from many others by Soviet writers throwing light on the process of collectivization was the narrowly-defined task Zalygin set himself when he wrote it—to depict the doubts and hesitations of the peasants in one village. How long are these crude concepts of norms going to be with us? Readers have been acquainted with them since the days of war prose—everything is wonderful everywhere in the USSR except this one village, factory, regiment, battery and so on. The author, it is claimed, has not the slightest intention of generalizing on the basis of one village. There is nothing wrong with the leading role of the Party either. The only problem is that the faithful Stalinist Koryakin "did not think deeply enough about the Party's orders."[4]

Again and again the critics refer piously to Sholokhov because the greatest danger for a truthful book is the world of Sholokhov's lies given legitimacy the the State: "Of course four days in the life of one village cannot eclipse what has been related in our literature about the first years of collectivization or conclude the discussion..." Time will have the final say. Lies have short legs.

3. BORIS MOZHAYEV AND CHINGIZ AITMATOV

*Whatever is alive and pure perishes, while the forces of death and
inhumanity triumph and their hatred for purity and truth grows from
day to day...*

Peasant prose led inevitably to the development of this theme in
Russian literature. By peasant prose I mean the works of modern writers
who have maintained their connection with their native village and the
patriarchal home and who write about them. Boriz Mozhayev and Chingiz
Aitmatov are possibly the most talented and, at least in their writings, the
most uncompromising of these true sons of the soil.

Aitmatov decisively crossed the boundary of purely national literature
long ago. Although himself a Kirgiz, Aitmatov's books have played a significant role in the formation of the ideas of whole generations of readers
who were beginning to think seriously about what was going on around
them. At first Aitmatov's "rise" was facilitated at official levels because
of his unusual talent and the fact that the problems he treated did not go
outside the framework of what it was permitted to discuss. An example is
his story "Dzhamilya." However, it was not long before this ideologically
impeccable author broke out of the permitted framework. He went so far
beyond what was authorized that it was difficult to force him back within
the accepted framework. The fact that in his public statements Aitmatov as
a rule was almost orthodox in what he said and toed the official line made
the task doubly difficult. Having redeemed himself in this way and appeased
his guardians, he suddenly wrote the story "Farewell, Gulsary," which became a talking point across the country. Later he wrote "The White Steamer,"
which was a poetic and strictly truthful work about the demise among the
Kirgiz peasants of all that was really pure and genuine.

This was the first time Kirgiz literature had known a trouble-maker.
With Tvardovsky to launch him he became a writer with a wide readership
in the Soviet Union far beyond the confines fo Kirgizia.

Aitmatov is hated by the obscure Kirgiz writers who are propped up
by the local authorities. As he once said to me, his position in his homeland
is a complex one. He is also hated by the Moscow Russophiles for whom he
represents "alien blood." The fact that he has talent and courage is quite
enough to lead to attempts to banish him from the scene.

Aitmatov is middle-aged, with a strong athletic build—he is an excellent
skier—and has a quietly ironic manner. He pays little attention to the malicious attacks of the Russophiles and local Kirgiz "princes." He now has a
defender of some weight—his huge Russian readership, which runs into
millions and seizes with impatience on each new work he writes.

There is much lyricism in Aitmatov's writing. His lyricism, which at first pacified the powers that be, eventually came to provide a striking contrast with the base behavior of human beings in his stories. It did not matter that despicable behavior had reached such levels in the country because half of Kirgizia is made up of mighty mountain ranges and from the peaks of the Pamirs all "high positions" appear lowly.

Gulsary is the name of an old horse on which old Tanabay Bekasov, the story's main character, rides around shakily. Bekasov is a herdsman. Neither he nor Gulsary likes bridles and Aitmatov writes about this as follows:

> *Through his sleepy day-dream Gulsary suddenly heard the trees rocking and rustling as if someone had suddenly started shaking and knocking them over... Lashing rain came pouring straight down. The horse bolted away from its tether as if it had been struck with a whip and began whinnying desperately with fear for its herd. The timeless instinct to protect his own from danger had been awakened. Instinct called him to them to help them. Maddened with fear, he rebelled against being bridled, against the bit, against the reins which held him there so firmly...*

Tanabay, an honest and upright character, attacks the scurrilous chairman of the kolkhoz with a rake for letting the lambs die. The soul of honesty is thus expelled from the Party. They shout at him that his right place is in prison since he "hates our system and the kolkhoz" and various other things. The old man's fate, like the fate of his friend Gulsary, is to finish his days in the hands of a "knacker." He is flayed alive.

Like "Farewell, Gulsary," Aitmatov's story "The White Steamer" first appeared in *Novy mir*. It appeared to have a bright transparent quality about it. At a forest inspection post near Lake Issyk-Kul in Kirgizia live three families. The authorities are represented by the forest warden Orozkul. He has working under him an old man called Momun whose grandson is the main character. It is around this grandson that the story's poetry and pain revolve. As he walks along the boy talks to all his favorite rocks which for him are living things called Wolf and Camel, for instance. His favorite rock however, is called Tank, an unassailable boulder on the bank of the river. Some of the other rocks are hostile, cunning and stupid as well as kind, just like the plants which he knows as no one but a solitary country boy looking for friends around him can know them.

> *The spiny bodyak bush was his main enemy. The boy fought with it dozens of times a day. But he could see no end to the battle because the bodyak bush just kept growing and multiplying. By day, usually around midday, he liked to make his way into the thickets*

270

of thick-stemmed shiraldzhin plants. They were tall and had no flowers although they were strong-smelling. They grew in small islands all gathered in a clump, keeping other grasses at bay. They were his true friends. They were the best place to hide, especially if your feelings had been hurt in some way and you wanted to cry without anyone seeing you. It was hot and still in there. The best thing was that they did not cover the sky. The thing to do was to lie on your back and look at the sky. At first because of the tears you couldn't make anything out. Then clouds would come floating across making any shape high up in the sky that you could think of. The clouds knew you didn't feel too good and that you wanted to go away or fly away somewhere no one could find you and everyone would then sigh and exclaim that you had disappeared and where could you be found... And so that this should never happen and you should never disappear anywhere but lie quietly and admire the clouds, the clouds would turn into anything you wanted...

However, the boy has his enemies. The greatest is Orozkul, whose ill-feeling towards him has its source in the fact that his wife has not given him any children.

The boy is swimming in his grandfather's pond, dreaming of turning into a fish so that he can swim to meet the white steamer he caught sight of once on Lake Issyk-Kul from the top of the mountain. He lived in a fairy-tale world and this was why he dreamed of swimming off to meet the steamer. He wanted to be a fish "all over—his body, tail, fins and scales—only his head would stay his on its thin neck, big and round, with protruding ears and scratched nose."

But his favorite story is one his grandfather tells about the antlered mother deer. He tells how once upon a time only one boy and one girl were left alive after the Kirgiz had all been killed. When they were about to be thrown off a cliff as well, the antlered mother deer came to the children's defense. She begged to be given the children. "My udder is full. My milk weeps for children. My milk begs for children." She was given them and she took them to Lake Issyk-Kul. This was how the new race began which regards the antlered mother deer as sacred. The people then became rich and forgot the past. They even killed all the deer. They liked to decorate their graves with deer antlers. The antlered mother deer was deeply hurt at what the people had done and took her last young away from Issyk-Kul. That was how Momun finished his tale.

But that is not the end of the tale. Deer reappear in the mountains all of a sudden. Momun is convinced that it is the deer which saved Orozkul from disappearing in the river when he fell off his horse. While Momun is happy for him, Orozkul despises him for feeling happy over a fairy-tale.

Momun bears Orozkul's disdain without complaint and only rebels once. This is on his grandson's account. His grandson does not return from school at the usual time one day and Momun sets out to look for him on Orozkul's horse which he takes without asking permission. Orozkul cannot understand this kind of human impulse. He is a bad-tempered and cruel man and has more power than anyone else in the inspection post in the mountains. He decides to get rid of Momun. The punishment he thinks up for him is a terrible one—he makes him shoot deer, the deer from his own happy fairy-tale. He does violence to all that is sacred and poetic in the old man's life.

His grandfather's treachery is a great blow to the boy. He is called to a feast where he sees a pile of meat and huge branching antlers which could only be those of the antlered mother deer. Orozkul enjoys Momun's shame and kicks the deer's head with his boot. Momun, drunk and barely conscious, just mutters, his face spattered with the Mother Deer's blood.

The boy begins to feel sick. He feels as if someone is aiming an ax at his eyes. He quietly goes out in a fever and goes down to the icy river. "I won't come back," he says to himself, "it's better to be a fish, better to be a fish..." He swims away never to return. "There's only one thing I can say—you refused to accept what your child's soul could not live at peace with. This comforts me... As I say farewell to you, my boy, I repeat your own words: 'Hullo, white steamer, it's me...'"

This is how the story ends. Chingiz Aitmatov as a writer joined the ranks of Isaak Babel and Sergei Zalygin despite the real differences in their themes, poetic devices, imagery and narrative method. These differences notwithstanding, they are united by the bitter truth of their times: whatever is alive and pure perishes, while the forces of death and inhumanity triumph, mocking the cherished fairy-tales of childhood in which generations of us believed.

Aitmatov, together with other Kirgiz writers, is also co-author of the well-known play *Ascent of Fujiyama* whose themes are similar. It has been produced at the Taganka Theater in Moscow and in the West.

Although I have a great liking for Aitmatov, my affinity for Boris Mozhayev is even stronger. He is a somewhat dishevelled, thin man with the features of a Russian peasant and the large strong hands of a tractor-driver. He appears incapable of observing social graces either in the speeches he gives or in conversation.

A story by Mozhayev came out in *Novy mir* in 1966 (No.7) entitled "From the Life of Fyodor Kuzkin." In the manuscript form it was called "Zhivoy"—literally "The Living" but in context meaning "Still Alive." Even Tvardovsky took fright at this title because it sounded like a challenge to the dead and lifeless who were coming into their own in 1966, the year before the fiftieth anniversary of the Revolution. The non-people were polishing up their trumpets for the big occasion. It was impossible to get hold of a copy of the issue of *Novy mir* containing Mozhayev's story. It was no coincidence that the Taganka Theater under the director Lyubimov mounted a play based on Mozhayev's story and that it was very soon banned.

The ban was put into effect with great cynicism. All the Moscow region's leading workers and peasants were brought to the theater for a discussion. The most exact description of what happened came perhaps from the poet Vladimir Soloukhin in a speech he made at the discussion itself: "It is very hard to imagine but not impossible, all the same, mayors being invited to a discussion of Gogol's *The Inspector General...*"

Mozhayev has his own solution to the problems posed by the main theme of the age—the triumph of anti-life forces: he takes the theme and stands it on its head. His main character is Fyodor Kuzkin who comes from the country and is nicknamed "Zhivoy"—"Still Alive." Although attempts are made to kill him, to starve him and freeze him to death, he survives. He comes back from the war an invalid. Despite all the bullet-holes and shell-wounds he is still alive. He spends five years in a camp for "spreading anti-Soviet propaganda"—throwing the kolkhoz chairman over his shoulder. Not much attention is paid to the camp inmates' health yet he survives. Kuzkin takes a philosophical attitude to his misfortunes. As he sees it, all the family misfortunes happened on St. Frol's Day—his brothers died from drinking bouts on that day and he caused the death of his horse at a race meeting on that day. It did not matter what you did. St. Frol's Day always brought disaster.

With the arrival of the new kolkhoz chairman Guzenkov and the district chief Motyakov a particularly difficult period begins for Kuzkin. He takes an immediate dislike to the new arrivals, and especially to Motyakov who acts the big boss and "keeps you standing like a post while he stays seated."

He is released from the kolkhoz as a war invalid. He would like to go to the city with his family but cannot, "due to lack of resources," as he puts it in his application. He makes the most desperate and exhausting efforts not to starve. He finds casual work as a reaper. He goes off to mow distant fields together with his grandfather Filat, where he sings away merrily as if he did not have a care in the world.

Suddenly those in power take an interest in him because he is not paying his taxes. A commission arrives with great fanfare. It pokes into every corner and is shocked at what it finds. It has seen empty cottages before, but it had no idea that such crying poverty existed. It is quite simply at variance with all the official documents and statements. "Against the background of the general rise in living standards..." and so on. But here conditions are reminiscent of those which prevailed during the Leningrad blockade.

Still Alive is lively here too. "Excuse me," he says politely to the visitors, "but before you came we had pancakes and turkey but now we only have fever left." The members of the investigatory commission register their astonishment and drive off to enjoy their free meal, immediately forgetting all about Still Alive. He has to remind them. A new investigatory commission drives up bringing with it a life-saving gift of three sacks of flour for him and his many children. It also finds him a job looking after rafts. He appreciates the good turn that has been done him and during the breaking up of the ice on the river he saves the rafts from being swept away.

He is in a position to overcome his difficulties at last, but Motyakov, who is a thoroughly nasty piece of work and a representative of the anti-life forces, rings around to have Kuzkin fired from his job because he is an "escaped" kolkhoznik. He knows perfectly well that this is a lie and that he released Kuzkin as an invalid but he cannot forgive him his lack of respect. He telephones offices all over the district raising the alarm as if Kuzkin were an escaped convict. He then rings the shop and orders them not to sell him any bread. If the authorities can telephone a shop and issue instructions not to allow someone to buy bread there there would seem to be no limits to the power they have over individuals in Russia.

There are, however, a couple of catches. Firstly, not all instructions in Russia are obeyed. The Russian people has always been kinder than its leaders, especially the old women who have felt pity for and been responsive to those struck down by misfortune. Secondly, a desperate man is a very slippery character.

When Kuzkin learns that he is not to be given any bread, he angrily exclaims in front of Motyakov's wife: "Likes being the big boss, your husband does, Nastyonka. A real skunk!" Nastyonka, a soft-hearted woman who works in the shop herself, takes fright and tells Kuzkin not to say such things. He replies calmly: "Don't be afraid, Nastyonka. As I've said, we've got nothing to lose."

Kuzkin is caught out by the authorities when he plows up his garden, something only kolkhozniks are permitted to do. He is taken to court, but wins the case. Those around him are amazed at his capacity to emerge from any situation unscathed, always living up to his nickname.

Kuzkin is then moved to a job at a wharf on the river where he manages to exist until winter arrives. In winter his luck turns sour. He cuts switches for baskets. He can turn his hand to anything. While coming back from collecting switches he slips and breaks his leg. He crawls towards the village on all fours and during the night is found near a farmhouse with his head poking into a gateway. It is thought that he has frozen to death. However, when he comes to in the hospital the first thing he asks is whether his switches are safe. Despite the strength of the opposition—the district authorities with their huge administrative apparatus, the executive committee chairman Motyakov, the public prosecutor, the chief of police and all their financial resources—Kuzkin survives. He comes out of the hospital well and truly alive.

The irony is that while Kuzkin survives, the district does not. It is merged with another district and ceases to exist. Motyakov is left without a job and takes to going fishing. No work can be found to suit him.

A kind of victory has been won. Sitting fishing with Motyakov, Kuzkin starts to philosophize. "A hen was hatching some duck eggs. When the ducklings hatched they made straight for the water. When they swam off, the hen started cackling away on the bank. She couldn't swim but that didn't stop her from giving orders—do this, don't do that and so on. Well, that's what our bosses are like."

Kuzkin, standing for the forces of life, philosophizes about the evil anti-life forces yet the latter continue to grow and prosper like weeds. Such are the times Kuzkin lives in. Motyakov is appointed personnel supervisor in the very office where Kuzkin is earning his livelihood. Motyakov immediately orders the wharf Kuzkin is managing to be moved away somewhere else. Kuzkin has to move away too. However, he does not give in to depression but thinks to himself: "We'll live through it."

The last words in the story seem to be for the censor's benefit, an assurance that what has been related refers to the years before 1956: "After that things went more easily." Like his hero, the author Mozhayev is a survivor. He is made of sterner stuff than to give in to fear. For this reason these words are followed by a completely unambiguous sentence: "I would have tried to continue my story but it didn't work out..." The Taganka Theater's attempt did not work out either. The anti-life forces grow from strength to strength.

4. FYODOR ABRAMOV

The peasant writers give each other support, regardless of whether or not they have any liking for each other. If one gets stuck in a rut, another will take over his load. For some reason the Vologda region has made a greater contribution in this direction than any other.

The Vologda writers have been spoken of with respect for many years—and with some surprise. When the grain harvest fails, there seems to be a bumper crop of writers. Perhaps Vera Inber was right when she said in a moment of bitterness: "When things are really bad for us, we write good verse."

Yet it is strange that there should have been such a stream of highly talented and courageous writers from Vologda, some of whom had their writings published in Tvardovsky's *Novy mir,* Russia's best literary journal in the sixties.

After all, it is not only Vologda which has suffered from bad times.

Perhaps the first to throw some light on the mystery was the grand old man of Vologda writers Varlam Shalamov. In his samizdat story "The Examination" mentioned above he told about the "particular moral climate which was a step higher than in any other Russian city" in Vologda, where so many exiles had settled in tsarist times. It was in Vologda that the hostage system was, if not actually initiated, at least developed. Humanity's short memory later identified the system with Hitler.

When it was forced to undergo the most incredible upsurge of brutality and terror, it was silent and bore it. It knew the meaning of the Leninist variety of Shigalyovism which lashed it before other areas and the second generation produced Varlam Shalamov who was thrown into the Gulag for calling Bunin a Russian classic. How many more were thrown into the camps and did not have time to reveal themselves? The next generation produced Alexander Yashin, poet and author of "The Levers." Following closely in Yashin's footsteps came Fyodor Abramov.

Abramov has a hard, thin face. It is the unsmiling face of a forthright and abrupt man. I have not met Abramov often. He lived in Leningrad and only made visits to Moscow on business. In 1965 soon after my fight with the Central Committee Secretary Demichev he came up to me in the writers' establishment called *Dom literatorov,* shook my hand and introduced himself. This gave me great pleasure because I had followed every line he had written for a long time, in fact since 1956 when a critical article of his had appeared in *Novy mir.* It had been hard and intelligent like his face.

The critical articles appearing in *Novy mir* were subjected to official attacks, which after the events in Hungary became particularly menacing. Abramov disappeared. Consequently, when his novel *Brothers and Sisters* about the terrible years of famine in the countryside around Vologda appeared, and the later his novel *Two Winters and Three Summers* about the no less famine-stricken post-war countryside, I did not immediately connect the critic who had disappeared with the new writer who rapidly joined the ranks of the foremost "village" writers in Russia.

Abramov, a talented and honest writer, although not favorably regarded by everyone for reasons which I shall touch upon, became the people's true defender.

Abramov writes about the sufferings and ruin of the countryside and the moral impoverishment of the peasantry. The action of his best-known novel *Two Winters and Three Summers* takes place on the river Pinega in the village of Pekashino. This is the far north. In winter there is a "dull daybreak after ten in the morning." The war is over. The village people press close to each other to survive. The Pryaslins and Stavrovs have lived communally together for virtually the whole war. Mikhail Pryaslin is the oldest child in his large family although he is still not eighteen. The children do not remember their father. To them Mikhail is brother, head of the house and provider. Everything rests on his shoulders. The kolkhoz chairman Lukashin forces him to work on the timber rafting and at the other heavy jobs. Fortunately Mikhail and Yegorsha manage to bring in some autumn hay, otherwise things would have looked very grim indeed for the family.

One passage from the story should be sufficient for a clear picture of life in the Vologda countryside to emerge. Mikhail brings some presents home. He gives his sister Lizka some material for a dress, which makes her cry out with delight. "Petka and Grishka accepted their present of dark blue flannelette for some trousers with little reaction but when Mikhail pulled out of his basket a whole heavy loaf or rye bread they got really excited." This takes place in a village where from time immemorial the peasants have been farmers, raising animals and growing grain and flax, the most profitable crop in the north. Fedka is growing into a thief and has the ways of a wolf. "His bare cracked feet seemed forged to order—they were strong and thick and the toes were bent under—he walked with his claws out..." Fedka walks like a wolf. His eyes are ice-cold. "And suddenly these pieces of ice were ablaze: they saw the bread... The children caught their breath when he took hold of the loaf of bread. It had been many years since they had had such a luxury in the house..."

All their life the children have known nothing but hunger and brutality. They are forced to work on the timber rafting as if sentenced to it, and they have become used to it. Brutality and callousness become the normal condition of their lives. Mikhail, although he is only eighteen, is made to report to the district authorities to the effect that so-and-so "left the forest without authorization and went to the district hospital without a medical certificate." A more precise report is written to the effect that a former prisoner of war had deserted the forest front under the pretext of being ill. At district headquarters it is decided to cure him by calling in the public prosecutor's office. Three days later the "deserter" dies during an operation for cancer.

Even such incidents as this come to be regarded as normal, a part of everyday life. The novel contains many of them. Strange as it may seem this makes the novel difficult to read in some ways. The uniformly dark coloring of the details and descriptions creates a long drawn-out impression and makes the story-line appear loosely strung together. The overriding impression is of the Prysalins' poverty and the brutality born of poverty, of completely impenetrable darkness and the absence of the kind of deeply penetrating analysis which made Yashin's "Levers" such an incisive literary event. Even Lukashin, chairman of the New Life kolkhoz, is a martyr who suffers. The district authorities all rush about as if possessed. Who is to blame? It is up to the reader to come to his own conclusions.

It took years for Abramov to write his novel. Everything hung on it— the family finances, the life they led, the children's health. It was not right that it should then lie somewhere unpublished and unread.

Abramov is no cynic. I am quite sure that his ideas and his writing were not molded in any way by need or fear. Abramov is a "tough nut," as we say, and he stepped with conviction across the line less talented or less resilient writers could never breach.

However, it is by no means out of the question that the heavy blow he received in 1956 left its mark on him. The pain from blows of that kind lasts a long time, especially when the cudgels keep raining down for a long time and it is the whole Central Committee Politburo, in this case panicked by the events in Hungary, which is wielding the cudgels.

It is also possible that the writer's worst enemy, the so-called "inner censor," also made himself felt in Abramov's case. In the stories he had published in *Novy mir* there is not a trace of the dreary uniformity in tone of the episodes and details of *Two Winters and Three Summers.* One of these stories, which is in some ways an artistic masterpiece, is called "Pelageya." It was published in the sixth issue of *Novy mir* for 1969.

Firstly, however, I should like to devote some space to Abramov's sketch "Around and About." I was once asked to read the manuscript for some publishers. My reaction to it was so ecstatic that it was rejected. However to placate the author, my comments were sent along with the manuscript to Leningrad.

"Around and About" only appeared once in Russia (*Neva*, 1963, no.1). Here in a slightly abridged form is the first page of the sketch which is dedicated to the memory of "my brother Mikhail, an ordinary collective farm worker":

> *Telephone calls from the Party District Committee;*
> *First call:* "Anany Egorovich? Hullo, how are you? What's the good news? A lot happening, you say? Everyone out in the fields?

Fine, fine. And what about the silage?"

Second call: "I don't see any mention of the silage in the report. Your kolkhoz is holding back the whole district."

Third call: "Comrade Mysovsky? [A form of address which bodes ill.] What am I to make of your stubbornness? Is it sabotage? Or is it a case of bungling and not understanding a basic economic task?"

Anany Egorovich loses his patience: "Just who in the final analysis is running the kolkhoz? The Party has given the kolkhozes their freedom but you keep sticking your poke in..."

The decision: "Comrade A.E. Mysovsky, chairman of the New Life kolkhoz and member of the Communist Party, is to be severely reprimanded for failing to appreciate the political importance of the silage as the foundation of the fodder base for stock-raising on the kolkhoz...

This is the way the economy is ruined in Russia. It has been going on for almost half a century. It is no accident that an Army officer in the Caucasus I know of once agreed to take on the chairmanship of a kolkhoz "on one condition," as he put it: "that the Party District Committee should not assist me for three years."

The first to speak honestly and bitterly about the hardships the peasants endured was Fyodor Abramov, himself of peasant stock. And he did not so much speak about it as cry out about it for all Russia to hear. How did he manage it? He did not have recourse to the Aesopian method, although Aesop taught Soviet writers many profound lessons. Despite his desperation and his pain, he did not seek a round-about way of saying what he had to say. The following passage from Chapter Four of the sketch illustrates the new strategy which genuinely came from the people for saving themselves from death by starvation:

As he lit his cigarette with a match, Anany Egorovich turned his back to the wind and then suddenly straightened up. Three women were tramping across the yard behind the Voronitsyns' homestead bending right over the baskets they were carrying.

"Stop!" he shouted...

The women ducked around the corner of the bath-house.

Although he could not see where he was going, he rushed after them across the potato field to cut them off, leaping over the fence.

"Working, are we?" He was out of breath from running and fury.

The women did not say a word. They stood wet and blue, as if crucified, thrown back against the wall of the bath-house, looking at him stupidly. Their big wicker baskets, filled right to the brim with red and yellow mushrooms, stood heaped up at their feet.

"I said, working, are we?" he repeated.

"Well, we're not the only ones."

"Who wouldn't go mushrooming if it meant an extra kopek for the kolkhoz, Anany Egorovich?" said Arafena in a tearful voice.

"And where does the extra kopeck come from? Does it drop from the sky?

The women became bolder. "We've been hearing that for the last fifteen years. I spent the whole summer out in the fields and how much do you think I got for it?"

"And my kids have to go to school soon and I haven't got anything to put on their feet or their backs. Do you think we enjoy wandering around in the forest? Your teeth chatter with the cold, you're wet through and you just keep wandering around. If you sell a basketful of mushrooms to the store you at least have an extra kopek or two in the house.

"Do we have to eat them ourselves?" said Olyona Rogalyova, suddenly breaking into the conversation in a rude, high-handed fashion. "I've been two years without a cow and I've had a hard time of it. I thought now there's a good pile of hay where I'd get a cow. A fat hope I've got of doing that."

Obviously considering any further conversation useless, Olyona hoisted up her baskets whose handles made a squeaking sound and strode off, bent under her load. Her companions straggled off after her with hesitant steps.

Anany Egorovich bit his lower lip in indecision...

I remember that at this point in the manuscript the editor-in-chief put a mark in the margin and the head of the prose section, whom I had let down, scribbled like a lackey inside it: "Does serfdom still exist here then? Why make shortcomings appear typical? This episode to be rewritten."

Abramov did not rewrite a single line. Not one word was altered, despite the fact that on the following pages the editor's marks turned into exclamation marks, which meant that he was sounding the alarm. But Abramov had by no means completed his analysis—he was in fact only beginning it.

Abramov artistically portrays the woes of the peasants, reveals the causes of Anany Egorovich's cruelty and unbearable anguish, and then concludes the page with a sentence which has particular import: Anany Egorovich "went around the Voronitsyns' homestead out into the street in front." What sort of "homestead" is it that the chairman walks around trying not to be noticed—a chairman who was once as quick to take punitive measures against others as they were against him. Who is it that he does not dare reproach? Before whom is he guilty?

In this house lives a peasant who was once hard-working and then suddenly began drinking himself to death, the father of three hungry children.

Not finding him at home in the morning, Anany Egorovich asks his wife if her husband is ill. It turns out he is suffering from several seeks of hard drinking.

> *Anany Egorovich asked her as if in self-justification: "What money is he using? I haven't given him any."*
> *Polina snorted. "What money? For these damned drunkards communism arrived a long time ago. I swear to God it did. They go to the shop and say: "Manka, give me half a litre, will you, and just jot it down." And at the end of the month Manka comes round the village collecting what's owed. "You owe me ten roubles fifty kopeks, Polina," she says... "What for? When did I run up a debt?" "Your hubby got some wine and wanted to pay for it later." He took it, so you get the money from him, I tell her. Do business for cash, not the communist way."*

Life in this village either brutalizes people or empties them of all feeling. Although he has a sense of guilt without being actually at fault, Anany Egorovich, to whom nothing is new, does not have the strength to drop into the homestead. There the cycle of spiritual and physical ruin has been completed. There is no point in going into it any further.

This sketch, for all its unevenness, is incomparably more valuable than the mountain of books about the countryside which fill the stands in Soviet exhibition halls every year. Its value lies in the fearlessness of its analysis of conditions in rural areas, in the colorfulness of the dialogue and the raciness of the language of the Vologda countryside, not yet deadened by officialese.

At a recent International Book Fair in Frankfurt the Soviet stands were crammed with empty books with tasteless jackets from *Molodaya Gvardiya* publishers and barely a single collection contained any stories originally published in *Novy mir*. There were piles of brochures from Novosti Press Agency about detente, the rise in living standards in the kolkhozes and the machinations of the Zionists. There were also biographies of the Party leaders in deluxe leather covers. Everything was on display except the truth and those books which will always remain Russia's pride. Naturally, Abramov's sketch "Around and About" was not to be found on the Soviet stands. Nor were any of his best stories such as "Pelageya," which had been so thoroughly mauled by Soviet critics.

"Pelageya," which was passed for printing by Alexander Tvardovsky just in time, is one of the most significant works on the subject of Soviet rural life, although the countryside is by no means all it is about. Pelageya is a woman who works to the limit of her endurance and she is also head of the household. Her husband Pavel Amosov, the only one of four brothers to return from the war, is not long for this world. In order to have enough to eat, Pelageya gets a job in a bakery. It is hellish work, and the heat is insufferable. When she gets home from work she collapses on the bare floor to cool off. She feels that the wooden floor draws off the heat. She lies there motionless for five minutes or so with her eyes closed, wheezing and breathing with difficulty. It is only then that she turns to her sick husband and begins to ask him about domestic things. When she has finished, she gets up painfully, drinks five cups of sugarless tea and then begins to busy herself about the house.

On one such day her husband's sister Anisya drops in and invites them to a name-day celebration. Although it is close by Pelageya does not go. She does not have the strength. She does not go to her closest relative's, her sister-in-law's, but when Pyotr Ivanovich, an inspector and her superior, calls, she drags herself off there, even though she is ill and weak. Who will the guests be, she wonders. Firstly, the top brass will be there—"the chairman of the town soviet and the chairman of the kolkhoz, then the chairman of the central store and his accountant, then the manager of the forestry depot—he'll certainly be there, Pyotr Ivanovich's son works for him. Then there'll be the small fry—the power-saw operator, the loading machine operator, Antokha the stable-man..."

Pelageya mentally goes through all the guests wondering why each one would have been invited. But she still forces herself to go, because there is someone there she must talk to.

This party is reminiscent of a similar episode in Dudintsev's novel *Not by Bread Alone*. Drozdov, the manager of a very large factory, has a "gathering of guests." None of them are his friends, just highly placed bureaucrats, those in authority. But in Dudintsev's novel the subject was the disintegration of the bureaucracy and the emergence of the "new class" which has elevated its isolation from the common people to a principle of self-enrichment and power-wielding—a principle of its way of life. Following in Dudintsev's footsteps, the Soviet press was obliged to write about the degeneration of the new class from time to time. I remember the sensation caused by some sketches with expressive titles such as "Mold." The press touches on these topics when it is impossible to pass over them in silence, as for example when the sons of highly placed officials murder the daughters of highly placed officials and both sets of parents are equally powerful and the whole affair comes to the surface.

"Pelageya" tells a much more terrifying tale. Self-interest, callousness and heartlessness corrode the very bulk of the ship and not only the superstructure. They eat away at the very foundations, the lowest of the low who earn their livelihood by laboring in infernal conditions. These are the depths plumbed by State immorality and affected by spiritual degeneration in Russia.

"Pelageya" is basically about the collapse of moral principles, even at the lowest level among the common people. Although a relatively short story, it is utterly fearless in its forcefulness and the depth of its analysis, full of pain, anguish and tortured musings on the future of the country in which the good soil has been blown away by the wind, dried up and made infertile.

Pelageya herself does not come under these influences all at once. It is life itself which warps her. In order to secure a job in the bakery and not swell up with hunger, Pelageya, a woman of strict principles who hates her sister-in-law Anisya for chasing after anything in pants, is forced to swallow her pride as a woman and spend the night with Olyosha. Olyosha, who is chairman of the Workers' Committee, says that if she will spend the night with him a job at the bakery is hers.

Pelageya's daugher Alka has completely lost all idea of right and wrong. A calculating sense of self-interest is all that she has left. When some soldiers are held up for a while in their village, she immediately latches onto an officer—she does not even glance at the ordinary soldiers. She runs off with the officer on a ship without saying a word to anyone. This is the final blow as far as her father is concerned and he dies three days later.

Pelageya falls ill from all the misfortunes heaped upon her. She goes to the bakery where it is dirty and nothing is ever cleaned up. At this point she has to be put in a hospital. Pyotr Ivanovich, the inspector, visits her, as she thinks just out of kindness and to see how she is. How wrong she is. As it turns out, his visit is prompted by the fact that his son has fallen in love with her daughter Alka and ever since she ran away he has been drinking heavily. "Pelageya," he says to her in an anguished voice, "didn't I once come to your rescue? You remember, don't you?... Now you can come to my rescue... This boy of mine is going to pieces... Why don't you write to Alka... What about it?" (The officer has already thrown Alka over, as Pyotr Ivanovich has found out on the side.)

That night Pelageya dies. In the morning she is found on the floor where she used to lie "to cool off."

Alka does not even come to her mother's funeral. She arrives a week later, sells up all her parents' thing and dashes off again so as not to jeopardize her enjoyable and advantageous position in the ship's cafeteria.

After Vladimir Tendryakov in his story "Creature of a Day," Fyodor Abramov was one of the most profound writers on these themes. Tendryakov presented the basic themes rather differently—in his story a woman from a collective farm who is being pushed into being a Hero of Animal Husbandry is quite simply corrupted and made to lie. Abramov's Pelageya, however, has no heroic potential. She is not one of Khrushchev's rural "beacons." She is a very ordinary honest woman, the spiritual bulwark of her family and neighbors. Yet she succumbs. Her daughter, of course, does much more than simply "succumb." The times leave their destructive and permanent marks even on people such as these.

There is a folk saying in Russia that if a claw gets caught, the whole bird is lost. It is the epigraph of Tolstoi's play *The Power of Darkness.* Tolstoi's painful reflections are filled out in a new and frightening way by the artistic skill and honesty of Fyodor Abramov.

Those who are partial to seeing conflicts between writers have hinted at a hidden polemic in "Pelageya" against Solzhenitsyn's "Matryona's Home." The suggestion was made even more forcefully when Abramov became a leading figure among Leningrad writers (in other words, a man with Party contacts) while Solzhenitsyn was sent into exile and reviled in *Literaturnaya gazeta* as a "monarchist chauvinist fascist," an abusive description which at least made a change from the usual one of being a lackey of the British, Japanese, Germans, subversives etc., etc.

Does this hidden polemic really exist? Both Solzhenitsyn and his Matryona, with the strength their faith gives them reject the regime—admittedly not in identical terms, but they do reject it. Pelageya tries to adapt to it, saying: "You've got to live..." This is hardly a "polemic." If one were to suppose for a moment that Matryona heard about Pelageya, the only thing she would say would surely be: "May the Lord forgive her!"

Matryona was killed by a train moving backwards, that is, by times of heartlessness and blindness. It is these very same times which laid Pelageya out on her wooden floor, not so much on account of poverty and illness—she could have come to terms with them—as of the amorality of those she was forced to come into contact with.

5. VASILY BELOV

Vologda's next gift to Russia was Vasily Belov. His "Carpenter's Tales" were published in the seventh issue of *Novy mir* for 1968 and were read to the accompaniment of the tanks breaking up the cobbled streets of Prague. For this reason the impression they made was all the stronger.

A note of irony was perceptible from the very start and grew stronger with each tale until it became dominant in *Tall Tales from Vologda* which came out a year later.

In his "Carpenter's Tales" Belov appears to be telling the rather slight, humorous story of an everlasting argument between two old men from Vologda, Aviner Kozonkov and Olyosha Smolin. They recall seemingly by accident the lies and injustice which have surrounded them since they were small. One had his ear tweaked by a priest for his honesty. "You should have said 'I've sinned, father!' " he said to me, but I had told the truth—I hadn't climbed into anyone else's garden." For his honesty he had his ear twisted. While still a boy he walked a hundred and fifty kilomenters to the town to get his birth certificate and was sent home again with nothing to show for his trouble. "We've got no papers on you at all," he was told, "So you weren't born. You don't exist." The old men weave their tales one after the other until the expected blow-up comes and they lose their tempers.

Aviner Kozonkov, an old dried-up kolkhoznik, is telling one of his stories over a glass of vodka. He is talking about his life of ceaseless activity. I've got a good head for heights... They had this campaign against religion. Who did they send up the bell-tower to pull the bells down? Me... Up and up I crawled and got to the very edge where I relieved myself—from right up there on the bell-tower..."

After relating his exploits he asks the narrator who is also from Vologda, if he could be given a "special" pension for his work on the bells and the jobs he did with his revolver and so on. While bidding farewell to the narrator, the two old men come together and this time immediately start squabbling. Olyosha Smolin cannot forgive Kozonkov his bragging about his "gun toting youth." "Well, you were once a class enemy and you still are!" retorts Kozonkov, raising his voice. They they start fighting. "I wouldn't spare my own brother if it was for the good of the collective!" shouts Kozonkov, raising his voice. They they start fighting. "I wouldn't spare my own brother if it was for the good of the collective!" shouts Kozonkov.

The narrator feels to blame for the fight. He should not have stirred up old animosities. Finally he goes to see Olyosha. The two old men are sitting there drinking tea as if nothing had happened, chatting peaceably: "According to my reckoning the coffin will need forty-eight nails..." One of them places an order with the other: "Will you make me a coffin with lugs, which is better than with nails. With nails it's more solid." Then they start singing a long drawn-out ancient song. That is all there is to the story. It appears to be about nothing in particular.

Yet in fact it is about something very serious. It is about Russian history as perceived by those who are young. Why feel proud of knocking down church-bells and going around with a gun in hand? It is not all the same whether a coffin is made with nails or lugs? So much blood was shed in Russia—half the country was swimming in blood—and to what avail? It should not be forgotten that the story came out a month before Soviet troops invaded Czhechoslovakia, at a time, in other words, when the Kozonkovs in the Central Committee were still engaged in cutting down bells, although in this case the bells were called "socialism with a human face." The irony, as can be imagined, did not escape the readers.

A year later when the days of Tvardovsky's *Novy mir* appeared to be numbered it was no time to be so light-hearted.

At a time of misfortune and woe it is not permitted to write tragedies. In 1939, for instance, a year of mass terror, an argument took place in the Union of Writers on whether or not the tragic genre could exist under socialism. The newspapers reported the discussion. Learned debaters, trembling at every knock on the door, naturally were inclined to the opinion that under socialism the tragic genre would die out. Towards the end of the sixties it began to die out again.

If in 1964 a story such as Zalygin's "On the Irtysh" could be published, and in 1966 Babel's "Kolyvushka" could slip into print, in 1969, a fatal year for *Novy mir*, serious and tragic subjects could only be touched upon by giving the story a title such as "Tall Stories from Vologda, faithfully recorded by the author from the account given by Kuzma Ivanovich Barakhvostov the baker." The extent to which these tall stories are light-hearted nonsense is up to the reader to decide.

"My biography. 1. I was born—just in time for the redistribution of land. 2. I lie with my umbilical cord still untied. They're still wearing the thread... 7. The "wealth" is divided: Half a cow to me and half to my father." Things get worse. After the kolkhoz is formed, the narrator's wife does not let him into the house. "You can spend the night in any house you like. That's what the kolkhoz is for." The collective life of the kolkhoz begins. "It was at that time that we all experienced an upsurge in nervous tension."

Then comes an episode which seems utterly trivial, something on the level of a music-hall routine. It is called "A father-in-law gives good advice." "While the cow was being milked, she hit you in the eyes with her tail. My father-in-law said we should tie a brick to its tail so that when she swished it she would hit you over the head with the brick." Quite unexpectedly the narrator then says: "People are odd nowadays. If you tell tall stories they're all ears and believe you. If you start telling the truth no one listens to you."

Perhaps that tells us something about the nature of the supposedly "tall stories."

The kolkhoznik finds life a battle for survival. The peasant cottage is a scene of complete chaos: it is like the storming of Berlin and the raising of a public loan both happening at once. Hunting provides the only solace. Suddenly a bear looms. " 'Stop!' I cried out, 'A step to the left or right is an attempt to escape!' I offered him a bottle of vodka and he drank it. I asked him how he managed to sleep through the whole winter without eating, not needing any food. Tell me your secret, I said. I've got a big family, it'd be marvellous for us to be able to go to bed for the whole winter."

Some hunters arrive from the city and soon afterwards there is an announcement in the newspaper to the effect that the "predator has been destroyed." The narrator cannot believe that his bear was a predator.

He goes on to give a further account of happiness kolkhoz-style. "There are no reins," he is told at the office. You can't do anything without reins. Nothing can leave the kolkhoz or be brought in. "I immediately thought of using a cobweb. I pulled a cobweb off some bushes. Now you can go where you like, I said to myself, take your pick."

The narrator introduces a somber theme, to the "bright memory" of Nikita Khrushchev. "I decided to die. I arrived in the other world. They didn't let me in. I knocked hard. 'There's no room!' I wondered if I'd go to hell or paradise. 'You should read the newspapers, citizen,' they replied, 'there hasn't been any hell or paradise for a long time. There's been a merging of departments.' "

The next theme touched upon is even more somber. The tall story in question is called "I get rich." Barakhvostov goes to buy a conscience. No one has one. Finally he finds one which he puts in his bag and takes home. Once home he puts the bag with the conscience inside it down in the cellar where it has been lying now for almost three years.

This theme is associated with the October Revolution and executions without trial. In the words of the poet Blok, "I slept badly today, citizen,/ I exchanged my soul for kerosine." The baker Barakhvostov comes to the same point fifty years after the Revolution. This is how Abramov's sorrowful theme from "Pelageya" takes shape in Belov's story: conscience is stored in the cellar because it is not needed—even in a distant village in the Vologda district.

Novy mir waited for the telephone call which would give notice that steps were being taken to close it down. This is in fact the topic of the "tall story" called "The ending is well-known." A directive arrives from the regional headquarters to "stop the squandering of tall stories and to stop Barakhvostov." Officials arrive with witnesses. " 'The order has been given to inventory all your tall stories and to have them signed for.' 'What do you mean?' 'Don't spread private property around.' There was nothing I could do, so I surrendered them. Now I just sit at home in the evening in silence..."

At *Novy mir* they imagined that their own end would be similar. They would discuss it with a little smile on their lips. They avoided facing up to the fact that when officials arrive with witnesses on such occasions it is no laughing matter. A year later they were burying Alexander Tvardovsky.

Legally recognized literature was approaching its end. Soon even "tall stories" were not to be permitted. Soviet writers were to bury in the cellar everything of talent, just as Barakhvostov had done with his conscience, for the future of samizdat.

Lest the impression be given that Belov is of interest principally as a writer in the "comic tall stories" mode and that it was as such that he came into his own, mention should be made of his bitter and clever story "The Rogue." It is one of his realistic stories whose publication placed Belov among the five top writers of the middle generation bemoaning the fate of the Russian countryside.

The main character in the story is Senka Gruzdev, a cheerful, carefree young man and a war invalid. He used to love and sing the praises of his beautiful wife Tayka, but she became a burden to him. While he was away fighting, she bore him twins after "making merry" with one of the officials, as the narrator tells us nonchalantly. Senka is also unruffled. He is no fool and foresaw what would happen. When he was leaving for the front, he performed a lively dance beside the cart that was to take him away and sang the following ditty over and over:

> The road to the Red Army, boys,
> Is wide.
> Enjoy yourselves, girls,
> Until forty.

He accepts the children as his own, although quite often he would abuse Tayka for giving birth to twins instead of just one child.

Before a year is up Tayka again gives birth to twins, although this time they are Senka's own. One of them dies. However he still has two of his own—one was born before the war—and two from "higher up." So he has four mouths to feed as well as his wife and this is no easy task. It is almost impossible to get a family on its feet in such a situation.

One night Senka steals a sheaf of barley to spite Ilyukha the brigade leader. "He wanted Ilyukha to come in the morning and see that the sheaf was missing. He wanted to do something spiteful to the brigadier who took a count of all the sheaves before going to bed." This last clause is highly expressive. Because the story was written under conditions of strict censorship, it concentrates on the character of Senka without generalizing as Grossman did. What Grossman in "Forever Flowing" could describe in great detail—the famine organized by Stalin, the peasants dying off village by village, the terrible life that the peasants lived, forced to steal in order to stay alive—Belov says in one short clause. There can be no doubt about Belov's skill as a writer.

As far as Senka's family is concerned, the sheaf could not have come at a more opportune moment. After a little indecision, Senka steals another sheaf, and then two at once. "Then Senka really got going: he became adept at making off with anything he came across—if he happened on a stock of corn, then he took that, or if it was a sheepskin, he took that. He started to live his life according to the principle that everything should be common property. He also went about his thieving cheerfully and was never caught although everyone knew what a rogue Senka had become." Senka also stole for the kolkhoz—it might be a new horse-collar which someone had left lying around or a whole wood-sledge to which he would harness his gelding.

Both the brigade leader and the kolkhoz chairman just laugh and with an eye to thrift add the booty to the credit side of the kolkhoz accounts. Every time it is Senka they send out as head carrier with women and boys following him. The journey is a long one—seventy kilometers to the station with nothing to eat on the way. To keep his own spirits up against the fierce frost and those of the boy with him on his last trip, he sings a merry peasant song of the region. The song is about the Aleksandrovsky central prison standing "between two enormous cliffs, skirted by a big fence." As always, he steals whatever comes his way, such as hay for the horses—they have to eat too.

"Dear, oh dear, Senka, what a rogue you are!" sighs one of the women sent along with Senka, "Dear, oh dear, you mustn't take what belongs to other people. They'll have your head for it." "There's no 'oh dear' about it—it's the times," Senka answers good-humoredly and without further ado steals a goat from the very woman who has allowed them to spend the night in her cottage. "You stupid stinking thing," Senka says, turning on the goat. "You should've said you belonged here and not to somebody else."

"There's no denying it—if it hadn't been for Senka, Borka and the women would have had a terrible time in the city... The horses snort, the sledge-runners don't speak today but make a groaning noise instead and the weather has become slightly milder." That is the story's conclusion. It takes up only ten pages in *Novy mir*.

During the firing-squad years, Emmanuil Kazakevich expressed his deep feeling for the officer condemned to death by a military tribunal. Kazakevich was obeying the dictates of his heart in taking this tremendous risk to his own life. Different times threw up a different kind of criminal. They were still guilty without blame. Belov's true peasant heart made him return to this theme.

Russia's prisons never empty. Stalinism has long been a thing of the past, its true nature uncovered. Yet even according to one set of figures there are a million people in Russian camps. According to another set of figures there are four million. Having travelled through the heart of Russia in 1969-70, visiting such places as Vorkuta, Norilsk, Krasnoyarsk and the Ukhta mines which are worked by prisoners, I find the latter figure more probable. Who are these three or four million criminals on whose account another million young men have been torn away from their families and productive labor, mobilized into serving as "convoy troops"? They include people such as Senka Gruzdev, a rogue for whom the narrator has deep feelings of sympathy and who is likely to be turned into a hardened criminal or even a murderer under prison conditions.

It was subjects such as these that Vasily Belov, a worthy successor to the Vologda literary tradition, broached in the censored press during the years of the excesses of the triple censorship in force at *Novy mir*. During this period the censors displayed an almost frenzied vigilance. There is a local expression quoted in the story to the effect that "the wood didn't burn but just sputtered." When the authorities forbid the thought of the nation to "burn," all it can do is sputter. Then Belov's ruse is to strike a blow by means of a "nonsensical tall story," apparently in jest. People cannot be punished for telling jokes.

6. VASILY SHUKSHIN

In the wake of Vasily Belov's literary successes came other writers such as Andrei Bitov, Viktor Astafeyev and Viktor Likhonosov. There were writers from the Vologda region, from Siberia and from the Kuban all mourning the fate of the countryside. Those of their works published by the obscurantist publishing house *Molodaya Gvardiya* are by no means their best. These young writers' books seem less substantial than Belov's. The ideas to be found in them are less probing than in Yashin's works and the themes somehow more shallow.

This does not necessarily mean that writers are declining in stature. From year to year the authorities arrange their meshes of censorship more and more densely and cunningly like the barbed-wire on the borders with unseen signal systems and trap-like instructions. In important anniversary years the publishing houses are so tightly ringed with solid meshes of this kind that not only the larger fish but even the small fry cannot get throught. The major works stay hidden in desk drawers and this also applies to the younger writers. Naturally literature becomes impoverished and superficial but this does not concern State officials.

Some small comfort may be gained from the fact that talent is not drying up in Russia, at least so long as there is no mass terror campaign. Evidence of this can be found in the phenomenon of samizdat, although there can be little doubt that only a small percentage of what is written ends up in samizdat.

One man of unusual talent, Vasily Shushin, who recently died, deserves special attention. His death was untimely and, as anyone who knew him or heard about what happened to him is aware, it was not a matter of mere chance that he died when he did.

Shukshin's talent was many-sided. He was a gifted writer and film director whose last film, *Snowball Berry Red (Kalina krasnaya)*, caused quite a stir and seemed tragically to foretell his own fate. He was also an outstanding actor who appeared in many films the last of which was based on the work of Sholokhov.

An honest, sensitive, vulnerable man, Shukshin had hardly had time to make a name for himself when he fell into a fatal trap. Various unsavory types quickly made it their business to assure him that he was really one of them, a real Russian from the timeless depths of the Russian countryside, and to marry him off to Anatoly Sofronov's daughter. He was also quickly introduced to Sholokhov. This vulnerable, honest man found himself caught between publishing with Tvardovsky in *Novy mir* on the one hand and being associated with Sofronov in his domestic life on the other. At some level he clearly inclined towards Tvardovsky, but Tvardovsky was disposed of and his journal beaten into submission as it became yearly more loathsome to the Sofronov element. With whom was he to side? Life itself, which as everyone knows is controlled by the Cultural Section of the Central Committee of the CPSU, nudged him in the direction of the Sholokhovs and Sofronovs, yet his heart strained towards the truth. Not surprisingly, by the time he was a little over forty he had developed heart disease and suddenly died. This was the tragic fate of a gifted writer to whose best stories we shall now devote some well-deserved attention.

I first became acquainted with Vasily Shukshin as a writer through some stories of his published in the second issue of *Novy mir* for 1963. The language in the stories was rich and colorful but on the whole they were cautious. The author skirted around any themes which were dangerous. For example, in "Grinka Malyugin," from the cycle entitled "They're from the Katun" we have the account of an act of heroism on the part of Grinka Malyugin who is a tanker-driver. By driving his burning petrol tanker into the Katun river he saves his load of petrol although he almost blows himself up in the process. This story is little different from any in the stereotyped Komsomol series of the "Our Heroes" type. It is the sort of thing magazines for soldiers publish by the hundred.

There was another story from the same cycle, however, which showed vastly more evidence of talent. It is apparent on the basis of this story just how gifted and perceptive a writer Shukshin was, and how authentic his descriptions were, although he avoided touching on deep social issues. This story, which attracted wide attention, was called "A Top Class Driver." A driver called Pashka takes a liking to an impressive-looking, educated girl called Nastya. Nastya is being courted by a rather indecisive young engineer who never gets around to doing anything. Pashka does not find this out until later, however. Meanwhile he sits down next to Nastya at the club and says to her with fateful results in an unsuccessful attempt to sound like a man of the world: "How about a little "tête-à-tête"? "My God!" Nastya sighs and moves to the other end of the room.

However, Pashka is not the sort of man to back down, especially when he is the object of ridicule. That night he sets out to abduct Nastya. She has obviously very much taken his fancy. He climbs in her window and she realizes that it is not her engineer. She delivers Pashka a tremendous blow across the face.

Pashka is taken aback and starts walking backwards and forwards across Nastya's room. Being a man of action he then shouts at Nastya: "Let's go, then!" and drives her off at full speed to her engineer boyfriend's—right up to the front porch. He pushes her in the back, and says: "Go on, make love with him, damn you, if you love each other!" And then drives off, sighing heavily.

The Solzhenitsyn decade had had its effect throughout the whole gamut of Russian literature. Shukshin could not write in the old way either and became bolder. He did not allow himself to pass over what he had earlier passed over without a backward glance. The very next year saw the publication of two of his stories: "Venom" and "Styopka." In "Venom" a young man is trying to obtain some snake's venom to help his dying mother. He scours the whole town but no one will give him any. In the last chemist's shop he is also refused, although he tells them in his desperation that his mother is dying. He looks at the chemist and says without concealing his feelings: "But I need it! I won't leave without it, do you understand? I hate all of you, you swine." Then some is found.

"Styopka" is even less ambiguous than "Venom," although neither the narrator nor his main character says "I hate all of you, you swine." One fine dreamy evening, avoiding the main road, Styopka Voyevodin arrives at his family's house. He is back from the correction center. His mother and father are happy and his sister is beside herself with joy. The neighbors gather and a celebration ensues.

All of a sudden a militiaman appears. Silently he beckons Styopka over to him so as not to disturb the festive mood of the family, and takes him off somewhere. His sister is the first to realize that something has happened. She rushes off after her brother to the police station. The militiaman is making a report. He is amazed at Styopka's stupidity. It turns out that Styopka escaped from the camp only three months before the end of his term. He did three years of his term—probably for brawling, since the sentence was so light—and then made his escape. Now he will be given a new sentence for absconding and have to begin from the beginning again.

"Never mind," says Styopka, "I've got my strength up again. I can put up with being inside again now. It was just that I couldn't get away from these terrible dreams—I kept dreaming about my village, every night... It's good here in spring, isn't it?"

There are great depths of bitterness in this story and impotent imprecations against the idiotic practices of the camps which entomb a living soul whether it is necessary or not. Even if a man becomes a saint, this is of no interest to anyone.

Even in 1967, the fiftieth anniversary of the Revolution and a fateful year for Russian literature as we shall see, Shukshin's "New Stories" are full of the most serious themes. An example is provided by the story "In Profile and en face." Ivan, who works as a driver, loses his license for a year. He starts drinking and making preparations to go away. His mother cries and tries to talk him into staying but he still leaves, although it is hard to part from his mother, his home and his dog. In fact he is himself pushed out like a dog. Just before he leaves he has a serious conversation with an old man who offers him some home brew since he's "such a fine lad," even if disrespectful towards authority.

"Life brings you no happiness," Ivan says to him. "Well, have you had a good life?" The old man is silent for a long time.

"When I was your age that isn't how I thought," he says quietly. "I was too busy doing the work of three people. The amount of grain alone that I grew!... Taken altogether you could feed the whole village for a year on it. I didn't have time to think like that."

"But I don't know what I'm working for," Ivan answers him. "Do you see what I mean? I got this job and I work, but if you asked me what for, I wouldn't know. Is it just to have enough to eat and drink? Well, I've got enough to eat and drink. Now what?... I just feel sluggish inside." The old man's explanation is that the young have grown too fussy. (This, by the way, is the explanation constantly voiced by the Central Committee's propaganda machine, all the newspapers and political instructors. Party thinking seems unable or unwilling to rise above this level. The old man is of no small significance in the subtext.)

Ivan sighs. "You've got to realize that you had no scope to do anything, so what you had was enough for you... You were living in the dark. I could live the way you did but I need something more." The old man gets angry. "You can't be bothered working for fifteen hundred a month while I broke my back all summer to earn that sort of money."

"But I don't need that much money... Can't you understand that? I need something else... As I said to you, I've got enough to eat. Now what? I don't know. But I do know that I don't like things the way they are..."

The same tone is dominant in "Thoughts," a story about an old kolkhoz chairman, a practical hard-working man whose life contains little joy— just drudgery on the kolkhoz. He abuses Kolka Malashkin for wandering around at night playing the accordion and disturbing his sleep. "Tomorrow I'll kick you out of the kolkhoz," he would say but he never does. The accordion brings back memories of a time when he was happy. He was riding his horse hard to fetch some milk for his dying brother. It was as if he was flying. "It was the longed-for moment of uncontainable joy. This was the memory the accordion evoked, as well as thoughts about what love can be like. But the rest of his life had been just work, work, work..." Then Kolka gets married and his accordion falls silent. The village becomes terrifyingly quiet.

At last a motif was found or perhaps suggested, which would satisfy on the one hand the former Smolensk peasant Alexander Tvardovsky whom the authorities had firmly in their sights and on the other hand the Sholokhov-Sofronov Mafia, whose thinking was a distillation of vodka and pogrom ideology. This was the anti-urban motif. Things were bad in Russia. However, this had nothing to do with the power structure or the regime itself and Stalinism was a thing of the past. What was to blame was the city, the accursed city, with its petty intelligentsia and its know-alls who were destroying the age-old rural way of life.

In Shukshin's stories published in 1970 (*Novy mir*, No.7) when Tvardovsky had already been dismissed, anti-urban motifs almost completely dominated his narrative, squeezing out the word of in-depth analysis which had been characteristic of his approach in his earlier works. In the story "Cutting Them Down to Size" ("Srezal"), for example, the main character is called Glep Kapustin. He is a thick-lipped, tow-haired peasant of forty, well-read, spiteful by nature and busy nursing his pride. His diversion and even mania is to cut his highly placed fellow villagers now living in the city down to size. When they come back, now colonels, pilots, doctors, and newspaper correspondents, and start telling their wondrous tales and answering the questions of their former fellow villagers who have come crowding into the cottage, Gleb Kapustin starts trying to catch them out and cut them down to size in the presence of all the honest folk there. Yet his merciless demagogy and ability to strike his opponents dumb with clever chatter— to "mow them down" as one of the characters puts it—have their origins in the city, in city meetings and city newspaper articles which Gleb has avidly lapped up in order to be able to stun the peasants. This then is the obnoxious calamity afflicting the countryside, something it had always been free of. The delusions of the city, in the guise of a new morality, sow the seeds of evil and bring misfortune.

This theme is also forcefully treated in the story "Matchmaking."

> *Old Glukhov lost three sons in the war. On 9th May, Victory day, the village would gather at the cemetery and the chairman of the village council would get up on a stool and read out the lists of the fallen. Among the multitude of others he would call out "Vasily Emelyanovich Glukhov, Stepan Emelyanovich Glukhov, Pavel Emelyanovich Glukhov." As the names of his sons were read out, the old man always felt grief gripping his throat with its hard fingers and found it difficult to breathe...*
>
> *People wept quietly at the cemetery. They really did weep quietly, into corners of shawls, into their palms, as if they were afraid of disturbing or offending the dignified silence so necessary at that moment...*
>
> *It was then that [Glukhov] noticed old Otavina in the crowd. She did not come from their village although she had lived there for a long time. Glukhov knew her. No one belonging to Otavina was in the list but she was weeping quietly and crossing herself together with everyone else. Glukhov respected religious people... for their endurance and steadfastness. He looked intently at Otavina and wondered whether he should marry her. It wouldn't be such a hardship. When you died, there'd be someone to bury you... And she wouldn't mind living somewhere cosier. Her own cottage was in a terrible state—a real hovel.*
>
> *Glukhov decided to have a talk about it with the widow of the commissar Malyshev. She had done some travelling with her husband and knew something about the world, and occasionally old Glukhov,*

297

after he had buried his wife, would sit with her on her verandah drink-ing tea with honey he had brought in a birch basket.

He didn't think there was anyone closer to him. He'd ask her advice... She invited both Glukhov and Otavina and then disrupted everything with a few malicious, sanctimonious words: "What sort of example are you setting for the young? Don't you understand your responsibility to the people?... You're being selfish. People are working hard without sparing themselves while you're amusing yourselves plot-ting a wedding."

"Who mentioned a wedding?" said Glukhov, trying to make her see reason. "We'd just move in together quietly and that'd be all. Who's talking about a wedding?"

"I see—like a naughty escapade, then. Pah!"

At this Glukhov flares up in anger, swears roundly at Malysheva and walks out slamming the door. His marriage plans have been shattered. If it weren't for the poison from the city seeping through, a couple of fine people could live out their days quietly, like two ordinary people, helping each other in lonely old age. In each successive story the accursed city poi-sons the Russian countryside with deceit, demagogy, hypocrisy, dead "norm-ative" morality and inhumanity. Yet deep in the subtext there may be found attempts at analysis and broader perspectives which question whether the city is actually to blame, and whether the city itself might also be suffering.

When he had his short tale "Mitka Yermakov" published, Shukshin appeared to be suddenly having second thoughts. In this story Yermakov lives beside Lake Baikal and one day sees some tourists standing at the edge of the lake resting and arguing in a learned way about something. Yermakov despises them. "These bespectacled types, all highly educated, read masses of books... standing around talking about how strong they are. But if one of them were pushed into the water, he'd be making bubbles all in no time. Their glasses would float longer than they did." Although it is only five degrees in the water and the water is choppy, Yermakov decides to demon-strate his peasant's daring and dives into a wave with a cry of bravado.

He keeps shouting out like this until he starts swallowing water because his mouth is open. He then has to shout out something rather different: "My trousers have come off! I'm drowning!" The bespectacled city folk save him by catching hold of him by the hair and rowing him in to shore. If it had not been for the despised, bespectacled city types he would have drowned.

This story provides some sort of key to the real Vasily Shukshin. This Shukshin seems to be winking at his city friends and saying: don't think that I blame you. I wrote like that for another reason—force of circumstances.

Alexander Bek wrote about such circumstances—which are unfortunately met with quite frequently by Soviet writers—in his story "A New Appoint-ment," which has been published in the West. Describing the misfortunes which befall his hero who thinks one thing, feels another and acts as he is instructed to act, Bek diagnoses his ailment as a clash. There is a clash be-tween his feelings and his sense of duty, his conscience and his calculations. Bek's hero dies through a clash, as did Bek himself after sending his manu-script to the West, unable to withstand the constant fear which began to accumulate around him. The heart says one thing and the head another. This is a clash.

It was from just such an inner clash that Vasily Shukshin died. He was a far-seeing, sensitive and nervous man. The Sofronovs and Sholokhovs killed him with kindness as they corrected the line he took. He himself felt that the vodka-sodden literary Mafia would finish him off eventually. It was no accident that his Mafia killed off the leading character in the film he had made just before his death, *Snowball Berry Red* which he scripted, directed and acted in. His hero broke free and escaped to the wide spaces of the countryside yet always felt a knife held over him. He waited for the knife to strike or the shot to ring out. Shukshin died at the age of forty-five, at the height of his powers and in the full flowering of his creative ideas, as was pointed out in numerous obituaries.

In the light of what has been said about so-called village prose here, the place of Vladimir Soloukhin in this stream must be obvious. Soloukhin is a sleek, well-fed man from the Vladimir district who loves to stroll around the writers' rest houses wearing enormous felt boots and a rustic sheep-skin coat à la russe, making a point of speaking with a northern accent, emphasizing the fact that he was, is and will remain a man with his roots in the Russian countryside. This undeniably talented writer is above all concern-ed with monuments of the distant past which are disappearing even in his native village near Vladimir. He makes only passing mention of his fellow villagers whether in his verse, his prose or in conversation. People seem very temporary inhabitants of the earth while these monuments of the past are somehow timeless. It is difficult to judge whether his particular talent is the result of some peculiar specific quality, hardness of heart or at least some lack of feeling. Whatever the truth of it is, the fact is that the misfortunes of his village in the Vladimir district which for years was half-starving and dressed in rags, in no less pitiful condition than the Vologda villages, did not become a leading motif in his works. Other writers have appeared on the scene to sing the praises of the countryside who are younger and energetically supported by the Komsomol Central Committee—people like Firsov and Lystzov who are always giving voice to the "age-old peasant" element, and Chuyev who wrote: "Return Stalin to his pedestal,/ We young people need an idea..."

This is why it seems to me that a carefully thought out selection of names of talented writers is so necessary at this point, writers who represent genuine Russian literature, and genuine peasant prose in particular: Alexander Yashin and Vladimir Tendryakov, Boris Mozhayev, Fyodor Abramov, Vasily Belov, Vasily Shukshin and those who followed them writing of the miseries of the countryside, sharing its pain, its deprivations and its cares.

Because the times allowed them to do so, it was these writers who broadened and deepened the first furrows plowed by Babel in the thirties, and later by Ovechkin, Troyepolsky and Dorosh, writing about the ruin wrought on the countryside by Stalinist policies and then the utter devastation caused by the war. Ovechkin, Troyeposky and Dorosh all did what they could and at times even went beyond what they had the strength to do, which led to Ovechkin's attempted suicide and Dorosh's early death.

The writers who took their place proved worthy of them and even more talented. In Russia there is neither shortage of talent nor shortage of hangmen.

7. THE HATCHET-MEN

The literature describing the misery in the countryside was subject to the same punitive campaign as the countryside itself. The greatest loss suffered by contemporary "village" prose was the early demise of Isaak Babel. For almost 30 years no one knew the real cause of his death.

In this connection, whenever he could, Konstantin Paustovsky would repeat his saying about Nikulin being Cain. Other writers did not altogether believe Paustovsky in this case. It was all too easy to accuse a colleague of murder. History would decide who was Mozart and who was Salieri. However, when Yuri Bondarev's story "Quietness" came out, the ageing Lev Nikulin immediately reacted with a denunciation running into many pages which he sent to the Central Committee and the KGB. Since times had changed, and it was a period of anti-Stalinism, his denunciation was shown to Bondarev. Now even the most cautious were convinced that Paustovsky was right about Nikulin. As soon as Nikulin appeared anywhere, the conversation would instantly shift to sporting or gastronomic topics. When his novel which was patriotically entitled *True Sons of Russia* came out, the following verse made the rounds of the Union of Writers:

> The most boring book without a doubt
> By the stooge Nikulin's just come out.
> All sons of Russia who are true
> Must read both volumes—right through.

> (Nikulin Lev, stukach-nadomnik,
> Skuchneyshy vypustil dvukhtomnik,
> I eto vse chitat dolzhny
> Rossii vernyye syny.)

However, as time was to show, Nikulin's denunciation of Babel was nothing more than a convenient pretext for dealing with Babel. It was not a matter of "foreign contracts" or of his friendship with Marshal Tukhachevsky—he was friendly with a number of writers. The point was that there was not room for both Babel and Sholokhov. If Babel's "Velikaya Krinitsa" had formed part of the literature of the thirties, then mendacious works of the type Sholokhov's *Virgin Soil Upturned* could not have appeared. "Kolyvushka" alone, which was just one chapter of "Velikaya Krinitsa," by the mere fact of its existence, would have cancelled out all Sholokov's fabrications with all their idiotic Shukars and given the lie to Stalin's historical opus "Dizzy from success," which brought such joy to the peasantry.

It was a clash of genuine literature on the one hand and anti-literature on the other supported by all the might of the State. The fate of Russian literature had been decided beforehand.

The obliteration of "Velikaya Krinitsa" and its author gave the green light to falsifiers of all stripes who then glorified the peasants' savior, their beloved leader leader Joseph Vissarionovich Stalin. Then a great wave of dirt and mud came flooding along the canal dug by Sholokhov, especially after the war. It consisted mainly of the type of thing churned out by Babayevsky which amazed the critics by its artful juggling with the facts and its utterly standard treatment of the subject-matter.

The critics had good reason to be dumbfounded. It was a resolution of Zhdanov, Secretary of the Party Central Committee, actually drafted on one of Babayevsky's manuscripts which gave the go-ahead for the standard falsifying work *Cavalier of the Gold Star*. This was the resolution to "obliterate" Zoshchenko and Akhmatova and at the same time to give Babayevsky enthusiastic support. Zhdanov was consistent if nothing else.

Not long after the death of Stalin and the Central Committee plenary session establishing that there were fewer cows in Russia than under Nicholas II, an article appeared in *Literaturnaya gazeta* virtually demolishing Babayevsky and all his works which had been full of glowing pictures of rural abundance. Later, at a meeting in Fyodor Panfyorov's office at *Oktyabr*, I learnt what Babayevsky's reaction had been. He threw the issue containing this article aside and said with sinister overtones through clenched teeth: "They'll answer for this with tears of blood. They'll publish me again, you'll see! In a gilt-edged edition." These hatchet-men were convinced that the need for them would not lessen.

The flood of works by writers of Sholokhov's and Babayevsky's ilk which cut off all paths leading to the truth about the countryside and then drowned it and washed it away, did not have merely a literary significance, strange as that may seem. Fyodor Abramov, one of the most trustworthy writers, writes about this in "Around and About." The women who have been picking mushrooms make off without waiting for Anany Egorovich to finish speaking.

    Anany Egorovich bit his lower lip in indecision. He should chase after and catch those women, tip over their damned baskets and march them straight off into the fields by the scruff of the neck!

    Eight years or so earlier there is no doubt what he would have done. There were examples to follow both in life and in literature. The story was told in one book, for instance, of how a kolkhoz chairman went about catching some obstinate farm workers while they were away from the village, and how another chairman took even more severe action, breaking into a cottage one morning and pouring water over the stove. Books such as these were used as weapons in the district. "That's how to do things," the district committee secretary would instruct the kolkhoz chairmen, taking the opportunity to make some reference to examples from literature. "Yet you bunglers can't even deal with women."

Yes, eight years earlier Anany Egorovich would have given those mushroom-pickers the fright of their lives. But now...

The "examples from literature" had been approved by Stalin and Zhdanov personally, as every single Party worker knew. It is possible that the uniformed hatchet-men and the literary hatchet-men never formed such a united front as in those years.

It is not difficult to imagine how many young writers' names they erased and how many talented books remained in their authors' desk drawers because of them. Editors-in-chief have consultative meetings in the Party Central Committee not once a year or once a month but every week. Every week these editors synchronize their watches, so to speak, as if they are about to launch an attack, and like wartime officers they are subject to certain threats. At one of these meetings of editors in the Central Committee Yakovlev, deputy chief of the propaganda section of the Central Committee, turned to the editors and exclaimed menacingly: "We'll shoot anyone in the back who tries to leave the trenches."

There is no need to examine here the Party machine which is on a higher level than Glavlit, the chief organization for protecting State secrets in the press, being attached to the USSR Council of Ministers. No one dares bypass Glavlit in giving permission for something to be published. Even Khrushchev who took the greatest possible liberties in what he did, only did so when forced to. In order to have Tvardovsky's long poem "Tyorkin in the Other World" published after it had been rejected by Glavlit, all-powerful Khrushchev passed it on to his son-in-law Adzhubey who was at that time editor-in-chief of *Izvestia*. Newspapers are subject to a different censorship body. Khrushchev was not able to beat Glavlit, so he cunningly bypassed it.

I have before me documents detailing what has been totally banned in literature in recent years. In 1971, for example, a censorship circular was sent around to all publishers, marked of course "Secret," adding the following subjects to the long list of those which could not even be mentioned in print: 1. 1937 (that is to say, Stalin's arbitrary rule); 2. prisons (that is to say, arbitrary rule today); 3. pollution of the environment.

To this rather vague document were attached new blacklists of writers. There was one list of writers who could not even be mentioned in print (of whom I noticed I was one), and another list of those who were to be penalized only in part—they could be printed but not under any circumstances mentioned in reviews or articles. Writers were also divided into those who could travel to capitalist countries ("vyezdnye") and those who were not to be allowed so much as to approach the border ("ne vyezdnye").

In addition, there are masses of circulars ordering the suppression of individual writers, indicating that the books of such and such a writer should be taken out of circulation. The instructions may run into several pages. Everything is subject to confiscation without recourse to legal processes and without trace—whether it be a novel published in 350,000 or 400,000 copies or a poem several hundred copies of which have been run off on a duplicating machine. It does not matter whether the material is in Russian or a foreign language. Fortunately Glavlit's power does not yet extend to libraries in Paris or the Library Congress in Washington, D.C. However, everything else is "scraped clean," as Russians say. Librarians who do not make haste to remove these books are dismissed and deprived of the right to work in any area connected with ideology or culture—they are "shot in the back."

There are yet other means of banning books with deadly effect. One book may be only read under supervision in a library, another may only be read with special authorization, another may be said to be "out" or "at the binders." Another method is to set aside two hundred copies of a book for Moscow, just to avoid possible scandal, and to pulp all the other copies in the edition. The order to pulp them is however marked "Secret."

Sometimes the opposite approach is cynically practiced. When Ivan Shevstov's book *In the Name of the Father and the Son,* written in the spirit of the crude anti-semitism of the Black Hundreds *(Moscow 1970)* came out, a scandal ensued which worsened when passages from the book were published in the Western press. The French and Italian Communist Parties started to ask questions of the Central Committee in Moscow. Then the Central Committee made a statement to the effect that the book had been taken out of circulation. It had indeed, but only out of the central libraries in Moscow. If you cared to go twenty kilometers outside Moscow you could buy copies of the book by the truckload. In fact, while working on my novel *Hostages,* I went to districts just outside Moscow and bought all the anti-semitic literature I needed, from historical texts to the most recent such as Kichko's and Shevstov's books which officially had been removed from circulation. These, then, in Pushkin's words, are the latest grimaces made by "the foolish, pious old woman of Russia's prim censorship." Over a century there were some important changes, However. The "foolish, pious old woman" was no longer pious or foolish. She became a murderer of the most refined cunning, hunting down all those who thought "differently."

The censorship machine is essentially a departure of the KGB. It is no coincidence that many of the Glavlit chiefs, such as its deputy head Nazarov, are former GPU and NKVD thugs. Formerly they shed the blood of innocent victims, deporting people by the village, by the district and even by the republic, while now, not through fear but as a matter of conscience, they are doing all they can to suppress the slightest mention of what they did in literature.

One might well wonder how it was that the faceless bureaucracy which at times was afraid of even a shadow of responsibility could bring a halt to the very flow of literature. How could it stop this flow of molten lava which as time was to show destroyed everything in its path? During the war in a village near Moscow I was told that while it was possible to hide from the German punishment squads—the SS and Sonderkommandos—it was impossible to escape the so-called Polizei or collaborators. The Polizei was your neighbor, someone from your own village who knew everything and everybody. He would track you down in the end. It is by precisely this kind of literary Polizei—from the same literary village—that literature has been persecuted over the last quarter of a century. Although their names occasionally appear in newspaper reports, all these Baruzdins, Alekseyevs, Stadnyuks and Ananyevs remain essentially nameless. Even names such as Sofronov and Gribachev, household words for many years now, are usually linked as one word because individually they sound strangely blank.

It is naturally the older generation which heads the march. At present their leader has life tenure. It is Mikhail Sholokhov who screams his orders at hatchet-men, mocks and pulls at his yellowish moustache. When others cannot manage, it is Sholokhov, the winner of the Nobel and various other prizes, who is called upon to flush out and eradicate divergent thinking. As is well-known, it was Sholokhov the "humanist" who demanded that Sinyavsky and Daniel be shot "on the basis of revolutionary justice" and would doubtless have had Solzhenitsyn shot without any reference to concepts of justice at all, since Solzhenitsyn had the audacity to question his authorship of *Quiet Flows the Don*. How this "humanist,"as he styles himself, would have dealt with Isaak Babel if he had had his way can be left to the imagination.

There are just two questions which remain to be answered. Firstly, how is it that the members of the "Red Hundreds," as they have come to be called, infiltrated with such ease into every nook and cranny of Russian literary life? They have become editors-in-chief, secretaries of organizations, official ideologues, established orators at conferences—in other words "true sons of Russia" armed to the teeth with all the right philosophical terminology and traditions of State. As soon as these ideologues of the "new culture" are given the signal, they appear, ready for action, with briefcases in their hands, like twentieth-century equivalents of Chernomor from Pushkin's *Ruslan and Liudmila*.

The question concerns the political, philosophical, national and psychological causes underlying their rise to the positions they have been firmly entrenched in for so many years. I shall attempt to trace the historical sources of the so-called ideological base on which the State has succeeded in legitimizing the existence of the Red Hundreds at the head of Soviet literature and turning them into a battering-ram to smash artistic talent in Russia. We shall work our way down through the years from the modern period to the distant past—Russia's subterranean depths.

1. The Red Hundreds armed themselves with the ideological heritage of the Black Hundreds of the Union of the Russian People and the Union of the Archangel Michael. It could be said that the stream of openly inflammatory literature over the last decade, seen in the books and pamphlets of Ivanov, Shevstov, Sakhnin, Kolesnikov, Begun and others, simply reiterates and dresses up with new examples the basic attitudes of the ideologues of the Black Hundreds. The lengths to which the modern Russian chauvinists have gone was proved at the 1973 Paris trial at which it was shown that the text of a chauvinistic article in the Bulletin put out by the Soviet embassies in Paris, London and Rome was identical with the text of the fourth edition of a viciously inflammatory pamphlet by Rossov published in St. Petersburg in 1906. The organizers of the latest hysterical outburst of chauvinism in the seventies simply took a photocopy of the yellowing pages of the Union of the Russian People pamphlet and passed it off as the very latest achievement of Soviet historical thought. In passing sentence, the court at the Paris trial in April 1973 caught the Soviet racists red-handed, something which had never happened before.

2. Another source of ideas for the Red Hundreds was the so-called anti-nihilist novel of the 1860s and 1870s. These works were for the most part published in Katkov's journal *The Russian Herald (Russki vestnik)*. The literary hatchet-men of the last century looked for the cause of all uprisings and disturbances in Russia, including the Pugachev revolt, in a "perfidious Polish plot." This was the stand taken by almost all patriotic writers such as Krestovsky, Count Salias and Boleslav Markevich, whom Chekhov once called "a police writer." According to Count Salias, for example, Pugachev was incited to revolt by a certain "half-blood, the grandson of a nihilist and a Polish woman called Ludwiga." When the valorous patriot Prince Danilo Khvalynsky in Salias' novel *Pugachev* meets the Pole Jan Brzezinski he threatens to punish him in the most degrading way possible—"to whip him to shreds in his own house like a yid." People of mixed descent and foreign blood have always presented the main danger to Russia in the writings of the Saliases in every epoch. This is a theme we shall return to. Was it not indeed a Persian princess who incited Stenka Razin to revolt?

3. The Red Hundreds' traditions find sure support in the ethical criteria of those of their predecessors who actively came to the defense of the throne, the police censorship. Notably among them were Faddey Bulgarin (1789-1859) and Nikolai Grech (1787-1867). Grech, for example, once wrote a denunciation of the journal *Annals of the Fatherland (Otechestvennye zapiski)* which was rejected at the highest levels. Bulgarin then rushed to Grech's aid, writing nothing less than a threatening letter to the tsar: if his

letter were not drawn to the tsar's attention, or if the tsar failed to answer it, then he, Bulgarin, would turn to the King of Prussia for assistance with the aim of having the King of Prussia inform Nicholas I of what Bulgarin himself wished to bring to his attention—in the name of defending the monarch and his realm.

Although he was not, of course, aware of it, being an exceptionally ignorant man, the writer Mikhail Bubenov, an abjectly loyal Soviet citizen, later acted exactly as Bulgarin had. He once wrote to the Central Committee saying that if they did not take steps against "Jewish domination" of Russian literature he would turn to "international public opinion" for assistance. Of course, Bubenov did not specify whom he had in mind when he spoke of "international public opinion."

The second question must still be answered. There are now more than eight thousand writers in the Union of Writers. Of those at least one thousand have some genuine writing ability and are therefore adversely affected and stifled by Glavlit and the literary hatchet-men. Why is it that under an avowedly elective system the same old faces appear more firmly entrenched with each passing year in the key positions? I remember an incident during some elections held in the mid-fifties when a bogus ballot-box was found hidden behind a door-curtain filled in advance with voting papers on which all the obscurantists had been voted for. Such a scandal broke out that the contents of the box were disregarded when the votes were counted. In 1957 they got by without tampering with the ballot boxes. This was the year of the massive influx of bureaucrats of all sorts into the Union of Writers, from those working in military publishing houses to those working on newspapers, foremost among whom was Yuri Zhukov from *Pravda*.

In the sixties came a variation on the theme. I have in my possession an interesting document recording the results of votes cast in secret ballot at a straightforward, democratic Union of Writers election. It was an election of officers to the governing body of the Moscow writers' organization. Not one of the nonentities, some of whose names are mentioned above, was voted for. The poet Sergei Vasilyev, the Party-affiliated critic Barabash and the literary scholar Dymshits received even fewer votes than one *litterateur* who was an acknowledged informer. Even those we termed collectively "the swamp"—those who would vote for anything or anybody—voted against the nonentities.

After the election every single one of those who had been defeated was appointed to the highest key positions. Barabash was transferred from *Literaturnaya gazeta* to the Party Central Committee and Dymshits was made "the eye of the State" to watch over the film industry. (His actual title was Editor-in-Chief of the Film Board under the auspices of the Council of Ministers of the USSR.) It was now up to him whether or not a certain film was made or a certain script-writer or director was allowed to work. No sooner had writers expressed their distrust of him and indeed made no secret of their contempt for him than he found himself with millions of roubles at his disposal.

As things have worked out in Russia, and not only in the Union of Writers, the principle of the electoral system exists only to demonstrate conclusively that no real electoral system exists.

PART V

THE JUBILIADA

1.THE OLD GUARD GOES DOWN FIGHTING: THE INGLORIOUS END TO THE POETIC RENAISSANCE OF 1956

Nineteen sixty-seven, the year the Fourth Congress of Soviet Writers took place, had all the appearance of being the year in which the Red Hundreds were finally victorious. The atmosphere was utterly stifling. In fact it was not the end, however, but only the beginning of the end.

The year heralded the opening of the much-trumpeted ten-year period Russians christened "the Jubiliada" because it was to see the fiftieth anniversary of practically everything in sight. At the end of 1967 there was a lengthy fireworks display in honor of the fiftieth anniversary of the October Socialist Revolution. Only literature which publishers considered "resplendent" was published. Writers bided their time, waiting for the "resplendence" to pass— after all, everything passes eventually. The next year, 1968, saw the jubilee of the Soviet army,which was to march into Prague the same year. The triumphal celebrations, fanned by massive coverage in the press, proceeded normally.

Writers were beginning to freeze up from the continual celebration of fiftieth anniversaries. However, 1969 had an even more notorious one in store: the fiftieth anniversary of the security services—the Cheka, OGPU, the NKVD, the MGB and the KGB. The atmosphere in the Union of Writers changed to such an extent that all the chekists involved in literature pinned on small blue anniversary diamond-shaped badges proclaiming the 40th and 50th anniversaries of the Cheka. Ten years earlier when the political prisoners were returning from the camps there could have been no question of such an open demonstration of one's affiliations.

However, the crowning jubilee celebration came the following year, 1970. Everyone prepared for it like sailors preparing for the admiral's review of the fleet. It was a hundred years since Lenin was born. The laudatory clichés automatically moved from Stalin onto Lenin and the ceaseless blaring of the radio on the subject eventually went sour even on faithful Leninists. Lenin jokes started to make their appearance in swarms. They were even told in schools and factories, something which had never happened before. The authority of the founder of the Soviet State was shaken. This could hardly have been the goal the Propaganda Section of the Party Central Committee had set itself, but then something might have been expected to go wrong where that body was concerned.

Nineteen seventy-two approached softly like a stealthy animal. It was the fiftieth anniversary of the formation of the USSR. It brought to a close the "jubiliada" which had torpedoed the ship of literature and sent it to the bottom with practically everyone on board. The older writers died standing at their posts like ships' captains. Some of them had their own jubilees, unheralded and without honor. One of the most important events of 1967 was the celebration in honor of the fiftieth birthday of Konstantin Paustovsky. The club rooms at the *Dom literatorov* (House of the Men of Letters) were packed full for the occasion. The crowds spilled over into the foyer and the smaller hall where the proceedings were watched on closed-circuit television. In the main hall people were standing in the aisles and along the walls and it was physically impossible to squeeze through. As far as I can remember, nothing like it had been seen before. A few of us who had been unwise enough to arrive just before things got underway had to be taken across the stage to a position on one side of the stage where we stood crammed up against one another in a passage for almost the entire evening. We realized that we were gathering all together like that without any official interference in the proceedings probably for the last time.

Paustovsky was not present because he was seriously ill. Consequently all the speeches were recorded on tape so that he could listen at home later to what was said about him. The proceedings were opened by Veniamin Kaverin, who was very thin and whose complexion had darkened in recent months as if he had been roasted over a fire. "The occasion of Konstantin Paustovsky's fiftieth birthday is a day of celebration for our literature," he said. "It cannot be compared with the Fourth Congress of Soviet Writers which has just taken place and which had no literary significance." Everyone caught his breath. No one had referred to officially sanctioned occasions like that for a long time. All the same, there could not have been any more exact description of the Congress at which anyone who might have so much as hinted by a slip of the tongue at the unhappy state of affairs in literature had been kept well away from the podium. Naturally, Veniamin Kaverin had not been allowed to speak. Fortunately, the speech he had prepared for the Congress was not lost but was distributed to Moscow writers and eventually found its way abroad where it was published.

It is now obvious that Kaverin's opening remarks at Paustovsky's anniversary celebrations were laden with ideas he had not been allowed to voice at the Congress. It was not his theoretical digressions which were so arresting as the frankness and bitterness of a writer who had not succeeded in suppressing the "inner editor" within himself. "I'm terribly envious of Paustovsky," Kaverin exclaimed. "I'm envious of his never having lied in his life. There is not a single false line in his works. The reason he has never lied is that he possesses a gift many have lost—inner freedom... What is inner freedom?" Here Kaverin placed his fists on the desk as if expecting an attack. "Why did Paustovsky beg us all his life not to lose it?... We writers of the older generation concealed the tragic situation literature finds itself in from ourselves for many years, became entangled in contradictions and had difficulty in distinguishing the rare notes of self-denial, sacrifice and vocation in the midst of the cacophony." Kaverin was gasping for breath. He moved his papers closer to him and began reading a passage from a letter Pasternak wrote to Tabidze: "Bore more deeply into yourself without pity or mercy—right into yourself. If you don't find the people, the earth and the sky there, then stop looking, there's no point in looking anywhere..." Then Kaverin went on: "The most important thing about this idea to which I have kept coming back in recent times is seeing the people in yourself, finding in yourself a reflection of its hopes, joys and suffering, its awakening and constantly growing aspiration towards the truth." As he spoke, he looked around the room as if looking for a particular person who needed to hear these words.

The next one to speak was the writer Boris Balter, one of the fledglings of *Pages from Tarusa* who began in the loud pushing way which was characteristic of him when he was nervous. "I am always being asked what sort of recognition Paustovsky has received in terms of awards or honors conferred on him. I always reply that as far as I am concerned, or anyone else, or even Paustovsky himself, this is of no importance. There is an old tradition in Russia that the more loved and recognized a writer is by the people, the less loved he is by the government." Everyone looked at one another and froze. Would he be allowed to continue? Would he be picked up as he went out?

Balter continued. He told about how Paustovsky had taught them. He spoke calmly although his calm did not come easily. He recalled in particular a seminar Paustovsky had conducted at which they had discussed a certain young writer's work in which a district committee Secretary was depicted. In order to emphasize the fact that he was a "positive" character, the young writer had described how he had gone into his sleeping son's room to kiss him goodbye just before leaving on an official trip. Paustovsky asked the young writer caustically: "Do you mean to say that the times are so cruel that to show ordinary human feelings is a sign of being 'positive' "? The young writer was so startled he was struck dumb.

There was something timeless about Yashin, who spoke next, with his tall broad-boned frame, which was reminiscent of the peasant stock he came from. "There are few poets present here this evening," he said screwing up his eyes ironically as he looked around the room, "so I wanted to speak as a poet. However, the thought occurs to me that I have the right to speak also simply as his friend—which it is my good fortune to be. Until I met Paustovsky, I was a successful young poet but one who walked on his hands rather than his feet and was convinced that that was the thing to do. ...I shall always be in his debt because he stood me on my feet when he had my story 'Levers' published in *Literary Moscow*... It is said that Paustovsky is not a Party member. What does it mean for a writer to be a member of the Party? Does it mean to cut yourself off from the people by means of a door—or rather two padded doors? Is this what it means to be a Party member?"

At this moment a terrible banging rang out in the room. Someone was hammering on the door. Yashin stopped speaking, waited for the noise to

313

stop and then went on with a bitter smile: "What is it? Am I being given a warning? If so, it's in vain. I've been through the mill. But I'm standing firmly on my own feet on this sinful earth..."

In conclusion he said that he wanted to recite a poem he would dedicate to Konstantin Paustovsky if he liked it. Although I unfortunately cannot remember it in its entirety, I remember its final two lines very well:

> I cannot get along with God
> Nor am I treading the same path as the devil...
>
> (Mne i s Bogom ne mozhetsya,
> I s chertom ne po puti...)

The next to speak was Ivan Semyonovich Kozlovsky, People's Artist of the USSR, who was known as a "model tenor." "My profession is to sing and not to speak, especially in front of an audience such as this," he began, "but I feel I must say a few words. Paustovsky is the intelligentsia's tuning-fork. He gives us all the note. We all love Paustovsky so much that even Sergei Mikhalkov turned up, although two hours late..."

At this point Mikhalkov leapt to his feet and began stammering that he wanted to give an explanation. Kaverin abruptly interrupted him: "Who gave you the right to speak? No one asked you to say anything. Why are you causing this disorder?"

It was not until Kozlovsky had finished that Mikhalkov was allowed to give his explanation. He rushed to the front. "My friend Ivan Semyonovich Kozlovsky will forgive me when he realizes that I came from a meeting with electors, which, as a deputy, I..." Here Kozlovsky interrupted him: "I have never been your friend and never shall be." He gave a wave of his hand and the boys' choir he had brought with him burst into song. It was the well-known "Slavsya!" and Kozlovsky immediately joined in singing with the choir.

This brought to an end the last open demonstration on the part of the creative intelligentsia which was officially praised and known to the whole country. We did not suspect, of course, that not only would Konstantin Paustovsky shortly die, but also the young looking writer Boris Balter and Alexander Yashin, a man of almost superhuman fortitude.

Yashin actually died just two days before Paustovsky and passed on the baton to the new generation which was to mount a protest on Red Square against the entry of Russian tanks into Prague. One of these protesters was Anatoly Yakobson who soon afterwards was to become widely known in the Soviet Union. He was a teacher of literature, author of a book about Blok and one of the country's most outstanding literary critics. His life was to end tragically. The other protesters were physicists, lawyers, and workers, who were soon mostly sent away to prison and psychiatric hospitals.

The young "revolutionary" poets did not, alas, follow in the footsteps of the protesters they had inspired. As everyone willremember,Yevtushenko, Voznesensky, Mezhirov, Vinokurov and Slutsky and a few others were not regarded simply as poets full of promise and resonance. In 1956 their names had been regarded as banners for the new poetry. Not one of these poets was repressed. Indeed, the times seemed particularly propitious for thim, filling their sails. Mezhirov and Slutsky had been in the war, as had Boris Balter, where they had distinguished themselves by their bravery and had not flinched in the face of death. What had happened to the banner of poetry from 1956, the year of anti-Stalinism? Why did it now find itself in the rear guard well behind the young poets who were so aware of what was happening and craved action?

The first to break was Boris Slutsky, who in 1956 had been the most courageous and mature of the poets. He was of the opinion that the publishing of *Doctor Zhivago* abroad and the resulting fury of the Party machine was undermining the newly emerging literature. Because of Pasternak, he considered, all writers would come under fire. He allowed himself to take part in the campaign of abuse against Pasternak in 1958. As a mark of their gratitude, the authorities promoted him to various positions of importance. In the Union of Writers it was said of him, without malice, that he was a "balalaika with one string." This single string was made up of Slutsky's military themes—the courage, forthrightness and purity of the soldier. When this string snapped, there was no other in his poetry to be found.

In contrast to Boris Slutsky, who for a long time was not published, Evgeny Vinokurov began easily in a clear, ringing voice. The day Stalin died, Vinokurov and another poet, Vanshenkin, went to see some friends. As former soldiers with parents in the Party, they had similar backgrounds. When they arrived at their friends' place, Vanshenkin was bellowing like a bull and Vinokurov was drumming on a bucket he had with him. "The tyrant is dead!" he proclaimed. "Mightn't things get worse?" someone asked in alarm. "They couldn't," Vinokurov exclaimed.

It was from Evgeny Vinokurov that I first heard of the literary method called "antabus." Antabus is a medical preparation used in extreme cases to frighten alcoholics into being cured. An alcoholic is given the antabus, knowing that if he drinks as little as a hundred grams of spirits while under treatment he will die. "But a Russian overcomes everything!" Vinokurov remarked cheerfully. "He'll even find a cunning way to get around a prohibition which carries the death penalty. The first thing he does to get around it is to add one drop of spirits to a glass of water which he then drinks without ill effect. The next day he adds two drops of vodka to a glass of water. He keeps this up until he reaches a dosage which is intoxicating. The same method is applicable to literature. You put one or two drops of social complaint into a glass of aerated water. It will immediately bubble up for a moment for the benefit of the connoisseurs, while by the time the censors come to their senses the bubbles have died down and the taste is quite bland—just like pure water!

Vinokurov is unfailingly true to himself. There are many examples of this in his later poems. The final lines of his poem "The Dances" in the collection entitled *A Human Face* (Moscow, 1968) are as follows:

> It's not such a long way
> From Voltaire's maxims
> To a Maxim machine-gun
> Ripping into the darkness from a cart.

What is the poet's position? Is it one of approval or condemnation? There is a brief effervescence, some lively discussion among some students, but when the authorities stretch out for it, it is pure water. In "Particular Cases" ("Edinichnosti") revulsion for philosophical systems shows through faintly. However, in the poem "The State System" ("Gosudarstvennost') the proportion of spirits to water is nearer to half and half. Here the poet makes no attempt to hide his horror at the advance of the State machine or his own persecution and repression. The ending is orthodox—the fledgling is safe under the State's wing. However, it is the opening lines which set the tone and the tone which governs the music.

In "Bathing the Children" it is again a case of a drop or two to each glass of water. Here the poet turns everyday life into something more philosophical—existence. He gives a poetic coloring to something Soviet poetry avoids, considering it private and therefore not worthy of being depicted.

The collection of Vinokurov's verse entitled *Gesture*, which came out in 1969, was another case of two drops of spirits in a glass of water.

In one of his latest poems Vinokurov exclaims: "Don't set me against the atomic state!" to which the Moscow poet Viktor Urin was not slow in responding in a poem well-known through samizdat:

> To be a screw
> In this rusty system
> And submissively whisper back:
> "Don't set me against the atomic state"
> —That's the way a slave thinks, not a poet.
> (Samizdat, *The Bridge (Most)*, no. 6, Moscow, 1977)

The profound post-war poets—Mezhirov and Vinokurov—killed the political poet in themselves. In Mezhirov's case there was no possibility of resuscitation whereas Vinokurov switched to the "antabus" method. This method was harmless for alcoholics but fatal for poetry born of liberated thought, hope and the thirst for freedom. More and more often not just the censors but the readers themselves nowadays cannot taste   the forbidden drops. They can only taste prolixity and monotony—just the usual tasteless water. What a tragedy it is when the battle flag and the bugle call sounding the advance turn out to be nothing more than a fading echo or a hallucination.

Be that as it may, a poet like Andrei Voznesensky, for example, who is extremely observant and has at times a supple, hard-hitting, aphoristic manner, would appear to have changed little. He roared across the landscape like one of his devils on a motorcycle wearing a chamber pot. Voznesensky's motorcycle knocked aside all the Dolmatovskys and Oshanins once and for all. Voznesensky was not the only one to play a part, of course—all the young bloods of 1956 had a contribution to make. Still, he played his part and cleared the air of the stink of Dolmatovskyism. Where is he now, the hope of his generation?

Time has shown what the answer to that question is. The key to Voznesensky's poetry is provided by the story of the non-conformist artist described by Daniel in his *Moscow Calling* who, "inspired by the declaration of an official Day of Open Murder, brought posters to the publisher's saluting it. Naturally, the posters had been executed in a non-conformist manner." The editor angrily sends him packing. "What do you think this is? *Life* magazine? You're a faddist!" he says. The artist leaves, complaining about the lack of creative freedom.

Daniel's artist was developed in an unexpected way. He kept serving up whatever was demanded and saluting in his non-conformist ("levy" in Russian—"left-wing") manner all the important dates. Then suddenly he applied his leftish poetic skills to a theme which would have seemed to exclude the possibility of a new approach: Leniniana. The icon genre is generally considered to be canonical. An icon needs the nimbus prescribed by tradition. Voznesensky did the same thing in his poem "Longjumeau."

Naturally no attempt was made to alter the content in a negative way— God forbid! Everything remained as it had been in the works of orthodox poets, except that it was done in a non-conformist manner. In "Longju-meau" Lenin is playing *gorodki*, a game like skittles, aiming his skittle at the future Berias and other scapegoats. It is tasteless and rather mindless but "levy"—non-conformist.

One's initial impression of this poet is a confused one. Is he a time-server, a coward, or a poet whose talent has been crushed by the times? With time it gradually becomes apparent that Voznesensky is completely insensitive to content. His main concern is that he should be spared any problems as a result of the content of his poetry. The important thing is to put on show the latest fashion in wine-skins without regard for the wine they contain—after all, he does not have to drink it. The reader eventually comes to the realization that the poet's passions are not genuine and his nervous energy is just a display. The simulated, almost drug-induced excit-ability, the shouting and the histrionic sweep of his performance no longer

317

deceive. Even his ability to depict pathological details from real life such as a deformed cripple evokes little sympathetic response—we have already seen what a wealth of meaning was concealed behind the cripples depicted by such authors as Babel in his "Kolyvushka."

I do not share the extreme view of some literary critics according to which Voznesensky is an antipoet and an antihumanist. All the same there is little comfort to be had from facts such as the following: Voznesensky dedicated one of his first poems to none other than Kornely Zelinsky, a literary jackal who was fond of orating at the funerals of his victims. At Pasternak's funeral, in front of the poet's anguished relatives, Voznesensky theatrically placed a copy of his collection of poems on the poet's grave—with the page containing the dedication to Zelinsky torn out.

On one occasion Voznesensky blurted out, perhaps in all sincerity: "My fate is deaf and dumb." How cruelly life had cheated him! Yet above all it was the reader who had been cheated. There is no country in the world apart from the USSR in the twentieth century in which innovations in artistic form are banned or cracked down on by the State. It is only in the Soviet Union that the paintings of non-realists are bulldozed away and pop music is regarded as political sabotage. It is not so long ago that even blank verse was regarded as something akin to anti-Soviet provocation, like stovepipe trousers, shorts or long hair in the hippie style. It is little wonder that the unusual verse form was greeted by young readers with ardent enthusiasm as a challenge to the authorities and as a courageous act on the part of the poets aimed at smashing the fossilized forms of socialist realism.

The Lithuanian poet Eduardas Miezelaitis and the Moscow poet Soloukhin, who sinfully began to write in blank verse, attracted attention. The mere fact that they wrote in blank verse was taken to be a mark of protest.

However as the years passed people grew accustomed to the new forms. Even the ever-watchful parrots on the Komsomol newspapers stopped attacking the "reformer poets." After all, the new form was unaccompanied by any new content, either philosophical or lyrical. This was also true of Voznesensky's poetry, which turned out to be insensitive to content. If form is considered as wings, then poetry's Pegasus, the winged horse, appeared now to be an empty body held aloft on its wings. The flapping of its wings ceased to evoke any fluttering in the reader's hearts. The readers turned away from innovators of the type described by Daniel and the poets, in Dostoevsky's words, "smudged and faded."

When a poet becomes virtually indifferent to the "what" of his poetry, the "how" becomes drab and bloodless. Yevtushenko and Voznesensky, who originally were at opposite poles in almost everything—their imagery, rhythms and aphorisms—now have much more in common.

Volumes of scholarly works have been written about Yevtushenko. It is a cliché to say that he is "poet tribun" (a public podium poet), a polemicist and a one-man show. In the social sense he represented at one time the opposition to all manifestations of Stalinism—"dirty hands grasped our flagstaff." He was sincere and his sincerity coincided with the main tendency of the epoch. He really was the opposite of Voznesensky. What was important to him was the sense, the content of his verse, even if the form suffered. As Boris Slutsky once correctly remarked, "out of his ten books time will choose one."

It was not only the young who rallied behind Yevtushenko. Once O., a literary editor on *Literaturnaya gazeta*, who was vigilant beyond the call of duty and was popularly known as the Iron Hardliner, told some of his colleagues after carefully locking the door of his office: "I've been to a party at Yevtushenko's. He made a tremendous impression on me. That man could head a provisional government." Even Yuzovsky, a wise and perceptive man, recognized something special about him: "Just look at his face," he said once, "he's a Savonarola!"

However, the times put a different complexion on things. The first thing that happened was that Yevtushenko's—and Voznesensky's—signature stopped appearing on protests. It transpired that he knew how to bend with the Party line. As one poet remarked sarcastically, he was "podvizhnik podvizhnoy morali" (selflessy devoted to a shifting morality—a play on the Russian words "podvizhnik" and "podvizhnoy"). Yevtushenko protested vociferously that it was not true. "I am a tactician," he said and wrote some verse about tactics in reply: "I make a career for myself by not making one!"

This was all just empty words. All over the country folk choirs began singing a new song to words by Yevtushenko: "Do Russians want war?" In this song he managed to combine the aspirations of the authorities and the war-mongering general staff on the one hand and the long-suffering Russian towns and villages on the other, where every family had had its losses. This sly mouthing of "patriotic" formulae fitted in with the official slogans ratified by the Central Committee and hung on fences all over the land. For example: "The people and the Party are one."

Yevtushenko no longer felt bound to experience a situation for himself, to go through the same emotions or to penetrate its meaning. It was enough for him to hear someone else's story or even just pick up a hint from someone else.

> No monuments rise above Babi Yar,
> Just a steep-sided gully like a crude head-stone.
> I'm terrified.
>> I'm as old today
> As the Jewish people itself.

No one remained unmoved by these courageous lines of Yevtushenko's. They were heard as a challenge to the ring-leaders of the tavern-building project who, of course, were enraged. Yet even as he worked on this poem which was to be such a landmark for him and which was sincere in the direction in which it pointed, Yevtushenko was nonchalantly leaving one set of symbols for another diametrically opposed to it. Just as he was finishing "Babi Yar," he called up the poet Mezhirov, the only Moscow poet who was truly educated, and said: "Listen, Sasha, when Moses led the Jews out of Egypt, was he guided by the star of Bethlehem?" Mezhirov was astounded. "That was on a completely different occasion, my friend, and concerns a different religion." "Then give me another image," Yevtushenko demanded. "Moses' rod..." Mezhirov started to say. "Thank you!" cried Yevtushenko without waiting for him to finish and hung up. He did not need anything more. Under the new simplified system of writing poetry, it was all the same whether it was Moses' rod, the star of Bethlehem, an image of the crucifixion or something else such as "the goodness of my land." It was all just window-dressing.

Yevtushenko's poetry expresses his immediate feelings. His early verse such as "Wartime Weddings" ("O, svadby v dni voyennye...") is excellent. However, he lacked the necessary qualities to become a citizen poet, a "sovereign of thoughts." He lacked the strength of spirit, the poetic rigor, and the willingness to give up cheap comforts. He lacked the strength of personality.

That people should talk about him constantly was for Yevtushenko a necessity. If he was not writing anything that would attract attention, then he found another way. For example, without thinking it through properly, he tried to have Sholokhov eliminated from the list of candidates for a Union of Writers election. Naturally, he failed. Yevtushenko was experienced enough to realize that Sholokhov could not be toppled by one rather childish outburst from a back seat. Everyone there was waiting for some kind of argument for striking Sholokhov off to be put up, but Yevtushenko had no intention of putting up an argument. Sergei Mikhalkov who was in the chair disposed of Yevtushenko humiliatingly, jeeringly. He gave him a good drubbing just as if he had been a four-year-old street urchin. Everyone felt aggrieved except Yevtushenko. The next day his name was on everyone's lips. He seemed unable to exist without being at the center of some row in the press. Sensation was to him like insulin to a diabetic.

The pattern that emerged in his output as a poet was utterly simple. The critic Benedikt Sarnov called it "the swings." Yevtushenko wrote some verse which contained a certain amount of truth, sincerity and "trendiness" which made his young readers wildly enthusiastic and infuriated the Party leadership. Then he was "unmasked," first by the gangsters from the Komsomol Central Committee and then by Yuri Zhukov, a *Pravda* big-wig. Yevtushenko then rushed off to Cuba where he sun-bathed on the beach with Fidel Castro, publishing on his return appallingly bad, featureless doggerel in *Pravda* which was on the level of something penned by Sofronov. Everyone was saddened, except Yevtushenko. He had risen up on the swings, then came down again. Then his poem "Stalin's Heirs" came out.

Once more the storm clouds gathered. The KGB had microphones installed in his apartment ("Don't stay in one place, keep moving," as a kindly janitor was to say to Yevtushenko and his wife Galya when they were moving to another apartment block). Political instructors from "higher up" alluded to certain ties Yevtushenko had with the West. As a colonel with the border guard in the Pamirs said to me: "We know all about him. That Yevtushenko of yours won't be chirping for much longer."

What should he do? How could he get out of the situation?

> I am like a train tearing for many years
> Between the city of Yes and the city of No.
> My nerves are stretched like wires
> Between the city of No and the city of Yes.

Once more a long line of colorless poems justifying the status quo and bearing an official stamp came out like a teletype tape—"Bratsk Hydroelectric Station" and "Zima Junction." Again, for example, although they were false in terms of situations and psychology, they were technically superb.

In "Bratsk Hydroelectric Station" Nyushka from the village of Velikaya Gryaz (Great Mud) becomes pregnant. The father refuses to have anything to do with either Nyushka or the child that is to be born. Nyushka is desperate:

> I ran up to the scaffolding
> To put an end to my life straight away
> But froze like a statue
> When I saw my Bratsk Station below.

Nyushka is stopped by the sight of the unfinished dam "covered in its steel framework and voices," and also by the fact that Lenin and the Chairman were "gazing through the wailing of the sirens and the confusion." She is saved by Lenin, who has obviously been lumped together with all the anti-semitic petty merchants from "Babi Yar" and the Nyushkas. It is Lenin who saves her, not Kerensky. So Yevtushenko soars skyward on his swing.

It was as if poor Evgeny Yevtushenko, like Pushkin's Evgeny in *The Bronze Horesman*, had been pursued and caught by the bronze horseman of the State system. He was on the point of calming down and became a habitue of the Writers' Club again, bringing along foreign friends and popping the champagne corks. Then the Soviet tanks roared into Prague and in just one day everything changed. The older writers had long felt the approach of

321

some change and it had not been a matter of chance that their last anniversary celebrations had been farewells. The poseurs faded away on the spot. It was now necessary either to collaborate with the regime and "unanimously approve" the occupation together with "the entire Soviet people" or else break with it.

Yevtushenko began rushing about in an agitated manner. He was very frightened. Like everyone else he realized that what Pasternak had foreseen had come to pass:

> Instead of idle chatter
> Rome demands not a read-through
> From an actor but
> His death, and not in jest.

No illusions were left in anyone's mind. If they could crush a whole nation with their tanks, then they would certainly bloodily suppress any attempt to "think differently" within the country. "Socialism with a human face," which had been our last hope, had turned out to be no less an illusion than Campanella's City of the Sun or Fourier's phalansteries.

The morning of the invasion a neighbor of mine who was a literary scholar came to report a "reliable rumor" to the effect that it was intended to arrest a thousand people with deviant views as a warning to others so that it would not occur to anyone to mount a protest. Some fifty people, including Lev Kopelev, Boris Balter and myself, were roughly treated and bullied by people from "higher up." "They'll take the three of you, no doubt about it," my neighbor said. "There have been two black Volgas outside since early morning and some toughs. Take a look yourself. Grisha, God helps those who help themselves."

I was frightened by what my neighbor said. I decided not to go to Koktebel, where I had already made a booking in advance, and decided to hide away somewhere on the Volga or in Siberia where I would wait for the round-up to come to an end. Then I found my own haste absurd. After all, it was not 1937 when millions of people were picked up and they often did not even bother to look for those who had disappeared, having other things on their mind. Nowadays if the KGB decided to put a writer away, it would find him even if he hid at the bottom of the sea. So I went to Koktebel, to the sea, I needed to relax a bit for whatever might be coming.

The next morning in Koktebel Yevtushenko called out to me. He rushed over to embrace me saying: "Another one of our expelled ones!" He asked me to join him in finding a beach as far away as possible from the main one where the Party-approved poets were letting the sun soak their sciatica. At first I declined, being apprehensive of going out in the hot sun on the first day, but Yevtushenko was insistent. There was a kind of uncertainty, almost embarrassment, in the way he asked me. When I looked at him closely I saw that he was trembling.

We went quite a long way, beyond Lyagushachyi Bukhty, where we chose a beach which was completely empty. After we had lain down on the rocks he began to recite poetry, asking me to "forget" it immediately. Naturally I complied. However, it was not long before the poems he recited began appearing in samizdat under his name, although as far as I know he never read them in public. The fact that they have come out in samizdat permits me to reproduce the first few lines:

> The tanks are rumbling across Prague,
> The tanks are rumbling across the truth,
> The tanks are rumbling across the boys sitting
> in the tanks...

> (Tanki idut po Prage,
> Tanki idut po pravde,
> Tanki idut po rebyatam, kotorye v tankakh sidyat...)

"I'm afraid to write them down or read them out," he said, nervously tossing pebbles at the water. "They'd never forgive me this. Listen!" He suddenly sat up. "Should I send a telegram or not? What do you think? On the one hand, I can sent it and they can go to hell. On the other hand, if I don't send it, how can I face Zikmund and Hanzelka again? They sent me a telegram—they really believe that there's something I can do." He sat clutching his knees and rocked from side to side. "I'm in a real corner... Tell me, should I send one or not?"

I replied that it is not right to advise someone to go to prison, and that he must make the decision himself. Later over lunch his wife Galya complained that her husband had gone mad. "He's spent forty roubles on telegrams."

However, in a sense, Yevtushenko was still playing on the swings. It was a game which had its risks but it was still a game. Some time later when Demichev, Secretary of the Central Committee, gave orders that Yevtushenko should not be sent abroad ("You do not share the views of the Party," the head of the ideological service said to him) Yevtushenko replied that he was in full agreement with those views and that he was ready to take back his telegrams of protest. He had no objection to "idle chatter" but drew the line at "death, and not in jest."

Not so long afterwards I saw Yevtushenko at the Writers' Club. At the table next to his sat Vasily Aksenov and Vladimir Maximov. Things looked bad for Maximov who had just received an order to go see a psychiatrist. No one knew what would happen, but we feared the worst. Yevtushenko called Aksenov over and said in a loud voice so that the whole room could hear: "Why are you sitting with him—he's anti-Soviet?" At this point it is only fair to remind the reader of the line from Yevtushenko's poem about "the tanks ... rumbling across the men sitting in the tanks," a line which has become part of the poet's biography.

Just as the paintings of the non-conformists had been swept away by bulldozers, so poetry was crushed by tanks, figuratively speaking. What happened was that one of Russia's most gifted poets, Oleg Chukhontsev, wrote a poem about Prince Kurbsky who took refuge in Lithuania from Ivan the Terrible. When the poem, which included the line "How to repay the tyrant tsar but by treachery?", appeared in the journal *Yunost (Youth)* almost the entire general staff of the Soviet army was roused to action. A whole cohort of generals hastened to sign a furious letter attacking Chukhontsev for "calling on the country's youth to betray it." Were they then aligning themselves with Ivan's *oprichniki*? In any event, Oleg Chukhontsev was exiled from the literary scene for ten years. Naturally, attacks such as the one the generals mounted on Chukhontsev in effect traumatized many of the other poets, including Yevtushenko, who had a very high opinion of Chukhontsev as a poet.

In his verse he angrily demanded that we "hear the groan beyond the wall of your own apartment," and not only in Vietnam. Yet he made no attempt to do anything on behalf of Zhores Medvedev who was put in one of the special psychiatric hospitals or General Grigorenko, or Vladimir Bukovsky.

Medical science has invented a machine which can carry out the functions of the human heart for a short time allowing the patient with heart trouble to remain alive although his heart has stopped beating. In poetry no such machine has been invented. The youth of Russia cannot forgive heartlessness. Nor can it forgive hypocrisy. In Moscow a few lines of verse purporting to be by the former poet Evgeny Dolmatovsky, whose name was a household word, became widely known:

> I am Evgeny, you are Evgeny,
> I am no genius, you are no genius,
> I am a shit and you are a shit,
> You're a new one, I'm an old one.

Thus it happened that it was the young poetry of 1956, the poetry of revolutionary ardor, which was the first to go sour in the soulless atmosphere of the Jubiliada.

2. YOUNG WRITERS' PROSE: RETREAT WITH RESISTANCE AND LOSSES; ATTACK ON THE AESOPIAN METHOD

Prose proved more resilient than poetry. Like infantry under attack, it flattened itself against the earth and kept up its fire. Some prose writers adopted an all-round defense position affording protection to each other. They did not surrender. Many of these writers were put out of action, others were intimidated by threats to deprive them of their means of livelihood, by the camps and the prison in Vladimir. Others fell silent of their own accord when they saw the fate of those who had refused to desist.

One of those who quieted down was Vasily Aksenov, one of the most popular and promising writers to enter the literary field after 1956 together with Yevtushenko, Voznesensky, Akhmadulina and Bulat Oku-dzhava. He felt constrained to write cautiously but all the same managed to say what he wanted to say. Like many other writers of his generation, he is most profound not in novels and longer stories which demand consider-able experience of life, but in his short stories where his writing talent and knowledge of modern usage find their fullest expression.

Perhaps his most significant and best-written story is "Halfway to the Moon" which first came out in *Novy mir* (1962, No.7). The main character is a worker named Kirpichenko whose childhood was spent in a children's home, and who was then in prison for some time and worked in a lumber camp. He has spent all his life in hostels and barracks. "Nothing but bunks, single-deck and double-decker ones, plank beds and lockers... He didn't have any friends, but plenty of 'pals.' People were a bit afraid of him, he wasn't one to fool around with. It didn't take much for him to up and give you a black eye." Kirpichenko works well and remembers the cars and trucks he has had like old friends. In the army he once had a jeep called "Ivan Willis," then a one-and-a-half ton haulage truck, a Tatra, and now a diesel truck he uses to cart logs to the pass. Like everyone else, Kirpichenko is a hard drinker, goes to see films and in summer drives to dances at the cannery. When he is in towns like Yuzhno-Sakhalinsk, Poronaysk or Korsakov he sometimes stops on a corner and looks in through the windows of the new apartment blocks at the stylish lamps and curtains, and this fills him with alarm. He did not keep count of how old he was and has only quite recently realized that he will be thirty in a few months' time. At work there is an exemplary worker called Banin. "They were always carrying on about Banin at the lumber camp: 'Banin! Banin! Follow Banin's example!' ... There were guys at the lumber camp who did just as good a job as Banin—in fact they left him for dead. But the bosses can always be relied on to pick out one man and kick up a great fuss about him. But there's no need to envy a fellow like that—he ought to be pitied."

The official critics did not find this sentence to their taste. With a flick of the fingers Aksenov seemed to be calling into question the very foundations of the regime's callous game of "exemplary workers" ("peredoviki"), "beacons," "shock workers" of Communist labor and so on.

The author develops this secondary theme at his own pace and in his own individual way. Banin drives Kirpichenko to Khabarovsk where he knows some "top-class girls" and has a sister named Lariska. He tried to marry Kirpichenko off to his sister, who is not yet thirty and "knows a thing or two." They have some fun together and then Banin suddenly says that it looks as if Kirpichenko has become "one of the family." Kirpichenko coughs on his gherkin juice.

> *"What?!"*
>
> *"You know what!" Banin suddenly roared. "Are you sleeping with my sister or aren't you? Come on, tell me when the wedding's going to be or else I'll report you for immoral behavior—get it?"*
>
> *Kirpichenko delivered Banin a blow across the cheek from the other side of the table and he crashed backwards into the corner. He jumped up straight away and grabbed hold of a chair.*
>
> *"You scum!" Kirpichenko snarled, advancing on him. "I'm not going to marry the first slut who comes along."*

There ensues an exchange of insults and blows. Kirpichenko remembers all this as he sits in a giant Tupolev 114 flying right across the country from Khabarovsk to Moscow on leave. His seat turns out to be occupied by some bespectacled character who refuses to leave it because it makes him feel sick to sit at the back. Kirpichenko without further ado takes the man's hat off and throws it towards the back of the aircraft, telling him to go after it and sit where the ticket says he should. When a stewardess approaches him to ask why he is causing a disturbance, Kirpichenko just tells her to "take it easy." A little later she comes up to him again:

> *"May I take your coat?"*
>
> *It was the same girl who had spoken sharply to him before. He looked at her and felt quite stunned. She was smiling. Her smiling face was bending over him and her dark hair—no, it wasn't black, it was dark—looked soft. It was done up neatly and firmly and looked like fur or fleece or even nylon—like all the precious things in the world. Her fingers touched the sheepskin of his coat—he'd never seen such fingers before.*
>
> *"Took my coat, see?" said Kirpichenko to the sailor sitting next to him with a stupid smile...*

Kirpichenko gets up and goes to look for the girl. He finds her chatting away in English to some capitalists.

> *Kirpichenko walked up and knocked the capitalist with his shoulder. The capitalist was taken aback and said "I'm sorry," by which he meant naturally, "Just watch it, fella, or you'll cop it."*
>
> *"Take it easy," said Kirpichenko. "Peace and friendship and all that." He knew his politics.*

The stewardess's name is Tanya and she is the first woman Kirpichenko does not want to be parted from. When he learns that the Tupolev 114 is flying back to Khabarovsk the next day he buys a ticket and flies all the way back across the country on it. Tanya, however, is not on board because there has been a change of crew, so he flies back again to Moscow again and again fails to meet up with Tanya.

> *He knew almost all the stewardesses on this route by sight by this time and quite a few of the pilots as well. He was afraid they might remember him, too.*
>
> *He was afraid he might be taken for a spy.*
>
> *He kept changing his suits. He'd make one flight in his blue one, the next in his brown one and the next in his grey one.*
>
> *He slit open his underpants, took out his travelers' checks and put them into his coat pocket. He had fewer and fewer left. There was still no sign of Tanya.*
>
> *... There was a moon which seemed quite close. And it really wasn't very far away.*

When he does finally meet up with Tanya in Khabarovsk, his money having run out, all he does is ask a friend of his flying back to Sakhalin with him how far it is to the moon. "Well, it's about 300,000 kilometers," his friend says. "That's not far," Kirpichenko thinks, "A piece of cake." He looks at the plane, that "flying fortress of his muddled hopes" and then at Tanya and imagines how he will remember her on the way up to the mountain ridge and once there how he will forget her because there will be too many other things to think about. Then when he gets back down again he will remember her again and will have her on his mind all evening and when he wakes up in the morning.

Although he is not yet free of the hardness—or the slang—that comes with spending time in the camps, this rather crude young man has a purity of soul which gives him a certain superiority over the officially promoted "exemplary workers" and this moral purity was seen as a challenge to officially promoted literature.

The use of slang gives penetrating authenticity to this seemingly innocent story about the life of a free man in Russia which is in fact little different from the life of the political prisoner. There are the same bunks, the same barracks, and the same work, sometimes accompanied by extreme danger, and the same unattainable dreams. All dreams unconnected with money are seen as unattainable and as far away as the moon.

In "Halfway to the Moon" Aksenov reaches his peak as a writer. In fact he was not allowed to reach any higher. His next book was commissioned by the *Polizdat* publishing house for the "Ardent Revolutionaries" series. Aksenov had to force himself to write in order to earn his livelihood and it is painful to read what he wrote. Aksenov started drinking heavily and it is only the warnings of the doctors which restrain him from drinking himself to death. Aksenov became acquainted with life's darker side too early—he is the son of Evgenia Ginzburg who was once a political prisoner and author of *Into the Whirlwind*. In the life he now leads, however, his hands are tied as is the case with many other artistically gifted people.

This story, like all of Aksenov's prose, is a rich source for research into modern Russian slang. There is nothing false about its use by characters such as Kirpichenko and Banin. It is as true to life as they are themselves. In his knowledge of contemporary slang Aksenov can only be compared to Alexander Galich, whose poetry sometimes sounds like a distillation of the latest slang expressions. Indeed, at Galich's performance in Paris in 1974 it appeared to some long-time Parisian emigres that Galich was singing in a foreign tongue.

The use of slang puts a stamp of genuineness on Aksenov's powerful story about the similarity between the life of a free man in Russia and the life of a prisoner. Both ways of life are characterized by plank-beds, barracks, work conditions which can sometimes endanger life, and the unattainability of any dream unconnected with money—the kind of dream which is as far away as the moon.

During these years Vladimir Tendryakov was still working solidly. At first his stories, such as "Bad Weather" and "The Fall of Ivan Chuprov" and some others, were subtitled "sketch" ("ocherk"). However, when they were republished this description was as a rule removed, A "sketch" in the sense of the Russian "ocherk" is a kind of literary foray and has no pretensions to being a general statement about the world at large. It describes in particular an incident and within that framework studies the particularity of that incident as deeply as it wishes. Tendryakov makes cunning use of the apparent limitations of this genre for his own purposes. As one critic has said, Tendryakov, in contriving to use the sketch in this way, was "instantly released like a spring." He sliced his way into literature. "A Tight Knot" and "Potholes" were not subtitled "sketches" although in each case the action had its source in an incident beyond the control of those involved. In "A Tight Knot" the incident is the downpour of rain, but the fact that the farm workers are forced to sow their crops in the cold rain when everyone knows full well the grain will not grow, is not a matter of chance.

328

The accident in "Potholes" is an incident but Knyazhev's refusal to made a tractor available cannot be construed as an accident.

One of the best students of Tendryakov's works, the *Novy mir* critic Inna Solovyova, has correctly remarked that "the concreteness of the fact and the concreteness of the thought content support each other. It is the tightly knit nature of Tendryakov's observations which forms the strength of his prose" (1962, No. 7). The tight binding together of fact and idea mark both the early stories of Tendryakov and those that follow. An example is "Three, Seven, Ace" in which representatives of the law take away an innocent man who attempts to defend himself against a charge of murder. In Tendryakov's novels written in later years this interpenetration of incident and idea is nowhere to be seen. In these large works he seems to take refuge from the world as people do when they go down into bomb-shelters during an air-raid.

One writer hated with particular intensity by the Red Hundreds is the *Novy mir* author I. Grekova. Her name is actually a pseudonym. In Russian it is pronounced like the mathematical symbol for an unknown quantity—"y." This gifted writer is actually E. Ventsel, a highly educated woman who has the rarely awarded degree of "doktor nauk," a prominent mathematician and former professor at the Zhukovsky Military Air Academy. The hostility towards her has been provoked by what she has written and also by the fact that she is independent of the literary hangmen. There was something untouchable about her—she seemed to float on the heights of her impenetrable probability theories, as untouchable as Mars. When she wrote she was not particularly concerned about "playing safe" or using any of the common Soviet "double insurance" techniques. Once when she was sitting next to Tvardovsky at an important meeting, he leant across to her and whispered to her that it was time she moved over into literature permanently. After all, she had been a professional writer for a long time. Grekova said something in reply and they both burst out laughing. It turned out that what she said to her editor was: "Me? Become a professional writer? That's no different from suggesting that I, as a respectable woman and mother of three children, go out on the streets!"

Grekova's first published story was "On the Inside" ("Za prokhodnoi"). The story tells how the young scientists in a secret laboratory wage a zealous campaign for the right to work a ten-hour rather than an eight-hour day. Everyone is involved in the campaign: Sasha—called Megaton Sasha—an enormous buffalo of a man and the cleverest of all after Clever Vovka who is "uncultivated, wild and hellishly clever"—a sort of "scientific battering-ram"; then there is the almost too beautiful Klara who is always dreaming of writing an epic poem on cramming. They argue about whether lyrical poetry is still needed and whether or not an engineer named Poletayev was right in declaring in *Literaturnaya gazeta* that lyric poetry was obsolete. They heap abuse on Ilya Ehrenburg and then all of a sudden one of them reads some of his verse: "Not until many, many years have passed/And it is time to give an answer/We will sift through the pile of words./The whole world is different—it isn't as it was." They all fall silent, thinking about something it is unusual to think about in this secret laboratory. The unusual slowly starts to show itself. Clever Vovka loses his sight while conducting some experiments. His young colleagues discuss how to behave towards him when they meet him—nothing is more terrible than pity. A romantic attachment is formed. Another character, Vovka the Critic, unexpectedly says about Klara: "She's like three... roses at once."

Everything would have been quite normal if it were not for the presence of an unusual element hovering in the background. The laboratory is under the control of Vikenty Vyacheslavovich Loginov, the "chief" as they call him in English, who is nicknamed the Black Box. The problem is not only that the chief is difficult to make out—he is not quite a scientist and not quite an adventurer—it is also that these fine young people's work is being used for modern barbarous purposes. The results of their heroic labor can be used to destroy the world. They are working for the Black Box.

None of the critics was daring enough to give this interpretation to Grekova's story but none of the leaders forgot that this was what she had written. They were in no position to forget—soon afterwards the academician Sakharov and dozens of other young scientists, his comrades-in-arms, left these "black" laboratories for the wide world.

Grekova's next story was "The Ladies' Hairdresser." It is one of her best stories and concerns the artistic hairdresser Vitaly who is not allowed to be creative in his work. It is demanded of him that he fulfill the plan and nothing else. Vitaly is a real creative artist, working miracles with women's coiffures, yet he eventually leaves to become a carpenter as far away as possible from the hack-workers and rogues. Apparently even a hairdresser finds it impossible to create—and he is not even working for the war machine.

This is a tragic story, although the cultural bosses did not understand what was tragic about it and left Grekova in peace, at least until she had the story "The Tests" ("Na Ispytaniaykh") published. Then she was repaid in full for all her sins—for her truthful uncovering of the roughness and dullness of life in an out-of-the-way garrison and for her heretical ideas. During the endless Jubiliada, which began in 1967 and passed into the continuing day-to-day violation of freedom and dignity, Grekova was expelled with great fanfare from the Zhukovsky Academy on the grounds of the whole complex of heretical ideas she held and expressed in her works. She was then subjected to harsh criticism at various meetings coinciding with the assault on *Novy mir*, and on special orders from General Yepishev, head of the military political administration, *Novy mir* was banned from being distributed in the army.

Novy mir's fate became her fate as a writer. Naturally, Grekova did not "go out on the streets" as a writer but went quietly off to take up a chair at a non-military institute. Grekova's is a genuine talent, however, and a talent such as hers cannot be simply ordered to fall silent. We may expect to hear from her again.

Two other writers who attracted a lot of attention were Vitaly Syomin and Yuri Dombrovsky. Syomin aroused interest with his story "Seven in One House" and some others, while Dombrovsky, a former political prisoner, a genial but vulnerable man, was author of a novel called *The Keeper of Antiquities* which was published in *Novy mir*. Anatoly Kuznetsov once achieved the distinction of publishing in *Novy mir* with his story "Actor with No Lines" ("Artist mimansa"). This was perhaps his very finest work. Soon afterwards he failed to return from London and the Soviet press hurriedly began to erase him from the public consciousness as a deserter.

In 1966 one of the year's most popular books was Felix Krivin's *Stories of the Divine,* despite the fact that it came out in the Ukrainian city of Uzhgorod. The more the censors went on the rampage and satire was crushed, the more eagerly Krivin's Aesopian stories were read. Aesop had, after all, written about the same thing—a bloody epoch which never seemed to end.

One of the "stories"—which were not so "divine" at all—included this entreaty from Alexander the Great: "Save me from my friends, God, and my enemies I'll deal with myself." He fights so assiduously against his enemies that God gets rid of his friends for him. The story called "Methuselah" is just as relevant to the present day: "Adam was the first man. Methuselah was not the first man. Moses was the first prophet. Methuselah was not the first prophet. This is why Methuselah lived for nine hundred and sixty-nine years and his obituary said: 'He died an untimely death.' "

Krivin does not spare his reader, either, who not long before had deified first Stalin and then Khrushchev and was now again ready to raise up and idolize a new "leader and teacher"—whoever it might be.

> *"Don't make idols. I won't for one. I don't really have the inclination."*
> *Moses' flock became noisy.*
> *"Did you hear what Moses said?"*
> *"How true!"*
> *"How right!"*
> *"Don't make an idol!"*
> *"Don't make one!"*
> *"Oh, Moses!"*
> *"Wise Moses!"*
> *"Great Moses!"*

The most surprising thing is that these "Stories" were published by the least adventurous of publishing house—*Polizdat*, presumably under the rubric of antireligious literature. Oh, Aesop, thou art truly great!

At this period Krivin was in some ways our chief literary mentor. Thanks to him, the truth occasionally seeped through onto the pages of *Literaturnaya gazeta*, as a rule onto page 16, the humor and satire page. The following aphorisms were among those which amused our readers:

> "*Dalshe yedesh—tishe budesh.*" (Literary: "*The further you go, the quieter you'll be.*" It is a play on the expression "*Tishe yedesh—dalshe budesh*"—*More haste, less speed.*)
>
> "*Lines will shorten if people squash up more.*"
>
> "*Even at Genghis Khan's funeral someone said what a sensitive, responsive person he had been.*"
>
> "*Remove these lines—they make it hard to read between them.*"
>
> "*Long live all that, thanks to which we, despite the fact that...*"
>
> "*It was a quiet St. Bartholomew's evening...*"

Humorists finally let themselves go to the point where at literary evenings they were coming out with aphorisms which they had not managed to have printed in the press. The editor of the humor and satire page, Ilya Suslov, is still able to enjoy these telling aphorisms as he is now living outside the Soviet Union.

One cannot help suspecting that in the Soviet context the words "comic" and "comedian" may be related to the Japanese "kamikaze."

Yuri Kazakov, a man of rare poetic talent, stands somewhat apart. His first stories appeared in 1956 and his first book *Manka* was published in 1958 in Arkhangelsk. In his stories Kazakov polemicizes openly with those who idealize life, simplify human nature and treat the complexities and contradictions of modern life in an off-hand way. In this he has much in common with other writers of his generation such as Shukshin, Belov, Maximov, Konetsky, Aksenov and Vladimov. Kazakov has published several collections of stories: "At the Siding" (1959), "On the Road" (1961), "An Easy Life" (1963) and "Smell of Bread" (1965). He would seem to be taking Turgenev's *Sportsman's Sketches* as a model for his narrative manner. Hence his attempt to avoid a strict framework for the elaboration of the story-line or for bringing it to a conclusion. The narrator happens to meet someone or hear something and simply describes what he has seen or heard.

The later Kazakov is essentially the same as the early Kazakov who is mentioned in the section on *Pages from Tarusa*. The action in his stories, both the early and the late ones, arises from real-life situations and incidents and develops naturally, seemingly without any principle of selection of details. His stories seem to grow naturally like grass. This is, of course, an illusion. In the background stand the stylists Turgenev, Prishvin and Paustovsky.

Kazakov has more than once been accused of being an imitator. The disciples of pseudo-social literature have been especially vocal in their accusations. In fact Kazakov's works display not an imitative approach but the restoration of lost values. Kazakov has the ability ot get right inside his characters, however unlike himself they are. This is a rare gift.

In "At the Siding" there is a young man who is "without roots" who breaks a record in weight-lifting and is spotted and lured away with promises of an easy life. He holds nothing dear—neither the past, home, nor love. His is like the youths who mill around outside the church in Solzhenitsyn's story "The Procession," smoking, laughing and spitting out sun-flower husks. They have no attachment to anything—either to good or evil. If anyone beckons, they follow.

Kazakov depicts this spiritual emptiness most strikingly in "Smell of Bread." Dusya lives a comfortable, easy life. Even the telegram telling her of her mother's death does not disturb her. "I won't go—why should I?... It's so cold there at this time of the year... Anyway, if there were any bits and pieces to take, the relatives will have got off with them by now, I dare say..." Then some humane impulse stirs underneath the deeply rooted frozen selfishness. When she gets to her mother's house, she finds it has a damp, unlived-in feeling about it, "but there was a smell of bread, a smell she had had an attachment to since childhood, and Dusya's heart started beating faster..." At her mother's grave, she feels the misery of being an orphan with all her heart, not just her mind. It is as if she were a defenseless child. She weeps uncontrollably for a long time, and then slips back into her usual self-satisfied state of mind. This time her heart hardens once and for all.

Kazakov is repelled by these deeply rooted qualities of mindlessness, cruelty and moral dullness, which he depicts with the great sensitivity of a genuine artist.

In "Trali-vali" Egor, who is a young buoy-keeper, is always half-drunk and has been turned into a indolent lay-about by his easy work. The first sentence touches on this directly as if it were the main note to be struck in the story: "Exhausted by the heat of the day and full of undercooked, under-salted fish, Egor the buoy-keeper is asleep in his watch-house. He has a lot of money. Whoever he ferries across, he relieves of a rouble..." While drinking and making empty conversation with some people who have just arrived, he all of a sudden starts singing, and there is silence all around. It is as if the soul of the people itself were singing.

> Across the sea,
> The dark blue sea
> Swims a swan with its young.
>> The swan swims by serenely,
>> The fine yellow sand
>> Is not ruffled.

333

The critics compared this story with Turgenev's "Singers" from *A Sports-man's Sketches* with its strong folk element and its breadth of feeling. Yet the fact is that although the character who forms before our eyes is supposed-ly in the traditional Turgenevan mold, he is actually an unreliable, inwardly lazy, "weak and ineffectual" sort of man. He cannot be relied upon for support and no trust can be put in him. The Soviet critics tried to ignore this highly significant departure from tradition and accused the author of being imitative.

Kazakov's last work, "Northern Diary," is also a vividly written, pene-trating work. After "Northern Diary" Kazakov seemed to have been swal-lowed up, so suddenly did he vanish.

Such subtle and sensitive writers as these have generally found the vi-olence done to them as artists by the Jubiliada more than they can bear. They have either taken to drink or hidden themselves away in the forest with a hunting gun. It is impossible to say whether Yuri Kazakov will reappear again as suddenly as he faded away. Meanwhile, literature is still in a frozen state.

3. THE DESTRUCTION OF CINEMATIC ART

Lenin once said, with reason, that "the most important art form for us is the cinema." While even a good book is read by tens or perhaps hundreds of thousands of readers, a film may be seen by tens of millions of people in the USSR today. There is a film show at least once a week in even the most out of the way collective farm, shepherds' settlement or border post.

The cinema was taken in hand long before the Jubiliada. The State Film Committee (Gosudarstvenny komitet po kinematografii), the supreme control and disciplinary body, was formed on 23 March 1963 at a special meeting of the Politburo of the Central Committee at which Khrushchev delivered a furious tirade, expressing his dissatisfaction with the then existing state of affairs. According to the official announcement, the Film Committee was equivalent in its powers to a Ministry. Consequently, it had at its disposal enormous ministerial salaries and special funds the privileged could tap. It is for the sake of these that bureaucrats in Russia cling so tenaciously to their positions.

A former KGB General, Romanov, was appointed Chairman of the Committee. During the war he had been one of the directors of Smersh (from the words "Smert Shpionam!"—"Death to spies!") as the cultural organization he headed was officially called. The editor-in-chief was Alexander Dymshits, the same "irreplaceable" Dymshits whom the writers had always angrily deleted from the list of candidates at Union of Writers elections. (Special mention was made of Dymshits in a satirical poem doing the rounds of Moscow at that time: "There's a short-legged Dymshits, a Jew thirsting for a pogrom...") He was always eager to please the latest petty tyrant from the Union of Writers, the Lubyanka or the Kremlin.

This was the period of Khrushchev's broadly based assault on art and his "meetings" with artists during which he railed at the sculptor Ernst Niezvestny in particular, and threatened the painters of abstract art, abusing them in foul language and calling them pederasts.

The basic element in Soviet films is the script. The films themselves have as a rule an ideological purpose as a form of propaganda, so the scripts are kept under tight control. At about that time the Soviet cinema had just begun to recover from the almost fatal blow Stalin had delivered it. Stalin had personally checked every film. Under Stalin only some eight films a year had been made and each one had been hailed in the press as a "brilliant achievement of Soviet cinema art" and then been immediately forgotten. However, by the mid-sixties cinema was really beginning to show signs of new life.

For example, in 1966-7 when a film I had scripted was being made about the war in the North, right next door in the Mosfilm studios the most talented and original films of the decade were being shot. These included Tarkovsky's *Andrei Rublyov* and Mikhalkov-Konchalovsky's *Lame Asya*. This director was the son of the poet Mikhalkov, and he did not conceal his contempt for his father. The film *Everyday Fascism* was also being made at this time. Its director was the ageing Mikhail Romm, one of the founders of the Soviet film industry. At the Gorky Studio a film about Herzen was being made at the same time.

What was the fate of all these films, two of which—Andrei Rublyov and *Everyday Fascism*—have remained, despite all the cuts made in them, outstanding films? *Andrei Rublyov* was banned in Russia for several years and did not reach the screen in its original form. Even while the film was still in production the sound-track was changed. I could actually never quite understand how the dialogue of a completed film could be changed since the actors often spoke facing the camera, and sometimes there were close-ups of an actor's lips as he spoke. How did they cope with this? I did not have long to wait to find out.

The sound-track of *Andrei Rublov* was almost completely re-recorded. The director general of Mosfilm, Surin, who was an orchestral trumphet-player by profession, looked at the film and ordered some cuts and changes to be made. Alterations were made to the script—it was "smoothed out," as they say—and part of the sound-track was cut out. Then it was taken to General Romanov who called in Dymshits and a few of the other more vigilant comrades.

It is difficult for the ordinary person to imagine how the Film Committee looks at a film. Once in the semidarkness of the auditorium I looked closely at the faces of those supposedly reviewing a film and was astonished to find that almost none of them was looking at the screen. Although their eyes were closed and they looked as if they were sleeping, they had expressions of concentration on their faces. It turned out that they were just listening to the sound track, trying not to miss a single word in case something subversive slipped through. As a result, they sometimes passed over silent episodes which were actually quite "subversive."

Dymshits had part of the dialogue in *Andrei Rublyov* cut out. The sound-track was then re-recorded. Eventually the mutilated film, now in a form acceptable to the Committee, was taken to the Central Committee Secretary Demichev. The sound-track then had to be re-recorded yet again. Fortunately, at this point a scandal broke out which saved the film. Foreign film-makers began asking what had happened to *Andrei Rublyov* at various international film festivals. In order to avoid "unnecessary explanations" one copy of the film was sold to a Western millionaire whom the Central Committee considered to be "loyal." He had it shown in an international film festival where it was awarded first prize. According to the conventions of the festival, the country organizing the festival was then obliged to buy the film. It was in this way that the world came to see this outstanding film—almost by accident. Film-goers everywhere saw the cruel boyar who considered the craftsman who had made the gigantic bell as just a peasant deserving neither a kind word nor even a nod. They saw the master's servants kill the cheerful buffoon in a brutal fashion for expressing himself freely. The film suggested certain analogies to Russian audiences, which is just what the master's servants in modern Russia were most afraid of. Consequently they tried to deal with Tarkovsky, the free-thinking director, as brutally as the servants in the film. *Lame Asya* could have become an extremely interesting and original film. The parts were taken not by actors but by the inhabitants of a village in the depths of the Russian countryside. I used to enjoy going to the studios to watch the film being shot and to talk with the peasants. It was a bold experiment in which the peasants were given the basic idea and allowed to develop it as they wished. The film was cut to shreds. In the final version it was meaningless and was released in an infinitesimal number of copies. Not that there was anything heretical about it—it just showed life as it really was.

Another doomed film was one about Herzen. In its conception it promised to be of great interest. In the event, however, what Herzen had to say about despotism—they were hallowed words—and the arbitrary rule of the tsarist monarchy caused horrified panic in the Central Committee. It was decreed that Herzen's words suggested an "undesirable subtext" which could lead to certain parallels being drawn. Substitutions were made to the point where Herzen's exposures exposed nothing. Herzen is tolerable so long as he is merely published in huge multi-volume editions and remains on the whole unread. On the screen where he could address almost every Soviet citizen he became an enemy of the Soviet State and was banned.

Romm's *Everyday Fascism* proved to be a more difficult case. It was a documentary film about Hitler and German fascism. Romm was Russia's foremost director and the recipient of numerous prizes. The film had to be released. Episodes such as the following demonstrate why this posed problems: Hitler visits a painting exhibition and wherever he looks he sees his own portrait looking back at him, painted by obsequious artists. Soviet audiences found this uproariously funny. Khrushchev had just made a visit to an exhibition at the Manezh in Moscow where he too had been surrounded on all sides by portraits of himself. The audience only stopped laughing and applauding when the Nazis began shooting women in the back of the neck and taking snaps of each other in the process.

The film Committee was in agony over what to do with Romm's film. No one had the courage to ban a film about Nazism simply on the grounds that it might call forth undesirable comparisons. As a result, the film did reach the screens eventually, although only after severe cuts had been made, particularly in the more telling episodes.

I remember one of the arguments Romm had with the Film Committee.

He was at the end of his tether. When they demanded that he make certain predictable adjustments, Romm grabbed at his heart and exclaimed: "For God's sake, this is art!" Baskakov, Romanov's deputy, retorted with calm sarcasm: "Who ever told you that our business is art?"

Film-goers went in enormous numbers to see such truthful films as *We'll Live till Monday, Three Days in the Life of Viktor Chernyshev, And if This is Love* and *Byelorussky Station*. It was during the last years of the Jubiliada. The bright yet thoughtful film *Aybolit 69* (Dr. Aybolit is a sort of Dr. Doolittle character) marked a particularly high point. In it the wicked Barmaley intoned what the boyars and present-day Party types had long said: "Normal heroes always take the long way round." Dr. Aybolit and his friends sang lustily: "How good it is that things are still bad." All over the country people repeated with a wry smile: "How good it is that things are still bad."

The part of Dr. Aybolit was played by the gifted actor, Rolan Bykov who had played the small part of the wandering jester in *Andrei Rublyov*. It was a role which allowed him to play someone who shared his own fate—he was playing himself.

In order that no doubt should remain about what sort of hands the fate of such talented actors was in, one small fact should be mentioned. Surin, the director general of Mosfilm, was found to have embezzled a gigantic sum of money in foreign currency while making a film with a foreign company. It became necessary to replace him. Extraordinary as it may seem the man chosen as the new director general of the Mosfilm film studios with responsibilities for judging the merits or otherwise of the films being made was none other than the chief of the Moscow militia, Sizov. Admittedly, he had risen by this time to the position of deputy chairman of the Executive Committee of the Moscow Soviet but even here his area of responsibility was the maintenance of public order. During his free moments he had been doing a bit of writing and was hastily accepted into membership of the Union of Writers as just the man they needed.

It is not difficult to imagine my feelings when the film I was involved in, *All Quiet Here (Mesta tut tikhiye)*, came up for scrutiny by the Film Committee. Although the script had been cut about, it had retained the essence of what I had wanted to say and it had been published in the journal *Cinema Art (Iskusstvo kino)* early in 1966.[1] It had been ratified by the Committee. However, that had happened in 1966, and this was now 1967 and the Jubiliada had begun. I shall confine myself to describing what it was that provoked such a hysterical reaction on the part of Romanov, who was, it should be remembered, a General in the film industry and the KGB at one and the same time.

The main character was Alexander Sknaryov, navigator during the war years and now a soldier in a punishment battalion. It was not long since he had been a Siberian peasant, and to the end of his days he remained a simple-hearted and kindly peasant. The script as I wrote it was based on actual events. In 1942 a large number of German submarines appeared in the north. They were sinking convoys of English, American and Canadian ships taking arms to Murmansk and Arkhangelsk. Crack airforce groups were sent to fight the submarines. The planes landed in Vayenga, the most northerly airforce base, under fire. Indeed, the bombardment almost never ceased. So that planes could land, a punishment battalion was set to work filling in the bomb craters.

Some airforce officers recognized an old instructor of theirs, a colonel on the general staff, in one of the prisoners. Now he was wearing a soldier's greatcoat and leg-wrappings and filling in a bomb crater with a shovel. The officers took him with them, after promising   the chief of the punishment battalion that they would return him in two weeks or else send a piece of paper to say that he was being sent to carry out further duties. On the first mission the group commander who took Sknaryov was wounded and eva-cuated. Sknaryov was left without the protection of his friend and while an inspection was being carried out, the chief of staff had locked him up in a barn with a goat. However, on his first sortie Sknaryov made an important discovery which changed the whole course of the operation. He discovered that the submarines in the Barents Sea were only small ones, incapable of getting there by themselves. Therefore, the thing to do was to look for the mother ship. "We're just knocking off the eggs one by one whereas we should blow up the whole incubator."

Despite his discovery, Sknaryov was returned to the punishment bat-talion again when a representative of the Special Section arrived. Thus Sknyarov left just as the Northern Fleet began its victorious operation based on his plan. Trucks carrying ammunition, torpedoes and sailors rushed past the unshaven, hunched figure of Sknaryov carrying his green soldier's kit-bag and trying to get out of the way of the speeding trucks whose drivers cursed him. The man who made the victory possible walked off into the distance unrecognized and unwanted.

Romanov's reaction to the film was predictable. The former Smersh chief who herded thousands upon thousands of people into punishment bat-talions and orphaned thousands of children gave an order that the character from the punishment battalion be taken out. "We have no punishment bat-talions. That's all a fabrication."

The most striking scenes in the film were, of course connected with the character Sknaryov. The staff officer who locked him in the barn and who was deeply afraid of him was played by the well-known actor N. Grit-senko, one of the leading actors at Moscow's Vakhtangov Theater. Sknaryov's part was played by another prominent actor, M. Gluzsky.

It is the final encounter between this staff officer and Sknaryov which provides what is possibly the finest scene in the film. The staff officer is having Sknaryov returned to the punishment battalion, but he is ashamed of what he is doing and admits why it is that he, an air-force pilot of long standing, now finds himself committing a cowardly act down on the ground. "There were twelve of us, all friends from Voronezh. One was killed in Spain and another in Finland. But where are the others? Where are they? Where were they killed? You're a prisoner in that battalion until you spill blood, but how long am I a prisoner for?"

Gritsenko, who made the director shoot that scene eight times, kept gulping down some medicine for his heart and he was overcome with the heat. He was wearing winter flying gear while forty spotlights were trained on him. Yet he did not leave the set. He kept saying the last line with different intonations—now shouting, now hissing it. The way he played his part was nothing short of heroic and the whole scene was acted brilliantly. Yet while watching it Romanov, on the point of yawning, intoned in his bored general's voice: "We had no punishment battalions. Get rid of that prisoner character."

All his underlings began chorusing: "Got to get rid of him! That guy with the kit-bag, wearing those leg-wrappings—get rid of him!"

But how was one supposed to get rid of the main character? The whole plot hung on him, all the psychological interest. Everything hinged on him—even the pitiless rocky landscape of the Kola Peninsula was geared to his character. How was it possible to get rid of the character the whole film was created around? I refused. I threw my studio pass on the director's desk and walked out.

The film was "put on the shelf," as it was called. This did not worry anyone even if it had cost seven million roubles to make. It was public money and the State treasury was a bottomless barrel, as everyone knew.

A month later the director came to see me. His eyes were moist and his hands were shaking. "Grisha," he said, "they're not going to let me make any more films, they're kicking me out. Please do something..." But what could I do? Throw out the main character? Then in his train the whole film crew started coming to see me—the lighting technicians, the wardrobe people, mothers with large families to care for. "What are you doing to us?" they said. "We went all the way up north. We were counting on getting prizes. Now we haven't got a kopeck. How are we going to get by?" It was the mothers who finally got to me. I began trying to think of a way out of the situation. Then I suddenly had an idea. I telephoned Romanov. "So I can't have the prisoner from a punishment battalion in it," I said. "Not under any circumstances," he said. "Where'd you see punishment battalions?" "All right—I agree. Could we have just an officer reduced to the ranks?" "I expect so," he said after some hesitation.

The film was saved. Naturally the sound-track had to be re-recorded— we did not manage to escape the common fate. Where there was a close-up of an actor saying "punishment battalion" ("shtrafbat") we then dubbed in "construction battalion" ("stroybat"). The articulation of these words was similar.

Some 400 meters of film were cut out. Scenes in which it was obvious that the action took place in a punishment battalion had to go. For example, one scene showed the wild joy of a soldier who had had half an ear torn off. Blood was pouring out of it while he was running across the airfield shouting exultantly: "I've been hit! I've been hit!" This meant that he was free, no longer a prisoner, not in the punishment battalion. He would be given papers stamped "Krovyu smyl" (Washed off with his blood) and released to join the regular infantry in the near-by trenches. Scenes such as this obviously had to be cut out. The director shouted and beat himself with his fists in a frenzy but he was powerless to do anything—so he kept on cutting. He felt he was slicing up his own child. Four hundred meters, the film's best scenes, became clippings on the cutting-room floor.

When Gluzsky saw the film in its truncated form he began weeping. The character he had created had effectively been destroyed. The director wept from a feeling of shame and impotence.

The film was passed and was released in an enormous number of copies, for both the wide screen and small screen. This is how I received my thirty pieces of silver. My apostasy consisted of betraying Sknaryov from the punishment battalion, for whom the whole film was first conceived. It was only eight years later when my novel *Hostages* came out in Paris that I was able at least in part to atone for my guilt before Alexander Sknaryov and others of my friends who died over the Barents Sea. Yet, who at the time could have imagined that this would be possible?

The Jubiliada rolled over me like a tank flattening the trenches. It was then that I decided that I must fire straight at it. It was gratifying to me to know that my shots—my curses—aimed publicly at the hangmen reverberated right around the country, thanks to the efforts of samizdat, and that they were printed in *Le Monde* and other Western newspapers.

Yet how many others were beaten into silence and were simply never heard of? A film based on Dostoevsky's *A Nasty Story*, made by the talented directors Alov and Naumov, was banned, and Askolodov's film *The Commissar* was simply erased. (Again the leading role was played by Rolan Bykov.) This happened despite the fact that the most influential writers and directors in Russia attempted to defend it. The list of banned and cut films would alone take up dozens of pages. Directors made films and Party watch-dogs now sat, in conformity with a new rule, right on the set so that the film could be "closed down" at an early stage if necessary.

The wholesale mutilation of films reached phenomenal proportions. The order went out that "deviant thinking" should be wiped out completely—even the slightest hint of deviant thinking. Hundreds of millions of roubles were written off without a moment's hesitation.

Just as the Tartar khans used to feast and carouse on top of their bound Russian captives, so the new khans celebrated the jubilee of the world's first socialist State with the bound and crucified body of the Soviet film industry at their feet. This was only to be expected. As Lenin said, "the most important art form for us is the cinema."

4. THE DEMISE OF TVARDOVSKY: THE REMOVAL OF THE LAST OBSTACLE IN THE WAY OF PULP LITERATURE

The cinema was crushed in Romanov's iron fist. However, it was difficult to keep a watch on the hundreds of journals and publishing houses scattered across the length and breadth of the country, and the tens of thousands of editors among whom were many honest people who found their vigilante tasks almost unbearable. Suddenly the Siberian journals *Angara* and *Baikal* broke free and the Alma-Ata journal *Prostor (Scope)* began to act up occasionally.

A detachment of Romanovs was detailed to make an assault on literature. Another Romanov happened to be Chairman of the All-Union Press Committee attached to the USSR Council of Ministers. The two Romanovs were christened Two Boots Make a Pair—or simply the Two Boots. The rumbling of the tanks on Wenceslas Square in Prague echoed through all the Romanovs' circulars on the press.

On the outside everything appeared normal in the arts. The Red Hundreds, whose members had occupied key positions in the arts, called meeting after meeting. These were not closed Central Committee meetings at which one did not have to choose one's words too carefully, but large, so-called democratic assemblies which were often held in a formal, solemn atmosphere. The lists of guest speakers would include well-known names whose prominence was the product of a selection process lasting many years. These people were asked to share their deepest thoughts on the fate of the modern novel and to do what they could to raise the theoretical level of the inevitable empty verbiage. They were also asked to remind writers among other things of their patriotic duty to the jubilees being celebrated.

Those who were obedient were rewarded handsomely and without delay. Their books were republished and they were sent on trips abroad. The way these things are organized in Russia with its hundreds of thousands of libraries provides manna from heaven for all the tamed and mediocre writers in the country. Even if a book is utterly worthless, just a hack work, it will be ordered in hundreds of thousands of copies if it is recommended to libraries.

These so-called "creative meetings" were publicized with much ballyhoo in the press and on radio and television. The pictures of smiling Gribachevs and Sholokhovs squeezed more serious items out of the newspapers. It was the custom in *Literaturnaya gazeta* to place these pictures in a strip around the edges of the page—"like a mourning frame," as Paustovsky said.

The corner-stones laid down by the Central Committee—such as the primacy of the leading role of the Party, which would be mentioned at the beginning of the book—were defined more precisely and polished up: "Every component of a book must correspond to the demands not of yesterday but of the present moment."

Editors started using expressions from accountancy such as "to balance the work" ("sbalansirovat proizvedeniye"). This basically meant to weigh up how many positive characters there were in a manuscript and how many negative ones, and to calculate whether there might not be too many negative ones, creating an atmosphere which was too gloomy. It would be considered that the balance had been dangerously upset, for example, if a positive character had an Armenian surname such as Karapetian while a negative, or simply unpleasant character had a Russian one, such as Ivanov.

There were others such as "bringing up to date" ("dovesti do azhura"), "to coordinate" ("soglasovat"), "to settle" ("utryasti") "to adjust the figures" ("podognat pod obshchuyu summu")— meaning here to adjust them according to the demands being made) and to "round off" ("obkatat"— here meaning to smooth over sharp edges). Socialist realism openly took on the form of juggled books in which everything had to "add up."

Editors applied themselves to doctoring texts and changing the language. In Paustovsky's reminiscences of Olesha mentioned above there are a couple of lines attributed to an old doorman wearing lilac braces: " 'Gratis!' repeated the old man. 'There's absolutely no one to pay. Intourist has been evacuated. I'm here for the watchman.' "[2] ("Gratis!—povtoril starik.—Platit absolyutno nekomu. 'Inturist' evakuirovali. Ya zdes za storozha.")

In 1972, four years after Paustovsky's death, a junior editor called Izgorodina corrected this passage. In the collection entitled *Alone with Autumn* (Moscow) it now reads as follows: "It's free because there's no one to pay. The trust has been evacuated. I'm here instead of the watchman."[3] ("Besplatno potomu, chto platit nekomu. Trest evakuirovali. A ya zdes vmesto storozha.") The image of the doorman, an impulsive old native of Odessa with little time for logical constructions of the "because" kind, has been completely obliterated by the editor. The style has been completely changed. The editor could not apparently see any reason to mention Intourist directly, either.

I could not help imagining what would have become of Babel if he had fallen into the hands of Izgorodina. If the classics, the most subtle masters of style, can be "corrected" in this shameless and insensitive way, it can be easily imagined how those writers who have not yet become classics are dealt with. It is now the normal practice on the part of editors to do violence to the texts submitted to them.

To describe the more difficult case where the author is still alive and stubbornly resists this editorial practice, the Russian language has come up with another expression which reveals the true nature of the despicable practice of "passing the buck": "to chase the hare further." This expression means to pass a manuscript from one reader in a publishing house to another. One of my early novels was published only after running the gauntlet of twenty-three such readers.

This cowardice on the part of editors costs the State a lot of money. It is instructive to consider the exact figures. In 1961 alone, a year of partial freedom for writers, one might almost say of unheard-of liberalism, in the *Sovetsky pisatel* publishing house 133,500 roubles were spent on "playing safe"—or "internal reviewing" as it is called. This was the price paid for the editors' fear of new manuscripts. If all the publishing houses are taken together—literary, political and scientific—then the price paid must have run into the tens of millions of roubles.

It need hardly be added that under the firmly entrenched system of "balancing the books," "passing the buck" and "ironing out difficult points" the most profound and mature works never reach the printing presses. The last of these to be rejected was Vladimir Maximov's *Seven Days of Creation*. If it had not been for tamizdat (having things published in the West), it would have vanished without trace like scores of other talented works.

Sometimes it is not easy for publishers to reject a work. The author may be famous or influential, or the book may be written in such a way that it is hard to seize on specific faults. Sometimes the book itself can be "passed" but the author is on the black list. Somewhere at some time he said something he should not have. Under these circumstances they play their unbeatable trump card: there is no paper.

As I remember, there was a paper shortage of this kind in Moscow for fifteen years in a row. "The Finns aren't selling us any, so there's no paper," someone in the Central Committee told us "in confidence."

In recent years up to eighty percent of books by professional writers have been denied access to the printing presses on the grounds of "lack of paper." Anything at all original has suffered in this way. Several of my friends decided to find out if there really was no paper available. In 1965 after Khrushchev had fallen, an official commission of writers was formed, after many difficulties, which established that the work of the publishing houses had never been limited by the unavailability of paper. This was particularly true of *Sovetsky pisatel*. "On 1st January 1963 the actual stocks of paper comprised 1,380 tons, while the norm was 1,000 tons," their report stated.

Deception was being practiced at every level. The director of *Sovetsky pisatel* publishing house N.V. Lesyuchevsky informed the Secretariat of the Union of Writers that he had 935 tons of paper left. When a check was made, it turned out that he had 1,250 tons. He had concealed the existence of 315 tons even from the Secretariat of the Union of Writers, the notorious Black Ten.

For all this, literature could not be completely routed while Alexander Tvardovsky's *Novy mir* was still in existence, "giving us the note," as the Russian expression has it. It is difficult to say whether Tvardovsky will "come to rest on the sandbars of time" or not as a poet together with his

345

cheerful Tyorkin and his earlier hero Nikita Morgunok, who screwed up one eye so as not to be able to see too clearly the destruction of the Russian countryside.

As editor of *Novy mir*, Tvardovsky is part of history. Even the rather distorted mirror of Solzhenitsyn's *The Calf and the Oak* reflects his place in history more or less correctly, despite the fact that Tvardovsky clearly saw that Russian prose had not begun with Solzhenitsyn and would not finish with him. Tvardovsky was not able to defend Bek and was not able to afford protection to Grossman, urgently begging him to take back his manuscript of the second part of *In a Just Cause* into his safe keeping. On the other hand he rescued Zalygin's "On the Irtysh" from oblivion and made it possible for Mozhayev's "Still Alive" to see the light of day. He literally tore Abramov's "Pelageya" out of Glavlit's hands. He printed the story by the then unknown author Natalia Baranskaya "An Average Week" (1969), which told the bitter truth about women's emancipation in the USSR. He published the best of Shukshin and Belov. *Novy mir* provided the sustenance for the growth of the whole stream of "village" prose. It was Tvardovsky who saved Vasil Bykov from extinction. And how many more manuscripts were awaiting their turn in his safe and in writers' desk-drawers? Tvardovsky knew who had which manuscripts put away and waited for the right moment, the right sign of light in the darkness, to do something about it. He always humbled himself before Furtseva and took his hat off to all the Polikarpovs at all levels of the Central Committee. He did this for the sake of every page, paragraph and line of truth.

Despite everything, *Novy mir* kept coming out every month, appearing on the newsstands in its restful blue cover. It was this journal, so hateful to the atomic-age State, which put the Jubiliada pulp literature in its place. It was cut about, held up by the censors, by the Central Committee, the KGB and the military Political Directorate but still it kept hope alive with every issue that came out. When the prose writings that appeared in it were grasped by the authorities in a strangle-hold, it went over into "small print," as the Russian expression has it—that is to say, it devoted itself to critical articles printed in small script. Paustovsky's experience in *Pages from Tarusa* came in handy here. The articles by V. Lakshin, A. Lebedev, I. Vinogradov, S. Rassadin and others were read with thoughtful and deep attention, even if they did not contain any particular allusions or subtext. Readers did not believe that *Novy mir* could have its corners "ironed out."

Inevitably the journal was moving towards its own demise, and lightly mocked its own fate in V. Belov's "Tall Stories from Vologda." *Novy mir* could not be like other journals and indeed did not want to be. If this meant it had to die, then die it must. It would be a glorious death.

It is well worthwhile devoting some attention to the writers and works which stood out in the final issues of Tvardovsky's *Novy mir*. These works were a pretext for reprisals long in preparation.

Fate decreed that *Novy mir*'s swan-song should be the works of the very courageous writer Georgy Vladimov and the very cautious translator and poet Lev Ginzburg. Vladimor became known to Russian readers when the seventh issue for 1961 came out containing his story "The Great Iron-Stone." This story provoked widespread comment in the press.[4]

The main character in the story is a driver by the name of Pronyakin. His life and death gave rise to discussions of the deeply buried processes taking place in the working class, processes which were at variance with the official doctrines making it possible for villains in secure and powerful positions to juggle for years with concepts such as "hegemony of the proletariat" and "dictatorship of the proletariat."

Vladimov's last book, *Faithful Ruslan*, which not long ago came out in the West, was written during the same period.[5] It was not published in *Novy mir*. In deference to Solzhenitsyn all books such as *Faithful Ruslan* were pushed aside, although there can be no doubt that one day they will become classics. This was done not, of course, on Tvardovsky's initiative— it was not a question of his failing to appreciate the worth of Vladimov's book—it was simply that under the slave-labor conditions which obtained, only one man was permitted to speak about convict life in *Novy mir*.

In 1969, the year of *Novy mir*'s demise, Vladimov's novel *Three Minutes' Silence* was published in one of the last issues to appear under Tvardovsky's editorship (nos. 7-9). It was uncompromising in tone and the language was rich and saturated with sailor's slang. Before he wrote it Vladimov got a job in Murmansk as a sailor on a fishing boat and spent several months sailing the northern seas.

Interestingly enough, Vladimov, like Abramov, first started writing as a literary critic. However, he found that as a critic he could not say what it was almost painfully necessary for him to say and so he moved over into prose, into the mainstream.

Although in this novel Vladimov's characters are sailors, the conflict could equally well have arisen on dry land or indeed in any Soviet household. There are many different characters in the novel and many reversals of fortune. We shall address ourselves only to the central ones.

The character holding the position of power in the novel is Grakov. His hollowness is revealed to the reader only gradually. During the war he had tried to have Grandad Alekseich, as the chief-mechanic is called by the crew, put away in a camp. On the boat's second-last trip it goes too close to some rocks and because its engines are worn out, it gets swept onto them and its hull is holed. Grandad Alekseich says that they must put in to port for repairs but Grakov says that "the country needs the herrings." Grandad objects that "the country needs the people who catch the herrings." Grakov radios back that they are cowards.

On the last trip they try to save a Scottish vessel. Then a big storm blows up and it becomes obvious that they will all soon go to the bottom.

347

The only one who shows abject cowardice on this occasion is Grakov himself, who happens to be on board. He drinks himself senseless and staggers to his bunk to die. It is Grandad Alekseich who takes control and saves the ship. Grakov's hollowness and moral bankruptcy is typical of the powerful who are only capable of goading others onwards and destroying them. *Three Minutes' Silence* sounded like a call to observe three minutes' silence for *Novy mir* which was about to sink below the waves itself and had already started taking in water.

The end came all too quickly. In the fifth issue for the year there appeared some stories by Fazil Iskander which aroused the ire of the authorities. Iskander was one of the country's most gifted satirists. His story "Capricorn" had won him recognition right across the country. The stories he published in 1969 were much more profound. The hero of one of them, Emil, is from West Germany but the reader realizes that the story is not about German fascism but the Soviet variety. This theme which was such a sensitive one as far as the Red Hundreds were concerned was developed in some depth in a work which appeared to be quite slight, without any subtext. Lev Ginzburg, a well-known translator of German poetry and a seemingly timid man, suddenly came out with a story in *Novy mir* (1969, nos. 10-11) called "Meetings on the Other Side—Notes from Munich" which astounded everyone.

As he read this work, the reader found himself developing second sight, however naive he may have been previously. He found himself reading about German Nazis but right from the beginning he realized that he was actually reading not about Germans at all but about Stalinism, and, what was more important, about the Stalinists of his own day. This was despite the fact that the author mentioned nobody but German Nazis.

Ginzburg recounts his meetings with surviving leaders of Nazi Germany including some of Hitler's friends. He talks with Herman Esser who possesses membership card no.2. Hitler himself had card no.7. Esser was a member on the strength of being an "old friend of the Fuhrer's." "Fear and calculated self-interest ruin people," says Esser."But self-interest is not the worst thing. The worst is mental paralysis, foolish rapture at base and vile acts." Ginzburg is then taken to see Hans Bauman, author of the Nazi anthem and now a poet and translator. Although he is not free of a sense of guilt, Bauman has developed a love for Russian poetry, some of which he has translated. It is sad to read what he has to say. In his words there is a sort of belated repentance and a half-hearted attempt to ingratiate himself: "The national anthem sealed my fate. I have accepted my fate as my due. But you must allow me to hope that you understand the tragedy of someone who, having been blinded himself, unintentionally blinded others." These lines brought forth howls of protest from the literary bandits in Moscow who were still engaged in blinding readers whose eyes had long since been open.

The reader is then introduced to a whole line of old men who were once important bureaucrats in the Fuhrer's government. Their thoughts and attitudes sound exactly like those of their Soviet counterparts still filled with reverence for the bloody excesses of omnipotence. One of them is Schirach, the founder of the Hitler Youth League. There is also Speer, Minister for Armaments, Minister for Total War, who in 1942 replaced Todt when he was killed. Speer is the cleverer and more cynical. He is also very frank: "Human lives and the fate of individuals, of course, interested no one," he says. "We simply did what had to be done." Schirach is still able to enjoy a little joke at the expense of a non-Aryan race. He has pleasure in remembering how at Spandau he stumped his Soviet guards when he said to them: "You know, Ivan, that Pushkin of yours wasn't of Russian origin but Ethiopian." Ivan is indignant and protests that he was not an Ethiopian but a Russian, a real Russian.

Although Schirach probably made the story up since it was strictly forbidden for the Soviet guards to talk to or have any contact with anyone, he had an unerring sense, proper in an old Nazi, of the chauvinistic spirit emanating from Russia and enjoyed playing on it. This is what makes the passage on Schirach noteworthy. In a similar vein Jalmar Schacht, the former Reichsbank president, is still obsessed with the idea of the influence of the Germans on Russia: "There's your capital, St. Petersburg. And what about literature? There's Khemnitser, Fonvizin..." The old Nazis cannot help tweaking Russian chauvinism by the nose and Lev Ginzburg assiduously reproduces all of it.

Ordinary generals and burghers openly regret the passing of the good old days. They praise Hitler. "He always put the interests of the people above morality and the law," one general recalls. Hitler executed 119 of his generals and some 80,000 soldiers. "He had a high goal," the general says by way of justification. "A high goal sometimes demands a lot of blood." The proprietor of a bar is even more frank: "Ever since Hitler we've been governed by a lot of mongrels... He was a real personality."

Ginzburg also quotes a line from a book by the German poet Hans Magnus Enzerberger: "Out of our national self-awareness exotic flowers sometimes grow."

Those of the young big-wigs with an education who could read between the lines—they were mostly from the Komsomol Central Committee (Young Communists, but actually people about forty years old)—raised a hue and cry. The metropolitan newspapers immediately published a few clamorous articles which made it perfectly clear that the last shot *Novy mir* had fired had been uniquely well aimed, hitting the Stalinists right between the eyes. They were too dim-witted to keep their silence. Anyway, why should they feel inhibited?

It did not take long to convince the Party Secretary Pyotr Demichev and the Secretary of the Union of Writers Konstantin Fedin of what had to be done. The noose had long been around Tvardovsky's neck. It was now

349

just a matter of knocking the stool out from under his feet. This they did. Tvardovsky was put in a hospital and a year later he died. *Novy mir*, the last legal bastion of the progressive intelligentsia, had ceased to exist.

5. THE TAPE-RECORDER REVOLUTION

To all appearances, the destruction was complete. The theater, the cinema and prose writing had all been decimated. The Jubiliada, like an executioner who had finished his day's work, could not hang up its uniform —the job had been done. Then, in the deathly silence, the sound of poetry set to music and the humming of tape-recorders became more audible. The singing of poetry had long since broken free of the control of the Union of Writers and it now took up a preeminent position in place of the art forms which had been crushed and stifled. It was heard as a challenge in the cities and in the remotest corners. Russia began to express herself through them.

In the depths of the countryside, with few exceptions, Alexander Solzhenitsyn's books, like the books of other *Novy mir* writers, and samizdat were unknown. The only work by Solzhenitsyn to reach library shelves in outlying districts was *One Day in the Life of Ivan Denisovich* which came out in 700,000 copies in the pulp digest *Roman-gazeta*. Apart from that Solzhenitsyn was essentially unavailable. Subversive journals with restricted circulation and thick samizdat manuscripts are not read in the back woods. They are simply unobtainable.

This is why it was easy to make Solzhenitsyn out to be a liar. It was much more difficult to misrepresent songs people recorded on their own tape-recorders, especially songs which belonged not just to their composers but which had become common property.

The verse set to music of Bulat Okudzhava, Alexander Galich, Vladimir Vysotsky and others went even further, becoming a symbol of free-thinking, which had been abusively dubbed by the State "divergent thinking." These poet-composers saved the poetry of resistance from a complete rout. What they wrote was genuine poetry, talented works of literature with their own long and bloody history, their own enemies and ardent champions.

The Romanovs did not immediately realize what was happening. Fortunately, it took some time for them to grasp how much these poorly recorded tapes of civil disobedience enriched the life of the average person. People did not repeat the text of official speeches, posters or calls from the Party Central Committee but were caught up instead in the revolution of taped songs.

The revolution began in an unhurried fashion and then turned out to be irreversible and all-encompassing. It was the returning political prisoners who brought these poems and songs back to the cities of Russia together with their camp slang. Some of them were naively sentimental, such as those of the common criminals, shot through with vulgar expressions and obscenities while others were full of wisdom, bitterness and poetry which gripped the heart. It was often difficult to establish who had written the songs and

351

poems—there would sometimes be several claimants to authorship but in most cases the actual authors had probably perished in Vorkuta or Kolyma or some other far-flung corner of the Gulag. Yet their songs and verse survived. One of the songs which has come down to us is the artless "Vorkuta-Leningrad," infused with Russian folklore. Another is a bitter song of accusation written by a poet who died in the camps. It hurls a curse at the Gulag. I shall quote it as I remember it recited to me by prisoners from Kolyma I once encountered:

> I remember the harbor at Vanin
> And the mournful roar of the steamer,
> I remember how we climbed aboard
> Into the cold dark hold.
> > The fog crept over the sea
> > And the deep seethed.
> > Magadan, capital of Kolyma,
> > Rose up ahead.
> The prisoners stood at the railing
> Embracing like dear brothers.
> Only occasionally someone would let fly
> With a curse at the guards.
> > Curse you, Kolyma,
> > From you there's no return.
> > You can't help going mad there—
> > What a planet they've turned this into!

There were not many songs, but those there were set the tune for the young performers armed with just a guitar. Songs such as this gave the note like a tuning-fork and the note they gave rang with the truth about the camps. The themes of these writers' poetry were diverse but they were unfailingly truthful. This stream from the camps washed away the official lies about national well-being. It merged with the stream of Russia's best poetry and the guitar-players began to put to music the best verse of Yaroslav Smelyakov, a broken and shattered man who returned from the camps while Stalin was still alive and never wrote camp songs.

> If I fall ill, I shall not turn to the doctors.
> I appeal to my friends—don't imagine that I'm raving—
> Spread out a steppe for me, hang my windows with mist.
> Take one of night's stars for me to rest my head on.

No one knew exactly how these new songs surfaced. They comprised an elemental, only half-conscious, growing protest on the part of the young against the emptiness of the songs they heard on the radio and against their soulless existence. There is an almost inexhaustible supply of these spontaneous hiking songs, marching songs and satirical songs which young people used to shield themselves from the officially sanctioned compositions which were dressed up to look like real poetry.

At first there were no acknowledged leaders of this new genre but eventually and inevitably they appeared. The first to stand apart from the others as a very individual talent was Bulat Okudzhava. We heard his first songs in 1959 or 1960, but only at friendly gatherings. The country at large still knew nothing of them.

Okudzhava's first public performance was close to a disaster. The habitues of Moscow's Dom Kino (a club for people connected with the film industry)—the stylized beauties and the dentists among whom there was barely a film actor or film operator to be seen—gave his songs a cold reception. After Okudzhava's performance, Vasily Ardamatsky, an utterly conventional type of man who was conducting the proceedings, came to the front of the stage, threw up his hands and said with a wry smile: "I take no responsibility." Okudzhava told me about this in 1967 and even though it was many years since his first concert his face went hard at the memory of it.

Only two or three years after his first concert his songs had captivated Russia. It was an unprecedented breach in the concrete wall of censorship. Just after Khrushchev had purged the arts in 1962-3 and prose writing had lain low like soldiers at the foot of some fortifications, these songs began to flood the country, washing right over the fortifications. The first were Okudzhava's, and then came Galich's, Vysotsky's and others'. As Galich wrote: "All I need is a Yauza tape-recorder, nothing else!"

A real tape-recording revolution took place. Okudzhava's and Galich's songs began to be heard in the log huts of workers' hostels, on construction sites in timber depots in the forest where collections of poetry might never be read. They were heard in the most out-of-the-way places where books did not even appear.

The popularity of Okudzhava's songs kept growing like an avalanche, burying beneath it not only the songs broadcast over the radio but also the widely known, naively poetic songs of writers such as Isakovsky.

Okudzhava jokingly refers to himself as "a Georgian bottled in Moscow." He spent his youth in Georgia which he left after his father had been arrested and shot. Yet his command of the Russian language, his native language, would be the envy of any modern poet with his roots deep in the soil of Ryazan or Kaluga. What is the secret of his popularity? Let us take one of Okudzhava's apparently simple and even primitive songs in an attempt to explain it.

> *Devochka plachet—sharik uletel,*
> *Yeyo uteshayut, a sharik letit...*
> *(A little girl is crying—her balloon has flown away,*

353

Poetically these lines are simple in the extreme. The couplet does not even rhyme and the idea is a simple one: people are born, live and die.

The poem repeats the words "sharik uletel" ("the balloon has flown away") and "sharik vernulsya" ("the balloon has come back"). The monotony this creates is the very monotony of life itself. Only at the end of the poem does the tone change abruptly: "sharik vernulsya, a on goluboi" ("the balloon has come back and it is sky-blue"). The significance of the color cannot be interpreted in one way alone. There is a subtext here which needs throughtful consideration. There is a mysterious element to it which the reader or listener gropes his way towards. At the same time this last line compositionally closes a circle.

It is a sad poem, but not a hopeless or tragic one. The tone is rather meditative and elegiac. The balloon's blueness seems to refer to the mystery of life, not to the balloon.

Even people who were normally uninterested in poetry became pensive when they heart this song. The reason is that its mysterious quality is not the result of metaphors as in "The Black Cat" where it is obvious that the Black Cat stands for the powers that be, Stalin or something of that kind. "The Blue Balloon" does not strike us by its intellectual profundity but by its tonality and mood. This is in fact one of the particular qualities of Okudzhava's lyrical verse: the confidential tone which seems to come from the author himself.

The ideas behind Okudzhava's songs became more and more challenging and the sense of their mystery more and more tragic and serious. They made his listeners and readers pause to think—whether they wanted to or not.

In his song "Like the First War" as usual Okudzhava does not speak in the name of the Russian people or a particular generation, as the poets he overshadowed were infallibly wont to do, but he gives voice to his own thoughts, his own experience, and has his own tone. The language is modern and colloquial, expressing only the poet's own feelings. It is this quality which found such a positive response among Okudzhava's contemporaries.

Apart from this, the poetry of folklore and the romance which are so deeply engrained in the Russian people have been organically developed in Okudzhava's verse, enormously enriching it in the process. The vocabulary and structure of the folkloric poetry and the romance suddenly became inseparable from Okudzhava's poetic voice. For example:

> *A kak pervaya lyubov, ona serdtse zhzhet.*
> *A vtoraya lyubov—ona k pervoy lnyot.*
> *A kak tretya lyubov—klyuch drozhit v zamke,*
> *Klyuch drozhit v zamke, chemodan v ruke*

When first love comes, it burns the heart
Second love—it clings to the first.
When third love comes, it's a key trembling in the lock,
A key trembling in the lock, a suit-case in the hand.

Here we have the traditional repetitions and parallel similies of Russian folk poetry.

In the following lines we have an example of the age-old motif of a series of three from folk songs.

A kak pervaya voyna, da nichya vina.
A vtorary voyna...
A kak tretya voyna—lish moya vina,
A moya vina: ona vsem vidna.

(The first war—no one's fault.
The second war...
The third war is my fault alone,
And my fault is obvious to all.)

For all his innovative and ultra-contemporary approach, Okudzhava observes the canons of poetry scrupulously. This does not refer to the semi-official stereotypes in the press which the average reader simply finds nauseating. The canons he observes belong to folk poetry, dear to the heart of Russian readers. He has the triple structure in the opening and a triple-line structure:

A kak pervy obman, da na zare tuman.
A vtotoy obman—zakachalsia pian.
A kak trety obman—on nochi chernei,
      on nochi chernei, on voiny strashnei...

(The first deceit is like mist at dawn.
The second deceit is rolling drunk.
The third deceit is blacker than night,
      blacker than night and more terrible than war...)

This contemporary poet's verse with its repetitions is infused with Russian folkloric song. The folk element is combined with feelings, experience, a confidential tone and openness which are genuinely his own. One feels that every single listener is a friend. The folk element gives Okudzhava's poetry in song a penetrating strength and a liberating radiance.

Even the well-worn theme of the individual's responsibility to history—a theme readers had grown to loathe, soiled as it is by the hands of all the

355

hack-workers and speculators—rings out with a new lyricism. Despite the civic theme, the formal elements in Okudzhava's song belong to lyricism.

Galich attained his lyricism after passing through a satirical stage. With the exception of "The Black Cat" and "The Fools," Okudzhava's satire itself is lyrical. The old folkloric *bylina* or song form has its limitations in Okudzhava's works as does the form of the urban romance. He imbues it with a tonality of his own.

> *Vot za blizhayshim povrotom*
> *Korolya povstrechayu opiat...*
>
> *(Just past the next turn here*
> *I'll meet the king again...)*

These are not lines to be shouted or recited in a loud voice. They are charged with a mood which is communicated to any listener who is receptive to moods and feelings.

Even the most stony-hearted listener was touched by the lyricism and transparent idea behind "The Last Trolleybus." It belonged to the years when life was being thought through anew, years of moral vulnerability and feelings of being unsettled, years of spiritual, moral and physical losses. This is why the whole country began murmuring and singing about the kind-hearted trolleybus which went round and round "picking up all those who had been wrecked in the night." The theme of being merciful and kind to the needy has a long tradition in literature and among the Russian people. "Your passengers, your sailors,/Come to the rescue..." The aid they give is very real: "I've avoided disaster several times thanks to them,/I've rubbed shoulders with them..."

Next comes the theme which is the most contemporary of all, one which earlier could not have been treated with the same burning urgency at a time when words and concepts had been devalued totally and all the official propaganda organs were assaulting the ear with their slogans. It seemed as natural as breathing: "Can you imagine how much kindness there is in silence, in silence..." The whole country dreamt of being able just to be silent, to say nothing and to think.

Okudzhava's late night trolleybus travelled all over Russia, from Minsk to Magadan. Its passengers were by no means all of one mind.   All of them wanted to be able to be silent for a while, to have time to think. This was true even of those who because of their high office had lost the habit of thinking, and had assistants and secretaries to do their thinking for them— even people such as these did nothing to stop the last trolleybus doing its rounds throughout the length and breadth of Russia. All those who had lost their way in the darkness needed the trolleybus—and there was no one who had not lost his way.

Okudzhava's strongest composition is perhaps "Francois Villon." It has the intensity of a curse. It is a plea to people to cast aside their intolerance, their narrowness and mutual destructiveness and to be themselves. There is something tragic about this work. It is a prayer, not a pitiful one, but one full of dignity, written by someone who belongs to the modern atomic age. The end of the world which has been foretold with such hysteria through the ages now becomes something tangibly real. The poet begs mankind to think again "while the world is still turning" however odd it may sound, to take a good look at one another "while the light is still bright," for the world will soon stop turning and there will be no more time or light.

This tragic and courageous work has a deep effect on the reader. There is courage, wisdom and breadth of vision in every line. It has the heroic stoicism of the all-comprehending poet. It begs generosity in the interests of happiness for all. This may well be Okudzhava's only direct treatment of the themes of life and death, God and mankind.

Russia—long-suffering and oppressed Russia—began to speak, feel and think in the words and thoughts of Bulat Okudzhava, who prepared the way for Alexander Galich's searing and sometimes brazenly social verse. The new talents which appeared by no means diminished Okudzhava's prominence. His verse stood side by side with theirs, enriching it and in turn enriched by it.

If it can be said that Bulat Okudzhava's lyricism established a secure bridgehead free from official versifying, then it was Alexander Galich's poetry which played the role of the shock troops thrown into the breach.

Galich stirred up the whole country. Suddenly the things on Russians' minds became the concern of the finest verse.

> *Where are the loud-mouths and prophets of doom now?*
> *They had their noisy say and rotted away in their youth...*

> *While the silent ones have become the bosses*
> *Because silence is golden.*

> *How simple it is to get to the top,*
> *How simple to end up a hangman:*
> *Stay silent, stay silent, stay silent!*

> *(Gde teper krikuny i pechalniki?*
> *Otshumeli i sginuli smolodu...*

> *A molchalniki vyshli v nachalniki,*
> *Potomu chto molchanie—zoloto.*

357

Vot kak prosto popast v pervachi,
Vot kak prosto popast v palachi:
Promolchi, promolchi, promolchi!)

It is no accident that it is this poem, "Goldpanners' Waltz," which opens the collection of Galich's verse entitled *Generation of the Doomed* which has not been published in the West.

The stirring effect of his verse was partly the result of Galich's technical brilliance. His verse has great strength and skill. On occasion a pause is as pointed and profound as a striking choice of word. His use of rhyme, as in the second stanza quoted where each line ends in a masculine rhyme ("pervachi," "promolchi,'"palachi"), fills his poetry with explosive strength.

The most important reason for the dramatic effect Galich had on his readers was that he spoke about Russia's greatest misfortune—the people's silence. He did so by using his full range of poetic skills: the accusatory force of his imagery ("The grinding toil of speeches has eaten away at us/ But beneath all the verbal pearls/Dumbness shows through like a black spot..."), a feeling for the historical, concrete reality of Stalinism ("Where are the loud-mouths and prophets of doom now?... The silent ones have become the bosses") and the constant use of terms from the language of the people ("pervachi," "mayata," "molchanie—zoloto"). Taught by all regimes not to think about the affairs of State, intimidated, herded together and hungry, the Russian people is silent. As one important Moscow bureaucrat once remarked to me with a cynical grin: "This is where all our strength lies. A worker needs another ten roubles, or even three or one rouble, to last him till pay-day and this keeps him busy. He hasn't got time for politics."

Galich struck at the "power of the people" at its most vulnerable point. However, it took him some time to reach the heights of his ironic, caustically satirical lyricism—if his verse can be called lyrical. This is a question we shall return to.

Surprising as it may now seem, Galich worked after the war in a completely orthodox fashion as a talented script-writer for the cinema. He scripted the comedies *To the Seven Winds* and *True Friends* which were long-running successes in Soviet cinemas. Galich was also a dramatist, although he certainly does not have the same importance as a dramatist as he does as the writer of film-scripts, poetry and songs. Yet for many years plays he had written such as *Taymyr Calling* (1948) (written together with K. Isayev) and *The Paths We Choose* (1954) were put on in Soviet theaters. Consequently, during the years literature was under siege (from 1948 to 1953), Galich was extraordinarily well-off.

Galich did not set out along the thorny road to the top immediately. The stages of his ascent are a faithful reflection of the changes in the state of mind in Russia. During the "years of half-open doors," 1962-3, when Solzhenitsyn appeared on the scene and the bureaucrats took fright as Russia began to lift her head, Galich began his *Simple People's Monologues*. These are songs of compassion and kind-hearted irony.

This master of modern Russian poetry, now in disfavor, began on a peace-loving note. In "Lenochka," for example, he tells of the hard life of a militiawoman on duty one April night: "A militiaman's fate is to abuse people all day./Whether you're shy or cheeky,/You must abuse people all day./You'd like to spend the day enjoying yourself with your friends/ Smelling lilac./But you have to abuse drivers all day." Then a handsome Ethiopian espies her from his car and a special messenger is sent from the Central Committee to fetch her because the Ethiopian is of royal blood and is even allowed the privilege of holding a model of the flag sent to the moon on the lunar module. What more could you want?

If we were to talk about the ideas in a poem such as this, we would probably mention a sort of benevolent philistinism maintaining order and socialist legality. This is expressed in the mildest and most inoffensive form. Nothing could be more straightforward—there is Lenochka dreaming of her handsome prince on the one hand and accursed reality on the other.

However, the times moved on and the bureaucrats were becoming more and more insolent. In March 1963 Khrushchev launched his assault on the artists exhibiting their pictures at the Manezh. He spent the whole month of May teaching them a lesson and trampling them underfoot.

Then Galich's "Tonechka," an "urban romance," came out. This poem has all the elements to produce a traditional lyrical effect—the basic elements of romance are there—wounded love, a parting. However, a satirical element soon breaks into the romance, and becomes dominant. He makes an attempt to stay within the bounds of the traditional romance but cannot. At the end he tries to reintroduce a note of romance by having his hero, still in love with Tonechka whom he has thrown over, tell the taxi-driver to take him to the Titan cinema at Ostankino where she works as an usherette, but the change in tone is unconvincing. The satirical passages are much stronger.

Although Galich continued to write his benevolently ironic verse and songs about painters, boilermen and the theory of relativity, it was in his cycle of prison poetry that the last vestiges of good humor were washed away. He can no longer compose romances even if he would like to. Instead he writes a song like "Clouds."

Professor Etkind has written a masterful analysis of this work.[6] In view of the fact that "Clouds" is the equivalent of Babel's "Kolyvushka" in terms of its maturity of ideas, it would not be out of place to quote from Etkind's analysis here, an analysis which throws light on the secret of the song's unprecedented popularity.

> Galich's well-known song "Clouds" begins on a note of un-
> hurried meditation, and the language is at first in a neutral literary
> register. At the end of the stanza it becomes colloquial: "Oblaka

plyvut, oblaka,/Ne spesha plyvut, kak v kino,/ a ya tsyplyonka yem tabaka,/Y konyachku prinyal polkilo." ("The clouds float by, clouds,/ They float by without hurrying, as if on the screen,/While I eat chicken tabak,/Having drunk half a kilo of cognac.")

The second stanza is constructed in a similar way but is at the same time opposed to the first. It begins with the same retarding repetitions ("Oblaka plyvut,,, ne spesha plyvut) but does not end in common colloquialisms. Instead, it ends in solemnly symbolic hyperbole. "Oblaka plyvut v Abakan,/Ne spesha plyvut oblaka,/ Im teplo, nebos, oblakam,/A ya prodrog naskvoz na veka." ("The clouds are floating towards Abakan,/The clouds float by without hurrying./ I dare say they feel warm, the clouds,/But I am chilled to the marrow for all time.")

The first stanza moves downwards and the second abruptly upwards while the third stanza combines the attributes of the first and second stanzas. It begins with a lofty symbolic metaphor, suggested at the end of the second stanza, and breaks off on the low colloquial note suggested at the end of the first stanza: "Ya podkovoy vmyorz v sanny sled,/V lyod, chto ya kaylom kovyryal./Ved nedarom ya dvadtsat let/Protrubil po tem lageryam." (I've frozen into the sled track like a horse-shoe,/Into the ice I've been picking at with a hack./So it's not for nothing that I blew twenty years/Suffering in those camps,")

These stylistic, inflectional zigzags continue. In later stanzas there are repititions of an elevated kind belonging to song ("Oblaka plyvut, oblaka..."), melancholy irony ("Ya v pivnoy sizhu, slovno lord, i dazhe zuby yest u menya") ("I sit in the alehouse like a lord and I've still got my teeth") and a prosaic, matter-of-fact date ("A mne chet-vyortogo perevod") ("I've got money coming on the fourth")... The interweaving of various styles has its own power to induce concentration... their merging is the very movement of life itself, embodied in the floating clouds which are at one and the same time real clouds, memories and both a symbol of the external world and a part of the inner world.

"Clouds" was the first song in a whole terrifying prison cycle which may have brought readers as close to the realities of prison life as *One Day in the Life of Ivan Denisovich*. The juxtaposing of different speech registers in these songs about the camps from subtle symbolism to low jargon gives "Clouds" the unexpected force of a sudden cry in the mountains which can even stir nature itself. This song became popular at all levels of the population. It is now sung by people who have never heard of Galich.

Other song-poems which became part of Galich's prison cycle included "It's Always the Wrong Time," dedicated to Varlam Shalamov, in which there is a guard who is annoyed at having to take prisoners to be shot during his lunch break, and "The Curse," in which a retired prison warder is furious with the Black Sea for not accepting regimentation. Another one is the poem "Night Patrol" which is a piece of bitingly satirical buffoonery about a monstrous parade of the stumps of broken statues which will one day "again acquire greatness... and beat drums."

In this last poem Galich passes through satire and the grotesque to achieve a certain "civic" lyricism with the element of high pathos proper to that genre. In lyric poetry we do not so much see the world through the eyes of the poet as in his eyes. This is true of Galich's lyrical verse. Yet his lyricism is not only characterized by pathos, but by philosophical preoccupations.

It was the terrible events of 1968 which led Galich to write these songs. His personal experience also played a part. He read and sang his verse in a club called "Under the Integral" in Akademgorodok near Novosibirsk. As a result the club was closed down and its director was sent to prison for seven years.

The invasion of Czechoslovakia led to the intensifying of social motifs in his works, while the callousness and mindlessness of half-drunk painters and sober taxi-drivers who complained that "we feed them and they turn around and...", the lack of feeling on the part of people at large for the anxieties and problems of their own Russian intelligentsia, sped up the process of Galich's switch to satire of a particularly biting, mocking kind in which there was no longer any place for feelings of good humor.

The early seventies, right up to the bitter moment when he was forced into exile as an emigre, increased his scorn of those who wash their hands of what is happening while remaining fully aware of it.

The story-line is always well worked out in Galich's verse. The satirically edged discourse and the fantastic, absurd situations are not perceived as fantastic or absurd because it is real life which is absurd.

In the sixties Galich's most common hero was the philistine worker who drinks half a liter of vodka with his companions and then goes to sleep on some boards or under a bridge "because healthy relaxation brings on healthy sleep." He sleeps for a year or two or even fifty years, then hands over his independence as an effective worker in its entirety to the blood-bespattered hangmen. However, in the seventies, a new main character makes his appearance—a petty bureaucratic boss, someone of infinitesimal stature, but a boss nevertheless. He does not simply sleep but in his timeless day-dreaming he actively participates in the crimes and deceptions of the regime. He is on the same spiritual plane as the common worker but has nicer things to eat and a position of power. He is surrounded by things from everyday life which characterize his moral and spiritual world. As in the case of Galich's previous heroes, he has a language all of his own. On occasion the narration is in the *skaz* tradition of Zoshchenko and the narrator speaks in his hero's language.

361

Regardless of whether the voice is the hero's or the narrator's, the language is not melodic or tuneful but conversational. Unlike Okudzhava, Galich is primarily a poet little inclined towards musical effects, except in terms of the rhythmical structure.

Eventually Galich's turn came to go to the so-called Oak Room—room no. 8 on the second floor of the Writer's Club in Moscow. This is where the endless closed sittings of the Secretariat of the Union of Writers took place. We have all been through the experience of the Oak Room. Now it was Galich's turn. His misfortunes had reached their climax when the tape-recorder had been switched on during a family gathering at the apartment of the Politburo member Polyansky, who was a notorious obscurantist, and a guest, Yagodkin, a young careerist who was head of the Moscow district committee of the Party, "exercised vigilance" and pointed out the harmfulness of the songs that were being played. The songs were Galich's.

Then it all started in earnest. As Galich wrote in one of his more recent and as yet unpublished songs: "Once I was given a flogging/In an oak lodge./And the faces I saw/Were more terrible than in a fun-fair booth…"

The attrition of the poet got underway. Galich held out for an amazingly long time. He was expelled from the Union of Writers, from "society" and finally from the country, but he continued to beat out the rhythm of his songs in every apartment or house where a tape-recorder was to be found: "I choose freedom,/Not to escape the fight, but to fight./I choose the freedom/Simply to be myself… I choose freedom,/We drink together as intimate friends./I choose the freedom of Norilsk and Vorkuta…"

"None of mine is personal poetry," he once said to me. "The personal element is surrendered to the consciousness of my involvement with my generation…" Yet that is what it means for poetry to be personal, to be about oneself and one's own personality. This is what the eternal rhythm of civic lyrical poetry means, poetry which gives strength to the heart.

In recent years, years of unbridled chauvinism, Galich wrote more and more often about racism, national arrogance and antisemitism. Examples are his ironic poem "Oh, Jews, do not sew a livery" ("Oke, ne sheyte, yevrei, livrei"), "Song of Exodus" (1971) which was inspired by a conversation he had in the Party Central Committee, and a poem entitled "The Train" in memory of Mikhoels ("Our train leaves for Auschwitz/Today and every day"). His poem "Kaddish," dedicated to the heroic Polish teacher Janosz Korczak, is a poetic chef d'oeuvre which he read out with the courage born of desperation in Moscow in 1970, the year of the hijack trial in Leningrad:

> I cry out to you/From 1970:/"Pan Korczak! Do not return!/ In this Warsaw you would feel ashamed!/…In this Warsaw you'd feel afraid…/The horde of speechifying scum/Rushes for unclean power…!/Do not return to Warsaw,/I implore you, Pan Korczak!/You would be a foreigner/In your native Warsaw!"

362

To read verse such as this in Moscow in 1970 meant you had to be ready to leave this vain world and prepare for death. Death could come any day.

However, what were all the others to do? Was there really no point in doing anything? The young poet Gananskov had died in a camp, General Grigorenko had suffered for years twisted into a straight-jacket, and there was a constant stream of fresh victims marching with raised heads to their Golgotha.

How did Galich view all this at a time when he was very ill, having suffered three heart attacks? He wrote a prophetic song called "The Ducks Are Flying." The last line is as follows: "If even one arrives it means it was worth it, it means that they had to fly." Yet the sense of the song is even more tragic: Even if none arrive, it is necessary to fly.

Galich's conviction gives his anger and sarcasm strength, especially when he concerned himself with the intelligentsia which has sold itself, as, for example, in the poem entitled "In Memory of Pasternak." The beginnings of this poem date from a visit Galich made to the township of Peredelkino near Moscow, where Pasternak is buried alongside Kornei Chukovsky in the sloping cemetary. Galich could not and did not forgive the villains who hounded Pasternak to death: "We shall not forget that laughter/And that boredom!/We'll bring to mind by name all those/Who raised their hand!"

The linguistic stream which nourished Galich deserves special and extensive research. Galich's language is the language of today's Russia. Attention should also be paid to the influence on his sung poetry of the folkloric tradition—in particular the dual voice device as in his "Fantasy on Russian Themes"—and the powerful influence of Alexander Blok in terms of both his vocabulary and themes ("Song of the Beautiful Lady," "New Year's Drinking Bout" and various epigraphs from Blok). Galich's verse appears as a kind of roll-call of the centuries.

The recent emigre to the West, Professor Efim Etkind has written a study which I consider to be the first piece of extensive research into such diverse aspects of Galich's work as his poetics and the sources of his language which is a particularly rich example of post-war Russian, from the level of slang and officialese to lyrical eloquence. In this article by Professor Etkind, who is a specialist in European poetry and verse translation, there is only one passage I find myself in disagreement with. "Okudzhava represents a Romantic period in Russian poetry," Etkind writes, "He squeezed out Lebedev—Kumach as Zhukovsky did Sumarokov... Galich's songs appeared according to the same law as realistic art did when it squeezed out classicism and the Romantics."

It seems to me that Professor Etkind has given too much weight here to a theoretical position which is not justified.

Okudzhava certainly prepared the way for Galich's appearance when he began some two years earlier. However Galich did not then squeeze

Okudzhava out. Both Okudzhava and Galich are manifestations of one and the same lyrical "break-through" which was to transform the inner life of a generation. This was a single tidal wave, sweeping away the officially approved optimistic clap-trap of poets such as Kumach, Dolmatovsky, Ostrov, Vasilyev and all the other purveyors of broadcasting material of the kind no objection was ever raised to. Galich's "Human Comedy" and Okudzhava's "Francois Villon" could be heard wafting in turns from the same windows. I do not recall another example from the history of 20th century Russian poetry of such a triumphant passage around the country of two such perfectly complementary poets as Galich and Okudzhava.

In Galich's poetic crucible Blok and Bulgakov, folk song and parody on the romance of middle class urban life, camp slang and the language of the street are all stirred together to produce works which will be studied by our children and our children's children. For ten years Okudzhava and Galich were Russia's life-blood, the whole country sang their songs thought their thoughts, repeating with a new awareness after them: "When we're old we'll sort out what color it was we perished for..."

The Solzhenitsyn period helped poets gain strength to such an extent that they were able to shoulder the problems of the neglected extended prose form.

There would scarcely have been any cause to speak of a tape-recording revolution if it had been confined to the songs and poems of only two poets, however brilliantly talented and original they may have been and even if, as Etkind says of Galich without exaggeration, they reflect almost the whole "comédie humaine." There was, however, another songster-poet who found acceptance at a deep level with the mass of the population: Vladimir Vysotsky.

Many of the songs attributed to Vysotsky are not actually his. This may be taken as some sort of sign of his enormous popularity. On Vysotsky's long-playing record which came out in the United States not so long ago the last song is Galich's "Clouds"—sung by Galich!

For those for whom Galich is sometimes too complicated, philosophical and clever and Okudzhava excessively subtle—and there are many such people—Vysotsky with his hundreds of ironical sporting songs, underground songs, tales in song and gushes of feeling provides relaxation and a kind of bitter joy. He sings his songs as he tears the shirt on his chest.

> I'm fed up to the neck, up to the chin,
> I've even started feeling tired of singing...

These are words which Russian workers have been familiar with for many years. In workers' quarters on the Enisei or in Murmansk people rarely gather without listening to tapes of Vysotsky's hoarse base—the voice of a hard drinker. However, it should not be thought that Vysotsky, the actor from the Taganka Theater, is just a "poor man's Galich," although for a long time the major part of his songs were inferior in their lyricism and satirical sharpness to those of Galich and Okudzhava. Then came songs such as "Moscow–Odessa" and "Learned Comrades." It is not only learned gobbledygook and current mores the latter mocks and satirizes. It presents a vivid picture of Russia's ruling class. It is a psychological portrait of those in power who permit themselves to pontificate about things they have no conception of. "Learned comrades! Professors and doctors of philosophy,/We're sick to death of your x's, confused by your zeroes..." The representative of the powers-that-be is of course an experienced demagogue and his speeches are full of promises to make scientists equal to the heroes of labor on the kolkhozes: "Your fame will spread almost right across Europe if/You show your patriotism with your spades..." There is also a reproach, partly menacing, to those who have forgotten about the Party's main concern while finding square roots "ten times a day": "Oh, while you're amusing yourselves and finding square roots/The potatoes are rotting and moldering on their roots..." There is also an element of frank flattery: "Precious Einsteins, beloved Newtons..." Subconsciously, however, it is only one step from flattery to using a word with quite another meaning—kahal (literally an assembly of Jewish elders but colloquially meaning a group), "a whole kahal of you attacked the tumor..."

Now suddenly the strict overseer armed with a whip is seen behind the good-humored figure with his exhortations: "So, we go as far as Skhodnya on the bus,/And then we go at a trot—don't groan!" You give an order, then you hesitate for a moment and all the "precious Einsteins" send you to the devil and start making all sorts of excuses for themselves.

He now starts mouthing whatever comes into his head. He begins to sound like Khrushchev who promised that the Soviet Union would outstrip America by 1960 in milk and meat production and that the present generation would find itself living under full Communism:

> Dear Learned comrades! Have no doubts
> If something doesn't go right for you, we'll put it to rights.
> We'll arrive in a flash with spades and pitchforks
> We'll work on it for a day and correct the defect.

It appears to be just a cheerfully satirical, uncomplicated song, yet what a precise portrait has been drawn of the representatives of "the people's power" who are ready to hitch the Einsteins up to a cart so long as their own position of power is not threatened.

In his latest songs Vysotsky has begun to have something in common with Galich, especially in his exposure of those who "wash their hands."

> ...They've some slight sympathy for
> Those who have perished, but from a distance...

In touching on this theme Vysotsky also has something in common with Yuli Daniel when he writes about "the non-conformists" and with Eduard Kuznetsov.

Those marching ahead, when they look round—not infrequently from behind prison bars—sometimes find just an empty space behind them. This tragedy of the present-day democratic movement which still lacks mass support is becoming a more and more frequent theme in poetry and prose.

In Vysotsky's verse there is much which has great social import—for example, "The Wolfhunt" in which as a poet he is in the front rank. He is one of three, but by no means superfluous.

Vysotsky began to feel increasingly alone. Not long before other poets had been standing alongside, perhaps just slightly in front, and then they were no longer there. Okudzhava took to writing prose and Galich was thrown out of Russia and died in a tragic accident. Obviously, Vysotsky felt very keenly the responsibility which had fallen on his shoulders. Radical changes began to appear in his work. Some of his more recent songs were devoid of irony and mockery. They were laments for Russia. This is certainly the impression given by "Black Eyes" which is his strongest and most terrifying song, a song of desperation. It contains the despair of the fighting man blocked off by the impenetrable wall of a forest, the despair of a hunted man and the despair of a native son returning to the depths of Russia which greets him with profound unshakeable silence:

> Is anyone still alive here? Come out! Help me!...
> Nobody. Just a flitting shadow in the shade
> And a carrion-crow wheeling lower, tighter...
>
> Is anyone going to answer me? What sort of house is this?
> Why is it darkness—as if plague-stricken?
> The lamps have gone out, the air has gone stale.
> Have you forgotten what it means to be alive?
>
> Your door is wide open, but your soul is locked up.
> Who is the master here? Why don't you offer me wine?
> The reply comes: "You've obviously been long away
> And forgotten us. We've always lived like this.
> We eat grass and have always eaten sorrel,
> We've gone sour in the soul, and are covered in pimples.
> And then we've sought comfort in wine quite a lot.
> We've wrecked the house, fought and hanged ourselves...
>
> I foundered the horses and galloped away from the wolves.
> Show me a land lit by bright lamps,
> Show me the place I was looking for,

Where people don't moan but sing and the floor doesn't slope...

We haven't heard of houses like that.
We've lived a long time in the darkness and got used to it...

Even the souls of the people have been ravaged and deadened. In touching on these themes, Vysotsky's poetry is linked with the writings of Fyodor Abramov ("Pelageya") and Yuri Kazakov ("Trali-vali" and "The Smell of Bread"). So many of these writers' characters suffer from sourness in the soul.

Russians sometimes do not even know the names of the writers of the songs they sing—for example, Klyachkin ("Don't look back, don't look..."), Gorodnitsky ("The sky over Canada is deep blue"), Vizbor ("Seryoga Sanin") and Ancharov ("The parachutes opened and took the weight..."). This last song contains very striking and unexpected imagery in its treatment of its unpoetic theme—the machine-gunning of an airborne landing party:

> *The guns whined*
> *   like bitches in the frost,*
> *The pistols fired point-blank.*
> *And the dead sun*
> *   on the shroud-lines of the birches*
> *Made talking impossible.*

Another writer who has been popular for a long time with romantic travelling songs is Kukin: "I'm following, following the mist. The mist and the smell of the taiga." The reason he follows the mist, Kukin explains in another song is that "fairy tales don't come true,/And fairy tales which don't come true are forgotten..."

Yuli Kim is unfortunately less well-known outside the main centers. Kim was the idol of student audiences, a wise, ironic and splenetic poet who once wrote a whole cycle of songs about informers. Few have held up the "spiritual monolith" of Soviet society to more caustic ridicule than Kim, especially the way that on special days "the intelligentsia and the militia demonstrate their unity." Few have penned a more devastating exposure of the Red Hundreds patriots who:

> *would accuse a babe in arms of lying,*
> *and expect thanks*
> *for not incinerating him as at Auschwitz.*

Every year new names appear of talented, self-sacrificing fearless people. Despite the inevitable casualties, there would appear to be no end in sight to the tape-recording revolution—the only "permanent revolution" left in this exhausted land.

6. VASIL BYKOV

The scratchy tapes of the tape-recording revolution eventually proved to be the salvation of millions of souls from the life-sapping Jubiliada. These tapes served as a kind of innoculation against the "verminous radio," as Eduard Kuznetsov put it.

The scorched earth policy had misfired again, and not only because of the flood of verse and songs on tape. Yet this spring flood would scarcely have been able to fill the spiritual vacuum left by the closure of *Novy mir* if it had not been for one important circumstance. During Khrushchev's assault on literature, it had been the resurrected Babel who had taken up the cause of resistance. Platonov had also been partly involved—"partly" because he had turned out to be stylistically complicated and difficult for the average reader in the fifties. One of the historical paradoxes of this period was the fact that the Jubiliada, while sometimes rattling like an empty tin can and at other times clanking like a tank, gave birth to the century's most heretical novel—Mikhail Bulgakov's *The Master and Margarita.*

The effect on the intelligentsia of its appearance in 1966-67 from the realm of darkness was astounding. One of my friends bought a copy of *Moskva* containing the last part of the novel at Ufa airport while waiting for his plane to Moscow. He opened the journal and became so engrossed that he missed the announcement of the departure of his own flight and the next one. Young students sometimes knew the novel by heart. Bulgakov's novel occupied the same place in the minds of the young generation as the satirical novels of Ilf and Petrov had for our generation, or perhaps Hasek, whose *Good Soldier Shweik* was a tonic during the era of the nauseating military propaganda of the Komsomol press: "Young Russians—join the artillery" and "The sea calls you!" and so on.

Another original Soviet prose-writer of the period who is less well-known or discussed than Bulgakov is Vasil Bykov. This Byelorussian writer ignores all threats and explores his themes tenaciously. At the moment he is living in the town of Grodno, although for a long time he has wanted to live elsewhere because of the way the local KGB persecutes him. Vasil Bykov has been called the Byelorussian Solzhenitsyn. Whether or not he has deserved this title, it is doubtful whether it has made his life any easier, especially now that Solzhenitsyn has been exiled.

Some years ago a correspondent from *Literaturnaya gazeta* came to see Bykov. No one met him at the station. There was a middle-aged man striding nervously around the platform dressed in an army greatcoat without any stripes, looking like a demobbed captain. He appeared to be waiting for someone but he did not at all resemble the writer the correspondent had imagined.

It was only some five minutes later when there was no one else left around that they approached each other. They began talking with some difficulty. Bykov was watching the newcomer with distrust and then suddenly asked him point-blank: "Which journal do you read—*Novy mir* or *Oktyabr*?" When he learned that the correspondent's favorite journal was *Novy mir* he softened somewhat and gave him an account of how attempts had been made to intimidate him.

The local KGB chief had recently called him in, kept him waiting three hours in the reception room and then, after having him shown into his office, had begun to tell the story of how he had personally shot one of Vlasov's men, shooting him in the temple at point-blank range so that his brains had splattered the wall of the barn they were in. "Do I make myself clear?" he asked when he had finished his instructive tale.

I have full confidence in the truthfulness of this journalist whom I have known for many years. His name is Shokhin and he has now left the Soviet Union. He is a man of unimpeachable honesty—indeed, it is because of his honesty that he could no longer stay on at *Literaturnaya gazeta*.

The story has a ring of authenticity because it is in perfect conformity with Anatoly Kuznetsov's account of his experiences with the Tula KGB. These provincial KGB officers could not care less about the nation-wide fame of a local writer or the fact that he had become the pride of the Russian intelligentsia and a much-praised writer. The local KGB chief, accustomed to taking the law into his own hands, continues to regard the writer as just another trouble-maker in his charge and here the degree of his arrogance and coarse power-wielding is directly proportional to his ignorance.

In what way had Vasil Bykov deserved such ardent hatred on the part of the local—and not only the local—KGB? Why was he persecuted in such base fashion and so consistently for many years?

Bykov's fame spread beyond the borders of Byelorussia in 1961 when his war story "The Third Rocket" came out. His next book *An Alpine Ballad* came out in 1963. These and his other early works contained nothing seditious. They were aimed against self-interest, at people like Leshka Zadorozhny in "The Third Rocket" who fled the trenches and the clerk Vasil Blishchensky in "Page from the Front," a demagogue and careerist. There is in this story a note of compassion for Lukyanov who escapes from captivity and is then not trusted. Bykov's lieutenant Klimenko successfully escapes from a trap although the staff-officer has begun to put together a case against him.

This happy ending is false in terms of the time setting. It was a period when millions were cut down indiscriminantly. It was this falsity which won the approval of the critics from the Komsomol press. They saw in Bykov their own man, not someone who would slander reality. "The Third Rocket" and *An Alpine Ballad* were immediately published by *Molodaya Gvardiya* publishing house and the author's star rose.

It then suddenly turned out that Bykov was not the "war patriot" or, more exactly, the stereotyped war writer which the Komsomol Press reviewers had presented him to their readers as being. He was a serious and profound writer with his own themes, his own voice and his own very purposefully defined hatreds.

Bykov first aroused widespread comment in Moscow in 1966 when *Novy mir* published his work "The Dead Feel No Pain" (1966, nos. 1,2).

The main character, Sakhno, is the chairman of a military tribunal. He is a cruel, heartless villain. A young soldier taking a German prisoner meets Sakhno and tells him that there are German tanks not far away in the steppe. Sakhno replies that his is not an anti-tank division and that he has his own tasks to perform. He tells no one about the German tanks. As a result, the company commander Krotov is killed by the tanks. In short, Sakhno causes much misery in the war—he shoots his own men and the enemy, under the impression that he has some kind of monopoly on patriotism.

After the war he changes his name. He becomes a legal consultant under the name of Gorbatyuk and receives a military pension. However, he need not have bothered changing his name because the dead take no revenge, or, as Bykov concludes, the dead feel no pain.

In 1969 another story by Bykov which developed a similar theme appeared in *Novy mir* (no.3). It was called "Kruglyany Bridge." The opening almost belongs to a detective novel. A partisan names Styopka Tolkach is sitting in a pit which the partisans are using as prison. He sits there like an animal which has fallen into a trap. His food is thrown down to him. Interest is aroused right from the beginning to why he is there.

Styopka is a good lad but not anyone of great importance and once he is simply forgotten at his post. He finally gets back to his own side where he gives the wiseacre Grushetsky from Polotsk a good drubbing to stop him mocking him. This makes people call him a madman.

Bykov is master of plot. While the action as such has not really begun, a secondary episode has already introduced the main conflict in which the principal questions of contemporary life, without digressions or rhetorical flourishes on the part of the narrator, are posed—questions of the great aims and the means used in the battle for those aims, of the indifferent murderer who is in his element when foaming at the mouth with "patriotic" phrases.

Themes such as these came to the fore in many books by writers trying to put the brakes on the return to Stalinism. They appeared in different versions in works published in *Novy mir*. They are expressed with particular courage and resoluteness in the stories of Vasil Bykov, every one of which provoked the fury of the bureaucrats.

The action of "Kruglyany Bridge" is simple. A partisan called Maslakov is forming a group with the task of blowing up the Kruglyany bridge which is being used by the German punishment squads. He takes along Styopka whom he remembers from previous occasions, Danila Shpak, a local peasant who wears bast shoes, a man called Britvin, the only one in the group who is like a real officer of the old kind.

On the way they pass the fresh grave of partisans who have been killed. The ground has settled. Maslakov makes a halt to build the grave up with turf, saying: "They were great lads." Britvin grumbles: "There's not enough time for all the 'great lads' ". He is dissatisfied with Styopka, too, whose rifle-sights have been knocked off. He would seem to have some justification for his dissatisfaction. A responsible task has been given to some blockhead of a kitchen-hand, who is also apparently a lunatic. Britvin also does not think they should have made a halt along the way. Admittedly he is not carrying the kerosene like the others. When it is his turn to carry it, he puts a stick through the handle and shares the load with someone else. He is no novice when it comes to playing war games.

Styopka is a far more likeable character as far as the reader is concerned, and being more human and warm-hearted is easier to understand. Yet in the circumstances of the cruel inhuman task the men are embarked upon it is still not clear who is in the right.

The action develops with great speed. Not wanting to risk other people's lives, Maslakov attacks the bridge himself. He is wounded and Styopka just manages to carry him away before dashing to the nearest village to find a cart to drive him away in. He comes back with a horse and cart driven by a fifteen-year-old boy. By this time Maskakov has unfortunately died. The men set about dividing up his things: Britvin takes his padded jacket and Danila Shpak, who has only bast shoes, his boots. Styopka watches this as if it were something completely natural: "as always in a war, things outlasted people and probably for this reason acquired a greater value than people."

There is something quite sinister about this sentence, especially since the operation is now to begin under Britvin's command. His ideas already cause some anxiety. "The one who takes the greatest risks wins. Whoever plays at having various principles ends up like this," he says, referring to Maslakov, who had not wanted to risk anyone's life.

The way he expresses his philosophy is revealing but for the moment he is in the right. It is true that the soft-hearted Maslakov is now in his grave and that they have not managed to blow up the bridge or even to set it alight. Britvin also condemns the action of a certain Lyakhovich he remembers who had not been able to bring himself to kill a traitor because at the moment he went to finish him off the traitor had been feeding a baby. Britvin with his hardness of heart seems set to be successful in blowing up the bridge.

The yount boy driving the cart turns out to be the son of the village

Polizei or collaborator. He despises his father for his treachery. It does not take Britvin more than a moment to take advantage of the situation. He asks the boy to load the explosives onto the cart and ram it up against the bridge and then make a dash for it with his horse.

After blowing up the bridge and escaping their pursuers, the partisans take a rest and take out the food the boy has provided. "Let's take a look at what the Polizei's son has gotten for us." Styopka abuses Britvin because he feels pity for Mitya who has been killed in the explosion despite their calculations and who is now suddenly referred to as the "Polizei's son." During the ensuing argument it is revealed that it was not the Germans but Britvin himself who caused the boy's death. When the horse ended up on the bridge, Britvin fired at it, and the boy, who had not foreseen such treachery, rushed onto the bridge to save his horse. When the bridge blew up he was killed.

"You bastard!" Styopka shouts at him, unable to restrain himself any longer. "You're a bastard, do you hear?" Britvin calls Styopka a sniveller and tries to take his gun from him. "You have a drink and think you can rebel, go against an officer?" "You're not an officer! You're a crook."

Britvin grabs his rifle and clicks the breech-lock but Styopka is too quick for him. He shoots him three times in the stomach. This is why Styopka is now sitting in the pit waiting for his fate to be decided.

Danila Shpak calls out to him to say that Britvin has sent him to tell him that the doctor says he will be all right and that there is no reason for things to end badly. He'll say the gun went off accidentally and nothing need be said about the boy Mitya. There was an explosion and that was all. Otherwise the commissar would come.

Styopka decides not to make peace with Britvin, even if it means facing the commissar. The final sentences in the story, with their carefully orchestrated intensity, create a deep subtext. Although they are perfectly orthodox they have another meaning which is completely the opposite to the orthodox one. Even the syntax reinforces the subtext. Each of the three final sentences is a separate paragraph.

> The commissar will sort things out.
> It is impossible for him not to sort things out.
> Let the commissar come!

As he thinks about it, Styopka is optimistic and defiant. But the reader knows with a sinking feeling that the times are in Britvin's favor. The moral norms of the times are on Britvin's side and Styopka is doomed. His fate will possibly be the same as the boy Mitya's.

A quite unorthodox sense comes through in Styopka's naively trusting declaration. This sense was immediately clear to everyone, including the apologists of Stalinism. From then on they had no doubts about "whose man" Vasili Bykov was.

The Union of Writers brings train-loads of completely untalented writers to Moscow, the sort of people who will vote for whatever they are told to—but for Vasili Bykov there is no place in Moscow. All his requests for permission to move from Grodno to Moscow have been refused one after the other over a period of many years. He is being taught a lesson.

Bykov's answer to this bureaucratic persecution was his story "Sotnikov." In this profound work he strikes out directly at the Stalinist-KGB "black and white" approach to literature and life. He analyzes the nature of betrayal in his depiction of the character of the partisan Rybak and the nature of a humanitarian way of thinking in the character of Sotnikov who is an artillery officer and *intelligent* who is hanged by Rybak so that he, Rybak, can stay alive. This particular twist to the plot was in itself equivalent to sedition. We shall return to it. However, it is Pyotr, the starosta appointed by the Germans, who turns out to be on the same moral plane as Sotnikov.

The action in "Sotnikov" is again uncomplicated, almost elementary. It concerns a partisan operation. This time, however, there are only two men involved, Sotnikov and Rybak, who are being sent to find food.

The first action Sotnikov's heavy artillery battery sees is also the last. His thoughts on the reasons for lack of success in military operations show that he is a perceptive and serious thinker. "The assimilation of the experience gained in the first war is not only an army's strength but also its weakness. The character of the next war is made up not so much of the typical regular features of the first as of its unnoticed or ignored exceptions." Now, encircled by the enemy, he has become a common soldier in a partisan detachment. He is following a wolf's track through the snow with Rybak—because a wolf knows where the snow is thinnest. Misfortune dogs their tracks from the very start. The first village they come to greets them with a gunshot. "They're turning the place upside down, the bastards. For mighty Germany," says Rybak.

Rybak is dependable and touchingly thoughtful. Sotnikov has caught a heavy cold and is coughing. He has the right not to go on the operation but he does not permit himself to take this way out. Rybak gives his comrade his towel in place of a scarf. He upbraids him for not managing to get a hat from a peasant. He gets a sheep for the detachment and hoists it up on his shoulders. Sotnikov is glad Rybak is with him. After the first raid they hide in the cemetery and then in Demchikha's house, which is the one closest to them. Demchikha is not at home—only her two children are there. When she does come back she does not chase the two men away. It is here in her attic that they are caught by the local Polizei Stas Gamanyuk when Sotnikov's coughing gives them away.

Gamanyuk's jeering and derision increase Sotnikov's resolution and inner strength. He is prepared for death and when they begin to interrogate him in the office of the police investigator Portnov he "began without being aware of it himself to speak ironically as he usually did when involved in unpleasant explanations about something to arrogant fools."

Since he can get nothing out of Sotnikov, Portnov calls in Budila, who is another collaborator, and the torturer and executioner. While he is torturing Sotnikov, Portnov occupies himself with Rybak. The hope of staying alive prompts Rybakov to start thinking along new lines. He suddenly realizes that if Sotnikov dies his chances of getting out alive will be improved. There are no other witnesses. "He understands how entirely inhumane his discovery was," says the narrator intrepidly. "He was making his calculations in a way which had nothing to do with any other considerations."

They are all together in one cell. A little girl called Basya is shoved into the room. "This is Meyer the shoemaker's daughter," they are told. Pyotr the starosta says pensively: "That's how it is. They began with the Jews and they're obviously going to finish with us." Basya had hidden in Pyotr's house because the village had decided that they would not look for here there. However, it was not on account of Basya that Pyotr was picked up. She was actually found later. He was picked up for killing the sheep for the partisans and not informing on them to the police. Rybak had wanted to shoot him on the spot but he just had pointed to some holes in the wall. "The polizeis have already had a few shots," he explained. "You're not the first."

Pyotr's wife had latched on to Rybak, explaining that he had not done it because he had wanted to."The peasants begged him until he gave in. Otherwise they'd have made Budila the starosta."

This story introduced into Soviet literature a completely new type which demolished the stereotypes created by earlier works and by the sentences handed down by military courts—in a word, by Stalinism. The most humane and self-sacrificing character in the book is the German-appointed starosta, Pyotr. There in the cell he quietly muses on the astonishing fact that people have turned into murderers.

Unreconciled, Sotnikov, who is an officer and a product of his times, asks him: "Have you been thinking like that for long? How is it then that you became a starosta?" It is only then that he finds out that the whole village had begged him to so that Budila would not be appointed—the same Budila who has torn out Sotnikov's nails. When Sotnikov grasps this, through the pain which is dimming his consciousness "a feeling came over Sotnikov that he had been somehow stupidly remiss in his attitude to this Pyotr."

Vasil Bykov was not afraid of saying this forthrightly, defiantly, realizing what he would call down on his rebellious head. He knew that he would be hated not only by the Grodno KGB but by countless ordinary Soviet philistines who would be incapable of parting with their black and white idea of truth.

The thoughts and feelings of having been "stupidly remiss" are those of the pure and saintly Sotnikov who after being tortured acquired "a certain special, almost absolute independence from his enemies." He feared nothing any more.

They are all taken to be executed—Sotnikov, Pyotr, Demchikha, Basya and Rybak. Seeing that his machinations have led to nothing, Rybak tells Portnov the investigator that he is willing to serve in the police. Rybak is given this opportunity but only on condition that he knocks the block out from under Sotnikov.

After Sotnikov's execution, Rybak decides to hang himself on his belt but forgets that his belt was taken from him when he was arrested. He is forced to go off with the police chief waiting for him outside. He is now "a free man."

Soon after this tragic story was published, the KGB "suddenly" found the man who had been depicted as Rybak, Eduard Kuznetsov tells about it in his *Diaries*. He once shared a death cell with this Lyapchenko who kept asking the guards to get him a copy of the fifth issue of *Novy mir*. Apparently, at his trial Vasil Bykov, who had been present, had gone up to him and told him to "read about himself" in *Novy mir*, although at the time Lyapchenko had not been in a mood for belles-lettres and had told Bykov to go to the devil. Later he had regretted it.

Bykov's story turned out to be factual and this gave added significance and indisputable authenticity to those aspects which an attempt had been made to ignore or denounce as a fabrication on the part of the author. The character of the starosta Pyotr as Bykov had drawn it became irrefutable, as well as Sotnikov's attitude towards Pyotr latterly—and not only towards Pyotr: "Now, in the last moments of his life, he unexpectedly lost his earlier confidence in his right to make the same sort of demands on others he made on himself."

These were the thoughts which occurred to Sotnikov as those who were being killed because of him and Rybak—Pyotr, Demchikha and Basya— were being hanged. Rybak did not want to die.

Two characters from the literature of the twenties became classic types: the *intelligent* Mechik and the peasant Morozko from Fadeyev's novel *The Rout*. In saving his own skin Mechik, the *intelligent*, betrays the peasant. Fadeyev's novel provided confirmation of Stalin's slanderous attacks on the intelligentsia, and it was not for nothing that Fadeyev became a favorite of Stalin's. For decades after this there was a flood of books, broadcasts and films in which the traitors customarily knew foreign languages and wore pince-nez.

This murderous slander on the intelligentsia was dispelled by Vasil Bykov. His traitor Rybak is a former army seargeant-major, a man of little culture, but reliable and of worker-peasant stock. In civilian life he no doubt was a shock-worker and a Stakhanovite. Brought up on the enthusiasm for labor and political hysteria of the thirties, what did he have left from those years? Just the notion of "looking after number one first" and cynicism

375

about the so-called principles of the educated?

Rybak might also be seen to be in the image of Britvin from "Kruglyany Bridge," a true son of his times. It was Britvin who ridiculed the principles of Lyakhovich who conducted himself with such dignity and pride while under interrogation "just like in the pictures." Lyakhovich was also hanged like Sotnikov and indeed he contains within him the seeds of the future Sotnikov. Similarly the patriot Britvin with his brutal Stalinist pragmatism had the potential to become the traitor Rybak.

Bykov was the first to make this kind of attempt to shake the very foundations of the moral order. For a quarter of a century Russians had been singing: "When our country gives the order for a hero to appear, any one of us becomes a hero..." Pavlik Morozov was still carrying out his heroic exploits. It was this kind of blood-thirsty Stalinist morality which several generations had imbibed with their mother's milk that Bykov now attacked with all the force of his extraordinary talent. It is not difficult to understand why bureaucrats of all ranks conceived such a hatred for him and why the Grodno KGB, with the tacit approval of the Union of Writers under the control of Fedin and his ilk, proceeded to hound him the way it did.

7. VLADIMIR VOINOVICH AND VLADIMIR KORNILOV

Whereas Vasil Bykov has been dealt a blow, blackmailed and broken but still published, Vladimir Voinovich has been dealt with much more severely. He has been expelled from the Union of Writers and an attempt was even made to poison him. The reasons for this treatment may appear from an examination of those of his works which have been published in the Soviet Union, works which have put him in the first rank of contemporary Russian writers.

Voinovich has not left the Soviet Union despite the persecution he has suffered.* It is doubtful whether he will ever leave. The reason is a simple human one: he has two children he loves growing up in Moscow. The day I left the Soviet Union I asked him if it might not be better for him to emigrate to the West, which would allow him to give material aid to his children, something which it is extremely difficult for him to do living in Russia, cut off as he is from any income from his work as a writer. He looked at me with a kind of anguish and said in a voice tinged with pain: "Grisha, but then I would never see them again!"

We have been friends for many years. Once when I dropped in to see him in his small writer's apartment on Aeroportovskaya Street in Moscow he was setting up a joiner's bench and vice in the entrance hall. I'm going to do some carpentry," he said in answer to my unspoken question. "Otherwise they'll just strangle me." Things had not always been like that, however. Once at a rally to honor some cosmonauts Nikita Khrushchev had suddenly started singing a song from the reviewing platform on Lenin's mausoleum to words by Voinovich: "On the dusty paths of far planets/ Our tracks will remain..." Subsequently Voinovich was set up as a sort of semi-official court poet or troubadour with an enormous salary. When that happened Voinovich stopped writing altogether. He was unable to write on command. It was contrary to his whole nature. He was tolerated for eight months and then banished from paradise.

In short, he was always himself wherever he found himself—either in the saddle or saddled. He was always warm-hearted, shy and trustworthy. He had a crystal-clear honesty about him. In fact, the first work of his to be published in *Novy mir* was entitled "I Want to Be Honest" (1963, no.2). In terms of his inner aspirations the main character can easily be identified with Voinovich himself.

Voinovich's hero Samokhin is a thoroughly likeable character. He is kind and has an ironical attitude to life, and particularly to himself: "I saw a plywood sign on a fence which read: 'Project 2. Construction work supervised by Comrade Samokhin.' Next to it was a poster which said: 'Helena Velikanova sings.' I am Comrade Samokhin. Helena Velikanova has no

----

*In December 1980 Voinovich finally did leave the Soviet Union. [Trans. note.]

connection with me." Elsewhere the hero is shaving and looking at himself in the mirror. "To be quite frank, the mirror brings me little joy. The man looking out at me from it has red hair, is partly bald, is fatter than he ought to be and has large ears sprouting a grayish fuzz. When I was little my mother used to tell me that Beethoven had big ears like mine. At first I drew some comfort from the hope that I might turn out to be like Beethoven."

The hero exhibits an ironical attitude to himself in every situation. Even when the woman he lives with praises him he shrugs his shoulders as if giving the reader an ironical wink: "She means me. Books will be the end of her."

He eventually arrives at his place of work where he is works supervisor. He is awaited by what the Soviet press likes to call "Its Excellency the Working Class." The first man he sees is the floor-layer Shmakov. It is at this point that the main theme comes to the surface:

> *"Shmakov," I say, "was it you who laid the floors in the third section?"*
>
> *"Yes, it was—what of it?" He looks at me with his usual insolence.*
>
> *"I'll tell you... The parquet is coming apart."*
>
> *"Don't worry, it'll be all right. Before we hand it over we'll wash it down with water and it'll join together again."*
>
> *"Shmakov," I say, asking him a question which is really pathetic... "Don't you have any pride in your work?"*
>
> *"We're an ignorant lot," he says. "All we want is money and plenty of grub."*

Another worker is hanging doors and hammering in the screws right up to the head. "Haven't you got a screw-driver?" "No." "Surely you know that you're supposed to screw them in with a screw driver?" "They go in all right like this."

When they get their pay they all go off to have a few drinks. The foreman goes with them. It is their custom to "wet the pay-packet," as they put it. It is not permitted to drink in the cafeteria and the militia and druzhinniki* see to it that there is no drinking where it is not allowed. When these guardians of public order suddenly appear on the scene, a worker called Sidorkin covers up the empty bottles standing on the floor with his wide canvas trouserlegs. Another man, Yermoshin, rushes off as if to get some tea. When the druzhinniki have gone, he comes back full of apologies:

*druzhinniki are ordinary citizens who patrol the streets on a voluntary, part-time basis in support of the militia.

"The thing is that I'm a public figure. People know me. They'll say: "On the one hand you speak at public meetings and then you...' " "Take your pick," says Sidorkin. "Either don't drink or don't speak at meetings." As everyone realizes, this demand cannot be taken seriously.

The rottenness goes deep, touching the very soul. This is the subject of peasant prose—Abramov's "Pelageya" and the works of Shukshin and Belov. It is also what the songster poets wrote about. (In Vysotsky's words, "What sort of house is this?/Why is it in darkness—as if plague-stricken?") This is what Voinovich too, with a deep apprehension which he endeavors to conceal behind his humor, writes about. People's very souls have been blighted and deadened. It is not just a question of the soul of the bureaucrats—that goes without saying—but of the workers, who are absolutely powerless. All they have in their hands are the hammer and sickle. It is Its Excellency the Working Class which has been destroyed most effectively.

In this atmosphere of widespread and legalized lying there is nothing unusual about the fact that the chief whose name is Silayev suggests to Samokhin that he hand over a certain building not by January, as the plan was, but by 7th November, the anniversary holiday of the October Revolution—even if it is not completely ready, even if it means practicing a deception. If Samokhin hands it over by 7th November he will be made chief engineer. If not, it could entail his being fired. (It is a common occurrence for jobs to be finished by some public holiday rather than at the projected time. Even cosmonauts are launched nowadays according to this principle.)

The demand made on Samokhin is a dishonest one but the threat is serious. If he stubbornly refuses to cooperate, Silayev will still make sure he does not disappoint the district committee or the city committee which have no doubt already promised people high up in the Party a nice little October Revolution anniversary present. If need be he will dismiss his foreman but will hand the building over by 7th November. The whole system from top to bottom is riddled with this kind of chicanerie.

Samokhin ends up in the hospital. His heart could not stand the strain. His thoughts turn towards how little he has managed to achieve in life just because all his life he has wanted to be honest.

The story has a burning truthfulness about it in terms of its ideas, which are unusual in censored literature about the working class, and of its language which is heavily laced with slang expressions and vulgarisms which leave not the slightest doubt that the author knows his workers at first hand. So much the worse for him.

After "I Want to Be Honest" had come out, Voinovich became a regular contributor to *Novy mir* which also published his second work to be passed by the censors—"Two Friends" (1963 no.2). The opening lines are worth quoting for their originality of style:

Our town was divided into two parts—the old part where we lived

379

and the new part where we did not live. The new part was more often called "past the Palace" because some sort of Palace was built on some vacant land between the old and new parts, one of the kind they call "the biggest in the country." At first it was to be the country's biggest Palace of Metallurgists and was in the style of Corbusier. It had almost been finished when it transpired that the architect had been under the influence of Western architecture. He got such a drubbing over this Corbusier fellow that it was a long time before he came to his senses again. By then new times were upon us and he was permitted to return to his interrupted work. But now he was much smarter and just to be on the safe side he had some six-sided columns added to the building which stood somehow apart. This structure was now called the Palace of Science and Technology—also the biggest in the country. When the columns were in place the construction was put on ice yet again because underneath they found the biggest subterranean streams in the area. A few more years went by and then the construction work was begun again—I don't know what they did with the subterranean streams—but this time it was to be the biggest Wedding Palace in Europe.

The ironical style caused the author quite a lot of trouble. Then those works of Voinovich which censorship had kept buried in Russia began to appear in the West. What followed was nothing less than phantasmagorical and can only be imagined by someone who has lived in Soviet Russia.

In the Union of Writers he was threatened with legal proceedings for having sent his works abroad. He was then told to write a protest against the illegal publication of his works abroad. "But you don't publish me!" Voinovich shouted. "My 'Two Friends' is still marinating at the publishers' ... and you want me to write a protest? That's like beating someone and not letting him cry." "If you write a protest, we'll publish 'Two Friends,' " said the illustrious personage from the Union of Writers and reached out for the telephone. "I'm being deprived of my innocence," Voinovich cried and darted out of the Secretariat office. During the next few days he was tortured by the decision he had to make. Should he try to be finished with the whole thing by writing a few well-phrased lines saying that they should not have published him without his permission? In the end he decided to do just that. Paris is worth mass, as the saying goes.

When the issue of *Literaturnaya gazeta* containing his protest came out, everyone including Voinovich himself was aghast. Several paragraphs in an official demagogic vein had been added to Voinovich's four lines, obviously written by someone well up in the hierarchy.

Voinovich created a great commotion, rushing around the Union of Writers showing everybody whose opinion he valued that it was not what he had written. But that was his personal affair as far as the authorities were concerned. Approval of the doctored protest had been given at the level which mattered and the author was suitably rewarded with the publication of his book in a handsome *Sovetsky pisatel* edition. Less than a year later things were to turn sour because bitter experience teaches an author to refuse to accept further compromises. But this was all to happen later.

Meanwhile, "Two Friends" came out, a book which, incongruously, was directed against cowardly hypocrisy and inspired feelings of precisely the opposite kind.

The main character has been friends with Tolik ever since they were small boys. One day they are caught by a gang of hooligans who force Tolik to beat his friend up. Later Tolik feels deeply upset about what he has done but he had been afraid of the hooligans. Their paths then naturally part. It is time to do military service and the main character joins the air force while Tolik becomes a general's batman and starts writing doggerel verse for the newspaper, thereby entering on two time-honored professions at once. When he meets his friend some time later, Tolik says to him: "It was better for you like that."

The main character is intrigued and astonished by this attitude on Tolik's part and finds it hard to fathom. "They would have beaten you up even worse," says Tolik, looking at him straight in the eyes. "This was a real philosophy. Later I came across it under other circumstances and heard more or less the same thing said by other people who were in a hurry to do what anyone would have done in their position."

The depiction of the violence is symbolic. Voinovich captures the stamp of Stalinism, which is alive even today, with great effect and realism.

Voinovich's five-part novel *The Life and Extraordinary Adventures of Private Ivan Chonkin* was announced in the tenth issue of *Novy mir* for 1968 but did not appear. Later there was nowhere for it to be published. At the end of 1969 Tvardovsky's *Novy mir* ceased to exist and when Tvardovsky himself died, Voinovich realized that the position was hopeless. Wherever you looked there were the Red Hundreds.

Although he had no hopes of having it accepted, Voinovich offered the novel first to one Moscow publishing house and then to another. Then suddenly it came out in the West, first of all in the journal *Grani* (Part I in No. 72, 1969) and then in a YMCA Press edition in Paris (1975).

At this point Voinovich fell into iredeemable disgrace as a writer. Yet, despite the persecution he suffered, he remained himself—shy, courageous, with an ironical good humor and love of life.

What the Central Committee thought would be Voinovich's final fall in fact gave him new impetus as a writer. *The Life and Extraordinary Adventures of Private Ivan Chonkin* begins with an "iron bird" crashing on a village. It turns out to be a PO-2 aircraft. The whole village rushes to the scene. Fedka Ryzhy, whose nickhame is Burly, feels the plane all over as if it were a mare. Someone should guard the plane but everyone in the local regiment is deeply perplexed about whom to send to guard it. Eventually someone thinks of Chonkin.

Chonkin is a kind of Russian Good Soldier Shweik, although he is a Shweik with his head on his shoulders. He is an artless, trustful peasant, and the beginning of the novel makes fun of the hallowed tradition of the war detective novel with its super-heroes, the kind of thing the publishers of books on military themes, *Voyenizdat* puts out in millions of copies.

> *Dear reader! You have doubtless already noticed that our soldier hero Ivan Chonkin who had one more year to serve was small in build, bow-legged and even had red ears. "What an absurd character!" you will say indignantly. "What sort of example does he set for the younger generation? Where has the author ever seen such a hero (in inverted commas)?"... "Could not the author have chosen some outstanding, politically mature student from a military school?"... I could have, of course, but I was not quick enough. All the outstanding ones were snapped up and I ended up with Chonkin.*

Even when Chonkin is on his guard duties and sleeping with one of the village girls a long way from his barracks, he is assailed by anxiety dreams. He dreams that someone steals the plane. Comrade Stalin comes down from the sky and asks him in severe tones with a slight Georgian accent: "Where is your rifle?" "My rifle?" "And where is the sergeant major?   Comrade, Private Chonkin abandoned his post and lost his combat weapon in the process. Our Red Army has no need of such men. I advise you to have him shot..." Chonkin wakes up in a cold sweat, afraid that the dream might turn out to be real.

Although Nekrasov's *In the Trenches of Stalingrad* and Voinovich's novel belong to completely different genres, the common soldier in both works is afraid not so much of the enemy as of merciless treatment at the hands of his own side's military tribunals, generals and beloved leader, Stalin.

It is not only Chonkin who is a prey to fear. The kolkhoz chairman is also afraid and confides to Burly that there is much more to Chonkin than meets the eye, that he has in fact been detailed to watch him and catch him in *flagrante delicti*. In their leisure moments the kolkhozniks talk mainly about conditions in prison where they all seem to end up spending some time eventually, one after another. As professional satirists in Soviet theatres know, to make fun of the manager of an apartment block, an accountant, some petty official or the kolkhoz stable-hand is permissable, but not of anyone higher up on the social scale. Those are the rules of the satire game.

Voinovich, however, makes fun even of Captain Milyaga who works for the Security Service and of an army general who throws the whole regiment into the fray against Chonkin, and, what is more, even of the Party big-wigs who cause all the commotion in the first place. They are held responsible for having reported over the telephone that Chonkin had not a "woman" ("baba") but a "gang" ("banda") with him. Voinovich, like his hero, seems to be totally unaware of the strict and onerous rules of the game which exist in the free socialist Soviet State.

The West has taken Voinovich's simple-minded hero seriously and there have been several penetrating pieces of research devoted to Ivan Chonkin. The author of one of them, V. Iverni, first made use of the "rules of the game" concept with reference to this novel.[7]

In 1973 *Grani* published a story by Voinovich called "Through Mutual Correspondence." It has an air of hopelessness about it, like the station at Kirzavod where the hero sergeant Altynnik arrives. His first impressions of the family he is to live with are very negative: "Is there a dog?" asks Altynnik as he comes into the yard. "No. Last year we had one called Tuzik but my brother shot him with his gun." "What for?" asks Altynnik in astonishment. "He'd bought a new gun and wanted to test it out..." This is the first appearance in the narrative of Boris, who is a Party member. As far as Lyudka, who first meets Altynnik is concerned, it is hard to say whether it is her moral turpitude or mean-spiritedness which is her most outstanding characteristic. "You must be the only fool in the whole Soviet Union who feeds strangers," she says to him. So much for the hallowed tradition of Russian hospitality!

Voinovich is a connoisseur of working class slang, that mixture of drunken swaggering, lack of education, cliches from newspapers and rural vocabulary—although it is in this case somehow sapped of all vitality, anemic, devoid of the rich imagery traditionally associated with it.

Once he has gotten rid of the dog Tuzik, Lyudka's brother turns his attention to Altynnik and marries him to his sister while he is in a drunken stupor. Altynnik naturally tries to escape from his captivity and the circle of deception he is trapped in. When he does so Lyudka starts a hue and cry and the local militiaman comes to take Altynnik in hand. "What did he do?" he asks severely. "He's leaving me... with a small baby..." The militiaman is disappointed that there is no more to it than that and regrets that he let himself get mixed up in the brawl at all. He tells them to sort it for themselves. Then he goes off, leaving Altynnik defenseless in the face of the violence threatening him, on the grounds that it is domestic violence. This theme imbues the whole story, right to the end:

> *When I went outside, they were already some way off with Altynnik walking out in front with his head down. With her left hand Lyudmila was holding him by the scruff of the neck and with the small fist of her right hand she was hitting him over the head with all her might. The militiaman was slowly cycling down the other side of the street with his trousers tucked inside his brown socks and was observing what was going on with interest.*

It is a horrifying story. What makes it so unbearably horrifying is that everyone who has lived in Russia knows that this is what it is like all over the country. If Aksenov's Kirpichenko in "Halfway to the Moon" had had a weaker will, the same fate would have awaited him. The triumph of evil over good, to which the guardians of public order are utterly indifferent, is to be observed anywhere. They only become alarmed if there is an actual murder in a family. This is one of the most horrifying angles on lawlessness in the USSR which has up to now been avoided by Soviet literature.

I listen to the news from Russia with increasing anxiety. I wonder what is in store for my gifted friend Vladimir Voinovich. More of the kind of persecution he described in his story "Ivankiada?" I also wonder what is in store for his friend Vladimir Kornilov who like Voinovich has also stepped boldly beyond the limits of what the State considers permissible, having decided to taste freedom for himself in the land of slavery.

Vladimir Kornilov is a rather taciturn, reserved, well turned-out man with the dashing appearance of a naval officer. For years he put what he wrote "in the drawer," as everyone knew. He used to be called "one of those who have been buried alive."

Kornilov made the decision not to attend his own funeral, figuratively speaking. The first issue of the Paris emigre journal *Kontinent* contained his story "Armless and Legless." His poetry is constantly being published outside the Soviet Union. People in the West often fail to realize that this involves real heroism.

At the same time I know no one more mild-natured and soft-hearted than Kornilov. He forgives his fiercest enemies. He feels saddened by their fate and feels sorry for them as he once felt sorry for the poet Yaroslav Smelyakov, who was a broken man as a result of his experiences as a convict and as a "free" man and eventually succumbed to drink.

In 1972 he wrote the following angry, bitter poem full of human feeling about the poet Yaroslav Smelyakov who died an alcoholic:

> *I was not there when you went to your new home*
> *and I imagine I can see you: bent and ill-tempered,*
> *You've gone for the fourth time...*
>
> *You've done with suffering and pining... Enough!*
> *You return a red coffin,*
> *As if all the coarseness and drunkenness*
> *And the obscenity of your interviews had not been...*
>
> *As if all of it—the craziness and brutishness,*
> *The tenacity of lies—were of no account!*
> *And you did not waste your claim to being first-born*
> *On rather paltry esteem.*

The squandering went to extremes—to Novodevichy
Cemetery,
Where like guards in prison towers
The marshals stick out—
Marshal after Marshal.

You'd have found worthier shelter
Half a verst from the Literary Foundation dacha,
You'd have left behind your delirium tremens
And scraped out of your black memory
How the guards walked around with sheep-dogs
And the soldiers threatened and snarled
and the cursed women screamed
And, leaving you, loved you...

And you'd lie, not at all like a poor relative
Living on charity,
In the quiet cemetery beside Pasternak,
In brotherhood.

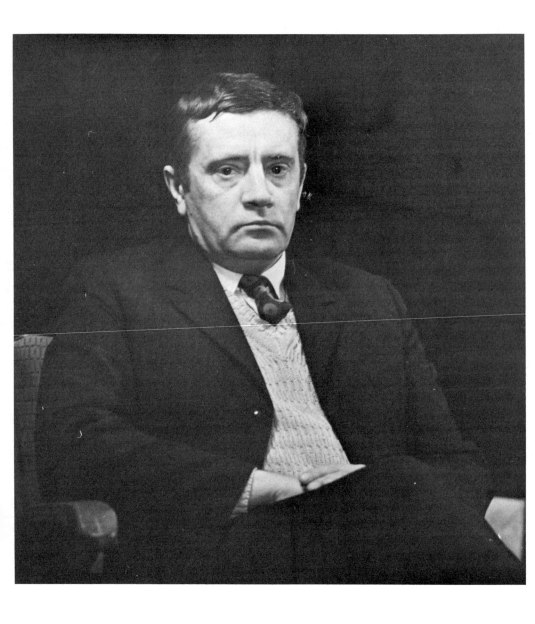

8. VLADIMIR MAXIMOV

I have in front of me the directive of the Presidium of the Supreme Soviet of the USSR depriving Vladimir Maximov of his Soviet citizenship. The State dealt harshly with Maximov, who was the son and grandson of workers and himself a worker.

Vladimir Maximov was born in 1932. He was sent to a so-called children's "colony" which was virtually a children's prison. He escaped from this "colony" and roamed around the whole country in railway carraiges—and under them—and hiding in packing cases. He found himself in the company of thieves, smugglers, vagrants and exiles. One of the exiles he met was Gekman, who had once been First Secretary of the regional committee of the Volga Germans. Gekman, whose life was fading and who looked at Maximov with sad sheep's eyes, argues with him that "I can't just cancel my life because some young Russian is not pleased with its results."

On another occasion the future writer met a young peasant who had done his time in a concentration camp and then had not wanted to leave. "For us kolkhozniks it's what a rest house is for you. You fulfill your norm and get your rations." As for freedom, he said he had no use for it at any price—"I've seen it lying in its coffin—what I want is to eat."

Until he was twenty years of age and Stalinism had come to an end Vladimir Maximov kept roaming restlessly around the country, a vagrant occasionally subject to harrassment. He spent a lot of time in the marshlands of the north where he suffered from the extreme cold and nearly drowned in the swamps. His first story, which was published by Konstantin Paustovsky, concerns his experiences there.

Before going on to other works by Maximov, I should like to quote something Maximov said to me after he emigrated:

> I don't reject anything I wrote earlier. Right from my first work which came out in Pages from Tarusa, my position in my writing has remained unchanged. No—to be exact, I did make one concession. In one of my stories some vagabonds working in a brick factory kill their foreman. The editors were horrified and wanted to know how I could show an innocent man being killed in the land of the Soviets. The publication of my story was in question... So I wrote in a small scene in which some vagabonds who have decided to kill their scoundrel of a foreman come across a militiaman and tell him all about what a beast their foreman is and the militiaman tells them to come to the militia if anything further should happen to talk about it, but it happened... It was the first and last time. In my prose writings I was not hypocritical. I can't say the same thing about my poetry. I wrote emp-

ty verse for official occasions, so as not to die of starvation. When I was an immature twenty year old I thought that this "kopek-counting cynicism" was forgivable. That's what I thought then but I don't think so now.

It was easy for them to push me around. I was a Russian, a proletarian, with a working class background, they said. They even appointed me to the editorial board of Oktyabr, *although I stopped going to the meetings and automatically dropped out, as they say.*

When the Sovetsky pisatel *publishers rejected my novel* The Seven Days of Creation *there was nothing left for me to do but to give it to samizdat. That's how it found its way abroad and came out in the* Possev *edition in 1971 and afterwards was translated into many languages.*

In 1973 *Possev* published *Quarantine* and in 1974 *Farewell from Nowhere.*

The Seven Days of Creation is the story of the Lashkov family. It is a working class family—in fact, a whole dynasty. It is the story of Pyotr Vasilevich Lashkov, a former political commissar, his daughter Antonina and his other children who for some reason prefer to live at some remove from their meritorious father and grandfather who is by no means the proud simple laborer he once was. There was an episode in his childhood which Pyotr Lashkov will never forget. It has a kind of primary symbolic force and becomes an ideological and psychological refrain in both the work itself and the character of Pyotr Lashkov who has seen his numerous working class family fall apart. It takes place in 1905 when there are disturbances and firing in the streets. A merchant's shop-window is shattered by bullets and a starving boy sees a ham behind the shattered glass. Although he is risking his life every second, he crawls up to the window to grab the ham and at last eat his fill. With the bullets whistling around him, he stretches out his hand for the ham and finds that it is made of cardboard.

The narrative, which virtually opens with this symbolic episode, is organized according to what I call the "literary binoculars" principle. When we look at the events of today like this and feel that we are actually taking part in them, it is like looking through a pair of powerful binoculars which bring people, actions and other details and psychological motivation close to us. Then we turn the binoculars around, as it were, and see events which took place long ago and enrich our understanding of the characters and explain the motivation of their present actions.

Grandfather Pyotr Lashkov appears to the reader sometimes as an old man wandering through the city in which he seems to be on familiar terms with everyone he meets, and sometimes, unexpectedly, he retreats into the distant past, to the time of the Revolution and the twenties. We are absorbed in his lucid, concrete reminiscences, his conversations and arguments and his despair. We seem to be looking at him through the reverse end of the binoculars, which distances us from him by some fifty years and at the same time helps us understand more fully why the Lashkov family fell apart and why this champion of justice is abandoned by everyone who is close to him.

This retrospective view of these episodes from different periods provides a wide-ranging perspective, the kind of overview we have of someone's life when we know its beginnings, its background, its upward movement on the wings of the paper glider of current faddish ideas—as happened in Lashkov's case and its conclusion.

The final social and psychological form the Lashkov family's life takes— which is the final form assumed by the whole generation of working people who brought about the Revolution—creates some impression of the final shape of the whole period. All the aspects of the collapse of Pyotr Lashkov's inner world and sense of cohesion become increasingly clear, as does the fate of his warm-hearted and unhappy daughter Antonina who leaves her father to join a religious sect. We are shown how his son-in-law, recently out of prison, lives, and a picture is drawn of a cynical Stalinist bureaucrat called Vorobushkin, who has an important position on the district executive committee of the Party. He was once one of Pyotr Lashkov's pupils and still will have a drink with his former teacher who has remained a worker, but he only drinks with him when something goes seriously wrong. His son was with the Soviet armed forces in Germany and tried to escape to the West and now his whole life is ruined—and not only his but his father's also. Until this happened Vorobushkin was hard and abrupt with everyone and was even unwilling to help Lashkov's son-in-law get a residence permit. Pyotr Lashkov himself without noticing it comes to share his son-in-law's feelings, although he himself is by no means an ex-convict but a proletarian who has lived a righteous life.

His feelings have been somehow turned inside-out. There is something not quite normal about it. "For the small children Pyotr Vasilevich did not feel exactly a lack of love but a kind of protective aversion." However, he takes in his grandson. Why does he take him in? Is it because there awakes in him some natural human feeling? Not at all. It is just that he derives pleasure from being able to humiliate his daughter-in-law who hated him. His feelings have been perverted by the bloody conflicts of the revolutionary years, although in his simplicity he takes no account of the fact.

The fate of Pyotr Lashkov's younger brothers is also examined in some detail. One brother, Vasily, did not want to take any kind of post and became the janitor in a Moscow apartment block. "Vasily considered that his whole life was ahead of him... but that he had been deprived of it. They started asking me for what I owed them and I still haven't paid off my debts. It turned out that I owed money all over the place... There were places I was always careful not to go, things I couldn't say and things I couldn't do. And the longer it went on, the worse it got." He says to his brother, now an old man: "We could have [lived by our own wits]. But you lot didn't let us. You just fed us that pap of yours. A step to the right, a step to the left is considered an escape attempt. That's the only tune you know. And when the time comes to die, we look back and see that we've been walking back to front all the way and it's you who have been driving us on." "As a result of this heart-to-heart talk Pyotr Vasilyevich Lashkov gained a terrible new insight. His own fateful involvement with everybody and everything, his own close relationship with them in their common and irreversible malady was revealed to him..."

We find ourselves, as it were, looking through the reverse end of the binoculars again at people who at the time of the Revolution were Pyotr Lashkov's fierce enemies, people who were the hated counterrevolutionaries, as Pyotr Vasilyevich the commissar then considered them. Then, for some reason, they began to catch him up and pass him and to become far more important and useful people in life than he was. One of these is a man called Gupak, who on checking turned out to be an engineer called Mironov whom he, Lashkov, had once ordered to be shot. However, the soldier who had taken him off to be shot had let him go. And now this long forgotten Gupak-Mironov, whom he had completely wiped out of his memory, has a kind of victory over him. He is a preacher among the sectarians his deeply unhappy daughter Antonina goes away to join.

After several meetings and conversations with people from his dead past, Lashkov again remembers the shattered shop-window on the square in 1905. "And what if everything turns out to be as they wanted it? If it turns out that everything we tried to do was actually in vain?"

There is one question in particular which gives this former commissar and working son of generations of workers no peace and saps him of his strength. It is the question of where, when and why he, Pyotr Vasilyevich Lashkov, surrendered what was the truth to him to all those Gupaks, Vorobushkins and Gusevs, by what shaky line he had cut himself off even from his own children. He remembers the words of his father-in-law Ilya Makhotin: "You're all dried up, there's a dried up air about you... The blood isn't flowing in a single one of your veins..."

This sudden illumination shakes Lashkov to the bottom of his honest, artless soul: "I got further and further away from them, not closer to them... None of them, in fact no one, got any warmth or light from me, so they flew away from me like moths towards whatever lights they could see flickering in the night."

In terms of the narrative, only one of Lashkov's "seven days" of creation has gone by, yet already the problem has been put in considerable depth and in fact resolved, and in Russian literature, which is mainly concerned with questions, not answers, this is rather rare. Any social revolution is doomed, regardless of the slogans which accompany it, if the doctrine turns out to be beyond the people involved.

This cardinal theme of the century is bathed in a new light—psychologically, morally and socially—by the way the narrative explores the seven days of creation.

During the war Pyotr Lashkov's second brother evacuates his cattle. However, this is only a small detail from everyday life. The questions which arise are still the same but approached from a different angle—this time the cattleman's: "the world suddenly appeared divided into those who are pursued and oppressed and those who pursue and oppress. The Lashkovs had always belonged to the second lot. And now suddenly he was struck by the searing question of why, and by what right."

In the chapter entitled "House in the Clouds" Maximov depicts with a maximum of artistic sensitivity and authenticity the dangerous unaccountability of the doctrines crushing people. Each new "day" of creation brings with it a further stage in the unfolding realization of the tragedy of what has happened.

The omniscient person in the overpopulated Moscow apartment block turns out to be the brother who is the janitor, Vasily, the one who first set Pyotr Lashkov thinking about things deeply. Vasily Lashkov was himself a soldier in the Red Army and himself once cut the throats of the lawless *basmaches* in Turkmenistan, so he knows the meaning of arbitrary rule. We meet him for the first time not long before he dies. A wiser man now, he is in a state of bitter sadness. The narrative then becomes retrospective, as is normal in Maximov, bringing the reader closer to the apartment block "house in the clouds" in which both the victors and the vanquished are for some reason cheated of their share of happiness. As Gupak would say, the doctrine begins to "play up."

The first one in the block to be arrested is Sima, a prostitute with the face of a cherub. But for some reason she is "isolated," as it was called, just when she has given up her time-honored profession and has settled down happily with an actor called Lyova Khramov. Everyone in the apartment block knows that it is unjust for Sima to be taken away, and even the local police-officer Kalinin sighs that her relatives denounced her and now nothing can be done about it because "there's an ordinance prohibiting it." When she is taken away all the residents grumble about what the "gangsters" are doing and say that "the girl had just got back on her feet." But it is only the peasant Ivan Levushkin who rushes from one to the other begging them to do something. "Tell me, citizens, what sort of murderousness is this? Is it Christian? All of us could get together and come to her defense... We can go higher..."

Gorev the carpenter is a Party member and Ivan pesters him to do something: "You're in the Party, you're in a position to help—do something for her. As a matter of conscience, do something to help her." But for some reason this Party member merely averts his eyes. Shtabel the plumber, a man of great strength, also remains silent. "Shtabel could bend pipes, but the authorities could bend him, Shtabel."

Coming to the moral defense of a prostitute who is trying to get back on her feet is a classical theme in Russian literature. Writers from Gogol in his "Nevsky Prospect" to Dostoevski in *Crime and Punishment*, Kuprin and Gorky, and from Nekrasov to Nadson among the poets, have traditionally raised their voices in defense of the downtrodden and broken. Only Soviet literature has maintained silence on the question because a pronouncement once came from the seat of power to the effect that "*that* does not exist here."

The first to break this hypocritical ban was Maximov. He touches on the perennial theme twice in this book, once in connection with the cherubic Sima, and then at the end of the book, in connection with the saintly yet not all other-worldly character of Mysya, the warder's moll, who says of herself: "I'm bad through and through." This is essentially a Sima who has lost her bashfulness and who has experienced the Gulag. The interesting thing is that although the classics examined this theme from what appeared to be all sides, these fallen women in Maximov's novel do not come across as "literary reminiscences" at all. It is not the milieu which has ruined them, nor desperate poverty, nor what Kuprin delicately called their social temperament, but revolutionary legality (as the doctrine of social equality was called in legal terms).

The residents put up with the first manifestation of lawlessness, brazen and obvious though it may be. Things go from bad to worse, however. They then come for Kozlov, a former tsarist officer who later worked for the Bolsheviks. Kozlov refused to shake hands with Nikishkin when the latter moved in with him. Nikishkin was in charge of security in Butyrki prison, and Kozlov's behavior towards him leads to his downfall. He leaves with his pride intact saying: "Russian guards officers try to die in clean undercollars."

Vasily Lashkov the janitor just sighs. He thinks of Kozlov as just an "inoffensive, slightly eccentric old man." However, when they take away the plumber Gorev, someone he feels close to, another worker like himself, his gorge rises and he feels "a gush of choking fury." He has the sense of having lost something far more important and irrevocable than simply Alexei Gorev. Elated with what has happened, Nikishkin barks out to Vasily: "We'll uproot the lot of them. We'll exterminate them. We fought and split our blood and they'll get it in the neck. If they don't like it, they can bite the bullet." Vasily is disgusted by him but makes no reply. The worker does not reply and the half-mad Nikishkin is victorious over him.

It is not long before the police officer Kalinin lets Lashkov know that he is being carefully watched too. This is natural because he has begun to think. He is not yet thinking deeply, but the process has begun. He starts to behave cautiously and warns the woman he loves, Grusha, that she should go away from him for a while for her own protection. It is in vain. Grusha throws him over saying: "You can live like a gopher if you like, but I'm going to look after myself. A real Red hero, aren't you!"

Eventually Shtabel is deported from Moscow because he is a German. Vasily tried to do something in his defense. "He's an Austrian, Alexander Petrovich," he says to Kalinin, tryint to talk him round. "He's an Austrian, it's in his passport that he's an Austrian."

"It's all the same thing, Lashkov. Hitler was also an Austrian..." It was difficult to make out Kalinin's face in the darkness, but because [he] was breathing in a broken, noisy way his burning obduracy could be felt. He hands over Shtabel's keys to Vasily.

The days fly by and Kalinin is again forced to come after someone. This time it is Semyon Tsygankov, Sima's brother who is a deserter. Kalinin would have caught him but Semyon fell off a roof to his death. Kalinin cannot bring himself to do any more killing. He comes to Vasily and commits suicide by shooting himself in the temple.

The millstones of the State are grinding to powder human happiness which is so fragile. Khramov, the hapless actor who is the son of a nobleman, philosophizes: "Russia has been lashed by Smerdyakovism. Make way for his Excellency Foma Fomich Smerdyakov!... Everything is possible, everything is permitted... The Smerdyakovs have emerged to meddle in politics... They'll set the world alight yet."

Sergei Lashkov rips open the collar of his shirt and shows the scars from old wounds. For what were they the punishment? "I didn't buy them" he says. "Nowadays I seem to need a special permit to breathe. Is this what order means?"

Levushkin starts crying in a drunken state. Khramov pats him on the head affectionately and tries to comfort him: "What are you crying for Ivan Nikitich? What are you crying for? You belong to the class in power. Everything is yours, yet you're crying. You should be dancing with joy and singing with happiness... But you're crying—why?... A Russian peasant is crying. Before it was from being flogged and now it's from inner anguish. What's happened to us, Ivan Nikitich? Tell me, what?"

Grusha, who left the cautious Lashkov, is brought back drunk in a car by a brigade commander. Everyone pokes his head out of the window to look and she shouts at them all:

> *What are you all staring at like a lot of screech-owls? Well, any of you who has a sinless soul can spit on me. What about you, Nikishkin? How many more souls have you sold? What about you, Tsygankov? Do you take parcels to your daughter? Or do you go to church like the Executive Committee, to ask for charity from God?*
>
> *The shutters were banging shut... As far as management of their personal moral lives was concerned, there were not too many people in that block who enjoyed public scrutiny.*

Yet this is the courtyard of just one old Moscow apartment block. As everywhere else, time has made a mockery of human dignity and of the human being's faithfulness to himself. Behind Nikishkin, the representative of death in the apartment block, stood the Leader of the peoples, who had declared to the whole world that the enemies of the people would answer for their crimes with gallons of blood.

The residents, like the country as a whole, lose all moral sense. It is as if a tornado had swept through the courtyard, leaving their souls morally debilitated and their spirit coarsened.

The narrative on this subject breaks off suddenly as if for no particular reason with a *chastushka* which underlines the senselessness of Russia's sufferings "to the glory" of this and "in the name" of that:

> *Vanya's sitting on the stove,*
> *Smoking a felt boot...*
> *(Sidit Vanya na pechi,*
> *Kurit valeny sapog...)*

For some reason Lashkov's grandchildren are no happier than their fathers and grandfathers although Stalin has long since rotted in his grave.

Vadim Lashkov poisons himself with gas and ends up in the Stolbovaya asylum. Who are the inhabitants of this asylum? As early as the end of the sixties, Vladimir Maximov told the world in his *Seven Days of Creation* the truth about Soviet psychiatric prisons, but few paid serious attention to what he said.

Nikishkin, who is actually mad, is still enjoying his freedom as before. But in the madhouse is a producer called Kreps who wanted to stage whatever plays he wanted as he wished. Naturally, a producer like this cannot be "normal." All the producers with the greatest conscience and intelligence are here. "So long as the feeling of personal guilt towards others is still alive in you, they can't make a pit of you," says Kreps. "The aim of art is... in giving yourself to others, not in sacrificing yourself," he says. Kreps is disgusted by the patriotism of the lackeys. He knows what life is all about: "They've taken the peasant's soul out and offered him nothing to replace it except drink." "The world should be grateful to Russia until Judgment Day for showing the rest of the world through its own hellish experience what not to do!

This is why Kreps is sent to Kazan to the most terrible psychiatric prison of all. The old doctor there, like the police officer Kalinin, can no longer bear to take part in the daily ritual of murder. He calls in Vadim Lashkov, Pyotr Vasilyevich's grandson, hands him his documents and tells him to make a dash for it. He then poisons himself. (Kreps does not want to escape—there is nowhere to escape to.) So yet another guardian of public security commits suicide. The times do not spare them either.

Vadim is swiftly recaptured on a ferry. At the moment he is recaptured he can see the red kerchief of the girl he loves on the shore. She is convinced that all is well at last.

The ending of this section again takes the form of a *chastushka*. This nonsensical folk form becomes a constant refrain, bringing out the loss of all hope and the mockery that has been made of human dreams—indeed of all ideas of a normal human life.

> *An axe floats down the river*
> *From the village of Unbelief.*
> *Where are you being carried to,*
> *You bloody great hunk of iron?*
>
> *(Po reke plyvyot topor*
> *Iz sela Neverova.*
> *I kuda tebya nesyot*
> *Zhelezyaka kherova...)*

There is not a single superfluous word nor a single superfluous digression in the narrative, although the story takes us to a far-distant small isolated Russian town and to Central Asia where Pyotr Lashkov's daughter Antonina and Osya, the son of a Dante expert called Mekler, go. Good people flee as fast as their legs will carry them as far as they can go from the bestiality of the State, and the bestial people who represent it. Yet even in Central Asia, surrounded by the steppe and the winds, the characters are bound tightly together by the threads of the narrative. At first glance they would seem to have been widely scattered but in fact there is no escape for them—the country is one huge camp. Osya Mekler, for example, thought that he would be building something of use to people there, but he then finds out that he will be taking part in the erection of a prison. "It turns out that you just can't get away from them," he says. Unable to bear the vile news, he hangs himself in a toilet, and Antonina, who loved him, finds herself alone again.

The book's leitmotif appears again but this time, by way of contrast, it does not take the form of a nonsensical *chastushka*—and for this reason is even more effective. " 'What I say is this,' sighed the commandant noisily, 'all your grandfathers achieved by starting this mess was to take the place of the guards.' " Almost all the novel's characters think along these lines. Even Pyotr Lashkov who has given his whole life to "the workers' cause" is gradually and convincingly brought to this conclusion.

The old man makes every effort to rescue Vadim from the asylum but without success. Perhaps for the first time in his life he:

felt the presence in the world around him of some dark and insuperable

*force which soundlessly and clammily like cotton wool snuffed out
any opposition to it. The most unbearable thing for Pyotr Vasilyevich
was the consciousness of his utter helplessness before this force. And
however much he contemplated it, his thoughts unfailingly came back,
after circling for a while in the labyrinths of his memories, to that
tumultuous morning on the market square when he found himself
in front of the smashed shop-window with the painted cardboard ham
in it...*

As he looks deeply into the abyss of misery and misfortune, he suddenly remembers the Cheka chief Avanesian. On one occasion Avanesian
took no action against a soldier called Paramoshin who killed a man in order
to steal his gold teeth. Lashkov said to Avanesian: "Are you afraid... of
Paramoshin?" "We'll deal with him when we need to," says Avanesian. "And
if we don't, that means we've taken on more than we can handle. In that
case he'll pay his debts together with everyone else—all his debts."

When his daughter Antonina returns from Central Asia with the son
she bore to Osya, Pyotr Lashkov asks his former enemy Gusev, who is a
casual laborer, to get a place ready for her to live in. While he is talking to
Gusev, "his whole destiny suddenly rose up in its entirety, the life he had
lived to no purpose, chasing a pitiful and intangible shadow. And Lashkov
burst into tears."

If *The Seven Days of Creation* had come out in the sixties when it
was written it may well have hastened the rate at which the Russian reading
public was acquiring new insight, even if Maximov's hopes for a religious
revival in Russia did not evoke the sympathy of the majority of his readers.

At least two more things need to be said. I shall return to one of them
in the section on nationalism but shall deal with one here. Certain misunderstandings arise not only from *The Seven Days of Creation* but from the
whole body of works by Vladimir Maximov.

There is unfortunately a negative side to samizdat, although samizdat
is, of course, a major factor in the preservation of Russian literature. The
samizdat author acquires a certain freedom but at the same time, with few
exceptions, loses touch with that wide professional milieu which is able to
be of real assistance to him as a source of impartial comment, advice and
sometimes even serious analysis of his work. As the director of the Central
Moscow Puppet Theater Sergei Obrastsov once cheerfully remarked, whoever
criticizes your work before it comes out is your friend—but after it comes out
he is your enemy.

The handful of friends who read a samizdat manuscript are concerned
above all with the writer's personal safety and the safety of the manuscript
itself, and not with stylistic points or flaws in the narrative. This fact could
not help having an influence on Vladimir Maximov. A certain insensitivity
to the sound of what he has written becomes observable, as well as the

growing intrusion of thieves' slang, especially in "Farewell from Nowhere." Fortunately, *The Seven Days of Creation* remains relatively untouched by the corrosion of tastelessness affecting his other works.

Quarantine is a wordy, unpolished and linguistically untidy book, written in haste and with a certain indifference to the finer points, although this is perfectly understandable in an author who, after publishing *The Seven Days of Creation* in the West, was expecting the KGB to burst into his apartment at any moment, a search of his apartment to be carried out, his own arrest and the confiscation of everything which had not been well concealed. Naturally these are not the best circumstances under which to write a book.

The circumstances under which "Farewell from Nowhere" was written would appear to have been less worrying and unsettling. It was begun in Russia. It denotes a return for Maximov to what we might term his literary assault position. This work is an extremely frank, intelligent and splenetic account merciless both to himself and to others, of his own life. Yet even here, especially in the opening pages, Vladimir Maximov loses his sense of moderation, let alone his sense of exacting standards of style. There is an excessive accumulation of linguistic stereotypes where elements of street jargon, official slogans, snatches from popular songs of the forties and verses from the Bible are all mixed up. Maximov has an uncertain sense of where to draw the line. He particularly overdoes the use of slang expressions.

The Seven Days of Creation is a unique achievement. It is a courageous and brilliant novel about the collapse of the Lashkov dynasty of workers—those workers for whom the October Revolution was brought about. It is a genuinely philosophical novel about the murderous fraud which by force of habit still goes under the name of the dictatorship of the proletariat, the Russian proletariat which fifty years after the final victory of the Revolution is still poverty-stricken, deprived of any spiritual life to the point of despair, brain-washed and reduced to a drunken stupor by this dictatorship. What was there the leaders of this dictatorship which had brought the Lashkovs to ruin could say to Maximov when he confronted them with *The Seven Days of Creation*?

The best thing they could have done at the moment of revelation would have been to reiterate the idea Gekman, the former Secretary of the district committee of the Volga Germans, voiced when he turned away from the truth once and for all, refusing to "cancel out my whole life." In fact, there was nothing they could say to Maximov.

The most valid proof of this is to be found in the directive from the Presidium of the Supreme Soviet of the USSR "divesting V.E. Maximov of his Soviet citizenship for acts besmirching the name of a citizen of the USSR."[5]

9. A NEW GENERATION OF RESISTANCE WRITERS: GINZBURG, GALANSKOV, AMALRIK AND OTHERS

The new phases in the development of samizdat—the contributions of well-known writers from Paustovsky to Solzhenitsyn, the tape-recording revolution and the stream of so-called prison literature—all evoked an immediate response among young writers. Here and there typewritten periodicals appeared which would have been indistinguishable from other student publications if it had not been for the fact that those responsible for them received prison sentences. There were many more of these periodicals than is customarily recognized. The country's youth could not and did not wish to remain silent. In one school publication known to me the lead article in a 1956 issue began with childish directness: "Stalin gad!" ("Stalin is a viper!") In 1956 all the frightened teachers could do was to throw up their hands. In the sixties, however, courtroom notes began to appear in these periodicals. They were some gauge of the extent of rebelliousness among the purveyors of these manuscripts.

The first typewritten youth periodicals were *Sintaksis (Syntax)* and *Bumerang (Boomerang)*. *Sintaksis* was put together by Aleksandr Ginzburg and *Bumerang* by Vladimir Osipov, a former history student who was expelled from the University in 1959 for a public protest he made against the arrest of one of his fellow students. *Sintaksis* came out in the winter and spring of 1960 and *Bumerang* in November of the same year. Soon afterwards the typewritten periodical *Feniks—61 (Phoenix—61)* appeared whose inspiration and editor was the young poet Yuri Galanskov. Issues of the periodical *Sfinks (Sphinx)* were also distributed at this time, as well as occasional collections of verse by very youthful poets with the somewhat pretentious title of *SMOG* (which stood for Sila—strength, Mysl—thought, Obraznost—imagery, and Glubina—depth).

Young people not only offered their acquaintances copies of their collections of verse, which were rarely seditious and more often than not unconnected with politics, but also went out into the streets—not, this time, the Senate Square as the Decembrists had done, but Mayakovsky Square in Moscow.

I happened to witness the breaking up of one such demonstration. After a public poetry reading on Mayakovsky Square a crowd of some two hundred people set off for the Union of Writers to declare their right to take part in the spiritual and literary life of the country. Unfortunately the leaders of the crowd of young people were so inexperienced that they led the crowd into Gorky and Vorovsky Streets where about ten foreign embassies are situated. (The Union of Writers has an entrance on Vorovsky Street.) As a result the guards posted at the embassy entrances who have special radio-transmitters that ordinary militiamen do not have became involved in breaking up the demonstration. Several minutes later a number of black Volgas drew up and the organizers of the demonstration were efficiently bundled into them and driven off. Without their leaders the other demonstrators were soon dispersed.

I managed to attract the attention of one of the fleeing demonstrators who had broken free from the *druzhinniki* and was dashing around trying to escape. I pushed him through the doors of the Writers' Club, led him through the building and let him out on the other side in Vorovsky Street. All he had time to tell me was that they had been at the monument on Mayakovsky Square. This was the beginning of the repressive measures taken against students, although at the beginning there seemed to be no hint of the turn of events which was to come.

The Mayakovsky monument was officially unveiled on 29 July, 1958 on Mayakovsky Square in Moscow. Mikhailov, the Minister of Culture, made a speech, the former poet Tikhonov, then chairman of some committee or other, cut the ribbon and in conclusion a number of officially recognized poets read their poetry. However, when they had finished, it became obvious that they were not the only ones who wanted to read their poetry. The number of people who wanted to recite their verse was overwhelming.

After many years of alienation from each other, this new and spontaneous interest people had in each other was encouraging. The young people decided to meet each month on the day the monument was unveiled at the foot of the statue to read their verse. Some of what they read was permitted and some was not permitted—Gumilev, for example, and Akhmatova. They recited their own verse, which was only occasionally of any outstanding merit. Discussions would develop, right there in the center of Moscow, of a kind which had not taken place for almost fifty years. Young men and women argued about the latest works to attract general attention such as Dudintsev's *Not By Bread Alone*, Tendryakov's "Potholes" and Pomerantsev's article "On Sincerity in Literature" which had been published in *Novy mir* at the end of 1953. There were certainly things to argue about. After all, most of those taking part had been born in the late thirties or early forties and had grown up at a time when the word Stalin was virtually synonymous with Soviet power and the hopes of the whole world for a better future. Then all of a sudden their idol had been swept off his pedestal.

The main thing these young people were rising in rebellion against was any kind of regimentation. Alexander Ginzburg, for example, declared that as a matter of principle he would print works of any tendency in *Sintaksis*. The mixture which in fact appeared was certainly of a kind never before seen in Russia. There were anti-Stalinist poems and patriotic pro-Soviet poems as well as religious and formalist poems.

Alexander Ginzburg managed to put out three issues before he was arrested in July 1960. *Sintaksis* contained no critical articles and barely any prose—it consisted almost totally of poetry. However, what it did contain proved to be sufficient ground for having him arrested.

It was not only poetry which revived, however. Young artists who did not wish to paint within the permitted framework of socialist realism began to exhibit their works in private apartments.

The poetry and the art were not always very good, but the important thing is that these paintings and periodicals constituted the first open attack on conformism in art.

The youthful protesters were still naive enough not simply to hold demonstrations on streets which were under particularly heavy guard but to try to prove to the KGB investigators that the arrests they were carrying out were unconstitutional and that Article 70, for example, of the Criminal Code of the RSFSR was contrary to the Constitution. It is certainly true that the Soviet Constitution allows freedom of speech. Vladimir Osipov who later became a neo-Slavophile and editor of the journal *Veche* tells how Ilya Bokshteyn who was arrested with him tried to convince the KGB investigators that Article 70 of the Criminal Code was unconstitutional when it defined "fabrications besmirching the Soviet social order" as a crime. Bokshteyn said that historically freedom of speech had always meant the right to criticize and that the freedom to praise the social order had been granted to despots.[10] The KGB listened carefully and took down what he said— to be used in evidence against him.

Although arrests had begun, the meetings on Mayakovsky Square continued. Now the leading organizers among the young were Yuri Galanskov, Vladimir Bukovsky and Viktor Khaustov. After their release these men were joined by Vladimir Osipov and Ilya Bokshteyn.

In April 1961, during the "universal celebrations" in honor of Yuri Gagarin's first flight in space, the poets who had gathered on Mayakovsky Square to read their verse were brutally beaten and dispersed when one of them began to read his verse critical of the regime. This critical note was considered to be intolerably out of tune with the dominant cosmic joy. Those arrested were detained for from ten to fifteen days for "petty hooliganism." Yet the activists in this persecuted "club" continued to meet. They included Eduard Kuznetsov, Anatoly Ivanov, Ilya Bokshteyn and Vladimir Osipov.

These young people could scarcely have suspected that once they had gathered together they were not simply people who held dissident views any longer. They formed a group, and for group discussions about the future of the USSR prison sentences were given of a type often reserved for murder in the West.

They were released after initial questioning, but not, of course, by mere good fortune. The aim was to lock them up properly later. Eduard Kuznetsov and Vladimir Osipov were each sentenced to seven years in prison and Bokshteyn for five years. Five years were considered enough for a tuberculosis sufferer. Although what they were accused of was tantamount to a terror campaign, it was perfectly obvious that they were being isolated from society for reading poetry on Mayakovsky Square and for their attempt to unite together in a State whose principal aim was to disunite.

The trial of Sinyavsky and Daniel only hastened the attainment of spiritual maturity by the young. Yuri Galanskov's typewritten periodical *Feniks-66* became strongly political. One editorial which was addressed to the powers that be, concluded with the words: "You may win this battle but all the same you will lose the war—the war for democracy and for Russia." This cost him his life. He was sentenced to seven years in prison and died in the camp. Although he was suffering from a stomach ulcer, no attempt was made to cure him and when he was eventually operated on he died on the operating table. Ginzburg was put behind barbed wire for five years and when he was finally set free he was chosen by the dissidents to be in charge of the funds coming from abroad to help political prisoners and their families. Once again he has become a victim, and once again he is in prison.

In a totalitarian society any thinking person represents a threat. He may become "someone who thinks differently" ("inakomyslyashchi"). An honest person, who will not make a deal with his conscience, is doubly dangerous. Anyone who is honest through and through is quite simply a sworn enemy.

The so-called people's power first of all took repressive measures against the very best people. Nikolai Gribachev explained in a lead article in *Literaturnaya gazeta* to those who were left what their position was. The article was entitled "What does it mean to be revolutionary in our times?" For those who found his explanations hard to follow he explained further in various public speeches he gave that in every stream there is some scum and that they, the stirrers and mischief-makers, were that scum—filthy scum. I once heard him myself speaking in this vein at a meeting at the University. He accused those students who had asked to be spared their dull and unimaginative Marxism lecturers of also being filthy scum. Only he, Gribachev, knew what it meant to be a revolutionary. Other writers were forbidden to so much as touch on this theme.

What themes were writers allowed to touch on at times such as these when young writers were being herded into prison camps? Publicists were permitted, for a short time, to support the saving of Lake Baikal from pollution (see O. Volkov's article in *Literaturnaya gazeta*, 6 February 1965), satirists were permitted to write about laundries (Likhodeyev, ibid., 3 March 1965), and prose writers were permitted to discuss the harmful effects of alcohol (N. Atarov, ibid., 11 January 1065). The most the authorities would allow was attempts to convince ones colleagues not to shake hands with base types (Natalya Ilyina, "And what if you don't shake hands?" ibid., 5 November 1967). Meanwhile the courts were hard at work and more and more often in secret.

The ideologists of the Soviet State did not even make any attempt to understand the kind of basic truths some of Nicholas II's ministers grasped. When Eduard Kuznetsov mumbled something during his interrogation about human rights and legality, his jailers answered with a sarcastic smile: "You talk about rights like a new bride... Now, you're not stupid. It's time you understood..."

However, young people did not at first understand who it was they were dealing with. After all, it is not easy to disentangle oneself from the sticky web of words with which the State binds a child from his earliest years. Yet when young people did understand, they did not become afraid.

On 4 July 1969 a young man who was at that time completely unknown, Andrei Amalrik, sent the manuscript of his book *Will the Soviet Union Survive Until 1984?* abroad. In December 1969 this book became a talking point all over the world. Amalrik was born in 1938, a year of mass terror. He was too young to be affected by the war with all its fears and blood-shed and the psychologically damaging experiences of a combatant. He grew up free, or at least with the conviction that he was as free as a bird. His first arrest and internal exile (for some plays he had written which had never been put on but were found during a search) put a more correct perspective on things. Amalrik could not be sent away immediately because of the heart trouble he suffered from and he was put in the care of various doctors for a long time. As he has remarked: "It may seem unnatural that someone should be glad that he has heart trouble, but then the conditions in which we live are obviously unnatural." This sort of idea has the ring of one of Shalamov's ideas. It is born of the camps. The new generation was assimilating the wisdom of the older camp inmates as it progressed.

His first arrest came as a shock, all the same. When "those people with faces like official reports" locked him up in a cell reeking of urine at the militia station, he remembered an occasion when the river had been in a flood near Smolensk and he had walked barefoot for several kilometers across the flooded meadows. When he remembered this, he felt more sharply than he ever did again his lack of freedom. He describes this in his book *Involuntary Journey to Siberia*.

What saved him during his exile was his well-balanced temperament and his ironic sense of humor, which colors his book about his exile so strongly. It was his job to graze cows and he found that while all the other cows plodded along in a disciplined fashion one of them was more fractious and kept wanting to leave the herd. "Then it was that I understood," writes Amalrik, "how our leaders must loathe individualism, even when it is not connected with any active protest... This cow kept me in a constant state of tension."

Andrei Amalrik was the first and to all intents and purposes the only person in the USSR to make a convincing and professional survey of the different opposition movements in Russia. He did not exaggerate his own importance, declaring facetiously that his "article," as he modestly called this piece of research, held at least as much interest for Western sovietologists as a fish which suddenly starts talking would hold for ichthyologists. Amalrik was also the first person to speak openly of the existence of what he calls a cultural opposition. He described the evolution of samizdat from belles-lettres to a documentary form of indisputable reliability which, given the level of the official ideology has presently sunk to, can say immeasurably more than fiction.

It was samizdat together with the cultural opposition, to use Amalrik's term, which prepared the ground for the emergence of the Democratic Movement. Amalrik poses the question as to how many people are involved in the Democratic Movement in an active capacity—not just making threatening gestures at the authorities while their backs are turned. The worrying thing as far as the writers and poets are concerned, Amalrik affirms after examining in some detail the samizdat manuscripts, is that only just over one thousand signatures appear on the letters of protest and other documents. Even if we take into consideration the fact that there would be several thousand more dissidents spread around the country whom Amalrik does not take into account, it is still obvious that the Democratic Movement is confined to the urban intelligentsia and is almost totally without support amongst the broad mass of the people.

After the shooting of the Novocherkassk workers on 2 June 1962 the authorities made strenuous efforts to find the instigators of the disturbances amongst the intelligentsia and the students—but without success. For the first time in many years they were forced to bring to court and to execute as the instigators the workers themselves, those who had made accusatory and incriminating speeches—speeches no record of which, unfortunately, reached the West.[11] Bloodshed of this kind could easily have been avoided if Soviet workers had the right to strike. People's so-called power took away this natural right from the workers.

However, these economic disturbances, which were crushed with the same degree of ferocity uprisings in the camps are crushed with, had no connection with the political protests of the Democratic Movement. This is why it was quickly smashed, with some of its participants being sent away to the camps and others being sent out of the country.

What were the ideas which were put up to counter the heterodoxy of the Democratic Movement? Amalrik's concise reply to this question is one which the left-wing movement in the West seems to find it difficult to come to terms with—or else is unwilling to come to terms with: the power structure and the forces of terror in the Soviet Union have no ideology at all. This phenomenon, at least on such a massive scale, must be unique. Incredible though it may seem, the Party elite in the USSR, whose influence is felt all over the globe from North Korea to Cuba, is still unable to work out any ideological system and still has as its foundation stereotypes which have not been confirmed in practice anywhere—not in a single socialist country. As Amalrik correctly observes, once having grabbed power, the Party elite has proved eminently capable of keeping it in its own hands —but to what aim? "We appear to have reached a kind of dead point," Amalrik concludes, "where the concept of power is connected with neither a doctrine, nor the personality of a leader, nor with tradition, but simply with power as such."

This lack of any ideological basis on the Soviet regime's part could have catastrophic repercussions for the world at large. This general notion of Amalrik's is being realized at a rate which even Amalrik did not foresee.

The regime's lack of any ideology could not help but alarm Amalrik. It was precisely this lack of any other ideological basis which led to the establishment of the ideology of great Russian chauvinism which was one of the banners raised by Stalin. The Russian people proved receptive to this ideology. It has always found notions of force and justice easy to understand.

However, the idea of force has hypertrophied and taken on monstrous, self-vaunting forms. The idea of justice has always been a highly individual one in Russia: Russia has no tradition of respecting the rights of the human personality. "The concept... that an individual's personality (in itself, not by virtue of intelligence of education) has some kind of value strikes Russians as strange in the extreme," Amalrik writes, echoing what Valentin Moroz has written with great precision. He explains why this concept is so utterly foreign to the Russian way of thinking, and his observations have been confirmed by the tragic events in Czechoslovakia which were accepted by the majority of the Soviet people as something entirely natural.

Since Amalrik's explanations are contained in his book, I shall confine myself to examining certain of his views as a historian, views which have led him to extremely dangerous conclusions.

The regime is becoming decrepit, according to Amalrik. This contention is based on the seemingly credible idea that the "any kind of internal decrepitude is linked with a tendency towards extreme self-aggrandizement in the external political arena." However, it is obvious that the source of such self-aggrandizement, aggressiveness and adventurism is not necessarily to be found in internal processes of senility. The leadership is certainly growing senile but it will eventually leave the scene and be replaced by people like Shelepin from the Central Committee of the Komsomol. Decrepitude and obsolescence are terms applicable only to Marxist ideology which long ago became nothing more than a tattered slogan in Russia. Amalrik has made a fatal mistake in ascribing "the continuing process of raising the levels of freedom—a process which gives rise to the illusion that things are being "humanized" simply to the growing decrepitude of the regime. Amalrik does the regime a grave injustice in suspecting it of "growing old and no longer being able to clamp down on everything with its former strength and passion." The experiences of Solzhenitsyn, Galich and thousands of other dissident thinkers who have been arrested and sent into exile, including Amalrik himself, give the lie to Amalrik's hypothesis about the absence on the part of the present regime of enthusiasm for repressive legal measures. On the contrary, the body which supervises repression, the Ministry of Internal Affairs, has never before been so mobile, or had at its disposal such sophisticated technology as now, nor have the techniques of disinformation and the repression of society ever been so highly developed and refined by the latest scientific achievements, including those in the field of psychology.

Some people have been crushed, isolated, and sent into exile, while others have sold themselves and become supporters of the regime. These are circumstances which Amalrik's explanations put a complicated construction on and at times intellectualize—indeed, idealize. "In our country," he writes, "since we all work for the State, everyone has a civil servant's mentality. This is true of the writers who are members of the Union of Writers, of scientists working in State institutes and of workers and kilkhozniks to the same degree as of those working for the KGB or the Ministry of Internal Affairs." As Amalrik sees it, the obscurantists are as much victims as the hangmen. Their thinking has become "bureaucratized" ("ochinovleno").

Fifteen years ago Kochetov, who in 1961 became editor-in-chief of the journal *Oktyabr*, told a writer whose manuscript he had rejected that any hopes of a return to "Leninist ideas" were childish illusions because "higher up" they had no ideas at all—and here he pointed to the ceiling. Having realized this, Kochetov served the authorities who were devoid of all ideas so faithfully that he even gained the reputation of being ideologically inclined. Yevtushenko's scurrilous "swings" and Voznesensky's Leniniana represent exactly the same openly mercurial approach.

In recent years public opinion has been particularly sensitive to the kind of smoke-screens, shows of repentance, grimaces and grand leaps, and to protestations of having been "reformed" which Amalrik tries to systematize.

It is in the second part of this book, the first part of which is based on observations made with great precision, that Amalrik makes his basic mistake, one which produced misunderstanding, alarm and eventually active protest on the part of the Russian intelligentsia. Here he claims that it is of no importance who starts the inevitable and totally destructive war between the USSR and China. It is true that there were a number of hotheads among the Soviet military leaders fifteen years ago when Khrushchev was at the height of his power who favored the idea of "fixing" China once and for all by throwing in the tanks before China became a nuclear power. But even at that time the idea was opposed by other military leaders who realized that after China had been "fixed" the Chinese economy would be in shambles, there would be wide-spread sabotage and insurgency and a hundred million people would take up arms—and 850 million people would have to be fed, like the Cubans. Since the Soviet Union could not feed its own people, how on earth would they manage with the Chinese? The whole idea was quickly dropped and became hopelessly outmoded when China became a nuclear power. Even as Andrei Amalrik was writing his book the idea was nothing more than a curisosity.

However, after Amalrik's book became widely known, it became one of the world's most dangerous curiosities. Europe has been lulled and demoralized by its conviction that a Russo-Chinese war is unavoidable, and this is what dissident thinkers in the Soviet Union desperately feared. The Soviet Union's iron-clad presence in Vietnam, Portugal, Angola, Mozambique, Lebanon and elsewhere will hopefully rouse those who are still lulled by a false sense of security.

In Russia no one has these illusions. There is a samizdat satirical review which gives a good idea of what the reaction was in Russia to the second part of Amalrik's book. It is called *Review of the Press for 1984*—the year by which according to Amalrik the Soviet Union will have ceased to exist. Here are some short excerpts:

Le Monde, *Paris 22 June 1984:*

Decree of the Presidium of the Supreme Soviet of the Socialist Republic of France:
The writer Jean-Paul Chartreuse is to be awarded the Order of Maurice Thorez (Third Class) on the occasion of his 80th birthday for meritorious contributions to the development of French literature.
Signed: Jules Porochais
Chairman of the Presidium of the Supreme Soviet of the SRF
M. Georgadze. Secretary of the Presidium of the Supreme Soviet of the SRF.
Versailles, 21 June, 1984.

John XXIV: Why I Rejected Religion Unita, *The Vatican, 13 July (Telephone report) Comrade Pinetti, until recently the prominent Catholic churchman John XXIV, and now a lecturer for the Society of Knowledge, gave a public lecture in the Grasia concert hall. With the words "Forward ever forward to Communism under the banner of Marxism-Leninism" Comrade John Pinetti concluded his lucid lecture, packed with interesting facts, to a thunderous ovation.*

"Passing the Buck"
The Times, *London, 5 January.*

*Last year toilers in the district of Scotland harvested an un-
precedented crop of cucumbers. Yet in London's fruit and
vegetable shops there are few cucumbers to be seen. What is the
explanation for this? "We've nothing to pack them in," answered
the Chairman of the Honest Way collective farm, Hero of Socialist Labour Patty Bridge.*

It seems, nevertheless that it was not Andrei Amalrik who was right
but George Orwell, who in his prophetic *1984* has described England under
socialism and foretold the basic elements of spiritual degeneration of a kind
long apparent in the USSR. The black humor of this samizdat document
can be attributed to an awareness of Orwell and of course to a close acquaintance with Soviet reality which is Orwellian in many ways.

Andrei Amalrik's second book contained letters he wrote to a number
of correspondents. The most interesting letter of all is perhaps his open letter
to Anatoly Kuznetsov in which he writes about internal and external freedom. Another important letter is one called "Foreign Correspondents in
Moscow" in which he argues that permanent correspondents in Moscow
actually have KGB connections. It cannot be just pure chance, Amalrik
contends, that a reporter refused to accept a letter from the only kolkhoz
chairman among the dissidents, Ivan Yakhimovich. All Amalrik is doing
here is informing the world at large of something known to almost all those
dissidents in Moscow who have ever tried to establish contact with the foreign press. Only a negligible number of foreign correspondents are willing
to have any contact with dissidents. The vast majority prefer comfort and
security to anything else.

It really was samizdat which gave birth to Andrei Amalrik. There was
nothing second-hand about the difficult and tragic experiences he described
and he wrote about them in the established samizdat tradition, the tradition
of Paustovsky, Bek, Shalamov, Evgenia Ginzburg and finally of Solzhenitsyn
whose manuscripts by 1969 were simply flooding Moscow and other large
cities. The new generation joined the samizdat tradition as if entering into
its very element. Sometimes it sent its manuscripts to the West openly and
fearlessly, like Andrei Amalrik, in youthful demonstration of its freedom.
In doing so it actually assisted its hangmen in tying its hands. However,
it also provided an example of civil disobedience, for which Russia in its
torment had a desperate need.

10. BEWARE OF TRAPS!

1. Police Literature

Nothing has worried the regime more than the self-sacrificing courage and new awareness of young people in the Soviet Union. They have tried everything—expulsion from universities and institutes, exile to Siberia, the Mordvinian camps and harsh sentences for nothing more than reading certain poetry. Yet their efforts have had no effect whatever. There can be little doubt that the authorities have now reached a state bordering on panic. Even cautious people like the First Secretaries of various national Communist Parties are announcing to Party congresses that there has been "a reevaluation and radical rethinking of its convictions on the part of a certain section of the population, and in particular on the part of young people."[1][2]

Realizing that it is impossible to intimidate the majority of Soviet youth—although the idea has not been totally rejected, as we shall see—the authorities are now hurriedly laying new snares on youth's path to maturity. Although the Mordvinian option is still made use of, a snare which is receiving great emphasis is police literature. The books which fall into this category are printed in vast numbers of copies and are important for any research into the general literary and moral processes taking place in the Soviet Union today. They light up the shadowy ins and outs of the State's Shingalyovism which Dostoevsky depicted so prophetically in *The Devils*.

Two novels came out at the beginning of the post-war stream of police literature which were greeted with reserved but suspiciously prolonged applause by the press. The two authors have already been mentioned here. One was Vasily Ardamatsky and the other Lev Nikulin, who was from the ranks of security investigators sent to work in the literary area. Ardamatsky and Nikulin were utterly dissimilar. Ardamatsky was a cheerful demagogue and teller of anecdotes, not averse to having a drink or two in the company of writers of his own kind. His novel *Vengeance* was timed to come out right at the beginning of the Jubiliada. His works then started to come out in such prodigious numbers that librarians began to measure Ardamatsky in meters as they had earlier done in the case of Babayevsky and Fedin.

The book's authenticity is attested to on the very first page. It reads:

> *From the minutes of the meeting of the Presidium of the Central Executive Committee of the USSR of September 1924.*
>
> *17. The award of the Order of the Red Banner to a group of OGPU workers.*
>
> *In consideration of the successful completion of their task, their assiduous application to their work and their manifestation of*

*complete dedication in connection with the carrying out of difficult
and complicated tasks for OGPU... the Presidium of the Central Executive Committee of the USSR decrees that Comrades V.P. Menzhin-
sky, A.P. Fyodorov, G.S. Syroyezhkin, N. Demidenko, R.V. Puzitsky
and R.A. Pilyar shall be awarded the Order of the Red Banner.*

    *M. Kalinin, Chairman of the Presidium of the Central
Executive Committee of the USSR.*

    A. Yenukidze, Secretary.

Why this fanfare? The fact is that OGPU concocted a bogus underground organization called L.D. which was successful in luring back to Russia
the elusive Boris Savinkov. As a result of this successful piece of provocation
Savinkov was murdered. Ardamatsky's enthusiasm knows no bounds and in
Vengeance he goes on to reveal the secret machinations which led to Sav-
nikov's murder.

In Dzerzhinsky's words, "When Vladimir Ilyich was still in good health,
I once told him about our plan for luring Savinkov back from abroad... Vladimir Ilyich looked on our plan with approval but said that the stakes were
so big that it was a gamble we could not be permitted to lose." Lunacharsky's
cooperation is sought and he is invited to a meeting. Ardamatsky leaves the
reader in no doubt: the Chekhists and literary leaders were working together.

This bogus underground organization set up by the Cheka did its job
well. Mountains of lies were thrown up. Savinkov and his closest friends make
their way to Minsk on horse-drawn carts and go right to the OGPU chief's apartment believing that it is a secret meeting-place, and there he, the friend of
Ivan Kalyayev and participant in the attempt on the life of Pleve and the
Grand Prince Sergei Aleksandrovich, is caught and bound.

The style of this novel is only worth mentioning by virtue of the fact
that stylistically it bore a close resemblance to official articles and court
sentences. It is as if they all had one author. It is dotted with phrases such
as "French militarism," "he took the money from the hands of the imper-
ialists" and "iron-willed Felix had the kindest heart, it was full of love for
people and the passionate desire to bring them happiness."

The other classic writer of police literature is Lev Nikulin, the house
informer for the KGB mentioned previously. His novel *Dead Ripples (Myort-
vaya zyb)* was published just slightly ahead of Ardamatsky's *Vengeance*.
It tells the story of how OGPU operatives penetrated the Supreme Monarchist Council in Paris. A Chekist by the name of Yakushev meets General
Kutepov and General Wrangel in Paris, purportedly representing an underground organization in Russia. Yakushev inspires such confidence that the
notorious Black Hundreds member Shlugin makes a visit to Russia incog-
nito, as he thinks, where his every step is naturally watched closely. It is only
in 1927 that the monarchists discover the deception practiced on them. Some
of them manage to escape through Finland while others are caught and

liquidated.

The Chekists who carried out these difficult "assignments" were all shot in 1937 and replaced by a new contingent of thugs, but Nikulin's book is not concerned with this.

Books such as these, displaying an inverted morality, are legion. They comprise a sinister anti-literature which for many years now has been eating away at the very moral foundations of the Russian people, representing espionage, mendacity and betrayal as heroic, an attitude rarely met with in Russian literature until then.

2. *Song Without Words*

In recent years one aspect of amoral literature has become predominant. It deserves special attention because the traps mentioned above are laid in great numbers in this area. Those responsible for laying these traps include both former investigators and those who were under investigation. The latter have at times been unaware of the fact that they have participated in the laying of traps.

Here are some excerpts from literary periodicals which illustrate this point:

> *Solomon's parents imagined his future each in a different way. His father dreamed of making a rich merchant of his son, while his mother saw her son in her dreams as a rabbi, or if the worst came to the worst as a tzaddik. Solomon, had his own thoughts on the subject. While still a young man he had demonstrated exceptional intelligence and an acute political sense and had joined the Bund. It was the same reliable political sense which helped him to get his bearings after the Revolution when he broke with the Bund and joined the Russian Social Democratic Workers' Party... he then began to make a career for himelf. As his model he took Leon Trotsky... He wore a service jacket with a military cut to it, and riding breeches tucked into box-calf boots he always kept clean and he always had certain revolutionary phrases held in reserve...*

> *I am tracing a line, working out a geneology—the dark geneology of the children of Israel in our times. And here it is: Solomon begat the commissars and the commissars laughed at the nakedness of his soul and his naive straightforwardness and had him put away in a madhouse. The commissars begat the people's commissars and they either had the commissars put in front of the firing-squad or else had them sent to the camps. Whom did the people's commissars beget? Bolotin, —who else? This Bolotin is the pitiful last-born in the line as it finally sputters out.*

411

... Apart from the fact that one of his arms was shorter than the other and deformed, Bolotin is lop-sided because he has a few ribs missing. I insist on describing his physical disabilities in this way because as I see it the type of person he was an example of is inseparable from his outer deformity. Two other Jews of a similar kind come to mind: one had two toes missing and the other was a hunchback.

Bolotin must have a field of activity dominated by absolute destruction and absolute evil... I go to visit Bolotin... the veneer is peeling off his television set and the divan is worn and dirty... To look at his apartment you would think he was having repairs done to it, but you quickly realize that in fact there are no repairs being carried out... You are then struck by the thought of the consistency of design *which has produced what is dominant here. It is the same zone of absolute destruction which affected Bolotin's precursors on a country-wide scale, reduced here to the proportions of a single apartment—and here I am face to face with the result! Ha ha! I would like to see Vasily Rozanov here with his apotheosis of the Jewish sense of home. Yes, Rozanov would throw up his hands, he would be able to fathom a few things about Bolotin!... How can you get away from Bolotin? How can you slip away from what surrounds you on all sides, hangs over you and crushes you?*

These quotations are not all from the same book, although they may appear to be. The first quotation is from Dimarov's openly anti-semitic novel published in the Soviet journal *Dniepro* (Kiev, 1963, N. 10, pp. 32-3), while the subsequent ones are from *Kontinent* (1975, No. 3, p. 91), the dissident journal published in Paris which Soviet sources unfailingly dismiss as anti-Soviet. Has an unexpected linking up of Soviet and anti-Soviet forces occurred on the so-called national question—one of the most pressing questions in Russia today?

The shift towards chauvinism in Stalin's policy in 1942 was made easier by the fact that, despite the established view to the contrary, evident in dissident literature also, internationalism has never existed in Russia. The much vaunted equality of workers of all races and nations has never existed and could not exist because respect for the human personality has not existed. This is true of the personality of the worker as well as of those who are not workers. During the Revolution there was no place for respect for the individual's inner world, especially if it did not correspond to the slogans of the moment. The writer Korolenko who was a great humanist was cast aside like carrion because in his letters he protested against the contemptuous treatment of individuals and against the reprisals taken without trial against Ukrainians, Russians, Jews, women and children.

This is all particularly true of the private spiritual world of the believer.

As I have already mentioned, Old Church Slavonic and Hebrew were banned in 1920 by special decree as languages connected with religious ritual and the languages of those connected with religious organizations.

That personality which in Mayakovsky's words "steps on the throat of its own song" once and for all with single-minded fanaticism is cut off from its own culture, its religion and its traditions, and thereby loses its spiritual identity—in other words, it dies. It becomes a mere cog.

It is not surprising that the Revolution led to a spiritual vacuum. It was this which was present in its very roots, rather than the chimeras of "international brotherhood," although all the faded slogans have been affirming the opposite for fifty years or more. The national Messianic myths were crushed out by the Revolution. The more the Revolution itself became Messianic and nationalistic, the more rigorously it attempted to shatter these myths—at least in words. By the beginning of the Second World War young people did not have the faintest idea about them.

I joined the army in November 1939 and well remember that the Red Army soldiers never talked about the taking of Lvov, Chernovtsy and Bialystok except in terms of cheerful irony as "freeing our blood brothers." The least sophisticated soldier knew that Stalin was pushing back the borders of the Soviet Union in anticipation of the war with Germany. The political activists brought this idea home to everyone. The Kremlin chimes were still ringing out the International as the Soviet anthem. It was only the newspapers which were prattling on about so-called blood brothers. The armed forces found some good-natured amusement in what was happening, not yet realizing that in two years' time the notion of the common brotherhood of all working people would be cast aside like the scenery of a play at the end of its run. Eventually in 1943 the State chimes on the Spassky tower of the Kremlin began to ring out not the International but the national anthem of the Soviet Union which in the mid-fifties Russians christened The Song Without Words.

Conscious of its ideological nakedness, the State donned the trappings of State chauvinism.

It should not be imagined that this display of buffonnery on the part of the almighty State has been accepted without a murmur by all sections of the Russian intelligentsia. The young poet Markov, who has never had the reputation of being a dissident, unexpectedly announced at a public discussion in 1968 that he was ashamed to be called a Russian. In scientific research institutes protests, totally unexpectedly for the regime, were voiced against the politics of tanks carried out in Czechoslovakia, Africa and the Middle East. In the factories workers began to complain openly about the fact that "we're giving aid to the black-arses but have nothing to eat ourselves." Even some of the KGB operatives stopped behaving like automatic machines. One young KGB lieutenant searching General Grigorenko's apartment kept asking Grigorenko what it was he wanted, whether he had a positive program of some kind. Questions such as these were not part of his duties which were quite simply to put everything he considered necessary in a bag and seal it up. Questions such as these were the interrogators' business. Yet this young KGB lieutenant was deeply interested as a human being in the question of what should be done and whether or not one could have a positive program of action. The same kind of questions were put to Krasnov-Levitin and Eduard Kuznetsov by their camp warders and their escorts.

When I was summoned to the Lubyanka in connection with statements I had made in the West and said while talking with the KGB plain-clothes "expert on the arts" that writers indeed had grounds for disquiet since a third of their number was in the camps, the young expert interrupted me to say with obvious sincerity: "Don't you realize that six whole layers of the Cheka-NKVD were wiped out? At times of repression it is always the little man who is blamed." Thoughts such as these scarcely arouse enthusiasm.

People were thirsting for ideas, it scarcely mattered what kind of ideas, and the gates were opened to total indoctrination of the population with the ideas of chauvinism, Messianism and duty to the "progressive peoples." The Soviet soldier, even if he finds himself sent to Tierra del Fuego, must feel that he has some right to be there, that he is there as a liberator.

The suggestion to inculcate these ideas into the new recruits in the Post-Stalinist era was first made to *Molodaya Gvardiia*. This occurred in 1967, the first well-planned year of the Jubiliada and it was part of an attack launched right across the ideological front. By a strange coincidence Chalmayev's article in *Molodaya Gvardiia* (1967, no. 10) appeared simultaneously with Ardamatsky's novel singing the praises of provocation planned at Central Committee level and virtually on the same day as S.V. Smirnov's poem glorifying Stalin was published in the journal *Moskva* (1967, no. 10):

Was it not his greatness we also proclaimed
Purposely, as we would a captain's?
He it was who at a time of trials
Did not leave his command post...

(...ne o nyom lik, kak o kapitane,
My trubili tozhe nesprosta!
Eto on v godinu ispytiany
Ne skhodil s komandonogo posta...)

It appeared not long after Part II of V. Zakrutkin's novel *The Creation of the World* had come out (*Oktyabr*, 1967, nos. 6-7). This is a novel in which the positive hero threatens his adversary: "Don't you touch Stalin... We know why Stalin stuck in your throat.").

Chalmayev's confused and practically illiterate article in *Molodaya*

Gvardiia was called "The Philosophy of Patriotism." Chalmayev was a critic who had been considered to belong to the *Novy mir* stable when he suddenly disappeared from the scene. He resurfaced as the ideological proponent of "internal patriotism." It was this rather gloomy critic who gave the Jubiliada its national profile, so to speak. Of course, as Solzhenitsyn suggested in *The Calf and the Oak* (266-7) "someone cleverer was standing behind him."

The joking ceased, however, when an article by the historian S. Semanov entitled "On Relative and Eternal Values" appeared in *Molodaya Gvardiia* (1970, No. 8) explaining the meaning of the onslaught of aggressive nationalism. According to Semanov, the really genuine and salutary revolution in the Soviet Union was actually the one which took place in 1937, the year the flower of Russian science and culture was slaughtered. "It is now clear that the watershed in the fight against destructive elements and nihilists came in the mid-thirties... after the adoption of our Constitution [on 5 December 1936] ... the equality of all citizens before the law was then established... These changes had the most beneficial effect on the development of our culture."

At the time Semanov's article appeared, Tvardovsky's *Novy mir* no longer existed. It was samizdat which wasted no time in delivering a knock-out blow to Semanov. Samizdat reminded him that it was the salutary thirties which saw the annihilation not only of Soviet culture but also of the culture which Semanov himself purported to be concerned about: It was not in the first years of the Revolution that the Church of Christ the Savior in Moscow was demolished. It was calmly demolished according to a plan ratified by Stalin during those same blessed thirties. The Church of the Savior in the Forest (14th and 15th Centuries) also in the Kremlin, and the Red Porch of the Faceted Palace were all demolished during the same period either with the blessing or on the direct order of Stalin. Where the Monastery of the Ascension had stood the completely useless and architecturally tasteless Kremlin Theatre was constructed. The author of the samizdat article goes on to explain angrily how it is possible for Semanov as a historian belonging to Soloukhin's cohort of "protectors of the monuments of antiquity" to date the beginning of the flowering of Russian culture from 1937. In doing so the author of the article claims that Semanov gives himself away:

> *For essentially he is not concerned with either the Russian people or Russian culture. The idea which is important to him and which he holds dear is that of Russia's greatpower status... Semanov, Chalmayev and the other neoslavophiles have every reason to be grateful to Stalin... At that time great-power chauvinism was declared by Stalin to be the sole unshakeably true Communist ideology and any disagreement with him to be anticommunist and anti-Soviet... When the lawgiver beckoned... the Black Hundreds not having any other opportunity to defend their views, are happy to take swift refuge within*

*the ruling ideology and to settle themselves cosily there and with the
passing of time to rework it.*

The Party leaders such as Suslov, Demichev and their associates could
not tolerate this wholesale baring of the shameful places on the body of the
Communist doctrine they espoused, so they ordered the lowering of the
great-power flag on the Komsomol ship and had the editor of *Molodaya
Gvardiia* severely punished. However, the same flag continued to fly over
many other State publishing houses, particularly *Voyennoye izdatelstvo*
and *Moskovsky rabochiy* which published one after another the openly
antisemitic and anti-intelligentsia books of Ivan Shevtsov. It also continued
to fly over the Novosti agency (APN) which publishes propaganda for consumption abroad, is a branch of and a cover for the KGB, one which railed
against the Prague Spring ("the Czechs are to blame for everything them-
sleves!")[3]

The flag of great-power status did not only fly over these publishing
houses and the Rodina Club, however. V. Osipov, the dissident and camp-
inmate who later declared that while in the labor camp he had reconsidered
his views on Dzhugashvili who had given the impulse for the rebirth of the
Russian national spirit, began putting out a "patriotic Russian journal"
called *Veche*, named after the popular assemblies in medieval Russian towns.
He published this journal, in which he called on his readers to continue along
the path mapped out by Dostoyevsky and the Slavophiles, in the town where
he lived just outside Moscow. As a former political prisoner with an anti-
Soviet past Osipov was, of course, kept under surveillance. As the reader
is aware, his samizdat journal *Bumerang* had been no less swiftly put out
of action than *Sintaksis* and *Feniks*. One whole department of the KGB,
armed with the very latest technological aids including laser listening devices,
was engaged on the task of tracking down the *Chronicle of Current Events*.
Hundreds of thousands of roubles were spent tracking down the culprits.

Veche came out for three years in a row, starting on 19 January 1971.
Its publication for all practical purposes was not concealed. Osipov gave his
home address in the journal so that manuscripts could be sent to him. After
all, he had spent seven years in the camps and was under surveillance. He
was being kept on a short leash. Let him experiment, if he had reconsidered
his views on Dzhugashvili.

Osipov was permitted to glorify the State on the grounds that power
is from God and to heap abuse on the "rotten West" in the words of one
of the founders of slavophilism, A.S. Khomyakov: "The European, who is
eternally talking about mankind, never quite comes to grips with man."
He is even allowed to argue with Lenin, although without mentioning him
by name: "It was Austria, and not Russia, which was the gendarme of Europe" (60). He contemptuously and arrogantly dismissed *Novy mir*: "the
success of *Novy mir* was short-lived and left no long-lasting trace. V. Bykov,

V. Syomin, V. Voinovich, F. Iskander and V. Mozhayev did not save the situation..." (No. 2, p. 70). His displeasure with Solzhenitsyn was even more legitimate. According to Osipov, Solzhenitsyn denigrates the tsarist generals in *August 1914*. "Right from the first battle the Russian generals' insignia are perceived as marks of their uselessness and the higher the rank the greater the futility, and there is almost no one the author can rest his gaze on with gratitude " (No. 4, p. 145.)

What an excellent turn of events this proved to be. Here it was stated not in some official organ, not in some hard-line periodical like Kochetov's *Oktyabr* or Sofronov's *Ogonyok* but in *Veche*, a dissident publication, run off by school-children at night, that the campaign against the cosmopolitans was of the utmost importance for the "revelation of Russia's calling" and that it was a failure only because "Stalin entrusted the intelligentsia itself with the fight against the intelligentsia's cosmopolitanism..." (No. 1, p. 16).

In return for this kind of material the authorities even found it possible to overlook the extravagant praise of the tsarist general Skobolev, who had subjugated Central Asia to Russian rule, in three issues of *Veche*. Unfortunately, however, these articles roused the ire of readers in Central Asia. A puzzled letter was sent to *Veche* which answered it with all the Great Russian arrogance and disdain which is permitted in relations with those of non-Russian origin: "Regardless of whether we like it or not, it is the law of might and not some abstract justice which holds sway in relations between different peoples " (No. 4, p. 154).

At this point Osipov broke the rules of the game. He seemed to lose his senses. He called the Central Committee Secretaries who had castigated the editors of *Molodaya Gvardiia* over the Semanov article "velmozhy" (grandees). "As soon as Russian patriots let their voice be heard in an official organ, the grandees were heard to intone: 'It is time to put an end to this Russophilism.' " The KGB immediately cut short the unsuccessful experiment. They began to search Osipov's house and to prepare a trial. This hapless and stubborn former political prisoner received a second term of imprisonment.

Osipov's latest boomerang had returned to hit those watching over him on the head and naturally they were annoyed about it. The last issue of *Veche* was above praise and was ecstatically quoted at the Rodina Club: "Is it proper to speak of *Russian* great-power chauvinism? Is it in the final analysis Russian? Who were the bearers of this chauvinism? Was it the bureaucratic machine of the post-Petrine epoch, crammed as it was with Germans? Was it Dzhuashvili and Dzerzhinsky? Would it not be correct to call this chauvinism simply great-power chauvinism? Or even better—the chauvinism of power without any particular national characteristics? Let all those remaining hotheads among the Ukrainians, Balts, Georgians and Kazakhs, who in their blindness vent their vain anger on Russia, take a better look at their offenders—was it Russia which produced them?" (*Veche*, No.6, p.9).

417

> *The march on Poland was the first not by Russian but by Soviet imperialist forces. The submissive troops of many nationalities were commanded by a Russian (Tuchachevsky), a Georgian (Stalin), a Hungarian (Bela Kun), a Kalmyk (Oka Gorodovikov), and a Jew (Yakir), and behind them stood the Poles Dzerzhinsky and Marchlewski, and the Jews Trotsky, Kamenev and Zinovyev.* (Kontinent, No. 4, p. 338)

After the appearance of the third issue of *Kontinent* in which the "dark genealogy of the children of Israel in our times" from Solomon to Bolotin was traced, I came to the conclusion that Maximov, the editor-in-chief, was actually just putting into practice the principle of freedom of speech—after all, I told myself, everyone has the right to his own opinion, including A. Sukonik, the author of the colorless story "Bolotin, My Consultant," who had left the USSR and escaped the dark genealogy of the children of Israel on a visa to Israel. I expected some sort of editorial comment of the usual kind to the effect that the editors did not necessarily share the views of the author. In due course it appeared in connection with a different article by the well-known Polish journalist Julius Mieroszewski in which he gave reasons for the Poles' fear of Russian imperialism.

The editorial comment appears in part above. The views of the editors are expressed very candidly. In marshalling their facts and in order to make their argument all the more convincing, they move up the Poles Dzerzinsky and Marchlewski to the front ranks together with other non-Russians as if to show that in fact the Poles were fighting each other and conveniently forget the Russian heroes of song and legend such as Voroshilov and Budyonnyi, although it was actually Budyonni's cavalry corps which had the slogan "Warsaw will be ours" painted on all its britzkas. However distasteful it may be to do so, it must be pointed out that the Poles, Jews, Kalmyks and other non-Russians who led their troops into Poland did so not as the representatives of their own minor nationalities, with which they had severed their connections, at times demonstratively, but as active participants in the Russian revolution.

For fifty years it never occurred to anyone in either the East or West to see them in any other light, with the exception of certain defeated members of the tsar's life-guard whose interpretation of events never went above the level of antisemitic ale-house jokes such as "the tea is Vystosky's, the sugar is Brodsky's and Russia is Trotsky's." (All three were Jews.)

New facts which illustrate a similar level of thinking have come to light. When Stalin found it necessary to prove the existence of a plot against the people on the part of the so-called doctor-murderers, the names of six Ukrainians and Russians were removed from the list of those accused "so that nothing should interfere with the clarity of the picture." It was only after Stalin's death when certain documents connected with the rehabilitation process were published that it was learned that these six names had been hushed up.

However, in the case of *Kontinent*, it is not simply a matter of preserving the clarity of the picture. The question before us is a far more serious one. After listing the names of all the non-Russian participants the dissident journal goes on to instruct its readers as follows: "As we can see, the author's very premise ('We are afraid of Russian imperialism') conceals within itself a major flaw, for to confuse Russian imperialism of the Pan-Slav kind of the last century with Soviet imperialism which has as its aim total world domination is to fail to make a distinction, albeit involuntarily, between two different concepts."

We might ask whether it was any easier for the Polish insurgents to meet their deaths because it was their blood brothers who herded them into the Siberian mines, shot and hanged them, and whether the fact that it was "Russian imperialism of a Pan-Slav kind" rather than Soviet imperialism which slaughtered them made it any easier for the Caucasian mountain people to die from General Paskevich's Slavic shrapnel, the Central Asians to die in General Skobelev's bayonet attacks or the Kalmyks and Kirgiz followers of Pugachev to die at the hands of Suvorov's wondrous warriors.

This is not to deny that there is any difference between Russian imperialism and Soviet Imperialism. The Pan-Slav troops moved on foot and their artillery and transport units were horse-drawn—they could simply never have reached Vietnam or Angola. Ivan the Terrible described the Sea of Azov and the Crimea in the Ukraine, Moldavia and Walachia, Livonia and the town of Verny in the Central Asian steppes as *dalnokonnyye*—at the limits of his cavalry's range. He was deeply aggrieved that the whole earth—Hindustan which was protected by the Pamirs and other distant, fantastic lands from Russian fairy-stories—could never find themselves beneath the hooves of his horsemen. Even the Dardanelles remained just a dream of the Russian Empire. Nowadays, however, the possibilites are different. An AN-22 transport aircraft can fly out of Moscow and unload tanks, rockets and troops in any corner of the globe the same day.

No sooner had *Kontinent* appeared with its revelation that it was not Russians but in the main Poles themselves—in friendly cooperation with other non-Russians—who had taken Warsaw than uproar broke out on all the other "continents." What about the murder of Poles at Katyn and the betrayal of the Warsaw uprising in 1944 when several armies with Red stars on their caps waited patiently for the Nazis to wipe out the Warsaw heroes? What of Nikita Khrushchev's hurried trip to Poland in 1956 to quell the workers' riots? By this time Dzerzhinsky, Marchlewski, and all the others had long since rotted in their graves, in most cases with a bullet in the back of the neck.

As a result of the embarassing situation which had arisen, the next issue of *Kontinent* (no. 5) contained an editorial signed by the entire editorial board and the core of writers supporting the journal: "With a sense of bitter regret and repentance we, the undersigned members of Russian intelligentsia, feel bound to accept some blame for all the grievous wrongs wrought against Poland and in Russia's name... it is our historical duty and obligation to expiate the blame of our *nation as a whole* for those marks which can never be erased."

The sense of bitter regret and repentance was so deep that in the next issue of *Kontinent* the penitents were joined by Alexander Solzhenitsyn: "I join you in the knowledge that Communism is not the invention of some particular nation but an organic gangrene which is affecting the whole of mankind... Wiser for our sufferings, we shall not allow our national sensitivities to dim the consciousness of our unity."[14]

A bad mistake had been made and had been corrected. A similar mistake would not be allowed to occur again. Yet in the very same issue— which Maximov considered to be the first issue of the real *Kontinent*—there appeared an article castigating not the Poles this time but our Ukrainian blood-brothers who published the *Chronicle of Ukrainian Resistance*. The indignation of *Kontinent* was aroused by its Ukrainian blood-brothers' desire for the complete independence of the Ukraine. The members of the Russian resistance movement had been upbraided for "delicately avoiding this question," including those who were in the West "with their hands untied." *Kontinent* could scarcely restrain its righteous anger as an elder brother in its reprimands to the Ukrainians: "a new tone must be found to conduct the discussion in... we must not engage in age-old feuds... At this tragic time when the whole world is faced with a deadly threat... Let us stretch out our hands to one another... We shall search for new paths..." Yet there was not a word about the right of the Ukraine to independence, even in the framework of the most insubstantial emigre fantasies.

Yet the choice is clear. Either it is a battle for human rights or for the unity and indivisibility of the peoples under which the free republics are permitted to display their own flags for decorative purposes alongside the flag of the Great Power.

In the same address quoted above, Solzhenitsyn gives an unambiguous explanation of his point of view: "By carelessly and ignorantly substituting the word Russian for Soviet... the crimes and latest designs of world Communism are ascribed to that people which was the first to suffer from Communism and which has suffered from it longer than any other people, and which together with its brothers in misfortune, the peoples of the USSR has lost through violence sixty million people."

The "brothers in misfortune" would appear to be mentioned here primarily for statistical reasons. They have nothing to do with Solzhenitsyn's basic idea which is to inveigh against any confusion of the Russian people with the concept of the Soviet people. What have the Russians to do with world Communism? Were they not its first and longest-suffering victims? As Stalin's deeply-rooted formula has it, the Russian people is the first among equals. This idea has been widely publicized for years by *Pravda*: first in labor and in the battle. *Kontinent* echoes *Pravda* in Solzhenitsyn's words: "first in its sufferings, in the number of victims and in its misfortune... the first to suffer from Communism and [the one] which has suffered from it longer than any other people..."

The impression to come out of all this is that *Kontinent* is wearing the Soviet Great Russian hat—it is just that it has been turned inside-out. Even the style of the article on the Ukrainians was reminiscent of the official *Pravda* style—"at this tragic time when the whole world...", "let us stretch out our hands to one another..." and so on.

There is surely something deeply amoral about the concern on the part of the ideologues on *Kontinent* with weighing up whose misfortunes are greater, whose pain is more unbearable and whose losses more irreparable. Some have achieved their national independence through great suffering while other must not even contemplate such wickedness. All that is needed is a promise that a brotherly hand will be extended.

Did the Crimean Tartars who lost half their numbers while being transported away from their homeland which they then lost suffer any less than the Russians? The Kurds fought for their independence for some forty years. Stalin had them deported like the Crimean Tartars. Brezhnev took the step of giving them arms but then recently when it turned out that there was oil under the mountainous areas they inhabited he betrayed them and played into the hands of Iraq which is exterminating the Kurds in massive numbers. Have the Kurds, who have been betrayed by everyone, suffered any less than the Russians? Have they suffered for a shorter time or less deeply?

The stance adopted by *Kontinent* on these questions is all the more offensive and unnecessary in the light of its many praiseworthy achievements in the battle for human rights. It resurrects works which might have been supposed to have moldered away in the basement of the Lubyanka. It publishes in every issue critical essays of a calibre possibly unsurpassed in Russian periodicals. It has become the rostrum from which the Russia denied all other public forums may speak.

The arrival of Viktor Nekrasov and Andrei Amalrik in the West and the freeing of Vladimir Bukovsky and other resistance heroes who are uncompromising opponents of nationalism, will no doubt eventually lead to the complete collapse in the West of the sinister mirages of Great Russian primacy among equals and its paradoxical collusion with Soviet Great Russian nationalism on the pages of journals which by no means have a pro-Soviet tendency.

Andrei Sakharov, Viktor Nekrasov, Andrei Amalrik and Vladimir

Bukovsky have all had a significant influence. In the ninth issue of *Kontinent* both Tatiana Khodorovich who has deeply-held religious views and her opponent Leonid Plyushch who is still a Marxist express equal disgust for the ethical goals Moscow has set itself—the extermination of everything human in man. "This is equivalent to the moral corruption of the people because the constant, gross, lawless and unrestrained abuse in the name of the majority directed at a national or intellectual minority deprived of the possibility of defending itself, cannot fail to lead to the bitter hardening and moral degradation of society." But when the next issue of *Kontinent* appears, the magazine severely enjoins Polish *samizdat* never again to mix Russian and Soviet, as though the bloody division of Poland had started under the Bolsheviks and not under the Russian emperors centuries earlier.

As if the Warsaw Governor-General, Muraviev, the pacifier of Polish revolts had never exclaimed: "I am not of the Muravievs you hang, but of those who do the hanging!"

But why speak about the Muravievs, the persecuters, or the above-mentioned Duke Saliases, the moral supporters of the executioners! The Russian national genius, Fyodor Dostoevsky, never even referred to Poles as Poles, but only, contemptuously, as "Polacks."

Raising nationalist or religious flags would do nothing to rid the peoples making up the USSR of what is abhorrent about the present system. It would only lead to bloodshed. If the banners of Orthodoxy were hoisted, certain dissidents would seek the unification of Central Asian peoples under the flag of Islam. The Balts would become Protestants and Roman Catholics, while the Ukrainians, even those who were Orthodox, would join the Uniates just to separate themselves as much as possible from the Muscovites. How long would it be before we were treated to the spectacle of the persecution and deportation of those of other faiths and the growth of territorial claims? Grossman called the frenzied nationalism of the popular masses "the nuclear warhead of the twentieth century." It threatens to explode so horrifically that there will be no pieces left to pick up.

According to the 1970 census Russians make up fifty-three percent of the population of the Soviet Union. In fact ethnic Russians almost certainly make up less than half the population because it can safely be assumed there are a million Russian Jews, and millions of Mordvinians, Komi, Chuvash and Karelians who register as "the first among equals." And although the champions of the united and indivisible land concept, listening to the subterranean roar of the nationalism of the non-Russian majority, instinctively cross themselves and hope to ward off the coming disaster, the fact is that when the "communal State" ("sobornoye gosudarstvo") is proclaimed non-Russians will go out and slaughter Russians and those who are considered equivalent to Russians without distinguishing between those who are guilty and those who are not guilty.

There is no more dangerous illusion than that of a "communal State" formed on a religious or nationalist basis. This traditional racism and nationalism which has spilled out onto the streets is loathsome to the best kind of Russian.

From camp Ya.O. 100/7 in the town of Sychevks in the Smolensk region the religious writer A. Krasnov-Levitin, a hero of the religious resistence about whom legends circulated in Russia, considered it a matter of crucial importance to send a letter reviling nationalistic hatreds disguised in the clothing of religion. "On the basis of the Church's teachings," he wrote, "these people represent a crucial danger because they are attempting to cover up their misanthropic ideology with the Gospel. This is not simply a matter of hypocrisy. It is the work of the Devil and abuse of the Holy Spirit when attempts are made in the name of Jesus Christ to conceal the preaching of hate, murder and cannibalism..."[15]

The direction present-day nationalistic hysteria on the part of so-called true Russians is taking has been noted in the West also. As early as 1972 Nikita Struve, editor-in-chief of *Vestnik RSKhD (Herald of the Russian Student Christian Movement)* published in Paris, wrote: "National self-awareness is necessary for rebirth to take place, but where it slides into any kind of nationalism or, more particularly, chauvinism, then it threatens to lead to utter disaster because it is here that it can become linked with the State machine—and there are already signs of this happening. National Bolshevism is one of tomorrow's most threatening perils." A writer in *Grani* (no. 82), Vladimir Pavlov, has also pointed out the "strange grimaces" of Soviet Slavophilism and some attention to the question has been paid by other scholars in a number of countries. A "communal State" in an atheist country is arrant nonsense.

Is some sort of Christian revival possible? *Kontinent* asked the opinion on this question of a leading authority, Bruno Kalnins who attended every Congress of the Socialist International from 1921 to 1972, and who has been imprisoned by both the Nazis and the Soviet regime and is now the Chairman of the Latvian Social-Democratic Workers' Party in exile. *Kontinent* wanted to know if the names of Solzhenitsyn and Maximov were known to people in Latvia and what their response was to these writers' call for a revival of Christianity. The reply Kalnins gave was a highly significant one, especially when it is considered that it was meant for *Kontinent*. Kalnins said that "the names of opposition writers are known in Latvia only through foreign broadcasts. The most popular... is academician Sakharov, particularly as a result of his statements in defense of the rights of national minorities. The call for the revival of Christianity does not meet with any particular response in Latvia."

There may be other opinions on this subject. It is, however, unlikely that anyone would wish to deny that in the Baltic countries, a third of whose population was deported to Siberia, there is a deep-seated hostility to Russians. This hostility has been expressed in the activities of the so-called "forest brothers" whom whole divisions were sent to crush, in the sabotage and mute hatred which any Russian-speaking settler there meets with constantly. There have been expressions of hatred for the "Muscovites" in the Ukraine as well. Nowadays, in every national republic Russians are associated with Moscow, Soviet power, lack of freedom, the high cost of living and the chronic food shortage. Nationalism has its own way of gauging these things. These problems cannot be simply passed over, warded off with pious hopes or prayed away. Fifty years have done their work.

An old doctor who had lived for most of his life in Central Asia and had been an officer in the border guards once told me in some detail of how the attitude there to Russians is changing. Once the Russian border post had meant salvation to outlying villages. This was where he had served as a doctor. Young people used to rush to him for help in the case of natural disasters or if problems such as rustling arose. Now he saw abundant examples of Russification and evidence of distrust for non-Russians. This distrust sometimes takes forms which are little less than dumb-founding. In Tadzhik-istan there is an *aul* or village whose inhabitants can only approach the river forming the border with Afgahanistan where they have gone to draw water for centuries by passing through a barbed-wire tunnel rather like the wire tunnels dangerous animals are led into the circus ring along. This is done to insure that these Tadzhiks do not try to escape from their own village. I was told by the officer in charge of the local detachment that this was the only thing to do and he quoted the old saying about however much you feed a wolf it will still hanker after the forest. There had apparently been one unfortunate incident... Hatred for those who come from elsewhere is raising its head in areas where it was previously unknown, for example among the Kazakhs, the Tadjiks and the Uzbeks who have always been famous for their friendly acceptance of outsiders.

However incredible it may seem, the border guards in the national republics are always of a different nationality from that of the First Secretary of the national Communist Party of the republic. At each border post it is permitted to have only one local man—"for purposes of contact with the local population," as it was explained to me.

Does the hatred for Russians on the part of these national minorities have any religious overtones, even involuntary ones? Are Russians to become involved in a vortex of religious wars which history has shown us are the most bloody? The road to hell is paved with good intentions.

No one doubts the integrity of the *Kontinent* writers. It would be highly desirable, however, if they could fearlessly think their thoughts through to some conclusion, not allow the pain of their nation's suffering to befuddle their thinking, or carelessly let slip phrases which can then be taken up and repeated by the propagandists of hate in every corner of the globe. An example of the latter is found in statements made by Alexander

Solzhenitsyn in Zurich in which he claimed that all through history people of foreign blood had managed to lead his great nation by the nose, even various half-breeds and quarter-casts having played the part.

"Yes, yes, it was they who led us," Stepan Zlobin used to agree sarcastically in "debates" of this kind. "On the one hand 'the Party leads,' yet on the other hand it is they who lead, and always have, in all ages from the Rurikoviches to the Kaganoviches, while we, great nation that we are, don't even answer for our own fate, like some madmen with a referral certificate..."

The Author's Index of Names at the end of *Lenin in Zurich* might have been written not by Solzhenitsyn but Sholokov. During the campaign against cosmopolitanism Sholokhov published an article under the heading "With Visor Closed" in which he demanded the disclosure of the real names of the cosmopolitan "imperialist agents" hiding behind pseudonyms. Solzhenitsyn seeks out his enemies in exactly the same place as Sholokhov. He discloses that these enemies of Russia, these revolutionaries and their associates were actually "Grigory Yevseyevich Zinoviev (Apfelbaum), "Lev Borisovich Kamenev" (Rozenfeld), and "Parvus" (Helphand), "Alexander (Izrail) Lazarevich." In those cases where there is no pseudonym, Solzhenitsyn informs his reader with scrupulous care for detail: "A Russian Pole," "an Estonian from Tallin," "daughter of a (Ukrainian) general and a Finnish peasant-woman"—all from foreign minorities, half-castes, quarter-castes...

"Can this be Solzhenitsyn?" The question means that each one of us, in his imagination, evidently had an image of Solzhenitsyn as a knight without fear or reproach.

It is particularly chilling and alarming to hear Solzhenitsyn resorting to such jingoistic insinuations and it makes us wonder again if this is the real Solzhenitsyn speaking... Yet wherever the paths of nationalism may eventually lead him, the immortal Solzhenitsyn has already taken vengeance on the mortal Solzhenitsyn a hundredfold, and put another nail in the coffin of the Soviet regime. This Solzhenitsyn will remain faithful to Russia wherever his completely understandable despair and the pain and impotence he feels at being an emigre may lead him.

One feels tremendous pity for young people in Russia who through their aspirations to oppose arbitrary rule have fallen prey to the State's neo-Slavophilism. As the great Russian philosopher Vladimir Solovyov once wrote, nationalism destroys a nation in the same way egotism destroys the personality. It is a shame this perceptive idea cannot be brought home to young Russians in the Soviet Union. The younger generation has certainly had far more opportunities to resist pressure than the older writers and scientists had. The young have not been organized into Unions created for the purpose of controlling thought, and have not been intimidated by Stalinism and are much more independent. Young people have even been ready for the sake of their convictions to go to the camp—and have gone. All the

425

same, *Molodaya gvardiya*, the KGB controlled Novosti Press Agency and the jailers have done what they could either to intimidate or buy the young, and if that has failed, they have attempted to deceive them by offering them the brutal State chauvinism of the new class in the guise of humane neo-Slavophilism, supposedly imbued with respect for all peoples.

11. CONCLUSION: THE NEW GENERATION OF RESISTANCE WRITERS–THE CHILDREN OF SAMIZDAT

While Soviet personnel officers and the Rodina Club were busy dividing the inhabitants of Russia up into the truly Russian, the half-breeds and the aliens, a group of young dissidents, without giving any thought to these racist games, took a step involving great self-sacrifice which shook the country. They mounted a demonstration in defence of Czechoslovakia on Red Square, and in doing so they upheld the honor of the Russian intelligentsia. This was the first political demonstration of a protest nature in Russia since 1927, the first demonstration not planned by the district committees of the Communist Party in forty years.

The trial of Pavel Litvinov and his friends who on 25 August 1968 held aloft banners saying For Our and Your Freedom, Free Czechoslovakia and so on is well-known. The poet Natalya Gorbanevskaya, who in an act of almost inconceivable courage took her baby along in a pram to the demonstration, prepared a record of the terror trial and had it sent to the West. It is very aptly called *Red Square at Noon*—the dawn of dissident thinking in Russia is well behind us.

Several years ago in Moscow I was asked to take on as my secretary a young writer the authorities wanted to have deported as a parasite. His name, Vladimir Bukovsky, did not mean anything to me as I noted it down on my calendar. When I handed the Secretary of the Union of Writers—and KGB General—V. Ilyin the piece of paper needing his signature, he turned it over in his hand and then looked at me sharply. "A writer has the right to a secretary if he earns more than 300 roubles a month," he said rapidly and got up. "Will you be handing in the form?"   He knew only too well I had been in disgrace for many years and could not hand in the form under those circumstances. Once I was home I jotted down the names of some writers who were rather better off than I was and at the same time prepared to take a risk. I regret to say they could be counted on the fingers of both hands.

Eventually a place was found for Vladimir Bukovsky through our combined efforts. Although we managed to find him a position, we did not, however, manage to save him from the attacks which were to come.

Now, fortunately, Vladimir Bukovsky is free and he will no doubt give an account himself in his forthcoming books of how he succeeded in outwitting the satanic designs of people like Snezhnevsky, Morozov and Lunts, the organizers of the psychiatric prisons for those who think differently. Thanks to Bukovsky, Plyushch and Gorbanevskaya were able to survive their terrible experiences and many others were spared them. Krasnov-Levitin, who has been imprisoned for three time for his religious activities

427

has written that Vladimir Bukovsky "is giving his life to the battle for truth and to assist those who are suffering, and in this sense, he, a non-believer, is a thousand times closer to Christ than the hundreds of so-called Christians whose Christianity only consists in hanging around churches. As a Christian I openly declare that I bow before the non-believer Bukovsky and the radiant acts of self-sacrifice which fill his life."

Bukovsky's pamphlet "I Managed to Do too Little" contains an account of his statements in court and must be regarded as a daring document of resistance. Although the prosecution was demanding the maximum punishment, which was death, Bukovsky, who had fallen ill in the camps, did not flinch before hurling the following words at his persecutors: "However long I have to stay in prison, I shall never give up my convictions... I shall fight for law and justice... My only regret is that in the short time I have been free—one year, two months and three days—I have managed to do too little towards this aim."

Several people have assisted Bukovsky in drawing the world's attention to Soviet psychiatric prisons. One of them is Viktor Faynberg who sent Bukovsky copies of medical records from a psychiatric prison hospital. Faynberg was the only participant in the demonstration on Red Square who did not appear before the court. When he was arrested he was so badly beaten up—while being abused in anti-Semitic language—that he could not be taken to the court. His nose had been completely smashed by a blow from a hobnailed army boot and where his eyebrows had been were just two bloody wounds. Since he could not be taken to the courtroom in his condition, the only thing to do was to put him in a special mental insitution. Here in the psychiatric prison Faynberg went on a protest hunger strike for 112 days. He was bound with a wet sheet and force-fed by thrusting a rubber tube up one of his nostrils because this was more painful than putting it in his mouth.

That battle for his release went on for three years. At the end of three years Academician Sakharov took up Faynberg's cause with the support of many people in other countries and eventually the KGB decided to let Faynberg go, on the condition that he refrain from speaking about his experiences. Faynberg was taken under escort to the Serbsky Institute. There the doctors whose white coats concealed their KGB epaulettes, leafed through their "cured" patient's records and asked him if he still held to his former errors now that three years had passed since the events in Czechoslovakia. Their intonation made it quite clear what answer they expected. At this point Faynberg, now terribly weakened by his experiences and anyway not of a robust constitution, realized that all was lost. He was utterly incapable of lying. He took a deep breath, bid freedom farewell and replied: "It is true that only three years have passed since the events in Czechoslovakia. But twelve years have gone by since the crushing of the Hungarian uprising and 112 years since Nicholas I invaded Moldavia and Walachia.

But that does not mean that these invasions have ceased to be violent acts of brigandage and occupation..." The order was given to put Faynberg away in the most isolated psychiatric institution of all and "extinguish his personality."

This latter term from Soviet psychiatry has become widely known in Russia. It has become the vital concern of the socialist State to extinguish personalities.

Shigalyov in Dostoevsky's novel *The Devils* is no longer a fictional character. His is a real life character in Russia. He believed that nine tenths of the people "would have to lose their personality and be turned into some kind of herd... We shall snuff out any genius in the earliest years. Everyone must be reduced to the lowest common denominator, there will be complete equality."[17]

The only reason Viktor Faynberg survived is that the woman psychiatrist who was put in charge of him as a dangerous and incurable patient fell in love with him and later became his wife. Both he and his wife now live in the West so mention of what occurred can now be freely made without fear for their safety. Faynberg was also able to arrange for various documents and records of expert opinion to be sent to the West where they aroused deep concern everywhere except at the World Congress of Psychiatrists in Mexico City which decided "not to become involved in politics." These documents and records were taken from the psychiatric institution by Faynberg's guards and passed on to the outside world as a result of the influence his heroic, warm-hearted and disarming personality had on them. The arrival of these documents and records in the West opened up a whole flood of documentation which has virtually pushed the works of recognized writers out of the limelight. The seventies have become the decade of documents—official records, open letters and records of minutes, all of which have uncovered facts revealing the true nature of the regime which claims to be marching forward to Communism under the Red Flag.

Perhaps the most philosophically profound and talented document of this period is Eduard Kuznetsov's work *Diaries* which he managed to get through the barbed wire of the Mordvinian camp he was in.

All those of us who are now free owe our freedom to Kuznetsov and his friends. I include the hundred thousand people who have found their way out of the land of victorious socialism—the Jews, the Russians, the Volga Germans, and especially the writers—Viktor Nekrasov, Vladimir Maximov, Alexander Galich, and Andrei Siniavsky who was let out "on the quiet," as he put it, along with the Jews. Those who arrive in the West in the years to come will also be indebted to Kuznetsov, as will those who are given the opportunity to say what they have to say about Russia, things which otherwise would never be heard. Few would have had the courage to write while in a camp as Kuznetsov did and to have what he had written published while still in the hands of his persecutors, locked up in a punishment cell, at times for long periods.

Eduard Kuznetsov and his friends were accused of attempting to hijack an aircraft in the hope of getting out of the Soviet Union. In fact he had no such hope. For him personally as a former political prisoner to take part in a mass attempt to cross the border was virtually to commit suicide. He knew he and his friends would be caught before the plane took off. It was the final gesture of someone tortured beyond endurance. Yet what other option did he have? "When there are no legal means for breaking through to some kind of real human existence, legalized illegality can only be exploded by an act of self-forgetful madness... It is always an explosion of despair."

He was aware that he and his friends were being watched, and knew full well what would follow. However he did not hesitate to continue with the plan which was doomed to failure. "The hijacking of an aircraft—or even the simple attempt to hijack one, if it does not remain a secret—not only gives a marvellous jolt to the calloused conscience of the Kremlin demagogues who publicly deny the very existence of an emigration problem, but represents a chance to be free for many thousands of people." This was the point of view he upheld in his arguments with his friends and he remained true to himself right to the end.

Kuznetsov and his companions threw themselves at the barbed wire enclosing them and were left hanging on it like soldiers coming under heavy fire during an assault. This is the story Kuznetsov tells in his *Diaries*.

Kuznetsov joins Amalrik in giving evidence of the disintegration of the regime's ideological basis. This is a theme he returns to constantly, aware as he is of its possibly fatal consequences for both East and West. With his eye on the future, he realizes that the Kremlin "cannot simply make do with giving the old idols a face-lift. The Kremlin needs an explosion of patriotism and the protracted inflaming of passions..."

Anything could be manipulated for these purposes—colonial wars under the flag of battles for peace, and carnage within the Soviet Union: "The pogrom mentality is not localized in time or space. There may be some abatement in the pogrom pandemic and its flare-ups may be dampened down but it is impossible to get rid of it altogether."

Eduard Kuznetsov arrived at the conclusions he did about the regime's lack of an ideology as a result of his prison experience. "The Cheka is very different now from what it was... You hear nothing now when under interrogation about the lofty happiness of being a Soviet citizen or the bright future of humanity... now the interrogators work you over as if you were in the kitchen of a communal apartment: 'The weakest go to the wall,' they say, and 'Why aim so high? Why not just live quietly'..."

Kuznetsov is too sober and caustic in his approach to idealize the dissident thinkers. He remarks that "the champions of all sorts of freedoms are extremely intolerant, especially in their own milieu." Here he arrives at the same despairing conclusion, although from a different starting-point, as the Strugatsky brothers in their portrayal of Perets who "thought differently" until he occupied the seat of power.

Kuznetsov feels an aversion for those who believe they are privy to the one truth. He has a much wider view than the all-knowing preachers of various truths such as Kreps from Maximov's *Seven Days of Creation*, a man of great moral purity by no means lacking in intelligence who attacks those opposed to the regime who do not share his mystical religious faith: "We signed no underground protests and made no attempt to solve our painful problems in above-board journals put out for the sake of the educated philistines in our society, yet we're sent away to Kazan. It's us they're sending away and not the highly placed liberal-minded active opponents of the government who are being paid a salary by the State! We are just the bearers of the light and word of God!" It may not have been Maximov's intention to emphasize Kreps' self-assertion while denigrating others but the portrait he has painted has turned out to be remarkably true to life. It is not the "frondeurs" in the Soviet Union Kuznetsov has no time for but those who merely play at being "frondeurs." In this he echoes some of the thoughts in Daniel's prison verse. "They are distinguished by an ability acquired over decades to sense where the line is which if crossed will today land them in prison... If samizdat is today to some extent ignored but tomorrow they start putting people behind bars for it, the *samizdatchik* will quickly switch to telling jokes and the day after tomorrow will confine himself to making concealed liberal gestures of defiance..."

Although they set out together on their chosen path by taking part in the public demonstrations on Mayakovsky Square, Eduard Kuznetsov and Vladimir Osipov later went each his own way. Their differences are fundamental. Osipov agitates for a return to Russia's sources and is ready to accept the rule of any State on the grounds that power is from God. Kuznetsov would like to see the State structure totally destroyed, founded as it is according to Kuzentsov on "blood, lies and inner emptiness."

Dictatorship is a kind of Mafia, although far more powerful than the Mafia as it exists in Europe and America. That is why dictatorship "regards organized crime as its own prerogative and brooks no rivals."

Vladimir Osipov calls for a return to national roots. Eduard Kuznetsov sees no hope of salvation here because, as he writes, "A handful of courageous opposition thinkers is as characteristic of Russia as it is alien to her national roots—it does not and cannot change anything." "We all come from Asia—those who have left and those who have remained. Asia is something subconscious... The crowd is always Asia."

These two courageous dissidents and writers, Vladimir Osipov and Eduard Kuznetsov, have divergent views on all subjects. They are now both behind barbed wire—and not for the first time. Osipov was sentenced to eight years. World opinion saved Kuznetsov from execution—he was given

431

fifteen years instead. Which of them is closer to the truth in his ideals? The arguments go on and will probably continue to do so. Nationalism is, after all, what we might call a gut feeling, quite deaf to reasoned argument. Is there a solution to the problems it raises? The supporters of the idea of Russia as one indivisible entity warn that if all the republics are given their independence according to the Soviet Constitution all that will be left will be Moscow and its kitchen-gardens. In all likelihood, however, economic ties and the danger of falling victim to those who are not averse to seizing whatever is left lying around will guarantee that the independent republics will be reunited in some way, but this time without being under Moscow's military supervision. They may have independent parliaments and differing social systems. Some may move towards socialism and others towards feudalism. Each republic should be free to choose.

If Russia is ever to escape the seemingly endless Tartar yoke, it must establish within itself a sense of law and justice to cancel out the ingrained obsessive ideas of first among equals, Gogol's flying troika, and Dostoevsky's seductive messianic call to return to the idea of the God-bearing Russian people. It will be necessary to give up the religious idea of repentence— the sons are not guilty for the sins of the fathers and everyone must be given the right to believe or not to believe as he sees fit. However, while repentance must be a matter of personal choice, it is imperative that questions of justice and of punishment should be taken out of the hands of Party committees and left to criminal and civil law procedures. The "law of the telephone" as it now operates, with calls from higher up dispensing justice in the land, hark back to the middle ages despite the fact that telephones are a modern invention. It is simply the modern version of the habit the powerful had in ages past of coming in person to mete out punishment to those who had disobeyed their instructions.

There is much wisdom in what Alexander Herzen once had to say about Westerners and Slavophiles: "Like Janus or the two-headed eagle, we were looking in different directions while the heart beating within us was one and the same."

The young dissidents I have been talking about are the children of resistance literature and the samizdat and tamizdat of different writers and philosophers. There can be no doubt that they have outgrown their teachers in terms of their heroism, their consistency and at times the depth and fearlessness of their ideas. Those writers who were formed—which means estranged from one another and alienated—during the Stalin era would never have had the courage to take the self-sacrificing step of publishing collectively the *Chronicle of Current Events*. Yet the young people of these times have had the courage. It was Natalia Gorbanevskaya who took the initial steps during the Prague Spring, as we called this time of hope in 1968. It was Gorbanevskaya who organized the publication of the *Chronicle* and took an active part in determining its overriding style, structure and editorial principles, as was openly stated in the *Chronicle* itself after Gorbanevskaya had left for the West.

Russia is no longer without a voice. How long this state of affairs can continue remains to be seen.

The heroism of Russian youth, which has been brought up on the literature and philosophy of resistance, and the personal acts of heroism of writers and scientists—and above all the heroic example of Andrei Sakharov—have had their effect on older recognized writers who have now begun in their turn to speak out bravely and without fear of the consequences in defense of the young. Lidya Chukovskaya, for example, is now writing much more hard-hitting, caustic articles on questions of public interest and has publicly lashed out at Sholokhov. People like Sakharov, Tverdokhlebov and Yuri Orlov, have made their positions much clearer and more well-defined as has Grigory Pomerants, the brilliant writer of philosophical essays. As they reach maturity these young people continue to produce astounding new works some of which have unfortunately been "written in blood" as is the case with A. Marchenko's *From Tarusa to Siberia* and the works of many other writers in Ukrainian, Lithuanian, Georgian and other languages who have insisted on being allowed to have their say.

Other developments began to take place which have received little attention from researchers.

Apart from books containing an open protest and a frank, in-depth analysis of the situation in the Soviet Union, there was also always a number of books by writers who wrote more cautiously. Their themes appeared to be fairly narrow—family quarrels, indifference towards the members of one's own family (as in Trifonov's "The Exchange"), the callousness of peasant children who abandon their mother as she is about to die (in a story by Rasputin) and so on. These writers seem to be merely showing the reader what happens. The Soviet reader, no innocent abroad, fills in for himself what has been left out. Yuri Trifonov is one writer who has gone some way towards speaking candidly to the Soviet reader who is now deprived of many of his favorite authors. Trifonov, in his story "House on the Embankment," courageously broaches subjects which have apparently caused him anguish all his life.

Initially Trifonov was subjected to fairly severe criticism, even if of a cautious kind, but later he suddenly became the object of praise and was elevated into a Soviet classic. His rather colorless prose, characterized as it was by indirect allusions and rather half-heartedly repentant heroes, once it had been "balanced out" and adjustments had been made to it by means of censorship cuts, turned out to be an unexpectedly useful lightning-conductor as far as the authorities were concerned. They much preferred Soviet readers to be fighting to get their hands on Trifonov's works than Solzhenitsyn's or—heaven forbid!—Zinovyev's.

Nowadays, Yuri Trifonov's and Valentin Rasputin's works are as a rule published in large editions and are eagerly snapped up by Soviet readers. With works such as *Farewell to Matyora* and *Live and Remember,* the young Siberian writer Valentin Rasputin is in some ways becoming the hope of Soviet literature. If he is not diverted into the dead-end paths of nationalistic writing—and strenuous attempts are being made to point him in just this direction—there is every chance that he will justify the hopes placed in him. Rasputin's unique place in the literature of moral resistance deserves our particular attention.

Rasputin's first collection of stories appeared in the 1960s. An urgent need was suddenly felt for a talented writer of pure Russian origins, from the depths of the Russian countryside, who had nothing in common with all these Grossmans, Voinoviches, Beks, "Solzhenitsers" (as Solzhenitsyn is sometimes mockingly referred to in an attempt to make his name sound Jewish) and all the other city-bred trouble-makers and half-breeds. Consequently, Rasputin was quickly snatched up by the most openly reactionary Stalinist publishers—the journal *Nash Sovremennik (Our Contemporary)* and the *Young Guard* publishing house, which is the organ of the Komsomol Central Committee.

Rasputin could not have appeared on the scene at a more opportune time. Among Rasputin's central concerns in his stories are questions of life and death. In "The Deadline" an old woman called Anna is dying. Her children come to say goodbye to her. When she sees her children, she miraculously revives and even tries to go outside. Her children feel almost let down. They have put everything aside—their work and their different affairs— and all for what? Her daughters leave on a convenient steamer and that night Anna dies, crushed by the heartlessness of her own children.

The death of Nastyona in *Live and Remember* is even more tragic. Nastyona is the young wife of a deserter who unintentionally gives her husband away. Her husband is hiding not far from the village. She becomes pregnant by him. No longer able to keep up the pretense and realizing that she is being followed, she jumps from a boat into the Angara River and drowns. Rasputin has said that the whole story was written around Nastyona and that the themes which inspired him to write his story were those relating to a woman's dedication and self-sacrifice, impulses which are stronger and higher than the regulations or the laws of the State.

Soviet critics saw only what they wanted to see in the book—the downfall of a deserter. This sort of theme is most important in a militaristic State such as the Soviet Union. The critics did not seem to notice that Guskov became a deserter only because of the excessive cruelty of the military authorities. Guskov had been fighting for almost the entire duration of the war and had been wounded three times. After being wounded on the third occasion, and this time seriously, he had begged permission to take home leave, if only for a few days. Permission was refused. In desperation Guskov simply went home without permission. He would have returned to the front if he had not known that he would be shot for desertion. However, in the Soviet press, it was not the causes, but the consequences of his action which became the subject of discussion. Naturally, a story describing the retribution for desertion was praised to the skies and the author became something of a celebrity.

His works were eagerly awaited by the journals and the critics, who gave encouragement to this talented and long-awaited son of the native soil. Rasputin, unlike the dissident writers, appeared to know the direction he was expected to take and how to walk in it.

Then he wrote *Farewell to Matyora*. It seemed to illustrate Saltykov-Shchedrin's remark that "Russian literature arose as a result of a lack of vigilance on the part of the authorities." In "The Deadline" the heroine is betrayed by her children. In this story it is the State which betrays the main character, an old woman dalled Darya, after first taking her son away from her. Darya is in some ways a further development of Anna from "The Deadline." She has had wider experience than Anna, and thinks more deeply and unforgivingly about things. Rasputin, in depicting Darya the way he has, knows that there will be no forgiveness for him, either, if he takes one false step, because it is he who must answer for what Darya thinks and says.

A genuine sense of history, with rare exceptions, is absent from Soviet historico-biographical literature. Exceptions worthy of mention are the works of Arkady Belinkov, Alexander Lebedev's *Chaadaev* and the historian Natan Eidelman's book *The Decembrist Mikhail Lunin*. These are the uncrowned kings of the contemporary historico-biographical genre and their best books have not been to the liking of either the Soviet or anti-Soviet camp. In juxtaposing as lucidly as they did the past and the present they showed extreme disrespect for the present as far as some were concerned and for the past as far as others were concerned.

It is in old Darya from the island of Matyora that this fierce, urgent sense of history finds a new lease of life. Her sense of history is natural and deeply ingrained.

The island of Matyora, which is her birthplace and home, is threatened with inundation as the waters connected with a new hydro-electric project rise and flood the surrounding countryside. Some workers arrive to prepare the town on the island for flooding. They begin with the cemetery. It never occurs to them that the children and grandchildren of those buried there are still living nearby. It is Darya who reminds them of this fact.

"You just clear off!" says Darya, advancing on one of the workmen. "You're destroying the graves..." Darya starts howling at him: "You haven't buried anyone here, have you? Are your father and mother buried here? Or your children? Scum like you had no father or mother. You're not a man. A real man wouldn't stoop to what you're doing." When the workman cites the order from the health inspection post (which in Russian goes under the clumsy name of "sanepidstantsiya"), the local inhabitants who have hurriedly assembled in the cemetery are even more infuriated. One spits back "sane-pidstantsiya" contemptuously at him in a garbled form ("samaspidstansy") and another suggests solving the problem on the spot by throwing the work-men in the river. "Into the Angara with them... Rid the earth of them. It will only thank us."

In isolated Siberian settlements the local people sometimes do take justice into their own hands. It is not unknown for a thief to be killed in this way, for example. Just when the inhabitants of Matyora are on the point of dealing out summary justice to the workmen one of the top men comes rushing up and explains that the whole area is to be covered by water, that holiday-makers and foreign tourists will be coming... how could they have crosses from the cemetery floating around for them to see?

One of the women calls out: "What about us? Did you give any thought to us? I just picked up my mother's photo off the ground after those pigs of yours had been there. Couldn't you have done this cleaning up without us having to see it?"

The theme which comes through so strongly in this and other passages is the main one in the work: in the enormous sea of socialism the human factor is engulfed and disappears. Socialism is built with callous disregard for either the living or the dead. All the various ramifications of this theme are brought out by Rasputin. One of them has been little remarked upon in the West: it concerns the regrouping of kolkhozes into sovkhozes and the consequence of this regrouping.

> Over on the right bank a new settlement is being built for the sovkhoz which is being formed by the merging of all the nearby kolkhozes—and some which are not so near... The old blacksmith Egor wants to join the sovkhoz but they will not take him.
>
> "The sovkhoz makes living space available to workers but you're not a worker, are you?" Vorontsov, the Chairman of the local soviet explains to him...
>
> "I've given my whole life to the kolkhoz."
>
> "The kolkhoz is quite a different matter. There's no kolkhoz now."

In approximately half of the administrative regions of the USSR the kolk-hozes have been merged to form sovkhozes. According to the Party leaders, this facilitates their operation. A sovkhoz is a State-run enterprise. There can be no question of democratic procedures, contentious issues being raised at public meetings or protesting voices being raised. An order is given and that is the end of it. However, on a sovkhoz the employees have a work schedule and receive a salary. Only some of the former kolkhozniks are taken on by the sovkhoz—occasionally quite a small number, perhaps four hundred out of two thousand—those in the best physical condition. As for the others who were also given land by State decree, they are left to fend for themselves as best they can.

In Rasputin's story the new sovkhoz houses are for some reason built on the northern side of the hill some five kilometers from the shore of the future lake. When the new settlers begin to store potatoes in their basements they find there is water lying there. "Why were they built like that?" Darya asks, puzzled. "Why on earth didn't they stick a spake in the ground?" Pavel, her only surviving son, explains to her that it was because "an outsider" was commissioned to do the building.

The old folk still cannot believe that they are going to be thrown off their own land just like that. "Perhaps they're just trying to give us a fright," remarks one of the old women. "Why give us a fright for no good reason?" asks Darya indignantly. "So there shouldn't be anyone who isn't afraid," comes the reply. Egor the old blacksmith gives way to tears. When they try to comfort him, he just shakes his head and says: "How can I help crying? How can I help it?"

How does the following generation greet these changes? It, after all, is educated and aware of the world outside. Matyora is not its only source of hope.

> Each time he came back to Matyora, [Pavel] was struck by how readily time closed in behind him. It was as if the new settlement did not exist and he had never been away from Matyora... His home was here and its's always better at home, as everyone knows... He had come home and the invisible door behind his back was already slamming closed... shutting off and removing him from all the changes which were to take place. And what about the changes? They themselves could not be changed and could not be altered...

It is at this point that Rasputin and Abramov, a writer who is no less gifted or sensitive to human suffering, may be seen to part company. The scenes described in Abramov's stories and novels are horrifying—scenes of famine and impoverishment in the Vologda countryside. Yet both Abramov and his characters would appear to offer some hope of change. The Siberian Rasputin would not seem to hold out any such hopes. "And what about the changes? They themselves could not be changed and could not be altered. There was no escape from them. It did not depend on either him or anyone else." This is how Pavel reasons. This former soldier from the front tells himself that "if that's the way it's got to be, then that's the way it's got to be." But in the course of the narrative he becomes less willing to accept this rather mindless formula for living. The narrator tells us that it is really only half clear to him—he can see that he has to move from Matyora. "But he did not understand why he had to move to that settlement... which had been set up with no concern for what was sensible or how people were going to live in it—all you could do was throw up your hands... But there it was—you could take it or leave it!"

Pavel then has thoughts which are even more heretical. He wonders if the new hydro-electric scheme is necessary at all? After all, it is not an unmitigated blessing—it is also causing people distress. "When he remembered that it was the very best land which was to be flooded, land tilled and enriched for centuries by his grandfathers and great-grandfathers before them, land which had provided food for many generations, he was overcome with anxiety and mistrust and his heart sank. Was the price too high?" Especially since the poor uncultivated land around the new settlement could not produce grain. Pavel's concern is not difficult to understand when it is remembered that the USSR has been buying grain abroad for many years. Siberia fears it might share the fate of famine-stricken Vologda.

At the same time, Pavel is envious of the young "to whom it does not even occur to have doubts. If things are done in a certain way, then that is the way they should be done. If the settlement has been built here, then here is where it should be... Everything that happens is for the best." This is reminiscent of the philosophy aired by Voltaire's Pangloss when faced with violent death: "All is for the best in the best of possible worlds." This same philosophy has been Russia's ruin.

What is Rasputin's attitude to these young people? He has nothing but contempt, for example, for the young man who is officially registered as Nikita although everyone, including his mother, calls him Petrukha because he is such a good-for-nothing. First of all he burnt down his own house, leaving his mother homeless, and then enthusiastically joined the professional arsonists, burning down the many villages on the Angara which needed destroying at that time. Rasputin regards another character, Klavka Strigunova, with a certain irony. It is her firm opinion that Matyora should have been flooded long ago. "She simply could not wait for the moment when she could set fire to her father's and grandfather's cottage and get the rest of the compensation for it."

At this point Pavel's son Andrei arrives from the city. He has spent some time serving in the army and working at a factory. He has turned out quite an impressive young man, strong and self-assured. He would appear to have all the makings of a positive hero. However, the narrator obviously has reservations even about him. The paragraph describing Andrei's departure for the construction site of Velikaya Stroyka resolves any doubts on this score. In the Newspapers Velikaya Stroyka is described as Communism's front line and that is where Andrei wants to be. It is of no importance to him that this "front line" of Communism will be responsible for Matyoras disappearance.

In the morning when he was leaving, Darya was hurt because Andrei started saying goodbye to her in the cottage and did not want her to see him off on the boat... But something more deeply and painfully

438

hurtful than that occurred, something it is impossible to give a name to because there is no word for it. It must simply be suffered, as anguish or sickness is suffered... She had not forgotten that since yesterday when he had arrived until this morning when he was going away Andrei had not gone further than the yard of his own house. He had not gone for a walk around Matyora or felt any secret sadness at never seeing it again. He had not troubled himself over it at all—yet he should have taken the trouble to take a last look at the island where he had been born and brought up. But all he did was pick up his case, go down to the shore by the path hear the house and start the motor.

Farewell, Andrei. Farewell to you too. May God preserve you from having a life which seems easy to you.

As it turns out, empty-headed, drunken Petrukha and dependable, ideologically motivated Andrei are both cut from the same cloth. They are both rootless and neither holds anything dear, although Andrei is a positive hero in the established Soviet tradition.

Just before his hurried departure, Andrei asks his grandmother why she pities everyone. "When you said he was a small man, did you mean he was weak, powerless or what?"

This conversation between Andrei and his grandmother is a continuation of the philosophical conversation which was interrupted in Russian literature over fifty years ago, partly thanks to Maxim Gorky who said well before the Revolution: "Man!... He must not be pitied... must not be degraded by pity... Truth is higher than pity..."

This is the first time the theme of pity—a peasant's pity, pity in the Christian sense—is brought out. Darya says:

How can I help being sorry for him, the poor thing? He hasn't changed. He had two arms and legs then and he hasn't got any more now. He's turned his whole life upside-down. It's terrible to see the mess he's made of it. He thinks he controls his life, but he lost control ages ago... I mean that about all of you.... You're not breaking your backs over anything, you take it easy, don't you, but you've wasted away your soul and you couldn't care less. Have you ever even heard that a man has a soul, Andrei?... You think you've got machines working for you. As if I didn't know that it's been a long time since they worked for you—it's you lot who work for them. You chase after them... You have no time for yourself or for people... You're going to lose yourself altogether soon the way you're going... Look at the toll your kind of life takes: we had to give up Matyora to it, it was hungry for it—but not just Matyora!... It demands more. And there's no escape— you'll give it more. Otherwise you'll have had it...

This man of your is an incredible muddler. If he muddles up

439

other people that's one thing—he'll answer for that, but he's got him-
self in such a terrible muddle that he doesn't know his right hand
from his left. He does everything round the wrong way, you'd think
he did it on purpose. The very thing he doesn't want to do he goes
and does... And when he talks... you don't know what he meant to
say. He doesn't say what he wants to say—he just says nothing... He's
up against so much, it's frightening to watch him. And he's always
dashing around all over the place—and to no effect either... Then there's
death... How afraid he is of it, the poor thing! You can't help pitying
him on that account alone...

Darya's monologue, which is only occasionally interrupted by the
self-confident Andrei's remarks, also introduces the theme of the lack of
continuity in Russia's spiritual life and traditions. Everything belonging to
the past has been cut down like grass under a scythe. This is why the pain
Darya feels is so unbearable:

It seems to Darya that there is nothing more unjust in the world than
when something—whether a tree or a man—outlives its higher use-
fulness, it becomes such a burden... Why look for some higher truth
when you can't be of any use either now or in the future? ... Truth
is in the memory. Whoever has no memory has no life.

However, the builders of the new life have no need of Darya's wisdom
or her experience, just as they have no need of the island with its rich, fer-
tile soil. In touching on themes such as this, Rasputin's work clearly goes
beyond the bounds of purely peasant or even Russian themes and assumes
a much wider philosophical and human significance.

In Soviet literature there is, of course, no recognition of the existence
of general "human truth"; this is attacked as "abstract humanism." The only
truth which is recognized is class truth. The truth being sought in "Farewell
to Matyora" by the narrator and by Darya whose thoughts are expressed
in an archaic form of Russian would seem to be that Russia has sunk beneath
the waters which now cover the memory, traditions, aspirations and native
kindheartedness of the Russian people.

The narrator has no mercy even for Darya's son Pavel, although he is
better than the others. "After the way it took a long time for him to return
to normal again and, as far as he could see, not many of those who had
fought in the war had returned to normal..." People were doing everything
that had to be done but "seemed to be doing it as if they were already dead
or else for the second time, always in a strained way, with a kind of familiar-
ity and patient submissiveness."

This becomes particularly obvious during the last days before Matyora
is flooded:

Pavel felt ashamed when he remembered how he had stood beside his burning cottage as the fire died down and tried to find and squeeze out of himself some heart-felt feeling of being strongly moved—after all, it was not just some stump burning but his own home—but he could not find anything to squeeze out of himself except an uncomfortable and bitter feeling of suprise at the thought that he had once lived here. This was the extent to which his soul had been obliterated.

Who then is in a position of authority in this world? Who gives the orders, makes the threats and controls the flooding operation? It is Vorontsov, Chairman of the local soviet at the settlement. Only Petrukha calls him by his first name and patronymic, everyone else calls him by his surname, Vorontsov.

The day before a State commission is to arrive to put its seal on Matyora's fate, Vorontsov starts behaving in his usual bullying fashion but this time it is from alarm because it turns out that there are still some old women on Matyora. That evening Vorontsov takes a launch and sets out to pick up Darya and her friends. However, the launch cannot find Matyora in the dark and the mist. Vorontsov becomes impatient and starts abusing the crew. He is told to stop shouting—"you're not at a meeting now." Surprisingly, Vorontsov restrains himself and says no more, realizing that giving orders would not help.

The book ends on a bitter note. The island is sunk in utter darkness.

"Is it night already?" asked Katerina [Petrukha's mother], looking around her.

"Well, it's not day." Darya replied. "There'll be no more day for us."

"Where are we? We're still alive, aren't we?"

"We might as well be dead..."

The old women started crossing themselves...

There is one more character in the work who should be discussed—the Master (Khozyain)—written with a capital letter. The real master in the story is not Vorontsov or Comrade Zhuk, the official in charge of the whole operation. The Master is a character of a type not to be found in the works of any other Soviet writer. The Master is an element in the islanders' personification of almost everything—the trees, the houses, the mill—are beings. The Master can be heard wailing, lamenting and farewelling the island.

When outsiders come to burn down the mill, Darya says to one of her friends: "Come on, let's go and say goodbye to the mill. There'll probably be none of us local people there. Imagine what it must be like for it surrounded by strangers—none of them will have a kind word to say... Think of all the grain it's ground for us, bless its soul. The least we can do is let it see us at the last."

The anthropomorphism in the work runs at a deeper level than this, however:

> *When night fell and Matyora went to sleep, a small animal, scarcely bigger than a cat and quite unlike any other animal, jumped out from under the bank on the mill canal. This was the Master of the island... If there are house-spirits in the cottages then there has to be a Master on the island. No one had ever seen him or come across him but he knew everyone and knew everything that was going on... That is what he was Master for—to see everything and know everything and not get in the way of anything. That was the only way he could remain Master—by not letting anyone suspect he existed.*

Running around the island at night the Master senses both what is happening above ground and under the ground. By the rancid, rotting odor around Petrukha's cottage, he knows that Petrukha intends to destroy it. It is as if he has set fire to it with a match no one has yet seen. The Master presses up against the dead, tinder-dry timber of Petrukha's cottage for the last time and can see through the walls what is going on inside.

The Master is obviously no ordinary animal. He is not afraid of other animals because they cannot smell him.

When Darya decides to leave, running along beside her is "a small animal never before seen, trying to look into her eyes." Darya is the only one privileged to see the Master—no one else can see him—because the Master recognizes that apart from himself only Darya can see everything and knows everything.

In Rasputin's work for the first time the supernatural element is not associated with devils, as in *The Master and Margarita*, but with positive life forces. The Master represents the spirit of the earth and the Russian way of life as it has existed for centuries, now to be destroyed by flood-waters. Rasputin's Master may be seen as an organic link with animate and inanimate nature, a link which vulgar atheism has annihilated. Genuine Russian literature is painfully aware of the loss brought about by atheism.

In order to break the chain linking the centuries through the age-old continuity in Russian spiritual life, traditions and ideas, it was necessary to drown Matyora-Russia over and over again in a sea of non-being and historical amnesia—in a sea of blood—depriving her of her very roots.

Writers in Moscow argued about what Rasputin's own views were, whether he was on the "right" or not, and whether it was just coincidental that he had been taken up and made a fuss of by the most reactionary publishing concerns. Was it possible that he was a neoslavophile? There appeared to be something extremist in the view that people "with something gipsyish about them," as the official in charge of the hydroelectric scheme is described, were responsible for drowning the Russian land, as if Russia were the victim of unsavory foreign types.

In Moscow they are still arguing about whether he is on the right or the left. Yet Darya herself said that man was a muddle-headed creature who didn't know which was right and which was left. "He does everything round the wrong way, as if on purpose. You think he's going left and it turns out he goes right..."

There can be no doubt that the heroism of the young in Russia has influenced those established writers who for years hid away in their desk drawers what they had written, putting off their attempts at publication until times were better. The times seem to be in no particular hurry to get better. Factors such as these brought about the publication of one of the wisest and most talented books of our time, Georgy Vladimov's novel *Faithful Ruslan*. This work has given the world a glimpse of the secret methods used to breed the species referred to ironically in the West as *homo soveticus* in the State's sheep-folds. This is also true of books such as Yuri Dombrovsky's *Faculty of Useless Things* and Alexander Zinoviev's profound, utterly despairing and mordant works *The Yawning Heights* and *The Radiant Future*. This well-known Moscow University philosophy professor's books will doubtless be the subject of debate for a long time to come.

The literature of moral resistance—or literature which includes "a moral factor" as the Soviet expression has it—has burst forth in a stream which may at times run shallow and at times burst its banks in springtime flood. But it is a stream which can never be staunched.

SELECTED BIBLIOGRAPHY

This bibliography is intended only for those who do not know Russian. Those who wish to read critical works, poetry, or fiction in the original, including the various periodical publications mentioned in this text, should consult the Russian edition of this book: Grigorii Svirskii, *Na lobnom meste: literatura nravstvennogo soprotivleniia (1946-76 gg.)*, London: Overseas Publications Interchange, Ltd., 1979.

ANTHOLOGIES

Blake, Patricia & May Hayward (eds.), DISSONANT VOICES IN SOVIET LITERATURE. New York: Pantheon, 1962.

Bochkarev, Yuri (ed.), SOVIET RUSSIAN STORIES OF THE 1960s & 1970s. Moscow: Progress, 1977.

Field, Andrew (ed.), PAGES FROM TARUSA. Boston: Little, Brown, 1964.

Glagoleva, F. (ed.), BY THE LIGHT OF DAY. STORIES BY SOVIET WRITERS. Moscow: Progress, 1968.

Ivanov, Y. (ed.), A TREASURY OF RUSSIAN & SOVIET SHORT STORIES. New York: Fawcett, 1971.

Kazakova, R. (selector), THE TENDER MUSE (SOVIET POETESSES). Moscow: Progress, 1976.

Kunitz, Joshua (ed.), RUSSIAN LITERATURE SINCE THE REVOLUTION. New York, Boni and Gaer, 1948.

MacAndrew, A. R. (ed.), FOUR SOVIET MASTERPIECES. New York: Bantam, 1965 [Vladimov, Voinovich, Aksenov, Kazakov].

Massie, Suzanne (ed.), THE LIVING MIRROR. Five Young Poets from Leningrad. Garden City: Doubleday, 1972.

Milner-Gulland, Robin & Martin Dewhirst (eds.), RUSSIAN WRITING TODAY. Penguin Books, 1977.

Niyazi, Shovkat (comp.), VOICES OF FRIENDS. Soviet Poets. Moscow: Progress, 1973.

Pomorska, Krystyna (ed.), FIFTY YEARS OF RUSSIAN PROSE FROM PASTERNAK TO SOLZHENITSYN. Cambridge: MIT Press, 1971. 2 volumes.

Proffer, Carl and Ellendea Proffer (eds.), THE ARDIS ANTHOLOGY OF RECENT RUSSIAN LITERATURE. Ann Arbor: Ardis, 1975.

Proffer, Carl (ed.), AN ANTHOLOGY OF CONTEMPORARY RUSSIAN PROSE. Ann Arbor: Ardis, 1981.

Reeve, F. D. (ed.), CONTEMPORARY RUSSIAN DRAMA. New York: Pegasus, 1967.

Scammel, Michael (ed.), RUSSIA'S OTHER WRITERS. London: Longman, 1970.

Whitney, T. P. (ed.), THE NEW WRITING IN RUSSIA. Ann Arbor: University of Michigan Press, 1964.

Yarmolinsky, Avrahm (ed.), SOVIET SHORT STORIES. Garden City: Anchor, 1960.

PERIODICALS

KONTINENT. Anthologies made up from the best-known emigre periodical are regularly published by Doubleday. To date 3 volumes have appeared, containing both fiction and non-fiction.

RUSSIAN LITERATURE TRIQUARTERLY. 1971- . Every issue of this journal contains translations of Russian poetry, fiction, and criticism, primarily 20th-century works.

SOVIET LITERATURE. Published in Moscow by Progress Publishers, the official Soviet propaganda publisher, the twelve annual issues of this magazine are the best place to see the conservative Party presentation of Soviet literature and politics.

ABRAMOV, F. A New Life. New York: Praeger, 1963.

AITMATOV, C. Tales of the Mountains and Steppes. Moscow: Progress, 1969.

———. Farewell, Gul'sary! London: Hodder & Stoughton, 1970.

——— and K. Mukhamedzhanov. The Ascent of Mount Fuji. New York: Noonday, 1975.

AKHMADULINA, B. Fever & Other New Poems. New York: Morrow, 1969.

———. [selected poems] , Russian Literature Triquarterly, No. 1 (1971).

AKHMATOVA, A. A. Selected Poems. Ann Arbor: Ardis, 1976.

AKSENOV, V. P. A Starry Ticket. Putnam, 1962.

———. The Steel Bird & Other Stories. Ann Arbor: Ardis, 1979.

———. It's Time, My Friend, It's Time. London: Macmillan, 1969.

———. Colleagues. Moscow: FLPH, n.d.

AMALRIK, A. Will the Soviet Union Survive Until 1984. New York, 1967.

ASTAFIEF, V. The Horse with the Pink Mane. Moscow: Progress, 1978.

BABEL, I. Collected Stories. New York: Meridian, 1960.

———. The Forgotten Babel. Ann Arbor: Ardis, 1978.

BALTER, B. Goodbye, Boys. New York: Dutton, 1967.

BARANSKAYA, N. "The Retirement Party," Russian Literature Triquarterly, No. 9.

BEK, A. The Volokolamsk Highway. Moscow: Progress, 1969.

———. And Not to Die. New York: SRT Publications, 1949.

BELOV, V. "Carpenter Stories" (excerpts), in Proffer (ed.) THE ARDIS ANTHOLOGY
OF RECENT RUSSIAN LITERATURE.

BITOV, A. Selected Short Stories. Ann Arbor: Ardis, 1981.

BONDAREV, Y. Silence. London: Chapman & Hale, 1965.

BRODSKY, Iosif [Joseph] , Selected Poems. Penguin, 1973.

———. Part of Speech. New York, 1980.

BUKOVSKY, V. To Build a Castle: My Life as a Dissenter. New York: Viking, 1979.

BULGAKOV, M. The Master and Margarita. New York: Harper, 1967.

BYKOV, V. The Ordeal London:Bodley Head, 1972.

CHUKOVSKAYA, L. The Deserted House. New York: Dutton, 1967.

———. Going Under. London: Barrie & Jenkins, 1972.

DANIEL, Yuli [N. Arzhak] , "This is Moscow Speaking," in Blake, P. (ed.), DISSO-
NANT VOICES IN SOVIET LITERATURE.

DOMBROVSKY, Y. The Keeper of Antiquities. New York: McGraw-Hill, 1969.

DUDINTSEV, V. Not by Bread Alone. New York: Dutton, 1957.

———. A New Year's Tale. New York: Dutton, 1960.

EHRENBURG, I. People and Life: Memoirs of 1891-1917. London, 1961.

———. Memoirs: 1921-1941. Cleveland: World Publishing, 1964.

———. The Thaw. London: MacGibbon, 1961.

EROFEEV, V. Moscow to the End of the Line [Moscow-Petushki] . New York: Tap-
linger, 1980.

ETKIND, E. Notes of a Non-Conspirator. Oxford University Press, 1978.

FADEYEV, A. The Rout. Moscow: FLPH, n.d.

FEDIN, K. Cities & Years. New York: Greenwood Press, 1962.

———. The Conflagration. Moscow: Progress, 1968.

GALICH, A. [Selected poems] , THE ARDIS ANTHOLOGY OF RECENT RUSSIAN
LITERATURE.

GINZBURG, E. Journey into the Whirlwind. Penguin, 196?. [Volume 2 is scheduled
for publication in 1981 as a Kurt & Helen Wolfe Book.]

GORBANEVSKAYA, N. Selected Poems. Carcanet Press, 1972.

GRANIN, D. Those Who Seek. Moscow: FLPH, n.d.

———. Into the Storm. Moscow: Progress, 1965.

450

GREKOVA, I. "One Summer Day," Russian Literature Triquarterly, No. 11.

———. "The Lady's Hairdresser," Russian Literature Triquarterly, No. 5.

GROSSMAN, V. Forever Flowing. New York: Harper & Row, 1972.

GUMILEV, L. Selected Works. Albany: SUNY Press, 1972.

ISKANDER, F. The Goatibex Constellation. Ann Arbor: Ardis, 1975.

———. Forbidden Fruit & Other Stories. Moscow: Progress, 1972.

———. The Thirteenth Labour of Hercules. Moscow: Progress, 1978.

———. "A Very Sexy Little Giant" and "Vengeance" in the anthology METROPOLE. New York: Norton, 1981.

KAVERIN, V. Two Captains. New York, 1942.

———. The Larger View. London, 1938.

KAZAKEVICH, E. The Blue Notebook. Moscow: Progress, 1969.

KAZAKOV, Y. Autumn in the Oak Woods. Moscow: Progress, 1970.

———. Going to Town & Other Stories. Boston: Houghton-Mifflin, 1964.

KOPELEV, L. To Be Preserved Forever. New York: Lippincot, 1978.

———. The Education of a True Believer. New York: Harper & Row, 1980.

KOZHEVNIKOV, V. The Strong in Spirit. Moscow: Progress, 1973.

KUZNETSOV, A. Babi Yar. New York: Dial, 1967.

KUZNETSOV, E. Diaries.......

LAKSHIN, SOLZHENITSYN, TVARDOVSKY & NOVY MIR. MIT 1980.

LEONOV, L. The Russian Forest. Moscow: Progress, 1976.

———. The Badgers. London: Hutchinson, 1946.

———. The Thief. New York: Dial, 1931.

MANDELSTAM, Nadezhda. Hope Against Hope. New York: Atheneum, 1970.

———. Hope Abandoned. New York: Atheneum, 1975.

———. Mozart and Salieri. Ann Arbor: Ardis, 1973.

MANDELSTAM, Osip. The Complete Critical Prose & Letters. Ann Arbor: Ardis, 1979.

———. Selected Poems. Trans. D. McDuff. New York: Noonday, 1975.

———. Selected Poems. Trans. C. Brown & W. S. Merwin. New York: Atheneum, 1974.

———. Stone. Princeton University Press, 1981.

———. The Prose of Osip Mandelstam. Princeton University Press, 1965.

MARCHENKO, A. My Testimony. New York, 1969.

———. From Tarusa to Siberia. Royal Oak: Strathcona, 1979.

MAXIMOV, V. A Man Survives. New York: Grove, 1963.

———. The Seven Days of Creation. New York: Knopf, 1975.

———. Farewell from Nowhere. New York: Doubleday, 1979.

NAGIBIN, Y. The Pipe Stories. Moscow: FLPH, 1958.

———. Dreams. Moscow: FLPH, n.d.

NEKRASOV, V. Front-Line Stalingrad. London: Harvill, 1962.

———. Kira Georgievna. New York: Pantheon, 1962.

NILIN, P. Comrade Venka [Cruelty]. New York: Simon & Schuster, 1969.

OKUDZHAVA, B. Sixty-Five Songs [bi-lingual edition]. Ann Arbor: Ardis, 1980.

———. Nocturne. New York: Harper & Row, 1978.

OLESHA, Y. Complete Short Stories. Ann Arbor: Ardis, 1978.

———. Envy. Ann Arbor: Ardis, 1975.

———. No Day without a Line. Ann Arbor: Ardis, 1978.

PANOVA, V. The Train. New York: Knopf, 1949.

———. Span of the Year. London: Harvill, 1957.

PASTERNAK, B. Doctor Zhivago. New York, 1958.

———. Selected Writings. New York: New Directions, 1958.

———. Poems. Ann Arbor: University of Michigan Press, 1959.

PAUSTOVSKY, K. The Story of a Life. New York: Vintage, 1964.

———. Selected Stories. Moscow: Progress, 1974.

PLATONOV, A. Collected Works. Ann Arbor: Ardis, 1978.

———. Chevengur. Ann Arbor: Ardis, 1978.

———. The Fierce & Beautiful World. New York: Dutton, 1970.

PLYUSHCH, L. History's Carnival. A Dissident's Autobiography. New York, 1977.

POLEVOY, B. The Story about a Real Man. Moscow: Progress, 1975.

RASPUTIN, V. Live and Remember. New York: Macmillan, 1978.

———. Farewell to Matyora. New York: Macmillan, 1980.

SAKHAROV, A. My Country and the World. New York: Knopf, 1976.

———. Alarm and Hope. New York: Knopf, 1978.

SHALAMOV, V. Kolyma Tales. New York: Norton, 1980.

SHOLOKHOV, M. And Quiet Flows the Don, with The Don Flows Home to the Sea, trans. of The Quiet Don. New York: Knopf, 1941.

———. Seeds of Tomorrow, and Harvest on the Don, trans. of Virgin Soil Upturned. New York: Knopf, 1935 and 1960.

SHUKSHIN, V. Snowball Berry Red & Other Stories. Ann Arbor: Ardis, 1979.

———. I Want to Live. Moscow: Progress, 1973.

SIMONOV, K. Days and Nights. New York: Ballantine, 1962.

SINYAVSKY, A. [A. Tertz], The Trial Begins. New York: Pantheon, 1960.

———. Fantastic Stories. New York: Pantheon, 1963.

———. The Makepeace Experiment. New York: Pantheon, 1965.

———. A Voice from the Chorus. New York, 1976.

———. On Trial: The Case of Sinyavsky (Tertz) and Daniel (Arzhak). Eds. L. Labedz & Max Hayward. New York: Harper & Row, 1967.

SOBOLEV, L. The Big Refit. Moscow: Progress, 1965.

SOLOUKHIN, V. White Grass. Moscow: Progress, 1971.

SOLZHENITSYN, A. One Day in the Life of Ivan Denisovich. New York, 1963.

———. Matrena's House & For the Good of the Cause. New York: Farrar, Straus, 1972.

———. The First Circle. New York: Harper & Row, 1968.

———. Cancer Ward. New York: Dial, 1968.

———. August 1914. New York, 1972.

———. The Gulag Archipelago. New York: Harper & Row, 1974, 1975.

———. Lenin in Zurich. New York, 1976.

STRUGATSKY, Arkady and Boris. Definitely Maybe. New York: Macmillan, 1978.

———. Prisoners of Power. New York: Macmillan, 1977.

———. Roadside Picnic and Tale of the Troika. New York: Macmillan, 1977.

SYOMIN, V. Seven in One House. New York: Dutton, 1968.

TENDRYAKOV, V. Three, Seven, Ace. London: Harvill, 1973.

———. A Topsy-Turvy Spring. Moscow: Progress, 1978.

TRIFONOV, Y. The Students. Moscow: FLPH, 1953.

———. The Impatient Ones. Moscow: Progress, 1978.

———. The Long Goodbye: Three Novellas. Ann Arbor: Ardis, 1978.

———. The House on the Embankment. New York: Simon & Schuster, 1981.

TSVETAEVA, M. A Captive Spirit: Selected Prose. Ann Arbor: Ardis, 1980.

———. The Demesne of the Swans. Ann Arbor: Ardis, 1980.

———. A Pictorial Biography, ed. E. Proffer. Ann Arbor: Ardis, 1980.

———. Selected Poems. Oxford University Press, 1971.

TVARDOVSKY, A. Vassili Tyorkin. Moscow: Progress, 1975.

———. Tyorkin and the Stove Makers. Carcanet Press, 1974.

VINOKUROV, E. Selected Poems: The War Is Over. Iowa City: International Writers Program & Carcanet Press, 1976.

VLADIMOV, G. Faithful Ruslan. New York: Simon & Schuster, 1979.

VOINOVICH, V. The Life & Extraordinary Adventures of Private Ivan Chonkin. New York: Farrar, Straus, 1977.

VOINOVICH, V. The Ivankiad. New York, 1977.
———. In Plain Russian. New York, 1979.
VOLODIN, A. Five Evenings. Minnesota Drama Editions, Univ. of Minn. 1966.
VOZNESENSKY, A. Antiworlds and The Fifth Ace. New York: Schoken, 1973.
———. Nostalgia for the Present. New York: Doubleday, 1978.
VYSOTSKY, V. [selection of poems and songs], Metropole. New York: Norton, 1981.
YASHIN, A. "The Levers," in The Ardis Anthology of Recent Russian Literature.
YEVTUSHENKO, Y. Bratsk Station & Other New Poems. New York: Praeger, 1967.
———. Stolen Apples. Garden City: Doubleday, 1971.
ZABOLOTSKY, N. Scrolls. London: Cape, 1971.
ZHDANOV, A. Speech on the Journals 'Star' and 'Leningrad'. Royal Oak: Strathcona, 1978.
ZINOVIEV, A. The Yawning Heights. New York: Random House, 1979.
———. The Radiant Future. New York: Random House, 1980.
ZOSHCHENKO, M. Nervous People and Other Stories. New York: Pantheon, 1963.
———. Before Sunrise. Ann Arbor: Ardis, 1974.

HISTORIES AND CRITICISM

Brown, Deming. SOVIET RUSSIAN LITERATURE SINCE STALIN. Cambridge University Press, 1978.
Brown, E. J. RUSSIAN LITERATURE SINCE THE REVOLUTION. London, 1969.
——— (ed.). MAJOR SOVIET WRITERS. Essays in Criticism. Oxford Univ. Press, 1973.
Brumberg, A. (ed.), IN QUEST O JUSTICE: PROTEST & DISSENT IN THE SOVIET UNION TODAY. New York: Praeger, 1970.
Gladilin, Anatoly. THE MAKING AND UNMAKING OF A SOVIET WRITER. Ann Arbor: Ardis, 1979.
Hayward, Max & E. Crowley (eds.), SOVIET LITERATURE IN THE SIXTIES. New York: Praeger, 1964.
Hingley, Ronald. RUSSIAN WRITERS AND SOVIET SOCIETY 1917-1978. New York: Random House, 1979.
Hosking, Geoffrey. BEYOND SOCIALIST REALISM. Soviet Fiction Since Ivan Denisovich. London: Granada Publishing, 1980.
Mathewson, Rufus. THE POSITIVE HERO IN RUSSIAN LITERATURE. 2nd ed. Stanford University Press, 1975.
Mihajlov, Mihajlo. RUSSIAN THEMES. New York: Farrar, Straus, 1968.
Proffer, Carl R. "Writing in the Shadow of the Monolith: A Guide to the New Russian Writers," NEW YORK REVIEW OF BOOKS. February 19, 1976.
Rothberg, Abraham. THE HEIRS OF STALIN: DISSIDENCE AND THE SOVIET REGIME 1953-1970. Ithaca: Cornell University Press, 1972.
Slonim, Marc. SOVIET RUSSIAN LITERATURE. Writers & Problems, 1917-77. Oxford University Press, 1977.
Solzhenitsyn, A. THE OAK AND THE CALF. New York: Harper & Row, 1980.
Swayze, Harold. POLITICAL CONTROL OF LITERATURE IN THE USSR, 1946-1959. Cambridge: Harvard University Press, 1962.

INDEX

454

JUN